PRAISE FOR *THE PUSHCART PRIZE, XV*

"The Pushcart Prize enters our cultural life but once a year yet never fails to enhance it in subtle ways. This indispensable compilation of quality poetry and prose recalls those traveling libraries the nobility carried with them in the 18th century, writings that were few yet choice. Get it, read it, lug it around with you: as always this book is essential."

—*Library Journal*

"Bill Henderson and his team of editors have consistently managed to put together remarkable collections of distinctive writing. The fifteenth edition is no exception. It is a true pageturner for fans of little magazines and obscure presses—and for anyone interested in fine writing in its shorter forms. The wonderfully diverse anthology is a tribute to the different ways that writing can move, instruct and entertain."

—*Booklist*

"The command and authority displayed at almost every turn are enough to convince us, once again, that these yearly volumes feature much of the best writing available in this country—and to make us thankful for them."

—*The New York Times Book Review*

"A national literary treasure . . . as usual, the offerings are a felicitous mix of fiction—usually short stories—essays, and poems, drawn from presses that serve as the American counterpart to the USSR's *samizdat*. . . . A noteworthy collection."

—*Kirkus Reviews*

THE
PUSHCART PRIZE, XV:
BEST OF THE
SMALL PRESSES

THE 1990/1991 PUSHCART PRIZE XV

BEST OF THE SMALL PRESSES

Edited by
Bill Henderson
with the
Pushcart Prize
editors.
Introduction by
Russell Banks
Poetry Editors:
William Heyen,
Elizabeth Spires
Essays Editor:
Anthony Brandt

A TOUCHSTONE BOOK
Published by Simon & Schuster
New York London Toronto Sydney Tokyo Singapore

Note: nominations for this series are invited from any small, independent, literary book press or magazine in the world. Up to six nominations—tear sheets or copies selected from work published, or about to be published, in the calendar year—are accepted by the November 15 deadline each year. Write to Pushcart Press, P. O. Box 380, Wainscott, N.Y. 11975 for more information.

Touchstone
Simon & Schuster Building
Rockefeller Center
1230 Avenue of the Americas
New York, New York 10020

10 9 8 7 6 5 4 3 2 1

Library of Congress Card Number: 78–58675
ISBN 0-671-73332-X

Acknowledgements

Introduction © 1990 Russell Banks
On The Zeedijk © 1989 The Georgia Review
What I Wanted Most of All © 1989 Massachusetts Review
Vital Signs © 1989 Natalie Kusz. Reprinted from *Threepenny Review* and *Road Song* forthcoming from *Farrar* Straus and Giroux, with permission.
I'm Having Trouble With My Relationship © 1989 Threepenny Review
More Room © 1989 Puerto del Sol. Also by permission of Arte Publico Press.
A Motiveless Malignancy © 1989 Ontario Review
Aliens © 1989 Threepenny Review
Hide-And-Go-Seek © 1989 The Georgia Review
What The Blue Jay Said © 1989 Ambergris
Dying In Massachusetts © 1989 Barnwood Press
Post-Larkin Triste © 1989 TriQuarterly
The Cave © 1989 Partisan Review
Captivity: The Minks © 1989 Colorado Review
What Is Beyond Us © 1989 American Poetry Review
Austerity in Vermont © 1989 Gettysburg Review
Hospice © 1989 Ploughshares
A Vacant Lot © 1989 Yarrow
Castrato © 1989 Ascensius Press
Ascension on Fire Island © 1989 Antaeus, reprinted from *The Zoo Wheel of Knowledge* (Alfred Knopf Inc.)
Heaven © 1989 New American Writing, also appeared in *Operation Memory* (Princeton University Press, 1990)
Dust © 1989 Agni Review
Hopkins and Whitman © 1989 Kenyon Review
Miles Weeping © 1989 American Poetry Review
For the Missing in Action © 1989 Ploughshares
Armageddon: Private Gabriel Wojahn, 1900-18 © 1989 Denver Quarterly
Cambrian Night © 1989 Poetry Northwest
Above the Tree Line © 1989 Shenandoah
Apologues of Winter Light © 1989 Poetry
For Anna Mae Aquash . . . © 1990 Joy Harjo. Reprinted from *Nimrod* and *In Mad Love and War* (University Press of New England), by permission.
Because © 1989 Teal Press
Miller Canyon Trail No. 106 © 1989 Carolina Quarterly
On The Life and Death of Stan Laurel's Son © 1989 Manoa
Rush Hour © 1989 Paris Review
Listening © 1989 Crazyhorse
At the IGA: Franklin, New Hampshire © 1989 Ontario Review
A Letter © 1989 Poetry
Zoe © 1989 Shenandoah
The David of Michelangelo © 1989 The Quarterly
Through and Through © 1989 Oxford Magazine
Astronauts © 1989 The Missouri Review

This book is for Harvey Shapiro

INTRODUCTION

by Russell Banks

HE MIGHT HAVE called it "the best of the literary magazines," and suggested elitism and the ivory tower; or "the best of the 'little' magazines", signifying cute, funky inadequacy; or maybe "the best from the alternative presses" or "non-commercial presses", implying a charitably maintained ghetto illuminated by a thousand points of literary light. But he didn't, and I'm glad. It's apt that, instead, Bill Henderson has persisted in calling this annual compendium, this huge and diverse gathering of the tribe, the "best of the small presses." And it's useful that he doesn't take care to distinguish neatly between the small, not-for-profit publishers of books and the so-called "little" magazines, as the IRS, National Endowment for the Arts, and Council of Literary Magazines and Presses are forced to do. For a long time (can this *really* have been going on for 15 years?), from the start, actually, Henderson has stuck with that one lumpy, somewhat vague term, "small presses", to cover the territory.

And it does cover the territory. When publishers are *presses*— not multi-national conglomerates, not family-owned media-empires, not magazines using words in narrow columns to sell four-color ad inserts, not even "periodicals", for that matter (which would oblige them, after all, to come out regularly and on time, and you know where that leads)—and also manage at the same time to stay *small*, then it's safe to assume that their commitment is to literature, not profit. Small presses, whatever they publish, books, chapbooks or journals, fiction, poems or essays, want only to find the stuff—literature (wherever and whatever it happens to be in our time and place)—and then print and distribute it.

11

And the word "small" is not really a diminutive here; it merely suggests one man or woman or family of collaborators; it points to solitude, independence, single-mindedness, a "lost colony of the saved," to use a Robert Bly phrase; it suggests someone with a *press*, by God, and a need to get the word out. So that, if you're interested in our literature and don't particularly care about tracking the New Thing as defined by *New York* magazine and *Vanity Fair* or even for that matter by Rust Hills' annual mid-summer roundup at the *Esquire* corral, then the "best of the small presses" ought to mean something.

And it does. When it comes to contemporary American litera-ture, this is where the action is. Understood correctly, under-stood Bill Henderson's way, it's our *samizdat*. I don't think I'm romanticizing the small press scene in claiming that; I'm fully aware that the large commercial publishers and magazines pub-lish more than docu-dramas, cat books and self-help guides (how could they avoid it?), just as I know about the *drek*, the merely competent and the self-indulgently incompetent, the reams of narcissistic self-expression that thrive in the pages of many small press magazines and books. I assume that a lot of crap has been published in the Soviet Union's *samizdat*, too; why not ours?

This doesn't for a minute take away from the importance of the small presses' adversarial relation to the *official* press, which in our society, all denials to the contrary, seems to be motivated by a love not of literature but of profit. I don't care what they say, those large commercial publishers and the so-called slicks, about their love of literature and the life of the mind. I know why they're in business and what they love, and so do you. Profit. Dividends. Increase. Is Rupert Murdoch interested in contemporary Ameri-can literature? Does Paramount Entertainment care about the in-tegrity of the language? Does S. I. Newhouse think Pantheon's list is crucial to our intellectual life? Or that our intellectual life is crucial to the culture? Of course not. In the 1980's and -90's there is essentially no difference between most of the large commercial publishers in this country and the three major TV networks, ex-cept that the publishers claim to have a love of literature, which to my mind only makes them the more invidious.

Now more than any time since back when I first started pub-lishing my own stories and poems in the small presses of the 1960's, there is need of a feisty, self-confident, pluralistic *samiz-*

dat. The official press is growing more official every year, and more monolithic. So that if you want to watch the trends in large scale publishing these days, you have to look in the financial pages of *The New York Times,* where my own publisher, William Shinker of Harper/Collins, recently lamented, "There is a dearth of people with a feel for books and a solid financial sense . . . People used to feel publishing was about a kind of mysterious alchemy, and we'd like to move away from that." The mega-agent Morton Janklow agrees: "Publishing is a badly managed cottage industry that now needs more Harvard M.B.A.'s."

I've got nothing against Harvard M.B.A.'s, you understand, but their under-representation in publishing is hardly the reason publishers are not making as much money as their stockholders and directors would like, any more than Medicaid is responsible for the federal budget deficit. Surely, it's no coincidence that half of all the M.B.A.'s ever awarded were made between 1980 and 1989, a decade with an average of 12 corporate mergers a *day,* with the result that by 1989, 71 per cent of the earnings of US companies went to interest payments on borrowed money. Consequently, in 1990, just as every US citizen has to bear part of the burden for the national debt, every writer has to bear some of the burden for the publishers' corporate debt. Even the late Sam Beckett at Grove Weidenfeld; even Thomas Berger at Pantheon.

The real problem in commercial publishing, from the literary writer's point of view, is the cash flow problem, caused by the mergers and take-overs of the last decade. The solutions to that problem, the quick-fixes, are like the federal buy-out (or payoff) of the Savings and Loan institutions. Ann Getty and Lord Weidenfeld may have managed to destroy Grove Press as a serious publisher in five years, but in the process they tried to turn their $2 million purchase price into a $10 million dollar sellout; Viking Penguin may have effectively dismantled Dutton, but they're no longer losing money there; and Random House's Reaganization of Pantheon, a $20 million dollar division in an $800 million dollar operation, will probably accomplish the same thing for S. I. Newhouse. A few more M.B.A.'s and a more widespread application of value-neutral bottom-line accounting, a few more multi-million dollar advances for a Sure Thing guaranteed to generate quick cash for interest payments, and publishing will no longer have to lose sleep over that "mysterious alchemy" and the "mis-managed cottage industry" that here and there validated the industry's claim to any useful connection to the creation of a literature.

This is not merely a collective abdication of responsibility; it's censorship as well. Speaking of Random House's blitz of Pantheon, E. L. Doctorow in his acceptance of this year's National Book Critics Circle award (as reported in *The Times'* financial section, naturally, in Roger Cohen's "Media Business" column) said, "Even if no censorship was intended by its application of its own bottom-line criteria to its Pantheon division, the effect is indeed to still a voice. To close a door against part of the American family."

We're seeing a lot of doors closed against parts of the American family these days. Sometimes in the name of the American family itself.

Directors of university presses like Wesleyan, Princeton, and Alabama make a long face, wring their hands, cite last year's losses (Wesleyan University's subsidy for its press last year was the same as its water bill, incidentally), and announce cut-backs and cancellation of their poetry series—as if the only responsibilities they bore toward the culture were the ones that could turn a profit, like men's basketball.

And when writers and the small presses, to avoid precisely this kind of censorship—which is to say, to survive as artists somehow, without being forced to apply that bottom-line criteria—turn to the NEA for financial help, they're met with yet another censor, the senior Senator from North Carolina and a supine Congress. Last year we all watched with dismay as Jesse Helms stamped his little feet over a couple of photography exhibits and got Congress to wake from its snooze long enough to punish the offending museums and restrict the grants-giving procedures of the NEA. Never again will the Senator and his Missus be offended if they happen to walk into the Corcoran after church one Sunday or receive in the mail a copy of a magazine funded by an NEA grant. Ed Sanders' *Fuck You: A Magazine of the Arts*, one of the highlights of small press publishing in the 1960's, would be stopped at the door today. (Or more likely at the gate, given the alacrity with which the director of the literary programs, Stephen Goodwin, sent up for special review the work of five writers whose work *might* have violated the guidelines.)

That's how far we've come in these two decades. It's the law now. Thanks to the Helms Amendment, all NEA grant applicants are obliged to promise not to be guilty of "depictions of sadomasochism, homoeroticism, the sexual exploitation of children or individuals engaged in sex acts and which, when taken as a whole, do not have serious literary, artistic, political or scientific merit." I don't know how many of you could sign that pledge in good faith, but I couldn't. (Actually, it's gotten so that I'd be worried if, regardless of what kind of sex act I depicted, Senator Helms and his appointees thought my work *had* merit.) Certainly, I could lie, take the money, and write or print whatever the hell I felt like, but as Richard Nixon said, that would be *wrong*, wouldn't it? Which is precisely the sort of cynicism that writers and small presses are expected to eschew. If you're going to be poor, you might as well be honest.

Increasingly, then, if we want to know what's worth reading of contemporary American letters, we must look to our small presses, our home-grown *samizdat*. These are the poems, stories, and essays that have been shut out by the official press—shut out by economics, by timidity, and by legislation.

It suddenly occurs to me that when I began this introduction I had no intention of making it a jeremiad. Besides, it's a beautiful spring day here in Princeton, New Jersey, where I'm writing— temperature in the 70's for the first time in five months, blue sky, soft breeze—and there's no large reason why I should grouse on about what happens in the world of big publishing, university presses, and the cloakrooms of Congress, when I could simply be singing the praises of the small presses. They are, after all, one of the few things in our literary culture that we can point to with genuine pride. For nearly a century, from the heydays of Harriet Monroe's *Poetry*, Martha Foley's and Whit Burnett's *Story*, and John Crowe Ransom's *Kenyon Review*, to the current season, with magazines like *Holy Cow!*, *Sulfur*, and *Witness*, the small presses have been responsible for finding and printing the best of our literature, the news that has stayed news.

And here, in the *Best of the Small Presses*, you will read this year's version, and you will find what, to my mind, is best about American writing today—pluralism without tokenism, controversy without containment, quality without chic. You will find little of this in the official press. That Bill Henderson and his co-

conspirators have been able to bring out this anthology annually for 15 years is a tribute, not only to their tirelessness and dedication, but to the abiding presence of an audience as well. I don't know the figures, but I would guess that it's the best *read* annual that is published—read and not merely sold and collected on a shelf. *Pushcart* readers are an opinionated, discriminating, and contentious lot; they're no easy victims of hype and rep and hullabaloo, no pushovers for the New Thing or the Big Thing or even for the Old Thing. Moreover, this is the anthology that the writers read, especially the young writers—perhaps because it's the only anthology whose contents have been selected by writers themselves, with Henderson and his staff editors, of course, making the final selection. Thus it's always a special privilege and a peculiar pleasure to have a story, poem or essay chosen for inclusion here: you know that it has been culled by your peers, your fellow tillers-in-the-field, and that now it's going to get read in a way that will test its mettle.

I speak as a writer who has been lucky enough to have been included here in the past, and thus will understand and forgive if you have skipped this introduction altogether (as I would have) and gone straight to the works themselves. If you haven't, please read on.

THE
PEOPLE WHO HELPED

FOUNDING EDITORS—*Anaïs Nin (1903–1977), Buckminster Fuller (1895–1983), Charles Newman, Daniel Halpern, Gordon Lish, Harry Smith, Hugh Fox, Ishmael Reed, Joyce Carol Oates, Len Fulton, Leonard Randolph, Leslie Fiedler, Nona Balakian, Paul Bowles, Paul Engle, Ralph Ellison, Reynolds Price, Rhoda Schwartz, Richard Morris, Ted Wilentz, Tom Montag, William Phillips, Poetry editor: H. L. Van Brunt.*

EDITORS—*Walter Abish, Ai, Elliott Anderson, John Ashbery, Russell Banks, Joe David Bellamy, Robert Bly, Philip Booth, Robert Boyers, Harold Brodkey, Joseph Brodsky, Wesley Brown, Hayden Carruth, Frank Conroy, Paula Deitz, Steve Dixon, Rita Dove, Andre Dubus, M. D. Elevitch, Louise Erdrich, Loris Essary, Ellen Ferber, Carolyn Forché, Stuart Freibert, Jon Galassi, Tess Gallagher, Louis Gallo, George Garrett, Reginald Gibbons, Jack Gilbert, Louise Glück, David Godine, Jorie Graham, Linda Gregg, Barbara Grossman, Donald Hall, Helen Handley, Michael Harper, Robert Hass, DeWitt Henry, J. R. Humphreys, David Ignatow, John Irving, June Jordan, Edmund Keeley, Karen Kennerly, Galway Kinnell, Carolyn Kizer, Jerzy Kosinski, Richard Kostelanetz, Seymour Krim, Maxine Kumin, James Laughlin, Seymour Lawrence, Naomi Lazard, Herb Leibowitz, Denise Levertov, Philip Levine, Stanley Lindberg, Thomas Lux, Mary MacArthur, Thomas McGrath, Jay Meek, Daniel Menaker, Frederick Morgan, Cynthia Ozick, Jayne Anne Phillips, Robert Phillips, George Plimpton, Stanley Plumly, Eugene Redmond, Ed Sanders, Teo Sa-*

vory, Grace Schulman, Harvey Shapiro, Leslie Silko, Charles Simic, Dave Smith, Elizabeth Spencer, William Stafford, Gerald Stern, David St. John, Bill and Pat Strachan, Ron Sukenick, Anne Tyler, John Updike, Sam Vaughan, David Wagoner, Derek Walcott, Ellen Wilbur, David Wilk, David Wojahn, Bill Zavatsky.

CONTRIBUTING EDITORS—Sandra Alcosser, John Allman, Philip Appleman, Jennifer Atkinson, Jimmy Santiago Baca, Jim Barnes, Rick Bass, Charles Baxter, Joe David Bellamy, Linda Bierds, Philip Booth, Marianne Boruch, Rosellen Brown, Michael Dennis Browne, Christopher Buckley, Richard Burgin, Michael Burkard, Kathy Callaway, Hayden Carruth, Kelly Cherry, Naomi Clark, Andrei Codrescu, Peter Cooley, Stephen Corey, Philip Dacey, John Daniel, Lydia Davis, Susan Strayer Deal, Carl Dennis, Laurie Duesing, Mark Doty, Rita Dove, John Drury, Stuart Dybek, Barbara Einzig, M. D. Elevitch, Carol Emshwiller, Jane Flanders, H. E. Francis, Stuart Freibert, Kenneth Gangemi, Reginald Gibbons, Gary Gildner, Barry Goldensohn, Pat Gray, Marilyn Hacker, Sam Hamill, Ehud Havazelet, Patricia Henley, DeWitt Henry, Brenda Hillman, Edward Hirsch, Jane Hirshfield, Edward Hoagland, Andrew Hudgins, Lynda Hull, Sandy Huss, Colette Inez, Richard Jackson, Mark Jarman, David Jauss, Laura Jensen, Julia Just, David Kelly, Carolyn Kizer, Yusef Komunyakaa, Dorianne Laux, Li-Young Lee, Gerry Locklin, Melissa Lentricchia, Denise Levertov, Stanley W. Lindberg, D. R. MacDonald, David Madden, Michael Martone, Dan Masterson, Cleopatra Mathis, Robert McBrearty, Lynne McFall, Jean McGarry, Kristina McGrath, Heather McHugh, Wesley McNair, Sandra McPherson, Judson Mitcham, Susan Mitchell, Jim Moore, Lisel Mueller, Joan Murray, Fae Myenne Ng, Sigrid Nunez, Sharon Olds, Greg Pape, Jonathan Penner, Mary Peterson, Robert Pinsky, Robert Pope, Joe Ashby Porter, C. E. Poverman, Francine Prose, Tony Quagliano, Bin Ramke, Donald Revell, Alberto Rios, William Pitt Root, Vern Rutsala, Michael Ryan, Sherod Santos, Lloyd Schwartz, Sheila Schwartz, Jim Simmerman, Arthur Smith, Chris Spain, David St. John, Maura Stanton, Pamela Stewart, Joan Swift, Ron Tanner, Peter Tysver, Lee Upton, Sara Vogan, Marilyn Waniek, Michael Waters, Gordon Weaver, Bruce Weigl, Susan Welch, Harold Witt, Christina Zawadiwsky.

ROVING EDITOR—*Lily Frances*

EUROPEAN EDITORS—*Kirby and Liz Williams*

MANAGING EDITOR—*Hannah Turner*

FICTION EDITORS—*Bill Henderson with Genie Chipps, Mary Kornblum, and Sally Wilson*

POETRY EDITORS—*William Heyen, Elizabeth Spires*

ESSAYS EDITOR—*Anthony Brandt*

EDITOR AND PUBLISHER—*Bill Henderson*

CONTENTS

THE
PUSHCART PRIZE, XV:
BEST OF THE
SMALL PRESSES

THE DAY I MET BUDDY HOLLY

fiction by KIM HERZINGER

from BOULEVARD

I MUST HAVE been about twelve, living in Eugene, Oregon and somehow I was by myself down at the train station. I don't know how that could have been, but I was down there anyway, and I saw this guy. He looked familiar to me, not familiar like someone I'd seen around town, but familiar in another way—a famous way. He had famous written all over him. He was just standing there, next to the tracks, smoking a cigarette and looking for the train. Once in a while he'd put his foot on his bag—he only had the one bag—and then take a deep drag on his cigarette and look down the tracks real seriously. I sat on a mail cart to consider him. He had the famous glasses on, black and thick—too black for an ordinary guy even in 1958—and he was wearing a kind of bluish checkered shirt that was open at the collar. His pants, I remember, were rumpled, as if he'd spent an awful long time sitting in the station, or if he'd slept in them even. Then he glanced over at me and gave himself away. It was the glance that tipped me off, just a flash of the eyes and something he did with his lips—he was through with his cigarette at that particular moment—and I could tell from that that he was Buddy Holly, the real Buddy Holly right there on the station platform waiting to catch a train. I don't know if you remember what Buddy Holly looked like, when he was singing his songs with The Crickets, but if you'd seen the way he glanced and what he did with his

27

lips you would have recognized him. And now everything made sense. His shirt was expensive, I could see now, but made to *look* inexpensive, like an ordinary guy's shirt except that it wasn't really. And his pants were the kind that gave him a lot of room to move around inside them, the kind that got rumpled because he was on the road and there wasn't anybody to iron them who wouldn't have paid too much attention to him and called up the newspaper and everything. It was pretty clear that Buddy wanted to be alone there—I looked around to see if I could see any Crickets but there wasn't anybody who looked like he could have been one—and the reason he was standing and looking so hard down the tracks was because he was composing something. Right there, on the station platform, composing a song that would maybe have this twelve-year-old kid in it, sitting on an empty mail cart, staring out toward the tracks. It's the kind of thing Buddy Holly would write about if he saw the right kid.

I sat for a long time trying to decide whether I should go up to him and tell him that I knew who he was and that I liked his music, and that I hoped he'd keep singing with The Crickets. I sat there trying to decide whether I should do that, and wishing that my friend Charles Kreitz was there, because he would do it if I didn't, and just wishing that somebody I knew was there so I could tell them about what I was seeing so I could feel famous for a minute. And then I thought maybe Buddy was unhappy because nobody had recognized him, that he had gone out among the people like a king to hear what they had to say about him, and nobody had said anything at all.

When I was ten a friend of the family had been involved in getting famous people to star at the rodeo; he was in charge of the Kiwanis Buckaroo Breakfast and Chuckwagon Dinner, where the star would sit up at the head table and sign autographs after the meal and, if he sang, sing. Lee Aaker, who played Rusty on "Rin Tin Tin," came to town when I was ten. He wasn't much older than I was and I couldn't understand why he got to be on that show and I didn't. Then I heard that he played shortstop for a Little League team in Hollywood. Now I was a pretty fair little ballplayer then, better than almost any of the kids my age—though I didn't have any power to speak of—and there wasn't any question in my mind that I was a better ballplayer than Lee Aaker, who just looked like a haughty little fat kid in a Fort Apache cavalry suit eating pancakes up on the stage at the Buckaroo Breakfast. So after he was through I went up there to talk to him. I was mad at him. I said, "So, you play baseball. Well, we got a pitcher could strike you out. Three pitches." And I held up my fingers to show him just exactly how many pitches it would take.

He just looked at me like I was nothing.

That was the last time that I'd talked to anyone famous, and I'd blown my chance. So you can see how I would be pretty nervous going up to Buddy Holly.

Now Buddy was beginning to look a little nervous, too. He was beginning to pace up and down the platform. I was worried because I imagined my chance to talk to him was going. When they get agitated, famous people don't want to have much to do with anybody who is not famous. I'd learned that from Lee Aaker, and you could see it on television any day of the week. But while he was pacing up and down I got a good look at Buddy Holly's shoes. They were wing-tips, but not like my father's wing-tips, which looked blocky and oversized, like orthopedic shoes. Everybody he knew wore those same shoes, walking around as if they lived in a town where everybody had foot problems, clumping around in shoes I said I'd never wear, ever. Buddy Holly's shoes weren't like that though. They were sleeker, and the tip seemed to shark out of the front of them like it had real wings on it, and the design was low on the sides and tense, sort of stretched out, like the orange flames on Charles Kreitz's brother's '55 Chevy. They were custom-made shoes, that was pretty clear. You couldn't go down to Kinney's and buy a pair of those. Even the soles were different—thinner, barely even there. Buddy Holly didn't look like he was walking on iron bars the way my father and all of his friends and business associates looked like.

Anyway, I thought I'd better do something, and quick. What I thought I'd do was to sort of saunter up near to where Buddy was pacing and wait for him to drop something, or hesitate, or maybe say something to me. If I said something first it would have to be *knowing*, like I knew who he was and that I liked him and The Crickets, that I wasn't one of those Christians who hated him and his music and thought he was a bad influence on youth, that I wasn't going to give him away, and that I could take talking

29

to him even if he was famous. All of this had to be done in a stroke. I didn't know how I would do all that, but I made my way over toward where he was anyway. Buddy Holly saw me coming, he looked right at me, took a deep drag on another cigarette—sort of sized me up in a glance—then looked down the tracks again. I looked at the tracks for awhile myself. I don't know what Buddy must have been thinking, seeing a little kid standing on the platform like that, looking down the tracks for the train as if he was going to be getting on any minute, but he didn't show any surprise or anything. Then I could see that Buddy was looking at a big old house on the side of Skinner's Butte, a sort of hill that stuck up right at the end of town and overlooked the train station, a place where teenagers would drive their cars up to the top of and make out, listening to his music.

The house was the pride of that butte. It was huge, bigger than it should have been, it had gables and towers, and no one seemed to know who lived in it. It was a great place for Halloween. Charles Kreitz told me once that he'd tried to rouse somebody in there on Halloween night, but no one ever even answered the door. He thought that the people who lived there had probably made sure that the police were watching it so kids couldn't come around and cause mischief. Buddy was looking at this house when what to say came to me.

"That's the Kreitz house," I said. "I know them."

Buddy smiled, but kept his eyes steady on the house.

"It's pretty old," I said.

Then Buddy Holly said, "How old is it?"

Now this is what bothers me. I'd just made up the people who lived in the house, but I couldn't think of a thing when he asked me how old it was. I suppose I could have said anything, 30 or 50 or 100 years old, anything—I doubt if Buddy Holly knew enough about houses to think I might be lying to him—but his question about how old it was stymied me.

After a long time, with Buddy and me both looking at the house as if it would get up off its foundation any minute and tell us how old it was, I said, "I don't know. It's old enough. I know that."

He said, "I've been through Eugene quite a few times, you know, but I've never noticed that house before."

Now I hadn't known that Buddy Holly had been in Eugene before, and I thought maybe he had performed over at the College and I just hadn't heard about it because I was too young then or something, or maybe he had been through town a lot before he had gotten famous. Being in Eugene didn't seem strange to me. I had lived there all my life. It seemed strange to think, though, that Buddy had been there a lot and I was evidently the only one who knew about it.

The sun was shining down onto the top of Buddy's head; like most of the rock and roll stars Buddy had sort of short hair, with just a tiny curl coming down in the front. I had to squint to see him.

"Well, usually the trains are here on time," I said.

He lit a cigarette. "Not today."

"No. Not today. There might be something wrong. Maybe a log problem or something. Sometimes we get a log problem in town because of all the lumber companies. There's a lot of them around here. You've probably smelled some of them. Maybe some logs have fallen off and hurt the tracks. That's lumber for you."

Buddy Holly shook his head. "Do they like living there? I'll bet it's kind of noisy."

Buddy was asking about the Kreitzes. It flustered me.

"I don't think it's too bad up there really," I said, and then I said, "You're Buddy Holly aren't you?" I was surprised at myself, and I thought for a minute that Buddy was going to turn and walk away from me. But he didn't, he took it in stride.

"I wish," he said finally. "My name's Tom Truehaft. I'm from Lake Oswego. I'm a barber."

I looked at his shoes. They were not the shoes of a barber. No barber would have ever known that they had shoes like that. I gave Buddy Holly a knowing smile.

"I think those shoes are pretty keen," I said. "Not like my dad's."

When I was seventeen I took a girl to a school dance who had the reputation of being impure. Her name was Tanya Vincent and she came from this crummy little town outside of Eugene called Coburg. We thought all the girls from there lived on farms; anyway, they all looked a little smudgy, like they didn't have much to

31

do and spent a lot of time out in the furrows reading magazines or something. My friend Scott Webber, whose father was a doctor and was rich, had had a date with Tanya earlier in the school year. It ended with Tanya running through their big ranch-style house in her panties, which were kind of rubbed-looking and gray, but still satiny, he told me. The picture of Tanya running around Scott Webber's living room in her panties was banging around in my mind when I told her about the time I met Buddy Holly at the train station. When I told her about it I changed the station from Eugene to Portland, after deciding against San Francisco at the last minute. I didn't think she'd think to ask me why I was waiting around alone at the Portland train station, and she didn't. Buddy was dead by then, of course. He'd died with the other two in that plane crash in Iowa. She said she liked Buddy Holly and that he reminded her a little of Roy Orbison. She didn't remember too much about him, she said, but her older brother—who was now a mechanic in Coburg and a guy I thought might be a major obstacle when I took Tanya back home after the dance—used to play his music a lot. I was trying to raise the stakes with Tanya. I was pretty popular in high school and played varsity basketball and baseball and she should have been happier about being out with me than she seemed to be. I thought maybe she had gotten a little jaded after her date with Scott Webber. So it made me mad to think that what she remembered of Buddy Holly was being strained through her hayseed brother, probably out in the family barn working on getting a tractor going. Somehow, her memory of Buddy Holly seemed to reflect on *me*.

So I told her that he'd given me his shoes. I didn't think that she'd ask me if Buddy Holly ended up just getting on the train in his socks, and she didn't. I told her that I had had the shoes until last year, and that I only showed them to my very best friends, and that I would have liked to let her see them, but that my mother had thrown them out when she had invaded my closet one day and thrown out a lot of stuff from my childhood days. I talked as if it didn't bother me so much except that now I couldn't show her that pair of Buddy Holly's wing-tips.

The dance ended with Bobby Vinton singing "Mr. Lonely" twice in a row. By then I thought Tanya Vincent was pretty much going my way, except that she said it was too late for her to go up to Skinner's Butte with me, and when I took her back to her house in the country it turned out to be low-slung, with that white gravel on the roof, and more modern than mine. Her older brother wasn't there, but everybody else in her family was. After she introduced me she told her mother that I had met Buddy Holly when I was twelve and that he had given me his shoes. Her mother thought that was nice of him and wondered what he had worn on the train.

That next summer, after I had started seeing Tanya regularly, she climbed up onto my roof in the middle of the night and knocked on my upstairs bedroom window and woke me up. She wanted to come in. She was squatting down on the slope of our roof and twisting around on her haunches. She looked excited, as if she was going to start giggling real loud any minute. The whole thing scared hell out of me, because there wasn't any carpeting on my bedroom floor and you could hear everything downstairs even if you walked on tiptoe. Mostly it was embarrassing; I had on my green pajamas with the beige piping and I was too scared to act like this kind of thing happened to me all the time. She spent about a half an hour in my bedroom, whispering the story of how she had been riding around with her Coburg girlfriends, how she had told them what she was going to do, how she had them drop her off at my corner, and that they were going to drive around the neighborhood until she came back down. Thinking of my mother, who was a light sleeper and who got up a lot in the middle of the night to wash or something, I told Tanya that the police patrolled the neighborhood all the time, and her friends' car would be suspicious. She said she didn't want her friends to get in any trouble and we went into a long kiss.

As she was climbing out the window, she said, "Could I see those shoes you got from Buddy Holly?" It really made mad. My parents were just downstairs, probably waking up now and rubbing their eyes and wondering why I was up so late, probably wondering if I was sick and Tanya Vincent was stuck halfway out my window asking if she could see some shoes that I had told her my mother threw away a long time ago. It really did make me mad.

Now what I told Tanya Vincent about the shoes was, naturally, not really what happened when I met Buddy Holly. I took in his information about being a barber from Lake Oswego and considered it for about a minute. Even though I had been flustered, I thought that I had asked him if he was Buddy Holly in a pretty casual way, casual enough not to make him think that I was going straight to a phone and call up the paper. But there wasn't any other reason why he would have told me his name was Tom Truehaft.

So I said, "Well, you really look like Buddy Holly. A *lot* like him."

"I wish I had his money," said Buddy. Then he sort of twisted around in his pants a little bit and looked down the tracks, flipping his cigarette onto the rails.

"Do you want me to check it out and see when the train will be coming in? I can find out inside." Buddy said thanks and I went in to find out. The train station in Eugene was one of the old kind, all wood and with the name of the town hung out in the middle of it. It wasn't orderly, but it made sense. When you were in there you knew exactly what you were supposed to do. A big chalkboard said that the train was supposed to be in at 12:17 and nothing said it was going to be late, although now it was 12:45. Nobody seemed surprised about it and nobody in the waiting room looked like he might have been a Cricket. The man behind the ticket counter wore suspenders and had a red face.

"What time is the train coming in?" I asked him. "Buddy Holly's out there and I'm checking for him."

The man smiled and told me it would be there in an hour or so.

That's what I told Buddy Holly when I came out. He told me thanks and said he was going to go over to the restaurant right next to the station and get some coffee and a paper.

It's true that when I told Tanya Vincent about the time I met Buddy I lied about getting those wing-tips. I suppose I thought that Tanya was a mouth-breather, and that I could put the shoes in the story and she'd believe me. And, of course, that's what she did. Later on, though, Charles Kreitz started taking her out—this was after I'd told him about how Tanya had climbed up onto my roof—and he wondered why I'd never shown him those shoes.

"I'm a good enough friend of yours, aren't I? I'm a good enough friend to have had a chance to see your own personal pair of Buddy Holly shoes." Charles thought Tanya was a little dim, too, but he said it didn't matter much to him. "Maybe your mother remembers about them," he said. "Maybe she never even threw them away, since they must have meant so much to you. Maybe they're still in the house somewhere. Maybe your mother is saving them for a special occasion."

I told Charles that I didn't think my mother even knew what they were.

"Seems like she would have," said Charles. "Seems like *I* would have. At least that's how it seems to me. You know what I mean?" I knew what Charles meant, all right, but it was too late to come clean about the shoes.

Charles always said that he really didn't care anything at all about Tanya Vincent, but when she dropped him for a guy named Mike, who lived out on some farm near where she lived, he came out against girls altogether for a while. Charles turned philosophical for a time about this, and he'd corner you and want to have long talks about women. He had never been dumped by a girl before and the experience had brought out a new side of Charles.

"What women want," I remember he told me, "is for guys to want to make out with them. They don't really want to make out, you understand—except sometimes, you know, when they do it just to keep up the image. No. They just want to make sure that you *want* to. We're talking barely human here. It's like when we drive down the gut on the weekend and see all these damn girls in their cars. *We* think they're down there for the same reason we're down there. *We* think they're down there *looking* for something. They get in their damn cars, and then stare straight ahead like they've got pretty important things to do just ahead of them—you know, as if they've got *big doings* waiting for them just down the street. And if they're not doing that they'll be putting on some of those damn toiletries they've got. They flash out these compacts, and they've got cotton balls all over the interior, and then they sort of apply this stuff with the most intense kind of concentration, as if this one last *dab* is the thing that's going to do it, you know, like this is the last little *touch* that's the only thing they need to make the sugar plums dance."

Charles was bitter because I'd been telling him that I thought that one of Buddy Holly's songs had it pretty close about women. I was thinking of when Buddy sang about "the dreams and wishes you wish in the night when lights are low." Charles was in no mood for this sort of thing, and said that he thought all the songs were stupid, although probably "Do You Love Me?" by The Contours had some truth to it.

"So we always roll our windows down, like fools, and make some kind of noise about how would they like to go somewhere with us or what high school do you go to or say something from a song. Then what do they do? They stare straight ahead of themselves and intensify their dabbing. And then they act like we've got hair growing out of our palms. A visible *pall* falls over their car. A goddamn *visible pall*. Then the light changes and they gun their car down to the next light, giggling like hell. Animals."

I told Charles that for women to stick with you that even money wasn't enough, that you probably had to be famous. I told him that I knew this from the day I'd met Buddy Holly.

"Or maybe being real good-looking," he said.

"Yes. Good-looking, too," I said.

"Only my mother loves me now," he said.

I had sat down on the mail cart for awhile and then I went over to the restaurant where Buddy had gone to wait for the train. It was just a little place called Thurber's with a counter and a few booths. The outside of it had some kind of covering that was supposed to look like red and black bricks. It had greasy menus and a little jukebox thing installed in every booth so people could play music without having to get up. When I visited Eugene again in the seventies I noticed that it had been taken over by some hippies. The sign was hand-lettered and so were the menus and the town sanitation board had given it a B rating—not very good. They had renamed it the Eugene Creamery. Later the hippies left and the place became part of a restoration project that swept the train station end of town. This was at the same time that the Smeed Hotel, which was just across the street, got turned into a toy store, a kite shop, and a place that sold Birkenstock shoes. During this time the restaurant was called The Buttery, and it always looked like it was just about to be open for business, but it never was. The last time I was there I saw it again, and it looked almost like it had when Buddy Holly sat there at the counter and had his coffee and read the paper. The individual jukeboxes were gone, though.

I was keeping an eye on Buddy from outside the restaurant when another kid I didn't know came up on his bike. Ordinarily I wouldn't have said anything, but this was too big a thing to keep to myself.

"Guess who's in the restaurant, at the counter," I said.

"Who?"

"Buddy Holly."

"*The* Buddy Holly?"

I nodded.

"Which one?" he asked.

"Right there, next to the pies, reading the paper. He's got a blue shirt on. I was talking with him earlier. He's waiting for the train."

The kid looked in through the window.

"Are you sure that's Buddy Holly?" he said. "It doesn't look like him."

"I asked him," I said.

The kid cupped his hands right up against the glass of the door and looked at Buddy. After a while he went for his bike. "I'm going to tell my friend, Darrell. He'd know. His sister's got all of Buddy Holly's records. She thinks he's cherry."

"I *asked* him," I said.

"I'm going to go get Darrell," he said.

While the kid went to go get Darrell, Buddy Holly ordered a piece of the Dutch Apple pie they had and I told some people going into Thurber's that they had Buddy Holly in there, eating a piece of the pie and drinking some of their coffee. The word started getting around outside, and then inside too. A few other kids joined me, and we took turns putting our faces up against the door window and watching him eat and drink. Somebody put on one of Buddy's songs from a booth, and everybody started tapping their feet and looking longingly over toward his direction. The people at the counter tried not to look at him at all, but most of them did it anyway, peeping over their newspapers or pretending to stare at the wall behind him where all the whole pies were stacked up in a refrigerator. Between the times she was refilling Buddy's coffee, the waitress would stand next to another waitress, and they would giggle and talk with their hands covering their mouths and then laugh hard and bump their hips together. Once, the waitress spoke in what looked like low tones to Buddy and pointed out somebody in a booth. Buddy turned around slightly and nodded and smiled when the man in the booth gave him a salute.

About the time the friend of Darrell's got back with some other kids on bikes, Buddy got up from his spot at the counter, paid the waitress, and came out. By now there were a lot of us outside of Thurber's and at first we all just stood back, gave him plenty of room, and watched him while he started to walk toward the station. He was tapping his newspaper against his leg and smiling. Since I had a special connection with Buddy Holly, I moved up next to him as he went toward the tracks.

"Thanks, buddy," he said, just before we got there. "This is great."

When Buddy got back to the platform, he lit another cigarette. I sat down on the mail cart again. By now all the kids had walked their bikes up to the edge of the platform, and people from the restaurant had trailed up behind them just to get one last look at Buddy before he got on the train. Some of them had bought coffee to go in cardboard cups, and drank it and talked and pointed with their elbows. A little wisp of a dust devil blew some bits of paper and cellophane and cut grass up and around, and it circulated through the crowd and the people stepped out of the way. It was as if they were all dancing. But they still kept their eyes glued on Buddy while he smoked his cigarette. Both of the waitresses stuck their heads out of the restaurant door, kind of stacked up like the pies, and Mr. Thurber stood out on his sidewalk and watched Buddy with his arms crossed and with a spatula in one hand.

This was all pretty amazing, of course, and not the kind of thing that you get to see very often. Fame up close rubs off on you, makes you feel that you're different and special just because you're *there*. I saw it again once when I was in Florence, Italy, on leave with some friends. One of my friends knew this girl from his hometown, and she was one of these girls who was so gorgeous it was like she was from another planet. She was a model for *Vogue* magazine and some other magazines, too, but she was in Florence cleaning art for the summer. She'd been on the covers of these magazines, but she was just as amazing in person. I felt that a girl like that must have feelings that were especially acute in order to go along with her looks, so everything I said to her sounded dumb.

Now this girl wasn't really famous. I mean probably nobody in Italy actually knew her name. But she was spectacular, so she didn't need to be famous, too. She must have felt famous just for being around herself. She had a favorite restaurant on a back street across the river and so the four of us—she was in the lead because she knew where she was going and she knew the Italian language—went on a long walk down there. So here I am, walking along beside this woman who's pretty obviously not from the world as we know it, looking as if the space has been cut out from around her, and I start seeing these Italian men begin to gather around doorways and windows, watching us as we come down the street. They start holding their heads and pretending to weep, they slap their foreheads and run inside and call for their friends to come out on the street. Some whistle and lay their heads straight back and howl. Men stick their heads out of bars and restaurants, still wiping away some sauce from their mouths. One guy reaches out from a window as if to shake my hand when I pass by him and says "Bravo, signor, bravo." He says this with his eyes big and a huge grin, like he's in awe. By now a pretty decent crowd is trailing along behind us, laughing and smacking each other and singing, holding wine bottles up to the great appreciation of all the people hanging out of windows and lounging outside of doors up and down the street. They take turns running up alongside of us, grabbing our elbows and jacking themselves down on their knees, giving out pleading sounds in Italian and clasping their hands and shaking them like they're praying. A few throw themselves in front of her and scuff along the street backwards on their knees. Some of them still have their dinner napkins tucked into their collars. They offer her flowers or wine or whatever they can find. One talks like mad and keeps pointing at an entire fruit and flower stand, wiping fake tears away from his eyes the whole time. And this lovely girl we're with walks on straight ahead, doesn't miss a beat; she just nods slightly and smiles at everybody as they howl and sing and whee like sirens.

It was pretty amazing. We ate and drank everything after we got to the restaurant. I told them about the time when I was twelve and Buddy Holly gave me a pair of his shoes. We made so much noise at our table that even the Italian waiters got a little nervous about us.

Just before the train came into view a sort of hush came over the station. Now I've been to a few train stations since and this is something that always happens. Nobody can see anything yet, and the train isn't blowing its whistle, but the ticket takers swivel around in their chairs, the porters start putting bags on carts, and people standing around begin to kiss each other or stand up straight and adjust their clothing. People begin to get out of cars and walk fast toward the platform. Maybe there's a deep hum in the rails or something. It's a special time. Buddy Holly flicked his cigarette onto the tracks, took a comb out of his back pocket and ran it through his hair.

When the train finally stopped at the station there were a lot of people around, more people than could possibly have been waiting for a train. I could tell from the way the porter said to get on board that he knew that he would be helping Buddy Holly, *the* Buddy Holly, onto his train. I moved up close to him again while he fixed his pants one last time. When he leaned down to pick up his bag, he put his hand on my shoulder. He shook his head slowly in a resigned kind of way, but he was still smiling. It was better than shoes.

"Son," he said, "son."

Then Buddy went inside and sat down.

I could see him from where I was on the mail cart. He looked outside at the platform but didn't seem to be focusing on anything in particular. Then he sort of nodded at all of us out on the platform, opened up the paper that he'd bought at the restaurant and started reading it. The train got going again after a little while and I watched it as it went up the tracks, toward Portland.

When the train was gone, everything seemed to relax, everybody went inside again. The house on the side of Skinner's Butte got a little smaller. The whole town let its breath go and settled back. Nothing had changed. Buddy Holly had been there, and now he was gone, and we were back to being what we'd always been.

Nominated by Boulevard

ON THE ZEEDIJK

by RICHARD WATSON

from THE GEORGIA REVIEW

IN LATE DECEMBER 1628, or early January 1629, René Descartes arrived in Franeker in Friesland. Just a few weeks earlier, he had had a private interview with Cardinal Bérulle, founder of the Oratorian teaching order in France, rival of the Jesuits, who was in the process of forming the Compagnie du Saint-Sacrement, a militant secret society of laymen to fight for the Catholic cause by eliminating Protestantism in France. The cardinal was a strange mixture of astute politician, courtier, and mystic. He talked familiarly with God, angels, and the Queen Mother every day. He had convinced the First Minister Richelieu to crush the last stronghold of Protestantism in France, La Rochelle, which fell in late October with Cardinal Bérulle marching triumphantly among the victors.

No one knows what Cardinal Bérulle, flushed with triumph, said to Descartes, but the result was that within weeks Descartes was about as far away from militant Catholicism as you could get in Europe in the seventeenth century, standing on the steps of a Protestant university founded in 1585 and known as a haven for persecuted Protestants from all over Europe. He did not return to France for sixteen years, well after Cardinal Bérulle was dead.

In Franeker—literally God's Acre—Descartes lived in a castle nearly as large as the Reformed church it faced down the wide main street. It was owned by the Sjerdemas, a prominent Catholic family. In this castle Descartes wrote the first draft of his famous *Meditations on First Philosophy* in which he bases certainty on the phrase "I think, therefore I am" and which earned him the title of The Father of Modern Philosophy. But in the winter of 1629, at the age of thirty-two, although he had a high reputation as a mathematician and philosopher, he had published nothing. He sat in his room, looking north out over the flat *polder* to the *zeedijk*, the low dike that held back the sea.

I sit now in an old fisherman's cottage under that zeedijk and look across the flat polder south toward Franeker just six miles away, visible only as points of orange light at night. I wonder why Descartes came here. I am writing a book titled *The Death of Descartes*. After it is finished I am going to write *The Birth of Descartes*. Yes, I know. But for most great men—perhaps for anybody—you have to understand their deaths before you can comprehend their births.

The Netherlands is a land of low relief but of infinite variation. When I was being shown around the grounds of Endegeest Castle near Leiden (a small but very elegant chateau that Descartes later rented for several years—servants, livery, and moat), my guide, Baron Schimmelpenninck, publisher of Martinus Nijhoff books, said, "See that large drop-off over there? We're on higher ground here. That's what protects the castle during floods."

I strained to see.

"There, at the line of trees."

Then I saw it. Eighteen inches. Actually, my guide said, it was slightly over three feet because it slanted down gently after the drop-off.

"You'll begin to see the differences after you've been here awhile," he said.

But I lived under the zeedijk for several months before I saw what someone pointed out to me, that inland was a parallel road that was in fact a lower dike, and beyond that another lower ridge, barely discernible at all. Three lines of defense are common against the sea. They are known as the waking dike, the sleeping dike, and the dreaming dike. Like Descartes, I thought, who was known to sleep late, to lie in bed of a morning meditating, and who found his profession as a philosopher in a dream.

Soon after we arrived in the Netherlands, my wife Pat and I went into a large cheese shop. "What shall we get?" she said.

On the shelves were perhaps a hundred large rolls of hard yellow cheese, six inches thick and nearly three feet in diameter.

We had just spent seven months in Paris, eating cheese. I looked at the array and smiled. "It doesn't matter," I said, "They're all the same."

The proprietress heard me and was outraged. First, they differ as to the farms where they were made. Then they differ in being young, middle-aged, and old. Middle age is actually *belegen* cheese, that is, cheese lying there, aging, between youth and old age, and this middle-aged cheese is also divided into young, middle-aged, and old. But more than that, in a fine shop like hers, we need not be restricted only to five ages. She could give us cheese of any age, month by month, from one to twenty-four. So what did I want?

"The oldest," I said.

She grumbled quietly as she cut a piece. It was the right choice, and the most expensive. This is plain cheese. It also comes, all ages, spiced with cumin or cloves or various herbs. Very old clove-spiced cheese is most Frisian, the finest product. The whole cloves have become soft, there are many of them, and you chew them up. Descartes must have eaten such cheese—he remarked on the pungent smell of spice in the Netherlands—and he must have been as bemused as we were.

Descartes said nothing about Dutch cheese in his letters, nothing about food at all except that he recommended that one should eat lightly—not easy in the Netherlands. And he once said that if the Netherlands did not have as much honey as God promised the Israelites, it was within the bounds of probability that it had more milk. He was said to be a virtual vegetarian, and like any Frenchman who has a piece of ground at least two-feet square, he kept a garden. Here in Friesland in winter he would eat carrots and cabbage, potatoes and parsnips, leeks and lentils, of which you can be sure there are many varieties.

The wind is almost always blowing in Friesland. In the dead of winter it reaches gale force for days at a time and will knock you flat if you are not prepared for it. We sleep in a loft under the eaves. The wind howls around our ears and the roof tiles clack and clatter. Like being on a ship in a storm on the North Sea, Pat says, without the inconvenience of a heaving deck. When we sit around the stove reading at night, outside the wind rages with such fury that you imagine you are on the Russian steppes. But if you step out the door, although the wind may take your breath

43

away, it isn't cold. All winter the temperature has ranged between 33 and 45 degrees Fahrenheit. It has rarely been below freezing, with ice on the pond in mid-December for only three or four days, and then not strong enough for skating. They say it has been an unusually mild winter—no doubt like the one Descartes complained of in 1633–34 when he was writing his *Meteorology*, during which he managed to study only one snowflake. When Samuel Sorbièrre visited Descartes in 1642, he characterized the Netherlands as four months of winter and eight months of cold. A neighbor says the prediction for this year is that it will warm up in July. He tells of the year you could eat outside from mid-April to mid-October. This mid-April the temperature continues the same, but the length of the day has increased from pitch-black at 4 PM in December to dusk now at 9 PM. The birds are nesting and the jonquils are in bloom.

There is not a lot of sun here. Pat marks time by referring to the day the sun shone all day. When the sun does shine on a warm day—which means no wind—everyone moves dinner tables outside to eat. In the towns where the houses are continuous and face right onto the sidewalks, at noontime you have to walk in the street because everyone is sitting at a table on the sidewalk in front of their houses eating dinner.

The weather changes a dozen times a day. Fog, overcast, light rain, heavy showers (squalls, actually, for we are in fact in the middle of the sea, held back by the zeedijk, our house a stationary boat planted on the sea bottom, nothing but the zeedijk keeping us from casting adrift in our bed), snow flurries, sleet and hail, and sun. The sky is enormous as are the clouds, and huge rainbows reach almost to the zenith. Sun and moon through clouds, spectacular sunrises and sunsets in tulip colors, rays of sun and shadow on the sky. All that billows and blows . . .

But on the ground all is straight lines. The green line of the grass-covered zeedijk, the brown reeds along the long blue pond, the green-and-brown fields beyond extending into blue haze on the horizon. Farmhouses, small villages, steeples rise tiny out of the flat polder in the distance. All colors shade into pastels. Out every window are Dutch landscape and skyscape paintings, always the same, always different.

Why did Descartes come here? He said he preferred living in a desert, where there are few people, where there is silence and

44

solitude so one can think. In Paris, the bustle and busyness of the city ran away with his thoughts. His friends importuned him. In Friesland he could escape.

"In what other land," he wrote in 1630 to his friend the poet Guez de Balzac, "can one enjoy freedom so entire?" He was living in Amsterdam then, but for him it was another desert. "In this great city," he said, "where everyone but me is engaged in commerce, each is so concerned for his own profit that I could stay here all my life without ever being noticed. I walk every day among the confusion of the crowds with as much freedom and repose as you would have in a park, and I pay no more attention to the people I see than I would to the trees and animals I might encounter in a forest." This is perhaps the first statement, not of alienation, but of the joyful anonymity one can have in a great city and nowhere else.

But most of Descartes' years in the Netherlands were spent outside small towns like Franeker, in isolated houses like our fisherman's cottage. He tended his garden, he dissected animals for his treatise on anatomy, he lay abed thinking and writing. In his leisure—but this was all his leisure—he rode, hunted, fenced, listened to music, and talked with friends. He claimed that he did not read books, but he did. He was enthusiastic about the use of the organ in the Reformed Church. He complained that country neighbors can sometimes be more bothersome than city friends. Did visitors then, as now, just drop in and think nothing of staying for four or five hours? Probably. Descartes apologized for his Dutch, although he wrote and spoke it fluently, and also knew Frisian. We know neither, but Frisian and English make up a subgroup of the Germanic family of languages, and since it is the closest relative of English, we often halfway understand.

Our closest neighbors are a retired zeedijk worker and his sister, about a hundred yards down the road. They loaned us a book on dikes. The land is sinking and the sea is rising and "a day will come when nothing more can be done. Then the time will have come for the Netherlands, like children's sandcastles when the tide comes in, to disappear from the scene." The first zeedijk here was built in 1570 and was 2.01 meters high. It was raised to 2.81 meters in 1571 and was at that height when Descartes was here. In 1930, it was raised to 5.25 meters, and then after disastrous storms and floods to 9.4 meters in 1975. It cannot be raised

45

higher because additional weight would just make it sink into the soft sea bottom on which it rests. Our house is a meter below mean sea level, the fields out there a bit lower. At night we can hear waves rolling onto the zeedijk.

We are from St. Louis, the home of Switzer's licorice, a favorite since childhood, so we were naturally attracted to the open bins of licorice in the stores here. Licorice is called *drop*. Drop ranges in color from light brown to dark black, and in hardness from very soft to crystal, but on first view they differ most obviously in shape. There is a bin of small cats, one of farmers and farmhouses, another of money—fat disks with a number impressed on one side and a dollar sign on the other—and many, many more. I picked up a licorice drop and popped it into my mouth and promptly spat it out. It was licorice, but . . .

Licorice drops come in mild, medium, and severe strength; these in plain, or in low sweet, medium sweet, and double sweet, and in low salt, medium salt, and double salt. I had made my first test on a double salt. Unbelievable. They differ also, of course, in brand name. My classification is the result of empirical tests, but I thought I might be exaggerating the number of kinds, so I asked a native Frisian. He was aghast.

"There are forty or fifty varieties, *at least*," he said. And this merely in taste alone. He warned me against getting an inferior brand of his favorite small cats. He also recommended laurel leaf licorice—not only in the shape of laurel leaves but wrapped around laurel leaves—that he particularly liked. Licorice also comes wrapped around mint leaves and with sal ammoniac. He also told me that I had missed a distinction in the cheese. All varieties come in either 48%, 40%, or 28% fat.

Two miles from our house in the village of Tzummarum there is an excellent bakery, Striksmas. (All Frisian surnames end in -ma, meaning of.) The bread comes with hard or soft crust in white, whole wheat, and rye; fine, medium, and coarse grained; and plain or sprinkled on top with oatmeal, poppy seeds, or sesame seeds. They bake all of these every day and all are delicious. When I remarked on this to our landlords who live in The Hague, they commiserated with us and brought us samples from their neighborhood bakery that produces a dozen different kinds of white bread alone, and varieties of another dozen different kinds of dark bread.

Sixteen years is a long time to stay away from your native land when it is virtually just across the border. In a few days Descartes could have been in Paris. He had spent over a year in the Netherlands when he was twenty-two, studying mathematics and architecture in the military school run by Maurice, prince of Nassau, the most brilliant military strategist of his time. Maurice is an excellent patron saint for Descartes. The prince loved mathematics. On his deathbed in 1625, a minister asked him to state his beliefs. "I believe," Maurice said, "that $2 + 2 = 4$ and that $4 + 4 = 8$. This gentleman here," referring to a mathematician at his side, "will inform you of the details of the rest of our beliefs."

For nine years between 1619 and 1628, Descartes had traveled in Denmark, Germany, Poland, Hungary, Austria, Moravia, Bavaria, Bohemia, Switzerland, Venice, Italy, and France. He had been in Paris much of the two years before his interview with Cardinal Bérulle, and had talked about locating in the country. The Descartes family owned houses and farms in Poitou, Touraine, and Brittany. He had wide choice and obviously enjoyed his stays in the French countryside. He apparently had said nothing about going to the Netherlands, although he had visited the Frisian Islands from northern Germany during his travels. But soon after seeing Cardinal Bérulle he packed up and left. These flat polders and this cool, even climate are an immense change from the hilly, wooded land where he grew up. I feel the difference because the landscape in southwestern Iowa where I was born is much like that in Touraine where Descartes was born. Did he miss the lack of mystery and hidden things, the continual change of prospect, that the flat, treeless polder rules out?

Descartes left his financial affairs in the hands of his closest friend in Paris, Claude Picot, later known as the Atheist Priest. This is probably because of the notorious story of Picot's deathbed benefice. Picot was traveling in rural France—this was long after Descartes' own death—when he was taken violently ill. Perhaps he had a stroke. They knew he was dying at the inn where he lay, so summoned the village priest. Picot said to this priest that he would bestow a very handsome benefice on the local parish, on one condition. No mumbo jumbo. No chanting, no last rites, no Latin. He was himself a priest. His conscience was clear. Just let him die in peace. The local priest was not happy with this, but agreed. Then when Picot seemed very near the end, in a coma apparently, the priest could restrain himself no longer. He began the incantation. Picot opened one eye and said, "I can still take back the money." So the priest fell silent and Picot died in peace.

Koek translates as gingerbread. It comes spiced mild, medium, and strong; fine, medium, or coarse textured; dry, medium, and moist; in loaves, long slices (called calves' legs), and cupcake. It also comes in the form of cake, brownies, cookies, and puff pastry. Also plain, with raisins, or with frosting. In fact, I am told that this is all wrong. Just because all these items are basically what I perceive as brown gingerbread, they do not at all belong to only one category. Mine is an outsider's empirical categorization that the Dutch do not recognize. But could an outsider ever get it right? Once I held up two packages of very dark, moist German rye bread and asked the grocery-van driver (he comes by our house once a week) if they were the same. He was scandalized.

"*Very* different," he said, but without enough English to be precise.

I bought them both. Indistinguishable.

Catholic commentators say Descartes would have been perfectly safe living and publishing in France. But Descartes opposed Aristotle, and the Parliament of Paris did pass a decree in 1624 forbidding attacks on Aristotle on pain of death. Vanini had been burned alive in 1619 for giving natural explanations of miracles—one of the advantages Descartes claimed for his physics—and more than a dozen heretics were burned alive in France during Descartes' lifetime. What is more, Descartes was making fun of astrology right at the time Richelieu was having horoscopes cast for making decisions of state.

In 1623, there was a Rosicrucian scare in Paris—placards appeared saying the Brethren were moving, invisible among the populace. Descartes was accused of being a Rosicrucian, and with mock indignation he defended himself by pointing out that everyone could see that he was not invisible. He rejected the magical and mystical beliefs of the Rosicrucians, but he took their motto as his own: *He who lives well hidden, lives well.* Like them, he practiced medicine without charge, tried to increase human longevity, was optimistic about the usefulness of science in improving the human lot, did not marry, and changed residences often.

During twenty-two years in the Netherlands he lived in at least eighteen different places. Having lived here awhile myself now, I suspect he was simply looking for a change. In any event, if it were not for the Saint Descartes Protective Association, Descartes might be known now as The Greatest Rosicrucian (just as Sir Isaac Newton might be classified as The Greatest Alchemist). We are so in need of squeaky-clean heroes that we present our great thinkers as Paradigms of Truth and Virtue rather than as the cranks they really were. Of course great men have to get only one or two major things right for people to forget the hundreds of things they got wrong.

Descartes' happiest time in the Netherlands was when he lived with Helena Jans from 1634 to 1640. He prepared his greatest works for publication during these years. He and Helena had a child, Francine, who died at the age of five of scarlet fever; she couldn't breathe, she turned purple, and she died. Descartes said her death was the greatest sorrow of his life, and that he was not among those philosophers who thought one must refrain from tears to prove himself a man.

A number of Descartes' biographers don't even mention his daughter. Or they speak of the deplorable incident of his illegitimate child. But Francine was baptized and is listed in the register of legitimate births in the Reformed Church at Deventer. What this might mean about Descartes' religious beliefs is more horrifying to good Catholic Cartesian scholars than illegitimacy.

The Dutch are precise. Our house is rented by the week, in seven-day measures, not by the imprecise month. That means that in twelve months there are thirteen four-week rent periods. (The Dutch have been the world's most astute capitalists for four centuries. Even the French still rent by the month.) It is a weekend house but it has everything we could want. First, no telephone. A grand piano. Good beds and chairs. It is the only house we've ever been in except our own where there is good light for reading everywhere and even a good light for the piano. We love it here.

Dutch houses have huge picture windows, and it is considered peculiar to pull the drapes or shades, day or night. In the seventeenth century when Descartes was here, foreigners commented on how beautiful Dutch interiors were, how elegant the furniture, how clean. The old paintings show it. You can still look in the windows to see. I run four or five miles every morning and cannot help but look into farmhouse windows as I pass by. Anyone inside looks back and waves. The window is not a barrier. I sit writing far back in a corner from the big windows facing onto the road, but everyone who walks by peers in, sees me, and waves. It is still surprising to me, but I wave back. The best views into houses are at night. We leave bare the windows facing the pond, but when we sit around the stove reading at night we pull the drapes across the windows facing the road. There really is no one out there, but it makes us feel more easy. We hope our neighbors will just think us foreign.

Is this openness a heritage of Calvinism? Nothing to hide in here? No one knocks when they come to the door, they just walk in. Neighbors, meter readers, postmen, repairmen, a schoolteacher from Franeker who heard we were here, and a newspaper reporter from Leeuwarden who learned from the schoolteacher that I was writing a book on Descartes. The schoolteacher stayed five hours. He was my informant about licorice drops. When the reporter left after two hours he asked if he could return to interview me.

"I thought that was what you were doing," I said.

"Oh no," he replied. "I wasn't taking notes."

Some days later he came and stayed the afternoon. The reporter warned me that after his story appeared, other reporters would come and disturb my solitude. I said I'd chance it. That was six weeks ago. The story has not appeared yet. He said when it did he would bring me a copy. Things are slow out here on the polder below the zeedijk. That's probably one good reason why Descartes came here.

The reporter had been a philosophy assistant at Groningen University, so he knew all about Descartes. There is very little hope of finding a permanent place in the Dutch university system these days, so he became a reporter. They are eliminating 250 teaching positions throughout the Netherlands just this year. The university business is shrinking all over Europe, but jobs of all sorts are scarce in the Netherlands. Government propaganda promotes the view that you have performed a national service if you are willing to go on unemployment, or to take early retirement, to allow someone else the opportunity to have a job. The retired dike worker down the way looks to be about fifty. He did not want to retire. He takes long walks along the dike half a dozen times a day.

"Its very difficult," the reporter said. "The Dutch like to work."

Storm warning! All out for the zeedijk! It is in their blood. The Netherlands is the grandest sandcastle ever made on a beach. Who would not cry at being drawn away from such colossal play?

Someone sent me a clipping from Ripley's "Believe It or Not": "René Descartes (1596–1650), the French philosopher and mathematician, learning that he would have to arise at 5 AM in a lucrative teaching position, warned that the cold morning air would be fatal to him—and died within four months."

Descartes hd been invited to the court of Queen Christina of Sweden. Why did he go? He had turned down very handsome pensions from several French noblemen. He said he did not want to be anyone's servant. He did not need the money. He went probably because Sweden had been a big winner at the end of the Thirty Years' War in 1648, and that made Queen Christina the most powerful and important (is there a difference?) monarch in Europe. She was accumulating great scholars and writers, so why not add Descartes to her collection? Descartes was like the professor in the sticks who waits all his life for the fabled call from Harvard. And lo, one day it actually comes. But it is too late, he is past his prime, he is an extinct volcano, recognition is as much a burden as a joy to him now. But he has to go anyway.

Descartes was fifty-three. Christina was twenty-two. She had a reputation for disconcerting the composure of dignified men. Once she taught her maids—who purportedly did not know French— to sing some dirty French songs, and then had them perform in front of the very old and distinguished French ambassador. She knew perfectly well Descartes' reputation for lying in bed until eleven o'clock in the morning, meditating, but she perversely had the great philosopher rise early enough to get dressed and ride in an open carriage across town—he was staying with the French ambassador—to give philosophy lessons to her at 5 AM. She had Descartes write the lyrics to a light ballet in which she herself danced the role of Pallas Athena. She had him write a five-act comedy. More reasonably, she had him write the

51

statutes for a Swedish Academy of Arts and Sciences. Descartes had already got the message. In the statutes he specified that foreigners could not be members of the academy. He wanted out.

It was while delivering these statutes, at five o'clock in the morning on 1 February 1650, that Descartes caught a chill. Ten days later, in a land where (he said) in winter men's thoughts freeze like the water, he died. This denouement is sometimes spoken of as Sweden's only contribution to Modern Philosophy. Descartes had often said that he expected to live to be a hundred. Christina quipped that the great mathematician miscalculated by nearly fifty years.

Queen Christina also said, "I love storm, and dread it when the wind drops."

On a rare day here when the wind does drop, the silence is deafening. Once I awoke in the middle of the night and it was the same sensation that I had years ago waking up in port with the engines turned off after having crossed the Atlantic on an ocean liner. The same thing—waking up in the middle of the night because it is suddenly quiet—happened to me a few times also in Paris. But there, after a few moments, the noise starts up again with the roar of cars and trucks. One is bombarded with noise in a city: construction, people, radio and television, the telephone, sirens, and bells—all jarring and startling, not like the wind. City noise, in itself and for what it draws your distracted attention to, is destructive of meditative thought. It can, perhaps, whirl you along in even higher flights of virtuosity. But city thoughts seldom come to rest.

The sugar cookies here are excellent—plain, or with peanuts, almond slices, raisins, or frosting on top. Yellow cake varies from bakery to bakery according to amount of butter, sugar, and eggs. Pudding is called *vla* and is sold in wide-topped milk bottles. It comes in plain, vanilla, lemon, chocolate, and strawberry. A pretty combination is half-and-half strawberry and chocolate, lengthwise in the bottle. Again, our city landlords scoff at this paucity of country flavors of vla. We should see the selection in The Hague.

I had the most difficulty working out the differences in *pap*, which is porridge that also comes in wide-mouthed milk bottles. Whole or skimmed milk or buttermilk, made with barley, wheat, corn or rice flour, with or without whole grains mixed in. Sweet or sour, plain or caramel flavored. Before I knew it was porridge that you were supposed to eat hot, I was testing it cold. The grocery-van driver set me straight. The next week I complained that when heated it is almost as runny as plain milk, not like porridge at all. He led me to understand, using a combination of English and Frisian, that any respectable family makes its own porridge at home, as thick as you like.

The days pass.

"In what other land," Descartes also said to Balzac, "could one sleep with such security?" Not in France where the windows are narrow and are shuttered at night like fortresses. Not in Germany. And I don't really understand why here. It is not as though these picture windows have not been smashed time and time again by invaders over the centuries, most recently less than fifty years ago. And the peace since World War II is the longest Europe has ever known. Perhaps it doesn't matter. There won't be a next time. Not another afterward, I mean.

A Sunday in the middle of March was still, and the sun was brilliant. Everyone was out in cars, on motorbikes and bicycles, or pushing baby strollers. Children of ten or eleven were walking across fields carrying poles eight or ten feet long that they use to vault across the ditches. They were looking for eggs. We know there are millions of birds here, we watch them all the time, but we still dislike this spring egg-hunting sport. A man and his small son come along the other side of the pond, beating the reeds with sticks as they do to scare up nesting ducks. I rushed out to try to warn them away from the lake coot nest I watch just by lifting my head and looking out the window.

"Nest? Where?" he laughed, looking closer and beating with his stick. The coot sat tight and he missed her nest.

The coots. I have lived in their midst all winter and have become so involved with their lives that I would have to write a book to explain. There are thirty-five of them on the pond, black and potty-shaped, about the size of guinea hens, with big white beaks that flare up on their foreheads. It has been a most frustrating obsession because they all look exactly alike—I can't even tell males from females. Pat says, "The coots know." I have no doubt that they differ from one another in many subtle ways.

There are both radio and television sets in this house, but we unplugged them when we moved in. We know the U.S. primaries

53

must be over now, but we don't know who the candidates are. Really, does it make any difference? My brother does send us clippings from *The New York Times*. They include a running documentary on the changing prognoses of the future of AIDS, which certainly will make a difference to the future of humankind. For a while government representatives such as Surgeon General Koop painted a very somber future for the human race because of the inevitable spread of AIDS throughout the population. But then in February, Admiral James D. Watkins, Chairman of the Presidential Commission on Human Immunodeficiency Virus Epidemic, assured us that the threat has been exaggerated and that we are not to worry. But only in January we had learned that "one of every 61 babies born in New York City last month carried antibodies to the virus, indicating that their mothers were infected and that many of the babies were also carriers." Where there are mothers and babies there are also fathers. When 2% or 3% of the population has a sexually transmitted disease, how long does it take for it to become 20% or 30% or 90%?

Pat and I are glad to see that Masters and Johnson are worried. That the health establishment is attacking them severely is a bad sign. Masters and Johnson are beyond the need of indulging in rabble-rousing just to create a sensation. When the government starts accusing people of causing undue alarm, one should be alarmed. And what is one to make of a silly article in which it is pointed out that leprosy was once feared and dreaded as AIDS is now? That's true, but leprosy seldom kills anyone and can be contained. People with AIDS almost always die and so far there is nothing we can do about it.

Descartes may have moved around so much to avoid the plague. In 1635, seventeen thousand people died of the plague in Leiden. It was thought at the time that bad air—like that in Italy—spread the plague. Descartes was wrong to think that bad air spread the plague, but he had the right idea when he moved away from infected areas. There isn't going to be any moving away from AIDS, however. It follows us right into our beds.

Descartes truly was something of a health nut. He told his friend Guez de Balzac that Italy was too hot. The Netherlands might be cold, but in a cold climate you can always get warm near a stove. In a hot climate there is no way to get cool. People like me who suffer serious heat debilitation in hot weather understand. Even air conditioning is inadequate. The body knows.

Descartes advocated government funding for cooperative research aimed at benefiting humankind. I don't believe the government needs to take as much of my income in taxes for my own good as it claims, but since it does take it, I'd like to see about half of what now goes for Defense Against Godless Communism transferred to research on AIDS. It is not that I do not fear the nuclear holocaust, but AIDS is a threat I can really believe in. We may all of us, like Descartes, be overestimating the amount of time we have left to live.

"I am out of my element here," Descartes said in the depth of the Swedish winter in the glacial atmosphere of a snow queen and a court filled with intrigue.

"But it doesn't make any difference that he had to be up at five in the morning," a Swede remonstrated with me. "It is dark all the time in Sweden in winter, so people don't pay much attention to the hour. It doesn't matter."

The wind blows, the light changes continuously, and the urgent clouds fly over the patient polder.

In Franeker, just over there on the horizon, Descartes wondered about the possibility that he might be deceived in thinking the world existed. There might be nothing but his own mind and a demon making him think he was experiencing a world. The town is built on a low pancake-shaped mound a few meters higher than the surrounding ground. You hope you can reach the church built on the highest part of the mound if the zeedijk breaks. One day it will. There are limits to all things. Descartes invented analytic geometry, the essential foundation of the infinitesimal calculus that operates on the principle that between any two points there are an infinite number of divisions. I sit here at dusk looking at the ever-changing sky. We all live between two points. Separated by infinite variations.

Nominated by The Georgia Review

A LETTER

by ALBERT GOLDBARTH

from POETRY

> *Number of direct-mail solicitations sent to Henry David Thoreau at Walden*
> *Pond this year: 90.*
> Harper's Index, 1988

At the end of a day that's rubble around me,
shrimp husks, tufts on a barber's floor, heaped circus doo,
at the burr tail-end, the tar tail-end,
the shitty piggy corkscrew tail-end of a day like that,
when all the dauby, wadded toilet paper staunchings of the
   shaving mistakes
of a lifetime buzz about this air like ghost wasps,
and to try to even say a word like *graciousness* or *honor*
coughs a bile-larded furball up into the throat . . .
at the end of a day like that, I pick you up,
Old Chisel-Puss, and head out to the last, thin brothlight
just to read some random observation you whittled,
cleansed in lime and ashes, then set on your simple sill
for the world to do as it will with it, yes,
Henry David, Old Man Applemash, Hardwood Grainface, you.
I like sometimes to take rank hold on life and spend my day
more as the animals do. You don't fail me
now and never have, Old Clever Clean Vinegar Eye.
There is no odor so bad as that which arises from
goodness tainted. Old Man Aphorism, Duke of Bean Rows, here
the lowered sun behind a lowered cloud rays out

56

in the shape of a clamshell—you
of all the boneyard might in one quick strike convince me
This is a delicious evening, when the whole body is one sense
and imbibes delight through every pore. Eventually
it's night, a little pearly murk and then the real
anthracite thing. This far into the blotto glow of the city,
there aren't many stars—enough, though,
for a small game of Commemorative Dot-to-Dot.
I'd like to place you among them: you'll shine
like a chart of the major nerve-ends.
I'd like to place you among them and ask you to peer down
once a night with your acerbic, well-intentioned gaze.
The horoscope zoo grunts, caterwauls, and burbles up there
uselessly—we could use some understanding
astral attention. I'd like to place you among them
just so we could point on cloudless nights: there's
Old Sufficience himself, the Scraggled Dour Lover of Stuff,
the Great Denouncer, Mr. Stickler, that Saint of Cheapskates
and Wonderful Phoney-Baloney of the Woods, the Lone Looker
who said *Every man has to learn the points of the compass again*
as often as he wakes. Who said *Olympus is but*
the outside of the earth every where. I'd like to constellate you
overhead. Don't tell me you wouldn't be pleased.
This far into the blotto glow of the 20th century,
your light isn't strong—but it's enough. I'm 40.
When I was 10, I wished on those stars. Oh
they might have been dead, but we corresponded.

Nominated by Philip Booth, Stephen Corey, and Philip Dacey

TYPICAL

fiction by PADGETT POWELL

from GRAND STREET

YESTERDAY A FEW things happened. Every day a few do. My dog beat up another dog. He does this when he can. It's his living, more or less, though I've never let him make money doing it. He could. Beating up other dogs is his thing. He means no harm by it, expects other dogs to beat him up—no anxiety about it. If anything makes him nervous, it's that he won't get a chance to beat up or be beaten up. He's healthy. I don't think I am.

For one thing, after some dog-beating-up, I think I feel better than even the dog. It's an occasion calls for drinking. I have gotten a pain in the liver zone, which it is supposed to be impossible to feel. My doctor won't say I can't feel anything, outright, but he does say *he* can't feel anything. He figures I'll feel myself into quitting if he doesn't say I'm nuts. Not that I see any reason he'd particularly cry if I drank myself into the laundry bag.

I drank so much once, came home, announced to my wife it was high time I went out, got me a black woman. A friend of mine, well before this, got in the laundry bag and suddenly screamed at his wife to keep away from him because she had *turned* black, but I don't think there's a connection. I just told mine I was heading for some black women pronto, and I knew where the best ones were, they were clearly in Beaumont. The next day she was not speaking, little rough on pots and pans, so I had to begin the drunk detective game and open the box of bad breath no drunk ever wants to open. That let out the black women of Beaumont, who were not so attractive in the shaky

58

light of day with your wife standing there pink-eyed holding her lips still with little inside bites. I sympathized fully with her, fully.

I'm not nice, not too smart, don't see too much point in pretending to be either. Why I am telling anyone this trash is a good question, and it's stuff it obviously doesn't need me to tell myself. Hell, I know it, it's mine. It would be like the retired justice of the peace that married me and my wife.

We took a witness which it turned out we didn't need him, all a retired JP needs to marry is a $20 tip, and he'd gotten two thousand of those tips in his twenty years retired, cash. Anyway, he came to the part asks did anyone present object to our holy union please speak up now or forever shut up, looked up at the useless witness, said, "Well, hell, he's the only one here, and *y'all* brought him, so let's get on with it." Which we did.

This was in Sealy, Texas. We crossed the town square, my wife feeling very married, proper and weepy, not knowing yet I was the kind to ,alk of shagging black whores, and we went into a nice bar with a marble bartop and good stools and geezers at dominoes in the back, and we drank all afternoon on one ten-dollar bill from large frozen goblet-steins of some lousy Texas beer we're supposed to be so proud of and this once it wasn't actually terribly bad beer. There was our bouquet of flowers on the bar and my wife was in a dressy dress and looked younger and more innocent than she really was. The flowers were yellow, as I recall, the marble white with a blue vein, and her dress a light, flowery blue. Light was coming into the bar from high transomlike windows making glary edges and silhouettes—the pool players were on fire, but the table was a black hole. All the stuff in the air was visible, smoke and dust and tiny webs. The brass nails in the old floor looked like stars. And the beer was 50 cents. What else? It was pretty.

She's not so innocent as it looked that day because she had a husband for about ten years who basically wouldn't sleep with her. That tends to reduce innocence about marriage. So she was game for a higher stepper like me, but maybe thinks about the cold frying pan she quit when I volunteer to liberate the dark women of the world.

I probably mean no harm, to her or to black women, probably am like my dog, nervous I won't get *the chance*. I might fold up at the first shot. I regret knowing I'll never have a date with Candice Bergen, this is in the same line of thought. Candice Bergen is my pick for the most good to look at and probably kiss and maybe all-you-could-do woman in the world. All fools have their whims. Should an ordinary, daily kind of regular person carry around desire like this? Why do people do this? Of course a lot of money is made on fools with pinups in the backs of their heads, but why do we continue to buy? We'd be better off with movie stars what look like the girls from high school that had to have sex to get any attention at all. You put Juicy Lucy Spoonts on the silver screen and everybody'd be happy to go home to his faithful, hopeful wife. I don't know what they do in Russia, on film, but if the street women are any clue, they're on to a way of reducing foolish desire. They look like good soup-makers, and no head problems, but they look like potatoes, I'm sorry. They've done something over there that prevents a common man from wanting the women of Beaumont.

There are many mysteries in this world. I should be a better person, I know I should, but I don't see that finally being up to choice. If it were, I would not stop at being a better person. Who would? The girls what could not get dates in high school, for example, are my kind of people now, but *then* they weren't. I was like everybody else.

I thought I was the first piece of sliced bread to come wrapped in plastic, then. Who didn't. To me it is really comical, how people come to realize they are really a piece of shit. More or less. Not everybody's the Candy Man or a dog poisoner. I don't mean that. But a whole lot of folk who once thought otherwise of themself come to see they're just not that hot. That is something to think on, if you ask me, but you don't, and you shouldn't, which it proves my point. I'm a fellow discovers he's nearly worth disappearing without a difference to anyone or anything, no one to be listened to, trying to say that not being worth being listened to is the discovery we make in our life that then immediately, sort of, ends the life and its feedbag of self-serious and importance.

I used to think niggers were the worst. First they were loud as Zulus at bus stations and their own bars and then they started walking around with radio stations with jive jamming up the entire air. Then I realized you get the same who-the-hell-asked-for-it noise off half, more than half, the white fools everywhere you are. Go to the ice house: noise. Rodeo: Jesus. Had to quit football games. There's a million hot shots in this world wearing shorts and loud socks won't take no for an answer.

And un*like* high school, you can't make them go home, quit coming. You can't make them quit playing life. I'd like to put up a cut-list on the locker-room door to the world itself. Don't suit up today, the following:

And I'm saying I'd be in the cut myself. Check your pads in, sell your shoes if you haven't fucked them up. I did get cut once, and a nigger who was going to play for UT down the road wouldn't buy my shoes because he said they stank—a nigger now. He was goddamned right about the toe jam which a pint of foo foo water had made worse, but the hair on his ass to say something like that to me. I must say he was nice about it, and I'm kind of proud to tell it was Earl Campbell wouldn't wear a stink shoe off me.

Hell, just take what I'm saying right here in that deal. *I'm* better than a nigger who breaks all the rushing records they had at UT twice and then pro records and on bad teams, when I get *cut* from a bad team that names itself after a tree. Or something, I've forgotten. We might have been the Tyler Rosebuds. That's the lunacy I'm saying. People have to *wake up.* Some do. Some don't. I have: I'm nobody. A many hasn't. Go to the ice house and hold your ears.

This is not that important. It just surprised me when I came to it, is all. You're a boob, a boob for life, I realized one day. Oh, I got Stetsons, a Silverado doolie, ten years at ARMCO, played poker with Mickey Gilley, shit, and my girlfriends I don't keep in a little black book but on candy wrappers flying around loose in the truck. One flies out, so what? More candy, more wrappers at the store. But one day, for no reason, or no reason I know it or can remember anything happening which it meant anything, I stopped at what I was doing and said, John Payne, you are a piece of crud. You are a common, long-term drut. *Look* at it.

It's not like this upset me or anything, why would it? It's part of the truth to what I'm saying. You can't disturb a nobody with evidence he's a nobody. A nobody is not disturbed by anything significant. It's like trying to disturb a bum by yelling *poor fuck* at him. What's new? he says. So when I said, John Payne, you final asshole, I just kept on riding. But the moment stuck. I began watching myself. I watched and proved I was an asshole.

This does not give you a really good feeling, unless you are drunk, which is when you do a good part of the proving.

I've been seeing things out of the corners of my eyes and feeling like I have worms since this piece-of crud thing. It works like this. I'm in a ice house out Almeda, about to Alvin in fact, and I see this pretty cowboy type must work for Nolan Ryan's ranch or something start to come up to me to ask for a light. That's what I *would* have seen, before. But now it works like this: before he gets to me, before he even starts coming over, see, because I'm legged up in a strange bar thinking I'm a piece of shit and a out-of-work beer at three in the afternoon in a dump in Alvin it proves it, I see out the corner of my eye this guy put his hand in his pants and give a little wink to his buddies as he starts to come over. That's enough, whatever it means, he may think I'm a fag, or he may be one himself, but he thinks you're enough a piece of shit he can touch his dick and wink about you, only he don't know that he is winking about a known piece of shit, and winking about a known piece of shit is a dangerous thing to do.

Using the mirror over the bar about like Annie Oakley shooting backwards, I spot his head and turn and slap him in the temple hard enough to get the paint to fall off a fender. He goes down. His buddies start to push back their chairs and I step one step up and they stop.

"What's all the dick and grinning about, boys?"

On the floor says, "I cain't *see*."

"He cain't see," I tell the boys.

I walk out.

Outside it's some kind of dream. There's ten Hell's Angel things running around a pickup in the highway like a Chinese fire drill, whatever that is. In the middle by the truck is a by-God muscle man out of Charles Atlas swinging chains. He's *whipping* the bikers with their own motorcycle chains. He's got all of the leather hogs bent over and whining where he's stung them. He picks up a bike and drops it headfirst on the rakes. Standing there with a hot Bud, the only guy other than Tarzan not bent over and crying, I get the feeling we're some kind of tag team. I drive off.

That's how it works. Start out a piece of shit, slap some queer-bait blind, watch a wrestling match in the middle of Almeda Road, drive home a piece of shit, spill the hot beer I forgot about all over the seat and my leg.

I didn't always feel this way, who could afford to? When I was fifteen, my uncle, who was always kind of my real dad, gave me brand new Stetson boots and a hundred-dollar bill on a street corner in Galveston and said spend it all and spend it all on whores. It was my birthday. I remember being afraid of the black whores and the ones with big tits, black or white, otherwise I was a ace. In those days a hundred dollars went a long way with la-dies in Galveston. I got home very tired a fifteen-year-old *king* with new boots and a wet dick.

That's what you do with the world before you doubt yourself. You buy it, dress up in it, fuck it. Then, somehow, it starts fuck-ing back. A Galveston whore you'd touch now costs the whole hundred dollars, for example, in other words. I don't know. To-day I would rather just *talk* to a girl on the street than fuck one, and I damn sure don't want to talk to one. There's no point. I need some kind of pills or something. There must be ways which it will get you out of feeling like this.

For a while I thought about having a baby. But Brillo Tucker thought this up about fifteen years ago, and two years ago his boy whips his ass. When I heard about that I refigured. I don't need a boy whipping my ass, mine or anybody else's. That would just about bind the tit. And they'll do that, you know, because like I say they come out *kings* for a while. Then the crown slips and pretty soon the king can't get a opera ticket, or something, I don't know anything about kings.

This reminds me of playing poker with Mickey Gilley, stud. First he brings ten times as much money as anyone, sits down in new boots, creaking, and hums all his hit songs so nobody can think. He wins a hand, which it is rare, and makes this touch-down kind of move and comes down slowly and rakes the pot to his little pile. During the touchdown, we all look at this dry-cleaning tag stapled to the armpit of his vest. That's the Pasadena crooner.

I was at ARMCO Steel for ten years, the largest integrated steel mill west of the Mississippi, a word we use having nothing to do

63

with niggers for once. It means we could take ore and make it all the way to steel. Good steel. However, I admit that with everybody standing around eating candy bars in their new Levis, it cost more than Jap steel. I have never seen a Japanese eating a candy bar or dipping Skoal showing off his clothes. They wear lab coats, like they're all dentists. We weren't dentists.

We were, by 1980, out of a job, is what we were. It goes without saying it, that is life. They were some old-timers that just moped about it, and some middle-lifer types that had new jobs in seconds, and then us young turks that moped *mad*. We'd filler up and drive around all day bitching about the capitalist system, whatever that is, and counting ice houses. We discovered new things, like Foosball. Foosball was one of the big discoveries. Pool we knew about, shuffleboard we knew about, Star Wars pinball we knew about, but Foosball was a kick.

For a while we bitched as a club. We were on the icehouse frontier, tent-city bums with trucks. Then a truckload of us—not me, but come to think of it, Brillo Tucker was with them, which is perfect—get in it on the Southwest Freeway with a truckload of niggers and they all pull over outside the *Post* building and the niggers whip their *ass*. They're masons or something, plumbers. A photographer at the *Post* sees it all and takes pictures. The next day a thousand ARMCO steel workers out of a job read about themselves whipped by employed niggers on the freeway. This lowered our sail. We got to be less of a club, quick. I don't know what any of my buddies are doing now and I don't care. ARMCO was ARMCO. It was along about in here I told my wife I was off to Beaumont for black chicks, and there could be a connection, but I doubt it.

As far as I can really tell, I'm still scared of them in the plain light of day. At a red light on Jensen Drive one day, a big one in a fur coat says to me, "Come here, Sugar, I got something for you," and opens her coat on a pair of purple hot pants and a yellow bra.

I say, "I know you do," and step on it. Why in hell I'd go home and pick on a perfectly innocent wife about it is the kind of evidence it convinces you you're not a prince in life.

Another guy I knew in the ARMCO club had a brother who *was* a dentist, and this guy tells him not to worry about losing his job, to come out with him golfing on Thursdays and *relax*. Our guy starts going—can't remember his name—and he can't hit the ball for shit. It's out of bounds or it's still on the tee. And the dentist who wants him to relax starts ribbing him until our guy says if you don't shut the fuck up I'm going to put this ball down and aim it at *you*. The dentist laughs. So Warren—that's his name—puts the ball down and aims at the dentist who's standing there like William Tell giggling and swings and hits his brother, the laughing dentist who wants him to relax, square in the forehead. End of relaxing golf.

Another guy's brother, a yacht broker, whatever that is, became a flat *hero* when we got laid off because he found his brother the steel worker in the shower with his shotgun and took it away from him. Which it wasn't hard to do, because he'd been drinking four days and it wasn't loaded.

Come to look at it, *we* all sort of disappeared and all these Samaritans *with* jobs creamed to the top and took the headlines, except for the freeway. The whole world loves a job holder.

One day I drove out to the Highway 90 bridge over the San Jacinto and visited Tent City, which was a bunch of pure bums pretending to be unfortunate. There were honest-to-God river rats down there, never lived anywhere but on a river in a tent, claiming to be victims of the economy. They had elected themselves a mayor, who it turns out the day I got there was up for re-election. But he wasn't going to run again because God had called him to a higher cause, preaching. He announced this with shaking hands and wearing white shoes and a white belt and a maroon leisure suit. Out the back of his tent was a pyramid of beer cans all the way to the river, looked like a mud slide in Colombia. People took me around because they thought I was out there to *hire* someone.

I met the new mayor-to-be, who was a Yankee down here on some scam that busted, had left a lifelong position in dry cleaning, had a wife who swept their little camp to where it was smoother and cleaner than concrete. I told him to call Mickey Gilley. He was a nice guy, they both were, makes you think a little more softly about the joint. How a white woman from Michigan, I think, knew how to sweep dirt like a Indian I'll never know. Maybe it's natural. I don't think it's typical though.

65

This one dude, older dude, they called Mr. C, was walking around asking everybody if this stick of wood he was carrying belonged to them. He had this giant blue and orange thing coming off his nose, about *like* an orange, which it is why they called him Mr. C, I guess. A kid who was very pretty, built well—could of made a fortune in Montrose—ran to him with a bigger log and took him by the arm all the way back to his spot, some hanging builder's plastic and a chair, and set a fire for him. It's corny as hell, but I started liking the place. It was like a pilgrim place for pieces of shit, pieces of crud.

Then a couple gets me, tells me their life story if I'll drink instant coffee with them. The guy rescued the girl from some kind of mess in Arkansas that makes Tent City look like Paradise. He's about six eight with mostly black teeth and sideburns growing into his mouth, and she's about four foot flat with a nice ass and all I can think of is how can they fuck and why would she let him. For some reason I asked him if he played basketball, and the *girl* pipes up, "I played basketball."

"Where?"

"In high school."

"Then what did you do?" I meant by this, how is it Yardog here has you and I don't.

"Nothing," she says.

"What do you mean, nothing?"

"I ain't done *nuttin*." That's the way she said it, too.

It was okay by me, but if she had fucked somebody other than the buzzard, it would have been *something*.

I was just kind of cruising there at this point, about like leg-up in Alvin, ready to buy them all a case of beer and talk about hard luck the way they wanted to, when something happened. This gleaming, purring, fully restored, *immaculate* as Brillo Tucker would say, '57 Chevy two-door pulls in and eases around Tent City and up to us, and out from behind the mirrored windshield, wearing sunglasses to match it, steps this nigger who was a kind of shiny, shoe-polish brown, an *exact* color and finish of the car. The next thing you saw was that his hair was black and oily and so were the black sidewalls of his car. Everything had dressing on it.

The nigger comes up all smiles and takes cards out of a special little pocket in his same brown suit as the car and himself. The card says something about community development.

"I am prepared to offer all of you, if we have enough, a seminar in job-skills acquistion and full-employment methodology." This comes out of the gleaming nigger beside his purring '57 Chevy.

The girl with the nice butt who's done nothing but fuck a turkey vulture says, "Do what?"

Then the nigger starts on a roll about the seminar, about the only thing which in it people can catch is it will take six hours. That is longer than most of these people want to *hold* a job, including me at this point. I want to steal his car.

"Six hours?" the girl repeats. "For *what?*"

"Well, there are a lot of tricks to getting a job."

I say, "Like what?"

"Well, like shaking hands."

"Shaking hands." I remember Earl Campbell not buying my stinky shoes. That was okay. This is too far.

"Do you know how to shake hands?" the gleaming nigger asks. Out of the corner of my eye I see the turkey buzzard looking at his girl with a look that is like they're in high school and in love.

"Let's find out," I say. I grab him and crush him one, he winces.

"You know how to shake hands."

"I thought I did."

Who the fuck taught *him* how? Maybe Lyndon Johnson.

He purrs off to find a hall for the seminar and the group at Tent City proposes putting a gas cylinder in the river and shooting it with a .22.

I've got my own brother to contend with, but we got over it a long time ago. IIe was long gone when ARMCO troubles let everybody else's brother loose on him. He, *my* brother, goes off to college, which I don't, which it pissed me off at the time, but not so much now. Anyway, he goes off and comes back with half-ass long hair talking *Russian*. Saying, *Goveryou po rooskie* in my face. It's about the time Earl Campbell has told me he won't wear my cleats because they stink, so I take all my brother's college crap laying down.

Then he says, "I study Russian with an old woman who escaped the revolution with nothing. There's only one person in the

67

class, so we meet at her house. Actually, we meet in her back-yard, in a hole."

"You what?"

"We sit in a hole she dug and study Russian. All I lack being Dostoevsky's underground man is more time." He laughed.

"All I lack being a gigolo," I said, "is having a twelve-inch dick." And hit him, which is why he doesn't talk to me today, and I don't care. If he found out I was in the shower with my shotgun he'd pass in a box of shells. Underground man. What a piece of shit.

That's about it. Thinking of my brother, now, I don't feel so hot about running at the mouth. I'm not feeling so hot about living, so what? What call is it to drill people in their ears? I'm typical.

Nominated by Pat Strachan

RUST

fiction by JOSIP NOVAKOVICH

from THE PARIS REVIEW

IF YOU WALK through the green and chirpy tranquility of the park around the castle at Nizograd, Yugoslavia, past the Roman Baths, you will come upon a monument that might appear unseemly.

Two dark bronze partisans are stuck on a pedestal uncomfortably high, back to back, one perpetually about to throw a hand grenade, another shoving his rifle into the air and shouting a most terrifying metallic silence from the depths of his chest, his shirt ripped open, challenging bullets to pierce his heart. Their noses are sharp, lips thin, cheekbones high, hands large and knotty; everything about them is angular—a combination of social-realism and folk art. This type of sculpture is common in most Eastern European towns; the larger the town, the larger the proportions of the sculpture. However, there is something unusually fierce in the grim faces of our monument.

The monument was done by Marko Kovachevich, a sculptor educated at the Moscow Art Academy who was a Communist before the war, when it was dangerous to be one, when you could be jailed or executed for it.

During the war, he fought as a partisan against the Germans and won several medals. After the war, the Communist Party commissioned him to erect the monument to those who had fallen. He received so little money for it that expenses for the materials were barely covered; his work was appreciated as a comradely contribution to the cause. Party members from the neighboring town wished to have an exact copy of the monument, and Marko asked them to pay in advance, which they did. The monument completed, there was a great ceremony—the uncovering of the monument by the mayor after speeches of great dignity. The crowd gasped at the sight of the bared monument; the partisans were as small as dolls. The crowd was about to stone Marko, but he said, "Comrades, small money, small partisans." The people laughed and the officials ground their teeth.

Marko excommunicated himself from the Party, flinging the red membership book into the garbage in town hall.

Since in a poor socialist country nobody can afford sculptures except the government, and he no longer wished to work for them, Marko could no longer make a living as a sculptor. He became a tombstone maker, specializing in the tombstones of deceased Party members.

He moonlighted as an art teacher and, as such, was loved and feared by children. His presence was imposing: tall and heavy-boned, a massive hooked nose, like Rodin's, and rising eyebrows like Brezhnev's. His hair, the color of steel, was cut several times a year to a centimeter's length, so that it looked like the bristles of a hedgehog. The hair grew quickly, obeying no conventions and leaping into various shocks and cowlicks. Even when it was long, his donkey ears stuck out, with some hair of their own atop each lobe. Whenever he entered a classroom—a room with greasy wooden floors in the castle, a huge building with thick walls, high ceilings and chandeliers—he would shout the assignment to us: to draw a tree whose branches in the wind scratched the windowpane, or the profile of our neighbor, or something out of our imagination, something we had never seen before.

Then he would pull four chairs together, take off his boots, put one beneath his head, the way Jacob put a stone beneath his, and soon the room resounded with snoring, as if a tank were tearing up the road, whereupon we would sneak out of the classroom into the park, to climb trees and dig with branches into the soil for small Roman and Turkish coins—the town was established 2,000 years ago as a hot springs spa and was renewed by the Ottomans. Waking up half an hour later, he'd shout out the tall baroque windows for us to come back.

Before the end of the two-hour lesson, he would stroll down the aisle, looking at our drawings.

"What's this?" he asked me.

"A tree," I answered proudly. I had paid painstaking attention to details.

"I don't see it. A tree lives, has a soul. Yours is a bunch of doodles."

He took a pencil and drew a line down the tree. The graphite pencil-tip broke, and flew off, hitting the window pane. Marko continued to draw the line, unperturbed, through the core of what the tree should have been, and sure enough, it began to look like a tree, irrepressible, ready to resist tempests, almost challenging them to arrive.

"See, you give it marrow. This is no beauty salon. First you make a tree, and what you do with it later—whether you put lipstick on it, eyelashes—that's incidental. But let it *stand* for Heaven's sake!"

By such a simple intervention he gave the tree character distinctly his: uncollapsible grand simplicity. How, I wondered, does one learn to impart character with one stroke? Can one learn that?

He often assigned us to print inscriptions: HEREIN LIES IN PEACE . . . The inscriptions he liked best, he used on tombstones.

Marko chewed gingerly, like an old wounded lion, telling us our region was poor in fluoride. I used to bring him apples from our garden just to see what trouble eating them gave him. But one day as soon as he entered the classroom he shouted for silence and stood on the table. In the posture of the partisan on the pedestal who is doomed to shove his rifle into the air for the remainder of eternity, or until a new regime comes to power, our teacher pulled out his front teeth and shoved them towards the gasping children.

"Comrades, asses! I have new teeth. They will give me no pain. If I get tired of them, I put them in a glass of water. When I need to chew or give a speech, I put them back in. Progress! Do you hear, that's called progress!" Then he fitted the upper teeth back into his mouth, and grinned through the pink and white plastic at us, closed his mouth, and masticated so that the muscles on his jaws kept popping, making a seesaw pattern, his jaw clanking. We watched silently, our eyes popping, disgusted.

Then, to demonstrate that the teeth were not only for show, he called my name and said, "Now bring me one of those apples."

I leapt to the window and lowered myself into the park and was soon back with a crunchy apple. Marko slowly chewed it in front of us, grinding the teeth sideways, the way a bull ruminates, turning his head a little to the left, a little to the right, so we could all see how it worked. "That's art, my children. It makes life good, that's what art should do. Now you can go home. You've learned enough for today."

One spring day, he stood on a chair and shouted, "Comrades, you need some real life, some hardship." He pointed at me and two other boys, because we were the largest in the class. "You go to the junkyard and ask for Marko's cart. Then pull it to my home."

As we pulled the laden cart, the junkyard keepers laughed at us, calling us donkeys. We heard chilling screams of pigs being slaughtered at a nearby slaughter-house. The cart squeaked under the weight of chains, parts of engines and crowbars of old school buses, whose blue and rusting bodies lay outside the junkyard, like tired elephants. Panting, we hauled the metal uphill, through and beyond the town, where the park turned into forest, on the edge of the cornfields.

His house was a grand sight—the redness of its bricks cried against the green forest in the background. Its massiveness cast a long shadow over the backyard, prostrate and vanishing in the darkness of the woods. What was in the shadow attracted even more attention, so much so that the bright house would sink into a shadow of your mind, while the darkened objects in the backyard would begin to glow—planks of wood with bent nails sticking out, bike chains, rusty train wheels, tin cans, cats, buckets, winding telephones, a greater disarray than Berlin on May 2, 1945. The backyard seemed a witness to the collapse of an empire. Marko seemed entrenched in a war of sorts, with chaos gaining the upper hand. That a teacher—the sort of being that teaches you cleanliness and orderliness—had such uncheckable, exuberant garbage made me shake for joy.

One half of the house was finished, the bunker-like downstairs with rusty rods sticking out, as if a cage had been cut through. The upstairs was empty, with large looming windows. As you approached the house, tripping over empty cans of paint, the door silently opened a little. A woman of wornout countenance peeped around the door, expecting nothing but evil from the other side. She wore black as if her husband, Marko, were dead. Perhaps she wore it for her mother and father, or perhaps because the Marko she had once loved was dead.

It seemed there had to be enough junk, but Marko kept hauling the rusty metal to his yard once a week for several years. Out of the junk he erected two iron pillars, connected on top by a steel beam from which hung a pendulum. A whole series of cogs and chains connected the pendulum to a motor emitting blue smoke. I thought he was building some kind of modern sculpture, something he had learned in Russia. The mechanism looked like an updated guillotine, its rustiness notwithstanding.

A large steel plate formed the base of the pendulum. He chiseled out a groove in a stone for the blade. The blade rasped over the stone, while he stood on the side, masticating contemplatively, constantly adjusting his teeth. Now and then he poured water over the stone as if baptizing it, though of course it was too late for baptism; it was a tombstone. His cats ran off into the woods, but returned, transfigured into hedgehogs, staring at the monster who ate stones.

Marko became a sort of town attraction. From the Roman baths in the park you heard the moaning and rasping of the stone-cutting machine from a mile away, like a steam engine gasping up a steep hill toward you. In the summer, idle adolescents, retired captains, crippled war heroes, children with jam moustaches, and even some tourists came by to take a look at him, most of them without a comment, as if observing an abstruse museum piece. Because of the noise, he could never hear your approach, and even if he could, he wouldn't bother to turn around and see if it was a stranger approaching, or merely his cats upsetting wood planks and buckets. Once, as I stole up to him bent over his stone, he said to me, without looking up, "Could you pour water over the stone once a minute?" and gave me an aluminum cup and a bucket.

On holidays, he took walks and attended public assemblies, where he often raised his voice, using folklore expressions like "Fuck the Sun," and some other ones involving various members of the Divine Family.

73

In 1971, on the Day of The Republic ("Commemorative holiday of the founding of the Socialist Federative Republic of Yugoslavia"), when there were nationalist tensions between Croatians and Serbs, he interrupted a vague ceremonious speech by the mayor, and shouted, "Comrades and Comradesses, enough bullshit. Our bureaucrats are liars and hypocrites. God has created us equal. In front of Him we are blades of grass and ashes. So, why all this nonsense, why do some of you shout, I'm Croatian, and others, I'm Serb, what the hell's the difference? Who should care? Let me tell you, God doesn't." And he proceeded to preach in the middle of the atheist, communist assembly and nobody stopped him. Religion and proselytizing were strictly confined by law to the churches; religion was considered a disease, a crutch for those who had no courage to face the finality of life. As a Baptist, I had seen many religious people of courage remain silent about religion in public. And here, a Communist whom I thought a nonbeliever spoke out, and I felt proud of our shared faith in God. Shivers ran down my body into my shoes.

When he sat down, there was a long silence, marred by throats clearing phlegm. Thick blue smoke hovered like a large wreath above the assembly. The mayor tried to go on with his speech as though nothing had happened, but nobody listened to him.

Because Marko Kovachevich had to work so hard as a tombstone maker, he took advantage of his job as a teacher, snoozing while he let the children raise hell, wrestle, and throw paper airplanes; but now and then he shouted: "Silence! Work!" If we ignored his shouts, he'd rush straight toward a boy—he always believed there had to be a gang leader—and grab him by the ear, twisting it. "Boy, I need to wind the clock. It's not break time, it's class time. Get it?"

Once seeing a girl crying, he asked her why, and she pointed at me and said, "He slapped me."

"Comrade," I said, "She spilled lemonade over my watercolor painting" (an eagle descending upon a rosy piglet).

Marko jumped over the table, grabbed the hair on the scruff of my neck, and shouted, "Painting you call it! Even if it was . . . " and he struck me with his fist—I saw stars and heard thunder even though my eyes were closed and my hands covered my ears.

"That'll teach you. I am beating a beast. You aren't the beast. You are a fine boy. But there is a beast in you. The only way I can reach it is through your skin. Let's hope some of the pain gets to that beast. Nothing is efficient in this life, I know, it's a waste of energy and pain, but . . . "And another slap. "Now repeat after me, Girls are to be kissed."

"Girls are to be kicked," I echoed. Whereupon Marko kicked me with his ox-hide soles fortified with iron crescent moons. I flew down the aisle, landing in a heap at the end. I limped for a week afterwards.

And when a boy released a stone from his slingshot, shattering a lamp on a post outside the window, Marko shouted, "Come here, beast!"

"No, Comrade, it wasn't me."

"Come here, I'll show you your God."

"But Comrade, I didn't . . . ah . . . do . . . I . . . "

If the mountain won't come to Mohammed, Mohammed will go to the mountain. The boy wouldn't come to the mountain, so the mountain rushed towards the boy. The boy leaped, knocking over several benches. Marko grabbed a coal shovel and hurled it at the boy. The weapon struck the wall a couple of inches above the boy's head, digging a hole in the loose mortar of the castle, while the boy rushed out the door. The mortar sand hissed as it trickled to the ground. Marko's gray eyes glared fierce and savage and he ground his teeth as if the boy's bones were there to be chewed—Poseidon chewing a member of Odysseus's crew fallen overboard. Had the weapon struck several inches lower, it would have cracked the boy's skull open; but, so far as I know, he killed no pupils. He was mostly pacific and ignored us the way a bull ignores flies. Of course, a bull's tail whips horseflies away now and then.

Visiting him at his home, and wishing to appear smart, I mentioned Aristotle and Plato to him once. He flung his hammer and chisel onto the ground, and gestured toward a pile of tree logs for me to sit on. He too sat down, and said, "Do you know the essence of Plato's philosophy?"

"Well . . . "

"It's the death of Socrates. You know why he was killed? He raised his voice against tyranny. That's how it was then, and that's how it is now. Nothing's changed. Our government is a bunch of tyrannical crooks."

"But there's more to Plato," I protested, though I hadn't read Plato.

"Yes, there's less to Plato. He had to write cryptically because he was surrounded by spies. You must learn how to read. There is politics everywhere."

"But here you have freedom . . . "

"In a manner of speaking. But do you think I like making tombstones? I used to hold a high post in the Party. I was about to be elected the Minister of Culture of Croatia, but I spoke freely against their Mercedeses and champagne. Since I had contacts in the Soviet Union, they discredited me as an informer. They sent me here into the province, behind God's back, so I wouldn't be in their way. This is my Siberia. But enough of this. There's a living to be made. I must support the old hag and the young hag. See, my daughter is pregnant, her fucker left her. I need to make her a room upstairs. She'll need the space for her bastard."

He spoke with acerbic, Serbian bitterness.

He walked back to his stone and paid no more attention to me. He hit the broadened head of the chisel with his heavy hammer, bluish steel cutting into bluish gray stone, stone dust flying up in a cloud. With his gray hair and bluish stubbly cheeks he blended into the grain of the stone; all you saw was a stone and a pair of upwardly curved eyebrows. The metal rang dully in a mesmerizing rhythm; your ears hurt as if you were descending in a plane, and you stared at the tombstone of a yet-unnamed dead man, whose face had no nose, no ears, no eyes, only stone and eyebrows. Passing by his house, people heard, saw, smelled work.

It seems to me I visited him often, but I did so only a few times, each of which left a strong impression that multiplied in my mind. Once, when I was depressed over having let loose my hawk, having failed to train it, I visited him and found him shoveling gray cement dust into a cement hole, into which he poured water. "Hello!" I shouted.

He didn't reply. I addressed him again and he turned round and looked at me as if I had misunderstood something.

"Why do you always work?" I asked, as if he had misunderstood. How could it be that the man whom I admired for his freedom was a slave to work, more than any other?

"God works six days a week, and who am I to work less? The whole creation labors, and so must I. Read Genesis."

"But if work is punishment, can't you avoid it?"

"No, you cannot run away from the wrath of God. You must work. If you don't, you grow weak, indulgent, slothful, and a thousand vices and vipers poison you."

"But can't you rise above that?"

"There's no rising above. Nobody can rise so high as to oppose God Almighty. In the sweat of your brow . . . that's how you have to live. If you fail to accept the punishment, God will destroy you."

He looked like a bleak judge pronouncing the sentence of life imprisonment, a whole life in the Siberian labor camps. He grabbed a shovel aggressively as if he would smash my skull with it. He strained his seesaw jaw muscles as he spoke. I shrank back.

"But isn't God love?"

"That's right, he wants you to stay out of the reach of the devil, and you do that by work."

I was more dejected than the young man who asked Jesus what more he should do to be saved and was told to give up all his riches to the poor. Homework, hauling wood and coal at home, all work I knew as a torment to my body and mind; the work interfered with my daydreams—mental loafing. My freedom.

"Is there heaven as a reward afterwards? Hell as punishment? Is that why you work?"

"God will not burn you in hell the way Italians grill frogs. He is no Italian. There is no hell. There is no heaven either."

"No eternal life?"

"One life is enough. If you love God, it is enough for you that God will live on. The Creator learns from what he creates. The more you work and create, the more He learns through you. Your eternity is in the knowledge of creation, which survives in God. As that part of Him, you live on."

I made no reply and daydreamed about my hawk—will it live on its own in the wild? Maybe I won't see it again. He gripped a heavy hammer and chiseled away the rough edges of a stone, refusing to answer any more of my questions. His hands were large, with thick cracked skin, and several of his nails were blue from the misses of his hammer. His tendons went prominently into his fingers, which looked like rakes with blue earthworms and snakes, his veins, twisting around each tendon like the emblem for medicine. The skin of his palm was like the skin on the soles of a barefoot boy in a mountain village in the middle of the summer. Layers and layers of blisters and dead skin, one atop another, burying one another, the dead burying the dead. The callouses were tombstones of the once-alive skin. The palm was a record of hard work. It could be studied archaeologically. Each layer of the skin signified a different stage of suffering: tombstone-making, sculpture, rifle handling in the army, ploughing in the fields in his youth. Chiseling into the stone, he wrestled with time, to mark and catch it. But time evaded him like a canny boxer. Letting him cut into rocks, the bones of the earth, Time would let him exhaust himself. He would run out of time and out of himself. He was being spent in epitaphs, which would remain even as he sank into the dank green earth. Gray widows would stare into the night, looking in the outlines of the epitaphs, for the ghosts of their beloved in the bleakness of the stone by faint moonlight, candlelight, expecting that by the shifting candle-flicker something in the stone would begin to move and flicker into life. Marko, and all of us, would be no more than the whistle of the wind in the pines, an octave higher than a screech-owl's.

But the idea of work disturbed me more than the idea of mortality. "But still, don't you relax and enjoy yourself?"

He took out his teeth, washed them in the aluminum cup, put them back in, and answered, "There. I've just enjoyed myself."

"But, can you just work? What good is life . . . what's there to life if . . . ?"

"This—work, eat beans, fuck, turn to the wall, fart and snore; work, eat beans, fuck, turn to the wall, fart and snore. That's the logarithm of life."

"Well, how about esthetic pleasures, music, art, literature?"

"The fiddle is of no use in the mill." He pointed at the stone-cutting machine. "This is enough music for me. Painting. Paint-smearing. Literature. Garbled words of sloth-ridden people who want to talk their way out of work."

As for TV, radio and the newspapers, he replied, "A bunch of propaganda."

"How do you keep up then with the news?"

"I read history."

"What does that have to do with the news?"

"There's nothing new under the sun. You can find out what is going on by reading about thousands of years ago."

"But what if a war broke out?"

"That would be nothing new."

"But you might find out too late and not have enough time to run away."

"In the war there's no running away. I would not stop working. Besides, war would be good for my business; tombstones would be in demand."

And he resumed work. Conversations with him could not last more than five minutes at a time. As I walked down the steep hill through the park, his machine roared on.

Marko Kovachevich respected the May Day. At night during the parades he stood in the shadows beside a kiosk, like Jonah awaiting the destruction of Nineveh. I greeted him, "Zdravo." He muttered in return, "Sodom and Gomorrah. Just look at it. All these girls running around naked and the guys don't even look at them." (It was the mini-skirt era.) "Look what it's come to. You lift the tiny cloth and stick it in! What godlessness!"

His mutterings surprised me; he had made several sculptures of naked women decades before. I had seen them in his cellar.

His daughter claimed he was strict and puritanical. Throughout her childhood, he'd kept an eye on her. In her teens, to keep her away from the town "dogs," he had locked her in for days, but it didn't have the intended effect on her. She eloped at the first opportunity, without examining the character of her lover. He left her pregnant after half a year of free love. Despite helping her out financially, Marko became extramoralizing, which made it no easier on his daughter. His influence was so strong that she too became an art teacher—a painter as well as a sculptor; but rumor had it that if you were a virgin, all you needed to do was visit her and she would initiate you. Her promiscuity hurt Marko's pride.

Marko looked aggrieved, like a medieval portrait on which there's not even the flicker of a smile. He grieved over what had come of it all: the country, and the family. I guess he was a bitter old man.

Seven years after graduating from the gymnasium and moving out of the country, I saw him on July 4, the day of liberation in Yugoslavia. How much he had changed! In his face there were still signs of strength, of his great strength, there in his glistening eyes, beneath the horned eyebrows. Something had changed in him though. His face was more sunken than before. His body had grown weaker and the stubborness in his eyes stronger. They were larger, more fierce. But no, it was not the eyes that had done it. It was Time. The old Marko had been buried in time. Time had chiseled into his face so steadily that you could tell how many years had passed just by looking there. His flesh had lost vigor and the vigor had moved into his eyes. Even his eyes seemed to have shrunk. They were a little grayer as if with glaucoma, as if the stone had entered them and had begun to turn him into stone, as Lot's wife was turned to salt. The work of time is black magic. Time drains a bit of tissue from under the skin and drains it down the lymphatic channels, out of the body, until only the skin and bones remain. But time does not stop; it thins the skin, empties the bones of their marrow. Only the skeleton remains under the tombstone. Seeing shrunken Marko, who had struck me as being as permanent as the tombstones he made, I was startled and afraid to look into his face. We shook hands. He masticated as he used to, his jaw muscles popping up, and said: "For God's sake, where have you vanished to?"

"I live in the States now. I'm studying philosophy for a Ph.D."

"Philosophy in the States," he said skeptically as if the choice of the continent was wrong. "They will teach you nothing. Come on, visit me in my workshop, and I'll show you what philosophy is!" He spoke in his take-the-whole-world-by-the-throat voice. "I'll tell you some things I have understood, something nobody here nor there understands. If you listen to me, you'll demolish all the philosophers over there by the force of your arguments. You'll sink them." He spoke calmly, spreading his arm forward and moving it level with the horizon, with a distant look in his eyes, as if he were leveling the American cities to the ground. I chuckled; he had become even more bellicose and preposterous than before.

Several years later, after abandoning my studies in philosophy, I returned to Nizograd. I walked through the park, to the periphery of the town, towards his old house. Where there had been piles of rust, there was a garden now, and in the garden sat his daughter, reading a book, and a child was swinging on a swing, hung on a branch of a large oak.

I walked in and asked about her father. The swing stopped, the child ran into the house, and bumblebees buzzed, bending stalks of flowers, as she closed her book and told me he had died several years before.

He had been ill for a year, skin and bone, and he had sunk, as unbelievable as it sounded, into the ground before his sixtieth birthday. In the war, in the mountain forests, sleeping in torn tents in snow, sleet, rain and mud, his kidneys had rotted. So, while he had appeared to be a man of steel, he had been instead a man of iron, rusted inside, though standing embattled and firm as if the war had not ended.

Jehovah's Witnesses wanted to bury Marko Kovachevich in their way, Serbian Orthodox priests in their way, and the Communists in theirs. Marko Kovachevich had left a spoken will with a friend of his who also had earned a couple of medals as a Communist partisan but had no faith in the Party. If somebody wanted credit for having a medal, Marko's friend would reply, "So? Even my dog has a medal, and you wouldn't vote for her as mayor, would you?" In the streets you could often see his bitch with a medal around her neck and a shopping bag in her teeth, proudly carrying groceries home. The friend and Mrs. Kovachevich warded off all the groups that fought for the right to bury Marko Kovachevich—no easy task since there was no written will that dictated how he should be buried. Now that Marko was dead, it was easy for the townspeople to claim he was one of them and to be proud of him. Kovachevich was buried according to his will, without a star, without a cross, without angels, and without food—as is the Serbian custom—on his tomb.

Atop his grave was placed one of his own products, a cubic tombstone from his own machine, formed by his own chisel, with the inscription cut by his own hand. His stone arose among many stones, sticking out of the ground like a tooth among many sparse teeth on the lower jaw of Mother Earth—a molar crown among crowns.

Nominated by The Paris Review

VITAL SIGNS

by NATALIE KUSZ

from THE THREEPENNY REVIEW

1. In Hospital

I WAS ALWAYS waking up, in those days, to the smell of gauze soaked with mucus and needing to be changed. Even when I cannot recall what parts of me were bandaged then, I remember vividly that smell, a sort of fecund, salty, warm one like something shut up and kept alive too long in a dead space. Most of the details I remember from that time are smells, and the chancest whiff from the folds of surgical greens or the faint scent of ether on cold fingers can still drag me, reflexively, back to that life, to flux so familiar as to be a constant in itself. Years after Children's Hospital, when I took my own daughter in for stitches in her forehead, and two men unfolded surgical napkins directly under my nose, I embarrassed us all by growing too weak to stand, and had to sit aside by myself until all the work was over.

It seems odd that these smells have power to bring back such horror, when my memories of that time are not, on the whole, dark ones. Certainly I suffered pain, and I knew early a debilitating fear of surgery itself, but the life I measured as months inside and months outside the walls was a good one, and bred in me understandings that I would not relinquish now.

There was a playroom in the children's wing, a wide room full of light, with colored walls and furniture, and carpets on the floor. A wooden kitchen held the corner alongside our infirmary, and my friends and I passed many hours as families, cooking pudding for our dolls before they were due in therapy. Most of the

dolls had amputated arms and legs, or had lost their hair to che-
motherapy, and when we put on our doctors' clothes we taught
them to walk with prostheses, changing their dressings with sterile gloves.

We had school tables, and many books, and an ant farm by the
window so we could care for something alive. And overseeing us
all was Janine, a pink woman, young even to seven-year-old eyes,
with yellow, cloudy hair that I touched when I could. She kept it
long, parted in the middle, or pulled back in a pony tail like
mine before the accident. My hair had been blonde then, and I
felt sensitive now about the coarse brown stubble under my bandages. Once, on a thinking day, I told Janine that if I had hair like
hers I would braid it and loop the pigtails around my ears. She
wore it like that the next day, and every day after for a month.

Within Janine's playroom, we were some of us handicapped,
but none disabled, and in time we were each taught to prove this
for ourselves. While I poured the flour for new playdough, Janine asked me about my kindergarten teacher: what she had
looked like with an eyepatch, and if she was missing my same
eye. What were the hard parts, Janine said, for a teacher like
that? Did I think it was sad for her to miss school sometimes, and
did she talk about the hospital? What color was her hair, what
sort was her eyepatch, and did I remember if she was pretty?
What would I be, Janine asked, when I was that age and these
surgeries were past? Over the wet salt smell of green dough, I
wished to be a doctor with one blue eye, who could talk like this
to the sick, who could tell them they were still real. And with her
feel for when to stop talking, Janine turned and left me, searching out volunteers to stir up new clay.

She asked a lot of questions, Janine did, and we answered her
as we would have answered ourselves, slowly and with purpose.
When called to, Janine would even reverse her words, teaching
opposite lessons to clear the mist in between; this happened for
Thomas and Nick in their wheelchairs, and I grew as much older
from watching as they did from being taught. Both boys were
eleven, and though I've forgotten their histories, I do remember
their natures, the differences which drew them together.

They were roommates, and best friends, and their dispositions
reverberated within one another, the self-reliant and the needy.
Thomas was the small one, the white one, with blue veins in his

forehead, and pale hair falling forward on one side. He sat always leaning on his elbows, both shoulders pressing up around his ears, and he rested his head to the side when he talked. He depended on Nick, who was tight-shouldered and long, to take charge for him, and he asked for help with his eyes half open, breathing out words through his mouth. And Nick reached the far shelves, and brought Thomas books, and proved he could do for them both, never glancing for help at those who stood upright. His skin was darker than Thomas', and his eyes much lighter, the blue from their centers washing out into the white.

When they played together, those boys, Thomas was the small center of things, the thin planet sunken into his wheelchair, pulling his friend after him. It must not have seemed to Nick that he was being pulled, because he always went immediately to Thomas' aid, never expecting anyone else to notice. Janine, of course, did. When Thomas wanted the television switched, and Nick struggled up to do it, she said: "Nick, would you like me to do that?"

"I can do it," he said.

"But so can I," Janine said, and she strode easily to the television and turned the knob to *Sesame Street*. "Sometimes," she said to Nick, "you have to let your friends be kind; it makes them feel good." She went back to sit beside Thomas, and she handed him the erector set. How would he turn the channel, she said, if no one else were here? What could he do by himself? And as the T.V. went unnoticed, Thomas imagined a machine with gears and little wheels, and Janine said she thought it could work. After that, Thomas was always building, though he still asked for help, and he still got it. Nick never did ask, as long as I knew him, but in time he managed to accept what was offered, and even, in the end, to say thanks.

In this way and in others, Janine encouraged us to change. When we had new ideas, they were outstanding ones, and we could count almost always on her blessing. We planned wheelchair races, and she donated the trophy—bubblegum ice cream all around. When she caught us blowing up surgical gloves we had found in the trash, she swiped a whole case of them, conjuring a helium bottle besides; that afternoon the playroom smelled of synthetic, powdery rubber, and we fought at the tables over colored markers, racing to decorate the brightest balloon. Janine's was the best—a cigar-smoking man with a four-spiked mohawk—and she handed it down the table to someone's father.

She always welcomed our parents in, so long as they never interfered, and they respected the rule, and acted always unsurprised. When Sheldon's mother arrived one day, she found her son—a four-year-old born with no hands—up to his elbows in orange fingerpaints. She stood for a moment, watching, then offered calmly to mix up a new color.

We children enjoyed many moments like these, granted us by adults like Janine and our parents, and these instants of contentment were luxuries we savored, but on which, by necessity, we did not count. I've heard my father, and other immigrant survivors of World War II, speak of behavior peculiar to people under siege, of how they live in terms, not of years, but of moments, and this was certainly true of our lives. That time was fragmentary, allowing me to remember it now only as a series of flashes, with the most lyrical event likely at any moment to be interrupted. We children were each at the hospital for critical reasons, and a game we planned for one day was likely to be missing one or two players the next, because Charlie hemorrhaged in the night, Sarah was in emergency surgery, or Candice's tubes had pulled out. I myself missed many outings on the lawn because my bone grafts rejected or because my eye grew so infected that I had to be quarantined. At these times, I would watch the others out the closed window, waiting for them to come stand beyond the sterile curtain and shout to me a summary of the afternoon.

In the same way that the future seemed, because it might never arrive, generally less important than did the present, so, too, was the past less significant. Although each of us children could have recited his own case history by heart, it was rare that any of us required more than a faint sketch of another child's past; we found it both interesting and difficult enough to keep current daily record of who had been examined, tested, or operated upon, and whether it had hurt, and if so, whether they had cried. This last question was always of interest to us, and tears we looked on as marks, not of cowards, but of heroes, playmates who had endured torture and lived to testify. The older a child was, the greater our reverence when her roommate reported back after an exam; we derived some perverse comfort from the fact that even twelve-year-olds cracked under pressure.

Those of us who did choose to abide vigorously in each instant were able to offer ourselves, during the day, to one another, to uphold that child or parent who began to weaken. If her need was to laugh, we laughed together; if to talk, we listened, and once, I remember, I stood a whole morning by the chair of a fifteen-year-old friend, combing her hair with my fingers, handing her kleenex and lemon drops, saying nothing. At night, then, we withdrew, became quietly separate, spoke unguardedly with our families. We spent these evening hours regrouping, placing the days into perspective, each of us using our own methods of self-healing. My mother would read to me from the Book of Job, about that faithful and guiltless man who said, "the thing that I so greatly feared has come upon me," and she would grieve, as I learned later, for me, and for us all. Or she would sit with me and write letters to our scattered family—my father at work in Alaska, my younger brother and sister with an aunt in Oregon. Of the letters that still exist from that time, all are full of sustenance, of words like *courage* and *honor.* It should have sounded ludicrous to hear a seven-year-old speaking such words, but I uttered them without embarrassment, and my parents did not laugh.

For most of us, as people of crisis, it became clear that horror can last only a little while, and then it becomes commonplace. When one cannot be sure that there are many days left, each single day becomes as important as a year, and one does not waste an hour in wishing that that hour were longer, but simply fills it, like a smaller cup, as high as it will go without spilling over. Each moment, to the very ill, seems somehow slowed down, and more dense with importance, in the same way that a poem is more compressed than a page of prose, each word carrying more weight than a sentence. And though it is true I learned gentleness, and the spareness of time, this was not the case for everyone there, and in fact there were some who never embraced their mortality.

I first saw Darcy by a window, looking down into her lap, fingering glass beads the same leafy yellow as her skin. She was wearing blue, and her dress shifted under her chin as she looked up, asking me was I a boy, and why was my hair so short. Behind us, our mothers started talking, exchanging histories, imagining a future, and Darcy and I listened, both grown accustomed by now to all this talk of ourselves. Darcy was ten, and she was here for her second attempted kidney transplant, this time with her father as donor. The first try had failed through fault, her mother said, of the surgeons, and Washington state's best lawyer would handle the suit if anything went wrong this time. This threat was spoken loudly and often as long as I knew Darcy, and it was many years before I realized that her parents were afraid, and that they displayed their fear in anger, and those thousand sideways glances at their daughter.

As a playmate, Darcy was pleasant, and she and I made ourselves jewelry from glitter and paste, and dressed up as movie stars, or as rich women in France. We played out the future as children do, as if it were sure to come and as if, when it did, we would be there. It was a game we all played on the ward, even those sure to die, and it was some time before I knew that to Darcy it was not a game, that she believed it all. We were holding school, and Nick was the teacher, and Darcy was answering that when she grew up she would own a plane, and would give us free rides on the weekends.

"What if," Nick said to her, "what if you die before then?"

Darcy breathed in and out once, hard, and then she said, "I'm telling my mother you said that." Then she stood and left the playroom, and did not come back that day. Later, her father complained to Nick's, called him foolish and uncaring, and demanded that such a thing not happen again.

After that, Darcy came to play less often, and when she did, her parents looked on, even on days when Janine took us outside to look at the bay. Darcy grew fretful, and cried a good deal, and took to feeling superior, even saying that my father didn't love me or he wouldn't be in Alaska. When I forgave her, it was too late to say so, because I was gone by then and didn't know how to tell her.

Darcy's absence was a loss, not just to her, but to us other children as well. Just as we had no chance to comfort her, to offer our hands when she was weak, we could not count on her during our worst times, for she and her family suffered in that peculiar way which admits no fellowship. I don't remember, if I ever knew, what became of Darcy, because I came down with chick-enpox and was discharged so as not to jeopardize her transplant. I like to think she must have lived, it was so important to her, and as I think this, I hope she did survive, and that one day she grew, as we all did in some way, to be thankful.

One of my smallest teachers during this time was a leukemia patient, just three years old, who lived down the hall. Because of his treatments, Samuel had very little hair, and what he did have was too blond to see. There were always, as I remember, deep moons under his eyes, but somehow, even to us other children, he was quite beautiful. His teeth were very tiny in his mouth, and he chuckled rather than laughed out loud; when he cried, he only hummed, drawing air in and out his nose, with his eyes squeezed shut and tears forming in the cracks where there should have been lashes. Most children's wards have a few favorite patients, and Samuel was certainly among ours. Those few afternoons when his parents left the hospital together, they spent twenty minutes, on their return, visiting every room to find who had taken off with their son. More often than not, he was strapped to a lap in a wheelchair, his IV bottle dangling overhead like an antenna, getting motocross rides from an amputee.

Samuel possessed, even for his age, and in spite of the fact that he was so vulnerable, an implicit feeling of security, and it was partly this sense of trust which lent him that dignity I have found in few grown people. His mother, I remember, was usually the one to draw him away from our games when it was time for treatments, and, although he knew what was coming, he never ran from it; when he asked his mother, "Do I have to?" it was not a protest, but a question, and when she replied that, yes, this was necessary, he would accept her hand and leave the play room on his feet.

I have heard debate over whether terminally ill children know they are going to die, and I can't, even after knowing Samuel, answer this question. We all, to some extent, knew what death was, simply because each of us had been friends with someone who was gone, and we realized that at some point many of us were likely to die; this likelihood was enough certainty for us, and made the question of time and date too insignificant to ask. I remember the last day I spent with Samuel, how we all invited him for a picnic on the lawn, though he could not eat much. He had had treatments that morning which made him weak, made his smile very tired, but this was the same vulnerability we had always found charming, and I can't recall anything about that afternoon which seemed unusual. The rest of us could not know that Samuel would die before we woke up next morning, and certainly some things might have been different if we had; but I tend to think we would still have had the picnic, would still have rubbed dandelion petals into our skin, would still have taught Samuel to play Slap-Jack. And, for his part, Samuel would, as he did every day, have bent down to my wrist and traced the moon-shaped scar behind my hand.

II. Attack

Our nearest neighbors through the trees were the Turners, two cabins of cousins whose sons went to my school. Both families had moved here, as we had, from California, escaping the city and everything frightening that lived there. One of the women, Ginny, had a grown son who was comatose now since he was hit on the freeway, and she had come to Alaska to get well from her own mental breakdown, and to keep herself as far away as she could from automobiles.

Brian and Jeff Turner were my best friends then, and we played with our dogs in the cousins' houses, or in the wide snowy yard in between. On weekends or days off from school, my parents took us sledding and to the gravel pit with our skates. Sometimes, if the day was long enough, Brian and Jeff and I followed rabbit tracks through the woods, mapping all the new trails we could find, and my mother gave me orders about when to be home. Bears, she said, and we laughed, and said didn't she know they were asleep, and we could all climb trees anyway. We were not afraid, either, when Mom warned of dog packs. Dogs got cabin fever, too, she said, especially in the cold. They ran through the woods, whole crowds of them, looking for someone to gang up on.

That's okay, I told her. We carried pepper in our pockets in case of dogs: sprinkle it on their noses, we thought, and the whole pack would run away.

In December, the day before my birthday, when the light was dim and the days shorter than we had known before, Dad got a break at the union hall, a job at Prudhoe Bay that would save us just in time, before the stove oil ran out and groceries were gone. Mom convinced us children that he was off on a great adventure, that he would see foxes and icebergs, that we could write letters for Christmas and for New Year's, and afford new coats with feathers inside. In this last, I was not much interested, because I had my favorite already—a red wool coat that reversed to fake leopard—but I would be glad if this meant we could get back from the pawn shop Dad's concertina, and his second violin, and mine, the half-size with a short bow, and the guitar and mandolin and rifles and pistol that had gone that way one by one. Whether I played each instrument or not, it had been good to have them around, smelling still of campfires and of songfests in the summer.

It was cold after Dad left, cold outside and cold in our house. Ice on the trailer windows grew thick and shaggy, and my sister and I melted handprints in it and licked off our palms. There had been no insulation when the add-on went up, so frost crawled the walls there, too, and Mom had us wear long johns and shoes unless we were in our beds. Brian and Jeff came for my birthday, helped me wish over seven candles, gave me a comb and a mirror. They were good kids, my mother said, polite and with good sense, and she told me that if I came in from school and she were not home, I should take Hobo with me and walk to their house. You're a worrywart, Mommy, I said. I'm not a baby, you know.

On January 10th, only Hobo met me at the bus stop. In the glare from the schoolbus headlights, his blue eye shone brighter than his brown, and he watched until I took the last step to the ground before tackling me in the snow. Most days, Hobo hid in the shadow of the spruce until Mom took my book bag, then he erupted from the dark to charge up behind me, run through my legs and on out the front. It was his favorite trick. I usually lost my balance and ended up sitting in the road with my feet thrown wide out front and steaming dog tongue all over my face.

Hobo ran ahead, then back, brushing snow crystals and fur against my leg. I put a hand on my skin to warm it and dragged nylon ski pants over the road behind me. Mom said to have them along in case the bus broke down, but she knew I would not wear them, could not bear the plastic sounds they made between my thighs.

No light was on in our house.

If Mom had been home, squares of yellow would have shown through the spruce and lit the fog of my breath, turning it bright as I passed through. What light there was now came from the whiteness of snow, and from the occasional embers drifting up from our stove pipe. I laid my lunchbox on the top step and pulled at the padlock, slapping a palm on the door and shouting. Hobo jumped away from the noise and ran off, losing himself in darkness and in the faint keening dog sounds going up from over near the Turners' house. I called, "Hobo. Come back here, boy," and took to the path toward Brian's, tossing my ski pants to the storage tent as I passed.

At the property line, Hobo caught up with me and growled, and I fingered his ear, looking where he pointed, seeing nothing ahead there but the high curve and long sides of a quonset hut, the work shed the Turners used also as a fence for one side of their yard. In the fall, Brian and Jeff and I had walked to the back of it, climbing over boxes and tools and parts of old furniture, and we had found in the corner a lemming's nest made from chewed bits of cardboard and paper, packed under the curve of the wall so that shadows hid it from plain sight. We all bent close to hear the scratching, and while Brian held a flashlight I took two sticks and parted the rubbish until we saw the black eyes of a mother lemming and the pink naked bodies of five babies. The mother dashed deeper into the pile and we scooped the nesting back, careful not to touch the sucklings for fear that their mama would eat them if they carried scent from our fingers.

The dogs were loud now beyond the quonset, fierce in their howls and sounding many more than just three. Hobo crowded against my legs, and as I walked he hunched in front of me, making me stumble into a drift that filled my boots with snow. I called him a coward and said to quit it, but I held his neck against my thigh, turning the corner into the boys' yard and stopping on the edge. Brian's house was lit in all its windows, Jeff's was dark, and in the yard between them were dogs, new ones I had not seen before, each with its own house and tether. The dogs and their crying filled the yard, and when they saw me they grew wilder, hurling themselves to the ends of their chains, pulling their lips off their teeth. Hobo cowered and ran and I called him with my mouth, but my eyes did not move from in front of me.

There were seven. I knew they were huskies and meant to pull dogsleds, because earlier that winter Brian's grandfather had put on his glasses and shown us a book full of pictures. He had turned the pages with a wet thumb, speaking of trappers and racing people and the ways they taught these dogs to run. They don't feed them much, he said, or they get slow and lose their drive. This was how men traveled before they invented snowmobiles or gasoline.

There was no way to walk around the dogs to the lighted house. The snow had drifted and been piled around the yard in heaps taller than I was, and whatever aisle was left along the sides was narrow, and pitted with chain marks where the animals had wandered dragging their tethers behind. No, I thought, Jeff's house was closest and out of biting range, and someone could, after all, be sitting home in the dark.

My legs were cold. The snow in my boots had packed itself around my ankles and begun to melt, soaking my socks and the felt liners under my heels. I turned toward Jeff's house, chafing my thighs together hard to warm them, and I called cheerfully at the dogs to shut up. Oscar said that if you met a wild animal, even a bear, you had to remember it was more scared than you were. Don't act afraid, he said, because they can smell fear. Just be loud—stomp your feet, wave your hands—and it will run away without even turning around. I yelled "Shut up," again as I climbed the steps to Jeff's front door, but even I could barely hear myself over the wailing. At the sides of my eyes, the huskies were pieces of smoke tumbling over one another in the dark.

The wood of the door was solid with cold, and even through deerskin mittens it bruised my hands like concrete. I cupped a hand to the window and looked in, but saw only black—black, and the reflection of a lamp in the other cabin behind me. I turned and took the three steps back to the ground; seven more and I was in the aisle between doghouses, stretching my chin far up above the frenzy, thinking hard on other things. This was how we walked in summertime, the boys and I, escaping from bad guys over logs thrown across ditches: step lightly and fast, steady on the hard parts of your soles, arms extended outward, palms down and toward the sound. That ditch, this aisle, was a river, a torrent full of silt that would fill your clothes and pull you down if you missed and fell in. I was halfway across. I pointed my chin toward the house and didn't look down.

On either side, dogs on chains hurled themselves upward, choking themselves to reach me, until their tethers jerked their throats back to earth. I'm not afraid of you, I whispered; this is dumb.

I stepped toward the end of the row and my arms began to drop slowly closer to my body. Inside the mittens, my thumbs were cold, as cold as my thighs, and I curled them in and out again. I was walking past the last dog and I felt brave, and I forgave him and bent to lay my mitten on his head. He surged forward on a chain much longer than I thought, leaping at my face, catching my hair in his mouth, shaking it in his teeth until the skin gave way with a jagged sound. My feet were too slow in my boots, and as I blundered backward they tangled in the chain, burning my legs on metal. I called out at Brian's window, expecting rescue, angry that it did not come, and I beat my arms in front of me, and the dog was back again, pulling me down.

A hole was worn into the snow, and I fit into it, arms and legs drawn up in front of me. The dog snatched and pulled at my mouth, eyes, hair; his breath clouded the air around us, but I did not feel its heat, or smell the blood sinking down between hairs of his muzzle. I watched my mitten come off in his teeth and sail upward, and it seemed unfair then and very sad that one hand should freeze all alone; I lifted the second mitten off and threw it away, then turned my face back again, overtaken suddenly by loneliness. A loud river ran in my ears, dragging me under.

My mother was singing. Lu-lee, lu-lay, thou little tiny child, the song to the Christ child, the words she had sung, smoothing my hair, all my life before bed. Over a noise like rushing water I called to her and heard her answer back, Don't worry, just sleep, the ambulance is on its way. I drifted back out and couldn't know then what she prayed, that I would sleep on without waking, that I would die before morning.

She had counted her minutes carefully that afternoon, sure that she would get to town and back, hauling water and mail, with ten minutes to spare before my bus came. But she had forgotten to count one leg of the trip, had skidded up the drive fifteen minutes late, pounding a fist on the horn, calling me home. On the steps, my lunchbox had grown cold enough to burn her hands. She got the water, the groceries, and my brother and sisters inside, gave orders that no one touch the wood stove or open the door, and she left down the trail to Brian's, whistling Hobo in from the trees.

I know from her journal that Mom had been edgy all week about the crazed dog sounds next door. Now the new huskies leaped at her and Hobo rumbled warning from his chest. Through her sunglasses, the dogs were just shapes, indistinct in windowlight. She tried the dark cabin first, knocking hard on the windows, then turned and moved down the path between dog houses, feeling her way with her feet, kicking out at open mouths. Dark lenses frosted over from her breath, and she moved toward the house and the lights on inside.

"She's not here." Brian's mother held the door open and air clouded inward in waves. Mom stammered out thoughts of bears, wolves, dogs. Ginny grabbed on her coat. She had heard a noise out back earlier—they should check there and then the woods.

No luck behind the cabin and no signs under the trees. Wearing sunglasses and without any flashlight, Mom barely saw even the snow. She circled back and met Ginny under the windowlight. Mom looked that way and asked about the dogs. "They seem so hungry," she said.

Ginny said, "No. Brian's folks just got them last week, but the boys play with them all the time." All the same, she and Mom scanned their eyes over the kennels, looking through and then over their glasses. Nothing seemed different. "Are you sure she isn't home?" Ginny said. "Maybe she took a different trail."

Maybe. Running back with Ginny behind her, Mom called my name until her lungs frosted inside and every breath was a cough. The three younger children were still the only ones at home, and Mom handed them their treasure chests, telling them to play on the bed until she found Natalie. Don't go outside, she said. I'll be back right soon.

Back at the Turners', Ginny walked one way around the quonset and Mom the other. Mom sucked air through a mitten, warming her lungs. While Ginny climbed over deeper snow, she approached the sled dogs from a new angle. In the shadow of one, a splash of red—the lining of my coat thrown open. "I've found her," she shouted, and thought as she ran, Oh, thank God. Thank, thank God.

The husky stopped its howling as Mom bent to drag me out from the hole. Ginny caught up and seemed to choke. "Is she alive?" she said.

Mom said, "I think so, but I don't know how." She saw one side of my face gone, one red cavity with nerves hanging out, scraps of dead leaves stuck on to the mess. The other eye might be gone, too; it was hard to tell. Scalp had been torn away from my skull on that side, and the gashes reached to my forehead, my lips, had left my nose ripped wide at the nostrils. She tugged my body around her chest and carried me inside.

III. Vital Signs

I had little knowledge of my mother's experience of the accident until many months afterward, and even then I heard her story only after I had told mine, after I had shown how clearly I remembered the dogs, and their chains, and my own blood on the snow—and had proven how little it bothered me to recall them. When I said I had heard her voice, and named for her the songs she had sung to me then, my mother searched my face, looking into me hard, saying, "I can't believe you remember." She had protected me all along, she said, from her point of view, not thinking that I might have kept my own, and that mine must be harder to bear. But after she knew all this, Mom felt she owed me a history, and she told it to me then, simply and often, in words that I would draw on long after she was gone.

She said that inside the Turner's cabin, she laid me on Ginny's couch, careful not to jar the bleeding parts of me, expecting me to wake in an instant and scream. But when I did become conscious, it was only for moments, and I was not aware then of my wounds, or of the cabin's warmth, or even of pressure from the fingers of Brian's grandfather, who sat up close and stroked the frozen skin of my hands.

Ginny ordered Brian and Jeff to their room, telling them to stay there until she called them, and then she stood at Mom's shoulder, staring down and swaying on her legs.

Mom looked up through her glasses and said, "Is there a phone to call an ambulance?"

Ginny was shaking. "Only in the front house, kid, and it's locked," she said. "Kathy should be home in a minute, but I'll try to break in." She tugged at the door twice before it opened, and then she went out, leaving my mother to sing German lullabies beside my ear. *When morning comes,* the words ran, *if God wills it, you will wake up once more.* My mother sang the words and breathed on me, hoping I would dream again of summertime, all those bright nights when the music played on outside, when she drew the curtains and sang us to sleep in the trailer. Long years after the accident, when she felt healed again and stronger, Mom described her thoughts to me, and when she did she closed her eyes and sat back, saying, "You can't know how it was to keep singing, to watch air bubble up where a nose should have been, and to pray that each of those breaths was the last one." Many times that night she thought of Job, who also had lived in a spacious, golden land, who had prospered in that place, yet had cried in the end, "The thing that I so greatly feared has come upon me." The words became a chant inside her, filling her head and bringing on black time.

The wait for the ambulance was a long one, and my mother filled the time with her voice, sitting on her heels and singing. She fingered my hair and patted my hands and spoke low words when I called out. Brian's grandfather wept and warmed my fingers in his, and Mom wondered where were my mittens, and how were her other children back home.

Ginny came back and collapsed on a chair, and Kathy, her sister-in-law, hurried in through the door. Ginny began to choke, rocking forward over her knees, telling Kathy the story. Her voice stretched into a wail that rose and fell like music. "It's happening again," she said, "No matter where you go, it's always there."

Kathy brought out aspirin, then turned and touched my mother's arm. She said that as soon as Ginny was quiet, she would leave her here and fetch my siblings from the trailer.

"Thank you," Mom told her. "I'll send someone for them as soon as I can." She looked at Ginny then, wishing she had something to give her, some way to make her know that she was not to

96

blame here; but for now Mom felt that Ginny had spoken truth when she said that sorrow followed us everywhere, and there was little else she could add.

The ambulance came, and then everything was movement. I drifted awake for a moment as I was lifted to a stretcher and carried toward the door. I felt myself swaying in air, back and forth and back again. Brian's whisper carried over the other voices in the room, as if blown my way by strong wind. "Natalie's dying," he said; then his words were lost among other sounds, and I faded out again. A month later, when our first-grade class sent me a box full of valentines, Brian's was smaller than the rest, a thick, white heart folded in two. Inside, it read: "I love you, Nataly. Pleas dont die." When I saw him again, his eyes seemed very big, and I don't remember that he ever spoke to me any more.

It was dark inside the ambulance, and seemed even darker to my mother, squinting through fog on her sunglasses. She badgered the medic, begging him to give me a shot for pain. Any minute I would wake up, she said, and I would start to scream. The man kept working, taking my pulse, writing it down, and while he did, he soothed my mother in low tones, explaining to her about physical shock, about the way the mind estranges itself from the body and stands, unblinking and detached, on the outside. "If she does wake up," he said, "she'll feel nothing. She won't even feel afraid." When Mom wrote this in her journal, her voice was filled with wonder, and she asked what greater gift there could be.

At the hospital, there were phone calls to be made, and Mom placed them from outside the emergency room. First she called Dick and Esther Conger, two of the only summertime friends who had stayed here over winter. We had met this family on the way up the Alcan, had been attracted to their madeover school bus with its sign, "Destination: Adventure," and to the Alaskan license plates bolted to each bumper. Sometime during the drive up, or during the summer when we shared the same campfires, the children of our families had become interchangeable; Toni and Barry were in the same age group as we were, and discipline and praise were shared equally among us all. It was never shocking to wake up in the morning and find Toni or Barry in one of our beds; we just assumed that the person who belonged there was over sleeping in their bus. Now, as my mother explained the accident to Dick, our friend began to cry, saying, "Oh, Verna. Oh, no," and Esther's voice in the background asked, "What's happened? Let me talk to her." Mom asked the Congers to drive out for my brother and sisters, to watch them until my father came.

Leaning her head to the wall, Mom telephoned a message to the North Slope. She spoke to Dad's boss there, explaining only that "our daughter has been hurt." Just now, she thought, she couldn't tell the whole story again, and besides, the worst "hurt" my father would imagine could not be this bad. The crew boss said a big snowstorm was coming in, but they would try to fly my father out beforehand; if not, they would get him to the radio phone and have him call down. A nurse walked up then and touched Mom's shoulder, saying, "Your daughter is awake, and she's asking for you." A moment before, Mom had been crying, pressing a fist to her teeth, but now she closed up her eyes like a faucet and walked after the nurse, pulling up her chin and breathing deeply in her chest. She had trembled so that she could hardly wipe her glasses, but when she moved through the door and saw the white lights, and me lying flat on a table, she was suddenly calm, and the skin grew warmer on her face.

Mom positioned herself in front of my one eye, hoping as she stood there that she wasn't shaking visibly, that her face was not obviously tense. She need not have bothered; as I lay staring right to where my eye veered off, the room was smoky grey, and I was conscious only of a vicious thirst that roughened the edges of my tongue, made them stick to my teeth. I was allowed no water, had become fretful, and when my mother spoke to me, I complained that the rag in my mouth had not been damp enough, and that these people meant to cut my favorite coat off of me. I have to think now that my mother acted courageously, keeping her face smooth, listening to me chatter about school, about the message I had brought from my teacher, that they would skip me to the second grade on Monday. Mom's answers were light, almost vague, and before she left the pre-op room, she told me to listen to the nurses, to let them do all they needed to; they were trying to help me, she said. A little later, after I was wheeled into surgery, a nurse handed her the things they had saved: my black boots, and the Alice-in-Wonderland watch Mom had given me for Christmas.

My mother made more phone calls, to churches in town and to ones in California that we'd left behind, telling the story over again, asking these people to pray. Old friends took on her grief, asking did she need money, telling her to call again when she knew more. These people knew, as my mother did, that money was not so much the question now, but it was something they could offer, and so they did. And for months and years after this they would send cards, and letters, and candy and flowers and toys, making themselves as present with us as they could. For now, on this first night, they grieved with my mother, and they said to go lie down if she could, they would take over the phones. And each of these people made another call, and another, until, as my mother walked back to the waiting room, she knew she was lifted up by every friend we had ever made.

The Turners had arrived, and for a little while they all sat along the waiting room walls, stuffing fists into their pockets and closing their eyes. None of them wanted to talk about the accident, or to wonder about the progress in surgery, and when my mother said to Kathy, "I just talked to some people in California who would never *believe* the way we live here," her words seemed terribly funny, and started the whole room laughing. It wasn't so much, she said later, that they were forgetting why they were there; in fact, they remembered very well—so well, that compared to that fact, everything else was hilarious. And they could not possibly have continued for long as they had been, she said, pressing their backs to the walls and waiting. So for hours after Mom's joke, and far into the night, the adults invented names for our kind—"the outhouse set," "the bush league"—and they contributed stories about life in Alaska that would shock most of the people Outside. They joked about styrofoam outhouse seats—the only kind that did not promote frostbite—about catalogues that no one could afford to buy from, but whose pages served a greater purpose, about the tremendous hardship of washing dishes from melted snow and then tossing the grey water out the door. From time to time, Ginny got up from her seat to walk alone in the hall, but when she came back in she was ready again to laugh.

99

My father arrived about midnight, dressed in a week's growth of beard and in an army surplus parka and flight pants. Mom met him in the hall and stood looking up; Dad dropped his satchel to the floor, panting, and he watched my mother's face, the eyes behind her glasses. He spoke first, said his was the last plane out in a heavy snowstorm. Then: "How did it happen," he said. "Did she fall out the door?"

My mother waited a beat and looked at him. "It wasn't a car accident, Julius," she said. She started telling the story again, and my father looked down then at the blood crusted on her sweater, and he closed his eyes and leaned into the wall. My mother told him, "You can't appreciate how I feel, because you haven't seen her face. But I wish that when you pray you'd ask for her to die soon."

Dad opened his eyes. "That must seem like the best thing to ask," he said. "But we don't make decisions like that on our own. We never have, and we can't start now."

Sometime after two a.m., my three surgeons stepped in. My mother said later that, had they not still worn their surgical greens, she would not have recognized them; during the night, she had forgotten their faces.

The men sagged inside their clothes, three sets of shoulders slumped forward under cloth. I was still alive, they said, but only barely, and probably not for long. I had sustained over one hundred lacerations from the shoulders up, and had lost my left cheekbone along with my eye. They'd saved what tissues they could, filling the bulk of the cavity with packings, and what bone fragments they had found were now wired together on the chance that some of them might live.

My father groped for a positive word. "At least she doesn't have brain damage. I heard she was lucid before surgery."

Dr. Butler brushed the surgical cap from his head and held it, twisting it in his hands. His eyes were red as he looked up, explaining as kindly as it seemed he could. A dog's mouth, he said, was filthy, filthier than sewage, and all of that impurity had passed into my body. They had spent four hours just cleaning out the wounds, pulling out dirt and old berry leaves and dog feces. Even with heavy antibiotics, I would likely have massive infections, and they would probably spread into my brain. His voice turned hoarse and he looked across at Dr. Earp, asking the man to continue.

Dr. Earp rubbed hard at the back of his head and spoke softly, working his neck. For now, Dr. Earp said, they had been able to reconstruct the eyelids; that would make the biggest visible difference.

On my parents' first hourly visit to Intensive Care, Mom stopped at the door and put her hand to my father's chest. "No matter how she looks," she said, "don't react. She'll be able to tell what you're thinking."

The nurse at the desk sat under a shaded lamp, the only real light in the room. She stood and whispered that mine was the first bed to the left. "She wakes up for a minute or so at a time," she said. "She's been asking for you."

"First one on the left," my father said after her, a little too loud for that place, and from somewhere inside a great rushing river I heard him and called out. At my bed, Mom watched him as he stood looking down, and when the lines in his face became deeper, she turned from him, pinching his sleeve with her fingers. She walked closer to me and held the bedrail.

IV. The Fear

It had to happen eventually, that I found a mirror and looked in. For the first days after my accident, I had stayed mostly in bed, leaning my bandages back on the pillow and peeling frostbite blisters from my hands. The new skin was pink, and much thinner than the old, as sensitive to touch as the nail beds I uncovered by chewing down to them. I had taken to running two fingers over stitches standing up like razor stubble on my face, then over the cotton that covered the right side and the rest of my head. The whole surgical team came in daily to lift me into a chair and unwind the gauze, releasing into the room a smell like old caves full of bones. And all this time I had never seen myself, never asked what was under there, in the place where my left eye belonged.

I had asked my mother once if I would again see out of that eye. It was an hour after my dressing had been changed, and the

101

smell of hot ooze still hovered in my room. Mom stood up and adjusted my bedrail. "Do you want your feet a little higher," she said. "I can crank them up if you like."

I said, "Mommy, my eye. Will I be able to see from it?"

"Hang on," she said. "I need to use the little girls' room." She started to the door and I screamed after her, "Mommy, you're not answering me." But she was gone, and after that I did not ask.

Later, when the light was out, I lay back and looked far right, then left, concentrating hard, trying to feel the bandaged eye move. I thought I could feel it, rolling up and then down, ceiling to floor, matching its moves with my other eye. Even after I was grown, I could swear that I felt it blink when I pressed my two lids together.

Men from down the hall visited me during the day, rolling in on wheelchairs or walking beside their IV racks. They all wore two sets of pajamas, one wrong way forward so their backsides were covered. The hospital floor was old, its tiles starting to bubble, and the wheels on my friends' IV racks made rumbling sounds as they passed over. If a nurse passed by the door and looked in, the men waved her away, saying, "It's all right, dear. I'm visiting my granddaughter." For a kiss they gave me a sucker and a story about bears, or they carried me to a wheelchair and took me around to visit. In this way, I passed from room to room, brushing at the green curtains between beds, pouring water into plastic glasses, gathering hugs and learning to shake hands in the "cool" way. I signed plaster casts in big red letters, and I visited the baby room, pressing my chin to the glass.

On a day when I felt at my smallest and was in my bed still sleeping, one of my favorite men friends checked out, leaving on my nightstand a gift and a note that said he would miss me. The gift was a music box in pink satin, with a ballerina inside who pirouetted on her toes when I wound the key. And behind her inside the lid, a triangular looking-glass not much bigger than she was.

My mother came in behind me as I was staring into the mirror, holding it first from one angle, then from another, and she stood by the bed for a moment, saying nothing. When I turned, she was looking at me with her shoulders forward, and she seemed to be waiting.

"My eye is gone, isn't it?" I said.

She kept looking at me. She said, "Yes it is."

I turned again and lifted the box to my face. "I thought so," I said. "Those dogs were pretty mean."

I didn't understand, or was too small to know, what my mother thought she was protecting me from. It must be something very bad, I thought, for her to avoid every question I asked her. "Mommy," I said once. "I don't *feel* like I'm going to die."

She looked up from her book and the light shone off her glasses. She said, "Oh, no. You're certainly not going to do anything like that."

"Then will I be blind?"

"Well," she said. "You can see now, can't you?" And when I pressed her with more questions, she looked toward the door and said, "Sh-h. Here comes your lunch tray."

It all made me wonder if my wounds were much worse than everyone said—and of course they were, but there were long years of surgery still ahead, and no one wanted me to feel afraid. I was angry, too—as angry as a seven-year-old can be—that Mom patted my cheek with her palm and said she'd be taking my malemute to the pound before I came home. I stared at her then with my head up and sputtered out a peevish tirade, telling her I didn't hate all dogs, or even most dogs, but just the ones who bit me. It didn't occur to me until my own daughter was seven, the same age I was when I was hurt, that Mom might have been sending my dog away for her own sake.

V. Small Purchase

I have bought a one-eyed fish. Drifting around the tank near my desk, his skin ripples silver like well-pressed silk, and he moves under the light and hovers with his one bronze eye turned toward me, waiting to be fed. His body is smooth and flat, like a silver dollar but twice the size, and his fins are mottled gold. He is relative to the piranha, a meat eater with a bold round mouth, but even when the smaller fish challenge him, swishing their tails at his eye, he leaves them alone and swims off. He has not eaten one of them.

I call him Max, because my sister said I should. She did not remind me, when I brought him home, that I had wanted no pets, nothing with a life span shorter than my own, nothing that would die or have to be butchered as soon as I had given it a name. She just looked up with her face very serious as if she knew well how one could become attached to a fish, and she said to me, Max. Yes, that should be his name.

I had told us both, when I bought the aquarium, that fish were low-maintenance animals, without personalities and incapable of friendliness, and if one of them died you just flushed it away and got another. And besides, I said, I needed a fish tank. I had begun to feel stale, inert. I needed the sounds of moving water in my house, and I needed, too, something alive and interesting to stare at when I stopped typing to think of a new sentence.

Last summer, when I was tired and the writing was going badly, I got superstitious about the sea and thought that the lurch and pull of waves would freshen my ears and bring on clean thoughts. So I packed some books and a portable typewriter, drove to Homer on the coast, and rented a cabin near the beach. Something about the place, or its fishy air, or my aloneness in the middle of it, worked somehow, and I breathed bigger there in my chest and wrote more clearly on the page. I had forgotten about tides and about the kelp and dried crabs that came in with them, and every morning I shivered into a sweater, put combs in my hair, and walked out to wade and to fill my pockets with what I found. I liked it best when the wind was blowing and the sky was grey, and the sounds of seagulls and my own breathing were carried out with the water.

Kelp pods washed up around my feet, and I stomped on them with tennis shoes to find what was inside. I collected driftwood, and urchins, and tiny pink clam shells dropped by gulls, thin enough to see through and smaller than a thumbnail. When the tide had gone far out, I climbed the bluff back to my cabin and sat writing in front of the window, eating cheese on bread and drinking orange spritzers or tea. The walls and windows there had space in between, and they let in shreds of wind and the arguing of birds and the metal smell of seaweed drying out on the

104

beach. When the tide started back in, I took pen and notebook and sat on a great barnacled rock, letting water creep up and surround me, then jumping to shore just in time. An hour later, the rock would be covered, three feet or more under the grey, and I would only know where it lay because of the froth and swirl of whirlpools just above it.

When I came home I threw my bags on the bed and unfastened them, and a thousand aromas opened up then into my face, drifting out from the folds of my clothes, the seams in my shoes, the pages of my notebook. I had carried them back with me, the smells of the wet sand and fish fins, of eagle feathers floating in surf, of candle wax burned at midnight and filled with the empty bodies of moths. I had grieved on the drive home for that place I was leaving, and for the cold wind of that beach, and I had decided that somehow water should move in my house, should rush and bubble in my ears, should bring in the sound of the sea, and the wind and dark currents that move it.

So I bought an aquarium, and fish to go in it, and a water pump strong enough to tumble the surface as it worked. I bought plants for the tank, and waved their smell into the room, and when I thought I was finished I made one more trip to a pet store, just to see what they had.

The shop was a small one, in an old wooden building with low ceilings, and the fish room in back was dark and smelled submarine—humid and slippery and full of live things. All light in the place came from the fishtanks themselves, and the plants inside them absorbed the glow and turned it green, casting it outward to move in shadowed patterns on my skin. When I closed my eyes, the sound was of rivers, running out to the coast to be carried away mixed with salt. And the fish inside waved their fins and wandered between the rocks, opening and closing their mouths.

I glanced, but didn't look hard at the larger fish, because I had found already that they were always very expensive. I browsed instead through tetras and guppies, gouramis and cichlids, trying to be satisfied with the small ones, because after all it was just the water and its motion that I really wanted. So when I saw the wide silver fish and a sign that said "$10," I assumed it was a mistake but decided to ask about it while I ordered some neons

105

dipped out. With my neck bent forward, I watched as fifty neons swam fast away from the net that would always catch them anyway. Was that big fish back there really only ten, I said.

The clerk said, "You mean the Metynnis with one eye. He's such a mellow guy."

I swung my head to look at her. One eye?

The woman stared at my face for a moment and opened her mouth. Her cheeks grew pinker, but when she answered me, her voice stayed even. She said, "Yes, his former owners thought he was a piranha and put him in the tank with some. They ate out one eye before anyone could get him back up."

"They go for the eyes so their lunch will quit looking at them," I said. I told the woman I would take the Metynnis. I thought we were a match, I said.

And I was right. As absurd as I felt about my affinity with a one-eyed fish, I found myself watching him for the ways he was like me, and I did find many. Max had already learned, by the time I got him, to hold his body in the water so that whatever he was interested in lay always on the same side of him as his eye. In the same way that I situate myself in movie theaters so that my best friend sits on my right side, Max turns his eye toward the wall of his tank, watching for my arm to move toward the food box. When I drop a worm cube down to him, he shifts his eye up to look at it and then swims at it from the side so he never loses it from vision. If the smaller fish fight, or behave defiantly around him, he turns his dead eye against them and flicks himself away to a further corner of the tank.

I don't know if it is normal to befriend a fish. I think probably not. I do know that as I sit by Max's tank and write, I stop sometimes and look up, and I think then that he looks terribly dashing, swimming around with his bad eye outward, unafraid that something might attack him from his blind side. I buy him special shrimp pellets, and I feed them to him one at a time, careful always to drop them past his good eye. My friends like to feed him, too, and I teach them how, warning them to drop his food where he can see it. Now one of my friends wants to introduce me to his neighbor's one-eyed dog, and another wishes she still had her one-eyed zebra finch so she could give it to me.

That's just what I need, I think—a houseful of blind-sided pets. We could sit around together and play Wink-um, wondering was that a wink or just a lid shut down over a dry eyeball. We could fight about who got to sit on whose good side, or we could make jokes about how it takes two of us to look both ways before crossing the street. I laugh, but still I intend to meet the one-eyed dog, to see if he reminds me of Max—or of me. I wonder if he holds himself differently from other dogs, if when he hears a voice he turns his whole body to look.

And I wonder about myself, about what has changed in the world. At first, I wanted fish only for the water they lived in, for the movement it would bring to my house, the dust it would sweep from my brain. I thought of fish as "safe" pets, too boring to demand much attention, soulless by nature and indistinguishable from their peers. Maybe this is true for most of them. But I know that when the smaller fish chase after Max, or push him away from the food, I find myself fiercely angry. I take a vicious pleasure in dropping down shrimp pellets too big and too hard for the small ones to eat, and I find pleasure, too, in the way Max gobbles the food, working it to bits in his mouth. When he is finished, he turns a dead eye to the others and swims away, seeking things more interesting to look at.

Nominated by Naomi Clark

ARMAGEDDON: PRIVATE GABRIEL CALVIN WOJAHN 1900–18

by DAVID WOJAHN

from DENVER QUARTERLY

> PAPER DEATH SHROUD: *German, c. 1918. To conserve cloth and timber, then in short supply, enlisted men were buried—usually without coffins—in such shrouds.*
>
> —The Imperial War Museum, London

They buried you in mud, in the standard issue
Paper shroud, like a tooth wrapped in tissue

And hidden by a child in a rain-drenched garden,
Somewhere on the Western Front, Flanders or the Somme.

No photos survive. Eighteen, illiterate,
From the family my family fled, God-mad zealots

Who beat you daily, kept all books but the Bible from your
    sight,
You signed your X, transcended to the State,

And a freight car to the trenches, the No-Man's-Land
Where your crazed, medieval eyes read signs,

Not words: Armageddon everywhere,
The Last Days, twitching on barbed wire.

Priests and Frenchmen served the Antichrist.
You divined the entrails of corpses, saw your fate

Augured in birds' flight, scarlet sunsets,
And one night Satan came in person to your tent,

Offering cognac, scented Parisian cigarettes,
A smoking jacket, spats, a wireless set.

You named it a *vision*, and not some dream.
You spoke of it in all the letters home

You dictated to your commandant, who'd dip your thumb
In his inkwell, press it to the thin

Blue paper. *They'll know you*, he laughed, *by your sign*.
Mustard gas killed your entire platoon.

Above the mass grave, a chaplain muttered scripture.
What survives of you? Neither words nor paper.

Nominated by Marianne Boruch, Mark Doty , Lynda Hull, Richard Jackson, David Jauss, Susan Mitchell, Arthur Smith and Maura Stanton

MY MOTHER AND MITCH

fiction by CLARENCE MAJOR

from BOULEVARD

HE WAS JUST somebody who had dialed the wrong number. This is how it started and I wasn't concerned about it. Not at first. I don't even remember if I was there when he first called but I do, all these many years later, remember my mother on the phone speaking to him in her best quiet voice, trying to sound as ladylike as she knew how.

She had these different voices for talking to different people on different occasions. I could tell by my mother's proper voice that this man was somebody she wanted to make a good impression on, a man she thought she might like to know. This was back when my mother was still a young woman, divorced but still young enough to believe that she was not completely finished with men. She was a skeptic from the beginning, I knew that even then. But some part of her thought the right man might come along some day.

I don't know exactly what it was about him that attracted her though. People are too mysterious to know that well. I know that now and I must have been smart enough not to wonder too hard about it back then.

Since I remember hearing her tell him her name she must not have given it out right off the bat when he first called. She was a city woman with a child and had developed a certain alertness to danger. One thing you didn't do was give your name to a stranger on the phone. You never knew who to trust in a city like Chicago. The place was full of crazy people and criminals.

She said, "My name is *Mrs.* Jayne Anderson." I can still hear her laying the emphasis on the Mrs. although she had been separated from my father twelve years by 1951 when this man dialed her number by accident.

Mitch Kibbs was the name he gave her. I guess he must have told her who he was the very first time, just after he apologized for calling her by mistake. I can't remember who he was trying to call. He must have told her and she must have told me but it's gone now. I think they must have talked a pretty good while that first time. The first thing that I remember about him was that he lived with his sister who was older than he. The next thing was that he was very old. He must have been fifty and to me at fifteen that was deep into age. If my mother was old at thirty, fifty was ancient. Then the other thing about him was that he was white.

They'd talked five or six times I think before he came out and said he was white but she knew it before he told her. I think he made this claim only after he started suspecting he might not be talking to another white person. But the thing was he didn't know for sure she was black. I was at home lying on the couch pretending to read a magazine when I heard her say, "I am a colored lady." Those were her words exactly. She placed her emphasis on the word lady.

I had never known my mother to date any white men. She would hang up from talking to him and she and I would sit at the kitchen table and she'd tell me what he'd said. They were telling each other the bits and pieces of their lives, listening to each other, feeling their way as they talked. She spoke slowly, remembering all the details. I watched her scowl and the way her eyes narrowed as she puzzled over his confessions as she told me in her own words about them. She was especially puzzled about his reaction to her confession about being colored.

That night she looked across at me with that fearful look that was hers alone and said, "Tommy, I doubt if he will ever call back. Not after tonight. He didn't know. You know that."

Feeling grown-up because she was treating me that way, I said, "I wouldn't be so sure."

But he called back soon after that.

I was curious about her interest in this particular old white man so I always listened carefully. I was a little bit scared too because

111

I suspected he might be some kind of maniac or pervert. I had no good reason to fear such a thing except that I thought it strange that anybody could spend as much time as he and my mother did talking on the phone without any desire for human contact. She had never had a telephone relationship before and at that time all I knew about telephone relationships was that they were insane and conducted by people who probably needed to be put away. This meant that I also had the sad feeling that my mother was a bit crazy too. But more important than these fearful fantasies, I thought I was witnessing a change in my mother. It seemed important and I didn't want to misunderstand it or miss the point of it. I tried to look on the bright side, which was what my mother always said I should try to do.

He certainly didn't sound dangerous. Two or three times I myself answered the phone when he called and he always said, "Hello, Tommy, this is Mitch, may I speak to your mother," and I always said, "Sure, just a minute." He never asked me how I was doing or anything like that and I never had anything special to say to him.

After he'd been calling for over a month I sort of lost interest in hearing about their talk. But she went right on telling me what he said. I was a polite boy so I listened despite the fact that I had decided that Mitch Kibbs and his ancient sister Temple Erikson were crazy but harmless. My poor mother was lonely. That was all. I had it all figured out. He wasn't an ax murderer who was going to sneak up on her one evening when she was coming home from her job at the factory and split her open from the top down. We were always hearing about things like this so I knew it wasn't impossible.

My interest would pick up occasionally. I was especially interested in what happened the first time my mother herself made the call to his house. She told me that Temple Erikson answered the phone. Mother and I were eating dinner when she started talking about Temple Erikson.

"She's a little off in the head."

I didn't say anything but it confirmed my suspicion. What surprised me was my mother's ability to recognize it. "What'd she say?"

"She rattled on about the wild west and the Indians and having to hide in a barrel or something like that. Said the Indians were shooting arrows at them and she was just a little girl who hid in a barrel."

I thought about this. "Maybe she lived out west when she was young. You know? She must be a hundred by now. That would make her the right age."

"Oh, come on, now. What she said was she married when she was fourteen, married this Erikson fellow. As near as I could figure out he must have been a leather tanner but seems he also hunted fur and sold it to make a living. She never had a child."

"None of that sounds crazy." I was disappointed.

"She was talking crazy, though."

"How so?"

"She thinks the Indians are coming back to attack the house any day now. She says things like Erikson was still living, like he was just off there in the next room, taking a nap. One of the first things Mitch told me was his sister and he moved in together after her husband died and that was twenty years ago."

"How did the husband die?"

"Huh?"

"How did he die?"

She finished chewing her peas first. "Kicked in the head by a horse. Bled to death."

I burst out laughing because the image was so bright in my mind and I couldn't help myself. My pretty mother had a sense of humor even when she didn't mean to show it.

She chewed her peas in a ladylike manner. This was long before she lost her teeth. Sitting there across the table from her I knew I loved her and needed her and I knew she loved and needed me. I was not yet fearing that she needed me too much. She had a lot of anger in her too. Men had hurt her bad. And one day I was going to be a man.

When I laughed my mother said, "You shouldn't laugh at misfortune, Tommy." But she had this silly grin on her face and it caused me to crack up again. I just couldn't stop. I think now I must have been a bit hysterical from the anxiety I had been living with all those weeks while she was telling me about the telephone conversations that I wanted to hear about only part of the time.

113

It was dark outside and I got up when I finished my dinner and went to the window and looked down on the streetlights glowing in the wet pavement. I said, "I bet he's out there right now, hiding in the shadows, watching our window."

"Who?" Her eyes grew large. She was easily frightened. I knew this and I was being devilish and deliberately trying to scare her. "You know, Mister Kibbs."

She looked relieved. "No he's not. He's not like that. He's a little strange but not a pervert."

"How'd you know?"

By the look she gave me I knew now that I had thrown doubt into her and she wasn't handling it well. She didn't try to answer me. She finished her small, dry pork chop and the last of her bright green peas and reached over and took up my plate and sat it inside of her own.

She took the dishes to the sink, turned on the hot and cold water so that warm water gushed out of the single faucet, causing the pipe to clang, and started washing the dishes. "You have a vivid imagination," was all she said.

I grabbed the dishcloth and started drying the first plate she placed in the rack. "Even so, you don't know this man. You never even seen him. Aren't you curious about what he looks like?"

"I know what he looks like."

"How?"

"He sent me a picture of himself and Temple together.,"

I gave her a look. She had been holding out on me. I knew he was crazy now. Was he so ugly she hadn't wanted me to see the picture? I asked if I could see it.

She dried her hands on the cloth I was holding then took her cigarettes out of her dress pocket and knocked one from the pack and stuck it between her thin pale lips. I watched her light it and fan the smoke and squint her eyes. She said, "You have to promise not to laugh."

That did it. I started laughing again and couldn't stop. Then she started laughing too because I was bent double, standing there at the sink, with this image of some old guy who looked like The Creeper in my mind. But I knew she couldn't read my mind so she had to be laughing at me laughing. She was still young enough to be silly with me like a kid.

Then she brought out two pictures, one of him and the other one of his sister. She put them down side by side on the table. "Make sure your hands are dry."

I took off my glasses and bent down to the one of the man first so I could see up close as I stood there wiping my hands on the dishcloth. It was one of those studio pictures where somebody had posed in a three-quarter view. He had his unruly hair and eyebrows pasted down and you could tell he was fresh out of the bath and his white shirt was starched hard. He was holding his scrubbed face with effort toward where the photographer told him to look, which was too much in the direction of the best light. He was frowning with discomfort beneath the forced smile. There was something else. It was something like defeat or simple tiredness in his pose and you could see it best in the heavy lids of his large blank eyes. He looked out of that face at the world with what remained of his self-confidence and trust in the world. His shaggy presence said that it was all worthwhile and maybe even in some ways he would not ever understand, also important. I understood all of that even then but would never have been able to put my reading of him into words like these.

Then I looked at the woman. She was an old hawk. Her skin was badly wrinkled like the skin of ancient Indians I'd seen in photographs and the westerns. There was something like a smile coming out of her face but it had come out sort of sideways and made her look silly. But the main thing about her was that she looked very mean. But on second thought, to give her the benefit of the doubt, I can say that it might have been just plain hardness from having had a hard life. She was wearing a black iron-stiff dress buttoned up to her dicky which was ironically dainty and tight around her goose neck.

All I said was, "They're *so* old." I don't know what else I thought as I looked up at my mother who was leaning over my shoulder looking at the pictures too, as though she'd never seen them before, as though she was trying to see them through my eyes.

"You're just young, Tommy. Everybody's old to you. They're not so old. He looks lonely, to me."

I looked at him again and thought I saw what she meant.

I put the dishes away and she took the photographs back and we didn't talk any more that night about Mitch and Temple. We

115

watched our black-and-white television screen which showed us Red Skelton acting like a fool.

Before it was over, I fell asleep on the couch and my mother woke me when she turned off the television. "You should to go bed."

I stood up and stretched. "I have a science paper to write."

"Get up early and write it," she said, putting out her cigarette.

"He wants me to meet him someplace," my mother said.

She had just finished talking with him and was standing by the telephone. It was close to dinner time. I'd been home from school since three-thirty and she'd been in from work by then for a good hour. She'd just hung up from the shortest conversation she'd ever had with him.

I'd wondered why they never wanted to meet then I stopped wondering and felt glad they hadn't. Now I was afraid, afraid for her, for myself, for the poor old man in the picture. Why did we have to go through with this crazy thing?

"I told him I needed to talk with you about it first," she said. "I told him I'd call him back."

I was standing there in front of her looking at her. She was a scared little girl with wild eyes dancing in her head, unable to make up her own mind. I sensed her fear. I resented her for the mess she had gotten herself in. I also resented her for needing my consent. I knew she wanted me to say go, go to him, meet him somewhere. I could tell. She was too curious not to want to go. I suddenly thought that he might be a millionaire and that she would marry the old coot and he'd die and leave her his fortune. But there was the sister. She was in the way. And from the looks of her she would pass herself off as one of the living for at least another hundred years or so. So I gave up that fantasy.

"Well, why don't you tell him you'll meet him at the hamburger cafe on Wentworth? We can eat dinner there."

"We?"

"Sure. I'll just sit at the counter like I don't know you. But I gotta be there to protect you."

"I see."

"Then you can walk in alone. I'll already be there eating a cheeseburger and fries. He'll come in and see you waiting for him alone at a table."

116

"No. I'll sit at the counter too," she said.

"Okay. You sit at the counter too."

"What time should I tell him?"

I looked at my Timex. It was six. I knew they lived on the West Side and that meant it would take him at least an hour by bus and a half hour by car. He probably didn't have a car. I was hungry though and had already set my mind on eating a cheeseburger rather than macaroni and cheese out of the box.

"Tell him seven-thirty."

"Okay."

I went to my room. I didn't want to hear her talking to him in her soft whispering voice. I'd stopped listening sometime before. I looked at the notes for homework and felt sick on the stomach at the thought of having to write a science paper.

A few minutes later my mother came in and said, "Okay. It's all set." She sat down on the side of my bed and folded her bony pale hands in her lap. "What should I wear?"

"Wear your green dress and the brown shoes."

"You like that dress don't you."

"I like that one and the black one with the yellow at the top. It's classical."

"You mean classy."

"Whatever I mean." I felt really grown that night.

"Here, Tommy, take this." She handed me five dollars which she'd been hiding in the palm of her right hand. "Don't spend it all. Buy the burger out of it and the rest is just to have. If you spend it all in that hamburger place I'm going to deduct it from your allowance next week."

When I got there, I changed my mind about the counter. I took a table by myself. I was eating my cheeseburger and watching the revolving door. The cafe was noisy with shouts, cackling, giggles and verbal warfare. The waitress, Miss Azibo, was in a bad mood. She'd set my hamburger plate down like it was burning her hand.

I kept my eye on the door. Every time somebody came in I looked up, every time somebody left I looked up. I finished my cheeseburger even before my mother got there, and, ignoring her warning, I ordered another and another Coca-Cola to go with it. I figured I could eat two or three burgers and still have most of the five left.

117

Then my mother came in like a bright light into a dingy room. I think she must have been the most beautiful woman who ever entered that place and it was her first time coming in there. She had always been something of a snob and did not believe in places like this. I knew she'd agreed to meet Mister Kibbs here just because she believed in my right to the cheeseburger and this place had the best in the neighborhood.

I watched her walk ladylike to the counter and ease herself up on the stool and sit there with her back arched. People in that place didn't walk and sit like that. She was acting classy and everybody turned to look at her. I looked around at the faces and a lot of the women had these real mean sneering looks like somebody had broke wind.

She didn't know any of these people and they didn't know her. Some of them may have known her by sight, and me too, but that was about all the contact we had with this part of the neighborhood. Besides, we hardly ever ate out. When we did we usually ate Chinese or at the rib place.

I sipped my coke and watched Miss Azibo place a cup of coffee before my mother on the counter. She was a coffee freak. Always was. All day long. Long into the night. Cigarettes and coffee in a continuous cycle. I grew up with her that way. The harsh smells are still in my memory. When she picked up the cup with a dainty finger sticking out just so, I heard a big fat woman at a table in front of mine say to the big fat woman at the table with her that my mother was a snooty bitch. The other woman said, "Yeah. She must think she's white. What she doing in here anyway?"

Mitch Kibbs came in about twenty minutes after my mother and I watched him stop and stand just inside the revolving doors. He stood to the side. He looked a lot younger than in the picture. He was stooped a bit though and he wasn't dressed like a millionaire which disappointed me. But he was clean. He was wearing a necktie and a clean white shirt and a suit that looked like it was about two hundred years old but one no doubt made of the best wool. Although it was Fall he looked overdressed for the season. He looked like a man who hadn't been out in daylight in a long while. He was nervous, I could tell. Everybody was looking at him. Rarely did white people come in here.

118

Then he went to my mother like he knew she had to be the person he'd come in to see. He sat himself up on the stool beside her and leaned forward with his elbows on the counter and looked in her face.

She looked back in that timid way of hers. But she wasn't timid. It was an act and part of her ladylike posture. She used it when she needed it.

They talked and talked. I sat there eating cheeseburgers and protecting her till I spent the whole five dollars. Even as I ran out of money I knew she would forgive me. She had always forgiven me on special occasions. This was one for sure.

She never told me what they talked about in the cafe and I never asked but everything that happened after that meeting went toward the finishing off of the affair my mother was having with Mitch Kibbs. He called her later that night. I was in my room reading when the phone rang and I could hear her speaking to him in that ladylike way—not the way she talked to me. I was different. She didn't need to impress me. I was her son. But I couldn't hear what she was saying and didn't want to.

Mister Kibbs called the next evening. But eventually the calls were fewer and fewer till he no longer called.

My mother and I went on living the way we always had, she working long hours at the factory and me going to school. She was not a happy woman but I thought she was pretty brave. Every once in a while she got invited somewhere, to some wedding or out on a date with a man. She always tried on two or three different dresses, turning herself around and around before the mirror, asking me how she looked, making me select the dress she would wear. Most often though she went nowhere. After dinner we sat together at the kitchen table, she drinking coffee, and smoking her eternal cigarettes. She gave me my first can of beer one night when she herself felt like having one. It tasted awful and I didn't touch the stuff for years after that.

About a day or two after the meeting in the hamburger cafe I remember coming to a conclusion about mother. I learned for the first time that she did not always know what she was doing. It struck me that she was as helpless as I sometimes felt when con-

119

fronted with a math or science problem or a problem about sex and girls and growing up and life in general. She didn't know everything. And that made me feel closer to her despite the fear it caused. She was there to protect me, I thought. But there she was, just finding her way, step by step, like me. It was something wonderful anyway.

Nominated by Boulevard *and Sandra McPherson*

THE CAVE

by MICHAEL COLLIER

from PARTISAN REVIEW

I think of Plato and the limited technology
of his cave, the primitive projection
incapable of fast forward or reverse,
stop-action or slo-mo and the instant replay
that would have allowed him to verify,
once and for all, *Justice* or the *Good*,

such as the way my family did, hour upon hour,
in the dark, watching films of my sister
diving, going over her failures and successes
like a school of philosophers, arguing
fiercely, pulling her up from the depths
of the blue water, feet first, her splash

blooming around her hips then dying out
into a calm flat sheet as her fingertips appeared.
Sometimes we kept her suspended in her mimesis
of gainer and twist until the projector's lamp
burned blue with smoke and the smell of acetate
filled the room. Always from the shabby armchairs

of our dialectic we corrected the imperfect
attitude of her toes, the tuck of her chin,
took her back to the awkard approach or weak
hurdle and everywhere restored the half-promise
of her form, so that each abstract gesture
performed in an instant of falling revealed

that fond liaison of time and movement,
the moment held in the air, the illusion
of something whole, something true.
And though what we saw on the screen would never
change, never submit to our arguments, we believed
we might see it more clearly and understand

that what we judged was a result of poor light
or the apparent size of things or the change
an element evokes such as when we allowed her
to reenter the water and all at once her body
skewed with refraction, an effect we could not save
her from, though we hauled her up again and again.

Nominated by Jane Hirshfield, Robert Pinsky, C. E. Poverman and Arthur Smith

I'M HAVING TROUBLE WITH MY RELATIONSHIP

by LEONARD MICHAELS

from THE THREEPENNY REVIEW

THE WORD "RELATIONSHIP" appears for the first time in the 1743 edition of *The Dunciad*. Pope uses it in a way both funny and cruel to identify his enemy Cibber with the insane. Cibber is said to be related to famous heads, sculpted by his father, representing despondent and raving madness. The heads were affixed to the front of Bedlam. Pope calls them Cibber's "brothers." Cibber and the heads have the same father; they stand in a blood, brains, "brazen," family "Relationship." The word effects a contemptuous distance between Pope and Cibber, and makes Cibber one with the sculpted heads. Funny in its concreteness; cruel in the play of implications; luminous in genius. Before Pope, "relationship" may have been part of daily talk, but until he uses it nothing exists in this way, bearing the lineaments of his mind, the cultural affluence of his self and time.

After 1743, "relationship" appears with increasing frequency, with no joke intended, and it not only survives objections to its redundant structure (two abstract suffixes), but, in the 1940s, it begins to intrude into areas of thought and feeling where it never belonged, gathering a huge constituency of uncritical users and displacing words that once seemed more appropriate, precise, and pleasing. Among them are "romance," "affair," "lover," "beau," "fellow," "girl," "boyfriend," "girlfriend," "steady date,"

123

etc. People now find these words more or less quaint or embarrassingly innocent. They use "relationship" to mean any of them when talking about the romantic-sexual connection between a man and a woman or man, or woman and woman. In this liberal respect, Pope's use of the word is uncannily reborn.

People say, "I'm having trouble with my relationship" as though the trouble were not with Penelope or Max but with an object, like a BMW, a sort of container or psychological condition into which they enter and relate. By displacing the old words for romantic love, "relationship" indicates a new caution where human experience is extremely intense and ephemeral, or a distrust of concrete words in which our happiness might suffer any idea of limit, or perhaps a distrust of words in general. It could be argued that "relationship" is better than the old words since it makes abstraction palpable, generously distributing it among four syllables; a feeling of love in the action of sex; or philosophy in desire; and, as love is various, so are the syllables of "relationship," not one of them repeating another. Though intended to restrict reference to a single person, the word has the faint effect of suggesting many persons. In its palpableness, syllables bob like Bedlam heads. Strange images of mind.

People also say, "I can relate to that," where no person is intended or essentially involved, just an idea of some kind of experience. The expression is innocuous, and yet it is reminiscent of psychopathic thinking. In the same modern spirit, people say "mothering" to mean no particular person is essential to the action; that is, "mothering" does not flow from a mother as poetry flows only from a poet, or life from the sun god. "Fathering" has a sexual charge different from "mothering" and cannot be used like this. We talk, then, of "parenting." The political necessity for "mothering" and "parenting," which justifies the words, doesn't make them less grotesque. But this sort of judgment is precious. The antinomies of our culture cling to each other like breeders in a slow, violent divorce, and aesthetic considerations are irrelevant. We have no use, in our thinking, for the determining power of essences, or depths of soul, or ideas of value that inhere, like juice in grapes, in the quiddity of people. Mom is not by any means an inevitable source of love. She might well be a twisted bitch, and many vile creeps are Dad. The words no longer pack

124

honorific content. Commitments built into blood are honored only by the Mafia. Philip Larkin writes:

They fuck you up, your mum and dad.

What conservatives, feminists, Marxists, and other contemporary thinkers have in common is the idea that value has fled the human particular. Larkin might agree. He might even say that, long ago, value went off someplace to vomit and it has not returned. If this is true, we have been abandoned to the allure of non-specific possibility, or the thrill of infinite novelty. A lexical whorehouse shines in the darkness of the modern mind. (The "new," says Roland Barthes, is itself a value. No big surprise to the automobile industry.) To descend again to my theme: Your hot lover has cooled into your "relationship," which in another aspect you have with your grocer or your cat.

This large disposition in our thinking and speaking arises from impersonal democratic passions, the last refuge of the supreme good. As Simone Weil says, thinking of God, "Only the impersonal is sacred." But it is a little crazy that "relationship," an uppity version of "relation," should be enormously privileged, lumbering across the landscape of English with prefix and two suffixes streaming from a tiny head of substance like ghostly remains of its Latin roots and Germanic ending (*referre*, maybe *latus*, and *ship*).

To have survived the guns of our grammarians and displaced more pleasant words in the natural history of English, it must answer to an exceptionally strong need. The other words may seem impossibly quaint, but it isn't only the sophistication of "relationship" that is needed. It is the whole word, including the four-syllable sound, which is a body stumbling downstairs, the last two—"shunship"—the flap of a shoe's loose sole, or loose lips and gossip. In fact, "relationship" flourished in the talky, psychological climate of the modern century as we carried it from the offices of our shrinks and, like a forgotten umbrella, left "romance" behind.

Notice well how the syllabic tumble of "relationship" makes a sound like sheer talk, or talking about something, emphasis on

125

"about," not "something." Exactly here, in the eternally mysterious relation of sound and sense, "relationship" confers the dignity of thought upon referential promiscuity, its objects graced with interestingness, a sound basis in indeterminacy for interminable talk.

Philosophers might complain that it is a word without much "cash value." Heidegger, on the other hand, might take it as an expression of "the groundlessness and nullity of inauthentic everydayness." He means the nonstop impetuous trivialization, in "idle talk," of *Dasein*, by which he means anything real, by which he means that thing of which anyone who "is genuinely 'on the scent of' [it] will not speak." Certainly, then, in regard to "relationship," Heidegger might say:

> Being-with-one-another in the "they" is by no means
> an indifferent side-by-sideness in which everything has
> been settled, but rather an intent, ambiguous watching
> of another, a secret and reciprocal listening in. Under
> the mask of "for-one-another," an "against-one-another"
> is in play.

By which he means, "I'm having trouble with my relationship."

"The secret king of thought," forerunner of deconstructionism, who spoke of the Nazis as "manufacturing corpses," Heidegger had the deepest grasp of what is authentic and inauthentic in human relations. (His literary descendants—as too often noted— manufacture "texts" out of "works.") But to feel what has been lost in thought, consider this text from a letter by Kafka to Milena, the woman he loved:

> Today I saw a map of Vienna. For an instant it seemed
> incomprehensible to me that they had built such a big
> city when you need only one room.

The incomprehensible city is "relationship," or what you have with everyone in the abstract and lonely vastness of our social reality. The room, all one needs, is romance, love, passionate intimacy, the unsophisticated irrational thing you have with someone; or what has long been considered a form of madness, if not the universal demonic of contemporary vision.

The city is also "relationship" in the movie *Last Tango in Paris*, where Marlon Brando texts to his lover, "Everything outside this room is bullshit." He makes the same point as Kafka, but the subtext of the movie is that, in our lust for relationship, we have shoveled all the bullshit into the room. This lust, which is basically for power, or control, or the illusion of possessing something that isn't there—*Dasein*, needless to say, but what the hell—makes us prefer Theory to novels, poems, and people, or flat surfaces in architecture to the various elaborations of material that once engaged our hearts.

Native speakers of Swedish say *förhallande* is close in meaning to "relationship," which suggests the Swedes are in the same boat as the English-speakers, especially since other native speakers say it is difficult to find a close equivalent to "relationship" in other European languages or in Asian languages. "Relationship," then, shouldn't be taken as a mere tendency of English where any noun might lust for sublimity in the abstract extension of itself. It isn't just another polysyllabic fascist on the left or right, but rather something that bespeaks a deeper tendency, in the soul, like what one sees in Andy Warhol's disquieting portraits of Marilyn Monroe and Mao, their faces repeating and vanishing into the static quality of their "look."

"Relationship" has a similarly reductive force, ultimately even an air of death worship. The "aura of death," says Georges Bataille, "is what denotes passion." It also denotes its absence, one might suppose, but this old notion isn't likely to seize our imagination, which is why "relationship" has slipped unnoticed into astounding prominence and ubiquitous banality. The word is no less common than death, and it is no less pathetically private; and we use it much as though, after consigning ourselves to the grave, we had lingered to love the undertaker, having had no such exquisitely personal attention before, nothing so convincing that one is.

Nominated by Sigrid Nunez

ASTRONAUTS

fiction by WALLY LAMB

from THE MISSOURI REVIEW

"NEXT SLIDE," THE astronaut says. For a second, the auditorium is as void and dark as space itself. Then a curve of the earth's ulcerated surface flashes on the screen and the students' silhouettes return, bathed in tones of green. This is the third hour in a row Duncan Foley has seen this picture and heard the smiling public relations astronaut, sent, in the wake of the Challenger disaster, to the high school where Duncan teaches. It's September; attendance at the assembly is mandatory.

A hand goes up.

"Yes?" the astronaut says.

"What did it feel like out there from so far away?"

"Well, it was exhilarating. A whole different perspective. I felt privileged to be a part of a great program."

"But was it scary?"

"I'm not sure I know what you mean?"

"Could you sleep?"

The astronaut's smile, which has lasted for three periods, slackens. He squints outward; his hands are visors over his yes. "Truthfully?" he says. "No one's ever asked me that one. I didn't sleep very well, no."

"What were you afraid of?" another voice asks. "Crashing?"

"No," the astronaut says. He has walked in front of the screen so that the earth's crust is his skin, his slacks and shirt. "It's hard to explain. Let's call it indifference. The absolute blackness of it. Life looks pretty far away from out there."

For five seconds longer than is comfortable, no one moves. Then ten seconds. "So, no," the astronaut repeats. "I didn't sleep well."

A student stands, his auditorium seat flapping up behind him, raising a welcome clatter. "How do you go to the bathroom in a space suit?"

There is laughter and applause. Relief. The astronaut grins, returning to his mission. He's had the same question in the first two sessions. "I knew *some*body was going to ask me that," he says.

Scanning his juniors in the middle rows, Duncan spots James Bocheko, his worst student. Jimmy's boots are wedged up against the back of the seat in front of him, his knees gaping out of twin rips in his jeans. There's a magazine in his lap, a wire to his ear. He's shut out the school and the astronaut's message from space. Duncan leans past two girls and taps Jimmy's shoulder.

"Let's have it," he says.

The boy looks up—a confused child being called out of a nap rather than a troublemaker. His red bangs are an awning over large, dark eyes. He remembers to scowl.

"What?"

"The Walkman. You know they're not allowed. Let's have it."

Jimmy shakes his head. Students around them are losing interest in the astronaut. Duncan snatches up the recorder.

"Hey!" Jimmy says out loud. Other teachers are watching.

"Get out," Duncan whispers.

"Get laid," the boy says. Then he unfolds himself, standing and stretching. His boots clomp a racket up the aisle. He's swaggering, smiling. "Later, Space Cadets!" he shouts to all of them just before he gives the door a slam.

On stage, the astronaut has stopped to listen. Duncan feels the blood in his face. His hand is clamped around the Walkman, the thin wire rocking back and forth in front of him.

Stacie Vars can't stand this bus driver. She liked the one they had last year—that real skinny woman with braids who let them smoke. Linda something—she used to play all those Willie Nelson songs on her boombox. Stacie saw Willie Nelson in a cowboy movie on Cinemax last night. It was boring. He wears braids, too, come to think of it. This new bus driver thinks her shit don't flush.

Nobody at school knows Stacie is pregnant yet, not even the kids in Fire Queens. She's not sure if they'll let her stay in the drum corps or not. She doesn't really care about marching; maybe she could hold kids' jackets and purses or something. Ever since she got pregnant, she has to go the bathroom all the time. Which is a pain, because whenever you ask those teachers for the lav pass, it's like a personal insult or something. She couldn't believe that geeky kid who asked the astronaut today about taking a crap. God. That whole assembly was boring. Except when Jimmy got kicked out by her homeroom teacher. She's not sure if Jimmy saw her or not when he passed her. He gets mad if she speaks to him at school. He's so moody. She doesn't want to take any chances.

The bus jerks and slows. Up ahead Stacie can see the blue winking lights of an accident. The kids all run over to that side of the bus, gawking. Not her; she doesn't like to look at that kind of thing. Jimmy says there's this movie at the video store where they show you actual deaths from real life. Firing squads and people getting knifed, shit like that. He hasn't seen it yet; it's always out. "Maybe it's fake," she told him. He laughed at her and said she was a retard—that if it was fake, then you could rent it whenever you wanted to. She hates when he calls her that. She's got feelings, too. Last week Mrs. Roberge called Stacie's whole science class "brain dead." Stacie doesn't think that's right. Somebody ought to report that bitch. Those police car lights are the same color of the shaving lotion her father used to keep on top of the toilet. Ice Blue Aqua Velva. She wonders if he still uses that stuff. Not that it's important. It's just something she'd like to know.

Duncan is eating a cheese omelet from the frying pan, not really tasting it. He's worried what to do about Jimmy Bocheko's hatred; he wishes he didn't have all those essays to grade. Duncan replays the scene from two days ago when he'd had the class write on their strengths and weaknesses. Bocheko had done his best to disrupt the class. "Is this going to count? . . . What do we have to write on something so stupid for? . . . "

"Just do it!" Duncan shouted.

The boy reddened, balled up the paper he'd just barely started, and threw it on the floor. Then he walked out.

The other students, boisterous and itchy, were suddenly still, awaiting Duncan's move.

"Okay, now," he said in a shaky voice. "Let's get back to work." For the rest of the period, Duncan's eyes kept bouncing back to the paper ball on the floor. The astronaut's assembly today was *supposed* to have given them distance from that confrontation.

At the sink of his efficiency apartment, Duncan scrapes dried egg off the frying pan with his fingernails. This past week when he did the grocery shopping (he uses one of those plastic baskets now, instead of a wheel-around cart), he forgot the S.O.S. Yesterday he forgot to go to a faculty meeting. He was halfway home before he remembered Mrs. Shefflot, his carpooler, whose husband was already there picking her up by the time Duncan got back to school. He knows three people his age whose parents have Alzheimer's. He wonders if it ever skips a generation—plays a double dirty trick on aging parents.

When the phone rings, Duncan tucks the receiver under his chin and continues his chores. The cord is ridiculously long; he can navigate his entire residence while tethered to the phone.

The caller is Rona, a hostess at the racquetball club Duncan joined as part of his divorce therapy. Rona is divorced, too, but twenty-three, eleven years younger than Duncan—young enough to have been his student, though she wasn't. She grew up near Chicago.

"What's worse than getting AIDS on a blind date?" Rona asks in her cheerful rasp. At the club, she is known as a hot shit. Kevin, Duncan's racquetball partner, thinks she's desperate, would screw anything.

Duncan doesn't know.

She is giggling; he has missed the punchline. This is the second AIDS joke he's heard this week. Duncan waters his plant and puts a bag of garbage on the back porch while Rona complains about her boss.

". . . to get you and me over the mid-week slump," she is saying. She may have just asked him out for a drink. There is a pause. Then she adds, "My treat."

Duncan has had one date with Rona. More or less at her insistence, he cooked dinner at his apartment. She arrived with two gifts: a bottle of Peachtree schnapps and a copy of *People* magazine. All evening she made jokes about his kitchen curtains being

131

too short. Fingering through his record collection, she told him it was "real vintage." (Her favorite group is Whitesnake, plus she likes jazz.) After dinner they smoked dope, hers, and settled for James Taylor's Greatest Hits. She didn't leave until twelve thirty, two hours after the sex. This struck Duncan as inconsiderate; it was a school night.

"I think I'd better beg off," Duncan says. "I've got essays to correct tonight." He holds them to the phone as if to prove it's the truth. Kevin is probably right about her. He's glad he used that rubber she had in her purse, embarrassing as that was.

"Oh wow," she says. "I'm being shot down for 'What I Did Over Summer Vacation.' " Duncan tells her he'll see her at the club.

Duncan's ex-wife used to love to read his students' work. She always argued there was a certain nobility amidst all the grammatical errors and inarticulateness. Kids being confessional, kids struggling for truth. After they separated, Duncan kept dropping by unannounced with half-gallons of ice cream and papers he thought might interest her. Then, when she had her brother change all the locks, Duncan would sit on the front porch step like Lassie, waiting for her to relent. Once she stood at the picture window with a sheet of notebook paper pressed against the glass. *Cut this shit out*, it said in Magic Marker capitals. *Grow up!* Duncan assumes he will love her forever.

Wearing underpants, sweatshirt, and gym socks, Duncan crawls between his chilly sheets. He snaps on his clock radio and fans out the essays before him. He'll do the worst ones first. The disc jockey has free movie tickets for the first person who can tell him who sang "If You're Going to San Francisco, Be Sure To Wear Some Flowers in Your Hair."

"Scott MacKenzie," Duncan says out loud. He owns the album.

Halfway through his third paper, he looks up at the radio. The announcer has just mentioned James Bocheko.

"Bocheko, a local youth, was dead on arrival at Twin Districts Hospital after the car he was driving . . . "

When the music starts again, Duncan turns off the radio and lies perfectly still, confused by his own giddy feeling. He leans over and picks up James Bocheko's paper which he took from the floor that afternoon and flattened with the palm of his hand. The wrinkled yellow paper is smudgy with fingerprints, the penmanship as large and deliberate as a young child's.

Strength's: I am HONEST. Not a wimp.

Weakness's: Not enouf upper body strength.

Duncan drinks bourbon from a jelly jar until the shivering stops. Then he dials his old telephone number. "Listen," he says to his ex-wife. "Can I talk to you for a minute? Something awful happened. One of my kids got killed."

At two, he awakens totally cold, knowing that's it for the night's sleep. When he rolls over, his students' papers crinkle in the folds of the quilt.

Stacie sits with her hands on the table, waiting for her mother to go to work.

"You ought to eat something besides this crap," her mother tells her, picking up the large box of Little Debbie cakes. She blows a cone of cigarette smoke at Stacie. "A fried egg or something."

It's the second morning since Stacie's felt like eating, but the thought of an egg puckering in a frying pan gives her a queasy feeling. She's eaten three of the cakes and torn the cellophane packaging into strips.

"Mrs. Faola's knitting a sweater and booties for the baby," she says, trying to change the subject. "Pale pink."

"Well, that'll look pretty g.d. foolish if you end up with a boy, won't it?"

"Mrs. Faola says if I wear something pink every day for a month, it will be a girl."

Her mother takes a deep drag on her cigarette and exhales. "If that wasn't so pathetic, it'd be hilarious, Stacie. Real scientific. I don't suppose you told the mystery man the good news yet."

Stacie picks at a ball of lint on the sleeve of her pink sweater. "You better get going," she says. "You'll be late for work."

"Have you?"

"What?"

"Told him yet?"

Stacie's cuticles go white against the table top. "I *told* you I was telling him when the time is right, Mommy. Get off my fucking case."

133

Linda snatches up her car keys and gives her daughter a long, hard stare. "Nice way for a new mother to talk," she says. Stacie stares back for as long as she can, then looks away. A ripple of nausea passes through her.

Her mother leaves without another word. Stacie watches the door's Venetian blind swing back and forth. God, she hates her mother. That woman is so intense.

If it's a girl, Stacie's decided to name her Desiree. Desiree Dawne Bocheko. Stacie's going to decorate her little room with Rainbow Brite stuff. Mrs. Faola says they sell scented wallpaper now. Scratch'n'sniff—she seen it in a magazine. Stacie might get that, too. She's not sure yet.

Everything is finally falling into place, in a way. At least she can eat again. This weekend, Stacie's going to tell him. "Jimmy," she'll say, "Guess what? I'm having your baby." She hopes they're both buzzed. She could very well be a married woman by Halloween; it could happen. God. She already feels older than the kids in Fire Queens. Maybe they'll give her a surprise baby shower. She imagines herself walking into a room filled with balloons, her hands over her face.

When the phone rings, it embarrasses her. "Oh, hi, Mrs. Faola. No, she left about ten minutes ago. Yeah, my pink sweater and pink underpants. No, I'm going to school today."

Mrs. Faola lives in Building J. She watches for Stacie's mother's car to leave, then calls and bribes Stacie to skip school and visit. Today she has cheese popcorn. Oprah Winfrey's guests are soap stars.

"Nah, I really think I should go today," Stacie repeats. She loves to see Jimmy in the hall, even though she can't talk to him. No one's supposed to know they're semi-going out. "When *can* I tell people," she asked him once. "When you lose about half a ton," he said. She's *going* to lose weight, right after the baby. Mrs. Faola says Stacie better get used to having her feelings hurt—that that's just the way men are. Stacie would die for Jimmy. Mrs. Faola had an unmarried sister that died having a baby. Stacie's seen her picture.

"Tomorrow I'm staying home," she promises Mrs. Faola. "Gym on Friday."

She guesses most people would find it weird, her friendship with Mrs. Faola, but she don't care. Last week they played slap-jack and Mrs. Faola gave her a crocheting lesson. She's going to give her a home perm when Stacie gets a little farther along, too. In her mind, Stacie's got this picture of herself sitting up in a hospital bed wearing a French braid like Kayla Brady on *Days of Our Lives*. Desiree is holding on to her little finger. They're waiting for Jimmy to visit the hospital. He's bringing a teddy bear and roses for Stacie. The baby has made him wicked happy.

Mrs. Faola is right about abortion being a fancy name for murder. Stacie won't even say the word out loud. At least her mother's off her case about that.

She stands up quick and gets that queasy feeling again, but it passes. She coats her mouth with cherry lip gloss and picks up her notebook. On the cover she's drawn a marijuana leaf and surrounded it with the names of rock groups in fancy letters. She keeps forgetting to erase BonJovi. Jimmy says they're a real suck group, and now that she thinks about it, they aren't that good.

On her way out, she looks at the cowgirl on the Little Debbie box. She's so cute. Maybe Desiree will look something like her.

Unable to sleep, Duncan has dressed and walked, ending not by design at an early morning mass at the church of his childhood. In the unlit back pew he sits like a one-man audience, watching uniformed workers and old people—variations on his parents—huddled together, making their peace. They seem further away than the length of the church. In his coat pocket Duncan fingers James Bocheko's list of strengths and weaknesses. The priest is no one he knows. His hair is an elaborate silver pompadour. From the lectern he smiles like a game show host, coaxing parishioners to be ready for their moment of grace when it comes hurling toward them. Duncan thinks of spiraling missiles, whizzing meteors. He imagines the priest naked with a blow-dryer, vainly arranging that hair. He leaves before communion.

This early, the teachers' room is more quiet than Duncan is used to. He listens to the sputter of a fluorescent light, the gurgle of the coffee maker. Jimmy Bocheko stares back at him indifferently, his eyes blank and wide-set. A grammar school picture. Duncan draws the newspaper close to his face and listens to his own breathing against the paper. The boy dissolves into a series of black dots.

135

At 8:15, Duncan is seated at his desk, eavesdropping. His home-room students are wide-eyed, animated.

"My brother-in-law's on the rescue squad. The dude's head was ripped right off."

" . . . No, that red-haired kid in our health class last year, the one with the earring."

"Head-on collision, man. He bought it."

A girl in the front row asks Duncan if he knew a boy named Jim Bocheko.

"Yes," Duncan says. "Awful." The girl seems disappointed not to be the one breaking the news. Then she is looking at his reaction. He thinks foolishly of handing her Jimmy's list.

The restless liquor night has already settled in Duncan's stomach, behind the lids of his eyes. The P.A. hums on. "All right, quiet now," Duncan says, pointing half-heartedly toward the box on the wall.

" . . . a boy whose tragic death robs us just as his life enriched us." The principal's mouth is too close to the microphone; his words explode at them. "Would you all please rise and observe a moment of silence in memory of your fellow student and friend, James Bocheko?"

Chairs scrape along the floor. The students' heads are bowed uneasily. They wait out the P.A.'s blank hum.

Duncan notices the fat girl, Stacie, the chronic absentee, still in her seat. Those around her give her quick, disapproving glances. Should he say something? Make her stand?

The girl's head begins to bob up and down, puppet-like; she is grunting rhythmically. "Gag reflex," Duncan thinks objectively.

Yellow liquid spills out of her mouth and onto the shiny desk-top. "Oh Christ, get the wastebasket!" someone calls. "Je-sus!" The vomit splatters onto the floor. Those nearby force themselves to look, then jerk their heads away. Two boys begin to laugh uncontrollably.

A gangly boy volunteers to run for the janitor and Duncan assigns the front row girl to walk Stacie to the nurse's office. "Come on," the girl says to her, pinching a little corner of the pink sweater, unwilling to get closer. Stacie obeys her, bland and sheep-dazed, her chin still dribbling.

Jimmy Bocheko's moment of silence has ended but nobody notices. The vomit's sweet vinegar has pervaded the classroom.

Windows are thrown open to the cold. Everyone is giggling or complaining.

" . . . And to the republic for which it stands, one nation under God, indivisible . . . " the P.A. announcer chants.

The first period bell rings and they shove out loudly into the hall. Duncan listens to the random hoots and obscenities and details of the accident. "If he gives us a quiz today, I'll kill myself," a girl says.

Duncan turns a piece of chalk end over end. He wonders if the decapitation is fact or some ghoulish embellishment.

A freshman thumps into the room, skids his gym bag across the floor toward his seat. "Hey, Mr. Foley, did you know that kid that got wasted yesterday? He lives next door to my cousin," he says proudly. "Whoa, what stinks in here?"

Stacie keeps pushing the remote control but everything on is boring. That Willie Nelson movie is on Cinemax for the one zillionth time. She wishes she could just talk to someone like that last year's bus driver—someone who could make it clear. Only what's she supposed to do—call up every Linda in the stupid phone book? It's *weird;* he never even knew. Unless he's somewhere watching her. Like a spirit or something. Like one of those shoplifting cameras at Cumberland Farms. She lies down on the rug and covers herself with the afghan. Her stone-washed jeans are only three months old and they're already too tight. She undoes the top button and her fat flops out. She can feel it there, soft and dead against the scratchy carpet and she lets herself admit something: she didn't tell him because she was afraid to. Afraid to wreck that hospital picture she wanted. Her whole life sucks. She could care less about this stupid baby . . .

She wakes with the sound of footsteps on the porch, then the abrupt light. She clamps her eyes shut again. Her mother's shadow is by the light switch. The rug has made marks in her cheek.

"What time is it?"

"Five after seven. Get up. I'll make supper. You should eat."

Stacie begins quietly when the macaroni and cheese is on the table. "I got something to tell you," she says. "Don't get mad."

Her mother looks disgustedly at something—a gummy strand

137

of hair hanging down in Stacie's plate. Stacie wipes her hair with a napkin.

"There's this kid I know, Jimmy Bocheko. He got killed yesterday. In an accident."

"I know. I saw it in the paper."

"He's the one."

"The one what?"

"The father."

Stacie's mother is chewing a forkful of food and thinking hard. "Are you telling me the truth?" she says.

Stacie nods and looks away. She hates it that she's crying.

"Well, Stacie, you sure know how to pick them, don't you?" her mother says. "Jesus Christ, you're just a regular genius."

Stacie slams both fists on the table, surprising herself and her mother, who jumps. "You could at least be a little nice to me," she shouts. "I puked at school today when I found out. It's practically like I'm a widow."

This makes her mother hitting mad. She is on her feet, shoving her, slapping. Stacie covers her face. "Stop it. Mommy! Stop it!"

"Widow? I'll tell you what you are. You're just a stupid girl living in a big fat dream world. And now you've played with fire and got yourself good and burnt, didn't you?"

"Stop it!"

"Didn't you? Answer me! Didn't you?"

"The jade plant looks nice over there," Duncan says. His ex-wife has rearranged the living room. It looks more angular, less comfortable without his clutter.

"It's got aphids," she says.

He remembers the presents out on his back seat. "Be right back," he says. When he returns, he hands her a small bag of the raw cashews she loves, and a jazz album. His ex-wife looks at the album cover, her face forming a question. "I've been getting into jazz a little," he explains, shrugging.

Although he would have preferred the kitchen, she has set the dining room table. The meal is neutral; chicken, baked potatoes, salad.

After dinner, he wipes the dishes while she washes. She's bought a wok and hung it on the kitchen wall. Duncan's eyes keep landing on it. "What's the difference between oral sex and oral hygiene?" he asks abruptly after an uncomfortable silence. It's one Rona has told him.

"Oh, Duncan, how am I supposed to know? How's your family?"

"Okay, I guess. My sister is pregnant again."

"I know," she says. "I saw your father at Stop and Shop. Did he mention it?" She hands him the gleaming broiler pan. "He was wearing a jogging suit. Gee, he looked old. He was mad at your mother. She sent him to the store for yeast and birthday candles and he couldn't find the yeast. Then there I am, the ex-daughter-in-law. He was having trouble handling eye contact."

"Did you tell him where the yeast was?"

"Yeah, then he thanked a pile of apples over my left shoulder and walked up the aisle." She turns to Duncan with a worried look. "How come he's limping?"

"Arthritis. It's weird, Ruthie. He and my mother are turning into little cartoon senior citizens. They go out to lunch every day and find fault. Last week I got stuck in a line of traffic; there's some slowpoke holding everybody up. It turns out to be my father. They're, I don't know, shrinking or something. She has a jogging suit, too. They wear them because they're warm. I can't help seeing them from a distance. It's bizarre."

Two years ago, when the specialist confirmed that his wife had indeed finally conceived, Duncan drove to his parents' house to break the news. His mother was out, his father in the back yard pruning a bush. "See what a little prayer can get you, Mr. Big Deal Atheist?" his father said, jabbing Duncan in the stomach with the butt of the clippers, harping all the way back to an argument they'd had when Duncan was still in college. When he went to hug him, Duncan drew back, resentful of his father's claiming credit for himself and his god. They'd been putting up with those fertility treatments for two years.

Duncan's ex-wife begins to munch on the cashews. "These are stale," she says. "Good. Now I won't pig out."

"I'm going out with somebody. She's divorced. Somebody from racquetball."

There is a pause. She pops more nuts into her mouth and chews. "Well," she says, "that's allowed."

"So when did you take up Chinese cooking?" he asks, pointing to the wok. He means to be nonchalant but is sounding like Perry Mason grilling a guilty woman. The wok is a damning piece of evidence.

"I'm taking one of those night courses at the community college. With a friend of mine from work."

"Male or female?"

She clangs the broiler pan back into the bottom drawer of the stove. "An androgyn, okay? A hermaphrodite. I thought you wanted to talk about this kid who got killed."

He takes Bocheko's paper out of his wallet and unfolds it for her. "Oh, Duncan," his ex-wife sighs. "Oh, shit."

"The kids were high on the death thing all day, exchanging gruesome rumors. Nobody wanted to talk about anything else. Do you think I should write them a letter or something?

"Who?"

"His parents."

"I don't know," she says. "Do what you need to do."

On TV, James Taylor is singing "Don't Let Me Be Lonely Tonight." On their honeymoon, Duncan and his ex-wife sat near James Taylor at a Chinese restaurant in Soho. Duncan and he ordered the exact same meal. Duncan is dismayed to see James Taylor so bald.

"You know my record collection?" Duncan says to his ex-wife. "Do you think it's real 'vintage'?"

"Real what?" she asks in a nasal voice. He realizes suddenly that she's been crying. But when he presses her, she refuses to say why.

Yellow leaves are smashed against the sidewalk. Duncan collapses his black umbrella and feels the cold drizzle on the back of his neck. An undertaker holds open the door. Duncan nods a thank you and sees that the man is in his twenties. This has been happening more and more: people his father's age have retired, leaving in charge people younger than Duncan.

He signs a book on a lighted podium and takes a holy picture, a souvenir. On the front is a sad-eyed Jesus, his sacred heart exposed. On the back, James Bocheko's name is printed in elegant script. Duncan thinks of the boy's signature, those fat, loopy letters.

In the main room, it's that pompadour priest before the casket, leading a rosary. Duncan slips quietly past and sits in a cushioned folding chair, breathing in the aroma of carnations. Someone taps his arm and Duncan sees he has sat next to one of his students, a loud-mouthed boy in James' class.

"Hi, Mr. Foley," the boy whispers hoarsely. Duncan is surprised to see him fingering rosary beads.

James Bocheko's family is in a row of high-backed chairs at a right angle to the closed casket. They look ill at ease in their roles as the designated royalty of this occasion. A younger brother pumps his leg up and down and wanders the room. An older sister rhythmically squeezes a Kleenex. Their father, a scruffy man with a bristly crewcut and a loud plaid sports jacket, looks sadly out at nothing.

Only James Bocheko's mother seems to be concentrating on the rosary. Her prayer carries over the hushed responses of the others. "Blessed art thou who art in heaven and blessed is the fruit of thy womb."

When the prayers are finished, the priest takes Mrs. Bocheko's wrists, whispers something to her. Others shuffle to the front, forming an obedient line. Duncan heads for the foyer. They will see his signature in the book. Mrs. Bocheko will remember him from the conference. "I know he's no angel," she said specifically to Duncan that afternoon, locking her face into a defense against the teachers and counselors around the table. Only now does he have the full impact of how alone she must have felt.

He sees that girl, Stacie, at the rear of the room. She is wearing a low-cut blouse and corduroy pants; her feet are hooked around the legs of the chair in front of her.

"How are you feeling?" Duncan whispers to her.

"Okay." she says, looking away.

"Were you a friend of his?"

"Kind of." She says it to her lap.

In the vestibule, the undertaker is helping the priest into his raincoat. "So who's your money on for the Series this year, Father?" he asks him over his shoulder.

Stacie walks past two other girls, representatives from the student council who stare after her and smirk.

The door is opened again for Duncan. The drizzle has turned to slanted rain.

141

Stacie is lying on her bed, wondering what happened to her notebook. She hasn't been back to school in over a month, since the day she found out about Jimmy—that day she threw up. She's not going back, either, especially now that she's showing. Let the school send all the letters they want. She'll just burn them all up and flush the ashes down the toilet. She's quitting as soon as she turns sixteen anyways. What does she care?

That Mr. Foley probably has her notebook. She's pretty sure she left it in his room that morning. Of all his teachers, Jimmy hated Mr. Foley's guts the most. He was always trying to get them to write stuff, Jimmy said, stuff that wasn't any of his fucking business. What she can't figure out is why he was at Jimmy's wake—unless he was just snooping around. By now, he's probably looked through her notebook, seen the pages where she's written "Mrs. Stacie Bocheko" and "Property of Jimmy B." and the other private stuff.

Being pregnant is boring. There's nothing good on TV and nothing around to eat. She wishes she and Mrs. Faola didn't have that fight. She still wants to get that perm.

She reaches back for her pillow. Drawing it close to her face, she pokes her tongue out and gives it a shy lick. She remembers the feel of Jimmy's tongue flicking nervously all over the insides of her mouth. She remembers the part just before he finished—when he'd reach out for her like some little boy. She gives the pillow several more little cat licks. She likes doing it. It feels funny.

Then she's aware of something else funny, down there. It feels like a little butterfly bumping up against her stomach, trying to get out. It makes her laugh. She kisses the pillow and feels it again. She begins either to giggle or to cry. She can't tell which. She can't stop.

"Why don't you ever make us write *good* stuff?" they wanted to know.

Duncan turned from the chalkboard and faced them. "Like what?" he asked.

"Like stories and stuff. You know."

So he gave them what they wanted and on Friday every student had a story to hand in. He has read them over and over again, all weekend, but has not been able to grade them. Each of

142

the stories ends in death; sentimentally tragic death, the death of a thousand bad television plots. Not knowing where to put the anxiety with which James Bocheko's death has left them, they have put it down on paper, locked it into decorous penmanship, self-conscious sentences they feel are works of art. How can he affix a grade?

The newspapers are full of fatal accidents. A bride has shot her husband. A girl choked to death in a restaurant. On the hour, Duncan's clock radio warns parents against maniacs, purveyors of tainted Halloween candy.

His wife is not safe. She could die in a hundred random ways: a skidding truck, faulty wiring, some guy with AIDS.

It was in a Howard Johnson's ladies' room that she first noticed she was spotting. "It's as if her body's played a joke on itself," the gynecologist explained to Duncan the next afternoon while his wife stared angrily into her hospital sheets, tapping her fist against her lip. "The amniotic sac had begun to form itself, just *as if* fertilization had occurred. But there was no evidence of an egg inside." Duncan recalls how she spent the next several weeks slamming things, how he rushed up to the attic to cry. There was no death to mourn—only the absence of life, the joke.

When he hears the knocking, he is sure it's his ex-wife, wearing her jeans and her maroon sweater, answering his need for her. But it is Rona, shivering in a belly dancer's costume. "Trick or treat," she says, holding out a tiny vial of coke. "We deliver." Inside, she lifts her coat off her shoulders and her costume jangles. She runs her chilled fingers over the stubble of Duncan's jaw.

* * *

The janitors have taken over the school, rigging the country western station through the PA system and shouting back and forth from opposite ends of the corridor as they repair the year's damages. It's the beginning of summer vacation. Duncan sits in his classroom, surrounded by the open drawers of his desk. He's in a throwing away mood.

What he should do is make plans—get to the beach more, visit someone far away. He should spend more time with his father, who is hurting so badly. Sick with grief: that phrase taking on new meaning. "You're not alone, I know what it's like," Duncan told him last week. The two of them were fumbling with supper preparations in Duncan's mother's kitchen, self-consciously intent on doing things the way she'd always done them. "When Ruthie got remarried this spring, it was like she died to me, too."

"Bullshit!" his father snapped. His grip tightened around a fistful of silverware. "That divorce was *your* doing, the two of you. Don't you *dare* compare your mother's death to that. Don't you *dare* say you know what it's like for me." That was six days ago. Duncan hasn't called since.

He's saved the bottom right desk drawer for last, avoiding it as if there's something in there—a homemade bomb or a snake. But it's the confiscated Walkman, buried under piles of notices and tests. Duncan sees again James Bocheko, crouched in the dark auditorium.

Tentatively, Duncan fixes the headphones to his ears and finds the button. He's expecting screaming guitars, a taunting vocal, but it's electronic music—waves of blips and notes that may or may not mean anything. After awhile the music lulls him, makes him feel removed and afloat. He closes his eyes and sees black.

The janitor makes him jump.

"What?" Duncan says. He yanks off the earphones to hear the sound that goes with the moving lips.

"I said, we're going now. We're locking up."

He drives to the mall for no good reason. It's becoming a pattern: tiptoeing in and out of the bright stores, making small purchases because he feels watched. At the K-Mart register, he places his lightbulbs and sale shampoo before the clerk like an offering.

Exiting, he passes the revolving pretzels, the rolling hot dogs, a snack bar customer and a baby amidst the empty orange tables.

"Hey!" she says. "Wait."

He moves toward them, questioning. Then he knows her.

"You're a teacher, ain't you?" She's flustered for having spoken. "I had you for homeroom this year. For a while."

Bocheko's wake. The one who vomited—Stacie something. It's her hair that's different—shorter, close cropped.

"Hello," he says. It scares her when he sits down.

The baby has glossy cheeks and fuzzy red hair that makes Duncan smile. He pushes the infant seat away from the edge of the table.

"Did you find a notebook in your class? It's green and it's got writing on the front."

The baby's arms are flailing like a conductor's. "What did you say?"

"My notebook. I lost it in your room and I kind of still want it."

There's a large soda on the table and a cardboard french fry container brimming with cigarette butts. Behind her, the unoccupied arcade games are registering small explosions. "I don't remember it. But I'll look."

"I thought maybe you were saving it or something."

Duncan shrugs. "Cute baby," he smiles. "Boy or girl?"

"Boy." She blushes, picks him up so abruptly that he begins to cry.

"How old?"

"Stop it," she tells the baby. She hooks a strand of hair behind her ear with her free hand.

"*How* old is he?"

"Almost three months. Shut up, will you? God," Her clutch is too tight. The crying has turned him red. "Could you hold him for a second?" she says.

Duncan receives the baby—tense and bucking—with a nervous laugh. "Like this?" he asks.

Stacie dunks her finger into her soda and sticks it, dripping, into his mouth. "This sometimes works," she says. The crying subsides. The baby begins to suck.

"Uh, what is it?" Duncan asks.

"Diet Pepsi, It's okay. He ain't really getting any. It's just to soothe him down." The baby's shoulders against Duncan's chest relax. "You have to trick them," she says. Then she smiles at the baby. "Don't you?" she asks him.

"What's his name?"

"Jesse," she says. "Jesse James Bocheko."

Her eyes are gray and marbled, non-committal. He looks away from them, down. "I'm sorry," he says.

It's she who breaks the silence. "Could you do me a favor? Could you just watch him for a couple of seconds so's I can go to the ladies' room?"

He nods eagerly. "Yes," he says. "You go."

The soft spot on the baby's head indents with each breath. Duncan *sees* his own thighs against the plastic chair, his shoes on the floor, but can't *feel* them. He's weightless, connected only to this warm, small body.

"Baby . . . " he whispers. He closes his eyes and puts two fingertips to the spot, feeling both the strength and the frailty, the gap and pulse together.

Nominated by The Missouri Review *and David Jauss*

THROUGH AND THROUGH

fiction by JOSEPH GEHA

from OXFORD MAGAZINE

BACK WHEN I was first on the lam from the Jackie Kennedy murder (the Toledo beer baron, not the other one) I spent some time in Damascus, Syria. There, not far from the house where my father grew up, is a street called Straight. *National Geographic* says it's the oldest continually inhabited street in the world—over five thousand years old—and my uncle took a day off work to show it to me. He was a bricklayer, helping to put up the new (then, in 1933) church commemorating the spot where Saint Paul was supposedly knocked from his horse and blinded by the light of Jesus. I remember how my uncle tried to put his arm in my arm and walk me along like a girl. I'd been warned they did that over there, men even holding hands. All pretty harmless, but I shrugged him off anyway. Twenty-two and on the lam, I'd just as soon keep my hands free.

(Yes, we really did say 'On the lam'—the movies got that from us, not the other way around.)

It was about noon when we reached Straight Street and the souk stalls were crowded. A metal framework stretched building to building over the street, supporting sheets of canvas that protected from the sun and wind, but which also trapped clouds of yellow dust that hung in the air as thick as cigar smoke back in the old Devon Club on a Saturday night.

Well, there I was, twenty-two, and I remember trying to grasp the whole five thousand years, imagining all the sweat, blood, and urine spilled on this one piece of ground, the semen and the spit and the tears. Not long ago *The National Enquirer* had an insert which I cut out and put in my wallet; it says that, per minute, a human being at rest sheds more than a hundred thousand microscopic particles of flaked off flesh, saliva, lint, sodium, dandruff, dead mouth tissue. Per minute. At rest. A slight head movement, and the number jumps to five hundred thousand particles. Five million when you walk real slow. Thirty million before you even get going good.

Five thousand years. Even now I try to grasp it. What the hell was I standing on?

Today, fifty-two years later, I am standing at a motel window with a view of a storage tank off Ohio Route 12, on the road to Toledo. It is night. There are crowds outside, people selling tee shirts and photographs of the storage tank, which is orange in the vapor lights. The *Review Times* says it is filled with soybean oil. I have prayed to Saint Helen, who first recoverd the True Cross, and to Saint Anthony of Padua, finder of lost things. I am not drinking. At first I saw only rust streaks and flaked paint, not even a pattern. The diagrams published in *Time Magazine* didn't help me any, even with these bifocals. I tried polarized sunglasses, and they were no help. I wished for those red-and-green lenses from the 3-D movies of the fifties. Then my eyes started playing tricks on me.

I suffer from poor eyesight. And from an ache in my hip. The doctor will probably say it is rheumatism. (But at night, alone in bed, I sometimes watch him shake his head and say cancer.) Only six of my own teeth remain in my mouth, and all six of them hurt. And I have gas. Everything I eat gives me gas. Which is particles that shoot out of you. Most people don't know that. Keep your nose clean, we used to say. We didn't know what we were saying.

I try opera glasses, but all they do is give size to what I think I see. The hard rainbow edges hurt my eyes and confuse me, all of it trembling because my hand won't hold still. In my other hand I hold the microphone to a portable cassette tape recorder. I tested it, and I sound just like me, whispering. Only younger. I even have an accent again, like when I was a kid, whispering.

In 1927, in the Detroit Pick-Fort Selby Hotel, Thomas "Yonnie" Licavoli, who was six feet tall and weighed 210 pounds and who never in his life talked above a whisper, told the Big Guy himself, Al Capone, "Stay the hell out of Detroit. It's my territory." The Big Guy agreed, and Yonnie's name—which is everything in this business—was made. At the time he was waiting for the Purple and Little Navy gangs to finish each other off in the war they were having. The famous Collingwood Avenue massacre was what finally ended the war. That, and the ten storey death leap of a beautiful young woman, a known campanion to one of the Purples. It seems that the *Detroit Free Press* somehow discovered that what the police were calling a suicide victim happened to've been bound and gagged at the time of death. Detroit put up its hackles, and things got too hot too fast, even for Yonnie Licavoli. It was right about then that Jacob 'Firetop' Sulkin made all those trips to Detroit he bragged about later, convincing Yonnie and his gang to set up in Toledo. The only problem, he told them, would be a minor one, name of Jackie Kennedy.

Was he in with the dicks? Yonnie wanted to know. In solid, Firetop said. And with the Irish politicians too. But Kennedy's only real connections were with Egan's Rats out of St. Louis. And Yonnie Licavoli knew all about them, their shooter with the smoked glasses, name of Browning. Yonnie was from St. Louis himself, dropped out of the Christian Brothers College there.

Me, my only school was what we called the College of Hard Knocks. My father enrolled me. He used to brag about how he'd lifted a sliver of the True Cross off a Turk who tried selling it to him. He always kept it wrapped in adhesive and slung around his neck on a string. He told people that if he ever lost it, he'd lose all his luck.

Back when I was about twelve or so I figured I'd need all the luck I could get. It took some doing, but I was already a good sneak. I managed to get it off him without his ever knowing what happened to it. Not long after that I said good riddance to my father's house and made it through Ellis Island in 1921, just under the wire of the Quota Act. Lucky me.

I traveled with 'relatives' from my village, and we wound up running a produce market in Toledo's North End. By that time word reached me that I'd left none too soon—it seemed my father's health was declining, and his feed and grain business wasn't feeling so well either.

Like most of my people, these 'relatives' I worked for were what was called industrious, but what I called penny scratchers. The North End was a clannish neighborhood—Little Syria—and in no time I'd developed a name for myself as something of a pickpocket. I took this as a compliment—I was a kid, what did I know?—but it was embarrassing to my adopted family who were straight shooters, doing their best by sending me to Catholic school and finding me work afterward (although it wasn't in school or in work but by playing hooky at the movies that I learned to speak English without an accent). So I moved on and ended up working on Canton Avenue in old Saint Patrick's Parish at the B and L Confectionery—a candy store where, on the QT, a Catholic could get himself a pail of beer after Mass. The beer was supplied by Jackie Kennedy, who wore pearl gray spats and a pinky ring. He was twenty-four years old and handsome and singing a love song to his sweetheart when they killed him. They put eleven holes in him. Jacob 'Firetop' Sulkin supplied the roscoes. I was the fingerman.

We really called a pistol a roscoe. It sounds funny now, after so many movies. It was at the B and L that I first learned to talk like that. I met Firetop there, and through him I got to know 'Chalky Red' Yaranowsky and 'Yonnie' Licavoli and 'Wop' English and the rest. We all really did use those nicknames. Firetop because of his red hair and Chalky Red because of his complexion and Joe English the Wop because his truename was Serifina Sinatra. There was even a Buster and a Blackjack in the old Licavoli Gang. Just like the movies. They called me 'Dip.' Somebody spread around a lie about me that I picked pockets. It was a bad name and a reputation I didn't deserve, as it was a knack I rarely used anymore, and only when I was desperate. Myself, I'd've settled for something like 'Shadow' or even 'Sneaky Pete' (my name was once Peter, in Arabic Boutros) but Dip was what stuck because the big shots, Yonnie and Firetop, made it stick, and there wasn't much I could do about it. Al Capone said once that there's nothing lower than a dip. (Well, 'rummy' would've been worse, which was why I did most of my drinking on the sly.) Capone himself never stood for being called 'Scarface'—he preferred 'Snorky', which in those days we used to mean a snappy dresser.

150

But nobody called him that, either. I saw him only once, on an elevator in Cleveland. He looked thick more than fat, back then in 1930, and on the short side, yet I could tell right off why everybody called him 'The Big Guy.' His reputation shone off him like a glow, like the golden light you see in holy cards. The Big Guy. He wore a cream fedora with the brim snapped down on the left to shadow the double razor scars. He nodded to me. Hasty, like somebody who didn't like to waste his time. Then one of his boys gave me the thumbs out sign, and I got off at the next floor.

For me it was pretty clear that if I ever did want a respected name, I'd have to work for it. So when Firetop called—I already knew what for—I was quick to be of service.

I uncovered Jackie Kennedy at a cottage over in Point Place, near Toledo. It took a sneak with talent to find and finger him. I learned that there was only one bodyguard, and that he was mostly kept busy playing babysitter to Jackie's four-year-old son. The time was right, I figured, even though Firetop wasn't around and Yonnie was in Detroit for his father-in-law's funeral. Chalky Red couldn't make it either, but his Ford V8 did. And me in it, sitting behind the wheel.

When the boys got out, they found Jackie strolling hand in hand with Audrey Rawls, a beauty contest winner. He was singing "Love in the Moonlight" to her, like in a movie. Afterward some of the papers called her the 'Tiger Woman' because they figured her to be the Judas. But she wasn't involved at all. I watched through the windscreen as Wop and Magnine shoved Miss Rawls out of the way and emptied both their .38 revolvers. One round blew off his watch. The other eleven were what coroners list as 'through and through'—in then right out the other side; clean, but they leave less evidence. Kennedy was tall and muscular and so strong his feet did the Jackson Shuffle for a full minute after he went down. That happened on July the 7th, 1933, a Friday.

Today is also a Friday, October the 3rd, 1986. My present name is John Doe. I deny all and any other appellations, true-names, nicknames, monikers, handles or tags. I am seventy-four years old, and this is my deposition which I give freely and without coercion or duress, without hope of reward or recompense.

The names I name have not been changed. Harry 'Chalky Red' Yaranowsky is a real name. So is Jacob 'Firetop' Sulkin. So is Thomas 'Yonnie' Licavoli. They are as dead as Jackie Kennedy. But they have not disappeared. They are in *The Toledo Blade*, *The Detroit News*, *The Cleveland Plain Dealer*, *The New York Times*. Me, I am in none of them. I got away. My current whereabouts are known only to the four walls of this room.

Until nine months ago my address was the same as that of my latest place of business, the English Language newsstand, mezzanine, St. Georges Hotel, Beirut, in what, as far as I know, is still being called Lebanon; my more recent names and addresses are too numerous to list. My father has been deceased for over sixty years; I didn't have a mother that I could remember. I never married, and currently I cannot be found.

Because they were so well known, Yonnie and Firetop couldn't get away after the murder. But they had the lawyers and the alibis. Now all they had to do was keep their mouths shut. Which they did until the Toledo cops sent to Detroit for a pair of dicks who specialized in extracting information. For some reason *The Toledo Blade* called these two the Clarke brothers, which anybody who knew anything knew wasn't their real name. But most people don't know anything. Most people think things like this happened only in the movies. But they should believe what they see in gangster movies. Who do they think made the movies? Anyway, the Clarkes figured Firetop to be the soft one since he bragged so much. One session with him lasted from after supper one night until 2:30 the next morning. His ribs were cracked and he couldn't walk because his groin hurt so.

Me, I'm hearing all this and I figure he'll spill in no time. Anybody would've. So if ever there was a time to take a fade, this was it.

I remember one night I'd sneaked out to eat at a place down the road from Toledo, in New Regal, Ohio. (The place still has a reputation for the best ribs around. I ate there two nights ago. Some things, like food, never change.) So there I was, fifty-some years ago, adjusting the napkin at my neck, the whole time thinking should I blow town or the whole midwest—in other words, how long is the long arm of the law?—when I happened to touch the lump of the True Cross where I kept it beneath my shirt. If anybody ever needed direction, it was me there and then. So I asked. Nothing. Okay. I started eating my ribs. Then, an instant later, I had my answer. There was a voice, not in my ears exactly, more like inside my head, telling me what to do.

I'd been an altarboy, but unlike most I took it seriously. I have always considered myself a spiritual person. To this day I believe that God speaks to us, and not just on the road to the holy city of Damascus, but on the road to Toledo, Ohio, too.

What the voice said was this: Do not blow town, My child. Blow the whole country.

Beirut would have been like heaven except that on the way there I discovered that my piece of the True Cross had been lifted from me. I was in New York Harbor, undressing in my cabin, when I felt, then looked and saw that it wasn't there. The last place I'd had my shirt off was in my flat above the B and L. So it had to still be in Toledo. But it was too late to go back. And too hot—Yonnie's trial had already begun. Being on the lam is like swimming underwater in the movies. You surface for air, see the patrol boat closing in behind you, and you go down again, deeper this time.

I had a couple of drinks, and after a while I said to myself Okay, it doesn't have to be the one great tragedy of your life. Go on, then, and make your own luck. I was surprised at how cocky I sounded. Besides, word had it that Lebanon, if not heaven, was a lot like home. A handful of family syndicates ran the whole place with defined territories, bosses and soldiers. Like the States, except it was called politics. Sure, vice was pretty much legal, gambling and prostitution, but there was the black market. And plenty of business from the hashish growers in Baalbek north of Beirut. Beirut Harbor itself was a conduit between the Turkish poppy fields and Marseilles.

Unfortunately, the luck I ended up making for myself over there wasn't too good, and before long I developed a liking for arraq (which is similar to absinthe, and because of that is illegal in the States to this day), but not so much that I got a name for it. The depression ended in the States and in Europe, but in the Middle East it lingered on into the war. Later, working with the heil Hitler Vichy Government was like doing business with the boy scouts. So our cheers were real when the Free French Sene-

153

galese marched into Martyr's Square to liberate us, their faces as black and shiny as their boots. After the boys in Italy finally did Benito (long overdue), the Mediterranean shipping lanes reopened and business started booming again.

The Bourj Plaza educated me. At one time I could speak French, Arabic, and get by in Greek and German. When I used to change money in the Ashrifiyeh District, the Armenians thought I was one of them. But I've lost all that now, all of it faded.

I worked on the up and up at hotel newsstands, and for real as a kind of errand boy for couriers who needed interpreting. In other words, one step above a dip. What I was called was Il Amerikain because my Arabic had developed an accent. You might say I didn't really have a name. Still, it became a life. I almost got married once but I sobered up and decided not to. There were even times luck came my way, as they say in the movies, and for a while I'd be what anybody'd call happy. Arraq stayed cheap, and even under the boy scouts the prostitute district remained open in Bourj Plaza, just behind the Gendarmerie. It was a life. If I had no name, at least I could say I was hanging on to the fringe, anyway, of the kind of work where a man might some day make a name. And, unlike Yonnie and Firetop, I was free.

Firetop served thirty years for his part in the Jackie Kennedy murder. He was granted parole in 1965, on his seventy-fifth birthday. Word reached me that he'd turned sour. Nobody feared him, calling him "Schmuck" to his face. He had to be strait jacketed, finally, and sent to the Toledo State Hospital for the mentally ill. He died there in 1971.

I took the news hard. It was, as they used to say in the movies, like losing a part of myself.

Beirut had a dozen or more picture shows called cinemas, and for a while I went to every American movie. In 1971 I saw *Easy Rider* dubbed in Arabic and subtitled in French. It frightened me. I was fifty-nine years old.

For me, the boom years—such as they were—ended with the Lebanese civil war. People got so they couldn't trust their own cousins, much less Il Amerikain. When the Syrians marched in with their half-a-goosestep clomp, it was like the boy scouts all over again. Car bombs went off sometimes twice a day, and I found myself reduced to working the crowds that gathered afterward. A dip.

Then, not long ago, I read in *Time,* in an article on organized crime, that Yonnie Licavoli was dead. Had been dead for over a dozen years. Nobody'd sent word. There was nobody left to send word. I closed the magazine and rolled it tight. I walked away from the newsstand without even bothering to lock up. The bottle of arraq sat uncorked on the counter. I left it there to evaporate. I began walking and I kept on walking, all the time twisting and choking the magazine. Those steps were the beginning of my journey back to Toledo.

Thomas 'Yonnie' Licavoli, while an inmate of the Ohio State Penitentiary, had been granted two first-place awards in international stamp collectors exhibits. He also won recognition for fifty songs he wrote under the name Tommy Thomas. Over the years three different wardens lost their jobs for allowing him special treatment. So for Yonnie too it had become a life. When he was sixty-seven years old he pleaded for release. "I have a daughter who was born three months before I came to prison," he wrote the governor. "Now she is married, with two lovely girls and a little boy of her own, and none of them have ever seen me except behind bars. My first born daughter was killed, along with my father, while they were on their way to visit me one day." The letter is public record. The only word that reaches me anymore is public record.

Yonnie Licavoli was released after serving thirty-seven years, one month and twenty-seven days. And he died less than two years later. His obit made *The New York Times.* The FBI attended the funeral in Detroit. A sixty-car procession followed the hearse.

Now they are all gone—Wop English, Chalky Red, Blackjack, Pimp Bruno, Buster Lupica. Johnny Magnine, like me, was never found. Word had it he died in Akron back in '35. A week ago I stopped there on my way back to check it out. Nobody knew. He was the other triggerman, but the memory of him had faded completely. For the first time in fifty-two years I felt free to surface. What was left of me.

155

It was while I was on my way back from Akron, almost to Toledo, that I read about the face of Jesus on a watertower.

Except that when I got here it turned out to be this soybean oil storage tank, and maybe it's the light or something reflecting on the rust and the paint that edges the rust, but whole crowds are seeing something there. I tried, and for the briefest instant I thought I saw something too. Yet what I saw—if I saw it—was nothing like the Image outlined in *Time*. What I saw had on a hat, a fedora, with the brim snapped down to hide the left cheek. Then the light began to hurt my eyes and The Image receded once more to rust stains and peeling paint and crowds of people looking. All of them faders. You'd think He wouldn't waste His time on faders. On sodium and lint and dead tissue that flakes away with every motion. Standing still even, I feel myself changing. The light blinds me the more I stare. I pull the drapes against it.

There's nothing left in Toledo, not after all this time. I can see that now. Now what I want to see is how much of me will be left when I get there, and what I'll be.

Nominated by Oxford Magazine *and Michael Martone*

AUSTERITY IN VERMONT

by T. R. HUMMER

from THE GETTYSBURG REVIEW

Astral blue of old mountains, ridge after rising ridge
Blurring the western horizon just after the sun goes down,
And there, up five degrees, the cold yellow evening star
My almanac says will be Saturn this month, the bastard god
    nobody
Wants for a father—not much light, but it's all Vermont
    conceives
Now that September's come and I feel like losing weight.
What is this voice I hear that tells me *Less flesh?*
Where does it go, the meat of the belly, when I stop
Drinking beer and run my groaning mile a day
Into the Yankee wind that articulates a whole
Future of frost in the darkening perpendiculars of maples?
All flesh has a fate, true enough, though it's clear no body
    believes
This moment's horoscope, Saturn in the sixth house descending,
Pissed-off cannibal planet of constipation and infanticide—
But what can you do if you're being born right now
In a ward in Burlington? They're about to cut the cord
Just as that point of luminescence the color of urine on snow
Crowns at the lip of the sky's birth canal. Will you scream
At the doctor to wait just five minutes more with his surgical
    steel—
Hold on, get back until that terrible light tips over the edge
And dissolves into somebody else's birthday? But look,
It's too late, there's a snip and you're bleeding, your flesh

157

And your mother's are suddenly lives apart,
And there you lie, naked in that planet's damning radiation.
That's how destiny works—you'll never be a stockbroker,
You'll have five kids of your own, you'll live on a farm in
    Vermont
Rolling stones up a hill for years until one afternoon you come
    home
And open fire with your old shotgun on everybody in sight.
Right at the moment, gasping for air, I'm trying to remember
How it felt when the doctor shagged me loose from the rope of
    blood
That strained me down toward the good sleep of the placenta,
And I was myself apart, zapped from a dozen angles
By all the essences of my future—Mercury, Venus, Mars,
The whole merciless pantheon of necessary acts
That impressed themselves in my blue flesh turning red
With its own bloody weight. And look at me now,
Out on a road in Vermont at sunset, running, trying to choose
To make the bulge in my belly disappear the way my mother's
    did
After the lying-in, after the labor, after the voice
In the anaesthetic stopped its mindless song, and some stranger
Lay there beside her with a body already growing
Ascetic, unbelieving, refusing her, demanding nothing not its
    own.

Nominated by Richard Jackson, Dorianne Laux, Judson Mitcham and Gordon Weaver

HEAVEN

by DAVID LEHMAN

from NEW AMERICAN WRITING

Once you lose it, it keeps coming back to you, forever.
A seductive notion: "now" is the price of eternal "then,"
A religious corollary to the theme of beauty and "easeful death."
And I suppose that's what we mean when we say
"This is what heaven must be like," or else heaven is the sum
Of all the comparisons that poets, writing with a gun
To their heads, propose in the terror of the moment.
But to recover the loss before suffering its absence,
To lose it on a yesterday that never was and have it back
On the endless plateau of today, is really what I had in mind,
That and the knowledge that something forgotten always has
A delayed echo, like an echo frozen on northern seas
To be released with the voices of winter mariners
In the summer thaw. In a dream, I forgot to write down
The words of the dream, and who had spoken them to me,
And what we were doing in this rented car we were driving
Across Los Angeles, from one end to the other, though
We knew this to be a physical impossibility: the end
Is what we cannot reach, or want to, Los Angeles being
One example. I turned to you in the car and said
I wanted to write a play called "The End of the World
In L.A." Somehow I knew that the world would end there
If an ending were possible. "If you're wrong," you said,
"It's a one-minute mistake." You didn't say what you meant,
Or you did, but I forgot to write down the words. In a dream,
I heard shots at ten-minute intervals. I turned to you

159

In bed but you weren't there: you were in Los Angeles,
Driving with me toward the end of the world
And the Pacific Ocean. In the infinite distance between
Here and there, the arrow paused without ceasing to move
Toward the moving target to the west of the horizon.
Only a second had gone by. And I knew I had you back, forever.

Nominated by Richard Burgin, Wesley McNair, Joyce Carol Oates and Lloyd Schwartz

FIELD OF FIRE

fiction by WILL BAKER

from THE GEORGIA REVIEW

W HEN THE SHOOTING started Raymond Walker shut his eyes but not the book propped comfortably on his midsection. The first report came from some kind of rifle, he supposed, since it was the flat whip-crack he remembered from western movies when men fired at each other from behind rocks, levering shells into their repeaters. Then came a series of fast pops, like a string of firecrackers. Then another rifle—this one a tremendous whack followed by long, rolling echoes.

Eyes still closed, Raymond moved his lips like a slow reader. *This is it,* he was saying. *Here we go. I knew.*

What he knew, among other things, was that Bea would now awaken from her nap and come forth onto this leaf-shaded porch. She would awaken in a state of fear and rage, of combat readiness. These days, as she often said, you had to be ready for anything. The worthless dollar and corrupt unions. Homosexuals and drug addicts spreading disease. A spineless judiciary.

In this case Raymond's responsibility would be central, because as a man he was supposed to know about other men. For example, about the men who had two hours ago driven their muddy pickup past the Walkers' new second home, a cunning cottage in the piney woods by an all-year stream (All on your own, wilderness-grade privacy, end of the line, the realtor had said, Bureau of Land Management on three sides and an abandoned ranch on the other.)

161

The big gun whacked again, followed by another string of little pops. It made no sense. One sounded powerful enough for rhino and the other had to be derringer class.

Raymond in fact knew very little about weapons. The flowering of his own manhood had fallen between Korea and Vietnam, so he had never served in his country's armed forces. Nor was he much of an outdoor sportsman, though as a younger man he had been included on a few trips, for professional reasons. Once in Oregon he caught a twenty-two-pound salmon, and another time—by what seemed to him a miracle—a duck had fallen out of the sky soon after he fired.

But he had no connection to guns, not even to the only one he owned. This was a thirty-eight-caliber revolver, a Police Special, duly registered, which lay in the bottom drawer of his dresser at home along with an unopened box of cartridges. He had stuffed them there eleven years ago after the naked body of a secretary had turned up in a ravine in a regional park downstate. The park was two hundred miles away, but the secretary had actually worked in an office in the same building that housed Raymond's medical supply company. That was enough to convince Bea that public order had disintegrated and the time had come for Raymond to arm himself and defend, at least minimally, his home and family.

The cry of outrage he now heard was not dissimilar to that of a matron molested in a parking lot after dark. This was daytime, of course, balmy and with a light breeze—an afternoon for relaxing after a busy and invigorating morning of spading up flower beds and scraping away old paint. He heard the slap of Bea's zoris crossing the living room and resettled himself in the deck chair, frowning as if at some authorial clumsiness in the pages before him.

"What in God's name is *that?*"

Raymond had already looked up, eyebrows hoisted in mild curiosity, before her question. "A rifle," he said cautiously. "Probably some hunters."

"It can't be a rifle. It's a cannon or a bazooka or something. My God, we paid a hundred and thirty thousand for this place."

She was imposing, even in her jeans rolled up to the knees and flannel shirt with the tail out, Raymond thought. A fine figure of a woman, as they used to say. Broad of shoulder and hip, almost an hour-glass. Her copper and silver hair was gathered in a purposeful ponytail secured with a wooden clip.

"After deer, probably. If they miss they'll move on—" The shooting exploded again, as if to refute him. Several guns were apparently firing at once. They heard a distant yell.

"Oh certainly," Bea said. "Of course they'll move on, Ray—right on over here. And then what?"

"Bea," he said, and tilted his head down so that he was looking at her from beneath his brows, a kind of genial glower. "Let's be calm here. They might be tracking some wounded—"

"It's only *June*, Ray. Hunting is in the fall. I thought all men knew that. And anyway, how could somebody shoot a deer this many times? It would be blown to smithereens. These are not hunters. Macho survivalist creeps, is more likely." She had walked down the front steps, talking louder, as if she hoped the men hidden somewhere in the trees would hear. "A hundred and thirty thousand. This is terrible."

It's a terrible life, Raymond thought before he could stop himself. But she was right of course. Of course she was right. To plant most of their savings into the unmovable earth, and then discover that the landscape was crawling with psychotics . . .

"For God's sake put that book away. We've got to do something."

He closed the book and set it carefully on the wicker table beside the chair. On the bright green jacket was a photograph of a billionaire, a man five years younger than Raymond. The man was wearing a dark suit and stood with his arms folded confidently across his chest. Over his shoulder loomed a great tower of steel and glass, and above that came the title in gold block letters: THE BUSINESS END.

"I'll call the sheriff," Raymond said. "See what can be done."

"Do that," his wife said without turning to watch him get up. "Do see what can be done."

Nothing, as it turned out. The deputy's voice, high and twangy, conveyed amusement. On BLM land any sort of weapon was permissible, except full automatic. There was only an old county regulation prohibiting the discharge of firearms within one hundred yards of an occupied dwelling. Raymond said that was a ridiculously short distance. The noise was deafening, a violation of all civilized standards.

163

"Well, now, Mister Walker, on that old Phillips place you won't find what you would call no habitable dwelling," the man said, and then laughed heartily to himself. "Anyways, the Phillips kids don't live there no more. They lease the ground to old Buck. And old Buck, he's quite a character. Rides in our posse ever year at the state fair. Loves to shoot."

Raymond's exasperation was submerged in a new dread. The deputy talked as if old Buck were an old friend, perhaps a relative. He recalled the couple who tended the tiny store, stacked with canned and packaged goods, at the intersection of the highway and their road. Also the man with the tremendous potbelly and absent smile who sold gas from two pumps in his front yard. These people seemed to know all about the Walkers' new property, where located and when purchased. Perhaps they too were related to the deputy and old Buck.

"So," Raymond said in his most aloof, professional tone, "it appears that you can't help us."

The deputy chuckled. "Long as Buck's within his rights, I surely wouldn't argue the issue. If I was you. Why don't you folks just take it easy now, and have yerselfs a nice day?"

On the next call Raymond's lawyer also recommended they wait a bit and see. The area *was* changing—many of the old ranches were selling to people like themselves—but these things took time. You needed a secure political base from which to argue for new zoning restrictions, bird refuges, and the like. For now, better to do as the Romans. Also these country types could be unpredictable. Every household had a shotgun, and what with moonshining and several generations of marrying cousins, you never knew what was behind the trigger.

Then for two weekends in a row they had the forests and mountains and all-year creek—now down to a trickle—all to themselves. They got a lot done. Bea created tidy, black rectangles of newly planted beds inside a spanking white picket fence. Raymond began painting the cottage a dusky rose with cream trim, and laid a curving pathway of flat stones to the front gate.

They allowed themselves an extravagant hope: that the shooting was a rarity, a fluke. Old Buck had moved on, or—better yet—passed away. But then for three Saturdays in a row the barrage

164

intensified, lasting from midday to dusk. Their immediate solution was to throw themselves grimly into new tasks. They worked in a fury so that they would not be conscious of waiting for the sound of the pickup or the thunder of the rhino rifle, and so that they would be too exhausted to argue.

Raymond scraped and painted; Bea, on her knees, threw clumps of weeds over one shoulder. Now and then they talked, mostly to themselves. "The Constitution," she would say, "apparently means nothing." Or, "Trip why don't you. Fall down and jerk the trigger and blow your own head off." Once she said, "I guess there are two kinds: pigs and ostriches." When Raymond figured out the analogy, he sulked for hours and made comments of his own under his breath. *The Golden Years. Retire to the country and go insane. The realtor. Shoot the realtor. An ostrich married to a hippo. Disney may be interested. Do some cosmetic work and sell out?*

He kept this last notion secret. It made good sense to him. He had even checked property values in the area with another realtor, and with all their improvements they might recover their one thirty and even part of the closing costs. But merely imagining the look he would get from Bea, if he proposed such a plan, was enough to twang his dormant ulcer. An inevitable alternative was looming closer, like a beefy dentist.

Bea had outlined it for him one evening after a day of deceptively light small-arms fire. Though they had electricity they sat at the kitchen table in the romantic glow of an Aladdin lamp, an heirloom from Bea's family. She was smoking one of her occasional after-dinner Schimmel-pfennigs. "The man has to be confronted," she said. "I assume you know that much, and have been avoiding it for your usual reasons."

"His name is Skinner," Raymond said, trying for the detached manner of a private investigator.

"Buck Skinner. How imaginative." She blew smoke in the direction of their neighbor's camp. "Who forced that information on you?"

"I asked the storekeeper a simple question."

"You need to ask Mister Skinner a few simple questions."

He didn't respond. She smiled and exhaled smoke at him through her nostrils, as if that were exactly the reaction she expected. A brief pause. What happens, he thought, when an undisguised contempt meets an inadequate object. She had already made clear that there was only one response he could make. He would have to drive up the road to the Phillips place, open the gate, and walk over an open field in the stark light of noon to meet Buck Skinner face-to-face, man-to-man.

On the following Wednesday evening Raymond dug the thirty-eight out of the bottom drawer and pulled it from its holster for the first time in eleven years. He was sitting on the queen-size in the bedroom, alone in their spacious townhouse. Bea had gone with girlfriends to work out at the club, and they would have a drink and a gossip afterward. He was surprised at how the leather had remained shiny and creaky as new. The pistol, on the other hand, looked dull and he found some freckles of rust on the barrel. He took a handkerchief from a top drawer and buffed the gun industriously for a few minutes and the blue sheen came back, though the spots did not disappear.

He would need a cleaner of some kind, he supposed. He seemed to remember the clerk at the sporting-goods store had given him a little brochure of gun-care tips, but he must have thrown it away. The whole thing had been only a symbolic gesture. It occurred to him that he had never once even loaded the weapon. Could he do that? He went back to the drawer and found the small, heavy box. Inside, the rounds were packed in neat rows, held upright by crosshatched cardboard partitions.

He shook out a handful and felt an odd thrill at the dense, magnetic pressure of them in his palm. They seemed old-fashioned, tips of pain, blunt lead and cases of dull brass, but they slid easily into the chambers, as if greased. Ray the Kid, he thought, smiling at his own absurdity.

As a boy he had read in some novel that the chamber under the hammer was always left empty. So he had five rounds. "Round"—the word took on a new dimension for him. Not symmetric anymore, it extended on its axis, a long, whining syllable ending in a deadly consonant of lead. *Roun-n-duh.*

He sat for a time quite still, the revolver on his knee, covered loosely by one hand. His eyes were open, but he was not seeing the dresser or the Klee print across the room. He was remembering another old movie, a memory he did not even know he had.

166

Barricaded in their log cabin, a man and his son were down to their last cartridges, while a savage horde of redskins rode at them with blood-curdling yells. A woman with a little girl, both in bonnets and aprons, cowered in a corner. Between shots through the window the man grimaced ferociously and said, "Save a cartridge for yer Ma *(POW!)* . . . and yer Sis *(BLAM!)* . . . and yer ownself *(KA-POW!)*."

Now there's a pretty pickle, he thought, and raised the revolver, apparently to aim at the three pairs of legs under one umbrella in the painting. A matter of timing. What if you pull the trigger on mama and just then you hear the bugle announcing a relief column? Surprise surprise. That's the drawback in taking these apocalyptic positions. Or the advantage. Hear the bugle, *then* pull the trigger.

When he heard the tires of their Prelude pad up the concrete driveway, he was already in bed, reading an Updike novel. The thirty-eight and the box of shells were packed in the handbag that would accompany him Friday afternoon, when they again took off for their country cottage. He felt lofty and at ease, bemused by the characters in the novel and their silly preoccupation with adultery. It seemed to him—and this was new—that he would know, were he in their shoes, what action to take, how to be swift and decisive.

Three days later Raymond had to make his move. On the dirt road, coming in, the pickup had run up behind them. It was a heavy vehicle with wide, knobby tires and a roll bar. Only one dark figure was visible through a windshield made milky by the spatter of insect collisions. When they turned into their driveway and the truck flashed by, Bea said matter-of-factly, cheerfully even, "Showdown, love."

He tried to look puzzled. She went on in the same light, hard-as-glass tone. "Tomorrow, Ray. The OK Corral. If you don't do it, I will."

After Saturday breakfast, which was late and monosyllabic, Raymond shed his robe and donned a clean workshirt, long pants, and his suede hiking boots. He removed the holstered thirty-eight from his bag and held it for a few moments, appreciating the weight, before putting it back under a folded sweater. He returned to the kitchen where Bea was finishing up the

167

dishes and stopped in the doorway. He prepared to clear his throat and announce, more or less formally, his intention to embark on the negotiating mission.

But before he could speak there was a rapid series of explosions from the direction of the Phillips place. It sounded to Ray like a burst from an automatic weapon. A Russian word came to mind, but he was not sure; it might have been the name of a famous ballet dancer.

Bea looked at him over her shoulder, smiling slightly. A bitter-sweet, female humor of acceptance. *Tanks? Grenades? Napalm? Of course.* In the charged silence after the shots there was no sound but the sucking and gargling of water draining from the sink.

Raymond knew better than to smile back. He did clear his throat, but then said nothing. After another moment's pause he turned and marched away, out of the house to the car, which he started, gunned, and put into reverse with a jolt.

He parked at the wooden gate, racing the engine once more before switching it off, in order to announce his arrival. The gate, a dilapidated assemblage of poles and wire, bore a large metal sign reading KEEP OUT. Several bullet holes were clustered inside the O. A cardboard poster forbade hunting or trespassing and noted that violators would be prosecuted to the full extent of the law. Fifty yards away the pickup was parked in front of a wooden shack.

The door of the shack stood open, but Raymond could detect no movement in the dark interior. The clearing around the little building was beaten bare, crisscrossed by tire tracks. Some of these tracks led away into the trees; other crossed a meadow toward a creek that wound along the base of a rugged ridge. Here and there he could see a disordered stack of boards or twisted metal roofing, old machinery or the shells of discarded appliances. Hidden in a tree, some bird was uttering an unnaturally shrill cry.

"Hello?" he called, "I say, hello!"

The gate was secured by a heavy chain and padlock, but the fence stretching on either side was in bad repair. Rotting posts leaned at all angles and rusty barbed wire sagged between them. After calling out twice more, Raymond pushed the top wire down gingerly with one hand and crossed easily with a scissoring maneuver of his legs.

He strode toward the cabin. Rough lumber, plywood sheets, and galvanized roofing had been slapped together to form the shell. A crooked stovepipe, streaked with rust, elbowed out of one wall, and over the doorway someone had nailed a jangle of deer antlers. A hand axe was buried in one block from a loose pile of firewood by the front door. It was a forlorn place, a pathetic hovel really.

"Mister Skinner," Raymond called. He was encouraged by the authoritative ring of his own voice. "I'd like a word with you." He stepped onto the narrow porch that protruded from the front of the structure and a plank squeaked. The door was ajar only a foot or so, allowing him to see the corner of a table and part of a shelf covered with magazines.

Raymond hesitated, listening. Could the man have fallen asleep? "Mister Skinner?" he said again, but softly this time. With his fingertips he pressed gently on the door panel. He saw first the whole table. It was positioned directly in front of a wide open window in the rear wall of the shack, beside a tiny black woodstove. On the table was a stack of small sandbags and a pair of binoculars.

Then he saw the cabinets against the left wall. They held guns in neat rows, behind padlocked crossbars. Long and short, black and blue and nickel-plated, some with curving clips and some with leather straps. Empty cartridge cases were scattered everywhere on the floor, along with scraps of paper and a few empty beer cans. Against the right wall, under the shelf piled with books and magazines, was a crumpled empty sleeping bag on a single cot.

"You'd be a dead man right now, iffen I was a mind."

The voice seemed to come from behind his left ear, and so shocked Raymond that he uttered a short, warped yodel and seized the front of his shirt in one fist. When he turned he saw, a half-dozen strides away, a man wearing a hat and holding a black, winged object in his two hands.

"Lookahere," the man said. He raised the object and turned a little away from Raymond. The wings flexed, there was a sudden loud hiss, and a metal rod sprouted, quivering, from the wood pile.

169

"Git clear through the vital cavity at this range," the man said. "Damn good tool for a close, quiet job." He stepped nearer and lifted the object into Raymond's chest. "See how she handles."

Raymond had raised his hands to protect himself, but found he was now holding the crossbow—a heavy, compact instrument, all metal.

"Walker, ain't ya?" The man held his head to one side and looked Raymond up and down. "Bought the Gill place. Good location, but she's water poor." He continued staring at Raymond, shaking his head. "Sorry," he said finally. "Resemblance there that throwed me plumb for a loop. Fella I ain't seen for . . . well, never mind. I'm Buck—Buck Skinner." He grinned wolfishly, his eyes only tiny glints of light in a tight bunch of sun-wrinkles. He was short and wiry of build, though his lumpy hands and long, craggy face seemed made for a larger man. That face, despite the shadow from the battered, wide-brimmed hat, looked vaguely familiar to Raymond.

"Yes, Walker," he said. "Ray Walker." He looked down at the crossbow in his hands. "I didn't mean to intrude. I tried to raise—"

"I seen what you done. Crosst the fence and pussyfooted up to my front door. Wouldn't make much of an Injun fighter, Ray. I coulda dropped you there with your ass astraddle of the bobwire."

"I only meant—" Ray began.

"Course I figured who you was. But technically you was trespassin'. You coulda been a armed assailant. I got the right to defend m'self. Same as you and your missuz."

Buck stepped onto the porch of his shack, and not knowing what else to do, Raymond followed him. "You *do* got pertection?"

"Beg your pardon?" Raymond was trying to compose a sentence, at once direct, unapologetic, and tactful, but felt himself distracted, still holding the crossbow awkwardly in his arms.

"You keep some kinda weapon in your home. You must. You don't look like a fool."

Raymond looked startled. "I own a handgun."

Buck laughed. "Might a fella ask what kind?"

"It's . . . uh . . . you mean the caliber?"

Buck paused in the doorway and turned to Raymond. His mouth was wide open, laughter erupting now like the cackle of wild birds. "Yeah," he got out finally. "Start there."

"Thirty-eight," Raymond said stiffly. He set the crossbow against the wall by the door. "However—"

"Old standby for years," Buck said, humor still detectable in his voice. "You probably got yerself a policer. They still make a lot of 'em, but you'd be better off with a .357 or a .44 Mag, a real manstopper. Even in former times, a P38 was way ahead of a policer." He cocked his head at Raymond again. "I see you're confused. P38 don't mean thirty-eight caliber. I'm talkin' about a Walther, the German military sidearm of choice. Pistolisher Actandryzig. Nine millimeter. Ever officer in Hitler's army wore one. Fantastic piece. But, hell, Ray"—Buck's voice now boomed hollowly from inside the shack. Raymond could hear the man rummaging along the cabinets against the wall and then a series of metallic clicks, something being unlocked—"A handgun's not much good for modern home defense. You want to hold up a liquor store or hit somebody on the sidewalk, then that's your baby."

Buck emerged again carrying a stubby, heavy gun with a wooden stock and a nickel-plated barrel that sent a lance of sunlight into Raymond's eyes. "You wanna deal with a close-quarter assault, like say a couple guys breakin' and enterin', you stick with a plain old gauge. A Browning pump fer example, double-ought loads. Lookahere."

Buck vaulted from the porch into the bare, rutted driveway. He hit the ground in a crouch, and Raymond was again reminded of the movies, of commandos or rooftop chases. With the odd, arthritic agility of a crab, Buck moved swiftly to his right and approached the carcass of an old refrigerator, which tilted aloft from a heap of refuse.

"Two of 'em, say. First guy in the kitchen—" The gun emitted a tremendous, thick noise along with a sharp tongue of dark fire. A cloud of dust flew from the refrigerator and it clanged. Buck's hand worked back and forth, a rapid, obscene movement along the column of the barrel, and there was a steady, heavy roar and flickering of the dark tongue. The refrigerator bulged and flakes of white paint showered from it. From the back flared streamers of insulation. One hinge was blown off and the door sagged away to reveal an interior of smoking, twisted aluminum, before the whole body toppled off the heap with a great crunch.

171

Buck wheeled around, facing the skeletons of abandoned machinery at the rear of the shack. "Other guy tries to get away in the car—" He fired twice more into the door panel of an old sedan with no hood, trunk, or wheels. The window blew out in a thousand glittering chips and a considerable cavity appeared in the door itself. "That's all she wrote for them two unwise sonsabitches," Buck said, nodding and winking at Raymond. He straightened and moved back to the porch at a brisk but casual walk. "You're good for up to twenty-five, thirty yards—you don't have to hardly aim and she's damn near as quick as semi-auto. That'll cover your average yard and patio and driveway and so forth. Out here, o' course, you gotta have an entirely different rig."

"I must discuss something with you." To his own ears Raymond's voice sounded high and rapid. The other man paused in front of him, the shotgun slung loosely in one hand, a faint ribbon of smoke still rising from the mouth of the barrel.

"Sure." Buck tilted his hat toward the interior of the cabin. "Have a drink. I got some other possibilities to show you."

"Really," Raymond began, trying to restore the depth and authority of his earlier tone. Much of the last five minutes seemed to him so preposterous that, despite the ear-splitting thunder of the gun, he felt himself locked inexorably in a dream.

"Come on, buddy." Buck waggled the shotgun near Raymond's feet. "I got a fair idea what's on yer mind. Let's sit down over a little bourbon. You look like a reasonable feller."

"No thank you. On the drink," Raymond said. His feet, however, were moving, responding to the motion of the shotgun rather than to his own will, carrying him over the threshold.

Buck came in behind him, leaving the door open. He dropped the shotgun into a rack, removed his hat and sailed it at a row of pegs on the wall. The hat ringed a peg once, then tumbled onto the bed below.

"How can a man shoot an inch and a half group with a open sight, at a hunnert yards, and not hang his own goddamn hat?" Buck shook his head in mock grief. He opened a cupboard above a tiny sink in a corner of the room and removed a bottle and two glasses. He went on talking as he inspected the glasses, rubbing each in turn on his shirt front before setting it down on the table.

172

"Because his life don't depend on a hat. If it did he'd get god-damn good at it, real fast. I'm pourin' you a hook, Ray, in case you change yer mind. Necessity, on the other hand, 'll make any dufus a sharpshooter. But most people don't see the need. Don't understand this goddamn screwed-up world they live in. Take yerself—and I don't mean no disrespect, pardner, here's to ya—" Buck had finished pouring an inch of topaz liquid into each glass, and now raised one of them in salute before sipping judiciously "—but I can tell you don't know jack shit about what yer up against. Ain't yer fault. It's what they feed you. Statistics. The anti-gun numbskulls and commies. Accidents in the home and so forth." He smacked his lips, sipped again. "So they sold you a little popgun. Just go beddy-bye all safe and sound with that un-der your pillow. Lordy, lordy, Ray." Buck exhaled, whistling. He indicated to Raymond the one chair by the table and, pushing aside the rumpled sleeping bag, sat himself on the cot. "Suppose some hard case really wanted to take you down. Now what's he gonna come with? An M-16 or a AK-47, common as dirt these days, with a .357 for backup. Or suppose some big darky pumped full of dope, steroids or whatever, takes after yer wife? Three, four slugs from that thirty-eight, even hunnert and thirty grain hollow points, might just slow the man down. You put a load of double-ought from that shortie into his chest, he's gonna go backwards. I guarantee you."

"Our concern," Raymond said, "is with the noise level. My wife—"

"Course she's worried. Christ a'mighty, *I'm* worried. These women, Ray . . . " He gave Raymond an odd, squinty wink. "They got no patent on fear. Especially in the big city. Damn war zone is what it is. Drug wars, gang wars, race wars. People wake up someday, and see what's become of this country . . . " Buck looked down for a moment between his boots, dejected. Then, suddenly, he was on his feet again and across the room in two strides.

"Right here. Right here is where she started, Ray." He pointed at a faded picture on the wall beside the tiny sink.

Raymond peered at the square of paper between thumbtacks, apparently a page torn long ago from some large-format maga-zine. A grainy blowup of a convertible, a woman in a pink

173

suit. . . . He recoiled, recognizing a frame from the notorious Zapruder film. The limousine was already blurring with acceleration, the President's head jolted to one side, hair disarranged.

"You 'member?"

"Of course." Raymond looked away. There was a pause, and he knew he was missing an opportunity to begin stating his case, but the old photograph had rattled him. His own concerns seemed petty and irrelevant in the face of national tragedy.

"A little six-five em em Manlicher. Jackrabbit rifle. He could've survived that first slug through the back. But with a lucky head shot. . . . Hell, even a twenty-two could do the job. Ask his brother. Anyway, that day in Dallas was the day we seen the handwritin' on the wall. All them FBI and Secret Service and Texas Rangers and what? One ex-Marine with a jackrabbit gun knocks off the big one. And damn near got away to boot. Now it was a terrible thing, Ray, ain't sayin' otherwise—I wisht I could've got little Lee Harvey in *my* sights—but the sonofabitch could shoot, got to give him that. Two out of three at eighty yards on a movin' target, in twelve seconds? Your criminal can shoot, don't think he can't. That's the goddamn problem." Buck looked at Raymond again with a meaningful squint of one eye, and again Raymond saw something oddly familiar in the craggy countenance with its light frost of beard. "All this propagander from the liberal media. People think guns are the problem. Hell, Ray, a gun ain't good nor bad. It ain't a damn *personality*."

Raymond's hands, not knowing what to do with themselves, had found the glass of whiskey. The urgency and sense of desperation inside him had reached a sort of equilibrium, like the vibrations of an engine running full throttle. *I'm here*, he told himself. *I'm performing my duty*. He lifted the glass to drink.

"Right. You see what I'm sayin'. They're tryin' to scare people away from their constitutional right to bear arms. And the NRA—them pussies with their safari coats and bumper stickers—they talk like the Foundin' Fathers give us that right just so we could hunt *ducks*. Ha! Them old boys was only interested in blowin' the redcoats clean out of North America, Ray. You think they wouldn't hand out all the grenade launchers and mortars they could git a hand on, in this present crisis? Shoot, Ray, we was born from a gun, us Americans. We come through 1812 and Bull Run and San Juan and the Argonne and Iwo Jima and Khe San the same way. I was on Kwajalein, myself. And I can tell you, war ain't all brass bands. If some Jap comes creepin' along with a grenade and you got a BAR, then you cut him in two before he does the same to you. It's ugly, but it's the goddamn world." Buck paused for a moment to drain his glass. "That BAR was a fine weapon for its time, by the way. I got one here I might show you a little later on." He reached to take the bottle from the table, but before he poured he hesitated, arrested by a new thought, "You, uh, see action in the service, Ray?"

Raymond watched the bottle resume its tilt, the rope of golden liquor drop into the glass. "No." he said, "Not really."

"Well," Buck said quickly, "that's all right. A lot of things I couldn't tell you, though. Nobody can tell a man, unless he's been there, and if he has then you don't have to tell 'im. But I'm gettin' off my subjeck." He ignored a protesting hand and topped off Raymond's glass. "Clears the sinuses. But anyhow, if citizens was exercisin' their rights, would they have let them guys on the grassy knoll sneak off, or let Lee Harvey run loose after he shot that cop? Answer to that question is another. You never heard of no assassination attempts on Andrew Jackson, did ya? Damn right. Them days men carried a gun everywhere but church. Anybody took a potshot at Old Hick'ry he'd be dropped in his tracks. A hunnert men could draw down on 'im in the first ten seconds. Them days a man was his own security, and his fella man's and ever woman and kid's too. And come to it, *that's* why Jack Kennedy died. The citizens of this country was unarmed."

There was another pause, and Raymond took a hurried gulp of the whiskey. How long had he been gone? Bea would surely have heard the blasts from the shotgun. She would be anxious, impatient. He had to speak succinctly, bring this thing to a head, now that the situation was more informal. He opened his mouth, and then left it open in amazement. A tear had cut a glistening, crooked track down Buck's cheek.

"And I think then of all the young boys who fought 'n died in the mud to pertect our rights," he said in a voice made rough with feeling. "An' it gets me, Ray. Really gets me." He looked full at Raymond and blinked out another tear, ridges of muscle standing out along his jawline. "I once knew a young feller . . . fine a boy as you ever saw . . . " He squeezed shut his eyes and with thumb and forefinger wiped away the tears. "But let that

175

be." He paused, worked to get a grip on himself, and then went on in a soft but intent voice. "The thing is, these people—these people that wanta take away our rights. Wanta turn us over to the dope dealers and crazies and communists." He shook his head slowly. "What are we gonna do with 'em, Ray?"

Raymond shut his mouth with a tiny, wet sound audible only to himself. "Well," he said, "gun control is a very complex issue. I must say . . . allow me, Mister Skinner . . . "

"Buck. I just met ya, Ray, but I know when I like a man. You got a way about ya—listenin' close, considerin' things—I like that. Maybe on account of I'm a born gabber m'self. Fact is, we're probably different as night 'n day, but the laws of physics say opposites attrack. Gabbin' along here, never thought to ask yer line of work, how many kids, and so forth. Drink up and gimme an earful." Buck reached out and Raymond had no choice but to clink glasses and sip again.

"I'm in medical supplies," Raymond said. "A small firm. Bea and I—my wife—are hoping to sell the business and retire here in the country—"

"Peace 'n quiet, a whole goddamn forest right on yer doorstep, plenty of game—wunnerful, ain't it?" Buck beamed at him, his eyes lost in the sun-wrinkles again. "Neighbor."

"Well, my wife . . . " Raymond looked out the big open window and saw for the first time the row of targets in the meadow. Three were life-size mannequins of some pale material, with large red hearts painted on the chest. " . . . has been a little unhappy here."

"No!" Buck leaned forward, concerned. "Your missuz is okay, I hope. Health-wise, I mean. 'Course God only knows how long any of us has got, but she looks healthy as a hog, Ray, from what a man can tell drivin' by, which ain't much I grant. Now, you bein' in the medical line—not a doc, are ya, by any chance?"

"Oh no." Raymond raised a hand in firm protest. "Just supplies. Wheelchairs, crutches, beds—that sort of thing. We serve the medical community."

"That's damn fine, Ray. An' I'm glad to hear it, tell the truth, because what was once a honorable perfession has got to be a gang of crooks. The damn doctors don't need no leeches, like in the old days, to bleed you nowadays. One look at the bill is enough to give a man leukemia." He winked significantly

176

again. "I'd thin 'em out pretty severe, by God, if it was left up to me. Anyways, I'm glad to hear the missuz is in good health. I hope—" He stopped, looked away, and shook his head. "Now just hold 'er right there, pardner. That's none of yer business. I'm sorry, Ray. I know city life puts a strain on folks. All I got to say is I hope you two work everything out. An' if there's anything I can do . . ."

"Oh no," Raymond said with a short, embarrassed laugh. "We're fine. Married twenty-three years. No, I meant, actually . . ."

Buck had finished his glass again and got to his feet. "Don't let me innerupt, Ray, but while we're talkin' here I want to show you a couple things. Collector pieces." He ran his finger along the row of barrels, like a man browsing in a library. "I was married a couple times my ownself, Ray. Never worked out, but I got a notion of what a man faces. Woman's an amazin' delicate insterment, God's special work o' art, but you know a little snit of a woman can break a man big as a bull, now ain't it so?" Buck laughed and pulled a gun from one of the cabinets, a rifle— Raymond presumed—longer than all the others. "We was speakin' of the old days a minute ago, the frontier times and so on. This here's the old .45–70, one of the first cartridge-load buffalo guns."

Raymond made as if to rise, saying quickly that it was time for him to be going, but Buck put an oversized, calloused hand on his shoulder and shoved him gently back. Then he laid the heavy rifle in Raymond's lap.

"I seen you lookin' out there at the target range. You go ahead and take a couple pops, get the feel of old Martha. She's one hell of a firearm." Buck pulled out a drawer in the table, a drawer crammed full of unopened and broken boxes of shells in all different sizes. "Think I got a few of these in here. Black powder stuff. Ah!"

He showed Raymond three of the cartridges in his open palm. They were huge, long, blunt things, penile and primitive. Raymond could not believe they were meant to fit in the gun, but Buck reached over him, tripped some catch that swung open the whole breech of the rifle, and sank one of the brass shafts into the barrel. The breech clapped shut, and with his thumb Buck drew back the hammer until it caught with a solid click. He

177

reached around then, as if giving a bear hug, lifted the rifle and settled it against Raymond's shoulder. "All ready," he said. "Getcher bead, Ray, before you put a finger on that trigger. She's real light."

"Listen," Raymond bleated, "listen Skinner—Buck—I appreciate what you are trying to do but . . . "

The alien weight of the rifle and the pressure of Buck's body against his back produced a disturbing thrill of new feeling, not exactly fear and not exactly curiosity. The barrel had lodged on the sandbags, pointing out the open window toward the pasture where the target dummies stood, and Raymond's hands clutched the stock automatically to keep the butt end from sliding from his shoulder.

"There is a problem—quite a serious problem—with noise. These shots right next door. My wife—" His hands had moved along the stock, finding a natural grip on the dark, smooth old walnut. He felt a ring of metal, tried to fumble around it, and the gun went off with a tremendous bellow, leaping back with a great jet of gray smoke to punch him painfully on the collarbone. He thought he cried out, but the whole shack seemed to throb and ring like his own skull, and he heard only a tiny, distant yelp of surprise. He remained paralyzed, his mind blank until he became aware that the barrel, where his left thumb just touched it, had grown warm.

"Sonofabitch, Ray!" Leaning over to peer out the window, Buck punched him in the other shoulder, but lightly. "You been a-funnin' me, you old so-and-so. Look at that!"

Raymond looked and saw that one of the dummies was swaying and nodding, anchored apparently on some sort of spring designed to give under impact. He must have hit it. Accidentally. His mouth was screwing into what he knew must be a foolish smile. Buck rummaged along the table with one hand and lifted up the set of binoculars. He crouched and fiddled with a knob, sighting. "By golly, Ray, you fooled me. Will you lookathat? Just a hair high, just a hair." He put down the glasses and beamed at Raymond. "Pop 'im agin."

"It was luck," Raymond said. "Entirely."

"Sure it was." Buck punched him again lightly and then flopped open the breech mechanism, still fuming from the explosion within. "Shoulda known when I seen you glancin' out there, sizin' up yer field. You're a deep one, Ray." He shoved another of the long, heavy cartridges into Raymond's hand. "Load up."

Raymond held the cartridge a moment, amazed at its weight. "Black powder? Really?"

"Oh yeah. Modern manufacture, acourse. More regular. But a lotta fellas hand load and stick to the genuine old stuff. They love that fire and gas. I've shot a lot of it m'self. In the Injun wars."

Raymond disposed of the bullet by sliding it into the chamber of the rifle. The breech plate, when he merely touched it, dropped neatly shut. He looked at Buck, eyebrows raised high.

Buck laughed. "In motion pictures."

Raymond made a loose fist and struck himself in the brow. "That's it. I knew there was something . . . "

"Yea, I seen you lookin' at me that way, like you thought you oughta know who I was. Happens to me a lot, with older folks. I was a extree in so many westerns for so long I lost track. Worked with the Duke and Randy Scott and Tim Holt and Autry and Wally Brennan and all them fellas. I been around a good while, Ray."

"Remarkable. I . . . I must have seen one of your movies." Raymond fidgeted with the hammer on the rifle, stifling the impulse to offer his hand to the other man in some gesture of recognition. His skull was still ringing from the blast of the gun, and his whole body seemed lighter than usual.

"Coulda been. *Cimarron, Red River, Guns Along the Pecos, Wagons West, Apache* . . . shoot, I done four or five a year for a while, I was usually the guy that come in all dusty and bedraggled on a wore-out horse to tell the star the Injuns was a-comin'. Or sometimes a little comic deal, like in *She Wore a Yaller Ribbon*, when Wayne says to the sergeant, 'I want these men on their feet and sober at dawn tomorrow, Sergeant Brady, and that includes you.' That's me, Brady, and I salute and say 'Yes sir' kind of unsteady-like, to show I've been drinkin'. That always got a laugh. Or in *Santa Fe Trail*, I'm the old guy who gets shot—I died a lot, too—on the ramparts of the fort, and the young kid who I have befriended is cryin', 'Don't die, Jake! Don't die on me!' and I says, sort of coughing, 'Git one o' them red devils fer me, Kid,' before my head falls to one side and I let this little stream of chocolate syrup outa my mouth to look like blood—this

179

was in the black-'n-white days, see. Lord! A million memories, Ray." Buck smiled and shook his head, blinking away what seemed to be more tears.

"Remarkable," Raymond said again, a thickness in his own throat. He thought he remembered the scenes Buck had described. From the time when he had slumped with the other boys in the front rows of the old movie palace. One hand foraged like a small, blind creature in a sack of popcorn while he gaped at the screen looming above. Tremendous currents of fear and exultation rushed through him as the riders thundered across this bright window, guns booming. Once he had been so enthralled he ignored the pressures in his own body and soiled himself.

How could he have forgotten that time, those sensations? The bugles blaring over the shots and screams and studio symphony, the regimental flags fluttering at a full gallop? And this man beside him had been there, one of those gruff, salty, loyal, tough-as-leather fighters. Earning his way with horse and gun. And not an arm's length away from the great stars. Of course. He understood now the gun collection, the weekend fusillades.

"But don't get me started on them old times. Sometimes I think I was really born a hunnert years ago, and them great old pictures is really real, whereas all this here is a dream. Felt like I belonged there. More vinegar in my veins—and lead in my pencil." He gave Raymond the squinty wink of light-hearted fellowship. "I always throwed myself into those pictures, Ray, tried to believe in everything. And ridin' around Monument Valley, with all them Navajos John Ford rounded up, it wasn't that hard to imagine. Always used authentic costumes and props, too, like old Martha here. Which brings us back to our subjeck at hand. It always helped me, Ray, to pretend I was firin' at real targets. I know them dummies don't much look like a redskin, but just imagine you got one of old Geronimo's thievin', butcherin' outlaws comin' fer ya and you can't afford no misses. Cock that thing slow and easy."

Raymond pulled back the hammer, using his thumb as he had seen Buck do. The mechanism seemed stiff and the effort made him clench his teeth.

"Now take a bead, breathin' slow and steady, until you got that gold ball right in the groove and right on that savage's heart. Don't try shootin' 'em in the head, not a big enough target. Can't afford to miss, with the old single shot. At this range he can come in on you hand-to-hand, knife or tomahawk . . . "

The beating of his heart made the little gold knob on the end of the barrel bob slightly, and the trigger guard, when he curled his finger tentatively through it, felt cold and slick. In his mind's eye, Raymond could see a cinematic figure from some long-ago drama. A dark, fierce face bearing slashes of paint, two or three white feathers, a brawny chest. The figure was crouched, ready to run. He exhaled and, between two heart beats, touched the trigger.

The blast was as deafening as before, and this time there was a stroke of fire out of the muzzle, along with the billow of smoke, but the shock to his right shoulder was not so severe. The dummy he had aimed at jerked and swayed on its mount with a loud *Sprong.*

"Hoo-eee! Got 'im, Ray! But—wait now—looks like a neck shot. Too high agin. Missed the spinal cord, so he's up and after you now! One ca'tridge left! Load up, man, load up!" Buck was pounding him on the back, excited. Raymond wrestled with the breech lock, managed to spring it open, and jammed in the last of the shells.

"Take him five minutes to bleed to death, and he's crazy for revenge—strong as a bear! You got to shoot straight, man!"

The breech snapped shut. Raymond wrenched back the hammer and snugged the old rifle into the cradle of arms and shoulder again. He was disoriented momentarily, expecting somehow that the dummy would have hurried nearer, like the lunging, bloody figure in his mind. In trying to bring the barrel back into line he unconsciously tightened his grip and nudged the trigger. The rifle bucked and bellowed, and Raymond shouted aloud in frustration. He had not been lucky this time, he knew. The bullet had gone wide of the mark.

"I'm sorry," he began, "I was—" But the sight of Buck's pale, set face shocked him back into silence. The older man had drawn back as if recoiling from something especially ugly or malodorous. There was a long pause.

Buck spoke finally, his voice gone flat. "You're a dead man, Ray."

"Well, not really," Raymond said with a little laugh that sounded, even to him, anxious and false. "I'm still here."

"No you ain't. That brave come right through the winder and tomahawked yer brains all over the floor. You had three ca'tridges and when the chips was down . . . I seen this happen to a kid once before, Ray." Buck shook his head and sat heavily again on the cot. "Goddamn it, that was once too often."

"I was trying to hurry," Raymond said plaintively. "I'm not experienced at this. And anyway, really." Gingerly he laid the rifle across the sandbags. The dejection and shame he had felt at first were interrupted by a pulse of anger. How absurd that he should despair over missing a plastic mannequin with some old blunderbuss. "It's just silly," he blurted.

"Silly?" Buck looked at him with a sudden, new hardness. "*Silly?*" Then his face underwent a convulsion, as if at a physical pain, real and deep, and he looked away out the window. "If yer life ain't worth livin', I guess maybe it is silly. But I'm surprised at you, Ray. Disappointed, I can't help from sayin'. You been funnin' me in ever direction. I thought, the way you got off that snap shot, you was a cool feller. A good eye to boot. But when you seen the situation as *real*, felt some pressure . . . well, you flubbed 'er, Ray. Come unwound. Cost us our lives. And now you're trying' to claim it don't matter."

Another silence, and now Raymond could hear the very faint hushing of a breeze through trees on the hillside. His match-flame of anger had extinguished itself in a deep gloom. Silly? No, it wasn't silly. It was all too profound a symbol of his whole life. He had never done well in pressure situations. Examinations in school. Coming to bat on the playground. Giving a presentation to his regional sales people. And Bea, of course. He was always on the spot, and never quite delivered. This feeling was so much worse, he realized, because moments before when he had hit the dummy twice and provoked Buck into jump-up-and-down enthusiasm, he had known a pure, powerful exuberance, a thrill that had been underground in him since childhood. *Freedom,* he thought suddenly: *this is what freedom is.*

Buck heaved a sigh and bent to reach underneath the cot. "I got to show you a couple more things, Ray. I wasn't gonna do this but maybe it's the only way to git my point across." He drew out a small cardboard box and then took from the box an album bound in ragged black leather. He flipped over a few pages, then reversed the album and shoved it into Raymond's hands. "Man

182

fergits he is always livin' in a jungle. He has to, acourse, to function. Otherwise he'd go nuts with the strain. But it's the truth. You oughta know that, Ray, livin' in the big city. Way it is now, the streets belong to the cocaine kings and them color gangs."

The album was filled with snapshots, some of them yellowed by time. They showed weary soldiers, faces smudged under helmets draped with netting and leaves, smoking and lounging beside heaps of bodies outside a burned-out bunker. In one photograph a much younger Buck faced the camera, beaming. Slung through one arm was a heavy gun with a long clip curving from its underside. One boot rested on the head of a corpse.

"I figure that's why you bought that old policer you was tellin' me about. Wanted to pertect yer home. Yer wife. Am I right?"

Raymond nodded, only half listening. He was staring at the photo of Buck and his kill. It was not the principal subjects, however, that attracted him, but another figure in the background, a GI who had turned partially away from the camera, laughing at someone outside the frame. The rounded shoulders, the head tilting slightly, the toes pointed outward in a duckwalk. . . . He sucked in a breath, suddenly unsteady.

"You seen that, eh? Jimmy was his name. Just a kid then. Better shot of him on the next page. Anyhow I'll go ahead an' say some more things I probably shouldn't. I bet it was yer wife's idea for you to slip up here today. Sent you off to straighten the situation out. The noise and so forth."

Raymond turned the page, still holding the breath he had taken. The sight of the younger soldier, head-on and without a helmet, was as physical as the kick of the rifle against his shoulder. The youth was arm-in-arm with Buck, both of them in dirty fatigues, grinning. Part of a palm tree was visible behind them, and the hood of a truck. Raymond was aware of moisture condensing on his face, like a chill mist. Buck, was still talking, was tugging another and much heavier box from beneath the cot.

"I got to tell you, Ray, even though it ain't none of my business, that I seen that when I first drove by yer place. She's a handful of woman, I thought to myself, and him—that's yerself I was referrin' to—now he's one of them nice guys, real lovable guys, that can't quite . . . Ah! Seen it too, right away, didn't ya? When I first spotted you out there crossin' my fence I near passed out. Like a ghost. Only a ghost wouldn't be thirty years older. But if Jimmy had of lived, you'd be a dead ringer fer 'im."

"He died?" Raymond whispered. But the young man was himself. The same broad forehead and slightly protuberant eyes. Even the crewcut (which he too had affected three decades ago). Fine pale hair glowing like a halo flattened on the skull.

"Oh yeah, he died," Buck said. "About three weeks after that picture. Come around a hill and run right into a Jap. Jimmy missed his first shot and the Jap got off a grenade. Blew 'im in two. I loved that kid, but he just couldn't keep good hold of hisself in a tough spot. Anyway, I wanted you to see them pictures, how there's some men on their feet, walkin' around and laughin', and there's others lyin' there with parts blown off, who ain't never gonna git up. And I'm tellin' you somethin', Ray. A woman knows that. That's why when she recognizes we're in a damn jungle, she makes a move right away fer pertection. It's natural. And yet—funny thing—she don't like to admit it. Don't like it to come too easy."

Raymond had closed the album and tossed it back on the cot. He felt completely unstrung. Tears formed in his own eyes and he had to dash them away furtively on a sleeve. The resemblance, uncanny enough, had driven him to imagine that he saw a pleading in the young man's expression, an intuition that in the future, beyond the grave, a man like himself—a double also hounded by hidden weakness—would have this second chance. A grenade awaited Jimmy, inexorable; yet the halo of sun in his hair suggested redemption. *Don't let me down*, the eyes said. *Don't miss*.

The large box was open now and Buck was taking black, oily metal parts from it. Swiftly he was assembling a gun: a chunky breech section, a folding metal stock and handle-grip, a barrel and sheath of perforated tubing. The parts slid and locked together with solid clacks. Buck kept his frank gaze on Raymond, hands working with swift autonomy.

"Funny critturs, women. But tough as steel under that froofroo, some of 'em. And yer lady, Ray . . . I'm sorry . . . " He cocked his head while with one hand he rammed a clip into the breech of the gun, which Raymond now recognized as a weapon like that pictured in the album.

"Bea."

"That's right." Buck laughed. "To Bea or not to Bea, eh? Now my guess is—beggin' yer pardon—she's got you a little shy of the quirt. Hey?" His grin was a touch sad.

Raymond could not speak. To his intense shame, the corners of his mouth jerked downward uncontrollably, his chin puckering. He felt exposed, with odd and terrible sensations running just under his skin. He might be on the verge of some kind of collapse.

With one hand Buck dragged from the bottom of the box a heavy canvas belt studded with cartridges that narrowed abruptly to sharp, copper-plated points. He lifted the belt and draped it loosely over Raymond's head, slanting from one shoulder.

"It's all right, buddy," he said. His voice was now quiet and kind. "Listen up. You're new to the jungle. Takes time to git adjusted. Me? Well, a feller told me once I was what they call an American ark type. A universal type of guy, he said. I guess like the critturs goin' into Noah's boat. My parts in the movies was all that way. All it means is, hell, I don't have to think about a lot of stuff, I just do it natural. Whereas an educated feller like you has a tougher time." He lifted out another belt and slung it, too, over Raymond's head, so the two crossed on his chest.

"But don't think about that. Just remember it's a jungle, and Bea knows that as well as you do. Maybe better. And we can't trust nobody but ourselves, Ray. I mean that. Not the damn govermint. You see how they lie and sneak around. One day hollerin' about terrorists and the next day sellin' plastic bombs to some madman. The CIA can't seem to get a slug between Castro's eyeballs, but they managed to let Lee Harvey slip by 'em, and if it wasn't for Jack Ruby, God bless 'im, that little bastard would probably be out on the street now on a furlough program."

Buck took a step backward and hooked one hand on a curved metal bar on the breech, which he jerked and then allowed to spring forward in a blur. There was a final, sharp clash of metal, and a slow grin spread across his face.

"So it comes down to a few good men, like they say in the Marines. The ark types, hey? First ones on the boat. Men, though. You got to be a *man*, Ray. And that don't mean size so much, any more. Authority is the thing. And this—" he tilted the barrel of the heavy gun and swung it in a slow arc "—has got

185

authority. Which these days is firepower. Plain, simple, goddamned firepower." He picked up his hat and threw it on his head with a practiced snap of the wrist.

"A woman respects that, Ray. She may *say* otherwise, talk about how much she abhors violence and so forth, but she respects it. You can tell when a couple walks into a room, whether the man exercises his right to bear arms, by how much easier and more at home his wife looks. Or, takin' the question another way, if a feller's lady is just a mite slow to demonstrate respect—" Buck turned to Raymond with both eyes squeezed shut, wrinkling his nose in a cute, animal expression "—it don't hurt to have a cabinet full of equalizers in the background when them little disagreements pop up, know what I mean? But keep the key hid good, buddy." He laughed and jabbed with the gun barrel toward the door. "Now let's step outside and I'll show you how to do-si-do with big Betsy. She's sweet and she's fast and she's full auto, Ray, so keep this confidential, but you're gonna see some chips fly. Gonna come a long way, baby, from Old Martha. Betsy's a modern girl and she can settle just about any argument that comes along. What say?"

Thirty minutes later they came around the corner of the shack talking animatedly. Raymond's sleeves were rolled up, his shirtfront unbuttoned, and he was sweating under the heavy cartridge belts. He carried the BAR cocked aloft on one hip, as Buck had shown him, and moved with a new roll and swivel in his gait. There was a stink of cordite behind them, and several of the hulks of abandoned vehicles were still smoking, everywhere ripped with new, bright-edged scars. What they were talking about was inconsequential—how the body was braced differently for short bursts as opposed to sustained fire—but beneath the commonplace words was an easy intimacy that should have taken years to form. Raymond felt loose and supple under the sweat and grit on his skin, like a newer and stronger and more capable version of the boy in the photograph. He knew that was why Buck had hugged him with one arm, eyes glistening, when he executed properly the crouch, wheel, and release maneuver.

They stopped when they saw Bea making her slow, sidewise goose step over the fence. Buck had been saying something about timing, about dancing with your weapon, with your adversary.

186

The sun seemed to brighten perceptibly, fixing everything in a hallucinatory light. Even from the distance Raymond saw the dark patches of sweat on Bea's shirt, a shoelace untied. She had walked, of course, the whole way.

"Okay, Ray," Buck said softly beside him. "Take charge, fella. Like to meet your lovely Bea."

They stood shoulder to shoulder while his wife began the fifty-yard journey. The sun was behind them and low in the sky, laying their elongated shadows at her feet. She was digging her heels hard into the earth and her mouth was open, her breathing harsh and quick. Raymond could feel the rage coming from her like a wind against his face, lifting his hair. But there was something else, too, in her eyes—a crazy, rolling emotion.

He shifted his weight from one foot to the other and resettled the BAR against his hipbone. The barrel was still so hot he could feel the warmth on his cheek. Betsy had been wonderful in his hands. Far-reaching and lightning quick. Responsive. You only had to lift a finger. Literally. *Reach out and touch someone.* He laughed aloud, a deep laugh from the center of himself.

Bea heard him and her pace seemed to slow, as if the atmosphere had thickened. Her hair was loose and there were damp strands of it plastered to her brow and neck. She was yawing a little to one side, gravity exerting itself unequally. Her mouth, also skewed, had begun to work, as if preparing to spit out something unchewable.

Raymond knew he appeared to her as a silhouette, feet spread wide and the gun glancing up at the sky. He could not remember ever seeing her so pale. She seemed smaller, too, and rounder. He thought of one of those silly bombs in comic strips, a bowling ball trailing a sparking fuse. She was in fact emitting a hiss, breath superheated beyond the tolerance of syllables.

Struck dumb, he thought all at once. *I struck her dumb.* He shifted his feet again and let the BAR swing lower, pulling it simultaneously a little to one side so she was not quite in the line of fire. He saw her eyes move with the gun, her face distorting in apprehension—and a spasm of exhilaration went through him.

She was not a half-dozen strides away, but her momentum was failing. The gun seemed to fascinate her like a bright light, to focus the crazy spinning in her eyes. *Go ahead*, he found himself thinking, *Go ahead and say it please say it and let Mama kiss you goodbye.* He began to tremble all over, on the brink of some unbearable joy.

First Ending

But it was Buck who spoke, moving between them. "Miz Walker, I presume," he said and then did something with his hat, a trick that sent it somersaulting down his arm to end with a flourish in his hand. "I've kep' yer husband hostage here, Ma'am, please excuse, but I just had to meet the lady I saw beside that little rancho down the road. He can't keep you a secret no longer." Buck dropped to one knee, the wide hat clapped over his heart.

Bea had come to a halt like a drunk abruptly confronted by a locked front door. She unhinged her eyes from the BAR and fixed them on the man at her feet. Her breath was still hissing in and out, but more slowly now. She lifted her hand in a vague gesture, as if to restore her balance.

Buck was on his feet instantly and picked her hand out of the air. "I was walkin' in the woods back there this mornin', Miz Walker, and I seen the first mountain bluebells comin' into bloom—dew sparklin' all over—and I thought to m'self now that's the purtiest sight a ugly ol' wrangler like me can ever hope to see. Yer bluebell, Ma'am, is kinda special—so big and sassy and bright as a piece of sky that fell down somehow. But I got to tell you somethin' Ma'am—beggin' yer pardon for talkin' so frank, but ol' Ray here will tell you it's my way—them bluebells don't come anywhere *close* to you, purty as you looked marchin' up here with yer eyes flashin' and that red hair in the sun." As he spoke Buck bent lower and lower, looking up at Bea from beneath his heavy eyebrows, and when the speech was finished he kissed the back of her hand. For a moment after he released her Bea seemed paralyzed. She looked at Raymond and blinked. Her mouth worked again. "Ray?" she said. There was a curious, petulant note in her voice that made him want to giggle. She looked at her hand, waggling the fingers experimentally, and then again at Buck.

He stood almost at attention, the hat still held over his heart. "Miz Walker," he said quietly, "you are one damn beautiful woman."

188

All at once two fiery roses bloomed on her cheeks and the hand flew to her brow to push back one of the damp curls. Raymond laughed. His own voice, when he spoke, sounded bigger and deeper, and—without thinking about it—he used words he had never heard himself say before. "Hi Hon," he said. "This's my buddy Buck. He's been around since Noah's ark, in the movies."

Second Ending

But then, two strides away, Bea seemed to recover. She straightened her body and aimed herself at her husband, not even glancing at Buck. "Isn't this wonderful," she said. "The little boys have a new toy." She laughed—a loud, clear peal that came back as an echo from the mountain behind them. "Oh you're impressive, Ray. A stone killer, isn't that the expression?"

There was a terrible cheerfulness in her manner as she pulled gardening gloves from a hip pocket and put them on. "You're really quite absurd," she said matter-of-factly. "You idiot. Now give that here." She reached out, quick and efficient and strong, and pulled the BAR away from him. Then she flung it from her, both arms thrusting out hard. Buck uttered a short, sharp sigh.

Bea looked at him finally, smiling widely. "You're under arrest," she said. She hiked up her shirttail and fumbled at the waistband of her jeans for a moment, coming up then with the revolver, Raymond's .38, which she manipulated rather clumsily with both leather-gloved hands. "Citizen's arrest. Disturbing the peace and firing an illegal weapon." She tipped her head toward the BAR in the dirt. "You're a criminal, armed and dangerous."

"Bea!" Raymond swayed away from his wife. "What—"

"Shut up, you ignorant baby. You're going to drive, and I'm going to guard this maniac while we take him to the state police. Put up your hands." The revolver wavered toward Buck like a compass needle in the vicinity of an iron deposit.

Raymond sagged at the knees. He wanted to fall face-forward onto the ground, but he feared losing sight of his wife. Buck did not move at first. He was staring at the .38. Raymond saw then that the hammer was not cocked, and he recalled that it required

189

a very strong pull of the trigger to rotate the cylinder and operate the cocking mechanism at the same time.

"Now Ma'am," Buck said softly and took a gliding step forward, lifting a hand, palm up, toward the gun.

Raymond saw her hands flex, the hammer lift a little and then fall back. Bea's mouth stretched with effort and he saw the tip of her tongue protrude a little. She had dropped into a crouch, an imitation of the stance favored on television police dramas. Her fingers convulsed again, the gun wobbling with strain, and the hammer lifted higher.

"Now Ma'am," Buck repeated, his voice sharper, and his hand darted forward to close over the gun.

She shot him, the bullet passing through his hand and into his chest. He started to say something more but his voice became only a buzzing and he sat down heavily, as if exhausted. After a moment he coughed and said "Ma'am," again, softly as before. They looked at each other and then Bea showed once more her tongue-tip of effort and concentration. Raymond heard the slight sound of metal parts moving. She shot him again, this time just under the chin, and he fell over on his back.

Raymond was on his knees beside Buck, hiccuping dry sobs, touching the other man experimentally on the shoulder and then jerking back his hand to cover his mouth. "Oh, oh," he was saying, "oh, oh, oh." Buck moved, but without purpose. One hand flapped at his face as if to brush away an insect and both legs flexed. There was suddenly a great deal of blood, and Raymond drew back, walking on his knees.

He looked up at his wife, her determined expression. "You didn't cock it, he didn't know," he said. "You shot him. My God, you shot him." He began to cry. "Cock?" Bea looked at him quizzically a moment, then at the gun in her hand. She fiddled experimentally with the hammer for a moment. Then, bracing herself, she got a grip on it and pulled it back with a loud *snick*. She smiled.

"My God, Bea, *you shot him*." Raymond's eyes strayed from hers and then along the ground to the BAR.

She watched him, examined him thoughtfully. She stepped nearer to him, coming between him and the gun on the ground. "No," she said. "*You* shot him."

He stared up at her again through a blur of tears, his head shaking, uncomprehending.

"Then you shot yourself," she said brightly, and lifting the revolver she put the mouth of the barrel above his ear and pulled the trigger.

Real Ending

This situation is preposterous. Raymond knows this, and so do Buck and Bea. That is why they behave so irrationally, so unpredictably. A couple nearing retirement buys a cottage on a remote road. Their neighbor is a funny old geezer fond of what is called "plinking." One thing leads to another and they find themselves in an absurdist nightmare. Is this credible? Of course not.

They are only creatures of paper, or rather sound—a barking the author has stirred up to draw attention to the fears that circle and wait in the darkness and silence of his own mind. Every alarm, every warning signal is similarly unrealistic, a harmless honking, a bit of red paint, a winking light. Its function is not to portray a real narrow bridge or smoldering cigarette, but only to startle the observer and refocus him on the advancing threat.

The difference here, of course, is that the sinister things that circle and wait are inside ourselves. Fifty years ago the comic strip *Captain Marvel* presented evil characters who were actually robots, directed by an inch-high, giggling psychotic who concealed himself in their skulls where he manipulated levers and knobs. Doctor Sivana's golems were completely convincing humans on the outside, like you and me. Only Captain Marvel could detect the presence of his minute adversary, peering through the portholes of the eyes. That was a simpler, purer time. We were at war with monsters, and every normal American boy yearned to bomb and strafe. We all had an arsenal of toy guns, and we used them in daily combat. It was many years before the awful thought came to me that there was no way of knowing whether Captain Marvel *also* was driven by a tiny mad jinni in his brain, and more years still before I entertained the notion that Uncle Sam himself, that gaunt graybeard Yankee in the star-spangled circus suit, might contain an analogous little

191

demon—an incubus that began to stir during my halcyon child-hood years of daily play slaughter.

For when the old guy stood tall and leveled his finger, saying he wanted *us*, we wanted to go. We loved him, not so much in the funny suit but in his other disguises: the Green Mountain Boy, the cavalry trooper, Sergeant York, the seasoned jungle GI. We wanted to go with an experienced teacher down in the mud under a hail of bullets until we could dodge and roll near enough to blast the enemy to bits, mow them down, torch them with flamethrowers.

Later I was taught to dismiss these early dreams as boyish fancy; and of course the nature of warfare changed too, becoming a kind of remote-control electronic pinball game. But surely we can all see that the seductive fever of violence has not been con-trolled in this nation. We revel in it as never before. Television. *Far-seeing*. But it is really deep-within-seeing. We watch over and over the image of the muscular arm contracted around the racketing machine gun, the muzzle flash, the bodies ripping and splattering and crumpling.

Or we don't watch that, expressly. We turn away after the first split-second shock (though that may be enough). We don't be-lieve in it. We believe in light comedy, or the Helen Keller story. Like Bea, we are disgusted by the gang and drug wars in our cities, also by the macho posing of big-game hunters. We hope that the police and the environmentalists are doing something about it. But men are so weak.

Ah, men. We are, indeed, the problem. Our dire urges. To *assert* (self, vision, principle). To *defend* (family, property, na-tion). To stand tall or ride hard as either asserter or defender one needs a measure of control, or authority. And as Buck has lamen-tably guessed, in this era of moral relativism and deteriorating trust, of unchained greed and paranoia, authority has come to be largely a matter of firepower.

The Big Guys are now very well equipped. Uncle Sam packs megatons in every chamber. He could, understand, wipe out *ev-erybody*. He thinks about it often, just as Big Bear does, so that his authority will have a real presence in our lives. The Little Guys go more for mobility and secrecy. Weapons have been designed that can spray a room with bullets, yet fit in a jacket pocket. Three pounds of an odorless explosive, pressed into a flat sheet in the wall of a suitcase, can blow an airliner out of the sky.

Then there are the Crazy Guys. All this firepower confuses them. A week ago, less than a hundred miles from my home, a young drifter went onto a school playground and shot thirty children with an AK-47. The five children who died in the first seconds were all Asians, born of refugees from the Vietnam War. The young killer affected camou garb and a flak jacket. In his room were hundreds of toy soldiers, all in neat rows. He appeared to have, the police chief deduced, a "military hangup of some kind."

So Ordinary Guys don't know what to do. Some remember the old days, simple and pure. They support a strong defense, join the NRA, and see every Dirty Harry movie made. (Like Buck they may even *be* in such movies.) Some, like Ray, make only a feeble gesture toward self-protection, often at the prompting of a strong and angry woman. They purchase a popgun and bury it in a drawer, hoping to move to the country one day soon.

The brain chambers of the Ordinaries may or may not have room for the tiny mad doctor. Now and then one unhinges, discovers that killing is thrilling, and does in a neighbor or spouse (or several neighbors and spouses), but the matter is not so serious as when one of the Big Guys turns out to be a Crazy. (That's the one that scares us all.) An Ordinary is more likely to muddle on to the usual end, wishing the world were a better and safer place, incapable of any vigorous personal effort to make it so.

What really happened here, then, is that there were tense words, a general embarrassment, banal nods and waves and grimaces to ease a hasty departure. Bea storming ahead to the car, Raymond drag-assing in guilt and humiliation, Buck cheerful and philosophical on his porch, already drifting off to muse over a .270 Weatherby he might pick up cheap.

Back in the cottage there is a scene, a funereal dinner, a restless night. But in the morning the sun shines and Buck blows by in his pickup raising a friendly two fingers to his hatbrim. Ray settles down to his book on corporate buccaneering. Bea in her jeans drives her hands into the earth. On the radio the news follows a sinus-remedy commercial. An airliner crash, the commissioning of a new superstealth nuclear sub, a mild-mannered electrician taken into custody after shooting his infant son in the head with an air-driven pellet pistol. The infant lives, a vegetable. Court battles are expected over the family's right to pull his plug. Other court battles may follow over society's right to juice the electrician.

Nominated by Stanley Lindberg

THE CENTER OF
THE STORY

fiction by LYDIA DAVIS

from GRAND STREET

A WOMAN HAS written yet another story that is not interesting, though it has a hurricane in it, and a hurricane usually promises to be interesting. But in this story the hurricane threatens the city without actually striking it. The story is flat and even, just as the earth seems flat and even when a hurricane is advancing over it, and if she were to show it to a friend, the friend would probably say that unlike a hurricane, this story has no center.

It was not an easy story to write because it was about religion, and religion was not something she really wanted to write about, though there was something about the story that made her want to write it. Thinking about it now, she does not know what that was. The story is not good, and there is a peculiar yellow pall over it, either because of the religion or because of the light in the sky before the hurricane.

She can't think where the center of the story might be.

She was reading the Bible in a time of hurricane, not because she was afraid of a major disaster, though she was afraid, or because these days also happened to be the High Holy Days, but because she needed to know exactly what was in it. She read slowly and took many notes. Outside her apartment, the weather was changing: the wind rose, the branches swayed on the young trees, and the leaves fluttered. She read about Noah and the Ark and tried to picture very exactly what she read, the better to understand it: a man hundreds of years old trying to walk and give directions to his family, the mud covering the earth after the flood receded, the stink of rot, and then the sacrifice of animals and the stink of burning hair, fur, and horn.

She did little else but read the Bible for several days, and she looked out the window often and listened to the news. Certainly the Bible and the hurricane belong in the story, though whether at the center or not she does not know. She had started the story with her landlady. Her landlady, an old woman from Trinidad, was in the downstairs hall alone talking quietly about the Mayor, while she was upstairs, thinking of writing a letter to the President. Her landlady said the red carpet remnant on the hall floor was given to her by her friend the Mayor. She will probably take out the President and the landlady, but leave in the Bible and the hurricane. Perhaps if she takes out things that are not interesting, or do not belong in the story for other reasons, this will give it more of a center, since as soon as there is less in a story, more of it must be in the center.

In another part of the story, a man is very ill and thinks he is dying. He was not dying, he had eaten something that poisoned him and drunk too much on top of it, but he thought he was dying, and telephoned her to come help him. This was at the very moment the hurricane was supposed to strike the city, and some of the windows in the neighborhoods between her house and his were covered with tape in the shape of asterisks. In his room, the blinds were drawn, the light was yellow, and the windows rattled. He lay on his back in bed with a hand on his bare chest. His face was gray.

It is unclear what his place is, in the story. Certainly his illness has little connection with the rest of the story except that it overcame him at the height of the hurricane. But then he also told her something on the phone about blasphemy. He had recently blasphemed in a dreadful way, he said, by committing a certain forbidden act on a Holy Day. What he realized as he did it, he said, was that for complicated reasons he was trying to hurt God, and if he was trying to hurt God he must believe in Him. He had experienced the truth of what he had been taught long ago, that blasphemy proved one's belief in God.

This man, his illness, his fear for his life, and the blasphemy that had caused his illness, as he probably thought, and also something else he said about God that she remembered later riding a train out of the city, could be at the center of the story, with the Bible and the hurricane at the edge of it, but there may not be enough to tell about him for him to be the center, or this may be the wrong time to tell it.

So there is the hurricane that did not strike the city but cast a yellow light over it, and there is this man, and there is the Bible, but no landlady, no President, and no newscasters, though she watched the news several times a day, every day, to see what the hurricane was going to do. The newscasters would tell her to look out the window and she would look. They would tell her that at that very moment, because the sun had just set, rams' horns were being blown all over the city, and she would be excited, even though she could not hear any ram's horns in her neighborhood. But though the newscasters serve to hold the story together from one day to the next, they are not in themselves very interesting and certainly not central to a story that has trouble finding its center.

In those days she also visited churches and synagogues. The last church she visited was a Baptist congregation in the north of the city. There, large black women in white uniforms tried to get her to sit down but she was too nervous to sit. Then she nearly fainted when a procession of women in red robes came at a stately pace, singing, toward her where she stood at the back of the crowded hall. She left quickly and sat in a stall in the ladies' room watching a fly, not sure she would be able to leave.

In fact, close to the center of the story may be the moment when she realizes that, even though she is not a believer, she has an unusual, religious sort of peace in her, perhaps because she has been visiting churches and synagogues and studying the Bible, and that this peace has allowed her to accept the possibility of the worst sort of disaster, one even worse than a hurricane.

She rides the train up along the river away from the city. The danger of the hurricane is past. The water in the river has not risen to cover the tracks, though it is close to them. As she rides, she suddenly remembers the devil and realizes she has not yet tried to make a place for him in what she might believe. She has asked several friends whether they thought there was a God, but she has not yet talked about the devil with anyone.

197

This comes close to the end of the story as it is now, but she can't really end with the devil and a train ride. The ending, though, is still less important than this matter of locating a center for the story. But there may be no center. There may be no center because she is afraid to put any one of these elements in the center—the man, the religion, or the hurricane. Or—which either is or is not the same thing—there is a center but the center is empty, either because she has not yet found what belongs there or because it is meant to be empty: there, but empty, in the same way that the man was sick but not dying, the hurricane approached but did not strike, and she had a religious calm but no faith.

Nominated by Barbara Einzig, Sigrid Nunez and Francine Prose

HOSPICE

by LYNDA HULL

from PLOUGHSHARES

Frayed cables bear perilously the antiquated lift,
all glass and wrought iron past each apartment floor
like those devices for raising and lowering
angels of rescue in Medieval plays. Last night
the stairwell lamps flickered off and I was borne up
the seven floors in darkness, the lift a small lit

cage where I thought of you, of the Catholic souls
we envisioned once, catechism class, the saint
in her moment of grace transfigured as she's engulfed
in flames. The lift shivered to a halt above the shaft
and I was afraid for a moment to open the grille,
wanting that suspension again, the requiemed hum

of one more city going on without me—Cockney girls
with violet hair swirling among the businessmen
and movie ushers of Soho, sullen in their jackets.
All of them staving off as long as they can
the inevitable passing away, that bland euphemism
for death. But I can't shake this from my mind:

your face with its hollows against hospital linen.
Newark's empty asylum wings opened again this year
for the terminal cases. Each day another
strung-out welfare mother, the streetcorner romeos
we used to think so glamorous, all jacked-up
on two-buck shots. It was winter when I last was home

199

and my mother found you on her endless dietician's
rounds, her heavy ring of keys. It was winter
when I saw you, Loretta, who taught me to curse
in Italian, who taught me to find the good vein
in the blue and yellow hours of our sixteenth year
among deep nets of shadows dragged through evening, a surf

of trees by the railway's sharp cinders. Glittering
like teen dream angels in some corny A.M. song,
buoyed by whatever would lift us above the smouldering
asphalt, the shingled narrow houses, we must
have felt beyond all damage. Still what damage carried you
all these years beyond the fast season of loveliness

you knew before the sirens started telling your story
all over town, before the habit stole
the luster from your movie starlet hair.
Little sister, the orderlies were afraid to
touch you. Tonight, the current kicks the lights
back on and there's the steady moan of the lift's

descent, the portion of what's left of this day
spread before me—stockings drying on the sill, the cool
shoulders of milk bottles—such small domestic salvations.
There was no deus ex machina for you, gone now
this half year, no blazing seraphim, finally
no miraculous escape, though how many times

I watched you rise again and again from the dead:
that night at the dealers' on Orange Street, stripping
you down, overdosed and blanched against the green linoleum,
ice and saline. I slapped you until
the faint flower of your breath clouded the mirror.
In those years I thought death was a long blue hallway

you carried inside, a curtain lifting at the end
in the single window's terrible soft breeze where
there was always a cashier ready to take your
last silver into her gloved hands, some dicey, edgy game.
Beneath the ward clock's round dispassionate face

there was nothing so barren in the sift from minute

to absolute minute, a slow-motion atmosphere dense
as the air of medieval illuminations with demons
and diaphanous beings. I only wished then
the cancellation of that hungering that turns us
towards the mortal arms of lovers or highways
or whatever form of forgetfulness we choose.

Your breath barely troubled the sheets, eyes closed,
perhaps already adrift beyond the body, twisting
in a tissue of smoke and dust over Jersey's
infernal glory of cocktail lounges and chemical plants,
the lonely islands of gas stations lining the turnpike
we used to hitch towards the shore, a moment

I want back tonight—you and me on the boardwalk,
the casino arcade closed around its pinball machines
and distorting mirrors. Just us among sea serpents,
those copper horses with mermaid's tails, porpoise fins,
and the reckless murmur of the sea. Watching stars
you said you could almost believe the world arranged

by a design that made a kind of sense. That night
the constellations were so clear it was easy
to imagine some minor character borne up
beyond judgement into heaven, rendered purely
into light. Loretta, this evening washes
over my shoulders, this provisional reprieve.

I've been telling myself your story for months
and it spreads in the dusk, hushing the streets, and there
you are in the curve of a girl's hand as she lights
her cigarette sheltered beneath the doorway's plaster
cornucopia. Listen, how all along the avenues trees
are shaken with rumor of this strange good fortune.

Nominated by Mark Doty, David Jauss, Susan Mitchell,
Maura Stanton and David Wojahn

A MOTIVELESS MALIGNANCY

by BARRY CALLAGHAN

from THE ONTARIO REVIEW

I T ALL BEGAN over a year ago. I was going in August to Saratoga for the horseracing season. Saratoga is magical: the best racing on the continent at the prettiest red-and-white-gabled track in the country. I had packed my working manuscript of new poems, *Stone Blind Love*, and my tinted prescription glasses so I could read the racing form in the hot mountain sun. Claire had packed steel tools and oblong dark bars of beeswax so she could work for a fall exhibition of her sculpture in Toronto. I went out the back door, through our small wisteria-covered courtyard (we live in a lean 1880s refurbished house in Chinatown), and decided to move the car forward in the garage, toward the lane. I liked our car, the way it held the road. I turned the key and the Audi 5000 shot backward, taking out the whole stuccoed wall, dumping concrete blocks and broken cement into the garden. I stared through the rear-view mirror into an emptiness, wondering where everything had gone, and heard the whisper of malevolence and affliction on the air but did not heed it.

The car was fixed and we drove to Saratoga, where we stayed in the house of an old friend, a retired dancer who had been with Balanchine. He has a house of many rooms and gardens and a broad veranda. Not long after, my father came down and sat on the veranda, finishing his new novel, *A Wild Old Man on the Road*. We were doing well at the track, and then one morning the phone rang and it was Claire. She had driven downtown along the tree-shaded side streets; there had been an accident.

When I got to the intersection I found our Audi had been T-boned by an elderly, absent-minded man from California who was driving a Budget car; he had gone blithely through a red light, driving our car up over a sidewalk and onto a lawn; smashed to a dead halt against a steel fence, Claire had stepped from the car unscathed but stricken; the car's frame was bent and twisted and it was towed to a scrapyard where it was cannibalized and then reduced to a cube of crushed steel, the whisper of malevolence and affliction on the air. I did not heed it.

Back home in Toronto I was sardonically amused by the gutted hole in my garden wall (nothing is what it's supposed to be: why shouldn't a car shoot backward when it's supposed to be standing still?), and we went on with life in our house and ordered a new Audi.

The house has always been open to writers who tend to drop in of a morning for coffee (and a little cognac in their coffee); sometimes I make pasta or a tourtière for two or three editors; and since Claire is a splendid cook, we have small suppers for poets from abroad; and we throw house parties, inviting forty or fifty people. It has been a friendly house, the walls hung with color—paintings, drawings, tapestries—all our travels and some turbulence framed, but one afternoon the front door suddenly opened and a young man walked boldly in, his eyes bleary, his shirt torn. He stared sullenly at me, spun around and walked out without a word.

I felt a twinge, a warning.

As a punter or poet, you learn to feel for signs.

But I was busy. After Thanksgiving, I was to give readings in Rome, Zagreb and Belgrade, and then go on to Moscow, Riga, Leningrad, and stay for a month as writer in residence in Bologna before coming home in late November for Claire's exhibition. We decided to celebrate Thanksgiving at the family farm near Mount Forest, with our sons and Morley.

As we packed my Audi in the lane (Claire's car was in the garage), I looked back through the broken wall, the jagged hole. There had not been time to fix it. I felt a sudden vulnerability, as if in the midst of my well-being, I'd forgotten to protect myself. I checked the locks on the doors. An old, fat Chinese woman stood in the lane watching me with a blank impassivity that made me feel strangely resentful. I knew she couldn't care what happened to me. I'd never seen her before, but she looked as if she belonged there in the lane.

Our farmhouse is on a hill surrounded by woods. The trees were red and gold. There were geese on the pond. We ate supper in a room that has old church stained-glass windows, under a candelabra that burns sixteen candles. For some reason, Morley and the boys talked about violence, whether it was gratuitous, or in the genes, or acquired, and whether there actually was something called malevolence, evil. Morley smoked his pipe, and we went to bed.

In the morning, the phone rang. It was my neighbor, Charlie Pachter. He sounded incoherent, as if he were weeping. "Come home," he said. "Come home, something terrible . . . the house, it's been broken . . . come home." I phoned my house. A policeman answered. "Yes," he said. "You should come home, and be prepared. There has been a fire. This is bad."

As we pulled into the lane behind our house (after two tight-lipped hours on the road), I felt a terrible ache in my throat: there, alone and in pairs and slumped in sadness, were several of our friends. . . . . What were they doing there? How did they know? They came closer and then shied away, the way animals shy from the dead. The police were surprised. They were expecting Claire's red car (it was gone), and didn't know who we were, but then a detective took me aside: "You should get ready before you go in . . . I don't know if your wife should go in, it's the worst we've ever seen." I looked through the gaping hole in the garage wall . . "She's not my wife," I said. "We've lived together for twenty years."

"Do you have any enemies?"

"I don't know."

"It looks like it."

"Why?"

"Because it looks like somebody's tried to hurt you."

"Really."

"We'll have to go around to the front of the house to get in. They never did break the lock on the back door."

"I've got a key," I said.

204

"Oh yes, sure," he said, and another policeman tried to lead Claire away, but she broke free; "No one's keeping me out of my own home." In the kitchen, a long black-handled carving knife had been stuck into the wall: two fires had been set, one on the floor, the other in the gas stove, and the house had the sour reek of smoke; papers and broken glass and crockery covered the tiles; the television set was gone. In the dining room, the armoire doors hung open, armloads of old family crystal and china had been swept out onto the floor . . . but I saw that a portrait of me by William Kurelek had not been touched, and I said warmly, "They're not after me, otherwise they would have slashed that."

"Don't be so sure. It doesn't look like you," a policeman said.

"The red car's been stolen," another policeman said. "It's just been reported in a hit-and-run accident."

We went into the living room with its high ceilings; the black sofa was hacked to pieces; an engraving by my old friend Hayter in Paris was smashed off the wall and scorched; a tapestry I'd brought from Cairo, through the Black September war in 1970 when I was a correspondent, was cut open down the center; the floor was littered with boxes, broken crockery, papers, broken frames, torn cloth, broken records and cassettes, a Chinese vase and ripped books; the curtains in the bay window had been set afire, blackened lace; in the vestibule, a turquoise funerary piece that had been in the pharaoh's tomb at the time of Moses lay broken, and beside it, a Phoenician bronze bull crushed under a heel, or at least there were worn black shoes beside the bull, and I realized my leather boots were gone.

"The son of a bitch," I said, laughing grimly, "he's not only smashed my house but he's gone off in my boots and he's left me his lousy Goodwill shoes."

"This is terrible," Claire said. We did not go near the grand piano. A fire had been set under it. I could see the charred veneer.

"It's worse upstairs," a policeman said.

"Well, lead on, Macduff," I said. He looked at me quizzically.

He was right; they'd torched a vase of silk flowers on the landing, my Philips word processor was stolen (a literary prize I'd never learned to use, didn't want to use, and was secretly glad to see gone); my library was overturned (they'd tried to set a fire using two books: *Child of the Holocaust*, by Claire's cousin Jack

Kuper, and A *Dreambook for Our Time*, by the Polish novelist Tadeusz Konwicki); in the bedroom, they'd thrown a chair through one of Claire's drawings, *Earth Mother*; Chinese porcelain figurines were smashed; and they had ransacked the bureau drawers for jewelry . . . all the gold . . . rings, charms, bracelets . . . all to be fenced and melted down by scumbag uptown swine who feed off junkie break-and-enter kids . . . melting down all our bindings of love. . . .

The third floor was blackened: dozens of Claire's frames and drawings smashed; an enormous painting by her friend Robert Hedrick—a homage to John Kennedy on his death—slashed; the sofa bed burned; plaster casts carved open or broken; and the floor covered by a sludge of burned and scorched and then doused papers . . . they'd started a fire in an armoire . . . it had burned through the roof of the house, the heat blowing out the windows . . . and all those papers, so assiduously kept: letters, manuscripts, transcripts . . . twenty-five years of intimacies, words chosen with care, exactitude. . . .

"We were here three minutes after the alarm," the fire chief said. "When we got here the whole house was full of black smoke . . . luckily, the front door was open, luckily a woman across the road saw the smoke coming through the roof. . . . "

A policeman waited at the bottom of the stairs. "Your father's Morley Callaghan?" he asked.

"Yes."

"He had that boxing match with Hemingway."

"Yes."

I got a book from the library and gave him a copy of *That Summer in Paris*.

"That'll tell you all about it," I said.

"Thanks," he said, lifted his cap, wedged the paperback into the crown, and put the cap back on his head.

"Who would want to hurt you?" Sgt. Hamel asked again.

"I don't know. All I know is the Dom Pérignon is gone."

Claire came into the room. There were tears in her eyes. She does not cry easily. "It's the piano," she said. The piano had been given to her by her father before he died of cancer, a cancer contracted during the First World War, when he'd enlisted too young, lied about his age, been gassed at Ypres and buried alive.

It is a 1912 Mason & Risch, a rich mahogany grand with a beautiful fiddleback grain and carved legs.

A fire had been set under it, burning into the hardwood floor, climbing up an antique silk shawl draped from the lid. When the lid was lifted, the piano was a burned-out, warped, gutted box.

"It's gone forever," she said.

"No it's not," I said.

A whalebone shaman, a drummer figure by Ashevak—the finest of the Inuit carvers—was standing on the piano, the drum broken, the beater scorched black.

"Don't you feel violated?" a woman, a friend who'd come in from the lane, asked. "Don't you feel raped?"

"No," I said.

"You don't?" she said.

"No, and as a woman you should know better. This is a house. No one has entered my body, no one has penetrated me. This isn't rape. . . . "

"Yes, but . . . " She was offended, as if I had been unnecessarily difficult, when all she intended was sympathy. I was being difficult, because I believe—especially in times of trouble—that exactness is how we make a last stand in the ditch against sentimentality, self-pity, falseness (remember the "apprehended insurrection" in Québec that Premier Robarts of Ontario eagerly called "war"—when there was no insurrection, no war).

"But the rage," she said. "Someone attacked your place in a state of rage."

"It looks that way."

"How do you account for such rage?"

"I don't know."

"Any ideas?"

"Motiveless malignancy," I said. An officer took me by the arm. He was smiling, a tight little angry smile. "We've got one of them," he said.

"You have!"

Police, driving down a lane behind the El Mocambo tavern, had seen a shabbily dressed man clutching two bottles of Dom Pérignon. "We knew something was wrong," they said. They handcuffed him in their cruiser. Strung out on drugs, he said he'd show them the house he had broken into that morning, and now he was in the backseat of the cruiser in the lane.

"I don't know whether I want to see him," I said.

"Oh, you can't see him."

"Why not?"

"I don't want an assault-and-battery charge on my hands, too."

But I did not want to beat anyone. I felt only the torpor that comes with keeping an incredulous calm in the face of brutality. Rage, imprecations, threats were beside the point. In fact, having seen what skilled and sanctioned thugs can do to a house—in Belfast, Jerusalem, Beirut—I felt curiously thankful so much had survived. . . . But people, and certainly some policemen, have their expectations: I learned later that for a while I was a suspect. . . . I was too cool, too detached; I had to be in on it, a policeman had told Sgt. Hamel, who tried to explain to him: "No, no. He's a writer. Writers stand back and look at things."

The suspect was named Lugosi ("a cousin of Bela Lugosi," a detective insisted), "of no fixed address." He fought in the cruiser, kicking out the rear window, punching, biting and spitting. He fought with them at the station. He seemed driven by rage. The officers went to the hospital for shots for hepatitis.

Sgt. Hamel, a quick, yet reflective man—who does not, like most cops, look at you as if you must have a criminal secret— opened the trunk of his cruiser. "They set seven fires," he said. "It *is* the worst we've seen." He reached into the bag and took out several small bronzes . . . more funeral ornaments from a pharaoh's tomb; a grotesque Phoenician clown's head, an alabaster fertility monkey from a scent dish. . . .

"These yours?"

"Yes."

"It's terrible, things like this being broken."

"Yes. Lasting this long, smashed on Sullivan Street."

"I want you to think about your enemies."

"I'm not sure I have any."

"You've written a lot."

"I'll think about it."

I did not think about it, not that night or the next morning, when we woke in the Hotel Admiral, on the waterfront. "We've got to go where there's water," I'd told Claire, and in the morning, with the dawn flaring red across the water as we sat up, we were suddenly full of the light on the water. "I had an old

208

philosophy professor," I said, "and he talked with his eyes closed, and when he forgot where he was going he'd open his eyes and say, 'Well, we'll lick the lips and start afresh.' "

We went back to the house. Standing alone in the sooty squalor of the rooms, I knew I had lost things that connected me to the past, but they would be nothing compared to the loss of the future. I wanted to sit at the piano, as I had on other morose days, and play in a minor key, on the black notes, singing, "If Beale Street could talk, married men would take their beds and walk . . . " but it was charred, and then the expert piano restorer, Rob Lowrey, came into the house, shook hands, and then shook his head as he lifted the lid. "Burned to a crisp. It'll cost more to fix it than it's worth, it'll cost $30,000 if we can do anything, and we can't." I talked, he listened; he hung his head and then opened his hands.

"The insurance will never pay for it," he said.

"I don't care," I said. "We'll work out something."

His men carried the piano out of the house. Lowrey said, "If we come back, it'll be in a year, and if we come back at all, it'll be a miracle."

"You bring the loaves, honey," I said to Claire as I closed the door, "and I'll bring the fishes."

We lived in the hotel for over two months. It is small and elegant, charmingly run by young women, and one wall of our room was glass facing over the water. Every day we came back to the room after sifting through rubble and refuse in the house, and we sat and stared as the sun leaked out of the autumn sky, and then we dressed for supper . . . a determined elegance of spirit, a determined refusal to yield to the lethargy of dismay, regret or self-pity, or blame (all questions asked by the police or insurance adjusters or oneself—even the simple question, Why?—contain a hint of blame, of accusation . . . it was even suggested by a friend that we had asked for it: our house had been too open . . . and another friend wondered whether we wouldn't at last learn that expansiveness was a vanity that was always punished), but we did not blame ourselves. We ate and watched the island airport lights on the dark water. There was a pianist in the lobby, out of sight, the ghost of our piano playing, our piano being rebuilt, and ironically, before our house could be rebuilt, it had to become the ghost of itself: walls were washed down, the quarry tile floors stripped, the broadloom ripped out, the hardwood floors sanded . . . as if a deep stain had to be eradicated, as if a cleansing had to be done (and all the while, we went through the dreary listing of each broken or missing thing . . . each thing the ghost of a moment from the past—like counting little razor cuts on the skin though the wound is deep in the bones). Papers had been hosed down by the firemen and letters turned to sodden ash in my hands; rolled drawings were scorched funnels that fell apart . . . a fingertip, a lip . . . all stacked in a hundred boxes piled in the basement . . . two lives, boxed and stacked, in stasis, and then, shortly after the police told us they had arrested a second man named Costa, in a gesture of dumb normalcy we put a new television set in the kitchen, a dead gray eye but a promise of sound. . . .

Then on a crisp December morning we ate breakfast and watched the long, lean harbor police boat leave on patrol. The lake was icing over but there were still geese on open patches of water. We went to the house and discovered the back door open, the television set gone, some jewelry and a fox fur jacket gone. We had been robbed again (when a house has been hit the word goes out on the street: they know television sets will be replaced, and an empty house is a sitting duck). So we were being watched, we were a word on the street, the word a whisper of affliction on the air again.

A policeman came by to dust for fingerprints. He was wearing a narrow-brimmed hat, a suit with narrow lapels. He was lean and close-mouthed, gruff and meticulous. Yes ma'am, no. Dust and fingerprints. For a moment, I thought I was losing my mind, except I couldn't stop laughing quietly, and I mumbled to Claire, "Go ask Jack Webb if he thinks we'll ever catch these guys."

"No," he said. "Not likely."

This affliction and folly was going to go on, I could see, for a long time. I went down to the water and sat by the hotel window, watching single-engine planes take off from the island airport. I worked on *Stone Blind Love:*

RESTLESS STONES

East of the waterfront grain silos
he was sitting on a stone.

210

"It's one of Lilith's eggs,
the beaches are strewn with the misbegotten."
A pearl of milk
on his lip was a fever sore.
"Stones never sleep, they grow,
they crawl up your legs,
the seeds
of all your misdeeds
until
you stand at last
with a stone
in each fist,
an enclosing wall your only
defense."

As I drove around the city, a rankling awareness grew in me. This tawdry, soft mockery of our life was going to last at least a year: we would of course outlast it because we could still laugh (grim men fear laughter because laughter dispels fear), but I was suddenly alive to all signs and signals of affliction: at Dundas and University, I saw through the car window the memorial monument to the poor dead airmen of the Second World War. I was suddenly enraged. I heard myself hissing. *Hal Jackman* . . . I hated that tasteless monument to his moneyed influence, *Gumby* . . . so contrary in every aesthetic sense to the lives and deaths it presumed to honor, to celebrate—an exercise in banality stuck in the city's eye. I could rebuild my house, and someday—if Rob Lowrey could work his miracle—I would play our piano, but I was going to have to look at *Gumby* for as long as I lived in the city. It was a permanent offense, a tin-soldiering view of life and death. What galled me was that Jackman would never understand my weary sorrow with those two addicts sitting in jail and my rage at him.

Just before Christmas, on a cold, clear day, we drove over to the old city hall for the preliminary hearing. I had not thought much about the two men doing dead time in the Toronto Jail (my own contacts on the street told me that six men had been in the house, that six men had been in Claire's stolen car). I wondered about their faces and pondered the old questions: Was this a

211

hired hit? And if so, who hated me so much? And if drug money were the motive for the break-in, was the raging destruction of the contents a malignancy without malice?

We sat in an overheated room with the fire chief, detectives and officers, a woman who said she was Lugosi's girlfriend, a Vietnamese bricklayer who had come face-to-face with Costa as he hauled suitcases full of our things out the front door, the woman who had seen the smoke, a stout woman who was the desk clerk at the Waverley Hotel, on Spadina Avenue. . . .

As we went up the marble stairs to sit and wait outside a courtroom, a courtroom next to the marriage bureau, I was told several things by several people: that when they were looking for Costa, two officers cornered a man in a cappuccino bar on College Street and the man flattened them both, driving one into the street through a plate-glass window . . . they felt sheepish about that, they said; also, Lugosi had checked into the Waverley Hotel before breaking into the house and he had checked in under my name; the house had been cased by a man, a light-skinned black man, named Bo . . . and Bo had probably been in the house at least once before it was hit; Bo worked for any "interests" who would hire him; Lugosi had come back into the hotel after leaving the house waving a blowtorch, threatening to set fire to the hotel "just like he had torched a house" on Sullivan Street; several men were waiting in a blue car at the hotel and got into Claire's car without Lugosi and drove off; Costa had made several trips to the fence during the night using Claire's car; Lugosi's old girlfriend, saying he had done her harm, not only wanted to testify to that harm but also said she could explain why he had savaged our house: it was all, she said, because of an incident in August when I was taking the ferry to the island and Lugosi, who worked with a punk rock band, had spoken to me and I had snubbed him: "He said he would get Callaghan for that." The only problem was I hadn't been on the ferry to the island for four years and in August I had been in Stockholm and then in Saratoga.

Why this determined fantasy? Were any of the little stories told to me true? Did it matter? Weren't all these people suddenly on stage for a moment? Wasn't this their time, not ours?

As the afternoon passed, as we waited to be called in the courtroom to at last look into the faces of the two men, to say to them and to the court what we had been through, what we had lost inside ourselves, what music had been stilled, we listened dryly to the sullying confidences of the street while very young couples—most of them black and surprisingly alone, without friends or family—strutted by, beaming, untarnished and newly wed. Then, after all the witnesses had been heard in the closed courtroom and the afternoon had waned, we sat alone on the bench, uncalled in silence: the doors opened and Sgt. Hamel, looking pleased as a newlywed, explained that everything had worked out, we were unnecessary. "They're being sent to trial." Lugosi was led to the elevator; slender, head bowed, penitential; Costa, less shrewd, smirked with bravado and stared brazenly at Claire. The elevator doors closed, so, with nothing left to do, we went Christmas shopping, and then on Christmas Eve, after the sanded hardwood floors had been stained, we stood at midnight in the vestibule, pleased with the wet, dark sheen. "It'll go beautifully with the piano," Claire said.

On Christmas Day, though there was no furniture in the house, we moved out of the hotel. Two old Chinese women stood in the lane watching me unload books and papers and clothes. They said nothing. I realized that in four years of living in Chinatown not one Chinese neighbor had ever spoken to me, not even the people who run the corner store, who sell me cream and paper towels. We had handed change back and forth, but I didn't even know if they could speak English. I was angry at Lugosi and Costa but loathed our political culture that encouraged people to close in on themselves like that.

Separate trials took place in February. The Crown attorney, a pert young woman, was eager; she had a solid case; break and enter, theft and arson, fingerprints and a witness. She thought she could get a substantial sentence. A plea bargain was struck: Lugosi would not contest his guilt if I would agree to five years. Yes, I said, I suppose five years will do. (But what did five years mean?—this curious attachment of penitential time to a crime . . . not the inflicting of corporal pain, but the religious notion of "serving of time" in a monkish cell; and I recalled the idiotic notions of my childhood catechism and the confessional—two years off in purgatory for going without candy for a week; four years off for . . . five years off for. . . .) We sat in an almost empty courtroom. A couple of men I'd seen around the Waverley

213

Hotel sat beside me, and a lone woman, and a detective. Lugosi sat in the box, head down. I looked at him for a while and felt little or nothing; no witnesses were called before Judge David Humphrey. Police photographs of our house were entered as evidence of wilful havoc and the seven fires. At the court's request, I had written a note about what it was like being a victim. It was for the judge to read. Time, I told him, was our punishment, too. Guilty of nothing, we were being punished. Time was the real bond between criminals and victims: "Having survived three months dislocation we realize how disruptive the devastation has been . . . the endless sorting through drawings, papers—charred, destroyed, these are the tissues of our life, our spirit. We have been robbed of time, it is a robbery that goes on and on. . . . Creative time, insights—those fleeting moments of inspiration—they are gone forever. . . . The dispiriting loss of time—and we cannot help each other—for Claire, as an artist, has suffered exactly the same loss as I have. We are doing time, and we get no time off for good behavior. The terrible irony is that these two men may well do less time than we will. For us, the loss of time spirals . . . each week implies a month of lost writing, sculpting . . . every two months a half-year, a half-year two years, a year will become five. Together, we may do more dead time than they will. There is the real crime committed against us. . . . " The judge expressed his stern dismay; we said nothing; Lugosi said nothing. He was sentenced to five years.

A few weeks later, Costa was tried. His defense was hapless: he said that all the damage had been done by Lugosi after he'd left the house for the last time at 9 o'clock in the morning. The fire alarm had been turned in at 9:03. That meant Lugosi had savaged the house and set fires on three floors in under three minutes. The judge shook his head, embarrassed by the ineptness of the argument. Costa was a young immigrant man, a drug addict, his life ruined, on his way to the brutality of prison. I wanted to say something but there was nothing to say. He was sentenced to two years in the penitentiary.

"At last," Claire said, "I feel safe." She stopped thinking about them at night. But we took no pleasure in the sentencing. It had to be; the arson demanded it, the police—for their own morale—needed it; as victims we were witnesses to it; but we took no pleasure. Vengeance, like jealousy, is a second-rate emotion,

214

which is why I have always found the old Jewish tribal stories of an "eye for an eye, tooth for a tooth"—charged with self-congratulatory moral delight—so twisted.

I am no pacifist, but vengeance gives me no pleasure, no satisfaction.

We felt only a hollow in the house, and the need to fill it with laughter, meditation and music. But every morning, all day, there was only repairing, hammering.

Drilling.

Waiting for workmen to show up.

Waiting. Life as repair.

Nothing on time, time meaning nothing, till in the summer we went to Rob Lowrey's to see the piano: it had become, in our imaginations, more than scorched fiddleback veneer and charred legs; after opening the lid on its inner parts, so scarred and warped and twisted by fire and supposedly beyond repair—it had become the embodiment of our own renewal. Mahogany can be turned and trimmed, as we had turned ourselves out for dinner every night at the hotel, but only we knew the ashes, the soot we could still taste on our breaths. So the piano had to be cleansed and brought back to life. The stillness that lies between the struck key and the string, the stillness that contains the note, had to sound.

Rob Lowrey, who had said in dismay that restoration would require a redeeming miracle, greeted us with a subdued eagerness, a caution that comes from dealing with damage. But he had a solid, rounded playfulness as he moved quickly and soundlessly into the aroma of varnish and glue in his workroom, standing in his white apron, obviously relishing his young workers' bashful way of laying their hands on wood. There were men at several pianos, each striking a note, listening, head half-cocked, then malleting a tuning peg into a pin plank, threading thin wire through the peg . . . slowly tightening, tuning the treble and then the heavier bass strings . . . twenty-four tones of tension in those strings, all our anxiety struggling toward the inner harmony that is always the mystery of the piano . . . the piano in tune with itself.

I stood staring into the hollow guts of our piano as if I were looking back into the months that had passed, the veneer peeled down to the glue-stained frame and new wood held by vises, the bridges and ribs, the pin planks all laid out . . . and Lowrey, smiling, said: "September. We've had to send the legs to Cleveland. No one here can carve those old legs. . . . "

"September?"

"Don't worry," he said. "It'll play like a charm."

"I'll have a party, then, open up the house."

"Why not?"

We felt safe: the lane and the garden were floodlit at night, the garage door could be opened only from inside, the garage wall was rebuilt, all the glass doors had jam-bars, the rooms had all been wired to an alarm system of motion detectors, and we were three: we had a young, powerful golden retriever who chewed our shoes as we retrieved our losses. We had been fortunate to have a good man—fair and accomplished—as our insurance adjuster: John Morris. His efficient cheerfulness puzzled me: more than a priest, it seemed to me, disaster rolled across his desk . . . an endless array of mishaps and malevolence that he adjusted. In his middle years, he had heard every story and dealt with every scam, yet, for all his rigor, he had been fair and sympathetic, and the insurance company had accepted all his recommendations. We would never recover all our losses, but the company was going to honor their obligations without argument.

But as we prepared to drive again to Saratoga, to renew the ritual, the hammer fell. Our insurance company, Trafalgar, announced it would not renew our coverage. They were shedding us, leaving us completely vulnerable. So be it, I thought. Our agent tried to make arrangements with other companies. To her astonishment, to my rage and sudden fear, no one would insure us. Not Trafalgar, not Wellington, not Guardian, not Laurentian, not any company approached. At the same time, the mortgage company wrote asking for confirmation of fire insurance, a condition of the mortgage. Without insurance the mortgage would be called. We would be broken by debt, driven out of the house. "Because," I was told, "you're high profile, you're a controversial journalist." This was worse than any street thuggery. Even our insurance adjuster, unbelieving, tried to get us insurance with his contacts: the answer was no. There was nothing to be done. Though I had paid house insurance into the industry for twenty-five years, as soon as I was hit—as soon as what I was insured against happened—those companies all closed down on me.

These men weren't junkies, strung out and hooked; no, these were the close cousins to the auto insurer for Budget rent a car in the U.S.—which still, years later, owes us $1,200, and refuses to pay . . . bigger thieves than any dipso break-and-enter kid: these were men who intended to leave us twisting in the wind, defenseless. I knew where I was. I was in the land of Erewhon, Samuel Butler's Erewhon, where "ill-luck of any kind, or even ill-treatment at the hands of others, is considered an offense against society, inasmuch as it makes people uncomfortable to hear of it. Loss of fortune, therefore . . . is punished hardly less severely than physical delinquency." We had committed an offense by becoming victims. The insurers—and who sits more at the center of our society than insurers?—were going to punish us more than any druggies had ever dreamed of . . . the motives behind this malignancy were clear. "The insurance companies are protecting themselves," a woman said with disarming openness. "If you weren't who you are there'd be no problem."

"If I wasn't who I am," I said to myself standing one afternoon in front of *Gumby,* "I'd blow you up."

Then, after talking to a sensible, experienced woman in the insurance business—who reminded me of the way good bank managers used to be: unafraid of their own judgment—the problem was solved.

"No, I am not a public personality," I agreed. "I write here and there and do a little television, but I am a professor. I have been a professor for twenty-two years."

The house was insured by Chubb.

On a September Saturday afternoon, two men levered the legless and lidless body of our piano into a sling and lowered it out of a truck onto a trolley and rolled the trolley into the house. They malleted the pins that hold the legs and set the piano in the bay window, all the light catching the grain, so that Rob Lowrey's brother, John, could tune the strings, and then in the early evening, Al Cromwell and Doug Richardson—friends for more than thirty years from the days when I used to go to the black dance halls—came in. Al is a guitarist. Doug plays flute and saxophone, and they had two pianists with them, Connie Maynard and Carlton Vaughan. "You get to christen the keys," I said as Connie sat down and worked through several songs, and then stood up, beaming: "Very nice. Beautiful sound. Quiet touch."

217

"Quiet, I like quiet," Doug, who has an impish wit, said. "I hate noise, noisy cars most of all. Expensive cars are noisy. Who'd want a Ferrari? How could you ever hold up a bank in a Ferrari?"

The house began to fill with friends carrying flowers and wine, crowding into conversation in all the rooms, friends who were writers and newshounds and gamblers, editors and the two carpenters who had meticulously trimmed the house, professors and maître d's and film producers, and after Claire said, "This'll be strange, being hosts at our own resurrection," I drifted happily from room to room pouring wine, all the slashes on the walls healed, hearing—I was sure—each note as it was unlocked from the stillness between struck key and string. Before reading my poems, which had just been published, I introduced Sgt. Hamel. Doug, playful as ever, stopped honking on his sax and spread-eagled himself against the wall. Everyone laughed, and curiously for me, it was a bonding laughter, an acknowledgment that there is a little larceny in all of us, and a cop, too. I read in the voice of a character of mine, Sesephus the Stone King, and then Al led us into a chant of "Stone Blind Love" in answer and call with Doug's sax, Vaughan on the piano holding it all together.

In the early morning hours, after everyone had gone home and Claire had gone to bed, I stood on the upstairs back porch staring down into the darkness of the back lane, the dark split by a shaft of light from the new high-beam lamp on the garage. The two thieves had come up onto the porch out of that darkness to break and enter into our lives, but as I stood there staring at the light I remembered my childhood and how at night when the light from a kitchen door fell across an alleyway, I'd crouch on one side of it—as if I were a mysterious traveller—and then I'd leap through the light and go on my way unseen, unscathed. The year had been like that light; we had leapt through it and, with our secret selves intact, we were now travelling on.

Nominated by The Ontario Review, *Philip Booth and Joyce Carol Oates*

ZOE

fiction by MOLLY BEST TINSLEY

from SHENANDOAH

S HE LIKED TO be the first to speak. It wasn't that she wanted
to be nice, or put them at ease; it was her way of warning them
not to be, of setting the tone she liked best: bemused, even
ironic, but formal. She didn't want any of them thinking she was
someone to cultivate. Whenever those voices, low and strained,
interrupted her life downstairs, whether they came late at night
from the front hall or mornings from the kitchen, she slipped into
the one-piece camouflage suit she used as a bathrobe, wrapped
the belt twice around her slim waist, and ascended to meet her
mother's latest. She liked to catch him with breakfast in his
mouth, or romance on his mind, and then before he could compose himself, announce, "I am Zoe, her daughter," offering a little bow and a graceful hand, limp as a spray of japonica.

It usually left him stammering, fumbling—this blend of child-
like respect and self-possession. If he'd already begun to imagine
her mother recharging his life with pleasure and purpose, Zoe's
winsome presence made such visions more intense, then tipped
them into unsettling. Though he'd never gone in for kids before,
he might find himself thinking at first how agreeable it would be
to have a delicate creature like her around, slender, long-legged,
with pale freckles across her nose. These days she has her auburn
hair bobbed at the ears so it curls up shorter in back above a
softly fringed nape. But if he thought for a moment how much
the child must know, her poise could seem ominous—all the
things *he* didn't know, was hungry to find out, but might not
want to hear.

219

"So what's it like, living with her?" one of them asked Zoe once, as if he expected soon to be sharing the experience, to be given exclusive credit for recognizing that her mother was an extraordinary woman. He reminded Zoe of a large rabbit—a confusion of timidity and helpless lust.

"There's never a dull moment," Zoe answered, sweet but nonchalant. "I meet a lot of interesting men." That was stretching things. Most were rabbits.

Often they felt called upon to tell Zoe, "Your mom's a great lady." Did they think Zoe was responsible for raising her mother and not the other way around? Or that she had a choice of mothers? Or that she couldn't guess what they meant, that her mother was something else in bed, that they'd never done it to a Sibelius symphony before?

Since the age of five when her parents split up, Zoe Cameron and her mother, Phyllis Rush, have lived beyond the D.C. Beltway in The Colonies of Virginia, clusters of townhouses subtly tucked into one hundred acres of rolling woods, whose inhabitants readily paid a little more to get aesthetic design and proximity to nature. Set against the ridge of a hill, with cathedral ceilings and an expanse of glass to the south, Zoe's mother's unit welcomes light, draws it in to challenge her work—heavy terra cotta, here and there a dull giant bronze—set off by white walls. Each piece has been given a woman's name, yet they are only parts of women, global buttocks and thighs, pairs of breasts larger than the heads mounted upon them—Leda, Electra, Helen, truncated. They are one reason Zoe stopped bringing home friends, who tended to stare about in stunned silence or whisper words like *gross* and *perverted*. Zoe has learned contempt for kids her own age, who cannot understand true art. Yet she hates her mother's women: fat, naked blobs. The bald definition of nipple or vulva makes her sick. There are more of them on exhibit in the local gallery her mother manages in The Commons. The public tends not to buy them, but Phyllis does enter them in shows and they have won awards, including a purchase prize at the Corcoran. After that a man from *The Washington Post* came out to photograph Phyllis at home in her skylit studio. Zoe declined to be in any of his shots. He took her mother to dinner in Great Falls. When Zoe came up the next morning to leave for school, he was in the kitchen alone making raisin toast. He offered her a slice, trying to act as if he owned the place, but she drank her sixteen ounces of water as if he wasn't there. It was easier than ever to resist that sweet yeasty aroma, tainted as it was by his male pride.

As far as Lucas is concerned, Zoe would give anything to go back and start over again with the moment she arrived home in the early afternoon to find his body sticking out from under the sink. Thinking her mother had finally called someone to fix the dishwasher, Zoe set her wide-brimmed hat down on the table and looked on absently as the body twisted and grunted with its efforts. Her hunger had been stubborn that day, conjuring extravagant food fantasies that almost sabotaged a test in pre-calculus. But she had conquered temptation, and now what she wanted was plenty of water and maybe a carrot to get through until dinner.

"Let me out of here," came a roar, all of a sudden, followed by bumping sounds and *great god's*, and the upper part of the man extricated itself from the cabinet. His knuckles were smudged with black, his once-starched shirt was sharply wrinkled, and he rubbed the top of his head ruefully, but when he saw Zoe, his expression flexed in a smile. "Well, look at you," he said. "Don't you look out of this world!" And not expecting such a remark from a repairman, Zoe, who was known to become transfixed by her own image wherever she found it reflected, who that day was wearing one of her favorite suits—broadly padded shoulders over a short slim skirt, a blue that turned her eyes blue—could not bring herself to disagree, nor think of anything to say back. She did try her ironic geisha bow, but in the same instant noticed the roaches hurrying over the sill of the sink cabinet and out across the kitchen floor in a dark stream.

Before she knew it she had emitted a soft scream, more out of embarrassment than fear. She had certainly seen roaches in the kitchen before, those nights when she gave in to temptation and felt her way up the stairs in the dark. Thinking it was almost like sleepwalking, she was almost not responsible for what she was about to do: forage for food, cookies, bagels, leftover pasta, cinnamon raisin toast drenched in butter. When she turned on the light, there they always were collected on some vertical surface in clusters of imperceptible activity, and she caught her breath in disgust, but went on to get what she had come for.

"They must have a nest under there," the man said, a little out of breath. He was somehow hopping and stooping at the same time, slapping at the creatures with one of his moccasions. "How about giving me a hand here?"

Zoe looked down helplessly at her clothes, her inch-high patent heels.

"How about insecticide, a spray or something?"

"If we have any, it's in there." She pointed to the cabinet from which they kept coming. The floor around him was awash with brown spots. Some had been hit and were finished moving. "Close the door," Zoe cried. When she realized the sense of her suggestion, she repeated it more calmly.

He smacked the door shut, and the stream was cut off. "Good thinking," he said.

She pursed her lips to hide her pleasure. Producing a fly swatter from the closet in the front hall, she commenced ceremoniously to slap at the remaining roaches from the comfortable distance its handle allowed. "Mother," she called.

"She went to the store," the man said, rubbing his bare foot along his pants leg, then replacing his shoe. "I thought I'd keep myself busy until she got back."

That was when Zoe realized he wasn't a plumber and that she had been inexplicably foolish. Her mother, who scorned home maintenance, who refused to spend any time on fixing things when she could be making something new—why would her mother suddenly hire a plumber? "I am Zoe, her daughter," she said, with a final stroke of the swatter, but it was too late.

"I assumed as much," the man said. "From the side you're a dead ringer." He introduced himself: Lucas Washburn. He had light, almost frizzy hair and eyebrows, no cheekbones to speak of, and his nose must have been broken once and never set straight. His skin was fissured from past acne, and his eyes were a flat, changeless gray. He was not handsome, Zoe decided, but there was something about him. His hair was cropped short, his skin evenly tanned, his khaki pants creased. Clean—in spite of his disarray, he seemed oddly, utterly clean.

"I assumed you were the plumber." Zoe pulled the broom out from beside the refrigerator and began with dignity to sweep roach hulls into a pile.

"I can see why. I hear you're down to one bathtub."

Zoe stiffened at the forced intimacy, the hint of sympathy. She normally did not interfere in her mother's affairs, patiently allowing what Phyllis would call nature to take its course. But this man, with his long cheekless face, who had poked around under their sink, discovered their roaches—he was not at all her mother's type, and the sooner he was history, the better. "And it happens to be my bathtub downstairs, which gets pretty inconvenient if you think about it. One of her quote friends pulled the soap holder off the wall in *her* tub and half the tiles came with it, and the guest tub has a leak that drips into the front hall. Actually, the whole house is a total wreck." She finished, and made herself laugh, but in the silence that was his reply, she heard her words echo like a blurted confession, false notes, as if something were playing in the background in a different key. Blasé wasn't working.

"If I had my tools," Lucas said, "we could get this sink to drain, and I could take a look at those tubs. Next time I'll bring my tools."

That is a lot to assume, next time, Zoe thought, and to her surprise, that was what she said.

Lucas nodded solemnly, then turned his back on her and began washing his hands. Should she explain that her mother had very liberal views, that if men and women were allowed to live naturally, without the inhibitions imposed by society, they would choose to spend their nights in each other's beds all the time, different other's beds as the impulse moved them, mornings parting, more often than not, forever? And that was all right with her, Zoe, for it was much worse when a man of her mother's showed up a second time, all twitchy and trembly, and suggested doing something that included her, and her mother, seduced by some transient vision of family, agreed.

"I appreciate the warning," Lucas said, drying his long hands finger by finger. Then he added, "Maybe I've got something in common with those guys in there"—he jerked his head toward the roach settlement—"I'm pretty hard to get rid of."

That night her mother and Lucas fixed strip steaks, steamed artichokes, wild rice. As she often did, Phyllis set up small folding tables on the balcony off the living room in view of the sunset, but Lucas moved the hibachi to the backyard below to

223

comply with the county fire code. ("What fire code?" Phyllis asked. She had never heard of any fire code.) Zoe went downstairs to change into a faded denim jumpsuit, espadrilles. She rolled a fuchsia bandanna into a headband and tied her curls down, Indian-style. She freshened the strip of pale blue shadow on her lower lids, all the while aware that Lucas was right beyond the glass door, the drapes that don't quite meet, calling arguments up to her mother in favor of well-done. Phyllis stuck to rare. Her face blank and impersonal, Zoe made a last appraisal in the full-length mirror. She pushed a fist into her sucked-in abdomen. *I hate my stomach,* she thought. You couldn't trust mirrors; they could be designed to make people look thinner. All the ones in stores were deceptive that way.

Lucas sawed off huge blocks of meat and swallowed them almost whole. Her mother plucked her artichoke, petal by petal, dragged each one through her lips slowly, her subtly silvered eyelids drooping with the pleasure. She had a strong jaw, and a wide mouth, with large teeth—but she knew how to recontour her face with light and shade, to make her eyes seem bigger, mysterious. Yes, Zoe had her nose, rising fine and straight from the brow, nostrils flared back, so that if you happened to have a cold or be cold, their moisture was open to view. Zoe had learned to carry her head tilted slightly forward, to make it hard for anyone to see into her nose.

To Lucas' credit he seemed not to be noticing Phyllis' sensual performance. He was expressing his suspicion that her clogged dishwasher and drain stemmed from a failure to scrape dirty dishes thoroughly; a small chicken bone in the trap, for example, was all it took to start an obstruction.

Phyllis threw her head back and laughed. "You sound like my mother," she said.

Lucas wasn't fazed. "You're talking to someone who's trained to eliminate human error." Lucas flew for Pan Am; Phyllis had picked him out of the happy-hour crowd in the lounge at Dulles Airport after dropping off a friend.

Phyllis stroked his closest arm. "That's mother all over again."

"Another word for it is *accident*."

"It's only a dishwasher," Phyllis said, sullenly, and the fatalist in Zoe settled back with the vaguest sense of loss to watch this man ruin things with her mother long before he could get the bathtubs fixed.

In a steady, almost uninflected voice, he was talking improvements. He could see a brick patio in their backyard, and redwood planters and a hexagonal redwood picnic table. Zoe saw clumsy strategy, tinged with pathos. He frankly admitted he was tired of living on the tenth floor of a condo in Hunting Towers. Between his job and the apartments he unpacked in, he never had his feet on the ground. "It's about time I got my feet on the ground," he said. Phyllis suggested he sprinkle dirt in his socks.

She was being strangely tolerant; maybe he had touched off an attack of what she called her *passion for reality,* when practical dailiness, what everyone else did, became the exotic object of curiosity and desire. Lucas was neither suave nor witty. If you sanded his face, he might be handsome. Zoe guessed he had what her mother would call a good body, though she, Zoe, had trouble looking at a male body long enough to form a complete picture of one. She tended to focus on them piece by piece, and they stayed like that in her mind, a jumble of parts. Her mother often said it was an insult to women the way men let themselves go after a certain age, after they had good incomes. Phyllis herself kept her weight down by smoking and thought women should band together and hold men to the same physical standards everyone held women to.

"Why me?" Phyllis asked Lucas, and seemed genuinely to wonder. "For how many years you've been tied to no place particular and been perfectly happy? Why pick on my place? Maybe I like it this way."

"Look at that," Lucas said, pointing above them at a strip of white streaks and blotches on the cedar stain. "Look at the mess those birds have made of your siding. Starlings. They must have a roost in the eaves. I'd have to take care of that before I'd put in a patio right under their flight lines!"

Phyllis pulled forward a lock of her thick dark hair. "I don't begrudge them that. It's nature." She gave a quick yank, then let the breeze lift an offending gray strand from her fingers.

"Like roaches under the sink."

Zoe held her breath as her mother lit a cigarette. Was he joking or criticizing? Either way he had no right; either way her mother would finally put him in his place. Then why was she stretching, smiling languidly at his rudeness? "Everyone has them," she said, blowing a plume of smoke. "They're a fact of life."

"You don't have to give in totally," Lucas persisted.

"It isn't in me to go around poisoning things."

Her mother's reasonableness was a puzzle to Zoe. *Why him?* she kept asking herself, until the answer came to her, all at once: it made her a little queasy. It was obviously something to do with sex that gave Lucas this power, this license. Wasn't her mother always declaring that everything came down to that? It must be something sexual he did to her mother or for her, which she, Zoe, for all her determined precocity, had not yet figured out. Then she felt very empty—empty as though she had failed an exam, empty because she didn't want to think of Lucas that way. In the back of her mind, she had been hoping he was different, and she didn't even know she was hoping until he turned out to be the same—just another male, who in the irresistible flux of life must soon disappear. Well, she could care less.

That night Zoe ate. Once dead silence told her Lucas and her mother had settled down, she stole upstairs in the dark, removed from the freezer a half gallon of vanilla ice cream and went back down to her room. She sat on the bed, and gazing at the photos of lithe models she had cut from her magazines, began to spoon ice cream into her mouth. Each mouthful hit her empty stomach like a cold stone. It made her feel a little crazy; she couldn't think straight anymore. She swung between defiance—when she agreed with herself that this was incomparable pleasure, no matter how high the price, this cool, bland sweetness, this private solitude—defiance, and despair. "Eat up," she heard her mother encouraging, as she had all evening, though never showing concern when Zoe didn't. "She eats like the proverbial bird," her mother told Lucas. And then Lucas had said, "Do you know how much a bird eats? One of those starlings, for example? They eat something like four times their body weight in one day."

Ah Lucas, the way he looked at Zoe then, as if he knew that sometimes she forgot she must be thinner. She forgot the terrible burden of stomach and hateful thighs, which kept you from ever being wonderful, and she ate, and having forgotten, she ate more, to forget she forgot. One hand around the damp, softening box of ice cream, in the other the spoon, hands like birdclaws, eating like a bird. Her stomach danced madly as if filled with birds. Her whole body felt in motion. She strutted across her own mind, plump-chested, preening; she opened her wings and

226

took off, soared and swooped above the balcony where Lucas, the flier, watched captivated. And then the ice cream was gone, and all that motion froze, like someone caught in the act. She looked down at her denim thighs spreading against the bed; she could barely get both hands around one. Her stomach was monstrous, almost pregnant. She was losing her shape. She would turn into one of those crude female blobs of her mother's. The thought alone was all it took to convulse her, as, eyes closed above the toilet, she imaged all the birds escaping from the cage of her ribs.

Afterwards she would not allow herself to sleep. Awake burned more calories, burned flesh from bones. She held one hand to the hollow of her throat and felt her heart beating fast and hot as a bird's.

This afternoon Zoe found her mother nestled in the wine velvet cushions of the sofa, her legs drawn up under a long Indian cotton skirt, smoking with one hand, sipping maté tea with the other. From the dull puffiness of her mother's eyes, Zoe could tell she had been crying. *It is all right to cry,* Phyllis has always said. *It is a natural response of the body. Holding it back is harmful.* Zoe hates it when her mother cries, hates to see the pain, the rivulets of mascara, the surrender.

"The bus was a little late today," Zoe says, hitching the knees of her linen pants and perching on the chair opposite.

Her mother pulled herself upright, bare soles on the floor, began carefully to shift the position of everything around her—the huge pillows, ashtray, teapot, the extra cup, which she filled and handed to Zoe. "You're not happy," she told her daughter.

"I'm not?" Zoe asked, with a careful laugh.

"Oh Zoe, you don't have to pretend. But why, when two people love each other, can't at least one of them be happy? You'd think they could pool their resources and work on one of them. Tell me something you want, Zoe, okay?"

"Kids my age just aren't very happy." Her mother was in one of her moods. "We grow out of it. It's no big deal."

"But what would make you happy? We could manage it."

"You must have had a bad day," Zoe said.

Phyllis took a long pull on her cigarette. "For six hours I have tried to work." She didn't exhale but let the smoke seep out as she talked. "I felt like any minute my hands were going to do something no one has ever done before, but they never did. Nothing. I might as well have been kneading bread. At least I'd have something to show for my time."

"Let's go to the mall," Zoe suggested. She and her mother have always had a good time shopping for Zoe's clothes. When Zoe was small, her mother said, it was like having a doll. Now Zoe has her own ideas, and Phyllis, rather than objecting, seems able to guess almost infallibly what they are—sophisticated angular lines, in pastels or white and black, plenty of defining black; Phyllis combs the racks, and brings a steady supply of possibilities into the fitting room for Zoe to try. Phyllis has always shopped for herself alone and piecemeal, at craft fairs, antique markets, Episcopal church rummage sales in Leesburg, Fairfax. She's owned her favorite jacket for over twenty years—brown leather with a sunrise appliquéd in faded patches and strips on the back.

"I'm going back to pots," Phyllis said dramatically. "Tomorrow I'm hooking up the wheel."

"Let's go to the mall." Zoe bounced twice in the chair to demonstrate eagerness. "I need summer things. That would make me happy."

Her mother paused, searched Zoe's face. "Lucas gets in at five," she said finally. "I think he'll be coming right over."

"Lucas?" Why the flare of panic? Zoe had not seen him since the afternoon of the roaches, assumed that, like one of her mother's moods, he had passed.

"That's what he said last week before he left. He had back-to-back European runs. He said he'd be carrying his tools in the trunk of his car." Her mother's voice quavered, as if she were afraid of something, too.

"What did *you* say?"

Her mother went into a prolonged shrug. "I said all right."

"Well, you must like him then," Zoe said dismissively, deciding it was all right with her, at least one of them would be happy.

"I don't know. I don't understand him. I don't know what he's after." She laughed nervously.

"Mother," Zoe said, stressing each syllable. This was no time for either one of them to act innocent.

"Do you know what he said to me? He said, 'Why do you women assume that's all you've got to offer?' " Phyllis shook her hair violently. "We shouldn't be talking like this."

228

"We always talk like this."

"I know, but . . . "

"Don't be weird, okay? You've got to tell me what's going on." That has been, after all, Zoe's main fare—knowing. "I can handle things."

"I was asking him to spend the night."

"So?" Zoe had handled that countless times. Then all at once question and answer came together in her mind. "He didn't spend the night?" A rush of feeling, worse than any amount of fear, washed away her strength. She fell back into the chair, crushing her linen blazer.

"He said, number one, it wasn't safe anymore and I should know better, and number two, that didn't matter because he'd promised himself the next time he met a woman he liked he would wait to sleep with her for six months." Her mother spoke haltingly, as though his reasoning mortified her.

"He said he liked you anyway."

"He said he'd been through enough relationships that began with great sex. He can't afford another."

Zoe pulled herself up straight again. "Did you tell him what you think, about tapping into the flow of nature, and creating the sensuous present?"

"I can't remember," her mother said faintly, then all at once roared angrily through her teeth. "Forget him," she said, bounding up, jabbing each foot into a thong. "Let's go. He's too damned controlled. Forget him."

"I don't mind staying here and waiting to see if he shows up." Zoe's voice was playing tricks on her, first whispering and then suddenly wanting to shout. "It would be nice to have the plumbing work."

Lucas arrived around seven, looking as if he'd never thought for a moment that he wouldn't. He was wearing fresh khakis and a white knit shirt, with the last of four neck buttons open. He had stopped somewhere to rent a giant ladder which he had tied onto the ski rack of his perfectly restored Karman Ghia. If there was awkwardness in the rather formal greetings he received from mother and daughter in the front hall, he didn't seem to notice; he was more interested in introducing the two of them to his plumber's pliers, assorted wrenches, a drain snake, a staple gun, and a roll of six-inch wide screening. He was ready to work.

"You must be hungry," Phyllis said. "I've got pastrami, swiss cheese. A wonderful melon. Aren't you too tired for this? I mean, what time is it for you? It must be after midnight. You ought to sleep. I can make up the couch," she added quickly.

He wasn't ready to sleep. He'd spent all that time in the air dreaming of feet-on-the-ground work, making mental lists of things to do. He had promised to return the ladder the next morning, and the sun was already dropping into the trees in back. "First things first," he said, unlashing the ladder from the car. He took one end, Phyllis and Zoe the other, and he led them back into the house, down the front hall, miraculously through the living room, without bumping a life-sized bronze of staunchly planted legs and hips—the Arch of Triumph, he had dubbed it last week. Out on the balcony, he passed his end over the rail and took over theirs.

He dug the ladder firmly into the grass below, then produced a shoelace from his pocket and tied one end around the staple gun, the other around a belt loop. He slipped the roll of screen up his arm, swung a leg onto the ladder, and descended. When he reached the ground, he stamped his feet a few times as if to get used to it. "Come on down," he called back to them.

Zoe had never been on a ladder before—the whole thing made her think of burning buildings, great escapes—she scrambled over the edge, linen pants, Capezios and all, and breathing deep against the slight sway, carefully eased herself from rung to rung. She was afraid of losing it if she looked down, so turned her eyes on her mother's face, where she found the blank patient expression of someone lying low.

"I think I'll use the stairs," her mother said, and disappeared. By the time she slid open the glass door, Lucas had extended the ladder twice to the impossible height of three stories. "It's simple physics," he had told Zoe, waving away her offer to steady the bottom. "It can't go anywhere." He had one foot on the first rung.

"Wait a minute, wait a minute," Phyllis said.

Lucas froze, eyes front, hands in midair.

"What are you going to do?"

"I am going to staple this stuff over the vents in the soffit, to keep the birds from getting up under your eaves and building nests and shitting on your siding." It took great control for him to speak that slowly, clearly.

"And you have to do it right now? I mean, it must be two in the morning."

Lucas looked at his watch and then back at Phyllis, stared at her as if he were having trouble translating her language. He didn't want to sleep, he didn't want to stop and wait for sleep to overtake him, he wanted to push himself until he dropped—at least that was what Zoe recognized.

Phyllis clenched her jaw, swallowed visibly. "I don't know whether I'm being pushed around or cared for."

"Give it a while," Lucas said, "and you ought to be able to tell the difference." Unblinking, he watched her, as she appeared to consider this. Then her shoulders fell forward.

"I'll be inside," she said.

Lucas was on the ladder, his feet over Zoe's head, when she realized that she must love him. She wasn't sure why—maybe because he didn't belong to her mother, maybe because there was something so definite about him, but it wasn't a boyfriend sort of love. He didn't have to return it; in fact she would rather he didn't. He just had to stay there, in her life, and let her watch him while he fixed things, and she would privately love him. The ladder flexed in toward the house.

"You sure this will hold you?" she called up to him. "What if the three pieces came apart?"

"I checked everything out," he called from the higher rungs. "But thanks for your concern."

She pursed her mouth. He was pressing the strip of screen against the eaves with the fingertips of one hand. With the other he tried to bring the staple gun into range, but he couldn't get it there: the shoelace was too short. He cursed and then tugged again, but only managed to hike his pants up the right side where he'd tied it. The ladder shuddered, and Zoe clutched it for all she was worth.

Then resolutely, Lucas climbed up a rung, and then another, until his head and shoulders ran out of ladder, the tips of which had come to rest just below the gutters. He wrapped his legs around the top rungs, twisted his right hip toward the house, and blindly felt the screen into place, firing the staple gun along its edges, clunk, clunk. He wavered precariously at each recoil. She gaped up at him in wonder, and not just his body at that odd foreshortening angle, but his whole heroic being seemed clear to her, shining. She was still afraid he would fall, but just as sure that there was a way to fall, a way to land so you didn't get hurt, and Lucas would know what it was.

In a few minutes he was down, and without pausing to comment or change the arrangement with the inadequate shoelace, had moved the ladder and mounted it again. He did this three times, four. And Zoe remained dutifully at its foot, face upturned, holding him in place with her eyes.

At first she thought her ears had begun to ring from craning her neck so long. She covered and uncovered them—the noise was outside, she had never heard it start, and now it had grown in volume to something shrill and unpleasant. Beyond the cluster of townhouses to the south, a long cloud of black birds hung in the pale violet sky. They were their own fixed path, funneling in from the invisible distance, spreading to rest in the saved trees at the base of the back slope. The shrieking came from the trees; when you looked closely among the leaves, it was as if each branch was thick with black fruit. Zoe had never seen anything like it.

When Lucas came down to move the ladder for the last time, she said, "They don't like what we're doing." It did seem their shrieking was directed at the two of them. "Maybe they think you've caught one of their friends up there behind the screen," Zoe said, to be amusing, but Lucas said it was just what starlings did, gather for the night in communal roosts. They had probably been there every night since early spring, carrying on, making a mess. She had just never noticed it.

"I guess I'd rather sleep under our eaves where I could get comfortable than have to balance all night on a tree branch," said Zoe.

"Starlings are the roaches of the bird world," Lucas called down meaningfully as he climbed one last time. A few minutes later he was finished, sliding the ladder back to carrying size with loud clanks.

"Could you see whether they've built any nests yet up there?" Zoe asked.

"Didn't look," Lucas said.

"Probably they haven't yet." She gazed skeptically at the streaks and blotches on the siding.

"Hard to say. It is that time of year. You know," Lucas went on, "being a pilot, there's no love lost between myself and birds. I could tell you a story or two about the accidents they've caused, hitting propellers, getting sucked into jet engines, gumming up the works. A couple months ago out of Kennedy a bunch of gulls sailed right up into one of my engines two minutes after takeoff."

"That's weird. What happened to them?"

"The point isn't what happened to them. The way a jet turbine works, it's got these finely balanced blades. A bird carcass gets in there and the engine chokes up." Zoe made a little gagging sound of revulsion. "Look," Lucas said, "that engine was ruined. I had to fly out over the Atlantic and dump 100,000 pounds of fuel before that jumbo was light enough to land minus an engine. That's good money down the drain, not to mention the danger. When you look at it that way; it's them or us."

Zoe could tell that she was being tested. She wasn't supposed to waste sympathy on the gulls, act squeamish at their fate. That was all right. She could see that a jumbo jet was more important than a handful of birds. Lucas was realistic. How much he knew about certain things—clear, definite knowledge. She searched her mind for something comparably definite to say, something to suggest she was in agreement with him on the issue of birds. But all that came to mind in that driving clamor of bird screams was a jumble of her mother's pronouncements, bitter and nebulous as a mouthful of smoke.

Lucas has showered in Zoe's tub and crashed on the sofa, which Phyllis fixed up for him. There was nothing for mother and daughter to do then but retire early to their own rooms upstairs and downstairs, leaving him the middle. Was it because Lucas was watching that Zoe hugged her mother before they parted, something she never did willingly, unless for a camera? And why her mother's body seemed so sadly appealing to her arms—her mother's odd scorched smell, so suddenly sweet—Zoe didn't know.

Zoe won't be able to eat tonight because she doesn't dare try to sneak by Lucas. That is all right. She would much rather know he is stationed there at the center of the house, a guardian of order. Stomach clenched around its treasured pain, she lies awake thinking about this man—his determination on the ladder, when he thanked her for her concern. She goes over and over these moments in her mind, savoring them. She imagines that she has emptied herself in order to be filled more purely and perfectly by his image. When she closes her eyes, he is all she sees, poised at the foot of the ladder, then at different stages of his ascent. *Give it a while,* he keeps telling her, and she knows that he does what he does because he cares.

He has climbed far above her now, and the ladder keeps lengthening. He is climbing far beyond the roof of the house, so far she can hardly see him. Her stomach begins to ache with worry. Then the dreadful noise begins—she knows even while it is dim and distant, it is dreadful. She tries to call a warning to Lucas, but he is too high to hear, and soon the noise is deafening, and the sky darkens with enemy starlings. Lucas is engulfed by a black cloud of them; Zoe screams as loud as she can, but nothing can be heard over that noise. Then as she looks up, something comes sliding down the ladder, something shapeless, shrunken lands at her feet. She wakes up in terror, the noise still in her ears.

She must calm herself. She is awake now. She is safe inside. There are no birds, they are all asleep in the trees, balancing somehow on their branches without falling.

But that noise still shrieks in her ears, and she must make sure. She turns on the light and stumbles to the window, pulls the drape aside, tries to peer beyond the glass, through the reflection of her own room, her own body, all arms and legs, wrapped in a large men's T-shirt. She is awake now, yet it seems the noise has filled her room, and she drags open the glass door to let it out. The night air flows in, chills her into alertness. The noise inside dissipates, met as it is by another sound from above, beyond the screen, softer, but as shrill and relentless, the sort of sound, like crickets, or running water, you could confuse with silence unless you had been warned it was there.

Nominated by Shenandoah *and David Jauss*

WHAT I WANTED MOST OF ALL

fiction by DANIEL HAYES

from THE MASSACHUSETTS REVIEW

I 'VE WANTED TO achieve things. I've wanted at one time or another to lose weight or increase my vocabulary or make a lot of money in a hurry, and when I was a boy I wanted most of all to stop masturbating. In short, I've wanted to change my life, I've always wanted that, and it's a hard thing to change your life, you think it's a matter of willpower, that the reason why your life has never changed significantly is because you've never really put your mind to it, you've never made the required sacrifices, but then you do put your mind to it, you become obsessed with changing your life and make a concerted effort, and your life doesn't change, not one bit, and that's not encouraging.

My father once told me a story about going into a public restroom and seeing a man with only one arm—he was standing at an adjacent sink—and my father realized that he'd seen this same man back at the urinal, only he hadn't noticed the missing arm, or he hadn't noticed that there *was* a missing arm, either because he'd seen only the man's "good" side or because he'd been too busy minding his own penis. My father felt sorry for the man and offered to help him wash his single hand, because it's not easy to wash your hand when that hand is your only hand, and the man was touched by my father's gesture, or at least that's what my father said. I can't remember my father ever describing the actual washing of the hand, but he was always a very thorough man, and I can imagine him sandwiching the man's hand between the two of his own, and scrubbing it first with soap, then rinsing it and carefully drying it with paper towels, though it's also possible that my father used only one of his hands and that he worked in conjunction with the man in washing his hand, that together they made up a set of hands, one squeezing the other or however it is that hands get washed, and either this strategy failed in its objective, because the man wasn't at all accustomed to the idea of hands working in unison since he'd never had two hands, or the strategy succeeded and yet reminded the man of a time when he *had* had both hands intact, which might've also led him to recall the way that the one hand had once worked, however unconsciously, in partnership with the other, and in that case I suspect that the man left the restroom not only with a clean hand but with a deep sense of sorrow, having been reminded in such a practical and sensual way of what was no longer his. I'm mentioning the breadth of possibility, I'm wondering what actually did happen, because I really don't know for sure, and because I think it's possible that my father made up the whole story, or maybe it was that my father did offer to help the one-armed man but was rebuffed, or maybe my father washed the man's hand but then couldn't help afterward washing his own two hands with unusual care, contagion no less compelling an idea than love. But in any case what now seems significant to me is that I never could believe my father's account, even at that age—I think I must've been twelve or thirteen—even then I knew enough to wonder why my father was telling me the story in the first place, and I knew the story threw my father in a favorable light and that what I wanted most of all—it kept coming back to this—I wanted a father who washed a one-armed man's hand and never told anyone about it and never gained any satisfaction from not telling anyone. But my father wasn't like that, maybe nobody's father is like that, and I've always thought of his story as the very beginning of doubt in me, the plight of never knowing for sure and never quite trusting what others say because there is always a story behind any story.

One time, ten or so years ago, I was sitting around with a group of people—it must've been at a dinner party—and one of them said that he had nothing in the least to hide, that he couldn't think of even one thing that would so embarrass him that it would stop him from telling us, from revealing the secret to us, and I remember immediately thinking of a number of possible revelations, things I knew about him that he didn't know I knew. In his mind he wasn't really capable of embarrassment, he was one of the lucky ones who can fool themselves into thinking of their lives as open to inspection, although it should also be said, it's only fair to say, that some people make up secrets and then act as though they've been burdened with them, and it seems foolhardy to think that so-called sensitive people have secret lives and that everyone else doesn't, both seem equally unlikely. Still, I've always suffered from this sense of having three hundred and seventy-one secrets and no place to keep them all, I keep spouting one leak after another. So maybe it was resentment that I felt toward that fellow at the dinner party, maybe I had it in for him because I couldn't be as carefree as he could, having secrets was too important to me, it gave me a mysterious quality that I thought others didn't have, and I imagined them the lesser for not having their secrets, for not having *my* secrets. It's always struck me as extraordinary that you can tell someone that you have a secret, let's say this *one* secret, and it absolutely takes the wind out of them if you don't reveal it right there on the spot, people think it's the height of impropriety if you say you have a secret and then don't tell it, but my feeling's always been that if you tell it, then you don't have it any longer, that's the nature of secrets, so it seems reasonable to tell someone that you have a secret—how would they know if you didn't tell them?—and then refuse to reveal what the secret is, that's the best way of creating and maintaining power.

The one I'm thinking of, she taught me the meaning of satisfaction and together we lived in a sheltered world, it wasn't my world and it wasn't her world, and it certainly wasn't *the* world, which is where you're really supposed to go with a woman, the two of you presenting yourselves as a couple for the scrutiny of others, an approach that was clearly impossible with the woman I'm talking about, and our failure in that regard was eventually our downfall. Every time we went out into public—even into a restaurant by ourselves, though I'm thinking more of certain occasions when we'd see other people in twos or threes or fours—it was a disaster, for neither of us had much aptitude for public talk, we both resorted to masks and couldn't so much as recognize each other, let alone prove ourselves recognizable to others, or at least to those who actually knew us, but when we were alone, just this woman and I, we stayed *inside* and created a world of games and names, it was all a matter of *keeping up* (not with the Joneses but with one another), and it was impossible to describe this world to anyone else (I can remember trying), though I guess that's what I'm doing right now, or taking a stab at it, for my benefit and edification as much as for yours. Feminine allure had always been for me a form of escape, a way of entering another world, I realize now that it was a way of gaining admission to the adult world, even after my status as an adult was secure, a foregone conclusion, even when I was an adult-and-a-half I'd still look at a woman and think she held behind her the key and if I could only wrestle it away from her I'd become something respectable, which was why those excursions into the public were so frightening and fraught with anxiety, they were supposed to show that I was an adult and that this woman was the reason why. Women were always coattails for me—I can see that now—and I always managed to find and sleep with women who saw *men* as coattails, I guess that was a little stupid of me, and together we were stepping all over each other, this woman and I, screaming at each other to grow up and take the initiative. As a boy I thought of sex as the quickest ticket out of the family, it was either fuck your sister or fuck someone else's sister, excuse the bluntness, and the latter strategy managed to get you the hell out of the family, and the family was in my view—and I'm referring now to my perspective as a child—a suffocating nest that offered only a mediocre form of privacy, and so the first girl I ever had sex with was an *out*, I used her in that sense, and I can still remember the thrill of having sex with her, doing what I knew my mother (not to mention *her* mother) would never condone, and this girl was willing to do anything, and we did everything, we even one time included her sister and a Siamese cat in the venture—two years younger and all legs is how I remember her, the cat didn't figure prominently—and the thrill of it was always to go on a kind of field trip unlike any other pre-adult field trip, and possibly, always possibly, to produce something new, some-

238

thing that belonged to a new kind of family, which gave me a power, so that if I was still under the authority of my father, I was also sleeping with a girl whom he couldn't sleep with, and I might just become a father myself. Of course I felt guilty about all of this, I was hardly *free* in my sexuality, there was always the guilt, always a parental figure to elude, or subvert, and my clearest memory is of being in the girl's bedroom, with the door open, in accordance with her mother's notions of modern chaperonage, engaging in cunnilingus and yet at the same time preoccupied with something else, and for that reason always staying alert, keenly listening for her mother's footsteps up the staircase, a kind of warning signal it was. No, not privacy by any stretch of the imagination but an idea of pleasure as coming from subversion, from doing what you weren't supposed to do, though of course there were church mice, and I would later become one for a spell, who saw it the other way, who couldn't understand it all as a game, as a way of creating excitement.

I visited his office twice a week for about five years, sitting in a chair—it was always the same chair, though the location of the office changed a couple of times—a chair that wasn't comfortable and it wasn't uncomfortable, and he sat across from me, his feet usually on an ottoman, legs crossed at the ankles, and a small white clock sat next to me on a table, it was facing Dr. Weiss, that was his name, and he'd look at the clock sometimes, I'd catch him, but he had to do that, there wasn't any other way to know that fifty minutes had elapsed, and for the first year I think I felt hurt almost every time he said, Well, our time's up, or whatever it was he said to end things, I can't remember exactly. Most often I'd leave the office in a depression, not so much from having brought to the surface certain facets of my life that I wished didn't exist, but from the embarrassment of having sat there and talked myself blue in the face for fifty minutes (as a rule, Dr. Weiss said almost nothing), talking about anything that came into my mind, or *almost* anything, and I worried most not about my own predicament, what had led me initially to seek psychiatric help, but about my performance in the office, as a patient, I worried whether my fifty-minute monologues had wowed the doctor or not, whether I'd come off as a fool or just what, and of course I had little indication one way or the other from Dr. Weiss, since he said so little, and if I asked, and in my weakest moments I did ask, he'd simply throw the question back at me, and he was right to do that, my doubts were at the heart of what needed investigation, and he'd say, Why would I think you're a fool? You'd think it, I'd say, because I'm squirming in this chair, I'm vomiting words and hoping against hope that the overall impression is favorable. I remember how I'd usually leave the office with a morbid sense that he was happy to be done with me, that after I left he'd open the door to another patient, a preferred patient, someone who talked eloquently for the fifty minutes, making sense and reaching significant conclusions, and I wasn't like that, I was always saying one thing and then immediately qualifying it with another, a zigzag that got nowhere, so that if you were to transcribe the whole thing and then whittle away the asides and qualifications, the prefatory comments and heartfelt vacillations, there wouldn't be enough left to fill even one lousy page. I can remember one time, with this failure in mind, deciding that I'd qualify nothing, that I'd be straightforward and that I wouldn't guess all the time at his secret reaction to what I was saying, and the next session took forever, more like fifty hours than fifty minutes, and I said almost nothing, I couldn't think of anything to say, it's a patient's nightmare, and Dr. Weiss simply sat and stared, and occasionally he smiled, I'm not sure why, either embarrassed for himself or feeling sorry for me.

I can't really remember any longer what it was like at the time, I'm forced to almost make it up as though it never happened, but it did happen, and at the time I was trying to put the pieces together, I know that, and most of all I wanted an anchor, I was in my early twenties and I wanted something that was stable and that I could call my own, or something that would call me its own. I'd attended Sunday school as a child, the church was never really pushed on me but it was there, it was a convenient place to begin the search. I wanted something solid then and I still want that, but I can't find it anymore, and I've grown accustomed to not finding it, I look around and nothing seems especially transcendent, nothing really fits the bill. I can remember as a boy how I'd find these rocks and I'd keep them, two or three at a time, I'd set them on the nightstand next to my bed, and I thought of them as precious, but eventually I'd take them outside and toss them just about anywhere, it really didn't matter, they'd become ordinary again. Now I'm left with the normal expedients, such as sex, it's this huge container into which you can throw just about anything, and in that sense sex is not unlike religion, since one of the things people do with religion is assume it as a ubiquitous category, which means that everything from this morning's rainfall to Aunt Betty's cancerous tumor becomes religiously significant, and that's how I used to think, it's shameful now to admit it, there was a time when I believed in God and even went to church, though attending services finally proved too disheartening, there was always this feeling afterward in the pit of my stomach, I couldn't ever get over that, the feeling afterward, it was the same feeling I'd felt as a child after being dragged to a Sunday service. Someone I once knew, an assistant minister at a Presbyterian church in another town, we were in his office one day and he said he wanted to say something to me, he had something important on his mind, but first there was a bit of gossip, a story about a man who was coming in for counseling and whose wife was truly beautiful, the minister referred to her as *comely*, that seemed a strange way of putting it, and the man was impotent, that was the twist, because somehow his wife's beauty intimidated him, and they prayed together—the minister and this man—right there in his office, week after week, eyes closed and heads bowed toward each other, they prayed for an erection is what it must've been, not a typical prayer request, not the kind you stand up and make in church when the minister asks whether there's any *special* requests—no, those are always reserved for some poor asshole who's dying and doesn't think it's his turn—and I think about that man from time to time, I don't know what's become of his wife's beauty but I wonder whether God ever answered his prayers. After telling me about the impotent man, that was just a teaser, this minister spoke frankly and said that it was his opinion that my main weakness as a Christian was in not loving my fellow believers, and of course he was right, people usually are when they say things to me, and eventually I did leave the church because of that weak link, my intolerance of others, and after that it was just God and me, as Protestant a religious experience as you're likely to run into, and we fought it

241

out, just the two of us, and then even that went away, I didn't believe in God anymore. It's a shameful thing to lose your faith. I can remember those first few days after I'd formally decided that I had nothing in me any longer, no belief whatsoever, I'd been drained of faith, it was like the end of a marriage, but it was also like being born all over again, it was somehow deeply religious I can't help but admit, and the world was completely new, and what before had seemed like too much confusion and chaos was now pure luster, not that things were necessarily better but the stage lights were shining a little more intensely on the surface of things, laying bare a new set of temptations, and I didn't feel myself so much drawn, I'd simply become a different kind of voyeur.

I felt no particular intimacy for any of the customers, except for this one, a man who always wore the same threadbare brown suit, who walked into the bookstore every Sunday night at nine-thirty, his hair slicked back with an oily substance or maybe it was just water, his skin as white as skin gets, a middle-aged man of small stature who suffered from a case of nerves, to say the least, and when he spoke, and he never spoke freely, he spoke as though he didn't want to speak, as though it made him twice as anxious to open his mouth as it did to keep it closed. He told me once, he whispered it as though there might be others interested to know, he said he worked for a gentleman's estate, that the gentleman was a bibliophile, that the gentleman never went out into public. That was the extent of what he said, but I felt lucky to be told anything, I knew he'd never told any of the other employees, he must've sensed their impatience with all that he asked of them, their unwillingness to cooperate with his vision of things, and it's my guess, I might be wrong, but I think that that's why he eventually came only on Sunday evenings, when I worked alone. He'd spend an hour walking around the store, deciding on the books he wanted to purchase, asking me occasionally to pull down a book that was beyond his reach, selecting maybe fifteen or twenty, mostly out-of-print art books—except for a few pocket-books on spinning racks, our stock was made up entirely of used titles—and when he was ready he'd bring them to the front counter, just before ten-thirty, that was when we'd close, and once at the counter, I'd be on one side and he'd be on the other, he'd insist, always with an economy of gesture, I never remember there being any words, he'd insist that he alone be allowed to touch the books, as though these used books had suddenly become clean and pure as soon as they'd been chosen, and so we came up with a procedure, I indulged his conceit, or maybe I indulged *in* his conceit, in any case he'd open each book to the first page and show me the price as marked, and I'd enter the price in the cash register, and then he'd place the book in a box (I'd have gotten one from the back room), which he'd already lined with brown paper bags, unopened and laid flat, and then he'd open the next book, I'd enter its price—in no time we'd be working as a team, taking satisfaction in the coordination of our efforts—and he'd stack each book in the box, one atop the other, but always with an unopened bag laid flat between the books, so that no two books ever touched once they were rung up, once they were officially his, and that made a kind of sense. One time he had two boxes of books, he'd bought more than his typical share, and he asked me to help carry them to his car, and together we went outside, it was an old Pontiac parked around the corner, and after he opened the door, just as I was beginning to set the box on the front seat, he slipped a paper bag between the box and the seat, he did it as though he had to. What I didn't sense at the time was the extent of this man's problem, the scope of what he was undertaking, which is to say I never realized that there was no gentleman, no figurehead of the estate, I never realized that this man was himself the bibliophile, the one who never showed his face in public, and maybe that's what we had in common, because at the time I never showed my face in public, appearances to the contrary.

It was in Dr. Weiss's office that I first spoke of sex, before that I'd never had anyone with whom to talk about it, I think it safe to say that I was mostly young and naive at the time, a wealth of adolescent sexual experiences notwithstanding, but during the last year and a half of my treatment we rarely spoke of sex but almost exclusively of one another, what was going on or not going on between us, though I talk about this as though Dr. Weiss were talking too, telling me of his own life, confessing to me his innermost doubts and desires, and of course all of that was very much off-limits. I remember once seeing Dr. Weiss on the street with a little girl, it must've been his daughter—I don't remember the color of her dress but I can still see the tiny pair of pink socks— and yet afterward, at our next session, there wasn't anything much to say, after I'd mentioned seeing him there wasn't anywhere to go with the topic, he simply stared at me and waited for some elaboration, and I think what I wanted most was to know something further about him, frankly I liked him, there was a kind of nervous restraint to his demeanor that I identified with, with which I could sympathize, and I tried at points to tell him that, that I liked him, and he'd stare at me, and I'd say, You probably think I don't know the first thing about you, but I really do, I can see by the way you hold yourself, it's in your gestures and your facial expressions, and occasionally you say something that gives away how you think, a disposition toward sadness is how I think of it, and by this point I know every tie you own and all your shoes, of which you have only two pairs, remarkable as that seems.

At one time I couldn't stand the idea of having another person living on the other side of my apartment wall, or living above or below me, and when I wasn't living in an urban setting I never had enough money to benefit from the privacy of a house, a single-family dwelling is what I think they call it, so I'd sit in some apartment, when I was younger, and I'd listen, and I'd figure they were listening too, and I'd walk around all the time as though there was someone else there listening to me, as though there were really two of me, one watching and one being watched, and I realize now that I don't do that anymore. I also don't have as many secrets, and I could be wrong, I'm really only guessing here, but I tend to think that when you're on your deathbed with your thirty-odd secrets, or however many you're left with at that advanced age, I'll bet those secrets melt away right before your eyes, one by one, and you're forced to do without any secrets at all—that is, without any sense of self-importance. It's a good thing to be less paranoid, even if you have to relinquish some of your secrets to get to that point, you never get something for nothing, it's one trade-off after another as far as I'm concerned, and the psychotic who finally decides that he *isn't* the king of Prussia is making a decision about what's more important, and what's always seemed most important of all, and I'm deeply convinced of this, I lose all cynicism when I get to this, what's most important is to keep making those decisions—however unconscious they may be, I'm not sure where intention comes into this—to keep making those decisions about what is and isn't important, realizing that what's important has a way of changing. When I was a young man, I wouldn't have liked the man I am now, or who knows, I might've been amused by him, but probably not, he probably would've struck me as someone I wouldn't want to become, and of course now when I think back upon myself as a young man I'm glad I'm not like that anymore, all nerves and misplaced intensity, though of course I *am* that person, we're one and the same, I guess we just don't always see eye to eye.

She was unabashed, I liked that about her, and she had a large mouth, it was huge, and when she'd smile she wouldn't so much smile as pinch her lips together and curl the edges of her mouth, so that she smiled when she tried not to smile, and when she actually tried to smile, then her mouth opened wide, it became a big dark circle that let out a laugh that caught like a cough, and I can remember kissing her, I remember wanting to kiss her and then getting to kiss her, being lost somewhere in that mouth, my eyes closed and my mind swimming. But things changed, and it was the mouth that changed first, or I changed it, the way I thought about it, it became a receptacle of ill-feeling, I began to see that when eating she lacked the oral coordination necessary to get the food into her mouth without smudging the edges, so that invariably I'd see food, little wet bits of food, stuck on her lips, and it bothered me to see food on the outside and knowing it should be on the inside, it was a problem of placement. I'd say, You've got food on your mouth, and then I'd take a napkin to wipe away the fleck of food and she'd react instantly, moving her mouth toward me, the way children sometimes do, as though hands were of limited usefulness, and it was that gesture—the mouth moving toward me, the chin slightly lifted—I could find no forgiveness for that gesture, and in my mind her mouth had become unwieldy and even ugly, it's a terrible thing to say.

I don't remember thinking about it until years after I'd left college, and then suddenly, it wasn't really a choice, or it didn't feel

245

like a choice, I realized that I wanted to do something with my life, I wanted to make a difference, however corny and foolhardy that may sound now, and I wanted to do it in the theater because that's what I knew something about, an inheritance from my grandfather, and it was in the theatre that my talents lay, if they lay anywhere—more often than not they seemed strewn everywhere in insufficient measure—but there's a difference between strongly desiring something and actually getting there, and I never did get there, I never got close. No one gets there without ambition, that's for sure, but there are ambitious people who never do get there, there are even ambitious people who never set one foot in front of the other, they sleep ambitiously and they'll die ambitiously, and that's sad but at least they know what they're missing, there's a kind of knowledge gained in wanting something and never getting it, it's called disappointment, and the people who get it don't always know what it's like not to get it and the people who never wanted it, or somehow judged the object of desire as beyond the realm of possibility, and therefore took the healthy route and expelled it from their minds, those people don't know what disappointment is, they've never felt it. Disappointment is knowing what the jacket looks like and knowing what it would be like to wear it, but then you never do get your hands on the jacket, and that's a shame, that's enough to make you realize what life's really about, it's about wanting I think, and everyone wants at least one thing and would give up just about anything for that one thing, but no one gets to live longer than the designated period, I don't care what the preachers say, and some poor suckers don't even get that far—a friend of mine drowned in a river when he was twelve, asshole couldn't swim (isn't dog-paddling some kind of survival instinct?). But even those people who live to be a hundred years old don't get a hundredth of what they really want, and that's disappointment whether you're still around to feel it or not, and a person must sense it, or at least fear it, when you're lying in bed, it's your last day on earth, forgive the morbidity, and you want *more* and you aren't going to get it, and years before, alive and healthy, you'd spent your adult life reading magazines and newspapers and watching television and hearing about it, right and left you'd heard about the people who had their fingers on the pulse, hands

246

on the ropes, you'd ended up worshipping those who got what you wanted, you'd been driven as much by envy as by anything else.

I was living in New York at the time, and I'd come home to my apartment, a sublet in Little Italy with wooden floors painted an institutional gray, it was a nice enough apartment, a few cockroaches but I'd seen so many terrible apartments and this one seemed a castle in comparison, and I went over to the sink to get a drink of water, it was the height of summer and oppressively hot, and I was at the sink, running the water, waiting for it to get sufficiently cold, it didn't always come out cold right away, and I looked out the window at an apartment building next door, and one floor down I saw into an apartment that had venetian blinds that were open and I could see a woman standing in what appeared to be a bedroom, she was wearing a teddy, I think that's what it's called, it was cream-colored and she was very pretty and I was watching and thinking that coincidence had somehow led to *this,* it wasn't the kind of thing that transforms your life but you take what you get. I was still holding the glass under the running water, or beside the running water, and watching this woman as she sat on the edge of a bed and she began rolling a pair of stockings up her legs and connecting them to the doodads at the top, attached to the teddy they must've been, and I stood by the window for a moment, then suddenly realized that I could also be seen, so I walked over and switched off the kitchen light and returned to the window, and by this time there was a man in the room as well, standing beside the woman and dressed only in a white T-shirt and darkly-colored socks that were limp around his ankles, and he picked her up, right off the ground, and tossed her on the bed, and the act of tossing—she flew through the air and landed on the bed, she would've broken a bone if there'd been no bed—that act of tossing, it was both aggressive and spoke of something between them, and that *something* was reflected as well in the look on her face after he'd tossed her, after she'd landed she was smiling widely, her eyes spoke excitement, and then the man lay down on the bed, too, and it didn't take long before they were fucking, though to tell the truth there was something wild and confused about the entire session, I quickly noted the conspicuous absence of sound, that would've helped,

247

and I felt—and maybe this always happens, maybe it's part of the price of admission—I felt *outside*, looking in, not knowing what was going on, and with the distinct impression that *this* was not how it would've looked if I'd been the man, and before long I was thinking another thought, I was thinking that maybe this thing had been set up for my benefit, or for someone else's, maybe it wasn't at all authentic, maybe they knew the blinds were open (as far as I could remember, they'd never been open before), and maybe they wanted to be seen, it was a show in some sense, and people have sex differently when they know they're being watched, or whether they know for sure or not they suspect or want to be watched, it's more like a pornographic movie, though of course it *would* look that way to me, since I was essentially looking at a screen, sitting in a theater, and how was I to doubt that this wasn't a true voyeuristic experience? But there are two kinds I think, two kinds of voyeurism I mean, one where you see something raw, pure, something not intended to be seen, and the other where someone is playing to you, giving you a wink of the eye the whole time, and I like the former and not the latter, because as I watched and eventually she began rubbing against him, that's really the only way I can describe what I saw, part of their bodies were by this time obscured by the edge of the window, at first I felt betrayed because it was made-up, it was almost an act of charity that I naturally resisted, but then everything changed, and the sex became something more private, it was a kind of rubbing for her, a secret way she achieved pleasure, and it was more pragmatic, not as pretty or picturesque, and at that moment I liked the woman, maybe I even loved her.

My grandmother used to talk to herself, she'd walk around her house and conduct elaborate conversations, and I grew up wanting to resist that impulse, I understood the desire and yet I was determined to conquer it, but all along I must've known there was a reason behind the impulse, a split in the mind I guess it's called. As a boy I sometimes had a habit, I couldn't control myself, I'd think about things I didn't want to think about, there'd be a voice inside that would say things I didn't want to hear, and I'd tell myself to stop thinking these things, but of course that didn't do a lot of good, and eventually I got so I didn't like the uncontrollable voice, I'd been fascinated but now I'd lost patience with it, I'd gotten scared is what it was, and so I began to say, Fuck you, I whispered those words to myself, a little snarl, and I can remember one summer—my sister and I were staying with our grandparents—I said this same thing, Fuck you, over and over, and after that things got easier, the other voice lost some of its authority and I became less afraid. Years later, after my mother died, I'd visit my father maybe once every two years, he was living then in a retirement community, and whenever I was around him I was nearly speechless, I could never think of what to say, it was a kind of power I had over him, he'd end up doing all the talking, an endless babble, and yet only a few hours later, after I'd left my father, someone would meet me at an airport and we'd be in a car on the way home and I'd be running at the mouth, rambling incessantly, there'd be this long string of words coming out, no hint of control, and I sounded just like my father, I was convinced of it—the same intonation, the same painstaking delivery.

Nominated by The Massachusetts Review

HOPKINS AND WHITMAN

by LYNNE McMAHON

from KENYON REVIEW

Hard to imagine two men more unlike, the one
a solitary wrestling in his cell with palpable Doubt,
the other striding the continent in great unbooted
certainty. And yet there was that kinship, pitched

past pitch of grief, and battlefield nursing—
"What is removed drops horribly in a pail"—
and Hopkins' own admission: "I know Walt Whitman's
mind to be more like my own than any man's living.

As he is a very great scoundrel, this is not
a pleasant confession." How magnetic the expanse
between fastidious and crude when cast
into the field of dappled things! For Hopkins,

the cows and finches and trout of a world whose
stippled shadows served to throw into relief
the Godlight, though his own scree of darkness,
the mountainslide, the mind's cliffs of fall,

was for days heaped on days impenetrable;
for Whitman, the skewed patchwork of criminal
and child twinned in one body and one land,
sending out its pied beauty in a cruel Morse—

blue/gray, blue/gray—horrible and redemptive
at once, for the Godlight shone through the stippled
bandages. . . . This was a man and country
straining to heal itself, something the English

priest in exile's Dublin knew something
about. Cold Ireland must have warmed a little
when the Classics Professor, Society of Jesus,
opened the newspaper to rawly dazzling American

nakedness. Unruly America would have bent
at once to the rigors of principle, had those
rigors been in print. But it was less their lives
which rang accord than it was their deaths,

though Whitman had his pharoahnic tomb,
secured with locks against robbers, and Hopkins
a bare-stripped room. It was their deaths
that knelled through the poems from the earliest

verses: Whitman, so much a part
of the sea he loved and feared, drowned
in the oceanic emphysema of his lungs. His last
day he was moved onto a sort of water bed

on the floor, "Oh I feel so good" his last words
when he heard the waves falling against
his sides. And Hopkins, spent with the typhoid
his fevered poems had long pointed to,

after great agitation, this clearing: "I am so happy."
And surely God stood at his pillow then.
And surely the sea made its smooth reclamation.
If we take heart in anything, it is a serene death

and the poems unfolding in reverse that we
might see death in all its guises, back to the first
awareness: "We hear our hearts grate on themselves:
it kills to bruise them dearer."

Yet they bruised them
again and again, in unlike piety,
to bring back to the world a praise
for the world, for which we give thanks.

Nominated by Christopher Buckley, Brenda Hillman, Donald Revell, Pamela Stewart

RUSH HOUR

by LAURIE SHECK

from THE PARIS REVIEW

These are the objects, the touchable—table, refrigerator,
   chair,
grease-splattered whiteness and woodgrain.
And here is the sound of the baby muttering and cooing,
background noise, static, the swish of cars outside
flashing by like an anger in the brain,
and the red-white-and-blue license plates with their
   picture of Lady Liberty—
she's holding up her torch
as she's swept on above the muddy roadway. What story
   would you see

peering into these lit windows?—
Mother and child, the fragile solidities
against the white wall, and the calendar where two bison
hunch like breathing hills
at the edge of the Firehole River, in the snow,
as the river, all slowness, all certitude, gleams and pools
   where it widens
round and smooth as handcuffs. The child is holding up a
   raisin
box, the mother turning from the child to the window
to the child. And the noise of the radio blurring

tomorrow's weather and the stockmarket's closing, the
   traffic report

that lingers there, hanging in her mind, until she sees
the slowed bunched cars bumper to bumper in the miles,
headlights on, stuck there and stuck there, and the
    featureless
trapped heads of the commuters staring through the small
strict windshields and the windows on either side where
    they can see
the gulls scavenging the landfill, and beyond that the
    smokestacks,
the metal-choked junkyards, the white aspirin-shaped oil
    drums
dotting the brown land. And in that noise, the child, all
    alone,

is leaning where the mother cannot follow,
into that separateness, that gash
where the world opens,
where pain and fear and beauty open. She leans and leans
in the sick fluorescent light, refrigerator hum, the clicking
of the oven as it cools. She can't
walk yet, she can't talk or even crawl.
So this is what it means to be *all eyes*
the mother thought in the blurred early days when she
    first held her,
this body that must learn to love the world
looking out at it with all of its small being, leaning in to
    where
all sound and shape and harm must smear itself,
a stain, onto the skin. The newborn child didn't even
    know

that it had hands; to look was all it knew of reaching.
And the world leaned its otherness down over it, blur of
    fragments
shifting and dividing, the audible grown loud then hushed
to a sound much less than softness. . . .
What the child saw then were the strange shifting shapes
that were the faces; mouths, eyes,

appearing, disappearing, light, light, and the darkness
splintering, wavering, unowned.
That's what she's leaning into now, the mother thinks,
that slurring she cannot imprison, cannot catch—
that splintering that will seep into her being
year by year by year, in the dark wordless place of her
    unknowing,
until one day she feels it rooting there and feels how it has
    claimed her,
and one day she will name it, calling it her body and her
    soul.

Nominated by Rita Dove

ABOVE THE TREE LINE

by KATHY MANGAN

from SHENANDOAH

Only the tenacious
reach this summit cone—scoured
to stone by eons of wind
and rain—that I climbed to
this day in my own time,
trying to surmount
something human.
I intended to carry
only what I could bear with ease,
yet I've hauled my tethered heart
one-half mile straight up
through densities of sun-
doused birches, fountains
of ferns that swept my knees—
clasped evergreens, then scrambled
over palm-rasping rocks
past stunted pine and scrub and
chalky, anonymous berry bushes up
to the gray, pocked surface
of this enormous glacial brain
in whose corrugations thistle
and lichen sprout. Strangely,
seeing birds circling
overhead, I don't yearn
for flight, or any fanciful freedom.
The world below is mine,

though ruthless. I lean
into the breeze sweeping
seventy-five miles from the sea,
anchored by an earthly sorrow,
rooted in grief,
the ground that will never give way.

Nominated by Michael Waters

INSTALLATIONS

fiction by ROBIN HEMLEY

from ANOTHER CHICAGO MAGAZINE

One of the first things the group did was to engage its film maker-associate Ken Kobland to shoot the beautiful surrealistic movie that concludes the piece. In the film, Mr. Vawter, outfitted in Arabic-bohemian garb, prods the flesh of an elderly dead woman with his walking stick.

Stephen Holden in the New York Times

FINDING THINGS. THAT'S what I love most about my job. Over the last ten years, I've found money, rings, wallets, knives, a couple of guns, umbrellas, pens, watches. Weird little statues. I have three Buddhas sitting at home, and a big African ebony thing with an hourglass in the middle.

A lot of things you wouldn't believe. A piece or two of men's or women's underwear almost every week, sometimes fresh, more often soiled. At 2 A.M., a cigarette lighter made out of a hand grenade rolls around in the middle of the car. No one even notices, or if they do, they just think, "Someone's dumb idea of a joke," and go back to sleep or look out the window, daring the thing to explode. After all, these people ride the el everyday. They've been around the block a few times. So have I. Some people would pull the emergency brake and yell, "Run for the hills!" But you can't faze *me*. Instead, I pick up the pineapple, see it's just a lighter, and stow it in my conductor's jacket. Now it sits on my coffee table at home.

Of course, I'm not supposed to keep anything I find. Regulations state you're supposed to turn everything into Lost and Found.

Yeah, right.

At rush hour, a guy wearing polyester pants with a pattern that looks like chain mail steps onto my car. A frilly straw hat covers his head, but I notice him because he's plastered with kooky buttons all over his chest like some Soviet field marshall. The buttons have sayings on them: "Are We Having Fun Yet?" "Instant Asshole . . . Just Add Alcohol," "Wake Me Up, I'm A Lot Of Fun," "Trust Me, I'm A Doctor," "Dain Bramaged," "Hallucination Now In Progress. Please Stand By," "Ask Me If I Care," "I'm The Person Your Mother Warned You About," and "Born Again Pagan."

A little guy with half yellow and half black hair accompanies the button man. An army poncho hangs from his shoulders and a cigarette sits behind his ear. He looks faithful but bored, like the body-guard of a low-level dignitary, and carries a book with a strange title, *Utopia TV Store.*

"It took me thirty-five years to overcome my disease," the button man tells me, "but I did it."

"That's good," I say. No big surprise that he wants to talk to me. I come from a family of authority figures, My Uncle Jerry's a priest and you can see my brother Ted on billboards all over the 'burbs. He's the model for Captain Safety Belt, wearing a hat like mine and two seat belts criss-crossed like bandoliers on his chest. I've dealt with plenty of people like the button man, people who latch onto the conductor because he's the Cardinal Bernardin of the rush hour chaos. They're always holding forth to me about something or other. The camera that follows them around their apartment. Or how they saw the Holy Ghost pissing on the station escalators.

"I learned how to make buttons all by myself," says the man. "No one showed me how."

"That's nice," I say.

I lean into the intercom and announce, "No smoking, littering, or radio playing allowed. Clark and Division will be next. Clark and Division." I run those words together, and emphasize the "Vision" so it becomes ClarkandiVISION, like I'm announcing some spectacular new movie technique.

"I'm a writer," the button man tells me. "I'm writing a novel right now about my experience, and I've also got a hundred poems about my disease. My novel's going to be called, *In It To Win.* That's because I stayed in it for thirty-five years and now I'm winning."

"That's nice," I say. The guy looks his age, which is remarkable for a loon. Most of them look about twice their actual age.

Yesterday, a guy told me the Shriners had vowed to make an example of him before his twenty-first birthday. (I've dealt with other people who think The Mooses, The Elks, or The Lions Club is trying to hunt them down. I wonder if they freak out every time they see a donation box by a cash register). The kid looked to be late thirties, but I saw he was still a teenager like he said, that the lines in his face were from lack of sleep, not age.

I'm younger than the button man, but I look almost forty. My hairline is eroding faster than the beach in front of some North Shore condo. My mustache is turning gray. My voice is losing its authority, becoming thinner. And my toenails have curled and yellowed like old people's. A couple of weeks ago, I found something on my big toe, and two of my friends told me it was a bunion. A bunion! I didn't think the word even entered your vocabulary until you were eighty. Presidents aren't the only ones who age in office. Conductors, too.

As we make the brake-screeching turn to Clark and Division, the button man's yellow-and black-haired friend drops his book at my feet. I wait for him to retrieve it, but he acts like it's just some litter he's not going to bother with.

"A movie company is going to interview me tomorrow," the button man says. "They want to do a video on me. In a little while *The Sun-Times* is going to do a story about me and my disease. Maybe not today or tomorrow, but soon. I'm that confident. I'm hot. Isn't that right, Gus?" and he nudges his buddy. "The *Sun-Times* is going to do a story on me."

"That's right," says Gus.

"He always agrees with me," says the button man and laughs.

We unload some people at Clark and Division and head off.

"It took thirty-five years out of my life."

"That's too bad," I say.

The button man starts making funny noises. "Coo Coo Coodle Coo," he sings.

After a few choruses, the button man stops abruptly, looks out the window, and shouts, "We're talking schizophrenia here." The commuters near him scoot away and look down their chests.

"This wasn't a good idea to take the el," the button man tells his friend. "Remind me never to take it again. It's too claustrophobic. It's counterproductive, and you know how I feel about things that are counterproductive."

"That's right," says his friend.

"Let's get some more buttons, Gus," the button man tells his friend. "I feel like some more buttons. How 'bout you, Gus?"

"Whatever you say." says Gus, and they both get off the car at Fullerton.

I'm a little sorry to see them go. People like them make the job interesting. I try my best to sympathize. You have to make these people feel appreciated. They lead rough lives, and besides, they're the CTA's most frequent riders.

We start up again. Gus has left his book behind. Each page has a little paragraph with titles like, "Kill Yourself With an Objet D'art" and "A Vegetable Emergency." I try figuring out a few paragraphs, but they don't make any sense. I'll turn it in to the Lost and Found.

Then, at Belmont, a girl about twenty flings herself at me and yells, "A prose poem fan. A kindred spirit."

At first, I'm thinking, "Great, another live one." She starts jabbering about the book in my hand. I'm about to tell her I just found it on the floor, but then I figure there's no harm in letting her talk. She's a runt: skinny with no hips and nubby breasts. He hair's black, short, and tufted like a boy's. But she's quick to smile and laugh, and she locks her eyes on me. A uniform freak, I figure.

Her name is Ivy, and she's from a small town about ten miles south of Beloit, Wisconsin. "Cody, Illinois," she says. "The Beefalo capital of the Midwest." She's twenty-one, a student at the Art Institute, where she's studying performance art.

"You mean like musicals?"

She laughs and says, "I mean like the Wooster Group, or Michael Meyers or Ethel Eichelberger or David Cale or John Kelly—"

"Never heard of them," I say and get up to announce the next station and open the doors.

When I return, she says, "Then you've probably heard of—" She pauses, puts a hand to her chest, and leans forward. "Laurie Anderson." She says this as though she's really saying, "Hemorrhoids." "Personally, " she continues, "I'd rather see *Beatlemania* or a strobe light flickering for forty-eight hours."

261

If you know what she's talking about, you've got me beat. But I pretend to understand her anyway, just like I did with the button man.

Ivy leans forward again. "Don't you think the el would be an ingenious place for an installation?" "Yeah, right," I say, "but not until they fix the air conditioners."

We sit across from each other other, Ivy huddles close to me, her eyes bright, and says, "I can be your accomplice."

"Sounds great," I say.

She tells me one weird story after another. A man and a woman are tied together by a three foot rope for a year. By choice. They have to follow each other everywhere. Even to the john. And they hardly knew each other before they tied the knot, so to speak. Of course, I know people who get into that sort of thing. Bondage. But Ivy shakes her head and says, "You're completely wrong and absolutely right. It's bondage of a different sort. They're making a statement about the bondage of male/female role-playing. And on the positive side, they're saying that the male and female parts of everyone are inextricably bound. The more we try to escape from the Other, the closer he/she follows."

Yeah, right.

When my shift is up, Ivy gets off with me at my stop. She seems completely oblivious to the fact that we've gotten off the train. She just keeps walking beside me and talking. Asking questions. Most of them she answers herself. I haven't figured her game yet, but I don't mind her tagging along.

I live in Wrigleyville, on Cornelia, a block from the Friendly Confines. That's my favorite neighborhood in the city. The best thing is summer. Sometimes I walk out on my back porch, and hear the national anthem shimmering from the park. You can't help but feel you're in a dream when you're doing something really ordinary, like taking a load of laundry down to the laundry room, and all of a sudden there's "The Star-Spangled Banner." Not to mention when you're sitting on the pot and a cheer of thirty thousand people comes out of nowhere. It makes you tingle. You feel like you're a part of something. Sometimes, when I hear the anthem or a cheer I drop whatever I'm doing, head over to Wrigley Field, and see if the scalpers have an extra bleacher ticket. Then I zone out in the right field bleachers for the rest of the day, drinking Old Style, getting a red nose from the sun, and yelling and screaming at the left field bleachers, "Left field sucks! Left field sucks!" One day, the Mets are in town, and Strawberry rocks one right to me. Naturally, I want to make this part of my memorabilia collection, but no way with the animals around me. "Throw it back! Throw it back!" they chant, and when I hesitate, someone sloshes beer on me. So I plop the ball back on the field, and Dawson picks it up and and tosses it to the side. Everyone around me cheers and the guy next to me gives me a nudge and belches. At that moment I feel like Strawberry's homer isn't worth diddly-squat.

At my apartment, Ivy won't stay in one spot for more than five seconds. The place is a sty, but she insists on checking out every room.

"You looking for something?" I ask. "You want something to drink? I've got Cuervo Gold and Old Style."

"I don't drink alcohol," she says, momentarily appearing in my bedroom door before crossing to the bathroom.

"Then all's I got is Tahitian Treat," I say, peering at the plastic liter bottle in my fridge. The only other thing to eat or drink is a two-foot-long summer sausage from Hickory Farms that my Mom bought me for my birthday. All the way in the back is my jar for Cubs tickets. I keep them there so that if the apartment burns up, it won't be a total loss. Right now, I have a ticket in the jar for Cubs Umbrella Day. It's a Dodgers game with Valenzuela pitching, but half of the reason I'm going is the free umbrella. I already have a Cubs AM/FM radio from Radio Day, a Cubs cooler from Cooler Day, and a Cubs briefcase from Briefcase Day.

"Tahitian Treat sounds luscious," she says.

I bring the drinks into the living room and start flipping through my records for something to play.

"What kind of music do you like?"

"You have any Sinatra?" she says.

"Does the Pope shit in the woods?"

I put on the album with "Witchcraft."

Ivy emerges from the bathroom and says, "I grew up with Sinatra," and walks to the couch and stands on top of it. She steps behind me to the end of the couch. I take a sip of Old Style. Ivy plops down and picks up her glass of red pop. She holds this out in front of her and says, "I never would have guessed Tahitian Treat looked like this. I've never seen anything so red, have you? Where do you think they get it from? Do you think there's a red dye mine in Tahiti? I bet the native miners have to wear dark goggles in the Treat mines."

"I guess so." I take another sip of Old Style.

"You've got a great view from your bathroom," she says.

"It's just the wall of the next building."

"You ever go to Exit or The Cubby Bear?"she asks.

"No."

"You know, Vacant Yellow's at the Cubby Bear on Saturday. Vacant Yellow's a group of ex-cabbies from Boston. I saw an interview with them in *The Face* this month. Can you believe Metro advertises in *The Face*? I don't go there often. Too much techno-funk. But sometimes if you just want to bop around, it's all right. If you're tired of staring into the abyss. I was in there last weekend with a whole crowd from London. They must have seen the ad in *The Face*."

Ivy takes a sip of her Tahitian Treat, and I nod. I imagine Ivy and the London crowd bopping around in the abyss.

She puts down her glass and sits back on the couch with me.

"You have an eclectic soul, don't you?" she says. "And old."

I've just finished my shift. I'm tired. I still have my uniform on. "Old King Cole was a merry old soul and a merry old soul was he," I manage.

Apparently, that's the wrong thing. Ivy slides away and gets up from the couch. She makes a slow circuit of the room. I pick up my grenade lighter from the coffee table and toss it from one hand to another for a while. Ivy ends up by my mantle and looks at me as though she's going to start a speech. I just watch her and finish my beer.

Then she picks up one of my Cuervo Gold bottles and turns it over. I have about a hundred and eighty empty Cuervo bottles around the house, fifty of them on my mantle. "What's this?" she says. "It says, 'Cicero. Sally and Mary Siriani, July 19, 1987.'"

"My Cuervo collection. It's something I started doing about five years back. Every time I finish one, I put the date I drank the bottle, and who I shared it with."

She picks up another one and reads, "Sally and Mary Siriani. Wrigleyville. July 20, 1987."

"The Sirianis and me go all the way back to kindergarten."

She picks up another one and reads, "Sally and Mary. In the gutter. July 21, 1987."

Ivy puts the bottle down, wanders back to the couch, and sits down next to me again. She sits with her hands crossed on her lap and her head tilted like a tourist listening to directions.

"Tell me about them," she says.

"There's not much to tell," I say. "They're sort of the party type. Sort of wild."

"Are you sort of wild?" Ivy says.

I half-shrug. "Yeah, sort of sort of," I say. "Let me tell you how I found that hand grenade lighter. It's quite a story."

Ivy grabs my hand grenade lighter. She knocks over the glass of Tahitian Treat. Crazily, she whips the lighter across the room.

"Duck!" she yells and buries herself in my lap.

The grenade slashes through the middle of my Cuervo collection, bounces off the mantle, and thuds twice. Two of the bottles shatter right off, glass spraying everywhere. Five others topple off the mantle, three bursting on the hardwood floor. Frank coughs into a new song. The two unbroken bottles roll toward us, one stopping against a leg of the coffee table.

Ivy stays in my lap, hands over her head.

Slowly, she raises her head and opens her eyes. She looks around the room like someone emerging from a bomb shelter.

"Sort of sort of," she says.

Sometimes I believe that people aren't nearly as bizarre as they let on. I imagine a date with the button man.

I reach for my can of Old Style on the coffee table and tilt it to my mouth. Empty. One warm drop, as refreshing as sweat, trickles onto my tongue.

I'm not easy to faze, but I don't expect this kind of behavior from a girl I invite over. Not that I invited her over.

I feel like I've just spent an afternoon in the bleachers. The way you get when you've been drinking beer in the sun for three hours. Bleached out. Completely in-between. Up for anything. That's how I feel right now, watching Tahitian Treat drip down the leg of the coffee table and onto an empty Cuervo bottle.

I'm not sure exactly how this happens, but we wind up slow dancing in the middle of the living room, which is a mess. We dance around the debris.

In bed, her breath catches when I touch her, so I take my hand away. Ivy goes to sleep right off, but I lie there for a couple of hours before stammering into a rush hour dream. Too many people stand in the small space in between the cars, and I can't get near enough to latch the safety chains. One by one, they fall off as we round the corners.

The next day, Ivy starts bringing stuff into the apartment. She says she's been staying in Wicker Park with some junkie friends of Phil, her ex-boy friend. A pan of beef stroganoff she made disappeared and turned up a week later under a pile of clothes in one of her roommates' closets. And Phil stabbed her with a fork. She rolls up a sleeve and shows me four red marks, closely spaced. "Phil's a tag artist," she tells me. "A good one, too. But he's awfully volatile. Besides, the landlord showed up today with a cop, and the two of them started putting our furniture on the front steps. I asked Gem what was going on. 'What happened to the rent money I gave you?' I said, 'I don't know.' she said. 'I been paying him every month. Maybe he don't remember.' I figured I could stay with you a couple of days."

Within thirty-six hours of our meeting, Ivy's completely installed herself in my apartment. I'm just a bystander. I don't say yes and I don't say no. But I'm curious.

We pass through a white curtain into this scene: a darkened room with a naked man and woman, thirtyish, lying like two sticks of old butter in the middle of the room. Either they're dead or manikins. The music in the room sounds like the part in *The Wizard of Oz* where Dorothy and her boyfriends are looking at the witch's castle, and the soldiers march around singing: "O-li-o-eyohhh-oh."

Ivy takes my hand and we approach the couple on the floor. A dozen other people saunter around as though nothing special's going on. We can't get any closer than five feet. The couple on the floor are surrounded by hundreds of apples in the shape of a cross. A ragged bat hangs above them, its ribbed wings stretching six feet. A sideways neon light sways between the wings and glows pale blue.

This is what Ivy calls an installation. This is what I call a fun house.

Up close, I see their chests, moving slightly, a small tremor from one of the woman's fingers touching the man's hand, a flickering eyelid. I study them and wonder if I've ever seen them on the el. I wonder if the woman's parents know this is what she does for a living. The man looks a little like the button man without his buttons.

Candles burn on their chests. Luckily the candles are in jars, or the wax would be excruciating. Still, the heat must get to them. Not that I can tell. They're not exactly your liveliest couple. I can imagine them showing up at Angel's Shortstop, my neighborhood bar, with them stiff as corpses on the bar stools, the candles still stuck on their chests. Angel would serve them up a couple of Old Styles, and squint at me and say, "They friends of yours?"

Yeah, they're installations.

We take the el back to Belmont and walk over to Clark Street. Everything seems strange tonight: a man waiting in the window of a tattoo parlor, the moan coming out of a storefront church.

Ivy asks me what I think about the installation. I don't know. I haven't thought about it. What are you supposed to think about a naked man and woman with candles on their chests?

"Everything," she says. "Adam and Eve lying in suspended animation beneath death and infinity. Christ figures surrounded by the forbidden fruit."

Yeah, well, I guess.

We turn the corner of Clark and Belmont, and two kids, one black and one white, not more than nine years old, slam into us as they tear through the parking lot of Dunkin' Donuts.

"Hey, watch where you're going," I say, touching the white one lightly on the shoulder.

"You watch where you're going, you fag." the kid tells me.

The black kid has a pizza box in his hands. He smiles and says, "You want some pizza?"

"Yeah, you want some pizza?" says the white kid.

The black kid opens up the box. Inside is a squirrel, its head smashed, its legs stretched out, its belly split open. At least a hundred cars have run over it. As flat as a pizza. A circle of dried tomato paste surrounds the carcass.

Before I can react, the kids run off shouting and laughing. They block one pedestrian after another yelling, "Hey, you want some pizza? Free pizza."

Ivy picks up a soft drink cup from the sidewalk and throws it after them. The cup, plastic lid and straw still attached, falls to the ground three feet away.

"You brats," she screams. "Come back here."

Ivy takes off. The white kid trips. She chases the other one. I can't make out much through the distance and pedestrians. A few minutes later, she comes smiling back with the pizza box in her hands, the lid closed.

"What do you want *that* for?" I say.

"Stealing is the most sincere form of flattery," she says. "Picasso did it. Every great artist does it."

"Throw it away."

"Are you kidding?"

"Throw it away."

"Don't give me orders. I had to fight them for it."

I don't say a word. I'm tired of her. I was curious before, but now I'm just tired. I head for Angel's Shortstop and Ivy tags along. I figure it's Ivy's turn to feel out-of-place. Not many out-of-place people ever wander into Angel's. If they do, they wander back out again in a hurry. The crowd at Angel's is as tight as a VFW post.

Ignoring Ivy, I sit down on a stool at the bar. There isn't one for her, so she stands in between my stool and the next guy's, and places her pizza box on the counter. Angel gives her a look. Then she looks at me. I order a couple of shots of Cuervo with Old Style chasers.

"I'll have to tap a new keg," says Angel. "How 'bout something else in the meantime?"

"How 'bout a mug of beefalo swill?" I say. "Come on, Angel. I'm talking brand loyalty."

"I'll go tap a new keg," she says. Angel is about sixty years old and has a white bubble hair-do. She comes to Chicago via the coal mines of Kentucky, and her husband's long-gone with black lung. Angel's jukebox has only the thickest country-and-western songs, with three exceptions: "A Cub Fan's Dying Prayer," Sinatra's version of "Chicago," and "Angel of the Morning." She's always pumping quarters painted with red fingernail polish into the juke-box and pushing those three tunes. I can't count the number of times I've come into the Shortstop and heard her belting, "Just call me Angel of the morning, baby. Just one more kiss before you leave me, darling." She thinks of the Shortstop as a family establishment, even though I'd fall off my stool if I ever saw a family walk through the door. Maybe a family of cockroaches or sewer-bred alligators. Definitely not a family of mammals.

When Angel returns with the Old Styles, Ivy pushes hers away and says, "I don't drink alcohol."

"Angel, this is Ivy," I say. "She comes from Cody, Illinois, the beefalo capital of the Midwest. It's ten miles south of Beloit."

"Blech!" says Ivy.

"What?"

"Beloit, I grew up with the name. It sounds like a quarter being dropped in a toilet. Beloit . . . Besides, I live in Chicago now."

"Yeah, she's a performance artist," I tell Angel.

"Pleased to meet you," she says.

"You want some pizza?" Ivy asks.

"No, she doesn't want any pizza." I say, and put my hand on the lid.

"Domino's?" Angel asks.

"It's not pizza," I say. "It's a squirrel."

"A squirrel."

"Yeah, a dead one."

"Pepperoni," Ivy says. "You want to see it, Angel?"

"Sure, why not?"

"No, you don't want to see, it," I say. My hand is still on the lid.

Ivy looks sideways and gives me a half smile, a dare. Her look says 'What's the big deal?' She's right. After all, Angel's not my mother.

With my job and all, I'm not easy to faze, but Ivy definitely fazes me. Not only her actions, but the way she dresses. An orange scarf as big as window drapes. Black fishnet stockings and metallic silver lipstick. Usually my life is pretty dull, but around Ivy, I feel the way I do when I'm sitting on the pot and I hear the fans cheer in Wrigley Field.

"You ever had squirrel?" says Angel. "Tastes just like chicken. Of course, there ain't as much meat on a squirrel."

"Do you always believe what you see, Angel?" Ivy says.

"Almost never," says Angel, leaning towards her, a look of concentration on her face. "A fella come in here the other day selling keychains. He had a metal man and a metal woman on the keychain, and when he wiggled a lever they started doing things. He said he had a whole trunk-full in his car, and did I want to sell some on a card behind the counter? I said, 'Look around, this is a family place.' He said, 'You'd be surprised. People just love them. I've seen grandmas and young girls go crazy over them.' 'Yeah, well this is a gay bar, buddy,' I said. 'That's fine,' he said. 'I can take off the woman and put on another man. I already did that with one gay establishment. I'll put on dogs. I'll put on a man and a horse. Even two Japanese girls and a rhinoceros if that's what you want. What ever turns you on.' Some people just want to shock you I could have called the cops, but I ignored him. Eventually, he just slithered back under his rock."

"You want some pizza?" Ivy says.

"Yeah, why not?" says Angel.

I take my hand off the lid and wait for Ivy to open up the box, but she doesn't move. What's she waiting for? I wonder if I'm going nuts. If Ivy's brainwashing me. I've known her two days, and suddenly I want to show Angel the dead squirrel in the pizza box.

"One object can have many functions," Ivy says. "Consider this pizza box. For you and me, it signifies food. For Rocky the squirrel, it's his final resting place. When you put the two together, it's repulsive. Why? Because food and death are opposites, right? No, not at all. Food and death go hand in hand, but our escapist society allows us to blithely ignore that fact. Hold the mayo, hold the lettuce, special orders don't upset us. Right, Angel? Next time you go to an open casket funeral, don't be surprised if you see a pizza with the works lying there."

I have a strange feeling in my mouth. My tongue seems to be getting bigger. I've gone through my life barely noticing my tongue, and now, all of a sudden, it seems humongous. I can't figure out where to place it. I try to settle it down by my cheek. I stick it between my teeth.

Angel tucks her chin into her neck.

My tongue has swollen to the size of a blimp.

Still, I manage to say to Angel, "Ya wa thom peetha?"

"Sure, why not?" she says.

I open up the box and Angel shrinks back.

She gives me a look and I can already tell that she's cancelled me out as a regular. Now, I'm just another bar story: "You remember Rick? He came in here with a squirrel in a pizza box. Yeah, it was dead."

Ivy shows up at work with me the next day. All she does is read poetry between stops, take notes, and draw sketches of the commuters. She's sort of nuts, but I like the way she looks at things. To her, everything's art. You can spit on the sidewalk and that's art. The commuters at rush hour are art, too. The way they crane their heads over the platform to see the train coming. They bob out as far as they can without sprawling onto the tracks. I've seen this sight everyday for ten years, but now Ivy tells me it's beautiful. All up and down the line, they wait, sticking their necks out. Ivy says they look like a bunch of pigeons jostling for breadcrumbs. All I see are some cranky people ready to be home.

When the doors open, they cram onto the car. At Washington, a couple more shove their way inside. At the next stop, Grand Ave., no one else can possibly fit, but a few try anyway, and the doors won't close. The button man and his friend are trying to jam on. He looks like he's added some buttons. Now they cover not only his chest, but his back, too. Over the intercom I say, "Clear the doors on car number five. Get in or get out and wait for the next train." Of course, no one except me has any idea which car's number five. But the button man and his friend are the ones who get off. As the doors close, I read some of his new buttons: "I Drink To Make Other People More Interesting," "No One Is Ugly After 2 A.M.," "It's Been Monday All Week," "Welcome To The Zoo," "The More People I Meet, The More I Like My Dog," "Beam Me Up Scotty . . . There Are No Virgins Left," "Only Visiting This Planet," "Art May Imitate Life, But Life Imitates Television," and "Time Flies when You Don't Know What You're Doing."

271

Ivy yells in my ear. "Now there's an artist! A walking circus."

"Yeah, a walking circus," I say, and laugh. "Las Vegas on a stick."

"That's perfect," she says, giving me a small hug. She puts what I just said into her notebook, writing in the tiniest print I've ever seen.

According to Ivy, my apartment is art, too, Or, at least she'd like it to be. I'm not so sure, but I give her the run of the place anyway. I figure it can use some straightening, but Ivy goes a little overboard. She spends one whole weekend rummaging through the apartment, throwing out some things and rearranging others. Half of my memorabilia collection gets the boot. I hate getting rid of this stuff.

"What about these?" I say, showing her my three Buddha statues that I found on the el. She points to the largest of the Buddhas and says, "That's a keeper." She's sitting in the middle of the living room floor sorting through my memorabilia. In the throwaway pile is my African ebony hourglass, my Cubs briefcase, my AM/FM radio, and my Cubs cooler.

"I kind of think this is artistic, don't you?" I say, picking up my Cubs briefcase.

"It's up to you," she says. "I'm just making suggestions."

She looks so disappointed.

Later, I put the throwaway pile in a box and set it downstairs by the trash bin with a sign that reads, "Free."

I still haven't got the hang of all this.

Ivy starts taking me to different installations. At one gallery a man toasts dozens of Pop Tarts while reading the constitution. At another, a guy sits in the fetal position inside a three foot tall box. Outside is a video screen which shows him sitting there. After that, a woman in black pajamas lectures on nuclear war while pelting us with eggs. Then there's the Mystery Installation. No one knows where it is, who's the artist, or what's supposed to happen. Only the date. The flyer says simply "Coming April 17."

One night, we're sitting in the living room taking target practice at my Cuervo collection with my hand grenade lighter. I've given up drinking, and now we shatter a few bottles every night before turning in. I'm down to about a hundred.

The phone rings and I answer. "Is Ivy there?" a man's voice asks hesitantly.

I point to Ivy and she points to herself. "Who is it?" Ivy says. In the five weeks that Ivy's been with me, no one's called her. She doesn't seem to have any friends. Only acquaintances. People in galleries who don't even seem to know her name, hug her and ask, "Where have you been hiding?" and move on before she has a chance to answer. Around most people Ivy acts stiff and angry, like she expects to be insulted. Only around me does she loosen up, though I'm not sure why. Sometimes I think we're pretty compatible, but sometimes I think she just needs a place to stay.

"Can I tell her who's calling?" I say to the man.

"Tell Ivy it's her parents," says the man. "We'd like to speak with her."

"Ivy, it's your parents."

"I have nothing to say to them," she says.

"Ivy, it's your parents," I repeat. "I can't tell them that."

Ivy shrugs. "Tell them I've turned into a dragonfly. When they learn to speak dragonfly I'll talk with them."

"We'd just like to speak with her, that's all," says her father. "Is she all right?"

"Yes, yes," I say. "She's fine." I put the receiver to my chest and say, "Ivy, please. Speak with your folks. You can't not speak with your *folks*."

"Okay," she yells and leaps up from the couch. She rips the phone away from me and puts it to her ear. "Okay," she says to the phone.

After that she doesn't say anything for a minute.

"Okay, I won't hang up," she says finally.

She stands there holding the phone about six inches from her ear, like a snake dancer with a coiled rattler.

As we're lying in bed that night, Ivy says, "I hope you're not too happy. I hope you're not enjoying yourself too much."

"Not in the least," I tell her. "I'm in agony. Don't touch me there. It's too agonizing."

Ivy takes her hand away.

"I was just kidding," I say. "I like a little agony from time to time."

One thing about this girl. She takes everything literally.

"The secret is staying off-balance," she says. "Whenever I start seeing someone, I immediately think of how we're going to break up. Then I'm happy. If I imagine the worst, then I can relax and enjoy myself."

"Here," I say, taking her hand. "Put your hand back there. I was just kidding."

"My parents think that it's wrong to cut yourself off from the people you've grown close to," she says, looking up at the ceiling and absentmindedly stroking me. "To me, it's just moving on, shedding skin."

"Yes, that's it," I say. "Yes, there. That feels good. No, I mean bad. It's right in between."

I start to give Ivy a hand with her installations. The first one's small, unplanned, but not quite spur-of-the moment. We head for the Loop on a warm Sunday afternoon with a Lady Remington razor. I shave Ivy's head on the steps of the Art Institute. Then she shaves my head. This is one of the parts I hadn't planned. At first I'm thinking, "Wait a second," but then I see the surprised faces of the spectators: commuters every one of them. *I'm* doing something crazy now. Let someone else be the authority figure this time.

We gather our hair and arrange it around the head of one of the stone lions in front of the museum. Our goal is to transform the lion into Moe of the Stooges, but it's harder to get loose hair to stay in place than you might think. The bangs are the most difficult. Unfortunately, before we can get the head in shape, the wind scatters our clippings.

We've got a pretty good-sized crowd around us, maybe twenty people. A puppeteer, with not nearly as many onlookers, stands jealously on the steps by the other stone lion. We ignore him as he goes through his routine with his marionettes. He swivels them around, and the two puppets point and jeer at us. They're not the only ones. The crowd is on the ugly side. "There are better ways to get attention," one marionette yells. "Why do you do such disgusting things?" the other says. Most people just walk by without looking at us. Ivy says they're the ones who worry her the most, the people who don't notice.

Sometimes Ivy starts shivering when it's not even cold. When I touch her, she says, "You're always touching. I feel like bruised fruit." So I stop touching and she says, "You're so distant. You're the worst lover I've ever had. I've been having a lot of dreams about women lately." I try touching her again, but she's restless.

"What's going to make you happy?" I say. "Sacrificing a beefalo? A vat of putrefying squirrels?"

She's alert again and smiling. I meant the question as an insult, but she looks like she expected it.

"Commuting at the speed of art," she says, like this is the only possible answer.

It's hard to tell the audience from the passengers tonight. They're all audience, I guess. I'm off-duty, but I'm wearing my conductor's uniform. I go up to the real conductor, a guy named Fred, and explain what we're doing. He just twists his mouth and stares at me. I ask him what his problem is and he says, "What happened to your hair? Didn't you used to have hair?"

"I shaved it for an installation," I tell him.

He twists his mouth again.

"Never mind," I say. "Here's twenty bucks. Just leave us alone for half an hour, okay?"

"Okay," he says, "but I still got to know what it is. I could lose my job. So could you."

"It's just art," I tell him. "Nothing to worry about."

"Well, okay, then," and he walks off with the twenty I've handed him.

The train's moving steady at about 30 MPH. I keep my hand on the back of one of the seats as we rock back and forth. We round a corner and sparks shoot up from our wheels.

I get on the intercom and announce, "Hello, you miserable commuters. This is Jason, your conductor from hell. No smoking, littering, or radio playing allowed."

About twenty of the passengers smile at me. The other ten keep their eyes in front of them as though they're soldiers in fox-holes waiting for an assault. Good, I've got their attention. Now I can tell who the audience is and who the real commuters are. One young child balances in the middle of the aisle. "*Carlos, ven aca!*" his mother yells from three seats back. She's got four other

275

children gathered in two seats around her. She's about seven months pregnant and wears a blue T-shirt with dark smears on it. The T-shirt has a picture of a bulldog and reads, "Yale."

Carlos doesn't hear his mother or doesn't want to obey. He bends down and picks up something invisible from the floor. Then he rubs it while squatting and rocking to the rhythm of the train.

"Carlos!" the woman yells again and darts out into the aisle and snatches the kid. She dangles him by an arm and swats him loudly.

Then she gives me a look like I was the one who made Carlos disobey. Like I want Carlos to be a juvenile delinquent. Like I was the one who just smacked him.

A little late, Ivy enters the car from the door at the other end. She looks as pregnant as the woman with the Yale T-shirt. She's carrying two shopping bags and she wears a platinum blond wig with a huge patch torn out of the scalp. Ivy closes the door behind her and starts waddling down the center aisle. Most of the passengers turn around and watch.

When she's halfway up the aisle, she squirms in her dress and moans. She reaches into one of her bags, takes out a turkey baster, and squirts it at the person sitting in the seat nearest her. A stream of milk trickles onto the man's crotch. The man looks at her and barks twice. Most likely he's one of the people she invited to the installation, but it's hard to tell. I've seen regular passengers bark before.

"Excuse me, miss," I yell down the aisle. "No smoking, littering, or radio playing allowed. No turkey basting."

The woman in the Yale T-shirt cranes her neck into the aisle and looks at Ivy. Then she puts her arms around her two closest children.

Ivy sticks her turkey baster back into her shopping bag and keeps walking up the aisle.

After she's gone about five feet, she moans again and starts rubbing her pregnant-looking belly, "Oh my," she yells. "I feel it! I think I feel it!"

She takes another step and something slips between her legs and plops with a wet slap onto the floor.

Ivy steps back and reveals a slab of uncooked liver lying at her feet. Quickly, she snatches it up. "Get back here, you little rascal. You ain't incubated long enough yet." She stuffs the slab of liver back into her dress.

"Miss," I yell. "No smoking, littering, radio playing, turkey basting, or liver deliveries allowed."

The train approaches the station. As it slows down, the woman in the Yale T-shirt gathers her children around her. She pushes the five of them in front of her, her arms sweeping them along, her eyes fixed on Ivy.

Ivy stands in her way. The woman, frantically trying to get around her as the train stops, knocks into Ivy, who loses her balance momentarily and staggers backwards as the train lurches to a standstill.

With a sucking sound, the rest of Ivy's fake pregnancy slithers out her dress. The whole mess slops on the floor. Chicken gizzards and bloody cow and pig entrails. Ivy looks as surprised as anyone because this was supposed to happen gradually.

The doors open, but the woman stands there a moment looking straight at Ivy and spits, *"Puta!"*

Then she herds her children out the doors. About five other people push through the doors with her. Undaunted, Ivy chases them off the train by squirting them in the back with her turkey baster.

Fred, in the next car, closes the doors and we start up again.

I hear someone pounding on the doors. The woman in the T-shirt raps with her knuckles, her face twisted, her mouth open, her eyes pleading.

"What is it?" I say.

We gather speed, and she falls away from the door like someone being hooked off a stage. As she crumples, I hear her scream. "Carlos!" she yells.

I turn around and see Carlos kneeling, playing with the fallen gizzards. He looks up and displays his hands to me as though I'm his father and he just washed up for dinner. He's covered with chicken and beef blood. The boy puts his fingers in his mouth and giggles.

Ivy thinks it's funny and stupid that someone would forget her own kid on the train. Ivy's friends think it's part of the installation. I take a minute to react, but then I pull the emergency cord. The brakes echo the mother's scream. I run to get Fred

277

and tell him to head back. He starts yelling and says he's going to report me, that I'm definitely going to lose my job.

After we reunite Carlos with his mother, Ivy and her friends traipse off to Angel's Shortstop for after-installation drinks. "You'll love this place," Ivy tells her friends. Poor Angel.

I'm left alone on the platform with the woman and her kids. The woman yells while her kids look up at me in awe. I listen even though I can't understand a word she's saying. I just stand there while she yells. She keeps this up for longer than is possible for one person to yell at another. The train leaves. Ten minutes later another train pulls into the station. She keeps yelling. But I stand here and take it. Finally, she herds her kids away and leaves me.

I stand alone on the platform at Addison for a while, facing Wrigley Field. I start pacing back and forth. I walk to the edge of the platform, where it narrows into a point and signs warn of the danger of electrocuting yourself. My life is ruined. In an alley below me a black dog trots between the garbage cans. Past the alley and before Wrigley Field, there's a large parking lot. A couple of apartment buildings stand on either side. A poster on one of the buildings shows Harry Caray with his butterball head, thick glasses, and uncontained joy, leaping through space. His arm is raised as though he's about to lead a crowd at Wrigley Field during the seventh inning stretch: "Okay now, let's hear it! Take me out to the ballgame!" Bold letters below him pronounce: "CUB FAN, BUD MAN."

A boy about ten, who's drunk or pretending to be, staggers down Sheffield, grabbing a lamp post and twirling around. He does a strange limbery Watusi down the sidewalk. No one else is around and he doesn't know I'm watching. Who does he think he's doing this dance for?

"Hey! You!" I yell, but he doesn't hear, or pretends not to. In a minute he's turned the corner and is gone.

A cannon burst, a sonic boom. Then the sound of thousands of wind chimes buffeted in a typhoon.

Glass is flying all over the parking lot from the building with the Harry Caray poster. It takes me a second to realize what's going on, but then I see the windows of the building have been blown out. A gas explosion, a bomb factory, a huge shotgun blast. Who knows?

A group of teenagers dashes out of the building and into the lot.

Someone runs from the building on the other side of the lot and yells, "Hey, is everything cool? Is everything cool?"

A man clambers out of a window by Harry Caray's knee. He swims, two quick overhead strokes before he hits the ground. Two kids climb over the fence at the back of the building. All over the parking lot, people are running around yelling, "What happened? Is everything cool?"

I hear a laugh, or maybe it's a cry. It comes from the building, and someone's yelling. "Did you call them? Are they coming?"

I feel so clear-headed as they run around. I look out towards the lakefront with its apartment complexes all lit up, and what am I thinking about? Water. A drop of it falling on the third rail. Worlds within worlds sizzling within that drop. A black dog trotting between cans, living off garbage. A drunken boy doing a strange Watusi. Harry Caray leaping joyfully through the abyss. This clear agony I'm feeling. I'm thinking about Ivy touching me, the rash she's given me, the skin I've shed. I feel like a tunnel with wind rushing through it. I feel like an underground test, a needle pointing to a zone past measurement.

I turn around again and lean over the railing of the el. Below me stands a cluster of kids, watching an orange flame bend a window.

"Hey. Hey you!" I yell.

All of them turn around at once and stare. They're looking up at me so expectantly, their eyes wide, their faces ready to receive.

"Did you see that?" I yell down to them. "Did you *see* that?"

Nominated by Another Chicago Magazine

SNUFF DIPPERS

fiction by SHAY YOUNGBLOOD

from THE BIG MAMA STORIES (FIREBRAND BOOKS)

I HAVE ALWAYS had a deep and undying respect for the wisdom of snuff dippers. Big Mama raised me in the company of wise old Black women like herself who had managed to survive some dangerous and terrible times and live to tell bout them. These were hard-working, honest women whose only admitted vice, aside from exchanging a lil bit of no-harm-done gossip now and then, was dipping snuff.

Big Mama and her friends was always sending me to Joe's grocery store on the corner to buy silver tins of the fine brown powder wrapped in labels with names like Bruton's Sweet Snuff, Georgia Peach, and Three Brown Monkeys. The summer I was six my mean older cousin, DeeDee, told me that snuff was really ground up monkey dust, a delicacy in the royal palaces of Africa. She told me to mix three heaping tablespoons of snuff with a glass of milk and to drink it through a straw fast like a chocolate milkshake.

"If you drink it all," she said, shaking her nine-year old hips, "you'll wake up and be real pretty like them African dancing girls we saw on TV. They drink it every day. It'll make your teeth white too."

"How come you know so much?" I asked suspiciously.

"Cause when I went to New York to see Aunt Louise she lived next door to a African dancing girl. She told me herself that's how come she was so pretty."

DeeDee was so convincing, especially when she made me promise on the Bible not to tell nobody.

I took one of Big Mama's good glasses with flowers painted on it down from the top shelf of the china cabinet. Then I mixed the milk and monkey dust, stirring it in the pretty glass till it made me sneeze. Holding my nose, I stuck a plastic straw into the foaming brown stuff and began to drink my way to beauty. Big Mama heard me coughing and crying and come in the kitchen. When she found out what I was doing she shook her head and tried not to laugh at me. She gave me some baking soda to rinse my mouth out and a lecture on not believing everything I heard. Said I was already pretty, and all the monkey dust in the world couldn't give me a good, kind, honest heart. I never forgave DeeDee for that trick. I was dizzy for hours, and the taste of the nasty, bittersweet snuff lingered on my tongue long after the humiliation had gone.

When I was a few years wiser and had the nerve to question Big Mama, I asked her why she dipped snuff. Big Mama leaned back, deep into her rocking chair. She slowly drew a fresh tin of snuff from her apron pocket. After opening the can, she took a big pinch of the brown stuff between her index and forefinger like I'd seen her do a million times. With her other hand she stretched out her bottom lip to take in the dip of snuff. She slapped her hands together and wiped them on her apron before she answered me. By the way she took her time I knew she was gonna tell me a story. Big Mama started out by defending herself.

"Snuff ain't no worse than them cancer sticks that be killing folks left and right. I ain't never heard tell of snuff harming nobody. But as I recollect, back in '57 when the only place colored folks could sit on a bus was in the back, Emma Lou came close to getting us killed on the #99."

Big Mama told me that over twenty years ago the #99 bus was known as the "maids' bus." It arrived downtown at the corner of Broadway and 12th Streets every weekday morning at 6:00 A.M. to pick up the Black domestic workers bound for the rich white suburb of Northend, ninety minutes away. The sun would just be creeping up behind the glass and steel office building to light the women's way. From a distance, the #99 bus stop looked like any other corner where buses stopped. Bout forty Black women stood there dressed as if on their way to a church social. They all carried shopping bags made of plastic, paper, or straw, advertising the names of places they would never see or stores where they weren't welcome. In the bags were maids' uniforms that pride prevented them from wearing outside the places where they worked in them.

Everybody had a regular seat on the #99 so that friends and neighbors could sit together recreating communities. Miss Emma Lou sat in the seventh row, right-hand side next to the window, and Miss Mary sat next to her. Seats weren't assigned, but all hell cut loose when the pattern was broken by a newcomer. Newcomers sat up front—period.

Big Mama said that conversations on the #99 went something like this.

Miss Emma Lou: "My lady asked me to come in on a Sunday afternoon, would you believe, to pour tea for some English foreigners visiting her mama. I told her that her mama was gonna have to pour that tea herself cause I had to go to church on Sunday. The Lord wouldn't preciate my missing a prayer service to pour tea for the Queen of England."

Miss Mary: "My white lady, bless her heart, is as simple as a chile. When the boss was near bout fifty years old he turn round and left the missus and two grown children to marry this girl right out of college. This chile, believe me when I tell you, sends her drawers to the dry cleaners. Ain't that nothin? A woman that cain't wash her own drawers."

Miss Mary and Miss Emma Lou lived in one-bedroom apartments on either side of me and Big Mama in the housing projects by the river. Miss Mary was a tall, straight-backed, thin Black woman, somewhere in her sixties, who looked like a gypsy. She wore big gold earrings and bright-colored head ties that matched her dresses. Sometimes in the middle of a conversation with her Miss Mary would see into your future and start to tell it if you didn't stop her. Folks said she come from a line of West Indian root women, seers and healers, and couldn't help it. Miss Emma Lou tried to convince her to charge for the privilege of knowing people's future, but Miss Mary said that would be highway robbery, charging money for a gift give to her by God.

Miss Emma Lou was Miss Mary's best friend. She was a short, heavyset brown-skin woman who was as bowlegged as Miss Mary was straight in the back. Unlike the other maids, Miss Emma Lou wore her white uniform most of the time—said it was the mark of a professional. She made her white folks refer to her as a domestic engineer and got paid a lil bit extra for it. Miss Emma Lou wasn't nobody's fool. And she was a snuff-dipping woman who said what was on her mind and emphasized her point by spitting snuff juice in a can she carried with her everywhere.

Then there was Ralph, a big, red-faced Irishman with laughing green eyes and curly blond hair, who had been the driver for the #99 since the service began in 1952. Dr. J. R. Whittenhauser, the millionaire doctor, had stopped Ralph's gypsy cab on Peachtree Street and offered him an easier job with a steadier income. All he had to do was pick up the domestic help for Northend by 6:00 A.M. Monday through Friday and pick them up again at 3:30 P.M. in a bus Northend residents bought for that purpose. Even if the city buses went on strike or riots broke out, white ladies in Northend would have their meals cooked, children looked after, and laundry done.

Ralph was one of the nicest white men she ever met, according to Big Mama. If one of the regular riders was late, Ralph would wait a few more minutes knowing that on Fridays Miss Lamama had to walk her grandchildren to school and on Mondays Miss Mary did a sunrise ritual. If it was raining real hard or the temperature was real cold, Ralph would drive some of the older women with arthritis, bursitis, and bad knees across town right up to their door. In return the women baked him cakes, brought him lunch, and treated him like one of them.

Big Mama said Ralph was like one of them cause white folks treated him the same as if he was colored cause he was a foreigner. She said he even stood up to a white man for them.

Big Mama's face got real serious when she started telling me one of her stories bout the not-so-long-ago days.

"As I seem to recall, it was a scorching hot day in the middle of July when Emma Lou liketa got in a whole heap of trouble over some snuff and Ralph stood up for us, like a soldier," Big Mama said.

"Not only was the weather hot, but colored folks was stirred up over the lynchings and killings of colored mens all over the South by evil white men. The whites was getting meaner as the summer got hotter. A colored woman had just been found dead. She was raped and sawed open by six white men who made her brother watch em ravish her. Some awful bloody things happened that summer." Big Mama closed her eyes and drew herself up like a chill had passed over her.

"What happened, Big Mama?" I asked impatiently, as children do.

"Hold on, chile, I'm getting to it. A story ain't something you just read off like ingredients on a soap box. A story's like a map—you follow the lines and they'll take you somewhere. There's a way to do anything, and with a story you take your time." She shook a finger in my direction.

"I'm sorry, Big Mama." I was afraid I'd messed up and she wouldn't finish the story. I promised to hush and not interrupt her again.

Big Mama shifted herself into a more comfortable position for storytelling and cocked her head back for better memory.

"As I was bout to say, the #99 was rolling toward town. Most of the women on the bus was talking bout how hot it was. Breakfast milk spoiling on the table, clothes drying stiff on the line quick as lightning strike, and lil babies crying all day long they was so miserable. We was all real hot, sweaty, and wore out. Emma Lou was sitting in her regular seat by the window, Mary was next to her, and I was sitting behind them at my window seat.

"I was sitting there listening to Emma Lou go on bout how her white folks was going on a vacation in Europe, or somewhere like that, and just looking out the window. We was still in Northend, where most of the rich white folks live, and I took notice of this brand new white convertible Cadillac cruising long side of the bus. It was a white man and woman in the car. She had on a pretty white dress and looked just as brown as your cousin DeeDee, but she had long yellow hair that was blowing all round her face. The white man was driving. He had yellow hair too, but he was real red; his skin was peeling off him like a boiled tomato. Look like he'd been to Florida and stayed in the sun too long. He had on a pair of them mirror sunglasses so you couldn't see his eyes like them small-town redneck sheriffs useta wear to scare coloreds. You can tell a whole heap bout a person by looking in they eyes. You can just bout see what's going on in they mind, and some people have some terrible things on they mind."

Big Mama stopped talking again, but I didn't say nothing, and in a minute or two she kept on.

"Well, you know Emma Lou got to have her a dip of snuff. Don't care where she is or who she with, she gonna have her a taste. That day wasn't no different, but that day Emma Lou didn't have her spit cup with her. She probably left it at her white lady's house. She asked Lamama if she could use her fancy Ethiopian handkerchief, but Lamama was offended. Told her to use her bag, but Emma Lou had her white folk's lace tablecloths in there. Wouldn't you know it, just as them white folks in they brand new Cadillac was passing the bus, Emma Lou stuck her head out the window and let out a long stream of thick, brown snuff spit right in that white woman's face and on her pretty white dress.

"When the other womens on the bus saw what had happened, they started falling off they seats they was laughing so hard. Ralph hear what happen and he laugh too, but pretty soon we all realize they wasn't nothing to laugh at. Them white folks drove up side the bus cussing and carrying on like I never heard and hope not to hear no more. All that white man could see was blood. Ralph got hold of the situation and threw the bus in high gear. That Cadillac speeded up too. Folks on the bus got quiet. All we could hear was the bus tires hitting the road and that raging white man calling us every kind of nigger he could think of. Ralph say, 'I'm trying to get rid of this fool. Hang on ladies.'

"For a few minutes we thought Ralph had lost them but before we got out of Northend a police car with flashing blue lights and a crying siren signaled for the bus to pull over. Ralph started cussing like a sailor, but he had to pull over for the law. Out of the corner of my eye I saw the colored Catholic woman from up North cross herself. I started praying myself cause I saw the white Cadillac pull up and park behind the police car.

"The white woman jumped outta that car looking ugly like somebody called her mama nigger. She had wiped most of the spit off her face, but she still had brown snuff stains on the front of her dress. The white man had evil and ugly wrote all over him. He was hollering at the policeman and waving his fist round. The police officer, a blond-headed boy with cold blue eyes, had to hold him back from getting on the bus. The policeman got on though and look us over like we stole something. He say out loud, 'Which one of you aunties spit on Mr. Roger's friend?' As if

285

we was children and any one of us could've been his mama, grandma, or help raise him.

"Nobody made a sound. Then he put his hand on his hip by his gun and say real nasty, 'I'm gonna have to lock every one of y'all up if don't nobody speak up right now.' We didn't hardly breathe. When he asked Ralph who spit on the white lady, Ralph say, 'Might be a pigeon thought he was flying over the ocean and took a notion to shit in the sea. Why you want to bother these nice ladies?' That made the police mad. He say, 'They a bunch of niggers and one of em spit on a white lady. I don't know where you from, but we don't tolerate disrespect from our niggers here in Georgia, or from nigger-loving foreigners.'

"When Ralph stood up in front of that policeman you could see the blood rush to his face. He was mad as all git out. The policeman back off the bus with his hand on his gun. He say loud, looking hard at Ralph, 'I want all you niggers to get off the bus. That mean everybody.' Ralph was the first one to get off the bus. Then we all got off and the policeman made us line up by the road in that hot sun like he was gonna let that crazy white man shoot us. Cars was passing long the highway with folks looking at us like we was from the moon. Then the policeman just left us standing there and went over to his patrol car and started talking on his radio.

"Before we knowed anything, that crazy white man was hollering at us, 'Somebody's gonna pay for this.' The white woman was leaning on the Cadillac looking hateful and mean as a snake. Then that fool white man started picking up rocks and dirt and throwing em at us. Mary still got a scar where one of them rocks split her knee. Ralph rush over to stop him, but the white man throwed dirt in his eyes. We all run screaming and hollering behind us into a patch of weeds and up against a fence a lil piece from the road till we couldn't go no further. I thought for sure we was gonna be killed. Finally the policeman see what was happening and pull the white man to the side. They look over at us standing in them knee-high weeds and briars and laughed at something that was said between em. Do you know that no-good policeman watch that crazy white man come over to where we was backed up against the fence like dogs and hark spit on each one of us. Lamama wiped our faces with her fancy handkerchief, weeping like a widow. Then the white man laughed and got in his Cadillac with his woman.

"Mary was behind me calling on her West Indian spirits and making signs. That white man pulled onto the highway, his tires kicking up dust every which way, right in the path of a tractor-trailer truck. I'll never forget it as long as I live. The sight of that big, brand new white Cadillac being knocked in the side and the surprise on them white folks' faces. It was a mess of twisted steel and burning white flesh. Mary was smiling. She crossed herself and said 'Thank you, Jesus. Thank you, Ogun.'

"Emma Lou turned to me and said, 'Ain't it a shame that folks can be so mean with the Lord watching they every move.' She clicked her tongue like she do and spit in the direction of the wreck.

"I said to her, 'Emma Lou, it be the truth. Folks act like God don't be on the case recording everything in his Book of Life.'"

Big Mama shook her head in wonder and spit in the big tin can with the yellow peach label on it, the one she kept under her chair, to let me know she was through. I went over and hugged her tight round the middle, glad she took the time to remember with me the way things used to be.

Nominated by Firebrand Books

ON THE LIFE AND DEATH OF STAN LAUREL'S SON

by WALTER PAVLICH

from MANOA

For nine days, two Stanleys, one funny,
one drowning, brain capsizing in its own blood,
lungs miscarrying air
from one breath to the next, a tenant
shut in its dissembling body,
incubator too much like a show room.

Stan's tired of crying on screen.
Off, that's all he can do. The night-nurse
steals his exhausted handkerchief, hides it
under her sleeve on her wrist-pulse.
Someday these tears might be worth something.

Stan Jr. dies without one chuckle
to smooth out its face, and is burned
into a little pile his father
pretends he keeps in a clear candy jar.
Every morning for luck Stan rubs
a fingerprint on the glass

cold as a spoon, his son
neutral inside. Then off to the laughter

works where he invents the same smile
each day, and that way of walking,
as if the ground were a ledge, and he's strolling
alone, three steps off the earth.

Nominated by Sandra McPherson

HIDE-AND-GO-SEEK

by JUDITH KITCHEN

from THE GEORGIA REVIEW

I AM SITTING on the deck of a house in Maine, overlooking the
Atlantic Ocean. Below me, lobster boats are making their daily
rounds—sputter of engine, flutter of gulls. It is supposed to be
beautiful, and I guess you could say it is. *I* could say it is. But I
am bored. I want something else, though I'm not sure what. Last
year was the same. I ran out of books to read and then I was
bored—ornery bored. The nearest bookstore is sixty-eight miles
southwest on Route 1, plus the seven miles over narrow roads to
reach Route 1, and the mile and a half of ruts from the house to
paved road.

So I bought puzzles at a local auction, 1,500-piece puzzles
spread out on the table—the kind where you have to make the
distinction between the thing and the shadow of the thing. Believe me, I know every nook and cranny of the Grand Canyon at
sunset, every shimmering reflection of autumn leaves in a New
Hampshire stream. But I was still bored. I spent time lying nude
on the deck, stretched out in the sun with my mind as blank as I
could make it. Little red swirls in front of the eyes, pinpoints of
heat. Nothing else. But my body resisted. I went home more red
than brown, more white than red, a patchwork of attempts to be
what I am not.

This year is different. I came armed with a box full of books,
something for every mood. *Love in a Time of Cholera. Songlines.*
Vivian Gornick's memoirs of life with her mother. Mystery. Poetry. Fiction. Today I brought my coffee out to the deck, along

with Tim O'Brien's *The Nuclear Age*. The steam from my cup rises, becomes a part of the fog burning off in the late morning sun. The open book pulls me into its pages. Catches me off guard:

> *Like hide-and-go-seek—the future curves toward the past then folds back again, seamlessly, always expressing itself in the present tense.*

I'm sure Tim O'Brien only wanted to repeat a line that sounded good, that gave him easy access to his next thought, that allowed him to move from where he was to where he wanted to be. Even so . . .

. . . *the future curves* and I am ten. It is late July, early August, the height of summer boredom. The whole neighborhood is waiting for something to happen. We spent the last days of June riding our bicycles up and down maple-covered streets, poking sticks into the muddy, overfull banks of the Cohocton, free from school and from parents, free to make the village our own. And July brought a smattering of one-week vacations—families stuffed into cars filled with camping gear, off to the Adirondacks—mosquitoes, canoe trips, outdoor toilets, those flimsy moccasins I bought every year hoping they might last. And then home to baseball games on the back lot, six or seven to a team, short tempers, the inevitable cheating, the heated shouts of "out" "no, *safe*" "no, *out*" until we all quit in disgust. By now I have picked quart upon quart of raspberries, carefully settled the slatted boxes into the bed of the red wagon, bribed my brother to knock on the doors, and sold them up and down the hillside. I've spent some of my earnings at Tombasco's fruit stand, a popsicle a day while the season lasted. I've eaten every flavor Basco has to sell. I've stood on his oiled wood floors, dripping sticky purple juice, watching the flies circle and circle the tomatoes and cucumbers, finally favoring the peaches and watermelons and the temptations of scent. I've grown sick of popsicles that never deliver what they promise, tucked in tantalizing rows in Basco's deep freezer. I've grown heartily sick of summer, and there is still a month to go.

A month of baby games: tag, kick-the-can, kick-the-can-in-the-dark, a dozen variations on hide-and-go-seek. "Draw a circle on the old man's back. Here's two eyes, and a mouth. Who will put the nose?" The quick stab of forefinger in the back. The whirling about to see if someone is still moving. The smug look on everyone's face. The guessing. "Donna." No, you're wrong. And the one who did it—Billy or Jimmy or George or Steve or Marilyn— giving you the penance: "Crawl on your hands and knees to Joel Sundquist's front steps, saying 'I love Joel' at each crack in the sidewalk, then get up and walk backwards to the tree, count to fifty, then you can look." Variations on humiliation.

. . . *toward the past.* It is the summer they built the Catholic church in town. Until now, ours has been a three-church town. A walk up Hamilton and there is the Presbyterian church, all cool brick and music and stained glass, a steeple that reaches for the sky. Turn the corner and it's Methodist, white painted wood, a rectangle, solid and simple. Simply there. And then on Water Street, facing the dike, the Baptist church—gray concrete, a sort of fake stone. It has two steeples, one shorter than the other, giving it the lopsided look of a man limping. That's what this town is like. Protestant to the hilt, but regular. Nothing fancy like Episcopal or Lutheran. Nothing too plain, like the Quakers. Which is why, during the summer months when people don't go to services so often, the three churches take turns holding them. For three months everyone is the same, then they break apart again into what they have always been because their mothers and fathers were before them. Catholics? Sure, they're here, but they've always gone over to the Saints—St. Joseph's in the next town, or St. Vincent's three miles further, because it has a school.

The bulldozer pulls up at the vacant lot on the corner of our street, stopping next to the sign that has been there all summer, meaningless: *Our Lady of the Immaculate Conception.* Suddenly, at the end of the summer, there is activity, something to watch, something to *do.* By evening there is a deep hole on the corner lot, and piles of dirt waiting for us to run up and down, in and out, in the long hours after dinner. The next day the dirt is trucked away and the hole is so huge and deep that our parents are telling us to stay away from it.

By the end of the week, the men have lined the hole with cinder blocks and poured concrete. By the beginning of the next, they are erecting cinder-block walls within the hole, an open maze of rooms with spaces left for doorways, an underground life

292

still open to the sky. The men place boards across these spaces so they will not have to walk around. Three, four, then six, seven feet from the bottom—the men crisscross the maze of cinder blocks, trowels in hand, smoothing and fitting. Then, miraculously, they stop work. They must be waiting for something— plywood or bricks.

For four days the maze is ours. By day we survey it, memorizing where the boards are placed, imagining our way across the planks, twisting and turning in a million intricate moves. In the thin evening light, we play the game we have invented: hide-and-go-seek-in-the-dark. We play it over the church cellar—those are the rules. We inch our way out onto the planks and move, foot by foot, to the next wall. We work our way out to the center, balanced precariously high over concrete. A fall could be fatal, or at least could put a stop to the game, so we are careful. Our parents do not know where we are—only that we are playing again, that we do not seem so bored, that they have another hour of peace before they must call us in for bed. They do not know that we are testing our bodies against our minds. That what is at stake is memory. That the one who knows best where each board is placed is the one who will win.

I am ten. I inch myself out onto the plank, pick up speed, scurry to the outside wall, veer left, hop out onto the next board, over the space left for a doorway, out and over the whole of the church, around and around, twist and turn, hardly groping in the dark, my feet full of instinct, my mind as alert as it will ever be. I hop over the last obstacle, reach solid ground, sprint for the big tree in front of Mrs. Hale's house, "Home free," and I'm first, I'm in safe.

. . . *folds back again.* But in the present I am sitting on the deck of a house in Maine, overlooking the Atlantic Ocean. Below me . . . I am bored. I am ten. But that is the past in the present, such intense boredom that it dares the mind to outflank the body. Is it the past curving toward the future I am sensing, or is it the present curving toward the past? What do I make of this memory—as real to me here, stretched out in sunlight, as it was then in the first hush of evening in the waning days of my last childish summer? Surely the past holds out something to the future as the loop shortens and folds. The present is tangential, touching only at this point, the here, the now. How can I dare to

293

admit to being bored? How can the present count for nothing, when this is all I have? Each moment finite. Half behind me, half stretching so interminably ahead.

Four days was all we had. After that, the bricks arrived, and the two-by-fours, and the hardwood and stained glass, so that by October there was an edifice where before there had been nothing. And by November we were not even surprised to see it, hardly remembered the vacant lot or the summer evenings or the games. We were eleven. We were busy belonging. We wore saddle shoes. We liked Ike. We were caught up in school, and something more. Boys. Not Billy or Steve or Gordie—not neighborhood boys. No, this was different.

I sat on one side of Mrs. Harrison's sixth grade and looked across the room to where John LeBarron pretended not to notice any of us. I thought about his dark hair, and the way he moved, and the mystery he brought with him down from the hills, riding the bus miles into town. In art class, we made identification bracelets. Narrow for girls, with roses engraved over our names. Wider for boys, with a sports motif. Each day a new girl would show up with a boy's bracelet on her wrist. I wanted John Le-Barron's bracelet—more than I wanted John LeBarron. What would I say to *him*? I wanted that bracelet more than anything in the world. And the world had changed. Looped. I felt my life ahead of me, a strand of desire, stretched thin and thinner, and there, always there, waiting, the present tense about to pounce.

Sputter of engines. The lobster boat turns sharply, homing in on the buoys. A tug and the trap seems to lift itself into the boat. Gulls swarm. A pause, engines almost off, as the trap is inspected, the lobster removed and measured, the trap baited and then, in a quick motion, it soars free of the boat, drops seaward. One flick of the wrist and the gulls go crazy, scattering over the sea, scavenging. Sputter of engines, the boat turns again, sets its sights, churns toward a small painted dot in the sea.

. . . *present tense*. Again and again, and I am familiar with the boat's pattern as though I had known it all my life. But I haven't. I have known it for precisely one year—from last summer to this. And yet the knowledge feels as solid as the knowledge of the Perseids, those showers of shooting stars I have watched each summer since I was eight. Or the knowledge of how to ice skate, one foot gliding out with such assurance, waiting for the other to pick up the cadence, begin its own thrust and glide, the two feet synchronized, out and over the ice, like wind. Or the knowledge of desire, which was swimming below my summer boredom waiting to surface in the guise of John LeBarron's surly indifference and swims now, in circles, asserting itself.

I am fourteen and it's there in earnest. High school is a sea of desire. I save my reading for home, for the quiet warmth of the hot-air registers and the cool privacy of thought. High school is where we test and retest our abilities to attract. No one is better at this than Mary Agnes, my new best friend. She came this year from St. Vincent's and has set the school on fire. She's short and dark and cute as a button, has been all her life. She knows how to use it—flash of black eyes, wrinkle of nose, flick of the skirt. She's a cheerleader, too, and seems to lead cheers all day long—everything needs to be whipped up to match her enthusiasm. To *hold* it. It's fun to swim along in her wake. Everything is new.

First cigarette. We're standing in October leaves behind Mary Agnes' kitchen window. The stale taste, the aroma of fall, the crunch of leaves underfoot, it's all one and the same. It's the glow of four cigarettes in the dark, pinpoints of light, flickering fireflies of evidence. And it's the furious flurry, the scuttle, the stamping of feet on dropped butts as the headlights swing into the driveway and her parents are home. It's the innocent way we all stand, pulling our identical blue-and-white corduroy jackets around us, laughing, practicing cheers as though that were our passion and we had been working through dusk. "One, two, three, four, who are we for?" We are for excitement. For something new. Something that will help the boredom of routine lives in a small town. Something akin to desire.

What do we know of desire? We know only what it is to want to be wanted. And we want to be wanted in the worst way, by the right kind of boys—the ones who will make other girls jealous. We want basketball stars, tall and smooth, the ball swooshing through the net without touching the rim. We want the good-looking boys, the ones who know they're cute. We want the older boys in the back of the room—we don't care if they've been held back. We aren't interested in their minds. We want the bored expressions on their faces. We want to feel our hearts beat as they pull us toward them, pull our faces deep into the fronts of their leather jackets, we want to smell hair oil and something sharper, more urgent. We want to have them kiss us with hard, angry lips. We want to feel our cheeks redden on the sandpaper of their cheeks. We want the stab of fear as they fumble for our breasts, pushing us back roughly against the pine trees. We want to be wanted. We take pains. We match skirts and sweaters, we pincurl our hair, we learn the new dances, the words to the songs.

We watch Beth Collins running around the block. Around and around, every night she runs and runs, exhausted. What is she doing? After four or five nights we figure it out. She is pregnant. She is trying to run her baby out of her body. We figure it out because, to us, it is clear. Close to us. To adults, it is not so clear. We watch for two more nights, holding our breath, feeling every inch of our bodies, how they fold inside themselves, secret and scared. By day, Beth drags herself through school. There are circles under her eyes, she looks bloated and sad and slightly desperate. What should we do? Mary Agnes has no doubts. She dials the Collins' number, puts a handkerchief over the phone, and in a deep voice says, "Tell Beth it won't work." Then we watch as Mrs. Collins throws open her back door, glances toward our window as though she almost suspects, walks slowly down to the sidewalk to wait for Beth to turn the corner. Two weeks later Beth is "visiting her aunt in Michigan" for the rest of the year. We are awed. Mary Agnes can get away with anything.

It's so real. I can see Beth running in her old white sweatshirt, her red hair weaving behind, her ponytail brushing first one shoulder then the other. I can hear Mary Agnes lower her voice and my own quickened heartbeat. What do I make of a past more real than the present? When it comes unbidden, like desire? What does it want? I have this sunlight stretching over waves, waves of heated air, my body stretched on the deck, my mind as clear and sharp as ever, ready for the future. But the future only curves *toward* and then folds *back*, not really touching. I am left with the future I am making now. How boring. A future of sitting in the sun over the Atlantic, remembering. My own inaction. My body's tense waiting. This does not make a memory, I'm almost certain of that. It will be just one of those ordinary days that recede and fade, that become the compost pile of a life. The hidden residue on which others grow. Unless something happens.

What usually happens, for me, is other people. They shape, through distraction. For instance, the man I am with is reading Virginia Woolf. Soon he will come out on the deck and read me a passage that interests him. I will have to admit to myself that I am not very interested in that passage—or any other. That I am bored by Virginia Woolf. It has taken years of composting to be able to say that. A woman is supposed to like Virginia Woolf. A woman is supposed to understand her feminine sensibility. But that's the problem, that's *why* she bores me. Women are not interested in other women. They are interested in men. And in themselves. Virginia Woolf is too much like me to interest me. I feel as though I could see things her way—*do* see things her way. Her thoughts *occur* to me.

He likes Virginia Woolf. She opens doors for him, puts a sentence together that twists and turns and takes him with her. I get tired of her incessant seeing, her ever-present *now* with its tidy observations. I get tired of Virginia the way I get tired of another woman on the phone when I am listening just to be polite, waiting for my turn to tell what's on my mind. I never feel that way with a man on the phone. I'm waiting for that little spark that says this conversation has undertone, and under-tow. My mind on alert.

In the end, I must come to the disturbing conclusion that I am interested only in *my* life. I wish that I felt more disturbed about this than I do, that it sent me into a novelist's version of panic— no more characters to people my deepest dreams. But I am satisfied with the characters who come, at random, into my life, and with wondering just what they mean, what they have meant, what they are about to mean in the drama that is mine and mine alone. I am satisfied to play this game of hide-and-go-seek. It's only the present that tugs at the body, saying "Get up. Get going. Make something of this day."

Make something. Make a phone call. Do. Act. Is memory made up of verbs? Perhaps. Verbs and adjectives. With the hindsight of memory, we paint in color and shape. Similes. At the time, we live only the moment, unaware of comparison, or the hint of connection. In memory we piece things together, give them the "that must be why" or the "now I can see" that sews up the seam of a life. Tim O'Brien is wrong. Life is not seamless, it's a myriad of seams, a patchwork quilt. But the seamstress is as quick and as accurate as my grandmother, who pieced together little octagons of colored cloth, flower after calico flower. They took shape in her fingers, a field full of wildflowers spreading over the bed, quilt after quilt, until her death left a box full of unfinished flowers—a lifetime of seams invisible to the unpracticed eye.

I am fifteen. The phone rings and it is Mary Agnes. "Come on over. Don't tell anyone." That's all she says. It's nine o'clock and I don't see how my parents are going to understand the necessity of going out. But I tell them Mary Agnes is locked out of her house and I'm going to help her get the cellar window open, and then, just for good measure, that we're going to the diner for a hamburger because she hasn't had any dinner. Fine, they say. They seem to believe whatever I tell them. I almost believe she *is* locked out as I run the three blocks to her house. There she is, standing with a set of keys in her hands, pacing the driveway. I almost say "You found them" before I remember.

"Come on. Get in." Her father's white Cadillac is parked in front of the garage. "Get in." The question goes underground, but it is still there. "They're out of town. Won't be back until midnight." But we are fifteen and we haven't taken driver's training and we don't even have a permit, let alone a license. We don't know how to drive.

Or rather, *I* don't know how to drive. What Mary Agnes knows never ceases to amaze me. She slowly backs the car up, turns it around, and noses it out onto the street, heading confidently out of town, stopping at each sign as though she had done it for years. Sitting next to her, in the dark plush of the passenger seat, I feel almost as safe as with my father. I don't relax, but I don't feel quite so nervous either. She heads for the back roads of the country around Gang Mills. The lights pry open the darkness, letting us own a small stretch of road. Up and down the dirt roads, dust spewing behind us, faster and faster—we begin to laugh, I stick my feet out the window, we wave as we streak past the mailboxes giving them at least four inches to spare. This is the limit of our world. We piece each stretch of the road to the next. We are the present—this motion, this exhilaration. A moving present, winding through the landscape.

At ten-thirty I am home. By eleven I'm asleep. The next morning Mary Agnes describes what I missed—how she went out again, driving the Cadillac up Rand Street where the railroad shunt cuts a lane of its own toward the factory. Straddling the rails, eighty miles an hour, right in town! I am not quite so taken with all of this as I pretend to be. I don't want to be left out, but I don't want to die. I want to come close, but veer off at the last minute. I'm not convinced Mary Agnes knows when to veer.

She's moving beyond us and we can feel it. She's finding new things to do—older, more experienced boys. I like it best when it feels familiar. Friday night, the diner after the basketball game, hamburgers and cokes. "Father Rogers would want me to eat this since it's already been ordered." Father Rogers is so understanding of her desires. I want a Father Rogers who knows what's best for me. I like Friday nights, all of us squeezed into a booth, Scott Dalrymple and his friends teasing, stealing our hats or mittens. But I can see it in her eyes. Boring. They glance over the formica table, the red vinyl benches, the confusion of teenagers, and they go distant. Darker. And suddenly it looks so ordinary, so hopelessly common.

Yesterday I picked blueberries and made my own pie. Fields of wild blueberries, the sun on my back. Blueberries staining my fingers and the promise of a pie. The sun like a compress. A bowl full of berries and a future tied to the present—no seams. And today I lie on the deck with the sure taste of the pie in my mouth—the taste of yesterday. No watch. No glasses. My body alive to the present. I close my eyes. The sound of sunlight is a deep rumble and intermittent churning of engines. Time is an ocean breeze that drops, suddenly, leaving a gap in the day. Whatever I am doing now won't count in that future. I am not here. I am alive in the greens and blues of the past. For this minute, or hour, there is no tense. I am on the underside of the quilt, moving with the thread that pulls it all together.

Desire does not rise as often in a life as we like to think it does. We spend our time waiting for it to reach out to us, wanting to be wanted. Real desire is the other side of that. It simply wants. It fastens itself on its object, unaware of self. It doesn't last—except in memory, where it rises again and again without warning. Always a surprise, always powerful.

I have five images of desire—only five times that *really* stand out. Count them on one hand. Maybe this is different for men, but I doubt it. I don't mean fleeting attractions. I mean the kind of desire that takes over and immobilizes. Five images that represent the spaces in my life where the focus is outward. Images. Held in the mind. Forever. Or revised, for common consumption. Real moments that stand for a succession of events or feelings. Real moments, although sometimes they happen only in the imagination.

First, nineteen, almost twenty, I turn a corner and can't go back. All night I wanted to be wanted, and then, on a hill in the Bronx, traffic making a red-and-yellow snake of lights below, I only want. What does he look like? He is twenty. Dark eyes, sardonic smile. Of course it can't work. His parents are threatening to cover the mirrors and say the prayers for the dead. So he dies, instead, for me. He will always be twenty, standing on a hill. Below him the weaving string of lights moves toward infinity.

Then I am dancing in the basement of St. Columba's Church in Edinburgh, Scotland. A young man with long curly hair is rushing down the stairs, rushing so fast he tumbles the last few, a blur of color and movement that I will interpret as love, and I am married and I speak in the first person plural and soon there is one son and then another and I rush on into a life my mother would surely approve. I am dancing in the basement of a church and there is nothing but color and motion, and perhaps some distant music.

There is one moment so fleeting I hardly know it was there, but I have evidence. A photograph. Not of him, but of me. A photograph I hardly recognize as myself, so unlike what I see in the mirror. But the mirror wants to be wanted, aids and abets. In the photograph, I am open to his lens: a woman with her hair to her shoulders, wearing white, holding a flower. Caught in the act.

The fourth is more difficult. Unfinished, and therefore open to revisions. Each day could become the image. For now, I choose to see a woman opening a letter, her hands tearing at the envelope, her eyes unable to read fast enough. She wants to know it all instantaneously. I see her open letter after letter, finding each time a mind that exists only for her. The letters lead, inevitably, to the moment when she sits on the deck of a house in Maine. They lead to Virginia Woolf and nights of Scrabble and never mind that in between there must have been pain and an intricate weaving of lives that must once have been simple.

300

The fifth is future. A future embedded in the past. It is why we go on. There is always $n + 1$ in the equation of desire. Fishing. Yes, I see a man with a rod, and time on his hands, casting the line. The sea both known and unknown, a moving bed of possibility.

This sea hardly moves. It could be blue flannel laid out on an ironing board, or corduroy. Boats skate its surface, leaving lighter lines, like scratch marks on ice. White sails stitch the sea to the sky. No, that's too poetic. The sky and sea meet and color has no meaning. They never meet, except to the deceived eye. And under the sea is a life we can only suspect. Lobstermen rely on that. The steady crawl. The traps, anchored to color. Flutter of gulls. What do they want? Each boat with its halo of wings. Groupies. Scurry and squawk. The noise of necessity.

Bad things come in threes. That's often the case. But that's because we look hard for the third when other things happen by coincidence. In the last few months, two of my friends have lost sons in their early twenties. I try on their lives. I cannot imagine them, though I try. What it must be like, at any time of the day, to feel the future snatched from you. The black shape that forms in the stomach and grows, branching out into artery and vein. The shape in the mind, the door that won't open to reveal that shape, the door that keeps on not opening.

My heart opens to them. And my fear. Where are my sons? One is in France, or is it England by now? One is working on Cape Cod, pulling lobsters out of boiling water and waiting for college to begin again. They walk through the door in my mind and it cannot stretch around their absence. Don't let me be third. Hedging of bets. Bargaining with fate. I leave the number where I can be reached, penance in advance—so it won't be needed. I can be reached here, in Maine. *Don't call. Don't die.* I am my own fear of the future.

. . . *always expressing itself.* The mind will not shut off. Close the eyes—still, the mind sees, hears, reacts, and moves effortlessly through its worries, back and forth, making plans. It knows what *could* happen. In and out, in and out, the mind expresses its sense of the self. On and on until I'm tired of it, my own internal voice with its interminable comments, its asides, its sarcasms and justifications.

A cloud, and the sun is snatched from the sky. Suddenly I am cold. I open my eyes. Several clouds, a slow-motion swirl, mixing then parting like lovers. Lingering. The sea is mottled with shadow and sun, a patchwork sea. The clouds are seamless—one large cloud where before there were many. No definition, and yet they had such distinct shapes, seen in an instant, frozen in the lens.

I am cold. My nipples stiffen. Do I imagine that the lobster boat circles one time too often, hoping for a glimpse as I stand to go indoors? "Jesus. Summer people. No shame." I doubt he cares what happens on shore, what women are sunning themselves on the decks. He's intent on the ocean. All present tense. Straight lines, therefore and thus. Male to the hilt. He's a fine-tuned machine, listening, working the boat close, a deft motion as he cuts the engine and reaches for the buoy. The trap reveals itself—his stock goes up or down in the blink of his eye.

My life loops and I sit, at its cusp, looking in both directions. Looking back is filled with people and events like a braid of colored ribbons. The future tails off and recedes into mist, the frayed end of possibility. I feel the burden. What do I make of the past, that the future may unfold with some definition? I am like anyone else. I want the end to complete the circle. I want to lay the incessant voice to rest. I want to know that life was not quite random—that I found a way to make some meaning. Like a good short story.

But if there is one thing the past has taught me, it is that our stories do not end. They intertwine. They are messy and incomplete.

I am fifteen and I do not know how to stop my grandmother from voting for Richard Nixon. It seems imperative that I do this, but I don't know how. I do not know that this will be one of my few memories of my grandmother—my agitation at her failure to like John F. Kennedy. That, and the inside of her refrigerator: Gouda cheese, lettuce, half a tomato—not the refrigerator of a grandmother, the refrigerator of a Republican. And the box full of flowers. A surprise, such bounty of color from such a spare life. And those stitches. The pinched, parsimonious workings of a lifetime.

I do not know how to end what is ending. Mary Agnes is reckless—with my feelings, with all of us. She drops us quickly, as though she can't be bothered with our silliness, our pitiful attempts to be daring, the cigarettes, the gossip. She spends all her time with Larry and his friends. Sometimes she drinks. We've smelled it when they come in from driving around. Wears a leather jacket. Acts loud. Acts as though she knows something we don't, and we're convinced she does. Sex. We're sure of it. Something changed and one day her eyes were different, as though they had been satisfied and then stoked—a fire waiting to burst into flame. She is brittle and beautiful and beyond us.

Tonight I am washing dishes when the phone rings. There's so much confusion on the other end. What comes over me now is not the present tense of what *was* but the past tense of what is. The phone rang. It was a friend: "There's been an accident." An accident at the lake, five or six kids, most of them dead. Mary Agnes was not dead—she'd been taken to the hospital. Her parents were on their way.

She would not die, of that I was certain. She had that kind of uncanny luck. Others would die, but she would live to make a story of it all. She was that kind of person.

She would not die, but she did. A screaming death, everything mangled and broken, her glasses embedded in the dashboard, her dark eyes riddled with glass. The imagination cannot go far enough with what happens inside a car that leaves the road at high speed and flies, at a thirty-degree angle, without a brake mark on the road, into a tree, shearing the roof and snapping the necks of four people in the back seat. The imagination cannot relive the moment of confusion when the girl who was steering realized that the boy who was working the pedals was not pushing on the brake. When she knew that she was out of control.

I am fifteen and my best friend is dead. The town is in shock. Six of its students are dead, and one of them is my best friend. My phone rings and rings. At school the kids swarm around me. My moods are measured. How am I taking it? How am I doing? It must be so awful. They try to imagine. They are so full of sympathy I am filled with it. I am so important. I have never been so important. I am full of something so powerful that I name it grief, although I had always imagined grief to be something personal and hard, like a fist. This is soft and cloudlike but spreads its own kind of clarity. I reel with my secret knowledge of what really happened. Of course it is not my secret alone—there are

303

others who rode with them while she steered, while he let the speedometer creep higher and higher, others who shrieked their new freedom and their reckless disregard into the night. But we see no point in telling adults. Her parents would only grieve more. No one would spring back to life. Our secret is ours, a whirling, heady part of our grief. We twist and twist it into a brittle strand of youth. They are ours. The loss is ours. We own it.

I don't know if what I am feeling is grief. There is no room to feel anything but this steady attention. I do know that this attention is close to desire—and that I want it more than I want Mary Agnes. That it brings with it relief. I will be her best friend forever.

In the past tense she died. I am the woman who lost her best friend, years ago, when she was fifteen. Her story ended. It was different from mine. My story goes on, carrying a small part of hers with me. But in *my* voice. Seen through *my* eyes.

This memory I am forced to reconstruct, brick by brick. Then he said. Then she came. Then they asked. Then we didn't. Today she dies in memory, and again I do not know what to make of it. It cannot be the simple narrative: *Once upon a time I had a friend. She was young and beautiful and a tiny bit reckless and that led to her death. The end.* If she had not died, she would have her own memory to pull out and mull over and then tuck away again and go on. She would see her life stretching before her, a future that curves back occasionally, like this, but holds out its essential promise with no strings attached. She would shiver slightly and stand up. Go inside.

The sea is deceptive with its surface of alternate sun and shade. Look, I say, what do you want from me? My hems are all straight. No stones in my pockets, I'm trying . . . trying to make sense of it all. Right now, George Bush and Michael Dukakis are beginning a campaign that will take them each around and around the country. Next year at this time, one of them will be president. Although it seems to me that it matters desperately which one it should be, next year, whoever it is, I will have gone on. The country will have gone on, just as it did when my grandmother put on her stockings and best black shoes and probably voted for Richard Nixon. The sea will rise and fall. The engines

304

will cut the morning in two, and I will see everything with a brief clarity, and then that, too, will cloud over. I will be one year older. Nothing else?

I am fifteen. In two months I will be sixteen, and in four years I will taste the first of those five desires. Three years after that I will have a son, and then another. I will nearly live the life my mother planned for me. I will watch her die slowly and I will wish for her another death, an alternate ending. I will plan my own as though such things could be planned. I will follow the thread that brings me here, above the Atlantic, as though this were ordained. I will feel the future riding the air, the way I imagine it must be to fish the surf. The wrist flicks, the line spins out and rides its own thermal, motionless for an instant before it settles, tugs against the current and is reeled taut.

I am fifteen and this is my first time inside a Catholic church, inside the deep vault of Our Lady of the Immaculate Conception. I sit nervously with four other girls. Self-conscious. Alive. We do not know what to expect of a requiem mass. We are not prepared for the chanting, the kneeling and crossing, the stifling odor of incense. Father Rogers intones the words he has memorized for such occasions. Father Rogers would not want Mary Agnes to be here, lying in the coffin in the front of the church, teasing us with her silence. I do not want to be here, wondering whether to kneel to something in which I do not believe. Little red swirls before my eyes. I sink beneath the hardwood floor where it is dark. Where night has fallen on the foundation of the church and children are calling—the high, chirping voices of children at play.

I inch myself out onto the plank and I run, all the old patterns intact, memory triumphant, turning and twisting through time, over the black cellar hole toward the maple tree. *Ollie ollie in free.* I am safe. My children are safe. It is now.

Nominated by The Georgia Review, *Marianne Boruch and Lisel Mueller*

THE MIDDLE OF NOWHERE

fiction by KENT NELSON

from GRAND STREET

T HIS HAPPENED JUST after I'd dropped out of high school, when I was seventeen and living with my father. We had this trailer southwest of Tucson about twenty-three miles, right at the edge of the Papago Reservation at the end of a dirt road which petered out into the Baboquivari Mountains. Across to the east you could see the Sierritas, which were a low rim of ragged hills, and to the south where there was not much of anything except saguaros and greasewood and mesquite and the highway that ran from Robles Junction to Sasabe on the Mexican border.

Our trailer sat on a hill above two sand gullies. The previous occupants had seen fit to throw their trash into the steeper ravine, but the other one was a nice broad wash, rocky in places, with good cover for deer in the thickets of paloverde and ironwood. There were a couple of other trailers back down toward the highway, their TV antennas and satellite dishes the main evidence that someone else lived out there. Now and then you could hear a dog barking at the coyotes at night.

By this time in my life I'd pretty much seen everything. I don't mean I had anything figured cold or that I possessed some ultimate knowledge. Pretty much the opposite was true. I mean, nothing surprised me anymore. When I was nine and ten I lived with my mother in Phoenix, and she had done about everything I could imagine. She drank and went on benders, leaving me in the apartment for two or three days at a time. Once she said she was going down to the Red Onion for some cigarettes and didn't come back for a week. I knew enough to go to a neighbor's place. People got beaten up there, and one man got killed. I remember watching him being carried out on a stretcher.

My mother had boyfriends. When a man stayed over, I slept on the sofa instead of in the one bed we shared, and I could hear through the thin wall my mother's calling out a stranger's name. When the man liked me, it was all right, but when he didn't, which was more usual, I got shipped down on the Greyhound to my father.

I didn't mind it in Tucson. My father had a house in the barrio then, and there were lots of people moving around the streets at all hours. I liked to watch them doing their deals and loving up and just walking around. I liked the sirens and shouts in Spanish and the music.

Sometimes I stayed a few days, sometimes a few weeks. But always a time came to go back.

"You sure you want to go?" my father used to ask.

"Why wouldn't I?"

"Your mother's not very well," he said. "She's fragile."

"I can take care of her."

The truth was I didn't know whether I wanted to go back. I didn't much like the apartment on the eighth floor or my mother's boyfriends. My father's girlfriends were much nicer. But I kept thinking of my mother's sad face and how much she wanted to be happy.

So it went that way for a long time, back and forth between Phoenix and Tucson. I tried to get my mother to take better care of herself—to go to sleep earlier so she could get to her job, which was in a plant nursery over in Mesa, to eat better, and not to drink so much. She did all right, too, for a while, until she met this man named Ray, who started her on some pills. He moved in, and I went off to Tucson, thinking I'd stay for good.

My father and I got along. He was a spindly man, wiry, very good-looking in a rough way. He had good hands and a sleek brown mustache, and he was a smooth talker. Over against him, I was softer like my mother, with a disposition more inclined to observation. We weren't close in the sense of camaraderie or

307

talking things out. Maybe he felt guilty about leaving. Anyway, we didn't discuss things much, so there were spaces around us unfilled, like something way late at night left unsaid.

I spent a whole school year when I was sixteen with my father, and only saw my mother once. In the fall she got sick and went to the hospital, and she called for me. I stayed up in Phoenix for three months until she died.

I guess I knew she was dying because I asked her questions I never had thought of before—what she used to be like when she was a girl in California, about her parents I'd never met (they owned a small artichoke farm), what she had hoped for in her life. She couldn't speak very well. By then she was sleeping most of the time, and she'd wake up only for brief glimpses of me. She'd start to talk and in the middle of a sentence, when she was describing a place she remembered or a special day, she'd drift off into a terrible stillness.

When she died, I was left hanging.

After that I decided not to go back to school. I wasn't a bad student or a troublemaker. I just didn't do anything. I wrote my homework but couldn't turn it in, and even when I knew the answer in class, I'd sit with my head down on the desk. The teachers didn't know what to do. They talked to me; they sent me to counselors. Why wouldn't I try? Why not cooperate? They even got my one friend, George White Foot, a half-breed Apache, to speak to me. But finally they gave up and let me seep down into groundwater.

About this time was when my father got hold of the trailer. He had been evicted from his house to make way for some renewal project, but I suspected he had other reasons for wanting to be out of town. He liked women. He had a way with them, too, but unlike my mother, he wanted the relationship to be simple. My mother was in love with every man she met, and she'd say "Stevie, he's so wonderful. He *feels* so good. What do you think?"

I thought she wanted love more than anything, but my father didn't. He liked things uncomplicated, and one way to keep them that way was to live out so far no one could drop by.

So pretty much I stayed out at the trailer for the next year. My father might have made me get a job, but in a way I had the upper hand there. My mother had left me a few thousand dollars, and I was able to pay my share of rent and food. Now and then I'd go into Tucson to the library or to a movie, but mostly I stayed home, as if I were waiting for something to happen. I didn't know what. It wasn't waiting, exactly, either. It was passing time. It was as if everything up to then had been a test of endurance, and I had to recover from it. I needed to rest.

I spent some time watching the cars float along the highway in the distance, imagining who was in them and what future they were headed toward. I could see pickup trucks coming from Mexico, red sedans, half-tons, vans. At night the headlights skimmed through the darkness like comets.

For a month I exhumed the trash in the ravine and tried to piece together the lives of the people who'd lived there before. I couldn't come up with much except they were poor and someone had done a good trade with whoever sold Jim Beam.

But mostly I took target practice with the .22 and I read. I read everything I could get my hands on. My father brought me books and magazines whenever he happened to think of me—from the 7-Eleven, from someone's house where he was repairing an air conditioner or a washing machine, from a friend's apartment, sometimes even from the bookmobile parked in the mall where his appliance repair company had its dispatch office. He never asked me what I liked, though. It was his idea that in the general variety he'd hit on something that would move me off high-center. He gave me manuals about engines, a history of Vietnam, a book on oil painting, porno magazines, English novels. I imagined him standing in front of a library shelf or a magazine rack wondering what to choose. What should he take home to a boy about whom he had not the slightest notion?

But I knew him. His whole life was women. He met women in bars or on the job or at diners, supermarkets, offices, even at the bookmobile. He had a gift for it, a genius. Educated or uneducated, black, white, Hispanic; tall or short; he could have charmed the underwear off a nun. But there weren't many nuns that made the long drive to the trailer.

He had a system worked out. He'd bring a woman for a night and take her back to Tucson in the morning. It'd be dark when they'd get there—a turn at Robles Junction, head west on gravel, keep left when the road forked, and so on. The woman would be riding blindfolded, so to speak. There was no telephone, so she couldn't ever call.

Sometimes he'd bring someone home on a Friday night, and she'd stay until Monday. I dreaded these times because my father worked Saturdays half-days, and often overtime, and he'd leave the woman, whoever she was, with me. On such occasions the woman usually slept late. One slept all day without stirring, and I was certain she was dead; and another one, when she woke up late and looked out the window, thought she'd been sent to hell.

But the worst thing was there were no introductions. Sometimes my father hadn't even told the woman I was there, and more than once a woman I'd never seen before came naked from my father's bedroom and, when she saw me, started screaming. After a few times, I made it a habit on Saturday mornings to take target practice with the .22 from the kitchen window.

Even that wasn't enough every time. Once, despite a half-hour's fusillade from the porch on a dead washing machine, a blonde came out half-naked. She was twenty-four or so, hung over, but still pretty, even with her make-up smudged. All she had on were a pair of green panties and a blouse with one button fastened.

"Who is the enemy?" she asked, shielding her eyes from the sun and peering off into the gully.

"Indians."

She moved to the rail of the landing. "Where?"

"You'd better go back inside," I told her. "We're the only wagon train in this circle."

She nodded, "You come with me," she said, as she walked by and dragged her fingers across my shoulder. "I'd feel safer."

But I didn't go. I spent the rest of the morning at the edge of the yard shooting the arms off saguaro Indians.

That wasn't the only incident like that either. I had the suspicion my father may have asked some of his lesser friends to flirt with me, but it was a suspicion I never proved.

One rainy afternoon when he was late, for example, I was reading in the living room, listening occasionally to the barrage on the tin roof. Out the window, little water-falls collected from nowhere and rushed into the gullies. The sandwash was a torrent. Then this woman, whose name was Jake, came to the window. Maybe she was watching for my father; maybe she thought

310

he'd never get there in the storm. Maybe she was bored. Anyway, she turned to me and said, "Steve, do you want to make love?"

"Who-what?"

"Don't you think I'm pretty?"

Jake was pretty. She had a smooth oval face and dark eyes, and nice high breasts which stood out under my father's shirt she had on. "I think you're very pretty."

"Well, then?"

"You're my father's girl."

She made a face that was supposed to show hurt or maybe defiance, but which made her look spoiled. "I'm not anybody's girl," she said.

I won't say I wasn't tempted. Under ordinary circumstances I wouldn't have cared whose girl she was, but these were not ordinary circumstances. I wanted to kiss her and slap her both. I wanted to shake her. What did she mean offering herself like that? But I didn't say anything.

She came over and put her hand on my arm, and I felt a terrible dark chill run through me like a sliver of cold steel. In that instant I knew what torture my mother must have suffered to be so helpless in desire. But the rain stopped abruptly. The drumming on the roof ebbed to a hum, and not far down the gravel road, the headlights of my father's truck delved through the steam rising from the hot earth.

There was one woman who stayed nearly a month. Her name was Esther, and she'd just been divorced from a doctor in Tucson and was waiting to hear about a nursing job in Los Angeles. She didn't have a place to stay, so my father said what-the-hell, and she came to the trailer.

She was not so pretty as most of the women my father had. She had curly hair and a broad face and rather sad blue eyes which looked right at you, which I liked. We used to drink beer together in the afternoons and play gin rummy at the kitchen table. She never asked about my father like some women did. Instead she asked about my mother: what was she like, what did she do, where was she? Why did she and my father get divorced?

I was usually a little drunk, and trying to answer was like exploring a region of myself I'd never encountered. I went down one wrong path after another, found dead ends, labyrinths. If I forced words too quickly, I missed details; if I labored too long, I became lost in a confusion of images. At the same time as it was hopeless to answer, I understood it was important to try. No matter what fleeting impression I gave, no matter how mystified I felt, I needed to know who my mother was to know who I was.

Esther didn't hurry me. She'd listen one day and the next. She'd fetch new beers. She was as solid as I was shaky. Her own divorce, she said, made her tougher, and she knew what she wanted. I admired her patience, and I remember it seemed hopeful to me at the time that someone could choose to change her life, get on a bus one day, and do it.

After Esther left for L.A., there was a month or so when my father didn't bring anyone home. During this stretch, George White Foot showed up one day with a bottle of tequila, which we took down into the sandwash, along with the .22. George said he'd run into my father in a bar, and my father said I was anxious for company.

George had quit school, too. He was bagging groceries temporarily at the Safeway and thinking of going over to Safford to work in the copper mine. "You want to go?" he asked. "I got Apaches who can get you in." He gulped the tequila.

"I'm not done here yet," I said.

George nodded. "What are you doing out here?"

"Taking notes."

He laughed and drank some more. "Taking notes on what?"

I didn't have an answer. I thought I was taking notes. I sighted the rifle and picked off a cholla blossom. "I bet I can outshoot you," I said. "I'll stand and you can shoot prone. A dollar a target."

"You have to drink some tequila," he said.

I drank some tequila, and George picked the targets, and I beat him five times in a row.

"Where'd you get the name White Foot?" I asked.

"Where'd you get the name Steve?"

He sat down in the sand and skewered the bottle down and took off his tennis shoes and socks. One of his feet was brown like his arms, but the other was albinistic—almost totally white up to the ankle.

I took off my boots and socks. "I got two of them."

We laughed and drank more tequila, and he called me Steve White Feet. "I'll bet the five dollars I owe you you can't give me the right question to the answer 'sis-boom-bah.' "

I pretended to think for a minute, but nothing came to mind. "I don't know."

"Guess."

I didn't want to guess. I was getting drunk and it struck me that George couldn't go to work in the copper mine in Safford, even though that was where the Apaches had their land. "Don't go, George," I said.

He stared at me. He was drunker than I was. "Don't you want to know the question?" he asked.

"I want to know every question."

"An exploding sheep."

He laughed, but it wasn't funny.

We finished the bottle of tequila, and after that we staggered up the sandwash to hunt rabbits. But by then the rabbits were safe.

It was late fall when something changed. The long-day heat was out of the rocks, and I had found a ledge behind an outcropping where I could sit and read and see nothing at all except the blue Sierritas and farther away the Las Guijas Hills and the Santa Ritas. Now and then through my binoculars I'd watch a hawk drifting on the updrafts which poured from the ravines.

Then one evening my father came home early with a stack of books from the bookmobile and some groceries. He actually sat down in the living room.

"I'm going to stay in town for a couple of days," he said.

"Oh, yeah? What's her name?"

"Don't be that way."

"What way? I just asked what her name was."

"Goldie."

I didn't think much of it at the time. My father didn't often stay in town, but that was his business, and it didn't matter to me one way or the other. He didn't give me the details, and I didn't ask.

"You be okay?"

"Sure," I said. "Thanks for the books."

A couple of days later I heard the horn of his truck. I was on the ledge, and I scrambled up to the ridge where I could see

313

down to the trailer. In the circle of my glasses, I made out my father standing on the porch beside a short-haired, dark-haired woman. He was waving to me to come down.

I figured this was Goldie, though I'd imagined her as a blonde. She looked tall from a distance, as tall as my father anyway, who was six feet. She wore fancy sandals, and he had on cowboy boots. She looked like some kind of real-estate person, dressed in a gray business suit, or maybe a social worker, and for a moment I wondered whether my father had some deal going, some scam. Then a piece of sunlight flashed from one of her earrings.

When I had climbed down into the sandwash and half-way up the hill, they appeared at the lip of the trail above me. I paused amidst the tangle of cholla and ocotillo and looked up. The woman's hair, which I'd thought was short, was pushed up on top of her head in a twist. The gray business suit was a sweater and slacks. I guessed she was about thirty, maybe a little older.

What impressed me most, though, was not the way she looked; it was the way my father looked. He kept motioning for me to hurry, and he had a grin on his face that seemed to say he had this secret he couldn't wait to tell me. He must have won the lottery, I thought, the way he was grinning.

"Steve," he said. "Come on up here. This is Goldie. Goldie, this is my boy, Steve."

I climbed the last few yards, and Goldie took a step forward and put out her hand.

I took her hand, felt her smooth palm. "You don't look like a Goldie," I said.

She squeezed my hand and smiled. "You don't look like a boy."

When I heard her voice, I knew she was not the lottery representative or a real-estate lady or like any of the other women who'd ever been to the trailer before. Her voice slid over words with a lilting inflection like water over slick rock, or maybe like the chinooks blow under the eaves of the tin roof.

"She's Irish," my father said. "I met her on a job at her uncle's place out Gates Pass. We've been up at the Grand Canyon for a couple of days."

"Your father rescued me," Goldie said. She gave a small, sweet laugh.

"I thought, if she wants, she might as well stay out here a while," my father said. "What do you think, Steve?"

314

He'd never asked me before what I thought. "Sounds all right to me," I said. "If she wants."

Right away it was strained. Goldie liked privacy, and in a trailer privacy's as scarce a commodity as snow in hell. From back to front there was a bedroom, a hall-way up one wall which joined the bathroom and a second small bedroom where I slept. The kitchen opened into the living room. Whenever Goldie wanted to use the bathroom, she knocked to make certain it was empty. And when she walked around the house, she had on at least a robe. In some ways it would have been easier having around a woman who didn't mind being seen half-undressed, even a flaunter, than one who was so prissy about things.

She also changed the hours of our days. My father didn't go drink in bars anymore, which was his usual habit. Even when Esther was here for that month, he might as well have been in a bar because as soon as he got home he took her to bed. But with Goldie it was more civilized. When my father got home and tried to talk her into going to bed, she'd laugh and say in a voice both teasing and gentle, "You're nothing but a rotten Englishman."

Goldie wanted to learn to cook—not necessarily fancy things, but something more substantial than hamburgers. She was anxious to try rabbit and venison and rattlesnake, and she liked Mexican food—burritos, jalapeño omelettes, enchiladas—which my father and I were pretty good at. So the three of us ate dinners at a normal hour. She called me Stephen, and I called her Blackie, and we talked about whatever happened to strike Goldie's fancy.

I could take the knocking on the bathroom door and the robe and the family dinners, but I chafed under Goldie's idea that the day started at five A.M. I liked to stay up late and read and then sleep in the next morning. So to hear Goldie making coffee in the dark drove me crazy. The kettle whistled, and she clanked silverware and unscrewed the jar of instant and got out the milk. Then the front door opened and closed. I'd lie there as the gray light seeped through the window, angry, unable to sleep. What was she doing outside? And how long was my father going to let this last?

Once I got up to see why she went outside at that hour. I expected to see her doing calisthenics or praying or something, but when I opened the door, she was sitting on the porch steps bundled up in a wool coat against the chill of the desert. Her coffee was steaming into the air.

"What the hell are you doing?" I asked.

"Sometimes I miss Ireland," was all she said.

For those first several weeks, she went into town with my father in the mornings. She borrowed his truck and toured the countryside—the Desert Museum, the mission of San Xavier, the university, the Pima Air Museum. She ranged as far as Phoenix and Nogales, even drove by herself through the Papago Reservation to Puerto Peñasco on the Gulf of California.

She asked me to go with her once. It was on one of those stormy days when low-flying clouds banked into the Baboquivaris and slipped over into the basin. I couldn't go up to my ledge, so I said all right, I'd go. She wanted to go into the Catalinas—to the top of Mount Lemmon. So that's what we did. The road started in ocotillo and saguaro along Tanque Verde Drive and wound up into oaks and sycamores. A warm misty rain was falling. But when we got higher into the pines it was snowing. I'd seen snow before, but I'd only been in it once up in Flagstaff when I was about nine. My mother had gone up to surprise a man—just the scene my father hated. This man said he owned a sporting goods store, and we went to every store in Flagstaff before we found him. It turned out he was a salesman, and he obviously wasn't expecting to see my mother. She sent me outside to play, and it was snowing on the streets. I remember how dirty the snow seemed, mashed down by tires and turning the buildings gray.

But at the top of Mount Lemmon the snow was clean. The pale trees were ghostly as the air, and even the road was white and unmarked.

"You should see the snow fall into the sea," Goldie said.

"I've never seen the sea."

"Oh, you must, Stephen. I live in Donaghadee, which is a fishing village near Belfast, and to watch the snow settle over the boats in the harbor and sweep across the gray water . . . it's lovely, really."

The snow was beautiful then, too, coming down through the huge ponderosas. We came out of the trees into a clearing where the whole world looked white.

"Stop." Goldie said.

I pulled over, though there were no other cars. Goldie got out and ran into the meadow full of snow. It was so white you couldn't tell where the hills were or how far the meadow extended into the whiteness. I didn't know what she was doing. She looked so frail, running like that into the wide expanse of nothing. It was eerie to see her fading behind the white sheen, as if the air were a deep hole and would swallow her.

I rolled down the window and called to her, but she didn't stop running.

Two months went by, right into December, and Goldie was still there. She had stopped going into town with my father. I guess she'd seen as many museums and churches as anyone could stand.

So she stayed at the trailer with me. Not that I found that a problem: by then I was used to the way she did things. When she was getting dressed, I stayed out of her way, and I developed a grudging respect for her five A.M. coffee. Sometimes I got up and watched the sunrise with her, and we all had breakfast together like ordinary people.

After my father went off to work, Goldie and I sorted out the day. Sometimes we hunted the wash. We'd go after rabbits or quail, and Goldie got so she could shoot a bird in the head from twenty-five yards. I showed her how to hold the dead birds tightly and break their skin at the breastbone so the skin and feathers peeled back like a jacket. We cleaned the quail and soaked them in salt water and made stuffing with bread and spices.

More often we just scouted the terrain. Goldie liked the desert because Ireland was cool and wet, the antithesis of the Southwest. She was fascinated how the ocotillo rolled its leaves in the dryness and the saguaros stored tons of water. We looked for animals—coatis, javelinas, snakes. She seemed to see things more quickly than I, maybe because the land was new to her. She picked out a stockstill deer on the hillside, an eagle sitting on rocks with a rock background.

"Do you think we could see a mountain lion?" she asked.

"Not in daytime."

"I'd like awfully to see one."

"They're here," I said, "but they hunt at night."

317

That night she begged my father to take her to look for a mountain lion.

"A puma? Hah! We wouldn't have the chance of a pimp at St. Peter's to see a mountain lion."

"Stephen says they're around."

"Oh, they're around. But they don't want to see you."

"We could drive the back roads," Goldie said. "Don't they hunt at night?"

"No way," my father said. He smiled patiently and pinched her arm, and every night for two weeks after that, they drove the back roads over in the Papago Reservation.

Something happened on these excursions. When they returned late at night my father looked haggard and drawn, and he'd sit down and have a stiff shot of rye whiskey. He wasn't angry or short with me or with Goldie. He'd talk normally, but I could tell the trip had exhausted him in a way that was beyond just the driving. At first I thought it was burning the candle late and early. My father wasn't used to staying up late and getting up at five. But it was more than that.

The next night, just as they were about to leave, I asked whether I could go along. "Do you mind?" I asked Goldie.

"You don't want to go," my father said.

"Why don't I?"

"You don't."

But he wouldn't give me a reason, and Goldie didn't mind. She sat between us in the front seat, her hands braced on the dashboard, her face pressed close to the windshield. We proceeded slowly, thirty miles an hour or so, the speed at which Goldie said she could see best. The headlights jerked over mesquite and saguaro and cholla, and sometimes we ran without a bend in the track for ten miles or more toward some village whose name was no name—Vamori, Idak, Gu Oidak.

All the while Goldie talked. The silhouette of her glassy forehead and her arced nose and her mouth blurred against the splayed light that moved in front of the truck, but she spoke without a pause, in that lilting voice. She recounted incidents from her childhood in Donaghadee. Her father was a fisherman, her mother a baker. They had a small house, old it was, she said, down at the rocks. She had got a scholarship to school, the first of her family to go away. They had all been fishermen laboring over nets and boats . . .

And I gradually began to feel the cloudy days over the sea, and to see the long sloping green farms bordered by gray stone walls. And I felt my father sink down gently behind the wheel.

We saw kangaroo rats, badgers, snakes, deer. Once a coyote crossed the tracks in front of the lights. But there were no mountain lions.

Not long after that my father stopped taking Goldie on those late rides. He said it was the expense of the gas; and finding a mountain lion was against all odds. But I understood it was something else that troubled him. He had come up against something he'd never faced before, which was what to do next. He liked Goldie. She was the first woman he'd cared about since my mother, or maybe ever, but she was a strain on him, too. Normally he was the one in control, the person to say yes or no to things, but with Goldie he found himself the one holding on. At dinner he'd stare at her, not listening to her talk, but looking at her as if he were trying to figure out something. From what I could tell, Goldie was satisfied with her life. She had no plans to leave. But the idea of her leaving was always there in the air like a hawk circling, throwing its shadow across the ground.

It was about this time, too, that I went to see George White Foot. He was on the last half-hour of his shift at the Safeway over on Speedway, and when I first got a glimpse of him—black hair in a pony tail, tall, slouched over the end of one of the check-out stands—he looked as though he were moving in slow motion.

"Hey, George," I said.

"If it isn't Steve White Feet," he said. "What you got, man?"

His eyes were glazed, and I could tell he was operating on batteries. "I was going to buy a six-pack," I said. "What kind do you like?"

"Anything."

I bought a double-pack of Miller and waited in the truck. When George finished, we drove out Tanque Verde. All along the highway huge divots had been scoured in the saguaro and greasewood for new houses. While one crew scraped the hillside, another was erecting frames for the families that would settle there.

"It makes you wonder, doesn't it?" I said.

"Wonder what?" George stared straight ahead.

"Look at the houses. Where's the water coming from?"

George wasn't paying attention to the houses. He was swilling beer and staring through the neon lights. "I'm going to Safford next week," he said. "Are you done out there yet with your old man?"

"Not yet."

"Shit," George said in a disgusted voice. Then he softened. "It's not bad pay. The union takes an interest."

"I'm not a copper miner," I said.

"Neither am I."

I imagined the daylight breaking across the huge orange copper pit, and men filing one at a time through a metal gate. All day they would chew the earth with huge machines, then go home and come back the next day. At the end of the week, they'd have money.

"You got to do something, Steve," George said.

He looked at me, but his eyes were blank. "Give yourself a break," I told him. "You don't have to go."

"A break? Like you? Give myself a break like you? At least I see my chances when they come at me. I got to jump."

"Jump where?"

"Fuck you," George said. He turned away and swigged the beer. He was afraid, that was all. But he wasn't afraid of Safford. He was afraid of the same thing I was: that dark land up ahead beyond the headlights where the highway went on into nothing.

In January my father became more distant, as if he were edging away from us. I didn't notice it at first because it was a gradual shift and day-to-day things didn't change much. He was often late for dinner—that's what I remember—and I began to wonder whether he was working late or going drinking or what.

One night Goldie and I had prepared a rabbit with gravy and rice and a nice salad. She'd dressed up for the occasion in a Mexican skirt and blouse she'd bought in Nogales as a souvenir, and she'd fixed her hair with turquoise pins. She'd put on perfume, too, which she seldom wore.

We were drinking Coors to tide us over, watching out the kitchen window at the gray dusk sliding down from the mountains. I was conscious how soft her skin looked above the scalloped neckline of her blouse, how her bare neck curved so delicately from her rounded shoulders. Her cheeks were flushed from the beer and from the heat of the rabbit's cooking.

"Where is he, do you think?" she asked.

"Looking for mountain lions."

She smiled but did not look at me. "They must be in caves all through these hills."

I nodded. The land out the window had faded. The Sierritas were lavender and blue, ebbing toward black, and in the yard the arc light had come on.

"You'd look for a mountain lion for me, wouldn't you, Stephen?"

"I would," I said.

She laughed and stood up and twirled around in the small space of the kitchen. Then she stopped and looked back out the window. "Do you know what he's really doing?"

"No."

"You do."

"He's looking for a place in town," I said.

Goldie seemed surprised. "What place?"

"Somewhere better than the trailer. He wants it for you."

We were silent for a long time, and the small space tightened up. Goldie didn't move from the window.

"Are you going to stay with him?" I asked.

That was the only time Goldie didn't say anything. She looked around at me with an expression so pained I couldn't move.

"Let's drink," she said finally. "The Irish are famous for drinking."

She got out the whiskey bottle from under the sink and poured two glasses and gave me one. Then she went into the living room.

A moment later, I heard the door open and close, and the trailer was silent.

That was when I knew how my mother had lived through all those years. I felt at that moment the weight of that emptiness of love, that terrible absence which wanted filling. Momentum was like wind seeking and seeking; even when it was invisible it was there, driving forward, unable to be calm. I held my breath for a minute, and then I followed Goldie.

321

I stood on the landing. Goldie was in the yard, illuminated by the arc light, holding her glass of whiskey above her head. She swirled through the light, lifting her skirt with one hand, twirling like a dancer across the gravel. She paused and drank and continued toward the rim of the trail into the sandwash.

"Stephen," she said. "Come on."

But she didn't wait for me. Her voice carried through the stillness and then she was gone over the edge and into the ravine.

I glanced down the dirt road toward the highway hoping to see the headlights of my father's truck sweeping up among the saguaros. But there was nothing there but the vacant dark highway and the barely perceptible ridge of the hills.

I went after Goldie, not knowing what else to do. By the time I reached the sandy wash, she had started upstream. Her dark tracks curved through the sand and around the first bend, and I called to her and heard my own voice echo against the rocks.

I knew she was waiting for me. I walked slowly, feeling my steps yield to the soft sand.

She was there, around that first outcropping of rocks. Her white blouse was vivid in the air. She had taken the turquoise pins from her hair, and it fell across her shoulder like black feathers.

I stopped and waited.

"Come here, Stephen," she said.

I went closer.

"Smell my hair." She bent her head back so that her black hair cascaded into her hand, and she held it up to me.

I breathed in. She pushed her hair into my face, across my cheek. Her hair smelled of apricot.

"Smell here," she said. "What does my skin smell like?" She pulled her blouse down over one shoulder.

"Cholla blossoms."

"Close your eyes."

I closed my eyes.

"Tight," she said.

I kept my eyes tightly closed, feeling my heart beat different colors behind the lids. The breeze smoothed across my damp forehead. In the thicket not far away, thrashers and quail were settling in. I heard the swishing of Goldie's skirt, the movement of cloth, the sigh she made when the cool air touched her skin.

* * *

In the early morning, while my father and Goldie were still sleeping, I packed the few things I had and coasted the truck out of the yard. About a mile down, I abandoned the truck where the sand gully intersected the gravel. It would take my father a while to understand, then at least an hour to reach the truck. I walked from there to Sasabe road, and sometime toward dawn got a ride north from a Mexican businessman. A Papago took me west on the main road to Sells, and by evening I was in Blythe, California.

I was going somewhere where it snowed into the sea—Northern California or maybe Oregon. I wasn't certain of anything. It was the beginning for me of a sadness which, I suppose, had to come to me sometime, an aching that lasted for years.

Nominated by Greg Pape and C. E. Poverman

CRAZY LIFE

fiction by LOU MATHEWS

from CRAZYHORSE

C HUEY CALLED ME from the jail. He said it was all a big mistake. I said, Sure Chuey, like always, que no? What is it this time, weed or wine? He said it was something different this time. I said, You mean like reds, angel dust, what? Chuey says, No Dulcie, something worse.

I said, So? Why call me? Why don't you call that Brenda who was so nice to you at the party. He said Dulcie. Listen. It's a lot worse. I got to get a lawyer. Then he like started to cry or something. Not crying—Chuey wouldn't cry—but it was like he had a hard time breathing, like he was scared. I couldn't believe it. I didn't do it, Dulcie, he told me. I didn't do nothing. I was just in the car.

I got scared then. Chuey, I said, Can anybody hear you? He said there was a chota—a cop—around and some dude from the D.A.'s office, but not close. I told him, Shut up Chuey. Just shut up. Don't say nothing to nobody. I'll come down. Chuey said, I don't know if they'll let you see me.

They'll let me, I said, Hang on.

I skipped school, fifth and sixth periods, just gym and home wreck, and hitchhiked up to Highland Park. I been there before, the Highland Park cop shop. Chuey's been busted there three or four times. Nothing bad, just drunk and one time a joint in the car.

This time it looked bad. They had a bunch of reporters there. This T.V. chick was on the steps when I come up, standing in

324

front of the bright lights saying about the police capturing these guys. She kept saying the same words, Drive-by murders. Drive-by murders. There was these two kids, brothers, and one was dead and the other was critical.

I walked up the steps and all these people started yelling. This one guy tells me, You can't come up here while we're shooting. I told him, You don't own the steps. The T.V. lights go out and the chick with the microphone says, Fuck. Then she turns around to me, real sarcastic and says, Thanks a lot honey. I told her, Chinga tu madre, Bitch, I got rights too. My boyfriend's in there. I got more business here than you. She gave me the big eyes and went to complain.

I went on inside, up to the desk and said I'm here to see Chuey Medina. Who? he says and he looks at the list, We got a Jesus Medina. That's Chuey, I tell him.

He looks at me, up and down, this fat Paddy with the typical little cop moustache. What's your name, he says. Dulcie Medina, I tell him. It's not, but if they don't think we're related they won't let me see Chuey. Dulcie? he says, does that mean Sugar? Sweet, I tell him it means sweet.

You related? he says. What the hell, I'm thinking, God can't get me till I get outside. I tell him, I'm his wife.

Well, sweetheart, he says, nobody gets to see Jesus Medina until he's been booked. He says it Jeezus, not Hayzhoos the way it's supposed to be pronounced, like he's making a big point.

He's *been* booked, I say. He called me. They wouldn't have let him call me if he hadn't been booked already. The cop looks real snotty at me but he knows I'm right. Just a minute, he says. He gets on the phone. When he gets off he says, You'll have to wait. You can wait over there.

How long? I say. He gets snotty again, I don't know, sweetheart. They'll call me.

Cops, when they don't know what to do, they know to make you wait. I hung out, smoking, for awhile. Outside on the steps, the lights are on and that same blonde T.V. bitch is holding a microphone up to a guy in a suit; he's banging his briefcase against his knee while he talks. I come out the door as the guy is saying about We have to send a message to gang members that we will no longer tolerate—blah, blah, blah, like that—and then all this stuff about the Community.

325

Hey, I tell him, are you the D.A.? They won't let me see my husband, Chuey Medina. He turns around. The blondie is mouthing at me GO AWAY. I tell the D.A. guy, They won't let him talk to a lawyer. Isn't he entitled to legal representation? Those are the magic words. He grabs me by the arm, Mrs. Medina, he says, let's talk inside. The blondie jerks a thumb across her throat and the lights go out. She looks at me and thinks of something. Keep rolling, she says, and the lights go on again. Mrs. Medina, she says, Mrs. Medina. Could we talk with you a moment? The D.A. still has hold of my arm and he pulls me through the door. She gives him a nasty look and then turns around to the lights again, I can hear her as we're going through the door.

In a dramatic development, she says, here at the Highland Park Police Station, the wife of alleged drive-by murderer Jesús-Chuey-Medina has accused the district attorney's office . . . The D.A. says, Goddammit. I don't hear what she says after that, my legs get like water and he has to help me over to the bench. Chuey didn't kill nobody, I tell him, he wouldn't. He looks at me funny and I remember I'm supposed to already know everything. I straighten up and tell him, Chuey wants a lawyer.

That's simply not a problem, Mrs. Medina, he tells me, an attorney will be provided. I *know* Mr. Medina has been offered an attorney.

No, I say, he wanted a certain one. He told me on the phone, but your chingadera phone is such junk that I couldn't hear the name. I have to talk to him.

He gives me another funny look and goes over to the guy at the desk. Look, he tells the cop, I don't know what's going on here, but I don't want *any* procedural fuckups on this one.

The cop says, Big case huh? and the D.A. tells him, This is the whole enchilada, Charlie. Where are you holding Medina?

Second floor tank.

Okay, he says, We'll use the conference room there. Call ahead. The cop looks at me and tells the D.A., We'll need a matron.

I know what that means. One time before, when I went to see my brother Carlos in jail, they gave me a strip search. It was some ugly shit. They put their fingers everywhere, and I mean everywhere, and the lady who did it, she got off on it. You could tell. My ass was sore for a week. I swore to God then that I'd never let anybody do that to me again.

Bullshit, I yell. No strip search. The D.A. guy whirls around. The cop says, If it's a face to face meeting with a prisoner, the Captain says skin search. That's the way we play it.

The D.A. tells him, I'll take responsibility on this one. We'll do a pat search and I'll be with her every step after that. I'm going to walk this one through. He holds the cop on the arm, We got cameras out there Charlie, he says.

The matron is waiting for me in this little room. Undo your blouse, is the first thing she tells me. I already told them, I say, I ain't going to strip. Just the top two buttons, she says, visual inspection, honey. I have to make sure your bra's not loaded.

I undo the buttons and hold the blouse open. Just some kleenex, I tell her. She checks me out and then pats me down. Then she starts poking in my hair. They always do that. Some pachuca thirty years ago supposedly had a razor blade in her beehive and they're still excited about it. They never do it to any Anglo chicks.

The D.A. guy meets me outside and we walk through the first floor jail. It's like walking through the worst party you ever been to in your life. All these guys checking me out. Putting their hands through the bars and yelling. Ola, Chica. Hey, Chica, over here, they keep saying, and worse stuff. This one dude keeps making these really disgusting kissing noises. Guys can be weird. I give the dude making the kissing sounds the finger and make my walk all sexy on the way out, shaking my ass. They all go wild. Serves them right.

Chuey is in this big cell, all by himself except for one other guy. When I see who that is, I know why Chuey's in trouble. Sleepy Chavez is sitting next to him. I don't know why they call him Sleepy. He's wired most of the time. I think he might have been a red freak once. Sleepy is one vato loco. The craziest I know. Everything bad that happens on 42nd Avenue starts with Sleepy Chavez.

There's this guy that shines shoes outside Jesse's Barber Shop. I thought he was retarded but it turns out he got in a fight with Sleepy in like sixth grade and Sleepy kicked him so hard in the huevos that the guy ain't been right since. And what's really sick is that Sleepy *loves* getting his shoes shined there.

Chuey doesn't look so good. He's got bruises on his cheeks, a cut on his forehead and his hand's bandaged up. He looks like what the 42nd Flats, that's his gang, call resisting arrest. He looks sick too, pale and his eyes are all red. Sleepy sees me first. He's chewing on his fingers, looks up and spits out a fingernail. Sleepy can't leave his fingers alone. When he was little, his sister told me, his mom used to put chili juice on them. He's always poking them in his ears or picking his nose or something. You don't want to be alone with him.

Chuey stands up while the cop is unlocking the door. He just looks at me and his eyes are so sad it makes me feel sick. He looks worse than when his father died or even when the guys from White Fence burned his car and laughed at him. Sleepy Chavez looks at me and chucks his head at Chuey. Watch your mouth, Medina, he says.

They take us in this big room. The cop stands by the door. The D.A. guy sits down at the end of this long table and we go down to the other. Chuey reaches out and touches my face. Dulcie, he says, Mi novia. Chuey only calls me that when he's really drunk or sentimental, he never has asked me to marry him. No touching, the cop says. Keep your hands on the table. I figure Chuey needs cheering up so I slip off my shoe and slide my foot up on the inside of his leg and rub him under the table.

Aye, Chuey, I tell him, all happy, que problemas you have, Chuey. My toes are rubbing a certain place, but Chuey surprises me he doesn't even push back.

Dulcie, he says, They think I was the shooter.

Keep your voice down, I say, What did you tell them? Exactamente.

We didn't say nothing. We got to stick together, like Sleepy says. They haven't got any witnesses.

Chuey, I say, one of those guys is still alive.

He sits up when I tell him that.

It doesn't matter, Chuey says, neither of them saw us. All the cops got is Sleepy's car. They ain't got the gun. Sleepy threw it out when they were chasing us. Chuey, I said, were you driving? he just looks at me for awhile and then he says, yeah. I ask, How come you were driving?

328

He had the shotgun, Chuey said, I had to drive.

I can tell when Chuey's lying, which is most of the time; I think he was telling the truth. Chuey, I said, you're crazy. They'll put you both away. You don't owe Sleepy nothing.

Chuey looks mean at me, his eyes get all skinny. It was my fault we got caught, he says. We should have got away. I hit another car and wrecked Sleepy's Mustang. We tried to hide and the cops found us. I owe Sleepy, so just shut up Dulcie.

It's hopeless to argue with Chuey when he gets like this. Muy macho. You can't talk to him about his friends, even the jerks. He won't believe me over them. Chuey says, I'm gonna need a good lawyer. Get me Nardoni.

Tony Nardoni is this big lawyer all the drug dealers in East L.A. use. Chuey I say, I don't think Nardoni does this kind of stuff. I think he just does the drugs.

Yeah he does, Chuey says, he's a lawyer isn't he? Sometimes Chuey can be just as dumb as his friends; it's not even worth telling him. Now he's all puffed up. You call Nardoni, Chuey says, Tell him I'm a compañero of Flaco Valdez. Tell him we're like this, Chuey holds up two crossed fingers, Tight. Flaco Valdez is like the heavy duty drug dealer in Highland Park and Shaky Town. As usual, Chuey's bullshitting. Flaco never ran with 42nd Flats and he deals mostly smack, so Chuey isn't even one of his customers. It's just that Flaco Valdez is the biggest name that Chuey can think of. O.K., I tell him, I'll call Nardoni. Now what about your mom?

Don't call her, Chuey says, all proud, I don't want her to know about this. Chuey, I say, Chuey you big estupido, she *is* going to hear about this. It's going to be in the papers and on T.V.

O.K., Chuey says, like he's doing me this big favor, You can call her. Tell her they made a big mistake. Right Chuey, I'm thinking. Smart, Chuey. Pretend it didn't happen, like always. That's going to be a fun phone call for me. His mom is going to go crazy.

I know better, but I have to ask. Chuey?, I say. Why did you do such a stupid thing?

They was on our turf!, Chuey says. They challenged us. Like we didn't have any huevos, Chica. We got huevos!

And whose smart idea was it to shoot those boys? As if I didn't know. Chuey just looks at me, he doesn't say nothing.

Chuey, I say, was you high? He looks down at the table, when he looks up again, I can't believe it, his eyes are wet. He sees me looking so he closes them. He just sits there, with his eyes closed, pulling on his little chin beard. God, he's such a pretty dude. Ay, Dulcie, he says. His eyes open and he gives me that smile, the one I have to argue to get, the one I love him for. What can I say?, Chuey tells me, La Vida Loca, no? La Vida Loca.

Right Chuey, I think, La Vida Loca. The Crazy Life. It's the explanation for everything on 42nd Ave.

The D.A. knocks on the table. Time, he says. I look right at him, I got to talk to you. Chuey cuts his eyes at me but I don't care. I never done anything like this, I never gone against him but now I have to. Sleepy Chavez could give a shit if Chuey takes the fall. Chuey doesn't get it, he thinks he's tough. If he goes to a real jail, they'll bend him over. They'll fry those huevos of his that he's always talking about.

I walk over to the D.A. and sit down. I tell him, Sleepy Chavez was the shooter. Chuey was driving and he was stoned. If Chuey testifies what will he get? That D.A. sees me for the first time. The numbers turn over in his eyes like a gas pump.

Mrs. Medina, he says, You are not a lawyer, I cannot plea bargain with you. If you were a lawyer I would probably tell you that your client is guilty and that we can prove it.

You got some witnesses? I tell him. He doesn't say nothing but the numbers start rolling again.

Chuey stands up and yells at me, Dulcie you stupid bitch, just shut up. He's all pale and scared. The cop walks over and sits him down.

I'm going to get him a lawyer, I say. The D.A. tells me, If you get a lawyer, we will talk. I would say better sooner than later— he has this little smile—before a witness shows up.

One other thing, I tell him, if I was you I'd put Chuey in a different cell from Sleepy Chavez.

Chuey won't kiss me goodbye. He pushed me away, all cold. He won't look at me. Out in the hall, he won't look at Sleepy Chavez either. Sleepy checks that out good and then when he sees that the cop is taking Chuey someplace else, he starts banging on the bars and screaming in Spanish. Hombre muerto, he's

330

screaming, Hombre muerto. The D.A. looks at me and asks, What's he saying? Dead man, I tell him, he says dead man.

The D.A. walks me back downstairs to the desk and shakes my hand. Thank you Mrs. Medina, he says.

I tell him, Look, don't call me Mrs. Medina no more. O.K.? They're going to check and find out anyway and it doesn't make any difference. It's not Mrs. Medina, I tell him, It's Dulcie Gomez. I'm only married in my mind.

I got what I wanted, I guess. Chuey's lawyer who was this woman from the Public Defender's office, and Chuey's mom, and me, we all worked on Chuey. We worked on him real good. Chuey testified against Sleepy Chavez. We talked him into it.

The D.A. wouldn't make any deals. The brother that was on the critical list recovered but he never came to court. He hadn't seen nothing and they didn't need him anyway. They done this test that showed Sleepy fired a gun and then they found the gun. Some tow truck driver brought it in. It was under a car he towed away. Sleepy's fingerprints was all over it. The only thing the D.A. said he would do, if Chuey testified, was talk to the judge when it was time for the sentencing. Ms. Bernstein, Chuey's lawyer, said it was probably as good a deal as we could get.

Chuey had to stand trial next to Sleepy. Every day Sleepy blew him kisses and told him he was a pussy and a maricon. Ms. Bernstein never complained about it. She said it might help with the jury.

I was surprised at the judge. I didn't think she would let that stuff go on. Every day Sleepy did something stupid. There was all this yelling and pointing, and she never said nothing. The judge was this black chick about forty. She wore a different wig and different nails every day. She sat there playing with her wooden hammer. It didn't seem like she was listening. If you ask me, she was losing it. She called a recess once when one of her nails broke. Ms. Bernstein was real polite to her. She said this was the best judge we could get because she was known for her light sentences.

Ms. Bernstein didn't even try to prove that Chucy was innocent. All she did was show that he didn't know what he was doing. She said that he was stoned that day and she said that he was

331

easily led. Even Chuey's mom got up and said that Chuey was easily led, from when he was a little boy.

It was weird to watch. They talked about him like he wasn't there. Ms. Bernstein would show that Chuey was a fool and then Sleepy's lawyer would try to show that Chuey wasn't a fool. He couldn't do it. Everybody in that courtroom thought Chuey was a fool by the time they got done. Chuey sat at that table listening and he got smaller and smaller, while Sleepy Chavez kept showing off for all the vatos locos and got bigger and bigger.

The jury said that Sleepy Chavez was guilty but they couldn't make their minds up about Chuey. They didn't think he was innocent but they didn't think he was guilty either. They didn't know what to do. The judge talked to them some more and they came back in ten minutes and said Chuey was guilty but with like mitigating circumstances.

The D.A. did stand up for Chuey when it came to the sentencing. The judge sent Sleepy Chavez to the C.Y.A., the California Youth Authority, until he turned twenty-one, and then after that he had to go to prison. The judge said she wanted to give Sleepy a life sentence but she couldn't because of his age. She gave Chuey probation and time served.

The courtroom went crazy. All the gangs from Shaky Town were there. 42nd Flats, The Avenues and even some from White Fence. They all started booing the judge, who finally bangs her hammer. Sleepy Chavez stands up. He makes a fist over his head and yells, Flats! La Raza Unida, and the crowd goes crazy some more.

I couldn't believe it. Sleepy Chavez standing there with both arms in the air, yelling, Viva!, like he just won something and Chuey sits there with his head down like he was the one going to prison.

I go down to kiss Chuey and Sleepy spits at my feet. Hey, Puta, he tells me, Take your sissy home.

I can't stand it. I tell him, Sleepy, those guys in prison are gonna fuck you in the ass and I'm glad.

Sleepy says, Bullshit. I'll be in the Mexican Mafia before I get out of C.Y.A. I'll tell you who gets fucked in the ass, Puta, your sissy, li'l Chuey. He yells at Chuey, Hey maricon. Hombre muerto. Chuey don't never raise his head.

I talked to the D.A. afterward. I said, You saw those guys. Chuey needs help. He helped you, you should help him. What about those relocation programs? The D.A. could give a shit. He cares for Chuey about as much as Sleepy Chavez. He just packs his briefcase and walks away, shaking hands with everybody. The T.V. is waiting for him outside.

Ms. Bernstein says she'll see what she can do about police protection. I tell her that ain't going to make it. The only thing that will make it is if Chuey gets out of East L.A. She says there's nothing to keep Chuey from moving, as long as he tells his probation officer and keeps his appointments. She doesn't understand, the only way Chuey will move is if they make him. She says they can't do that.

I tried to make him move. I tell him, Chuey, they going to kill you. Sooner or later. He doesn't want to talk about it, all he'll say is, Forget it. Flats is my home.

The night he got out, Chuey came to my sister's house where I was babysitting. I wanted him so bad. After I put the kids to bed we made love. He looked so fine, even pale and too skinny, but it wasn't any good. It wasn't like Chuey at all. He hardly would kiss me. It was like I could have been anyone. After we made it all he wanted to do was drink wine and listen to records. Every time I tried to talk he got mad.

On the street, the first month after the trial, the cops were doing heavy duty patrols. It seemed like there was a black and white on every corner. They sent the word out through the gang counselors that Shaky Town was going to stay cool or heads would get broken. They busted the warlords from the 42nd Flats and The Avenues for like jay-walking or loitering.

None of the 42nd Flats would talk to Chuey. They cruised his house and gave him cold looks but there was too many cops to do anything. Chuey went back to work at Raul's Body Shop. Raul said he didn't care about the gang stuff and Chuey was a good worker, but then things started happening. Chuey was getting drunk and stoned every night and then he started smoking at work too. Plus windows got broken at the body shop, then there were fires in the trash cans and over the weekend someone threw battery acid on a bunch of customers' cars. Raul told Chuey he'd have to let him go. He didn't fire Chuey, he just laid him off so Chuey could collect unemployment.

The night that he got laid off I took him to dinner and a movie, Rocky something, I forget the number. I didn't want him to get down. After the movie I took Chuey to the Notell Motel in Eagle Rock. It cost me all my tips from two weekends. They had adult movies there and a mirror over the water bed.

Chuey got into it a little. He'd been smoking weed at the movie and he was real relaxed. He lasted a long time. It wasn't great for me. I was too worried about what I wanted to ask and also he wasn't really there. Maybe because of the weed, but it was like that time when he first got out of jail. I could have been anyone.

When he was done I turned off the T.V. and laid down next to him with my head on his chest. We had a cigarette. When I put it out, I kissed his ear and whispered, Chuey, let's get out of this place. You got a trade, I said. We could move anyplace. We could get married. We could go to San Francisco or San Diego. We could just live together if you want. I don't care. But we got to get out of here.

Chuey sat up. He pushed me down off his chest. Flats is my home, he said. Chuey, I said, They're going to kill you. He looked at me like I was a long way away and then he nodded and his eyes were just like that D.A.'s. With the numbers. That's right, Chuey said. They're going to kill me. The numbers flamed up in his eyes like a match. You did this to me, bitch.

Chuey, I said, I love you. He said it again, You did this to me, bitch, and after that he wouldn't talk. We didn't even spend the night.

After he got on unemployment, he filled up his day with weed and wine. I seen him walking right on the street with a joint in one hand and a short dog of white port in the other. Chuey's color T.V., he calls it. I had to be in school, I couldn't babysit him. On the street, none of his old friends would talk to him and there was no place he could hang out. Even people who didn't know him didn't like him around. White Fence had put out the word that they were going to do him as a favor to 42nd Flats. No one wanted to be near Chuey in case there was shooting.

When I got out of school every day, I'd go find him. I tried to get him interested in other stuff, like school, so he could get his high school diploma, or a car. I was even going to front him some of the money, but he didn't want it. All he wanted was his weed and his wine. I even set him up for a job with my cousin who's a plumber but Chuey said no, unemployment was enough. He just kept slipping, going down, and I couldn't pull him up. There wasn't nothing I could do.

He started hanging out with the junkies. They were the only ones, except his family and me, that would talk to him. The junkies hang out in this empty lot across from Lupé's Grocery Store. A Korean guy owns the store but he's afraid to change the name. He's afraid of the junkies too. They steal him blind and shoot up in his alley. They got some old chairs and a sofa in the lot and they sit there, even when it rains. It wasn't too long before Chuey started doing reds. If you ask me, reds are the worst pill around. Red freaks are like zombies. They talk all slurred and spill things. The only thing that's good about them is they don't fight too much, like a white freak, and if they do, they don't hurt each other.

It was hard to be around Chuey once he started doing reds. He'd want to kiss me and his mouth was always full of spit and then he'd try to feel me up right in front of other guys. I hated it, even if they were just junkies.

Then I heard he was doing smack. Chuey didn't tell me, his uncle did. They were missing money from the house and a stereo. They found out Chuey had done it and they found his kit. The only thing I'd noticed was that he wasn't drinking so much and he was eating a lot of candy bars.

The weird thing was that once he got to be a junkie, the 42nd Flats stopped hassling him so much. Gangs are funny that way. They treat junkies like they was teachers or welfare workers. They don't respect them. It's like a truce or like they're invisible. I don't know now whether they're going to kill him or not. Maybe they think the smack will do it for them or maybe they're just waiting for the cops to go away or maybe they're saving him for Sleepy Chavez's little brother who gets paroled out of Juvie next month. I don't know. They still come by the junkie lot. We'll be sitting there and a cruiser will pull up with like four or five dudes inside and you'll see the gun on the window. They call him names, Calavera, which is like a skeleton, or they whisper Muerto, hombre muerto. But it's like they're playing with him. The other junkies think it's funny. They started calling him Muerto Medina. Chuey don't care.

335

Sometimes I skip sixth period and come down and sit with him. That's the best time of day. He's shot up and mellow by then. I cut out coming by in the morning 'cause he'd be wired and shaky and if he'd just scored he'd want me to shoot up with him. But by late afternoon he's cool. It's real peaceful there in the lot. The sun is nice. We sit on the sofa and I hold his hand. I like to look at him. He's getting skinny but he's still a pretty dude. Chuey nods and dreams, nods and dreams, and I sit there as long as I can. It's what I can do.

Nominated by Crazyhorse *and Lynda Hull*

MILLER CANYON TRAIL
NO. 106

by MICHAEL BOWDEN

from THE CAROLINA QUARTERLY

All morning & early afternoon clouds swell the sky
with their gray-and-white architectures,
labor toward rain. I hike alone into the mountain,

harder edges coming back in the effort of thigh
against trail—a path's shifting debris—
when I think of you, water broken, entering the tunnels

of pain which issue a son or daughter, childhood's
beatification. Often it's difficult to understand
our lives on this planet, as when we weep through bliss

at some particular sorrow's palpability: new mother
behind a curtain in the next bed, delirious, slurs
names through anesthetic for the stern-faced priest

with his gesture & sudden baptisms. I could see him,
later, from the grounds, hunched over in the rescue
helicopter as it ascended & thrashed toward Tucson.

I watched the swirl of clouds over the community hospital,
the state flags limp at their staff—navy blue &
copper, a rising sun's overconfidence. I'd like to say

I learned what makes a difference in this life
the day my boy went down into his nap & ceased breathing—
how quickly all we care about can collapse—but it's not

as easy as that. I had his sister to take home, dinner
to prepare—something simple enough for a father
to fix. I'm still unashamed for the way I dissolved

into the details of its assembly, the minutes I wasted
trying to find her favorite cartoons—my weak
gratefulness for small things. Like this year

the summer rains came late & I stayed away from my dad's
old blue Safari, its *clack, clack*, its vanity.
It doesn't make sense, but there it is: I felt my pride

could kill him. Unlike the child without a throat
or anus, my son reclaimed his life, as if he'd forgotten
something he wanted to grow up & tell us. Patty it's crazy

how once-fierce borders grow fuzzy, merge our hands
with spoons of puffed wheat, iridescent
green shoestrings—how the loss of such ordinary tasks

can ruin us. Here, where the trail runs out
in a wood too fire-damaged to be a proper forest
of legend, I remove my shoes & set them under foliage.

I drink from my face, my lips touching the cold
reflection of my lips. What's less substantial than
memory—the dozen blue moths which break from a pool's

surface, shatter into brush & pine like a present moment?
The hand's impromptu cup of water, its ten million
invisible creatures? We want it, whatever it is.

Nominated by The Carolina Quarterly

BELIEVER'S FLOOD

fiction by RICHARD CURREY

from STORY

M Y STORY IS no regal tale. Take my word for it. I sit here on this derelict front porch struggling for just one breath at a time and at sixty-two years of age I am not that old a man though my years shifting coal have rendered me such, taking my air and the kind of days I once had. I made twenty-four years underground before I strangled on the way they make the dark down there, before I was a lost soul in a glider on a summer morning waiting every day for the mailman to come, just that one extra person to talk to. Except I cannot talk, not well and not for long. I'm too busy breathing. Got my lips pursed, rounded, that's the way I was taught by the doctors up at the university. Lean forward on my knees they told me, make like I'm about to whistle and let the air come short and sweet, do the least work possible keeping it there, go on and let it push itself. *Black lung. What we doctors call silicosis. What it really means is you can't breathe too well.* Which I did not need a doctor to tell me. You can sit in my shoes and feel for just one moment the pressure of unadulterated air all around you, genuine air thin as a clean knife up against your eyes and in at your throat and you'll know what I mean, you'll know how it is to be a cat on a hook and coal dust hovering in your chest like a down of rime, lungs dropsied and purple in a bed of old blood and walking away from the light. A lifetime in a coal mine frees me to this. Working a long heat wave for what I could never have, and I'm told to be happy with what it's come to. Go home at last and sit in a chair and try to breathe, testament to a

339

lifetime's plain glory: sitting in a chair and working to draw one good breath, one decent breath. One clean simple breath.

I am Raymond Dance, born and raised in Red Jacket, West Virginia. My father worked for the Red Jacket Coal and Coke Company though not underground, lived what appeared to be a happy life, modest and without ceremony, straight-through and reliable. Everybody here then worked for Red Jacket Coal and Coke. The company owned the town. The storekeeper took company scrip and turned it over to a man in a tired suit who came around once a week. I remember trying to talk to my father about all of this and it's where a son hesitates, having spent so many years in the older man's shadow one way or another. You reach a point where you can't help but wonder if the old man has ever considered what you've thought about so long, what has come to dominate your way of thinking. My father never approved of my union work, never seemed to understand it or what we aimed for, and he listened silently while I told him of a battle for a better life, for wages and rights and a thimble-full of self-determination. A lofty speech.

My father grunted, glanced at me full of contempt as if he pitied me for some wholesale foolishness, got up and went inside the house, let the screen door slam behind him.

That was that. The first and last time the subject was to come between us. We stayed friendly enough to his death. Now I can look at the ground he's buried in and wonder why I never got so much as a go-to-hell when I claimed that we could someday pull out of the grip of the coal operators. When it came to my father I was always looking for myself in the wrong direction.

We had a movie theater in town—another thing owned and operated by the company—that by no real shift of the tongue could be called a theater, being an old grange hall outfitted with folding chairs and a whitewashed wall. They showed movies once a week, every Friday night and as far back as I can recollect I was there in a hardback chair staring up into that wall like it was heaven's gate for sure. It wasn't exactly that I wanted to be like those people, just that I wanted to know who they were, where they came from, what they were thinking. I suppose if I hadn't been that kind of boy I would never have been the sort to give my father his confusions about me. But I was that kind, edge of curiosity killing the cat and enough imagination to always want to see how the story comes out in the end. You have to remember these were silent pictures. Nobody played the piano. The projector clicked along, prophecy and wide-open promise, that ray of light cutting just over my head into another life where the poor and the hopeless always managed to locate a solution of some kind, or laughed their way through hell. The actors spoke without making a sound, and I never saw a picture that was about anybody I could possibly know, yet I still found a comfort there, a belief in the sanctity of what might come to pass, and when the union organizers arrived I was ready as any man could be.

The mine wars were like nothing we had ever seen. Godawful, bloody, terrifying to the bone. Red Jacket Coal and Coke showed their colors well enough and, just like we expected, hired in hoods and killers, Baldwin-Felts detectives for the most part. We all went at each other, baseball bats and rocks and knives and finally guns. I lost teeth and busted my nose, and my wife Edie was calling me off the whole affair. She reminded me there were miners who were not union: they kept clear of trouble and hoped they'd be alive and still have a job when the smoke cleared and she was telling me to take their example, stay home and wait. But I had too much taste for it, I was too sure it was the right thing to do and that I couldn't live with myself if I wasn't out there in the fray, going to meetings, saying my share. I've never felt different and I've never had a regret.

There was the night me and Wilbur Landown took on three Baldwins out in the Williamson field, the two of us standing vigil on picket, thinking we had a quiet shift, an easy time of it in the middle of the night sometime in June of 1920. The scabs were inside working the mine at about a third of what a real force of men could do, but nobody had come up to the line on foot and we knew we had trouble when these three yokels sauntered out of the dark, big hats and looking like brothers on the lam from daylight. There was no conversation, no negotiating with these boys. They sauntered awhile but as they came in close they started to run at us. Two of them were over me like a blanket drawn across my head, flailing, pounding my chest with so much force you'd think I was carrying a Congo gorilla on my back. I heard Wilbur screaming, and I heard the soft grunt of fists

341

coming into flesh and I was rolling around, taking a bruising but the Baldwins were in too close for real damage, more like wild boys in a schoolyard. I pulled loose and scrabbled backward in the dirt; one old boy was standing over me and in the downswing with a club the size of a bull's hind leg. I got to my knees and coupled my fists and brought my arms right up into the bastard's crotch: that stick still hit me broadside across the shoulders but there wasn't much punch left in the blow and my man fell down on his butt with his hat across his eyes. I stood up and took a sucker punch to the upper lip that knocked me straight flat; for a minute there I didn't know a thing. I came to in a haze with Wilbur pulling me upright. Wilbur looked in at me and his face was the grandest goddamn mess you've ever seen: teeth gone in front, nose bent sideways, cheeks and hair smeared with dirty blood. He looked at me and his eyes were bright and full of good times and he was grinning as if he'd heard the best joke of his life. Come on, he said, let's send these fellas down the chute. My mind wasn't any too clear and Wilbur held me up by a shoulder, saying, You don't look too good, know that? I told him he was handsome as ever, and got to my feet. One of the Baldwin men was gone, run off; the other two were on the ground and for all I knew were dead. Wilbur was already dragging one toward the mine gate, motioning me to do the same with the other. I got my man at the ankles and pulled him along; he started groaning and his eyes fluttered. Wilbur pressed the elevator call switch and I heard the old metal cage clanking up the shaft. My man said something blurred by a mouthful of swollen tongue, tried to lift his head to no avail. I got worried the elevator would come up filled with Baldwins and we'd be dead for sure, but the cage scraped into moonlight empty. Wilbur opened the gate, drug in his man. I did the same, closed the gate and sent them both back down.

When I got home I told Edie we'd run into some trouble at the picket line. She dabbed my wounds and frowned, didn't ask for details.

Next morning I had Edie and the two babies with me at the train station. Edie was grim, thin-lipped; the new sky overhead was wild as fire and water and in the time we stood on the platform we didn't speak. All I wanted was to board a train with all of us in one piece.

The northbound came in and took us out and we were a good seven miles from town when Edie said we shouldn't come back. Not for a long while, she said.

I looked out the window with my older daughter on my knee. Well, I said, I'll have to come back.

Edie stared at me with a look that held every insult I could hear. After a moment she told me I was like all the rest, just a damned fool.

I was scared and empty-handed and wanting nothing more than to agree, to stay on with her family near Welton, help around her father's farm. Let it all blow over.

She asked me exactly what had happened, and I told her.

She took off her hat and pushed at her chestnut hair. They'll be waiting for you, she said.

I told her I was sure they would be.

The whistle blew as the train slammed through a water crossing. I'll stay a spell with you at your folks' place, I said. And then I'll come back. I can't just disappear.

Edie looked at our daughters, each in turn. The baby in Edie's lap began to cry and I remember to this day the sound of that cry and the shape in Edie's eyes, washed-away, proud and cold as ice. My god, she whispered.

I came back into Red Jacket at dusk three days later, thinking our house would be gone, burned out or vandalized. It was our own home, land that had been in my mother's family, outside town limits and it was there, still standing pretty as you please, that old coat of ivory paint peeling black under years of coal soot. They had been there, somebody had: the front door stood open. It had rained in; dead leaves blew straight into the parlor. I went through every room, every closet, cupboard, shelf. I looked under beds and up the chimney until I was satisfied nobody was waiting for me. By then it was dark, and I turned on all the lights downstairs, drew the curtains to give the place a warm and homey look from the road. I locked the front and back doors and all the windows, and took the shotgun from the hall closet corner. Upstairs I pulled off my boots and socks, loaded the gun with two shells full of number six buckshot and sat in my bedroom in the dark, shotgun in my lap, terrified for every little sound I heard. I had the time, sitting there, to think about my situation, to

consider the plight of a man who dispatches his family to innocent country and sits afraid for his life in his own home simply
because he wants to trade his labor for a decent wage, and the
Baldwin men stepped up on the front porch. Knocked politely at
the front door. I kept my seat.

I heard them speak to each other, quietly, then one said my
name, calling me Mister, still polite as Sunday morning. He tried
the front door, rattled it gently against the latch, then walked
sideways along the porch, a heavy pair of boots under the room I
was sitting in. After more than a minute of silence I heard the
back door window shatter. A moment later the door squeaked
open and the boots were inside my house.

That was the meaning of forever, listening to those boots from
room to room, slow as honey on a cold morning. Closet doors
opened and closed. He went into the kitchen, seemed to stay
there a full minute or two. When he crossed into the front hallway I got to my feet and came to the side of the bedroom door.
He started up the stairwell and I was useless for any purpose but
holding my breath and staring into that patch of invisible future
that stands directly in front of a man's eyes. It is peculiar now to
recollect that in a moment of such overriding danger a man's
imagination might rise like water to fill that place and show him a
field of snow he last saw in his childhood, a frozen lake on a
mountainside. In such a moment one might think nothing would
move in a man except the trace of his fear, the taste of his own
salt burning his tongue and the corners of his eyes, and to this
day I remember the brief light of that winter memory, traveling
to see my grandparents in a sleigh, horses steaming and trees in
silver freeze. The road was disappeared, rivers snowed under and
the forests lost in the white. I could hear my visitor breathing as
he reached the top step.

The smell of slept-in clothes and poor man's tobacco was strong
on the landing. He stepped into the doorway and stopped.

He was not a large man and looked as if he might be quick as
he waited for his eyes to come around to the darkness in the bedroom. I pushed my shotgun's muzzle up against his neck.

He let out a small cry and stifled it. For a moment he didn't
move, then he made to turn suddenly. I shifted the muzzle to
just beyond his head and let go one barrel into the empty hallway
and my visitor fell flat.

The echo boomed around the house and I heard plaster and woodwork splinter and fall. My friend on the floor quivered face down; I smelled him as he soiled himself. He had been armed with a big Colt .44. The pistol was out in the middle of the bedroom floor. I straddled his body and lay the two barrels in at the base of his skull and I swear I have no idea what I said to him. In the years since I've imagined every manner of remark but the truth may be that I said nothing at all. I let him stand up—he thought he was mortally wounded—and walked him back downstairs with shit oozing in his trousers and the shotgun steadied between his shoulder blades. I directed him out the back door and onto the porch and his man was standing there and I know I told them both to start running. The partner was gone like a rabbit. I shoved my visitor with the shotgun and he fell off the porch into the mud and got up and ran like a cow into the field, grunting, slipping and whimpering. I lifted that old 12-gauge and fired the second barrel into the stars.

I had my fill of heroism, the home-grown war survived, fighting to work on in a trade that would leave me breathless. As if, in the end, there was no way to win, no way to go home a satisfied man. Always something to hold you back, tear you down, work at killing you. So I take a fresh breath with all my mind on it, every bit of concentration, small rivers of air drawn along the edges of my nostrils, cool, a glide of vanishing light drawn into the darkness of my body. I do without the oxygen bottle as much as I can, as often as possible, a half-assed notion that the more I go without the more I can do without. It does not happen that way, but a body hangs on to a vision of itself whole and intent on another good day just around the corner.

Out on an early morning drive. Winter, and the air cold enough to burn. The mines around Red Jacket are gone now, exhausted, folded, shut down. Phantom holes in the ground, mineral seeps and ruined tipples hanging off the black landslide out along Route 16. Away in the distance you can smell the past moving around, the years riding alive. I can run down that thicket of a past always trying to lock it out or bring it up again, make it dream right in front of my eyes, hear my mother's voice again in the still afternoons of summer, back when summers were long as a year. *Raymond Dance, I will not have you talking that way.* And

345

I'd call back, *What way, Mama?* and she never answered that I can recall. That's the story of the past: what you remember best is what was not said. What I remember best turns like the silent pictures we watched in that grange hall years ago, a world going on with nothing to deliver it forward but a double-bladed shadow and the salvation of time. Thinking of days gone before from the front seat of my truck—air bottle beside me like a friend coming along for the ride—and remembering is an act of farewell in itself, a goodbye to whatever belief in simplicity I might have had. God help us in the mouth of memory, on the last road home and free of any voice except our own.

I pass the big switching yard east of Red Jacket, a no man's land of grown-over track and drifters' fires. My Dodge pickup slips into the valley against a rush of flurried snow, out Main Street with the single row of houses hung on the ridge line above town, everything waiting for the beginning of time or the end of the world. One or the other. Whichever comes first. The one stoplight in town moves through its changes out here in the cold, running the affairs of an empty street. I bring my truck into the parking lot at May's Diner and check my watch. Ten minutes past five. Edie says she simply cannot fathom, for the life of her, why I've taken to wandering around the countryside at the crack of dawn. I've told her why: to tell my story to myself, to get it straight in my mind, once and for all. I've explained that, in order to do this, a man needs space and time and quiet. Well, she said, flat-voiced, I guess it's better than going out drinking at roadhouses till all hours of the night. I let it go at that. Inside May's I take up a position at the counter with my oxygen bottle occupying the stool next-door. May and I trade pleasantries before I ask for two eggs scrambled and a cup of black coffee. May nods and moves into the kitchen and I watch her go, knowing the picture that always comes back hardest is the night alone in that upstairs bedroom, waiting for all I knew to shoot a man dead next to the bed I shared with my wife, where our children were born. It had been my original intention to never tell Edie what had happened. After I sent the Baldwin boys off across the field I walked back upstairs and stopped in front of the piece of wall my shotgun demolished. There was no way I could pretend that was an accident. I stood there in front of that big ragged hole thinking of Edie and the kids and I was overcome, sobbed with the shotgun cradled in my arms and my life seemed nothing more than a broken-down passage stained by chance and mishap, backroad losses and good blood in turn, all of us surrendered naked and never for what we know. As if there is a place in your life when the future is your best friend, the very thing that can save you. Whatever's possible will surely come to pass if you're patient, life will redeem itself and you are carried on with a young man's certainty. May brings the eggs and pours a cup of coffee and I thank her. Outside the frosted windows it's dawning and I can see the shape of the country that started it all. I take a sip of coffee and watch the mountains sail away toward Kentucky, and south.

Nominated by Story

MURPHY'S ANGEL

fiction by THOMAS E. KENNEDY

from NEW DELTA REVIEW

M URPHY WALKED SLOWLY from the bus, smiling lazily into the calm evening sunlight. He yawned, shifted his briefcase to his left hand, flexed blood back into the fingers of his right. He fished a Pall Mall from his shirt pocket, lit it, filled his lungs. As he exhaled the smoke, he whispered an ejaculation: "Lamb of God who taketh away the sins of the world, hear my plea." Which he had learned as a child was good for a sixty-day indulgence from the sufferings of purgatory for yourself or the deceased of your choice.

On his street, a neighbor lady, middle-aged and blond in snug red shorts, stood watering her roses from a yellow plastic sprinkling pail. She smiled with her eyes at Murphy.

"Nice day," she said and bent to pluck a weed.

"You bet," said Murphy, his eye following the turn and pull of red terry cloth.

Lamb of God who taketh away the sins of the world, hear my plea. Another sixty days. If he kept it up, the accounts might soon balance out. There was an even shorter aspiration (*Lord have mercy on us!*) which could be ejaculated four or five times in the same breath space as the *Lamb of God* one and was said to be worth as many days off each time, but he thought it wiser to hold to the more demanding course. As a hedge against it all, he also prayed to the stars and burnt seasonal offerings of fruit and vegetables from his garden in honor of unknown forces of cosmos and chaos. His right hand never knew which god's back his left was scratching.

348

As he approached his own lawn, the shadow of a bird glided across the sunlit grass. He paused on the sidewalk and surveyed the house. *Who would know?* The house *looked* healthy. The egg-cream beige stucco was freshly painted, the shingles free of gaps, rain gutter and window frames glistened with white acrylic. The pink flamingo lawn ornament lent an innocent, fairy tale air to the scene.

He sucked the last drag off the cigarette and flipped it into the gutter, strode past the side stoop to the basement window, squatted and lifted away the wooden skid which he had placed against it some weeks before. Peering in through the bars into the shadows of the vast dim cellar room, he could discern the water tank like some extraterrestrial insect on its four tall spindly legs, the powerful squat-bellied furnace, the clotheslines, his tool-bench. A discarded, hingeless, knobless door lay on its side, propped at a forty-five degree angle to the wall beside the sewer lid, bolted down since the rat infestation two summers before. There, seated on the floor between door and sewer, was the angel. Its wings had molted and lay forgotten beneath the clotheslines, golden black like desiccated banana peels. It was clutching the backs of its biceps, where the wings had hinged, fingering them as though they itched or ached, and its knees were drawn up to its breast.

Alerted perhaps by a shadow, its pale face turned toward the window and saw Murphy's face there, then ducked away, pressing to the wall, gaze locked toward the floor molding as it tried to squeeze in beneath the lean-to formed by the abandoned door.

Idly, Murphy tapped at the window glass. The angel slouched tighter to the wall. Murphy noticed that the poor thing had found his old Wellingtons and drawn them on over its swollen, chapped, bare feet. Other than the boots, it was naked, and very pale. In the beginning, when they were still on speaking terms, the angel had told how its feet had been ruined in the Russian campaign. *Never go into Russia,* it said. *It'll be the end of you. If the peasants don't kill you, the elements will.* The angel had never explained its role in the campaign or even which campaign it had been. Murphy had never asked. Only now, when it was too late, did the question even occur to him. It saddened him that he had not extended more interest to the poor creature.

He stared hard at the bent figure, hoping for movement, some sign of activity, intention, but the angel knotted tighter, drew closer in beneath the angle of the leaning door like a shy, diseased fish in a tank.

Murphy drew the skid back over the window. His knees popped as he rose, and the blood rushed to his brain, dizzying him for a moment. He blinked, shook his head as the world dissolved and reappeared before his eyes, then lifted his briefcase and mounted the stoop to his front door.

Inside, in the living room, his little girl was dancing a mambo in front of a sleek, black sound system. Trumpets blared "Cherry Pink," and the girl swayed there, running her fists beneath first the one, then the other elbow. She was quite good for a five-year-old.

His eldest boy sat sprawled across an easy chair, staring intently into a *Dungeons and Dragons* comic book; on the cover a Dragonmaster in flowing cape manipulated a series of strange creatures like marionettes on strings of fire which extended from his fingertips. Murphy's eldest was an enormous boy of sixteen, six-five at last measure with fifteen-inch biceps. He wore an armless tanktop shirt and shorts which stopped midway down red-haired thighs thick as hamhocks. Murphy was always awed when he gazed upon the boy, that such a giant could evolve from his and his wife's loins.

"How'd the game go, son?"

The boy looked up and smiled with little white teeth. "We creamed them to bloody pulp."

"Great! You score?"

The boy's protruding brow clouded. "It's a team sport, Dad. That's what matters."

"You didn't score." Murphy wondered, looking into the boy's blazing eyes, whether he had ever killed anyone when he and his friends went out prowling on weekends seeking good-natured brawls like you see in the movies. But the boy had good manners. No one could deny that. It was a great comfort and consolation to Murphy whenever he observed the dignity with which his eldest son comported himself on social occasions.

"Want to watch the Movie of the Week on Channel 7 with me, son? Starts at eight."

The clouds passed from the boy's brow. His eyes grew placid once again. His little white teeth smiled. "Thanks, anyway, Pops, but I got practice." He stood and rolled his comic into a tube and

350

stood beating out the mambo rhythms against his thigh with it. "See you later, Daddy," he said and affectionately palmed Murphy's balding pate as though it were the curve of a B-ball. To his little sister, he bent and said, "Keep shaking that thing, Sis. Make you a fortune some day," and let himself out the front door.

Murphy shook his head after the boy, placed his briefcase on the floor, took off his summer jacket and began to slip it onto a hanger. A figure, his younger son, darted in between his legs and grabbed the briefcase, backed out, and dodged down the hall again. Murphy heard the boy's door smack to, heard the click of a padlock mechanism meshing shut. He chuckled, then frowned: the boy had been so contrary and belligerent lately. Murphy had thought it a mere phase, but his wife was beginning to talk about a psychologist for the boy. Maybe she was right. After all, there was no stigma in it, not anymore: everyone was crazy now. But how could you be sure you didn't get a crazy psychologist? That was what stumped him. Only last week, he had read in the papers about a psychologist who had hypnotized his patients and performed pagan rituals on them.

He hung his jacket in the closet with the animal skins, and called out "Hi honey! I'm home!"

From the sewing room, his wife's voice snapped, "Don't you start with me now."

Murphy's lips parted. "All I said was . . . " He felt a geyser of indignation boil up through his trunk. He pictured himself bounding in slow motion down the hall, shouldering in the sewing room door and grasping his wife's slender shoulders, shaking her until the expression on her trim, heart-shaped face rattled, watching her river-green eyes open wide with fear, dropping her roughly down into her chair again and leaping out like a TV narc to kick his younger son's door off its hinges, seize his briefcase from the fragile, agile, undersized little monkey. Saw himself call a conference of dependents: *All of you. Out here. On the double! Now behave! Do you understand me?!*

No! he could picture his wife shouting back. *I never have and I never will!*

Murphy stomped his heel on the parquet floor to vent frustration. In the basement, the angel groaned, shouted curses, wept.

"Shut up!" Murphy bellowed and clutched his head, thinking about how reasonably most of the people in his office behaved,

351

how sweetly the neighbor woman had smiled and bent to pluck that weed so he could view the glory of her bottom. If only people would be more manipulative and false at home as well as out in the world.

His little girl mamboed over to him, smiling, running her fists under her elbows. Her lips were rouged, her cheeks and eyelids glitter-striped. She was wearing a tight Latin skirt with a split down its front, a strawberry-patterned bra that sat flat against her young ribcage, and a Chiquita Banana fruit bowl hat on her head. She danced on stacked, shocking-pink espadrilles, while Perry Como sang, "Papa Loves Mambo."

Murphy beamed down at her. "Say, those lessons are really beginning to pay off."

His wife stormed into the room and tore the phonograph arm across the record. The needle zipped crazily over the grooves, amplified through the sleek black speakers. His little girl stopped dancing and glared.

"Mother and Father need time to *talk* to each other!" Murphy's wife shouted.

"Oh, *boy*," the child shouted back and stomped off down the hall.

Murphy's wife slumped into the easy chair. She pinched the bridge of her nose, a crumple of kleenex like a paper flower ready in the other hand to catch any tears that might fall.

He said, "All I said . . . "

"Sure," she said, "Alleluia. You're home. Roll out the red carpet. Strike up the band. Serve the martinis. Shake out the olives. The hungry hunter returns. And what about me? What about us? Have you considered how it is for me to watch my own son masturbating at the breakfast table right before my eyes?"

"Oh that. So that's what it is. Honey, it's natural. We have always encouraged the . . . "

"It is not natural for a thirteen-year-old boy to masturbate at the breakfast table. Masturbation is a private act."

"It's just a phase."

"Just a phase. That is you in a nutshell. *Just a phase. Give it time. Wait and see.*" She pinched up her mouth, mimicking with an unkindly nasal voice. "And *what*," she demanded, "I ask you for at least the fiftieth time this month, do you propose to do about that angel in the basement?"

352

"I need more time to think about it."

"You have had *more* than enough time to think. Now it is time to act. I want that thing *out* of my house. *Out.*"

Murphy glowered at her to indicate that his patience was reaching its limits. "What do you want me to do? *Kill* the poor thing? Shall I *drown* it like a barncat? Set a trap?"

"What you do is your business. Just do it, so I can be free of its whimpering and groaning and foul language, and its *stink*. And the embarrassment of being the only house in the neighborhood that has an angel in the basement!"

"Yeah. Sure. That's what matters, right? The neighbors. The neighborhood. Fine. *Great! Typical you.*"

"Fine," she mimicked in the unkind nasal voice. "Great."

The unkindness of her tone cut him, and he bled anger, fury. His passion crested. He opened his mouth to bellow, but saw reason: his rage would only fuel hers. There would be no end to it. The evening would follow as a stream of skirmishes, screaming, sarcasm. Nothing would be accomplished. They would all be miserable. He would miss the Movie of the Week, which was starting pretty soon. He closed his teeth. "Honey," he said, "I'm sorry. You're right. I'll talk to the boy."

"*Sure,*" she said. "*Sorry.*"

He allowed a tiny flare of anger to burn off before he spoke again. "I'll talk to the boy now. And I'll get cracking on the angel after that."

"I'll believe *that* when I see it."

"You'll see it. Just watch. You'll see it."

She snorted, but said nothing more, and he knew he had won the peace. "I'll just change my clothes," he said.

She followed him into the bedroom. He pried off one shoe with the toe of the other and kicked them across the room, unstrapped his shockproof wristwatch and let it fall to the floor, broke open his necktie and dragged it off, flinging it toward the bed. His wife picked up after him, smirking.

"Men," she muttered. He unbuckled his trousers and let them pool at his feet, stepped out of them. She touched the small of her back as she bent to retrieve them. Her white denim bottom caught his eye. It looked good. He would never have known it was hers if he hadn't been aware for a fact that her head was on the other end of it. He laid his palm against the pleasing white contours, embraced her from behind as she stood, pressing against her, thinking, *Just think, this could be the bottom of a completely strange woman.*

"Your butt makes me feel so young," he whispered into the small of her neck. "It's worth more than the Pope's brain." He nibbled her ear. "More than existentialism itself. It precedes essence by a long shot." She nuzzled against his mouth, smiling, allowing him his fun while she went through his trousers. Her hand came out of one pocket with a thick crumple of bills.

"My God?" She said and stepped away from him. "What is *this*?" She sat on the edge of the bed, deftly smoothing and sorting the bills: tens, twenties, several fifties. "Where did you *get* all this money?"

He gazed curiously at her. "Why I stole it of course."

"You could get in trouble, honey," she said, stacking the edges of each little pile.

He turned up his palms, offering honesty in a bid for reason. "It's my job."

She cocked her head. "All the same," she said, busily arranging the bills again so the portraits of Hamilton, Jefferson, and Grant all faced in the same direction. Watching her fingers move, the obvious tactile pleasure in their long, slender ministrations to the bills, pleasingly unctuous from the caress of hundreds, thousands of strange fingers before hers, Murphy became excited. He grabbed the little pile of fifties and stuffed them down the neck of her blouse. She closed her eyes and smiled, letting him do it. Then he buried half a dozen twenties in a crumple down the front of his jockey shorts and smiled demurely at her. "Shall we go fishing?"

This was their signal.

She chuckled and waved him off mildly. "You promised me something. *Two* somethings. Or have you forgotten already?"

"Will you go fishing afterwards then?"

Her smile was teasing. "I don't have a rod," she said and pouted up her lips. Murphy had to breathe through his mouth. "You can use mine."

Her eyes twinkled at him until he began to move closer again; then she said, "My goodness, we haven't even had dinner yet."

"*After* dinner then," he said.

"And what about the Movie of the Week?"

Murphy hesitated, considered, panted: "Between dinner and the film." Abruptly, from the living room, Perry Como began to sing "Papa Loves Mambo." Murphy rotated his fists under his elbows, swaying before his wife. She watched him with a private smile for a moment. Then she stood up and said briskly, "You go get some clothes on and have that talk you promised to have with your son and with the angel while I put dinner on. *Then* let's see." She kissed him briefly and ducked under his arm. His palm closed over a breast of air. He squinted and gritted his teeth, punched himself a glancing blow in the chest.

Lamb of God who taketh away the sins of the world, hear my plea. Another sixty days respite from the furnace.

Murphy donned his velour smoking jacket and fez, stepped into his slippers and padded down the hall to knock on his son's door. He could hear rustling, breathing, a groan. "Go away," the boy muttered breathlessly, "you'll ruin my climax."

"Don't mess up my new *Penthouse*, son," Murphy called through the door. "I haven't even looked at the centerfold yet." He stepped away, but turned back to say, "Come on into the study when you're free. Like to have a word with you."

In his study, Murphy sat in his five-footed safety chair and lit a Pall Mall. The cigarette's extra length seemed to filter the smoke and make it mild as milk. The milk of death, he thought idly as he tore another match from the book and struck it, touched the flame to a pellet of incense in a shallow jade ashtray on his desktop. He drew smoke deep into his lungs, set down the cigarette on the edge of the desk, bowed his head, raised his palms, turned them to face one another, said "*In hoc signo vinces per aspera ad astra.*" Bowed, clasped his hands over his groin and said, "*Oremus,*" and, in alternating voices of celebrant and responder: "Nomini gomini. *Nomini gomini.* Nomini gomini. *Nomini gomini.*"

From the basement, he could hear the angel caterwauling, smashing things. Then it fell silent and began to sing in a cracked distracted voice: "*Tantem ergo*/Makes your hair grow . . . "

Murphy slid the concealed leaf out from the end of the desk; a laminated sheet of paper was taped to it. He read aloud from the sheet:

"O Nosey who comes forth from Hermopolis, I have not been covetous without cause.

355

"O His-Eyes-are-of-Flint who comes forth from the slime, I have not caused crookedness of any real importance.

"O Eater-of-Entrails, I have not practised usury to a significant extent.

"O Wanderer who comes forth from Bubastis, I have not gossiped unduly.

"O Serpent who writhes forth from the place of judgment, I have not committed adultery beyond the privacy of my heart.

"O Hot-of-Leg who strides out of the twilight, I have not swallowed my heart except in deference to men who could bring me to disadvantage.

"O Dark One who comes forth from the black hole, I have not been abusive of those who did not request abuse by their low cunning or unpleasant manner.

"O Flowing One who streams forth from apertures, my voice has not been loud except to rise above noisy backgrounds."

From the basement, the sound of the angel's shriek raised the hair on back of Murphy's neck. He slumped shut the leaf, raised his face and recited loudly, from memory: "Evil will never happen to me in this land of the Two Justices because I know the names of these gods who are in it, and the sins which are repugnant to them."

He stood, genuflected, chanted:

"May the god who is not known be quieted towards me.

"May the goddess who is not known be quieted towards me.

"May the god whom I know or do not know be quieted towards me.

"O my god, my transgressions are many, great are my sins.

"O my goddess, my transgressions are many, great are my sins.

"O my god and O my goddess, my transgressions are nul, I have not sinned more than the next man and in

356

many cases perhaps less to the best of my knowledge. "The prohibited place on which I have set foot indeed was unknown to me."

The angel was coughing loudly, causing the floorboards to shudder, as though its mouth were pressed up against the ceiling beneath Murphy's feet. Murphy raised his voice:

"How long O my goddess and O my god whom I know or do not know ere thy hostile, majestically vicious heart will be quieted toward me and turn instead upon others whom I do not like.
"Man is dumb. He knows nothing.
"Whether he has committed sin or done nothing, he does not even know.
"The sin which I have done I beg you turn into goodness.
"The transgression I have committed, I beg you let the wind carry away.
"My misdeed I beg you strip off me like a garment and let my nakedness be innocent as a babe's.
"The transgression I have committed, I beg you let the wind carry away."

Then he knelt and bowed his nose down to the dusty parquet floor, rose again, fighting a sneeze, and bringing his palms together and apart again, said:

"Free my house of this angel. Deliver this house from the angel. Invite this angel from my house into the place of the noseless one to leave us at peace with our humanity. We are but poor creatures, O majestic forces of the cosmos and the chaos! We have a hard time upon the earth. We are worms beneath the feet of giants. Spare us this troublesome presence. Let us be humans among humans, for no man is an island unto himself. We despise one another, but we cannot be alone. Therefore, deliver us of this foreign angel. Amen forever, sow without anus, goodbye."

357

He finished just in time to retrieve his cigarette from the edge of the desk before it scarred the wood. He puffed the last drag off the butt and stubbed it out in the ashtray beside the ashes of the incense. It squeaked against the polished surface of the jade, and the sound caused the hair on his arms to lift. The angel had fallen still. Murphy stared at his own face reflected in the black glass of the window above his desk: the eyes and nose and mouth were hollow in a pale, transparent oval. He blinked, snorted the thick sweet scent of the incense from his nostrils, wondered who he was, what he had done, why. He blinked again. A tear beaded on his eyelash.

Lamb of God who taketh away the sins of the world, hear my plea.

"Dad?"

Murphy turned to see his boy in the doorway.

"Dad, I'm sorry."

Murphy smiled. "What are you sorry for, son?"

"That Jesus had to die for my wickedness."

"Son, no one knows for sure why Jesus died. It is a matter of speculation."

"Dad?"

"Yes, son?"

"Is the Movie of the Week rated okay for kids this week?"

Murphy smiled, opened his arms, and the boy rushed into them. They embraced. "Dad?" the boy whispered. "Am I a midget?"

"Why, no son, you're just petite."

The boy was rubbing his palm with the fingers of his other hand. "Can that be caused by masturbation?"

"No way, buddy. Why just look at your brother. He jerks off like crazy and he's as big as a house. Course, he does it in private and keeps it secret."

After a silence, still looking into his palm, the boy asked, "Dad? How do you confess masturbating?"

"Masturbating is not a sin anymore, sonny."

"But when it *was* a sin."

"Well, I used to confess it as an act of impurity perpetrated upon myself by myself when in my own company."

"Do you still masturbate, Dad?"

"Practically speaking: never."

"Well, uh, do you and Mom, you know: get it on?"

"Yes, my boy, we do *get it on,* as you put it."

"Do you go down on her, too?"

"Let me put it this way, son: when you love a person very much, you wish to kiss them everywhere. 'Nuff said on that, I guess."

"Dad?"

"Yes, son?"

"What's on the Movie of the Week this week?"

"I don't know, son. But it's usually good. What do you say we two pals watch it together?"

"*Yeah!*" the boy said with an enthusiasm that warmed Murphy's heart.

"There's just a couple of things I've got to do first, son, so you run along now and I'll be with you in a snap. Why don't you set the table in front of the TV."

He watched the boy move off to the task and felt blessed, loved, graced by good fortune. Then he remembered the angel and felt cheap again, dirty, false. He doffed his fez and lay it on the desktop. Then he opened the center drawer, took out a tiny heart-shaped tin and pried off the lid, removed a key from inside it.

At the end of the long hallway, he ran the key into the lock of the basement door, twisted it, heard the bolt fall away. The staircase was dim. Peering down into the darkness, he experienced scraps of memory, a heap of broken moments from his childhood, stray fleet glimpses of remembrance swimming at him swift as fish up out of a black sea. He thought of his father, dead these half-score years; his mother dead but one; his brothers and sisters with whom he ate roasted turkey twice a year, grilled beef and boiled corn once a summer. He thought of Jesus who some believed had died for the sins of men and of how he had lost his love for the Lord when finally he had embraced the conditions required of him to engage in human love. He sighed. Climbed slowly down the stairway into the cellar.

The angel lay on its back beside the extraterrestrial insect of the water tank. The furnace growled as it burnt black gold within its powerful belly. The angel's breathing was unpleasant to listen to. *Die then. Die now and be done.* Murphy took out his handkerchief and blew his nose, honking like a duck into the cloth.

359

He knelt beside the pale, fading creature. Its eyes rolled toward Murphy's face.

It said, "Death stands before me today as a man longs to see his house after he has spent many years in captivity. The light in the west is lovely, burning gently in that place beyond which the darkness has been smothered by the dark itself. The light is lovely. I shall sleep. You, old friend, shall continue a time in black darkness after I am gone."

Murphy asked, "Will it be tonight?"

The angel's only response was a hissing, labored breath.

Murphy heard the clock in the living room chime the quarter hour: almost time for the Movie of the Week. He asked, "Can I bring you something? Water? Food? Something to read?"

The angel inhaled sharply, jetted dead air from his nostrils. His skin glowed brighter for a moment, dimmed again. "I truly used to feel that you loved me, Murphy. At certain moments. When you smelt the rain, heard jazz, tasted gin. When you kissed your children or your wife, when you bathed your head in water. I truly believed that you loved me from the root of thy heart."

Murphy spoke softly. "I did that, angel."

"You do not love me now, Murphy, and I am sorry for you. I shall die, but you shall live without that love. With nothing but the other so-called love."

Murphy bowed his head. "You never wore the skin of a man, angel. You tried so hard to make us into radiant creatures. You . . . " Murphy stopped speaking and looked more closely into the angel's open, staring eyes, its slack mouth, its still, unlifting breast. The light of its body was dimming rapidly, fluttering up for a moment, dimming again, glowing like a phosphoresence shedding the last fuel of light absorbed over many years.

A sob croaked in Murphy's throat. He hiccoughed. Shook his head and wiped the corner of his eye. He whispered, "Angel, what did you do in the Russian campaign? What did you learn there?"

There was no answer.

He crouched to lift the naked, cold body in his arms, but the first contact of dead flesh against his living fingers had him leap back in horror. The feel of lifeless flesh, he thought, is *dreadful*.

Up above his head, he heard the basement door open, and his younger son called down furiously, "Dad, the Movie of the Week is with Bing Crosby? I *hate* Bing Crosby, and I think it all *stinks*! I'm going to *bed*!" he punctuated the declaration by slamming the door so hard that flakes of plaster jumped from the basement wall. Murphy didn't much care for Bing Crosy either, though he would have gladly pretended to enjoy the film for the sake of his boy's company. Now he hardly knew what to do. His wife would be furious with the boy if he didn't join them at the table for dinner. And then she would be in no way inclined to play go-fishing with him afterwards. Not that he was much inclined now either.

Murphy put his face into his hands. Upstairs he could hear Perry Como singing: "Papa loves mambo:

Mambo, papa.

Mama loves mambo:

Mambo, mama."

He could hear the tiny feet of his daughter on her stacked es-padrilles, dancing one-two, one-two-three. He pictured her sweet young face, thought, *The future, sweet child is yours: please be happy.*

He crawled on his knees across the concrete deck-painted floor to the wall, laid his back against it, drew his legs to his chest. He stared at the fading radiance of the angel's body. From upstairs, he smelt the roasted pleasures of supper, heard Perry Como's voice, his daughter's feet, saw her face, his wife's face, his young-est son's, his oldest's, the neighbor lady's snug red bottom, his wife's broad white one.

In a moment, he would climb back up the stairs and back into their lives. In a moment. For he needed them now, more than ever, needed to be close to them. But first he thought it only right and fit that he should witness this fading of the angel's light.

Lamb of God who taketh away the sins of the world, hear my plea.

Nominated by New Delta Review *and Gordon Weaver*

FOR ANNA MAE AQUASH WHOSE SPIRIT IS PRESENT HERE AND IN THE DAPPLED STARS

by JOY HARJO

from NIMROD

For we remember the story and must tell it again so we may all live

Beneath a sky blurred with mist and wind,
                        I am amazed as I watch the violet
heads of crocuses erupt from the stiff earth
                           after dying for a season,
as I have watched my own dark head
                     appear each morning after entering
the next world
              to come back to this one,
                        amazed.
It is the way in the natural world to understand the place
                         the ghost dancers named
after the heart breaking destruction.
                 Anna Mae,
                 everything and nothing changes

You are the shimmering young woman
                                        who found her voice
when you were warned to be silent, or have your body cut away
from you like an elegant weed.
            You are the one whose spirit is present in the dappled stars.
(They prance and lope like colored horses who stay with us
    through the streets of these steely cities. And I have seen them
            nuzzling the frozen bodies of tattered drunks
                                        on the corner.)
This morning when the last star is dimming
                                        and the buses grind toward
the middle of the city, I know it is ten years since they buried
        you the second time in Lakota, a language that could
                                        free you.
I heard about it in Oklahoma, or New Mexico
            how the wind howled and pulled everything down
    in a righteous anger.
    (It was the women who told me) and we understood wordlessly
the ripe meaning of your murder.
    As I understand ten years later after the slow changing
                                        of the seasons
that we have just begun to touch
        the dazzling whirlwind of our anger,
we have just begun to perceive the amazed world the ghost
dancers entered
            crazily, beautifully.

*Anna Mae Aquash, a young Micmac Indian activist, was mysteriously
murdered, her body found in February 1976 on the Pine Ridge Reservation in
South Dakota.

Nominated by Jim Barnes, Naomi Clark, Marilyn Hacker and William Pitt Root

WHAT THE BLUE JAY SAID

by FRANKIE PAINO

from AMBERGRIS

There's a stranger inside him. Each time he wakes,
a flutter, or a pounding. Something within him wants
release, and always that pink cord, like an arrow
shot from the base of throat through sternum.

They opened him like a book, cracking bone,
spreading ribs, great wings of blood and flesh.
They buried a secret inside him. Lying awake
at night he thinks it must be a bird, the way

his chest rises, falls, his pulse quickens.
He made love, at 18, for the first time. He remembers
that night, the only time in his life
when he flew out of his skin, looked down

on himself, on her on top of him. It was the same
pounding then, hooves in his chest. He traces
a finger over the smooth lines on his chest,
tries to believe he'll grow to love this marriage

the way saints come to love pain. He dreams
of a dry place, sun beating down on a young woman
who strings feathers, azure beads in her hair,
her breast an empty monstrance. She cleaves

his chest with a flash of silver blade.
Every day he stares at the pine bough outside his window
where a blue jay cries, "Thief! Thief!" One night,
he knows, he'll finish the dream. He'll bury

his fist deep in his chest, tear out the living heart,
raise it towards the woman, the blue jay, the girl
he first loved whose name he can't remember. He'll shout,
lungs bellowing his final breath, "Take it back! It's yours!"

Nominated by Ambergris

MORE ROOM

by JUDITH ORTIZ COFER

from PUERTO DEL SOL

M y GRANDMOTHER'S HOUSE is like a chambered nautilus; it has many rooms, yet it is not a mansion. Its proportions are small and its design simple. It is a house that has grown organically, according to the needs of its inhabitants. To all of us in the family it is known as *la casa de Mamá*. It is the place of our origin; the stage for our memories and dreams of Island life.

I remember how in my childhood it sat on stilts; this was before it had a downstairs—it rested on its perch like a great blue bird—not a flying sort of bird, more like a nesting hen, but with spread wings. Grandfather had built it soon after their marriage. He was a painter and housebuilder by trade—a poet and meditative man by nature. As each of their eight children were born, new rooms were added. After a few years, the paint didn't exactly match, nor the materials, so that there was a chronology to it, like the rings of a tree, and Mamá could tell you the history of each room in her *casa*, and thus the geneology of the family along with it.

Her own room is the heart of the house. Though I have seen it recently—and both woman and room have diminished in size, changed by the new perspective of my eyes, now capable of looking over countertops and tall beds—it is not this picture I carry in my memory of Mamá's *casa*. Instead, I see her room as a queen's chamber where a small woman loomed large, a throneroom with a massive four-poster bed in its center, which stood taller than a child's head. It was on this bed, where her

366

own children had been born, that the smallest grandchildren were allowed to take naps in the afternoons; here too was where Mamá secluded herself to dispense private advice to her daughters, sitting on the edge of the bed, looking down at whoever sat on the rocker where generations of babies had been sung to sleep. To me she looked like a wise empress right out of the fairy tales I was addicted to reading.

Though the room was dominated by the mahogany four-poster, it also contained all of Mamá's symbols of power. On her dresser there were not cosmetics but jars filled with herbs: *yerba* we were all subjected to during childhood crises. She had a steaming cup for anyone who could not, or would not, get up to face life on any given day. If the acrid aftertaste of her cures for malingering did not get you out of bed, then it was time to call *el doctor.*

And there was the monstrous chifforobe she kept locked with a little golden key she did not hide. This was a test of her dominion over us; though my cousins and I wanted a look inside that massive wardrobe more than anything, we never reached for that little key lying on top of her Bible on the dresser. This was also where she placed her earrings and rosary when she took them off at night. God's word was her security system. This chifforobe was the place where I imagined she kept jewels, satin slippers, and elegant silk, sequined gowns of heartbreaking fineness. I lusted after those imaginary costumes. I had heard that Mamá had been a great beauty in her youth, and the belle of many balls. My cousins had ideas as to what she kept in that wooden vault: its secret could be money (Mamá did not hand cash to strangers, banks were out of the question, so there were stories that her mattress was stuffed with dollar bills, and that she buried coins in jars in her garden under rosebushes, or kept them in her inviolate chifforobe); there might be that legendary gun salvaged from the Spanish-American conflict over the Island. We went wild over suspected treasures that we made up simply because children have to fill locked trunks with something wonderful.

On the wall above the bed hung a heavy silver crucifix. Christ's agonized head hung directly over Mamá's pillow. I avoided looking at this weapon suspended over where her head would have lain; and on the rare occasions when I was allowed to sleep on that bed, I scooted down to the safe middle of the mattress, where her body's impression took me in like mother's lap. Having

367

taken care of the obligatory religious decoration with the crucifix, Mamá covered the other walls with objects sent to her over the years by her children in the States. *Los Nueva Yores* was represented by, among other things, a postcard of Niagara Falls from her son Hernán, postmarked, Buffalo, N.Y. In a conspicuous gold frame hung a large color photograph of her daughter Nena, her husband and their five children at the entrance to Disneyland in California. From us she had gotten a black lace fan. Father had brought it to her from a tour of duty with the Navy in Europe. (On Sundays she would remove it from its hook on the wall to fan herself at Sunday mass.) Each year more items were added as the family grew and dispersed, and every object in the room had a story attached to it, a *cuento,* which Mamá would bestow on anyone who received the privilege of a day alone with her. It was almost worth pretending to be sick, though the bitter herb purgatives of the body were a big price to pay for the spirit revivals of her storytelling.

Except for the times when a sick grandchild warranted the privilege, or when a heartbroken daughter came home in need of more than herbal teas, Mamá slept alone on her large bed.

In the family there is a story about how this came to be.

When one of the daughters, my mother or one of her sisters, tells the *cuento* of how Mamá came to own her nights, it is usually preceded by the qualification that Papá's exile from his wife's room was not a result of animosity between the couple. But the act had been Mamá's famous bloodless coup for her personal freedom. Papá was the benevolent dictator of her body and her life who had had to be banished from her bed so that Mamá could better serve her family. Before the telling, we had to agree that the old man—whom we all recognize in the family as an *alma de Dios,* a saintly, soft-spoken presence whose main pleasures in life, such as writing poetry and reading the Spanish large-type editions of *Reader's Digest,* always took place outside the vortex of Mamá's crowded realm, was not to blame. It was not his fault, after all, that every year or so he planted a baby-seed in Mamá's fertile body, keeping her from leading the active life she needed and desired. He loved her and the babies. He would compose odes and lyrics to celebrate births and anniversaries, and hired musicians to accompany him in singing them to his family and friends at extravagant pig-roasts he threw yearly. Mamá and the oldest girls worked for days preparing the food. Papá sat for hours in his painter's shed, also his study and library, composing the songs. At these celebrations he was also known to give long speeches in praise of God, his fecund wife, and his beloved Island. As a middle child, my mother remembers these occasions as a time when the women sat in the kitchen and lamented their burdens while the men feasted out in the patio, their rum-thickened voices rising in song and praise of each other, *compañeros* all.

It was after the birth of her eighth child, after she had lost three at birth or infancy, that Mamá made her decision. They say that Mamá had had a special way of letting her husband know that they were expecting, one that had begun when, at the beginning of their marriage, he had built her a house too confining for her taste. So, when she discovered her first pregnancy, she supposedly drew plans for another room, which he dutifully executed. Every time a child was due, she would demand, *More space, more space*. Papá acceded to her wishes, child after child, since he had learned early that Mamá's renowned temper was a thing that grew like a monster along with a new belly. In this way Mamá got the house that she wanted, but with each child she lost in health and energy. She had knowledge of her body and perceived that if she had any more children, her dreams and her plans would have to be permanently forgotten, because she would be a chronically ill woman, like Flora with her twelve children, asthma, no teeth; in bed more than on her feet.

And so after my youngest uncle was born, she asked Papá to build a large room at the back of the house. He did so in joyful anticipation. Mamá had asked him for special things this time: shelves on the walls, a private entrance. He thought that she meant this room to be a nursery where several children could sleep. He thought it was a wonderful idea. He painted it his favorite color—sky blue—and made large windows looking out over a green hill and the church spires beyond. But nothing happened. Mamá's belly did not grow, yet she seemed in a frenzy of activity over the house. Finally, an anxious Papá approached his wife to tell her that the new room was finished and ready to be occupied. And Mamá, they say, replied: "Good, it's for *you*."

And so it was that Mamá discovered the only means of birth control available to a Catholic woman of her time: sacrifice. She gave up the comfort of Papá's sexual love for something she deemed greater: the right to own and control her body, so that she might live to meet her grandchildren, me among them, so that she could give more of herself to the ones already there, so that she could be more than a channel for other lives, so that even now that time has robbed her of the elasticity of her body and of her amazing reservoir of energy, she can still emanate the calm joy that can only be achieved by living according to the dictates of one's own heart.

Nominated by Stanley Lindberg

FRANCIS: BROTHER OF THE UNIVERSE

fiction by RODNEY HALE JONES

from ANTIETAM REVIEW

I WAS IN love with Maura's mother, Lucky.

Lucky McGovern. She's twice my age, over six feet tall and has high Irish cheekbones, deep-set gray-blue eyes. The knobby joints in her shoulders and arms look like clenched fists rotating under the thin jerseys she wears. I'm in love with her body—not in the usual way—but an aesthetic way. She is the most photogenic woman I have ever seen. The thought of the shadows the right lighting could produce around her elbows and knees makes me shiver. But Lucky is shy. "Point that camera at me and I'll rip your heart out," she says.

Maura and Lucky moved in a couple of months ago to the basement apartment underneath my one-and-a-half-rooms-and-a-shower on W. 14th St., where I've lived for the past six months. Before that I lived in my mother's house, a narrow, wood fame job just behind Utopia Parkway in Queens. On the day I left with my records and my father's old Rolleiflex, she cried for hours, then stood on the porch and sang "Won't regret what I did for love" at the top of her lungs, so guys driving past on the parkway blew their horns. She always had a thing for *A Chorus Line*.

"The City will gobble you up," she screamed after me.

She was wrong.

Contrary to my mother's suspicions, I am blessed with a secret weapon. I'm protected by the wide twin lens of my father's

371

Rolleiflex around my neck. Without it I'm skinny, nineteen-year-old Francis Abatti who flunked gym twice at Utopia High and broke his mother's heart because he never learned to say the "Hail Mary" and didn't want to go to college. But with the camera hanging from its worn leather strap against my chest like a baby, I become powerful. I become St. Francis of Assisi as he appeared in a Marvel comic book my mother gave me when I was ten. The comic was called *Francis: Brother of the Universe,* and my favorite picture was of St. Francis taming the wolf, petting it the way you'd pet a Siamese cat. A bubble from his mouth held the words: "What a disgrace it is, you killing people for food!" That's how I feel, magical. With my father's camera whatever is in front of me is made tame and tiny in the little glass square that stares up at me.

It works too. People treat you differently when you point a camera at them. It's the fear of the Lord.

It also gives me a way to pay the $450 a month rent on my coffin-sized apartment. I work for 12th St. Novelties Ltd. photographing furry animals for calendars, naked women for decks of playing cards, and typical tourist scenes of New York City for postcards, posters and matchbooks. Those guys will put a picture of Lady Liberty against a sulphur sunset on anything they think will sell. I got the job through my cousin Mario, a cop in the hundred and first precinct, whose girlfriend, a billowy redhead, sometimes models for the company. She appeared as the four of clubs in the most recently released plastic-coated pack of fifty-four beauties. 12th St. Novelties Ltd. violates city ordinances by housing its studios in a sooty cave of a building near the docks which it's supposed to use only as a warehouse. Across the street is a disco bar called "The Anvil" frequented by men.

I had the camera around my neck and was setting out for Central Park to shoot some "Greetings, from New York" postcards, on the day Maura and Lucky showed up. They pulled to the curb in a green Plymouth Fury packed full of furniture and cardboard boxes. Lucky stopped too late and collided with a metal garbage can, sending a fanfare of crashing cymbals into the street.

"Damn." Lucky climbed from the Fury like a shaken pilot.

It was a cold fall day, but all she wore over a magenta jersey was a blue hooded sweatshirt that revealed her broad, swiveling shoulders. Maura, the kid, wore a silver ski jacket with black triangles and the words: I Want Complete Control. She had electric green Nikes on her feet and Devo-style mirrored sunglasses and looked like she had complete control the way she sure-footed out of the car. A regular bass beat came from the tape player that dangled from her left arm like a briefcase. While Lucky loomed over the pile of beer cans and orange peels spilled onto the sidewalk, Maura trotted to the rear of the car and with a Swiss Army knife, started sawing at an old shoelace tying the trunk lid down.

Lucky stared at the sidewalk and shook her head. My heart swelled and the leather lens cover of my camera popped open. They always paint the Madonna as pale and frail, like she's made of china, but this is the way Mary must have been—raw-boned with black hair, tired looking, but so big she seemed capable of carrying the whole world on her broad back. Mary must have been one tough lady.

I was just about to snap the first shot of my "Madonna of Manhattan" series when Lucky looked up, not at me, but at the eye of my camera, as if it were a pistol. "You do, and I'll call the cops. Pervert." She pulled her hooded sweatshirt up and hurried into the building. The short stairway led to the apartment of Herr Krebs, the super, a fat German who I suspect was a Nazi criminal.

Maura followed, carrying a wilted potted plant in one hand and her blaring boogie box in the other. In the doorway, she paused, turned to me and said, "She's a little on edge today."

I don't give up easily. I waited for them to come back and when they did, I flashed Lucky my best I'm-gonna-make-you-a-star look, handed her my business card and said, "You ever think of doing modeling on the side?"

"Beat it, creep," she said and hustled back inside carrying a table lamp. Maura looked at me and shrugged. She turned up the volume on her tape player and screamed over the blades of an electric guitar, "Do you like the Psychedelic Furs?"

Later, on my way home, I stopped on McDougal to order a cookie-gram for my new neighbor: an eighteen-inch chocolate chip cookie shaped like a camera with the words: THINK IT OVER in script of white frosting.

At home, I pressed my ear to the floor to make sure the new tenants were there, then cranked up my RCA Hi-Fi with the

Talking Heads singing "I Need Something to Change Your Mind," to plead with Lucky:

Time won't change you.
Money, won't change you.
I haven't got the faintest idea.
Everything seems to be up in the air at this time.
I need something to change your mind.

From upstairs Herr Krebs pounded on the floor with the heel of his boot; I paid no attention. The Talking Heads kept talking:

Drugs won't change you.
Religion won't change you.
And it comes directly from my heart to you . . .
I need something to change your mind.

Suddenly, as if in answer to my plea, a knock sounded at the door. I swung it open, hoping to see Lucky, loosened up and ready to pose, but instead it was twelve-year-old Maura, still wearing her mirrored sunglasses, with polyester pajamas. She held my cookie-gram in a flat open box in front of her like a pizza, stuck her gum-coated tongue out at me and said, "My mother said to tell you that we don't eat sugar in our household. She says sugar is a drug and people shouldn't be able to get it without a prescription."

"Come in, come in," I said. "You can't walk around the West Village like that. You wanna be kidnapped?" The thought occurred to me: why not get the kid to convince her? My mother always told me that a good mother will endure practically anything for the sake of her children, and, with a face like Our Lady, how could Lucky not be a good mother?

Maura blew a pink bubble and walked into my apartment, dragging her slippered feet along the floor. She went for the orange crates where I keep my records and started flipping through them.

"Does your mother let you walk around in public like that?" I asked.

She lowered her sunglasses and glared at me. Herr Krebs stomped on the floor above. "You sure play your music loud."

374

"It's a habit I got into when I lived with my mother's singing."

Maura pulled a pink album from the crate, held it before her sunglasses, replaced it.

"You should have used psychology," she said coolly. "That's the way I handle my mother."

"What kind of psychology?"

"The regular kind." She sighed, as if I were the stupidest person she'd ever met. "Give them what they want. She wants to sing, let her. They always get over it when you give them what they want." She leaned her back against the wall, drew her paja-maed knees to her flat chest and gazed around my room—the kitchen sink full of developing trays, stacks of magazines and contact sheets piled in the corners, the wooden crucifix that my mother made me promise to hang above the bed wherever I slept. Finally her eyes rested on my father's Rolleiflex on top of the bureau.

"Would you rather be blind or deaf?" she said.

"I don't know. Neither."

Maura frowned and stared at the camera. "I'd rather be blind." She spoke with certainty. "One of my mom's patients, Mr. Sven-lov, is deaf. He's got cancer, but he can't talk about it. He talks with his hands. Did you ever see that?"

I nodded. Maura shivered.

"It gives me the creeps. I could never be deaf. But if I were blind, I could at least be a singer. Like Stevie Wonder. Blind people make better singers because they have to feel the music in their bones."

I wanted to get her back to the subject of her mother.

"Your mother has patients?" I asked.

"She's a nurse," Maura pulled off her sunglasses, and her eyes took another tour around my room. They were blue-gray dittos of her mother's eyes. "You sure are disorganized."

"A nurse?"

Of course! I thought and imagined the woman I had seen earlier that day dressed in white, standing big and benevolent as the Statue of Liberty in a ward of suffering men. The deaf don't have it so bad, but pity the blind who don't see her starched white glory.

"She's a private nurse." Maura was gazing curiously at the bureau. "That's a weird camera."

"Yeah," I picked it up and carried it over so she could see it more closely. As she reached for it, I pulled it back. I don't let anybody touch my camera.

"I won't break it," Maura said, but she didn't reach for it again. I snapped open the metal flap that covered the viewfinder and showed her a corner of my apartment projected into a two-inch glass frame.

"Far out."

"My father used to photograph fires. He would sit in the kitchen listening to his CB radio, and as soon as he heard about a fire, he'd grab his camera and rush to where it was. He even sold a picture to **The New York Post.**"

Maura didn't seem interested in my father's career, she kept looking at the camera and twisting the sleeve of her pajamas with her pencil-thin fingers.

"Is your name really Francis?" she asked.

"Why not?"

"It's a girl's name."

"For your information, Francis was the name of a famous saint. A guy saint."

"Francis? Take my picture, willya?"

"Sure," I said. "How about a family portrait. You and your mother, the nurse."

"Nope just me. Willya take it now?"

"Okay, okay," I said. "Don't rush me." I stepped a few paces back and in the viewfinder saw Maura crunched up and leaning against the wall. "Could you at least smile?"

She didn't. She didn't change her expression or position and after I clicked the shutter, she bounced up off the floor and headed for the door. She turned, her hand on the knob, and looked at the crucifix above my bed.

"Do you believe in God?" she asked. "I mean, do you believe that God exists?"

"Who doesn't?"

"Oh." She nodded and disappeared into the hallway.

That's how I got to be friends with Maura. Lucky would hardly speak to me, much less pose for me. Maura started hanging around my apartment every day after school, listening to Iggy Pop records or standing silent next to me in the red light of my cramped bathroom which I use as a darkroom. After two months and a hundred pictures of Maura—Maura sitting atop the lion at the Public Library, or break dancing in front of the Shubert Theater, or petting a horse in Central Park—Lucky still refused to pose for me. I never asked Maura to try to convince her mother; that would be crude and unsubtle. I figured that I'd get to be part of the family, Uncle Francis. How could she say no then? You've got to use psychology.

Lucky didn't take me seriously, she treated me like Maura's seventh grade friends. I began to understand the frustration in my mother's voice when she sang about what she had done for love.

Finally, the day after Thanksgiving, I got my chance to convince Lucky of my sincerity.

Maura had the day off from school, and we were going to spend it together while her mother visited patients on the Upper West Side. I thought we could go to a place I knew on E. 30th, where, for twenty-five bucks a pop, you can take a helicopter ride over Manhattan. I'd been saving for weeks for that helicopter ride, but Maura wanted to go ice-skating at Rockefeller Center. Certain things I refuse to do for love, and ice-skating is one. With a helicopter ride, if you crash, you know it's not your fault. But when you fall and break a leg on the ice at Rockefeller Center with everybody watching, you have to take responsibility.

"It's no fun to skate alone," Maura said. "My God, Francis. You're such a dweeb."

She was right. The reason that I failed gym twice in High School was that I didn't go. I didn't mind dressing out and shooting baskets, but the gym teacher, Mr. Snyder, was a sadist. He made us play this game called war. Practically every gym period he would put one-half of the class on one side of the gym and the other half on the other side and make us throw hard rubber balls at one another.

My mother thought athletics would be good for my character, and encouraged me to sign up for the Catholic Youth League teams, softball, football, ice hockey! "What are you going to do?" she asked. "Sit up in your room the rest of your life and rot? Listen to me, Francis. There are two kinds of people in the world: Those who get out and do things and those who sit around

377

and watch." I decided pretty early on that I was going to be the latter kind of person. Watching is important too.

"I swear," Maura said. "You can be so close-minded."

I finally convinced her that the helicopter would be educational. She could write a report about it. She said, "That just makes it sound worse."

That morning I slept late. I had gone to my mother's the night before for Thanksgiving dinner with her and Mrs. T., her bowling partner, and my head buzzed with too much chianti. At ten-thirty a firm knocking woke me. For a while I thought the building was under construction. I finally answered, wrapped in a yellow blanket, my head buzzing like an electric saw, I opened the door. Lucky, dressed in her nurses uniform, held out a picnic basket.

I wrapped the blanket tighter around me and motioned her and her picnic basket through the doorway.

"This is some lunch for you and Maura." Lucky put the basket on the floor and, like a magician, pulled from it a long white scarf. "And make sure she wears this." Then she stood looking down at the scarf that trailed from her big-knuckled hand down along my gray-green carpet.

"You want some chianti or something?" I asked.

But she kept standing there, then looked up and said, "Listen Frank . . . "

"Francis."

"Francis, listen. I need a lawyer. Do you know a lawyer? Mine stinks, I've got to get a new one."

I thought about my cousin, Dominique. He chases ambulances out on Long Island.

"Who do you want to sue?" I asked. To tell you the truth, I couldn't keep my eyes off her.

"I don't want to sue anyone," she said. She reached into the pocket of her white uniform and took out a letter, folded in thirds like a real letter, and handed it to me.

It was written on one of those script typewriters, that make the letters come out in neat, snobby script. I wonder about guys who use typewriters like that. There was a dove on the letterhead with rays of light coming from it, and underneath in bold, holy looking letters: CAMP EMANUEL.

"Maura's father," Lucky said. "He runs a Christian day camp in Suffolk County. He divorced me because he believed I was possessed by demons."

She explained to me that Maura had spent Thanksgiving with her ex-husband and his new wife out in Suffolk County and had returned with this note sealed in an envelope:

"Dear Lucky:

This festive time with our daughter has given me the opportunity to become acquainted with her living conditions. Is it not enough that you choose to bring her up in a section of New York notorious for sexual perversion, that you house her in property supervised by a suspected Nazi, as Maura refers to him? Apparently not. What Maura told me shocked me, to say the least. And right under your nose. The role of a parent is to give moral guidance, as a shepherd guides sheep. But some people are bad shepherds. They let the sheep roam free to be eaten by mountain lions. In view of this, I find myself forced to engage the services of Steckler, Riley and Wise with the intention of suing for custody. I have already spoken to Mr. Steckler on the phone, and he assures me of the viability of my case. You shall hear shortly from Mr. Wise.

Regards from Gwen.

Yours
In Jesus Christ,
Claude."

Reverend Claude. What a jerk.

"What did Maura say to him?" I asked.

"That's it," Lucky said. "She won't tell me. I called him up, and all he would say was, 'right under your nose,' as if it had been a snake it would have swallowed me."

Then I had an inspiration. "Don't worry about a lawyer yet," I reached up and put my hand on her shoulder. "I'm sure it's something she told him to make conversation. Something she made up like kids do." This was my chance to weave my way into the family web. I'd get Maura to tell me what she said to her father. She tells me just about everything whether I ask or not. I would be the hero. I'd preserve the family unit, and Lucky would be indebted. She'd ask, "How can I ever thank you?"

379

"I'll find out," I said. "I'm sure it's nothing. We'll worry about a lawyer later."

Lucky looked skeptical, as if she wondered why anyone would tell me anything.

"Give me a chance," I was already thinking how I would arrange the lights around Lucky's scantily clad body.

"Well," Lucky shrugged. "Maybe she will tell you. She calls you Saint Franklin."

That's Saint Francis.

Saint Francis received the mark of the stigmata, his big miracle. The day after he came down from the mountain, he got a fever and went blind. I still remember the comic book picture of a guy in a cloak standing over Saint Francis and cauterizing his eyes, and Saint Francis lay there talking to the fire. "Fire," he said. "You have been my brother, and I have blessed you. Don't cause me pain now." And you know, Francis didn't feel a thing.

Lucky wasn't the only one to remind me of Saint Francis of Assisi. Thanksgiving dinner the night before was full of religious allusions. My mother and Mrs. T. compete at being Catholic. One or the other has been the annual bingo champion for as long as I can remember. They try to beat each other to the hospital when they hear a member of the parish is about to die. But last night Mrs. T. had one that my mother couldn't beat. A real live miracle.

Mrs. T. has enormous teeth and she uses the word "wonderful" a lot. You could tell her that you're living in a cave by the East River selling heroin for a living, and she would say, "Isn't that wonderful!"

All she could talk about while we were eating my mother's turkey parmesan was how her granddaughter's polio vaccination scar had changed its shape to resemble a Latin cross after the little girl took her first communion. "It wasn't always that shape," Mrs. T. said between bites of turkey and stringy cheese. "It just got that way. So I told my son, take her to the priest before it changes back."

I don't know if you've ever had turkey parmesan. My mother makes it every Thanksgiving, and every Thanksgiving she tells the story about how her father wouldn't let her get married until she learned how to make spaghetti sauce. But she didn't tell the story this Thanksgiving. She couldn't get a word in edgewise with Mrs. T. telling about her granddaughter, saying her daughter-in-law took the kid to Father Antoloni and that Father Antoloni was going to write a letter to Bishop O'Connor.

"Bishop O'Connor?" My mother was jealous. She didn't eat after that and kept looking at me with a strange, disappointed look. I didn't feel hungry, myself, so I poured myself another glass of chianti from the gallon bottle next to my plate. Mrs. T. didn't stop eating, and she didn't stop talking either. "I'm not surprised," she said. "Things like that always happen in my family. My grandmother in Sicily had a scar on her stomach from a caesarian that they say looks like the face of St. John the Baptist."

All the time my mother was getting edgier. I could tell she was jealous because she was quiet and stared down at her plate.

Suddenly Mrs. T. turned to me as if she had just noticed I was there. She looked at me hard, maybe making sure I didn't have any disfigurements that might be taken for stigmata or something. "So Francis. Still not married. How many girlfriends do you have now?"

"Fifty-two," I said. "That doesn't include the jokers of course." I don't know why I said that, I was getting pissed off at her and her damned granddaughter.

"Isn't that wonderful," she said.

That's when I took it too far. I'd had a bit of wine by that time, and I pulled out a pack of the 12th St. Novelties plastic-coated playing cards from my jacket pocket. I peeled off the jack of spades and handed her to Mrs. T. . . . It was a crude thing to do, I admit.

The jack of spades was Fasha Johnson, a tall black woman photographed on a bed of sand in front of a sky blue background to make it look like she was at the beach. She held a pail and spade, the kind that kids have. I remember Fasha because she was one of the few models who took her work seriously. She wanted to feel like she was at the beach, so she closed her eyes and imagined smelling the salt air. It was ten minutes before she would let me start. But she kept shivering. That warehouse is pretty drafty. "Can't you turn up the heat in this place?" she rubbed goose bumps on her dark skin. "How the hell am I supposed to look like I'm at the beach?"

Mrs. T. held Fasha's picture way out in front of her. She had been ready to say, "How wonderful," but her face froze in a tight smile she couldn't get rid of. Her eyes glazed over, but she kept smiling.

My mother reached over the table and snatched the remaining fifty-three cards from my hand and flipped through them, one at a time. All fifty-three of them; Mrs. T. sat there with Fasha grinning in spite of her goose bumps, kneeling in the sand with this big pail right in front of her. Mrs. T. grinned back. When my mother finished looking at all the cards, she turned to me and said, "You will be damned."

Nobody had ever told me I'd be damned before. It kind of scared me.

I got up from my seat. I must have staggered. I tucked the half-gallon of chianti that was left under my arm and headed for the basement. The basement is always a good place to hide.

Everybody in the world has a box in his mother's basement with stuff in it from when he was a kid, that you don't want and your mother doesn't want to throw out. My box was underneath my mother's pool table, bulging and papered with tape, POMPE-IAN OLIVE OIL in red letters on the side. I couldn't have gone near the thing if I hadn't been drunk and a little sad too. I took a swallow of chianti from the jug and started crawling through the box underneath a bare, sixty-watt light bulb while upstairs Mrs. T. was trying to console my mother by telling her gossip about the sons of the other women on their bowling team. Everything had the musty smell things get when they haven't been touched for a long time. Old finger paintings. The robe I took my first communion in. A rock collection, a green spiral notebook from when I was eleven. I opened it and read the first page.

RULES TO FOLLOW
1) Always take pictures with the sun behind you.
2) Don't use Tri-X film in bright sun.
3) Don't use panatomic film inside.
4) Don't

I had never finished number four. I took another gulp of wine and turned the page.

FACTS ABOUT SAINT FRANCIS

1) More books have been written about Saint Francis than about any other Saint.
2) Many historians trace the origins of Renaissance (hence, modern) poetry, art, drama back to Saint Francis.
3) The city of San Francisco is named after him in Spanish. Also, in Arkansas, both a river and a town bear the name of Saint Francis.
4) His followers were the first missionaries to go to China. Franciscans were with Christopher Columbus when he voyaged to the New World.

Then I started to cry. I kept thinking about being damned, then thought about Paul Simon's song, "Kodachrome." It was my favorite song in high school.

Mama don't take my Kodachrome

Leave your boy so far from home,

Mama don't take my Kodachrome away.

When Maura showed up at my door about an hour after Lucky left, I had loaded my camera and was ready to go. It was my last roll of film before I got paid on Monday, that is if I wanted to afford the helicopter ride. Twelve exposures to find out what Maura had told her father, and if I ran out of film before she let me in on her secret, I'd never know.

Maura was wearing her silver ski jacket and a POLICE tee-shirt, and she was still trying to get me to take her ice-skating instead of on the helicopter ride. "Where's your holiday spirit, Francis?" she said. "Skating at Rockefeller Center is just about the most holiday spirit thing in the whole world."

She talked about it all the way to the subway station. "You can do that anytime," I said. "How often do you get to go up in a helicopter?"

"Helicopters suck." She adjusted her sunglasses as she went through the turnstile. "Let's take the E train to the Port Authority. I've got something to show you."

"The Port Authority's in the wrong direction. The helicopter is on the East Side."

"It'll only take a minute," she said, walking fast a few paces in front of me. "It'll only take a second."

383

On the E train she sat close to me and put her arm around my shoulder. "Let's make up," she whispered, "I hate to fight."

"Sure thing," I said. The train wasn't crowded, so I moved to the seat across from her and took a few flash shots: Maura against a background of black glass and graffiti.

"Hey, that'll look real punk," she said. "That'll look great on an album cover." She lay the length of her body along the seat and looked up at the dirty brown lights on the ceiling. "Trains bore me. But they don't bore me as much as helicopters."

I moved back to her side of the train. "Hey," I said tentatively. "How was Thanksgiving with your father?"

"Okay," she sighed.

She picked up the picnic basket and put it on her stomach. "Ever since he got to be a minister my dad has been real weird. And his new wife wears too much make-up. It makes her look dead. She always wants to know how many boyfriends I have."

"I know the type," I said.

"I'm not a person who has a whole bunch of boyfriends anyway. What kind of person does she think I am? I'm practically a virgin, you know."

"Me too."

"I believe in monogamy. Don't you?"

"Absolutely."

I followed her through the doors of the train and down the long corridor of the bus station. She knew where she was going. We came to the place where they have lockers and Maura stopped. She fished in her tight jeans pocket and held up an orange key. "I carry this with me all the time," she said in a low, James Bond voice. "Just in case."

"In case of what?" I whispered back.

"All out war." She walked to one of the lockers, locker number 121, and opened it. Inside there was a big blue suitcase with frayed luggage tags and a sticker from Atlantic City. She let me get a peek at it, and then slammed the door shut.

"It has everything in it I need to survive," she said. "Clothes. Tapes. Dried fruit."

"Where are you planning on going?"

"I didn't say I was planning on going anywhere. I said it's just in case. Okay?"

I took a picture of the locker with Maura standing in front of it. Number 121.

"Why did you take a picture of that?" she asked.

"Just in case," I said.

Our helicopter pilot's name was Burt. He wore pink coveralls with UNITED AIR TOURS in red script on the back. He had four earrings in his right ear, each one shaped like a letter of his name: B, U, R, T.

"You think the guy's a pilot?" Maura asked. "He doesn't look like any pilot I've ever seen."

"Don't worry, Hon," Burt said as he led us out to the pad where his helicopter sat like a huge glass insect. "This is going to be a thrill. It's going to be a thrill such as you have never known."

You can't talk in a normal tone of voice in a helicopter, the wind of the blades is so loud, you have to shout. Maura, wedged between Burt and me, looked straight ahead through the glass bubble, her hand clutching my knee.

"Relax, Babydoll," Burt yelled as we wobbled into the air. "This is going to be the thrill of your life."

Maura didn't look thrilled.

We flew uptown, crossed the reservoir in Central Park, dipped down near the Hayden Planetarium, then sped east over the Hudson. I snapped a couple of pictures. It was worth the fifty bucks, let me tell you. Burt played tour guide, calling out names of landmarks and every once in a while patting her leg and saying something like, "Don't worry, Babycakes. I won't fly upside down until you give me your okay."

The Hudson stretched out below us like a plowed field, like you could ride a mule straight across to New Jersey.

Suddenly Burt yelled. It was no tour guide yell. I turned. Maura, pale and shaking, held the blade of her Swiss army knife close to Burt's neck. "Take this bird down," she shouted. "Let's bring it home, Burt."

Burt screamed back. "Don't kill me kid. I'll take you anywhere you want."

"I want to go down!" Maura said.

When I reached to grab the knife, Maura jerked around and caught me across the palm with the blade. A trail of blood grew from my hand. I thought Burt was going to cry. "Don't kill me," he said.

"What is this shit?" I licked blood from my wrist. Maura shook like she had a fever, staring through her sunglasses at my hand.

"Fuck you, Francis," she said. "Just fuck you. You're the one afraid to go ice-skating."

Burt got us down damn quick and said if he ever saw us again he'd call the cops. Maura crawled out over my lap, and, without a word, walked across the concrete pad towards the terminal.

"Listen, I'm sorry about all that," I said to Burt and handed him a fifty and an extra ten, my last ten.

Burt pocketed the money. "If I were you, Honeybunch," he said, "I'd put that kid on a leash."

"Shut up," I said.

I got to the terminal building, and Maura was nowhere around. She wasn't on the street either. I walked a block up 2nd Ave., then a block in the other direction. By this time I was scared and feeling a little sick with that cut on my hand and my hangover still buzzing. I heard my mother's voice saying, "the City will gobble you up." I was sweating. Some Uncle Francis, I thought. I kept on walking south on 2nd Ave., thinking that I only had two pictures left. It was stupid to think about, but I couldn't help it. Two shots left before the City gobbles her up, I thought.

I walked all the way to 14th St., and, seizing on a hunch, took the double L train across to Chelsea and changed to the 8th Ave. Local. An old lady across from me shifted her seat when I sat down; there was blood on my sleeve, my palm was still bleeding a little, I guess I looked dangerous.

At the Port Authority Bus Terminal, there were a million Santa Clauses milling about, a sort of Santa convention. They all wore buttons with the name of the state they were from: Arizona, Texas. Only two shots left, and me jogging through this sea of Santas.

Port Authority isn't the safest place in the world, even with Santas hanging around. If my hunch were right, she came back here, but anything could have happened by now. I thought of the pictures of missing children on milk cartons. Two shots left, Francis Boy. Santas everywhere.

Then I saw Maura sitting on the floor leaning up against locker number 121. I pulled off my lens cover and caught her in the viewfinder before she saw me. I wanted to hold Maura forever, strong and lonely in her silver ski jacket. Click.

386

One shot left.

"Hey little girl," I yelled, "Want your picture taken with Santa Claus?"

But she hid her head in her knees. I walked over and sat next to her We didn't say anything, a Santa with big red boots walked past. Maura shifted her knees. "Francis, why won't you let anybody touch your camera?"

"That's a good question," I said. I was still shaken. "When it was my father's, he wouldn't let anybody but me touch it. A camera's special, like a violin. It can only belong to one person."

I paused, then went on. "I was only five when my father died, so I don't remember a whole lot about him. Remember I told you he liked to take pictures of fires?"

"Yeah."

"My mother thought he was crazy, said he'd get killed hanging around fires like that. She doesn't appreciate fires. But she was right. One night, a couple hours after he had left to catch this warehouse fire in Brooklyn, three firemen showed up at the house, holding his camera. They said that they had tried to stop him but hadn't been able to. He died inside the warehouse of smoke inhalation. My mother didn't understand. She thought it was dumb to walk into a burning warehouse. But I know why he did. It was a good shot. You're willing to do stuff like that for a good shot."

"Francis?"

"What?"

"It's empty."

"What's empty?"

"That suitcase. There's nothing inside. It's just to scare my mom. I'd never really split. It's just psychology, you know?"

I told her yeah, I knew. "Hey Maura," I said, remembering Steckler, Riley and Wise and only one shot left, "when you were over at your father's yesterday, did you tell him something that pissed him off?"

"Everything pisses him off."

"But did something especially piss him off?"

"No."

"Are you sure?"

" What?"

Maura hesitated. "It wasn't a lie or anything. I just told him that we were lovers. I thought it was time to get it out in the open." She took her sunglasses off and looked at me with her mother's gray-blue eyes. "Well, we are, aren't we?"

I looked down at the gash in my hand. It was beginning to swell and turn purple around the edges. But the funny thing was, I didn't mind the hurt. I thought of Saint Francis receiving the stigmata, cartoon laser rays coming at him from a huge image of Jesus Christ in the sky, piercing his palms and ankles. It must have hurt like hell for him too, but when you're receiving the stigmata you don't complain.

There were a couple of things I could have done next. I could have called up my mother and recited "Hail Mary." I could have gone to Camp Emanuel and asked Reverend Claude to forgive me for my sins. I could have called Lucky and told her to forget the whole thing and given her my cousin Dominique's number. What am I supposed to be, the kid's godfather or something?

But I didn't do any of those things. I went ice-skating at Rockefeller Center with rented skates Maura got me with some extra cash she had stashed away in her sock.

There I was, in the middle of the ice with people circling around me like a frenzied wagon train. I looked for an opening where I could break in and join the circle. At the edge of the rink Maura stood with her white scarf flapping in the air like a flag. She had my camera around her neck, her head pointed down into the viewfinder. I was about to fall when I felt the click. It was like I really felt it. Time stood still for a second, then the slippery ground fell out from beneath me, and I remembered. The last shot.

I still have it. Me, skating at Rockefeller Center. The thumb covering half my face is Maura's. But it's not a bad action shot. My legs are pulled up, my eyes squeezed shut. I still remember how it felt, not the falling, but the starting to fall. I felt it in my bones. I had no choice. Can't stay in my room all my life.

Nominated by Antietam Review *and Greg Pape*

DYING IN MASSACHUSETTS

by DONALD W. BAKER

from THE DAY BEFORE (Barnwood Press)

I think I should like to die in Massachusetts,
wading Parker's River in sneakers at slack water,
my wire basket a quarter full of blue crabs,
and I easing my long-handled net towards a big one.

The sun is shining as hard as it can, for it is August.
Clamshell clouds are crowding over the western horizon.
I mash a green-head fly against the nape of my neck,
and the big crab scuttles away under the peat.

No matter. Because I am thinking of what I read
last night in Van Gogh's letters: *I am in it*
with all my heart. I must become more skilled than I am
before I can be ever so slightly satisfied with myself.

And so at that moment the sun collapses into the river,
the crabs are spilled, the net, the fly, the collecting storm
plunge through a canvas of reds and yellows and blues
into the still, cool, clouded poem my life has written.

I'm the old white-bearded geezer they find,
floating face-down, two guys in a rented skiff,
with beer and sub sandwiches and Saturday off,
who on Sunday read about themselves in the Boston *Globe*,

and at night tell their wives about it in Worcester,
and on Monday their buddies down at the station-house.
So the rumor of Donald Baker's death ripples
into the neighborhoods where he was born and grew up.

It passes 14 Reed Street, riding no-hands on a blue bicycle,
and Red Logan's mother peers through her parlor curtains,
saying: *all that expensive college education*.
It rings a doorbell at 282 Chandler Street,

and Alice Crowe's father takes his pipe out of his mouth,
saying: *a good thing you married the dentist*.
And for about ten seconds the streets light up
with the glances and ball games and arguments nobody remembers.

Now the tide turns, a cold stream flooding in
from Nantucket Sound nudges the body upriver,
and the majestic voyage begins, through the grief
of sister and daughters and wife, across the promotion,

with tenure, of junior colleagues, beyond Life Insurance
and Supplemental Retirement Annuity, to a Free
Government Marker and Eternal Care in the plot
in Pine Grove Cemetery behind the Tastee Freeze on Route 28.

My friends, there's a lot of genetic dignity here.
Those oaks are rooted in great-aunts and great-uncles,
that headstone shadows the secrets of my mother's bed,
and my father's electrons waver forever in this loam.

It is March 26th. I am in it with all my heart.
I must try to become more skilled than I am before I die.
For the titles of a thousand unwritten lives
are circling overhead on the gray sails of the gulls.

Nominated by Barnwood Press *and Sherod Santos*

LISTENING

by DAVID MURA

from CRAZYHORSE

And from that village, steaming with mist, riddled with rain,
from the fishermen in the bay hauling up nets of silver flecks;
from the droning of the Buddhist priest in the morning,

incense thickening his voice, a bit other-wordly, almost sickly;
from the oysters ripped from the sea bottom by half-naked women,
their skin darker than the bark in the woods, their lungs

as endless as some cave where a demon dwells
(soon their harvest will be split open by a blade, moist
meaty flesh, drenched in the smell of sea bracken, the tidal winds);

from the *torrii* half way up the mountain
and the steps to the temple where the gong shimmers
with echoes of bright metallic sound;

from the waterfall streaming, hovering in the eye, and in illusion, rising;
from the cedars that have nothing to do with time;
from the small mud-cramped streets of rice shops and fish mongers;

from the pebbles on the riverbed, the aquamarine stream
floating pine-trunks, felled upstream
by men with *hachimaki* tied round their forehead

and grunts of *o-sha* I remember from my father in childhood;
from this mythical land of the empty sign and a thousand-thousand manners,
on the tip of this peninsula, far from Kyoto, the Shogun's palace,

in a house of *shoji* and clean cut pine, crawling onto a straw futon,
one of my ancestors lay his head as I do now on a woman's belly
and felt an imperceptible bump like the bow of a boat hitting a swell

and wondered how anything so tiny could cause such rocking unbroken joy.

Nominated by Crazyhorse, Kathy Callaway and Fae Myenne Ng

AT THE IGA: FRANKLIN, NEW HAMPSHIRE

by JANE KENYON

from THE ONTARIO REVIEW

This is where I would shop
if my husband worked felling trees
for the mill, hurting himself badly
from time to time; where I would bring
my three kids; where I would push
one basket and pull another
because the boxes of diapers and cereal
and gallon milk jugs take so much room.

I would already have put the clothes
in the two largest washers next door
at the Norge Laundry Village. Done shopping,
I'd pile the wet wash in trash bags
and take it home to dry on the line.

And I would think, hanging out the baby's
shirts and sleepers, and cranking the pully
away from me, how it would be
to change lives with someone,
like the woman who came after us
in the checkout, thin, with lots of rings
on her hands, who looked us over openly.

Things would have been different
if I hadn't let Bob climb on top of me
for ninety seconds in 1979.

It was raining lightly in the state park
and so we were alone. The charcoal fire
hissed as the first drops fell. . . .
In ninety seconds we made this life—

a trailer on a windy hill, dangerous jobs
in the woods or night work at the packing plant;
Roy, Kimberly, Bobby; too much in the hamper,
never enough in the bank.

Nominated by Maxine Kumin

WITH PAT BOONE IN THE PENTLANDS

Fiction by KEN CHOWDER

from NEW ENGLAND REVIEW/BREAD LOAF QUARTERLY

UNTIL THE COMING of my countrymen, I had every good reason to be happy. I was twenty-three and not in New Jersey. I was living a romantically-bleak existence in the perfect spot for it—West Penicuik, Peeblesshire, Scotland.

West Penicuik was a village much favored by an apt and icy wind and rain. Above, a string of barren treeless hills, the Pentlands, swept by on their way to Edinburgh like a series of sheep-infested moonscapes. Many of the town's ancient stone houses sloped picturesquely toward ruin; my own house, Dalgleish Cottage, was wonderfully protective of the cold and damp within its walls. The downstairs bedroom sported a hole through which the coalshed and flourishing rhubarb—which grew like a weed, because it *was* a weed—could be glimpsed, or even watched. Late afternoons, cup of bitter Typhoo tea in hand, I watched the rhubarb grow beneath the rain.

I even had a job. Twenty hours a week I fed chickens, gathered eggs, and sometimes cleaned the two stench-filled sheds at Brae Farm, run by the McAllister family. The McAllisters had a twenty-year-old daughter, Fiona, who was the only pretty girl in Scotland. Admittedly, I was, at 50p an hour, underpaid; admittedly, I hated chickens, if not at the job's outset, then shortly thereafter; admittedly, Fiona was a fiercely proud girl, whose primary response to my existence was an occasional uncomprehending stare.

Outside of these few drawbacks, my life was arranged ideally. My conversations with shopkeepers were of maximum terseness. "How much are your oranges today, please?" "Five pence apiece." "Two, please." A half pint of milk arrived on my stone doorstop daily in a little pyramidal package that was impossible to open without spilling; each little spill seemed to speak of Scotland, of the blessed foreignness of my life.

I spent Friday evenings in the pub above the greengrocer's, so as to admire the publican's plain but bountiful daughter. I did not speak to her except to place my order for a pint of McEwan's Export. One evening I found myself in conversation with two gigantic Scots, who spoke a sturdy brand of Glaswegian and drank pints of Heavy at a stupendous rate. They drove to this pub every Friday for a few wifeless hours, and so felt compelled to exercise fully their intemperance. They sang cheery song without key and took turns passing out in the toilet, their rowdiness not at all checked by their mutual profession, that of interior decoration. The publican gave us peas and chips to enable us to stay legally a half-hour after the ten-thirty closing time. Shortly after eleven I found myself losing these same peas and chips on the street, in front of the butcher's shop.

"That's all right," one of the decorators said. "Everyone does it here."

"In front of the butcher's?" I asked, miserable.

"Well, perhaps not in front of the butcher's," he said, and I never went up to that pub on a Friday again.

My felicities were extracted in solitude; this was, I believed, the way it was done. I strode on hillsides, disengaging my feet from the clawing heather, listening to the piping of lapwings, wrapping my woolen scarf tighter around my own neck.

I had been in West Penicuik for ten months when my father came to visit in early August. He had never been east of the Atlantic before; grimly I watched him step down from the plane in red plaid pants, of no recognizable tartan, beneath a chlorinated-swimming-pool-blue blazer with gold-colored buttons. He regarded my tweed, suspicious but impressed. "Hey, bud," he said. "You're looking kinda . . . *distingué*, unh?"

I showed him Dalgleish Cottage. "This place is no cottage," he said, "It's a whole damn house." He looked nervously around him. "No shower, unh?"

"No shower."

We took a walking tour of West Penicuik; my father's comments alternated between the only two American plaudits: "Nice" and "Great." At the end of the walk he said, "So where's the laundromat, bub?"

"No laundromat. That's part of the idea."

"Where do you get your clothes washed?"

"There is this sink in the bathroom," I said, with the satisfaction of someone who was not born poor.

Mornings, my father rose early to wash his socks and underwear in the sink. He hung them, perhaps distastefully, on the line above the booming rhubarb, then set out for a shopping excursion that I imagined terrorized the village. He bought a loaf daily, taking perverse delight each time at how swiftly it went stale. Every day he hunted a new curiosity. He would request "something really Scotch" from the dazed butcher, Mr. Gunn, or the appalled grocer, Mr. Stevenson. One day Mr. Stevenson recommended oatcakes; another day Mr. Gunn black pudding. Finally my father bore home the haggis. He came in, rain streaming from his cotton porkpie hat, holding the haggis in his two red hands like a treasure. I told him the ruthless truth— which parts of the sheep were inside that little pouch, and what that little pouch itself was. I was trying to acquaint my father with something I considered to be reality. He said he was sure this haggis stuff tasted okay, but it was placed, and resided for months thereafter, in the bottom of my small, tepid refrigerator.

Once I went with him on his daily rounds. My father walked into the greengrocer's, tossed off an unanswered "Hiya" to Mr. Johnstone, then began waving his arms and gesturing at fruit. "I'll take a coupla grapefruit, half-dozen oranges, few apples, some bananas, and . . . what else?" he asked me. "Whadda ya say to a pineapple?"

"Oh no," I said. I had never ventured a pineapple.

"Okay. So a heada lettuce and some of those little tiny potatoes you got and carrots and maybe some broccoli and a cuke and a couple pounds tomatoes. Got any corn?"

"No sir," Mr. Johnstone said. As Mr. Johnstone went around his shop slowly gathering fruit and vegetables, noting their prices with pencil on yellow notepad, I thought I saw him shake his head, and

I imagined I knew why: because a man who did not ask the price of his purchases had surely, long since, secured his place in Hell.

Somehow I made the mistake of telling my father about the one relatively celebrated resident of West Penicuik, Titus Griffiths. Griffiths Press published beautifully designed, printed, and bound chapbooks of poetry from the exalted likes of Edwin Morgan and Claire Burke—just holding those books made poets feel much, much better. But it was bruited about West Penicuik that Titus Griffiths himself was an arrogant loner. I had never even seen the man, but the moment my father heard about him, the decision was made. My father owned a quickprint shop in Passaic. "I'm a printer," he said. "He probably needs somebody he can talk to about ink."

With many misgivings I pointed out the path to Titus Griffiths's door. An hour later, by arrangement, I came back to pick my father up, but he waved me inside instead. "We're havin' us a great time here," he said. "Turns out Titus has never even heard about rubber-base ink."

Mr. Griffiths looked like a short and slightly drunken version of Santa Claus. He'd given my father a wee dram, and they sat together on an overstuffed floral sofa beside a peat fire, dramming and dramming again, my father in two opposing plaids and Mr. Griffiths in three shades of grey. "Havin' a great time," my father said again. He admired several times the smoothness of the single-malt whiskey in his hand, then moved on to more general admiration. "I mean," he said, "this is a great little set-up you have here, Titus. Really nice."

"I wish that were true," Mr. Griffiths said. "But there's not a great deal of life in it. Sometimes in winter I get so lonely I go out to the highway just to watch cars pass by."

"Hey, it can't be that bad, Titus," my father said. "This is a really great little town. Only thing it actually needs is a good laundromat."

"We could use one of those, at that," Mr. Griffiths said. "After a time a man tires of washing out socks in the sink."

"I know exactly what you mean," my father said.

My father had a wonderful time in Scotland. He bought himself three Shetland sweaters and an Atholl curling bonnet; he played golf at nine different courses, some famous and one historic; he sampled a dozen malt whiskies and did not have to eat the haggis. The sun even shone for one and two hours at a stretch. He had a wonderful time, he kept saying, but after eighteen days he wanted to go home. This was five days before he was scheduled to go.

He said he missed my mother. They'd been married for twenty-eight years and had never before spent three nights apart. "A guy gets so he can't sleep by himself any more," he said, dipping his socks in the sink. "Know what I mean?"

No, I did not know what he meant. Furious, I watched him twist the moisture out of his socks. "You should never wring wool," I said.

"Is this wool?" he said. "Oh, hell with it," he said, wringing.

To me it seemed he was forsaking his single chance to experience Not-New-Jersey; he would never have a chance to get outside his own little world again, see himself as a foreigner, see himself truly. I was twenty-three; I did not temper my words. "You have the patience of a flea," I said. "And the sensitivity of a brick."

My father let the sock drop back into the blue water. "Sometimes you say mean things to me," he said. "You know what I mean?"

I knew what he meant, and I had to let him go. I let him go home to Passaic, to my mother, and to the months that, as it turned out, he had left to him.

It was only a week after his departure, when I was still slightly panging, that I was invited to dine at the home of the McAllisters, my employers, for the first time. I am Jewish, which had been, I suspected, the reason for their hiring me: they were born-again Christians, and hot to convert. So far, I had not been convinced.

The McAllisters all had red hair and referred to Jews as Israelites. There were seven children, all tall, but only Fiona was handsome. Mrs. McAllister was protypically powerful and bucktoothed. She told me luringly that afternoon tea would feature both a silver-side roast and the presence of "Mr. Pat Boone, your countryman."

The McAllisters picked up Pat Boone in Prestwick and drove him to Brae Farm by Saturday noon. He was to be the featured speaker, and for all I knew the top-billed singer, at a big meeting for Born-again Christians in Edinburgh on Sunday night. In the meantime the McAllisters apparently thought he might be of use in the battle for the soul of a single Jew.

I was not so much curious about Pat Boone as interested in Fiona and the roast. I swathed myself in three pieces of tweed and walked through a negligible rain up the hill to Brae Farm. I considered walking around to the sheds to insult my antagonists, the chickens, but I did not: I was on best behavior.

Pat Boone was not wearing either saddleshoes or white trousers. He was in tan corduroys and a herringbone jacket with elbow patches. He looked, as the saying goes, taller than on television. He seemed older too, and was less bent upon smiling. He hardly smiled at all, in fact; but perhaps even people who sang on television were subject to jet lag.

Mrs. McAllister placed me next to Pat Boone at the table, a long way away from both Fiona and the roast. Mrs. McAllister herself kept hopping up to deliver more food; she wore a long white dress that looked oddly bridal, and her always-remarkable energy had doubled. Every time she sat down, she said something with the word Jesus in it.

Pat Boone began sawing gingerly on a slice of beef and said he understood that I was American. Reluctantly I said I was, yes. "Why are you here?" he asked, folding his hands expectantly.

I had the brief urge to tell him: Because I never want to watch you sing again. I didn't say that, and I realized with some shock that it was not even true. For some reason I didn't hate Pat Boone. He was a man like any other, aging more rapidly than anyone had thought possible, a tired man, probably unaccustomed to washing socks out in the sink.

And I found I didn't know the answer to Pat Boone's question. Why was I here, anyway? "I came here for the waters," I said, lamely, and then, embarrassed, I didn't even wait for the Claude Rains reply. "But there are no waters in West Penicuik," I said. "I was misinformed."

"I see," Pat Boone said. His gaze became locked on the gray juiceless slice of roast and the indistinct green or greenish vegetable on his plate.

At the other end of the table, Fiona appeared bored with life. She dabbled her fork in vegetable and didn't look at either me or

Pat Boone. Meanwhile, I devoured roast beef; I had known it would be gray and blamed no one for that—not Mrs. McAllister, not Jesus, and not even the chickens.

Pat Boone said nothing more to me while we ate. He answered Mrs. McAllister's questions without irony, even questions about What it was Like to be a Star. "I'm really not a very big star," Pat Boone said.

Mrs. McAllister was taken aback only for a second. "Of course," she said. "Just a servant of Jesus, like us all."

Pat Boone was looking dazedly at his plate. A quarter of roast potato hung on his fork; he seemed suddenly surprised to see it there. He looked over at Mrs. McAllister and rid his face of dullness. "Excuse me?" he said. "Did you say something?"

After apple crumble sodden with custard we all trooped outside for a McAllister ritual—the family football game, which they called The Big Match. They didn't ask if I wanted to play, but simply handed me an absurd old pair of baggy shorts. Pat Boone was made Nonplaying Captain of one side. I was his first selection; I felt unfathomably flattered. I asked if I could be goalkeeper. "You bet, buddy," Pat Boone said.

Fiona captained the opposing side. The instant her foot touched the ball, her face took on an eagerness I had never seen in her before. Her long red hair was held in place by a snapping elastic band, but the tail of it whipped behind her like a lash as she ran. She gave up the ball unwillingly, even to her teammates, for she was its rightful owner. As I watched her play, seeing her for the first time as something other than a static image, I began to believe that my feelings for her were more than simple crush; it was possible that I was well and truly in love with her.

Pat Boone stood on the sidelines. In the game's first minute he shocked me by calling out, "Way to go, Joel!" when I had stopped a meek shot by the youngest McAllister. But the next time I looked over to the sidelines, Pat Boone had disappeared. I had the irrational sense of loss. I wanted to invite him to visit me at Dalgleish Cottage; I could picture him there, carrying home the haggis, wishing for a laundromat, not asking Mrs. Johnstone the price of oranges. The vision, this time, was a warm one; but I was, to put it simply, too late.

Moments later, Fiona gathered in a stray pass and came darting upfield on her own, well in advance of any teammate. A brother came charging toward her, but with a catlike pounce she leapt around him, even as she pushed the ball cleanly between his open legs. She eluded a younger sister almost disdainfully, and came clear to me. I ran out to smother her shot with my hands. Just as I dove at the ball, everything held still for a moment. There was the ball, its white hexagons shining, leaving behind a darker wake where it had just skidded along the grass. The tops of the clipped blades of grass acquired a sudden sheen under a little spate of sunshine. I saw the Pentlands in the distance beyond, the heather just going from black to purple under the bright sunlight. I could see the end of Fiona's tigerish ponytail flying behind her, and then I could even see her eyes, burning bright. Fiona looked at me for the smallest of moments; her eyes were cold and alien, hardened toward me, and in that instant I could see another in the uncomfortably close future: the moment when I would be getting up off the ground and be walking back to pick the ball out of the net, the moment when I would finally realize that I was alone and deservedly alone in the world, with no father, no Pat Boone, no countryman, no Fiona, when all my desires would boil down to just the one: the simple desire to get back to even in this game.

Nominated by Joyce Carol Oates

CASTRATO

by KENNETH ROSEN

from THE HEBREW LION (Ascensius Press)

The Angel of Rome was a male soprano
Named Alessandro Moreschi. He was,

They claim, the last of the castrati.
I heard him do the Bach-Gounod "Ave Maria"

On public radio, static rattling like glass
Beads of a curtain parting, Professor Moreschi

Coming out to sing, record made in 1902.
I was deaf to his skill, and could hear

Only castrato sorrow, a music-is-my-life
Sort of bleating. This practice, securing

The boy's voice at soprano, this cast,
So to speak, of the dice, as the sacrifice

Does not guarantee ability at song, began
Among Spanish monks five hundred years ago,

Drifted to Italy, Germany, catching fire,
Passing away, leaving us Alessandro Moreschi

Singing with his high notes held overhead
As if barbells with eery tremolo. You know

How it goes: ah-vey mah-REE-EE-ahh. I had
To leave my chair to walk around my room to

Keep from turning it off, trying to listen,
Trying to figure it out. It was illegal,

But begun to keep women off the choirs,
And I don't know a woman who'd approve

Of this, or who would treat Alessandro
Unkindly. Remember the way the ladies

Loved Liberace, say, and maybe the famous
Farinelli flouted himself so, all heartache

And complaint, as Elvira in Mozart's
Don Giovanni. But Alessandro fluttered

On approach notes like a wounded loon,
Not weird in my ears alone, but who knows.

In this case I discover my vulgarity.
Faulkner says Benjy cried missing his,

And the boy manhandled by monks before
His larynx broke, was he so wise

As gifted boys are sometimes, to know
Was this a loss, a liberation, a slit

With a stilleto after a bath, thumb
Pressure enough to pulp him free from

What's ordinary. At a bris the mohel
Passes and shatters a whiskey glass,

Seizes the foreskin between his teeth
And saws it away with a sharp splinter,

Blood on his lips, whiskey in his breath.
When the baby cries, as if suddenly awake,

He's in the tribe. It's a trade, a tool
Being a scar of wood or iron, a plumber's

Ball pein hammer: a chimney-sweep gives up
His hair, a cormorant gets to wear a brass

Ring on his neck, and a castrato loses
His family jewels, and with luck he sings.

Nominated by Sherod Santos

405

MILES WEEPING

by MICHAEL WATERS

from AMERICAN POETRY REVIEW

To hear Miles weep
    for the first time, the notes bent
        back into his spent frame to keep
    them from soaring away—
I had to click the phonograph off
    and hug myself to stop the shaking.
        I'd recognized a human cry
    beyond any longing given a name.
If ever he let go that grief
    he might not touch his horn again.
        That cry rose in another country,
    full-throated in awkward English.
I still have the envelope, unstamped,
    addressed to "Mother/Father," its oily
        scrap of paper torn from a primer,
    the characters like the inky
root-hairs scrawling the washed-out soil.
    Lek—every boy's nickname—
        wrote he was "to be up against,"
    meaning, I guess, that his future
was end-stopped, one unbroken line
    of tabletops waiting to be wiped.
        He'd walked miles along the coast
    to find us combing the beach, then
stood, little Buddhist, with bowed head
    while we read his letter, composed

with the help of the schoolmaster.
How could we deny the yearning
ambition to abandon the impossible
land of his fathers, to begin again?
We could only refuse in a silent way.
When someone asked Miles Davis
why he wouldn't play ballads anymore,
he replied, "Because I love them too much."
All that we never say to each other.
The intimacies we can't complete.
Those ineluctable fragments. To be up against.

Koh Samui Thailand

Nominated by Laura Jensen and Michael Ryan

ALIENS

by SHARMAN APT RUSSELL

from THE THREEPENNY REVIEW

In 1986, ALMOST two million illegal aliens were arrested as they crossed the sometimes invisible line that defines and encloses the United States of America. In the El Paso sector—a pastel-colored desert stretching from Van Horn, Texas to the western end of New Mexico—hundreds of thousands of "undocumented men and women" are caught annually by the Border Patrol, with an estimated twice that number passing through undeterred. A small percentage of this traffic will come through the Mexican border town of Palomas, which in English means dove and which lies ten miles south of Columbus, New Mexico. Most Mexicans crossing through Palomas are seasonal workers who expect to return via the same route. Thus, over the years, what has come to pass for industry in this village is a strip of adobe store-fronts, brothels, and hotels used by men coming home with new-won wages sewn in the hems of clothing or shoved deep into pockets. From nearby ranching and mining communities, Anglos have helped build up this trade in sex and recreation. Although Mexicans entering the States are not likely to partake of the town's luxuries, this is not to say that they don't plan to on their return.

From Palomas, an even smaller percentage of *mojados* or "wet ones" will choose to walk up through the sparse creosote and yucca of the Chihuahuan Desert, past the town of Deming on Interstate 10, past—walking steadily on, in their fifth day by now—the jagged volcanic fang of Cooke's Peak with its barrel cacti and hidden shelves of pictographs. Under the shadow of this mountain, these men will gravitate to the green-lined Mimbres River and follow its cottonwoods up a narrow valley of irrigated fields and apple orchards. Here, sometimes alone, more often in groups of two or three, they might begin to look for work. By the time they reach my house, at the northern end of the valley, the memory of Palomas belongs to another life, another country, and they will have walked over eighty miles.

When I first came to the Mimbres in 1981, I often saw illegal aliens traveling purposefully at the edge of the highway and my peripheral vision. I did not recognize them as such, although in definable and undefinable ways they seemed out of place on the black-topped road that wound efficiently through the mountain curves. As I drove past in my rusted Volkswagen Bug, silver mail boxes flashed by with the inevitable dirt road, adobe home, or aluminum trailer attached. Cattle and horses grazed on the brown hills of grama grass, while fields blazed startling green along the banks of the river. Against this setting, there was something odd about the isolation of these men dressed in polyester pants and invariably carrying a paper sack, small bag, or bundle of clothing. Miles from any town, they did not hitch-hike and did not seem to be walking from a car or to a car. Strangely detached, they kept their gaze directed ahead to a focus which resolved not on the highway but at someone's door. The door opened, and the man or woman inside had something for them to do: adobes to make, walls to lay up, fences to fix, or—less satisfactorily—a garden to weed.

In my late twenties and by all standards an adult, I had never thought of myself as an employer, much less one who would require euphemisms to describe her employees. So when the men began to appear at my house with their diffident smiles and gestures, I felt uneasy. I did not know how to respond to their questions, how to supply food or even water. Not speaking Spanish was my excuse. But the truth lay more in the way they looked. They looked different. They looked poor. And they were, after all, men. I imagine that in the 1930s other women shared my feelings when the first hobos began to appear on porchsteps. Like these women, I eventually adapted, and in surprisingly little time, to the stranger at the door.

As the crow flies, the Mimbres Valley lies over one hundred miles north of the nearest metropolis (El Paso), thirty miles east of the nearest town (population 12,000) and directly south of the Gila National Forest. It is hard to make a living in this valley, and we miss the proximity of bookstores and corner cafes. In this rural area, our neighbors divide neatly into those who live here because it is familiar and those who came here because it is not. Most of my friends fall in the latter category, and for us the subject of illegals is new and interesting. One friend, who speaks French and Spanish and who has tried unsuccessfully to serve his workers borscht, describes the knock at the door as an informal "cultural exchange program." He writes down the addresses of those he likes and assumes that one day he will visit and be welcomed. Another neighbor argues that hiring aliens takes jobs from Americans who would work for less if the welfare system were suitably altered. To this, a third friend responds that Mexicans need to work as much as anyone else and that she hires for humanness, not nationality.

Some of us theorize that the flow of unemployed and ambitious out of Mexico gives that beleaguered country a necessary release valve and prevents political turmoil—i.e., revolution. This idea, too, divides into two camps: those who think it is good to prevent revolution and those who think it is not. From a rather different viewpoint, many of us believe the system wrong, because it permits so much abuse and, for this sinsoaked country, more guilt. We all know ranchers like the one who turned his workers into the Immigration Service the day before payday. Other employers withhold pay until the job is completed, a not-so-subtle form of blackmail. It is easy to see how racism flourishes where the employed have no avenue of complaint or redress. On the other hand, we also all know of some decent someone—a farmer in Deming or Hatch—whose small business depends on alien labor. More to the point is the Mexican couple who had dinner with us one night before Christmas. She was eight months pregnant, he was desperately seeking work. We told them that with the layoffs at the copper mine, unemployment in our county had reached forty percent. He replied that it was eighty percent where he came from. They had just walked nine days in the rain: we did not suggest they turn around and go back. Increasingly, it seemed that the problem of undocumented men and women could only be examined one focal length at a time. There was the

410

big picture and there was a man and a woman with a bundle of clothes. As one came into focus, the other blurred.

In any event, for my husband and me, the discussions were academic. We learned to give food. We pointed directions. We sometimes chatted. But when asked about work, we spoke without thinking, without hesitation, "No trabajo." No work here.

Then we began to build a house.

In southwestern New Mexico, building an adobe home is an intense rite of passage which requires, in its purest form, no previous construction experience. For financial reasons, we started with one room, fifteen by twenty feet. After the kind of research that involves a lot of driving and staring at other people's houses, we decided to make a traditional mountain adobe altered by passive-solar, south-facing windows. As teachers, we had the summer to make the bricks, lay up the walls, and put on the sloping hipped tin roof. This was traditional "wetback" work, but we never gave a thought to hiring someone else. We would do it together, alone.

It began well. Although a good *adobero* can talk importantly and at interminable length about R values and thermal efficiency, he or she knows that transmogrification is the truer miracle. A patch of soil becomes a bedroom. Solid ground is transformed into a window sill. An unsightly hole will be a wall nine feet high. For us, such magic depended upon a borrowed and ancient cement mixer whose idiosyncrasies were my responsibility as I shoveled dirt and sprayed water into its maw. The mud was then wheelbarrowed away by my husband and poured into a wooden form for three bricks fourteen by ten by four inches.

Adobe is a cunning mixture of clay and sand. Too much clay and the brick cracks while drying, too little and it lacks strength. We tested the proportions of our soil by throwing handfuls of dirt into a jar of water, shaking vigorously, and noting the stratification. Amazingly, our land appeared to be a kind of huge dehydrated adobe mix—add water, stir, and pour. This we did, every day, ten hours a day, for three weeks. It was hard work, but not unpleasant. Transmogrification! Magically the ground formed into squares that we set on their sides to dry and then gingerly stacked. On one good day, eighty new wet-looking bricks lay in soldierly rows before us; on most days, there were only sixty or

411

fifty or even less. We ended up with thirteen hundred adobes: a hundred less than we thought we should have, a hundred more than we would actually need.

While we waited two weeks for the bricks to dry, we began to dig the foundation footings, which had to be rather large to support the heavy walls. In a matter of days, etched deep in the ground, our room became defined. Into these holes, we inserted stakes of metal to which we fastened the longer slim poles of steel called rebar. There was something elegant about these complex metal layers running in their rectangle of fifteen by twenty feet, and I almost hated to cover them with cement. I hated it even more as we began to do it, for cement is nothing at all like adobe. The magic was gone, or rather, reversed. It had become bad magic. At the mixer, I glumly shoveled in heavy gravel and two buckets of cement. Moistened with water, the back-breaking load was then dumped into the wheelbarrow, which my husband manfully directed in tottering form to the foundation's edge. The stuff slopped out to disappear into the earth. Again, the process was repeated and another load swallowed without any sense of progress. Again, another load, and another, as our muscles strained and our skin split from the alkaline lime.

At this point, things really went to hell. There is a Mimbres Valley saying that the couple who builds together divorces together. As our visions of the house altered, diverged, and then collided, as our bodies reminded us that we were only getting older, we moved from bad temper to the kind of free-floating anger hidden since childhood. Through a haze of misunderstandings, we peeled pine logs for vigas, built forms for the next step of the foundation, and eternally mixed more cement. At night, bone-tired, we talked about the house, instead of sensibly talking about other things. One day, I left for a brief respite in town. On another day, so did my husband.

When the dust finally settled, we began again.

Down the road, our neighbor has a small trailer where he houses Mexican workers who come every year and build what seem to us a dizzying array of fences. That summer, two young men in their twenties were busy digging holes on his land, erecting posts, and nailing up expensive-looking wire. They began each day at eight and when they stopped at five the afternoon still stretched before them, light and long and empty of things to do. One evening, in the cooling hours of mid-summer, they wandered over to watch us lay our sixth course of adobe. With finicky nicety we placed each brick flush to the outside string that served as our level. At intervals, we also put wooden blocks where we wrongfully estimated heavy pictures or cupboards would go. At that time we agreed, quite incorrectly, that it would be easy to install the electrical wires later.

My husband, who speaks some Spanish, offered our visitors a beer and halting conversation. He inquired as to what part of Mexico they came from. Chihuahua? A nice city. He had been there. He wanted to know the current exchange rate for pesos. He asked how many adobes they could make in a day. Four hundred! We looked at each other. He asked the Spanish word for hammer. He told them he was a high school teacher.

At five the next afternoon, they showed up again. This time they clambered into the room like a crew just hired. One took over my task of lifting up the thirty-five-pound brick; the other elbowed my husband aside and demonstrated the proper way of setting the adobe in its mortar of mud. They stayed until the sun tipped over the ridge of our western hills. They had taken pity on us.

Although we offered, neither Mañuel nor Gabe wanted money. Of course, they liked the slide of our beer at the end of the day. But more, I think, they liked the companionship of working with equals. This was their free time, their gift. For two more weeks, they came uncalled when their own day was through—and we, who had also been working since eight and who would work on until dark, were in their debt. The conventional relationship between American and wetback turned on its head, abolished, and some tension in us relaxed. That next summer, we understood perfectly well that we had plenty of work for a skilled *adobero* and so began our career of hiring illegal aliens.

Effrem and Jesus sat rather stiffly on the edge of the couch while Amanda Johnson—ex-jockey, architect, and mother of two—spoke swiftly to them in Spanish and then as swiftly to us in English. Amanda knew Effrem well—he was an "old friend"—and we were letting her handle the negotiations with our first employees. At that time, in 1983, the going rate was eight dollars a day, plus food and board. In the next four years, the price would rise to

413

ten or twelve dollars; strenuous work on a farm or ranch pays fifteen and more. (As I write in 1988, most Mexicans in Mexico earn three or four dollars daily.) Feeling uneasy, we offered nine and consulted with Amanda as to what constituted board. Beans, she said. Beans, meat, tortillas, eggs, potatoes, coffee, and canned food. Effrem, she noted, preferred white Rainbow bread to tortillas. Employers also had the option to provide such amenities as cigarettes, beer, and the occasional pair of socks. We would do that, we said quickly. At nine dollars a day, we believed in keeping Mexican wages out of the American economy.

I was never to know Effrem or Jesus very well or, for that matter, any of the men who eventually worked for us. Each morning, my husband and they conferred, gathered tools, and went off together making more adobes, stuccoing walls, or digging ditches. I went inside our now-completed room to my household, and, later, child-rearing duties. At lunchtime I cooked a hot meal of beans, eggs, and tortillas which the three men ate outside in the shade of the patio. Then I washed the dishes. In the late afternoon, I prepared a bag of dinner and breakfast food for the workers to take and cook in our neighbor's trailer. My husband and I assumed these segregated roles because we believed the men would be more comfortable if we did so. Certainly, I felt a need to appear "traditional" and not, for example, to publicly contradict my husband's building ideas (something I did in private) or to wear short shorts while hanging up the laundry. My job, as I saw it, was to oil these days, in which we were getting a miraculous amount of work done, with a flow of domesticity.

What I learned, I learned in the evening, second-hand. Effrem, my husband told me, had four children and four hundred acres of land in Chihuahua. Most of his land was as worthless as our own yucca-and juniper-studded twelve acres; the rest was a small but viable apple orchard. Early in the summer, before his own harvest, he fell short of cash and came up to the States for employment. In his late forties, his dark hair touched by gray, Effrem proved to be slow, reliable, and meticulous in his work. His gentle manners and soft voice made him seem a very serious man, a family man, sensitive and thoughtful.

Jesus provided a contrast. While Effrem looked broad and solid, Jesus had a tall skinny frame that alternated between nervous energy and an indolent loll. With the dapper moustache and groomed hair appropriate to a twenty-two-year-old, Jesus was full of plans, the owner of a future in which the strokes were broad and the details still vague. Already, he boasted, he had traveled as far south as Nicaragua and as far north as Washington. He was out to see the world, on a young man's lark that required financing along the way. More voluble than Effrem, he enjoyed talking and came up with a running series of deals. Would we contract to lay the tiles instead of paying an hourly wage? Would we sell his cousin in El Paso our old car? Would we hire another worker, a good friend of his, who could do the finish work that Jesus thought we needed? When it came time for him to go, he asked us for a pair of Converse tennis shoes. No matter the cost, he said with largesse, he would pay. We shopped around and came up with a better price, not a Converse, but a good shoe. No, he said. The brand name was important.

Effrem and Jesus promised to return the next summer. Effrem did and first went to work for one of our neighbors, whom he didn't much like. After two weeks he moved on and settled further north as a ranch hand. From another young man who stopped at our house, we were shocked to learn that Jesus had been shot to death in a Palomas bar. The young man added that Jesus had been a coyote, a descriptive term for those who take money from illegal aliens—often refugees fleeing Central America—in exchange for transporting them across the border.

The same grapevine that spread the news of Jesus's death also put us on the circuit as a place to stop for information, food, and a day or two of work. By now, we knew that though it was illegal for an alien to work for us, it was not illegal (at that time) for us to hire an alien. We knew that there were serious penalties for transporting an alien north—possible fines, imprisonment, and an impounded car. There was little risk in taking an alien in a southerly direction. We knew that, on their way home, some aliens liked to be picked up by the green trucks bearing the Immigration's seal—*la Migra*, as we called them. Depending on their home, this would save them a walk and usually meant they wound up in an American cell overnight, where their money would be relatively safer than on the road. On the other hand, it could also mean being turned over for a shakedown to the Mexican authorities. We knew that some workers liked their pay put in a postal order they could send home. Others didn't.

That was the summer Ernesto and his "son Luis" came to help us put on an adobe floor for our second room. Ernesto would continue to come help us in various tasks for the next three years. He is a small man, possibly in his sixties, with gray stubble and ropy muscles. Each season he comes accompanied by a male relative whom he always refers to as his son Luis. Sometimes, it is his son. As likely, it may be a grandson, a cousin, or a son-in-law. Once, too, the man's name was actually Luis; for the others, their real names only emerged gradually in conversation. This simplification of relationships and names was, I think, Ernesto's version of making the Anglos "comfortable."

Ernesto's forte is stonework, and although we didn't plan on terracing our back yard with dry stone walls, his expertise convinced us. Like Effrem, he works slowly and steadily. The younger relative plays the role of helper, fetching the stones in a wheelbarrow and then lounging, bored, while Ernesto makes his selections. If necessary, Ernesto will trim the stone with a sharp blow of his hammer before fitting it carefully in its arranged niche. The result is a layered geologic work of art, which Ernesto will want to cap with cement. This practical touch we always veto since we prefer the natural stones.

In our longer relationship with Ernesto, we have learned more about familiar patterns and life in Mexico. We watch the pecking order that is quickly established between relatives, the respect due Ernesto as a skilled worker, and the way in which he jealously guards his skills. No hands but his place the stone, for he does not jeopardize his livelihood by teaching it—at least, not yet. We know that by extending our house into three rooms— 1000 square feet—we are reaching twice the size of Ernesto's home. By now, we have worked twice with the son-in-law whose name is actually Luis. He is a genial but restless man with six children, widowed when we first met him and newly married the second summer. His first wife, Ernesto's daughter, had died in childbirth and the son-in-law was coming to the States to pay off the doctor's bill. "I was a pubic hair for marrying again," he says in Spanish to my husband, and Ernesto agrees.

Because of our growing sense of familiarity, even friendship, it remains a shock when the morning comes that we do not see Ernesto and his relative trudging up the hill to our house. By nine o'clock we know that they are not coming, and we realize that once again they have left suddenly without telling us. We understand now, but do not condone, why some employers pay at the end of the job. It is to insure that the job gets done, that the adobe bricks are not left unfinished in the rain or a wall half-stuccoed or a floor half-laid. Here, at least, unreliability is the alien's trademark and privilege. His abrupt departures illustrate how tenuous the relationship really is and how unbound by social rules. Sometimes the explanation gets back to us: a brother has fallen ill or a child is born. Sometimes the men leave because they had an argument in the trailer, or because they are tired of working, or because they are homesick. Since Ernesto doesn't trust the postal system, he will be carrying all his money in a handkerchief wadded tightly in his pocket. If he has worked as long as two weeks, that will be $120 in savings—a substantial sum in Mexico, approximately equal to two months' work. If he is lucky, Ernesto will avoid La Migra's green trucks. If he is lucky, he will catch a ride on the highway and spend the night, not on the road, but in a Palomas hotel.

Any story of Ernesto, Luis, or Effrem requires as a postscript mention of the recent Immigration Act. Previous to the act, employers of illegal aliens were not subject to prosecution; today, the law requires any employer to ask for some documentation—a birth certificate, passport, or driver's license—before hiring. If the employer does not and hires an illegal alien, he or she is liable to a civil fine ranging from $250 to $2000. First offenders were forgiven until June 1988. For a second offense, the penalty rises to $2000 to $5000 per worker. A third offense can mean a fine of $10,000 a worker, in addition to a criminal penalty of six months in jail. There are, however, so many exceptions to this law (workers in certain crops, for example, are exempt) that such figures almost become comforting; they represent, at least, something understandable in the general confusion. The law also includes an amnesty provision which allows aliens who have been living in the country since January 1982 to seek American citizenship. Of course, this does not affect the men we know since they do not want American citizenship; they want to work here seasonally and then return to their own country. How the act *will* affect them is unclear. It depends, in large part, on how it affects us. Now that we too risk being illegal, will we stop hiring those men who pass through the valley looking for work? Will they themselves become fewer or more desperate? We don't know. We never did know, really, what we were doing; we never found an answer, right or wrong, but in the end responded to personal needs, ours and theirs. We let the big picture blur and focused on the small.

It seemed to work for a time.

Nominated by Julia Just

BECAUSE

by CHRISTOPHER MERRILL

from FEVERS & TIDES (Teal Press)
variation on a theme by Yannis Ritsos

Because the Dead Sea released its hostages—the taste for salt, a
    rudder and a sail;
Because a band of Roman slaves, disguised in their master's
    robes, fled across the Continent;
Because one manuscript, one waxen shoal of words, burned a
    monastery down;
Because the sun spurned the Black Forest, and windmills
    ground the peasants into the earth, into the air, into the voice
    of the boy who cried wolf;
Because the crowd hissed at the empty stage, and the prompter
    drank himself to sleep, and the diva hid in the pit;
Because we let barbed wire replace our wooden faces and
    fences;
Because a scream left a trail through the ruined air;
Because I followed that trail into the woods, where my hands
    dissolved in smoke and rain;
Because I wandered for days, weeks, until I found myself
    outside a walled city, a city abandoned hundreds of years ago;
Because I couldn't scale the walls, nor could I find a way to
    return to my homeland, and so I settled along a river in the
    desert;
Because the river changed course, and its banks crumbled into
    the dry bed, where I was on my knees, speechless and afraid;
Because whenever I hike into the desert I talk and talk and talk;
Because I have never been to the desert;

Because I refuse to follow any trail whose markings are not
    completely clear;
Because I distrust signs, guideposts, land and sea marks;
Because on my single visit to the ancient city I rifled the ruins
    for potsherds and stone tools, and was warned never to return;
Because I heed all warnings, all directives from the crowd;
Because I won't listen to anyone but myself;
Because I love to cry wolf;
Because everything I read smells of smoke;
Because sometimes I wake at night to find my hands covered
    with salt, my sheet wrapped around me like a sail;
Because I can't tell if this is the desert or the sea;
Because I never learned to read the stars, and don't know where
    we're heading;
Because of this and more, much more, I hid your name in the
    well . . . and here it is again, filling my cup.

Nominated by Teal Press

CAMBRIAN NIGHT

by JAMES SOLHEIM

from POETRY NORTHWEST

At 3 a.m. the first trilobites swim out
Over the reefs of Chevies on Third Street—out
Across the abandoned sidewalk
And through the window of Mrs. Gray.
Out they come, down the alley
And through the back of the volleyball court,
Through the shirts and underwear someone
Forgot to bring in from the clothesline.
Out they come, through the professional
Airbrush van, through the mirror and the
Letters and the pink kiss decal.
Uninventing legs, unremembering us
In the century where we fell asleep,
The crinoids break from the fossil stone,
Push up through the dirt and concrete
And dressers and beds, and Main
Creaks open for the primitive sponge.
A pizza place tilts, sign
Conceding its letters to salt.
Bryozoan and arachnid twine
Around the televisions we fell
Asleep to, and the water
Crusts our rooms with brachiopods
As it seeps into the all-night
Station's broadcast (sent
From a distant city, where someone

Is still awake), the picture
Sizzling into dark.

* * *

Algae parts for first light.
Mrs. Gray feels the headboard
For her glasses
As the last of the trilobites
Dives beneath her denture water,
Goes through the floor,
And dips ten feet through dirt
To rest in stone.

Nominated by John Allman

POST-LARKIN TRISTE

by MARY KARR

from TRIQUARTERLY

The day you died a cold New England wind
stung the air I breathed, and on the street
faces erased themselves as I approached.
For several blocks, I shadowed a big

round-shouldered man built like a pear,
plaid scarf and tweedy overcoat.
Sir, I almost said a hundred times,
but he escaped as you escaped:

my one, careful fan letter returned
unopened; the night I'd hitched
the length of England under thunderheads
your window glowed pure rose.

There you stood wiping off a plate,
the last romantic, a blade of fire
flickering in your eye. I didn't knock
or climb your stair. When you carried

your milk bottles to the stoop,
you briefly stared my way as if you knew
I crouched there in the mud,
my vision starry with the sleet,

your old sad music streaming through my head.
Then stepping through the door,

you sank from view, and later from our lives.
What might I have said to you?

That you were loved perhaps; that love's
a cure. I wanted to hold
your large white hands in mine
and say I understood until you yielded

all your pent-up hurt and wept
as you once said you did alone
safe in the bubble of your car
hearing Wordsworth read on the radio.

Instead, I watched you glower at the night.
The cloudy, dread-locked moon reflected
in your spectacles was a face
I didn't dare to meet, the face of someone

rushing to tell us something terrifying, true.

Nominated by Michael Dennis Browne

WHAT IS BEYOND US

by KAREN FISH

from THE AMERICAN POETRY REVIEW

(For Tim)

Above the meadow of pain, the pins of Queen Anne's lace,
black-eyed Susans and tall silver grass, the moon lifts large,
white a lake.
The midwife instructs me to remember something pleasant.
She is raising her voice, calling my name.
I don't remember anything.
My grandfather and I played a game called, "hand over hand."
First, he placed his large hand palm down on the tablecloth,
my hand went on top, our hands alternating till we had a little
hill of hands. The hand on the bottom was pulled out and slapped
on the top of the stack—and so it went.
We played till our hands were a blur, till dinner.
Tickle, tickle on your knee, if you laugh you don't love me.

I don't believe this. I don't believe this.
That's what I tell you, my voice a dark wing moving over us.
I am on a sailboat, standing on the bow, looking ahead,
spotting for rocks, shallow water, a ridge of sand. We drift
past the jetty of rock, past the marina, the stranded skipjack
of boyscouts who wave and laugh with embarrassment.
I'm in a dinghy alone, on my knees, paddling to shore,
toward birch and scrub pine.
Near the beach the lilies' closed white fists float on the surface
of the water. Two herons pedal and lift into the sky.

The air is pink, the water violet-green.
The midwife tells me to think of pain as constructive.
This pain is the best kept secret in the world.
My father died late at night, young and alone in some hospital
after drinking and drinking. Your father came from Ireland
in the late twenties and even when he had the chance,
didn't return. We suppose he wanted to go back too badly
and like the man who loves a woman too much, he pushes her
away.
I'm not remembering any of this because I'm on an opposite
shore,
under a hectic moon, the birches just doors of moonlight.
I'm in a darkness I won't remember.

This is the best kept secret in the world;
we've dropped anchor, the low clouds are, in this almost
darkness
the color of pearls. There are acres of reeds, a few startled birds,
trees. And when they hand you the child,
our daughter, you look at me with a face I've never seen before.
I've heard—sometimes, its what we've never seen before
that we recognize.

Nominated by Michael Burkard, Henry Carlile and David St. John

BROKEN HEARTS

fiction by SARAH GLASSCOCK

from SONORA REVIEW

T HE FIRST TIME I ever sang in front of a crowd was in 1964 at Anita's wedding. When the song ("Soldier Boy") was over, Charlie clapped his hands once, slapped his wallet pocket once and shouted, "Hot dog! Is that little Angela Conway?" without even losing the ash off his cigarette. Bobby Darren could have put his arm around me then, and I'd have shrugged him off to go with cousin Charlie.

"Such a big voice for such a little girl," Anita's new mother-in-law said. "Such . . . maturity. Such understanding of a woman's *pain* for a ten year old." She smoothed her peridot shantung silk suit across her hips until we could all see the dent of her belly button.

"Connie Francis," my mother said. She grabbed me and herded me away from the applauding crowd. There was champagne and sherbet punch dripping on my head from somebody's crystal cup. "She listens to Connie Francis records. She's a born mimic. She doesn't know what she's singing about."

"And I hope to *God* she never does," Aunt Claire said. Underneath her eyebrows were black dots of mascara left behind by her overcurled eyelashes. All her lipstick was already eaten away, but she kept working on her bottom lip and latched onto my mother's arm. "Don't let her ever, ever, ever understand what she's singing about."

"Why are those always the best songs?" Anita's mother-in-law asked.

Mother steadied Claire with one hand and looked for my father with that "your sister" look in her eyes.

Charlie snuck up from behind and swooped me up into his arms. "Angelina, Angelita, Angelide! Yo-de-oh! We are going places!" His sideburns hit his ears halfway then, but you could tell they wanted to go further. From either side Charlie's face looks fine. It's when you meet him head on that he looks off kilter, like somebody put their hands on his cheeks and the right hand pushed up and the left pulled down, but just a little. He hiked me up until our shoulders were level and away we danced. My feet were kicking against his knees, and he was humming "Chapel of Love" off-key.

During the third song, Anita came up behind Charlie to match her arms to his. Her veil poked my face. "Dance with me, Charlie," she said. She sounded sad for a bride.

"Come on then," he said. "Get on the other side of little Angela Conway. We'll all dance together."

"I want to dance with you. Alone," Anita insisted. "For the last time." She pulled the collar away from Charlie's neck with her teeth. They were small and rounded, but they left a string of dashes on the material. "For our very last time."

Charlie tightened his hold on me. "I'm dancing with my favorite girl. I can't give her up now, not when I've found her again after all these years."

"You gave me up," Anita whispered.

Charlie's neck was warm and smooth, not anything like I expected a man's neck to be. Anita's head was resting on his other shoulder so I couldn't see her face, but her voice went right through his neck, into his blood. With my ear against Charlie's throat, I felt what she said. I could hear her words in his blood. Her voice would never leave him.

That's when I understood what the songs were all about, and I knew then that in six or seven years, when I was old enough for Charlie, my voice would be more powerful than Anita's.

* * *

Charlie convinced my parents that I had a career that he needed to manage. He was a good manager, hustling dates at weddings and anniversary parties and guest appearances in choirs

428

of any denomination. By the time I was twelve we were making weekend trips to sing at dances after football games and rodeos. As long as it was only one night away from my father, my mother would come with Charlie and me. To this day we still don't know where he dug up some of the relatives we stayed with on those trips. As Charlie expanded the territory that the Little Angela Conway Band covered to include the whole state of Texas, we picked up Uncle Buddy, who was married to Claire, as a steel guitarist and we got a pair of chaperones in the bargain.

Buddy was Claire's first and third husband, and they were on their second go-round. During the day he kept books for the dimestore, on weeknights he was the Countrypolitan disc jockey, and on weekends he traveled with the Little Angela Conway Band. Daddy was general manager at the radio station on the weekends, and Mother had sworn never to go more than a day without seeing him, so Buddy and Claire became the chaperones. Mother never trusted Claire, and I still don't know if it was love or distrust that kept her so close to Daddy, but she liked Buddy. Her sympathies are with any man Claire marries.

Claire's second husband, the one sandwiched in between Buddy, had been a merchant seaman she met one weekend in Corpus Christi. He visited her for a week in Seminole, which is close to the Panhandle on the Texas side of the Texas-New Mexico border, and said he'd never been in a more land-locked place. Claire never saw him again, but she still maintains that a week with some men is worth more than a lifetime with others.

I liked Uncle Buddy. He had an understanding of the music that Charlie didn't. There was a communication between us onstage. Charlie never listened. He just galloped along on the drums and never let the rhythm of the music affect his direction.

When I was fifteen, I sang at ten proms in three weeks. I wore the same short yellow taffeta dress that Aunt Emory had made to every dance we played. Aunt Emory made all our costumes. Charles and Buddy wore yellow brocade jackets with thin lapels made of black velveteen. At the end of every show, Charlie would flourish the drums, and I'd twirl and say, "Dress by Emory—Fashions Unlimited."

It wasn't till the last prom in Carrizo Springs, which is starting the western slide into South Texas, that I finally got to dance. Uncle Buddy was playing "You're So Far Away" on his pedal

429

steel. Charlie and I had the whole slick and sticky gym floor to slow dance across, but instead he whirled me past the collapsed bleachers and underneath the suspended basketball backboards. The janitors were folding the chairs and throwing wadded up paper cups at each other. The principal was wiping his eyes with an ice cube, like he was hot, so nobody would know he was about to cry. "How did you know?" he kept asking. "Who told you about 'You Made Me Love You'?"

"Little Angela Conway goes for the heart every time," Charlie said. "She just knows."

Neck hair was beginning to hide the collar of his shirt. I remembered Anita biting into his collar and wondered if it would ever come to that between us, or between me and anybody. I wanted him to say the thing about the heart and mean it like a man would, not like a manager would say it. But that dance, the closest I got was when Charlie pulled me out of a dip and his lips skimmed my cheek. "I'm starved!" he said then. "Let's go get something to eat!"

We went to a hamburger place in Uncle Buddy's car. There was a tarp-covered U-Haul trailer attached to it that held Charlie's drums, Buddy's steel guitar and my bass, which they usually never bothered to plug into the amp. Onstage, I'd end up filing my fingernails down on the strings.

We ordered three hamburgers with everything. I traded my lettuce to Buddy; he traded his tomatoes to Charlie and Charlie traded his pickles to me. We all kept our onions. Aunt Claire always ordered a fish sandwich—it didn't matter if we were a day's drive from a body of water—as if that would be enough to trick the merchant seaman into coming back for her.

At the Carrizo Springs motel, Claire scooted Buddy and herself out of the backseat. "Charlie, be a doll and unhook that trailer thing. Buddy's tired." They disappeared into the room she and I were supposed to share.

Charlie honked the horn. "She's got herself a real winner there. A real *wild* man."

Buddy felt more like my uncle than Claire had ever felt like my aunt. He was the one who made us a band. I didn't understand the bad feelings between him and Charlie. "Why don't you like Buddy?" I asked.

"He doesn't know how to handle women," Charlie answered. He puckered his mouth and looked like he wanted to spit something out.

I snuggled into the front seat upholstery. "Let's drive around. I'm not tired."

"I'll give you one beer," Charlie said, "but don't open it until you're inside and the door's locked." He pulled his hair back into a ponytail and tried to stuff it into his collar.

"I want to go with you," I said, trying to make my voice go sad like Anita's. She was still married to another man and Charlie was still going out with her.

Charlie examined his cigarettes in the glow of the radio until he found the one with the green dot on the filter. The white paper skin was lumpy. He wet a place where a stem had punctured the paper.

"I know what you've got in there," I said. "Let me have some."

He stuck the cigarette into the corner of his mouth and grinned. "You're catching up to your voice."

What happens then, I said to myself, until I thought I had it down the way Anita would say it. "What happens then?" I wanted to move closer to make sure the words took hold and would haunt him forever.

"Watch out world!"

I kicked at the hump in the floorboard and banged my elbow into the passenger door. "You'd give some to Anita if she asked you. If she bit your collar like she did when she got married."

"When you fall in love," he said, making his voice go soft and warm, "the one thing you never want to do is give somebody what they want. Remember that. You're mine, little girl, all mine."

"Then take me with you," I pleaded. I didn't want to be alone after singing all those songs. As far as I was concerned, I'd already caught up. I knew more than they all thought I did. I knew what love was. I knew what everybody was rushing off for.

Charlie opened his car door. "Don't waste your voice." He caught my arm when it looked like I was heading for Claire and Buddy's door. "You know enough not to bother them right now."

I snatched my arm away. "I'll go where I want to and I'll sing what I want to and maybe somebody else'll discover me and it'll be too bad for you!"

"You're already discovered. Here, little girl, take your beer."

I slammed the motel door against his laughter and sat at the end of the bed sipping beer through a straw and watching TV until I began to think I could hear Buddy and Claire in the next room and I turned up Creature Features against them.

The phone on the laminated nightstand rang, but nobody answered when I picked it up. Little snatches of breath came through the receiver. I got my voice ready to go low and sleepy like Rita Coolidge's. "Hello?"

In a congested voice that nobody believed anymore, Claire said "Sing 'Crazy' and don't stop until I tell you to."

I fit a pillow into the headboard's cut-out designs to protect my head and leaned back and sang 'Crazy' straight through five times till somebody on the other side pounded the wall.

*　*　*

In the late winter of 1970 we graduated to the stock show circuit and wound up the season in San Antonio. Girls my age, sixteen-years old, wore turquoise or red leather belts and had hats and tight pants to match. Charlie had had Aunt Emory run us up long fringed vests out of a patterned vinyl that made me think somebody somewhere was missing some seat covers.

Charlie spent the mornings sitting at radio stations until they took our demo tape. Daddy had contributed a stockpile of general managers' cards that he'd gotten at radio station conventions. Afternoons, Buddy and I would play with musicians that Buddy had found while Charlie tried to jockey us up the list of opening acts for Johnny Rodriguez. When we performed at the Coliseum in the evenings, Claire would sit below Buddy with one of her elbows on the platform, reading magazines and filing her nails to keep any women from getting close to him and to showcase her own loneliness. At night I'd brush the dust and hay out of my hair and stare into the mirror until my nose started to flatten out like a championship lamb's.

The next to last night in San Antonio there were two baby-fat blondes to the side of me, bouncing their thighs against the platform and smiling at Charlie. I cut the blondes' boyfriends out of the crowd and started singing to them. The boys pushed each

432

other and turned red and started a game of Chicken by spitting tobacco juice at each other's boots. One of them had ears that curled under the brim of his gray felt hat and his eyes were as light as his hat. When he got close enough, I pulled the hat off and plopped it on my head. I danced away from the microphone to see what Charlie was up to. The drumsticks twirled through his knuckles and he gave me the eye.

The two blondes went back to bookend their boyfriends. They reeled in gold necklaces out of their sweaters. Huge ruby and gold senior rings dangled from the chains, and they ran the rings along the chains in warning. While Charlie trotted along in a drum solo, the baby-fat blonde with the ponytail reached for her boyfriend's hat, but I held it above her head and let her jump.

"What's your name?" I asked the boy with the curled ears and light eyes. He had clear, clear skin and a tiny mole under his right eye. I could see the flow of blood beating down his throat.

"Walter." He smiled and slipped out of his girlfriend's arms.

I whispered the name of our motel and the time that night I knew Charlie would be gone by into Walter's ear. Charlie tripled the tempo to get my attention and Buddy made his pedal steel go loud and plaintive, but I ignored them.

"Is that okay with you, Walter?" I asked.

He nodded and looked so hopeful that I forgot about Charlie. For the first time I felt like I had an audience. Instead of my voice sending people into each other's arms and dancing away, there was somebody listening and watching me. I wanted to sing a song for Walter the way he wanted to hear it sung. I almost felt like I had when Anita's voice traveled through Charlie's neck and vibrated into my cheek. Only this time there was nobody between me and the possibility of all that love and sadness.

"Can I sing a song for you?" I asked.

" 'Crazy'," he said. "Could you sing 'Crazy' for me?"

We never ever performed that song; it always set Claire off. But I pulled myself hand over hand up the mike stand so I could start the chords on the bass for 'Crazy'.

Claire sent her magazine skidding into Buddy's feet. "Don't you dare play that song!" Buddy slid into 'The Last Thing On My Mind', but I sang 'Crazy' for Walter. It was time I had my own

433

memory to attach to a song. And despite Claire's warning and his own best intentions, Buddy ended up playing what I sang.

That night Charlie had me and the trailer load of equipment dumped at the motel by one-fifteen. Claire and Buddy were next door; Buddy was pulling down the shades and Claire was crying and still saying, "You promised me. You *promised* me."

So Charlie wouldn't think tonight was any different and so I wouldn't be able to hear what was going on next door, I begged, "Come on, take me with you. I don't want to be cooped up here all by myself. Claire's going to be crying all night long. I won't be able to sleep."

Charlie pooled after-shave in his palm, letting the warmth of his skin melt the alcohol. With the lightest touch, he brushed his hands above his ears. "You shouldn't have sung that song. Old Bud's got his hands full tonight—thanks to you."

"It's just a song," I said. The tongue of the snake that was tattooed along the length of his spine flicked his neck, and I tried to imagine the coil that must sit in the well of his backbone below the low ride of his blue jeans.

Pounding the connecting wall twice, Charlie shouted, "I'm gone. Watch her!"

I beat Charlie to it before he even had time to start his wink. "Don't do anything I wouldn't."

"She's catching up," Charlie said into the mouth of his wallet and was gone.

"She's passed you," I said into the mirror.

There wasn't a moon that night. I went out five minutes early to get used to the dark so I would spot Walter. Through the television noise coming out of Buddy and Claire's cabin, I could hear Buddy still apologizing. "I'm sorry. Claire? Honey? I'm sorry."

It was just a song. Claire would never be happy, and Buddy, believing it was his mission to make her smile, would wind up thinking he was a failure. I didn't want to hear what went on between them anymore. Maybe Walter would take me to the market and buy me a Mexican blouse embroidered with red and purple flowers. Then we'd sneak into one of the big hay stalls at the Coliseum. Tomorrow we'd rent a paddle boat and paddle down the river. He'd follow me west, to the next livestock show in Odessa. Or maybe I'd stay here with him. I'd start my own band and Charlie could eat his heart out and try to find himself another Little Angela Conway.

Outside the last cabin in the next row a lighter flared. Walter passed the flame in front of his face and waved. I was halfway across the strip of grass when the high beams of a car cut through me. "Where do you think you're going, little girl?" Charlie called.

The lighter went out. I kept heading for Walter, but Charlie drove between us. One of the baby fat blondes sat beside him. "Go back inside," Charlie said.

"No!" I slapped the windshield and tried to get around the front of the station wagon, but the left fender kept nudging me back to our cabin. "It's not fair! You get rid of HER!"

"It's not the same thing, little girl."

"I'm not a little girl anymore. You can't keep me inside." The blonde was hanging on to Charlie's arm. I reached through the window and banged on the horn so he'd have to drop her arm and take mine.

Charlie rolled up the window enough to catch my arm. "I can keep you inside for as long as I need to. I know what you're about to get yourself into—you don't. It's not like some love song out here." He let down the window some and looked past me. "Buddy—do something right for a change. Come over here and get her."

I climbed onto the hood of the car and scooted to the other side. "Let's go, Walter," I whispered, but he wasn't there anymore. Buddy knocked lightly on the back of my head with his knuckles. "I know he was here," I said. "I saw him."

"You got her?" Charlie yelled and then drove off.

Buddy see-sawed my shoulders. "The music's got you hopped up."

"I'm sick of music!"

"It's not the music you're sick of. Let's go back and work on 'Good Night, Irene'."

I knelt in the grass and looked for the shine of tobacco and spit, but there wasn't a sign that Walter had been standing there. "I bet in fifteen minutes Claire bangs on the wall and you go back to her."

"I bet you've got the song down by the time that happens," Buddy said.

* * *

The next summer, my seventeenth, we toured the Texas Gulf
Coast all the way from Boca Chica in the south to Chocolate
Bayou in the north, outside of Galveston. We played in huge
roofless rooms with concrete floors that had been tacked onto
community swimming pools, and we played in country clubs that
had spongy tile floors and ceiling fans, and we played in tiny little clubs that always had fish nets hanging from the ceilings. On
free nights, Charlie would plug in the generator he carried in the
back of the station wagon and we'd park on the beach and play
from the back of an open U-Haul trailer.

Claire and Buddy still camped out next door wherever we
spent the night. Charlie still left me at night, but he started staying within eyesight of our room. I caught him once when I was
sneaking out. He and another baby-fat blonde were parked across
the street between sand dunes. I walked toward them, not being
particularly quiet, and leaned against a mailbox to watch. They
were both facing me; the blonde's eyes were closed, but Charlie's
were on me. Open your eyes, dummy, I thought. She didn't even
know when she was playing to an audience.

In an imitation of what Anita had done to him on her wedding
day, Charlie bit the collar of the blonde's shirt. That made my
stomach go hollow. I was relieved when he let the collar go and
started unbuttoning her shirt. The blonde turned around to face
Charlie. As they kissed, her head blocked my view of his face,
but I felt him waiting for me to do something. It was a standoff
until the blonde's shirt came off and Charlie's hands were dark
against her broad back. His head reappeared over her bare shoulder to watch me. I think he wanted to hold both of us, but finally
he stopped the blonde by whispering something into her ear. To
hide herself from my eyes, she pressed herself closer to him.

"This is the way it is out here, little girl," Charlie said.

He wasn't protecting me from anything by staying away at
night, or by letting me see that love and passion had nothing to
do with what he did.

"It doesn't have to be."

"I've got my eye on you, Little Angela Conway," he squinted.
"Don't think I don't."

436

"Why don't you just come in and use the bed?" I asked. "Don't you think she's worth it?"

"That's your room. I couldn't do that."

My voice hadn't gotten into Charlie's blood. He didn't hear my voice—he saw it. He saw what it could do. Make him some money. Give him an opening to any sad-eyed woman in the room. He could offer himself as a temporary protection against everything I was singing about. Once the song faded, he'd be gone. What I was singing about was him.

The night at the wedding, I'd felt Anita's voice. I'd thought she was becoming a part of Charlie. I thought she'd had the power of love, but her voice hadn't stayed with Charlie any longer than anybody else's had—it had gone right through him.

"Sing for me, little girl."

I'd make him feel my voice, but not now and not like this. I walked back to the cabin, turned on the TV to Chiller Thrillers to fool Buddy and Claire and climbed out the bathroom window to find my own station wagon and my own blonde hidden somewhere in the sand dunes.

One morning a few weeks later I was still in bed, rolling the sand down the length of the bed with my bare legs. The mornings were always hard. All the music was drained out of me. I couldn't believe that the night before I'd put my mouth close to somebody's skin and fed my voice into their blood. Their skin was always solid and thick again when they left in the morning.

The door banged open. "Get out of bed, lazybones!" Charlie shouted. "Go out there and get yourself some sun!"

"We're practicing this afternoon."

"You and Buddy practice way too much. All you need to do is get some color into your face and listen to that Linda Rondstadt tape. You two act like you think it's talent and not top flight management that's going to get us anywhere. Wrong again! I am conferring this afternoon with the Houston hotel man, and tonight I want you looking good and sounding even better."

"Don't come out till I'm dressed," I warned as he disappeared into the bathroom, hoping the suggestion would inflame him. I fished my damp suit out from under the bed and was just easing the shoulder straps on when Charlie barreled out of the

437

bathroom. He rubbed my back and smelled his palms. He lifted up my hair and smelled my neck. There was no romance in his hands, but I leaned against him anyway. To my surprise, he let me.

"Little Angela Conway," Charlie sighed. "What am I going to do with you, little girl?" His breath ruffled the hair over my ear.

I shivered and moved closer, My lips were close to his neck and my arms met behind his back. We danced to music from the radio in Buddy and Claire's room. Charlie's arms were like steel springs giving way but never letting me get close to him.

"What am I going to do with you?" he murmured again and moved his body close to mine. The pressure of his hands against my lower back was slow and steady as we moved toward the bed. This is it, I thought. And all I'd had to do all along was keep my mouth shut.

"Little girl," Charlie whispered. "Who's been using my after-shave? Who's been leaving little blond hairs in my comb? Who's been sleeping in my bed?"

I tried to pull away but Charlie rolled us onto the bed. "Who does this pillow smell like?" he asked.

"I sprinkle after-shave on it and pretend it's you because you're too chicken to stay."

Charlie rested his forearms on either side of me. "You're not ready for me. Almost, but not yet."

There was no way I'd let him use that voice of promise on me anymore. As far as I was concerned, it was time; he'd seduced me in every other way. "I want to go home. I don't want to sing anymore."

"Uh-uh. I've just about got that Houston deal sewn up. Plus— that keyboard player is very interested in becoming a part of the Little Angela Conway Band—he's been to see us every night for three weeks. We'll cut Buddy loose and he and Claire can go on a second honeymoon, try to patch things up."

"What makes you think it's the band he's interested in?" I slid out from under Charlie's arms and sat up. "Buddy thinks we should go to Austin."

"Buddy does not manage Little Angela Conway—I do," Charlie said and ran his knuckles down my bare back. "Old Bud better just keep his eye on his wife and stop trying to slip his friend's original songs into the set."

I moved away, a little. "Buddy says Austin's the best place for music."

"I don't care about music. All I care about is Little Angela Conway's voice." Charlie slid a hand around my waist and pressed my stomach. His hand was warmer than the swim suit was cold. "There won't be anybody else in Houston besides you and me."

"It's my voice. It comes out of me," I said stubbornly. "I know what it does to *some* people."

"I know where it comes from." His hands made circles on my abdomen. "We'll have us a suite at the hotel. You'll go down and sing in the club and I'll take care of everything else. Haven't I always? Haven't I, little girl?"

I wouldn't answer. I didn't want to be a hotel singer, always listening to other women's records to learn my songs. His hand started to roam my stomach, but I wouldn't move. Then the mattress shifted and I felt his mouth moving along my backbone. "Haven't I always taken care of everything, little girl?" Charlie whispered. "Haven't I?" He fit his free hand underneath one of my shoulder straps and slid his fingers along the low cut back.

"Yes," I finally answered and relaxed against him.

The cold swim suit snapped against my skin as Charlie released his hold. "Won't I always?" He bounced off the bed and went back into the bathroom.

The smell of his after-shave was so strong that it felt like he should still be there beside me, but he wasn't and I didn't think he ever would be.

"I'm not going to Houston with you," I announced, and it was the first decision about singing I'd made that wasn't a threat aimed at Charlie. His wallet sat open mouthed on the dresser. I took the Little Angela Conway Band Visa card out of the wallet and slid it under my pillow.

"Claire's taking you to a doctor tomorrow to get you outfitted with passion pills. Nobody wants to see a whale up there on the stage," he said on his way to the dresser.

"Is that what you're waiting for? For me to get protected?"

"I'm the best protection you've got, little girl." Charlie slipped on a T-shirt and tucked the after-shave into his back pocket. "Keep your boyfriends away from my stuff," he said and was gone.

439

That afternoon I took the Visa card to a music store and started piling sheet music on the counter. "Tell me when I hit the limit," I told the cashier and handed her the card. A bass with a cream-colored body and a mother-of-pearl neck caught my eye. Sound-wise, it wasn't much better than the crummy bass I already had, but I liked the way it looked. I could see myself on stage with it, which just shows how much of Charlie I still had in me.

A man with white hair, a bow tie and nose like Lyndon Johnson's, who was polishing the bodies of guitars and basses that were standing in the window and then sighting down their long necks, turned around. "There's no limit on Angela Conway's credit in my store."

"You know who I am?" Charlie was the one who always made the introductions, but this man, a *music* store owner, already knew who I was. It was the first time I'd ever been recognized on my own.

"I know your voice," the man said. "I know your voice."

The cashier took a Polaroid of me and the owner and the bass to stick in the window. When the cashier's husband came to take her out to lunch, I autographed his shirtcuffs and then signed the charge slip. Charlie's signature was on the back of the Visa card, but the raised letters on the front read LITTLE ANGELA CON-WAY BAND and who was that anyway?

When I drifted back to the motel, Buddy and Claire's door was open and from the porch I could see Buddy sitting at his pedal steel. He was clipping the strings with wire cutters. Each string lashed the air, then whipped back to coil on the bridge like a snake. Once there were no more strings to cut, he stropped the cutters along each one; the sound was so terrible it made me want to cry.

I stood in the doorway and waited for him to stop, but there was no break in the music. "Buddy—what is it?"

Charlie came out of Buddy and Claire's bathroom. He was carrying a trash can and searching through it. "There's nothing in here—no telling where they've gone off to. You better not get too close to him, little girl, I don't think Uncle Bud's too fond of the female race right now. Claire's split with our potential keyboard player."

"Oh, Buddy." I saw that Claire had left her nightgown underneath a pillow on the unmade bed. He couldn't stay in the room. "Come on, we'll switch rooms."

"Oh no, he's going back where he came from," Charlie said. "What has he ever done for us? And now he's lost us a keyboard player *and* a chaperone. What has his contribution to Little Angela Conway ever been?"

"Oh, Buddy," I said and worked the wire cutters out of his hand, "don't love her so much."

Charlie snapped his fingers in front of my face and opened his palm. "Credit card," he said. "You are Little Angela Conway—I am the Little Angela Conway Band. Remember that. Everything's going back."

"You don't even know what a band is," I said. "You're not my air and water. And I'm not taking anything back."

"You better throw a little more Linda Rondstadt into it out there tonight, or we're going no place," Charlie advised. "I've got a lot invested in you."

Buddy wrapped lengths of the steel strings between his two fists and twisted them into a figure eight. "She's not going anywhere if she doesn't throw a lot more Angela Conway into it," he said.

"Help him pack up if you want to, little girl, but he's on his way home tonight after our last set. Credit card. Now."

I got out the card and cut it in half with the wire cutters before Charlie could stop me. "Either we all go home or we all go to Austin."

Like I said, Charlie was a good manager. It didn't take him a second to start negotiating. "You and I are going to Houston," he promised. "Just the two of us." He used his fingers to comb the hair off my neck and then kissed the newly cleared skin. His promise sat on my skin. Before I'd had a chance to move toward him, or away, Charlie had picked up the new bass and was walking toward the door with it. I couldn't believe that part of me still wanted to go with him. The chances were good that I'd end up singing about heartaches until my dying day, and I might want to do that, but looking at Buddy—and Charlie—there was no way I wanted to live those songs and get trapped between being loved too much or not enough. "I'm not going with you."

Charlie held out his hand to me. "Come with me right now, Angela. We won't go any further than our room. Just you and me, nobody else. We'll stay there all afternoon."

Buddy had reached under the bed and pulled out his guitar. " 'Good Night, Irene'. Hit those chords, Angela. Let's see how the new bass sounds."

Charlie walked up behind me, and I could feel his hands on my shoulders. "Sing 'Crazy' for me, in memory of Claire." I could feel his breath on my neck and then the pressure of his stained teeth on my collar.

Buddy grabbed a fistful of Charlie's ponytail. "Let her go."

Charlie's head jerked back, but his teeth held onto my collar and the top button of my blouse popped off. 'Crazy' might be the song that would break his heart in the way I always thought I'd wanted to break it. In the way that Claire had broken Buddy's heart, and that was nothing I wanted to sing about.

I unbuttoned my blouse while there were still buttons left and then let the force of Charlie's teeth pull the sleeves off my arms, and I was free. "I'm going to Austin," I said and walked into the other room. Before shutting the connecting door, I looked back and saw Charlie still standing there with my blouse hanging from his mouth, and knew I'd broken his heart in another way.

Nominated by Samuel Vaughan

THE DAVID OF MICHELANGELO

fiction by DENNIS VANNATTA

from THE QUARTERLY

[1] DAVID

"I know your pride, and the naughtiness of your heart," says Eliab, his brother.

But David is not listening.

"I killed a lion and a bear that stole one of your sheep," he says to Saul, whose eyes have already begun to glaze over with wonder and madness. "I chased them down. I hit that bear so hard he dropped the sheep right out of his mouth. The lion came for me, and I grabbed him by the beard. I said, 'Whoa, old fellow!' Then I killed him with one blow."

The circle of warriors tightening around Saul and David push Eliab farther back, until soon his mutterings can no longer be heard.

David does not think himself vain. He believes that he has simply told a truth the King will surely be glad to hear.

He does not yet understand the madness in the King's heart.

But David does know that his moment is at hand. After a lion and a bear, a fat Philistine will make a short morning's work.

(He does not have to go naked into the valley of Elah. He could have worn the brass armor, weighing two thousand shekels, provided by Saul—could at least have worn his shepherd's smock, his sandals, and his goatskin cap against the sun. But no.

He goes naked into the valley, and just before killing the giant, he turns back toward Saul and Jonathan and Eliab—his white young manhood shining in the bright morning light like polished stone—and almost smiles. He looks as if he might be posing.)

[2] GOLIATH

He, too, was a shepherd. On his wild rocky hillside in Gath, he would cradle the little lambs gently against his huge chest and nuzzle his face into their necks and breathe the rich, warm, heady odor of young wool. He would study each newborn lamb, rubbing his chin, until he had thought of a suitable name: Wildflower, Mothersmilk, Raincloud. His tender ankles could only painfully support his bulk, so he could not have pursued a strayed lamb far beyond the slope rising above the hut where he lived with his mother. The sheep seemed to know this and would stay near and always come when he called them by name. When it came time for a sheep to be slaughtered, Goliath would weep. But even this the sheep seemed to understand, and they would turn their necks lovingly toward the knife.

When the King's men came to gather recruits for the war against the Israelites, Goliath's neighbors sent them to him as a joke.

"Go to the hut where the widow lives, at the foot of the rocky slope, and there you will find a giant who will slay all your foes," they said, pushing their beards up to hide their smiles.

"Mama!" he cried.

They pounded his fingers with the butts of their spears to make him release the roof pole, and it took six of them to load him into a dung cart. No horse could carry him, and they knew that he could not walk all the way back to camp.

He sat weeping and reciting, without hope, the names of his sheep as they hauled him off down the road. His mother wept long after he had passed from sight.

She knew she would never see him, or the dung cart, again.

At the camp of the Philistines, the training captain would slap Goliath's fat buttocks with the side of his sword and squeeze his huge quivering tits, crooning, "Ooo, baby, ooo, baby, ooo," while Goliath bawled and the men chortled.

In his coat of mail weighing five thousand shekels, Goliath could not even stand up without help, much less walk from the camp at the top of the hill down into the valley, where he was to shout his challenge to the Israelites. So they built a frame atop a small wheeled platform, all of gopher wood, and tied Goliath upright to the frame, which they concealed as best they could under his long scarlet cloak. Two long ropes were tied to the frame and then passed through the hands of two files of soldiers, whom Goliath seemed to be pulling down the hill after him. It was they, of course, who were letting him roll down slowly to the bottom of the valley, where Goliath stood, a strange, monstrous vision before the Israelites, who cowered before his challenge for forty days.

"The fattest scarecrow in the world," wheezed the general of the Philistines, holding his sides and laughing to see Goliath pinned to the frame.

Goliath's voice was high and girlish, and he could not have made himself heard to the Israelites trembling in their camp at his approach, were it not for the dwarf hidden under his cloak, who, at the proper moment, rammed into Goliath's anus the sawed-off end of a shepherd's crook. Goliath would bellow then, yes indeed.

"Send me your champion, that we might fight together!" he would bawl.

"They will never send a champion," the Philistine general said. "They will cower in their tents a few more nights, then give over all to me."

When Goliath saw the naked boy stride down the hill toward him, he thought of his mother, and of his lambs, and he smiled.

"Shepherd!" he shouted, with no encouragement from the dwarf squatting under his buttocks. And as the boy began to spin the sling faster and faster over his head, Goliath shouted once more, "Savior!"

[3] MICHELANGELO

Michelangelo has caught him in all the arrogance and cruelty of youth.

His left knee is canted delicately forward and in, almost girlishly—this for Jonathan? His left arm curls upward, holding the sling draped over his shoulder loosely, insolently. His right hand hangs heavily at his side, huge, blood-gorged. There the white marble is almost dark with blood. Though the legs, arms, and torso slant languidly this way and that, the head is perfectly erect, his gaze flat and direct, leveled at Saul, who, just across the valley, writhes in an agony of prescience. Saul knows: the old king under the pitiless gaze of the new.

It is not until a moment later, when he turns from Saul, that David first thinks of the giant. David does not think much of him even then. Hasn't he killed a bear with one blow and bearded the lion?

It is strange, though.

A handful of Philistine soldiers run up behind the giant and seem to give him a shove, then run off up the hill with the rest of their fellows, laughing. The giant seems to glide slowly toward David without moving his arms and legs. He smiles and shouts two words. A Philistine insult, no doubt.

But David does not think much about this, either, and it is not until after he has cut Goliath down from the wooden frame that it occurs to him to hack off Goliath's head and feed his carcass to the fowls of the air, the beasts of the earth.

Goliath surely did not know that his part in the divine plan was to grow fat, so that one day he could have his head bowled down the valley of Elah for the glory of a minor god, bloody and vengeful, bent on hegemony.

And David—a good man, by all accounts, from then on—did not realize that he was doomed to be frozen in stone at a moment of stupid, ruthless vanity, forever, in the Accademia, in Florence.

Nominated by The Quarterly *and David Jauss*

446

CAPTIVITY: THE MINKS

by TOI DERRICOTTE

from COLORADO REVIEW

In the backyard of our house on Norwood,
there were five hundred steel cages lined up,
each cage with a wooden box
roofed with a sheet of tar paper;
inside, two stories, with straw
for a bed. Sometimes the minks would pace
back and forth wildly, looking for a way out;
or else they'd hide in their wooden houses, even when
we'd put the offering of raw horse meat on their trays, as if
they knew they were beautiful
and wanted to deprive us.
In spring the placid kits
drank with glazed eyes.
Sometimes the mothers would go mad
and snap their necks.
My uncle would lift the wooden roof like a god
who might lift our roof, look down on us
and take us out to safety.
Sometimes one would escape.
He would go down on his hands and knees,
aiming a flashlight like a
bullet of light, hoping to catch
the orange gold of its eyes.
He wore huge boots, gloves
so thick their little teeth couldn't bite through.
"They're wild," he'd say. "Never trust them."

447

Each afternoon when I put the scoop of raw meat rich
with eggs and vitamins on their trays,
I'd call to each a greeting.
Their small thin faces would follow as if slightly curious.
In fall they went out in a van, returning
sorted, matched, their skins hanging down on huge metal
hangers, pinned by their mouths.
My uncle would take them out when company came
and drape them over his arm—the sweetest cargo—
He'd blow down the pelts softly
and the hairs would part for his breath
and show the shining underlife which, like the
shining of the soul, gives us each
character and beauty.

Nominated by Marilyn Hacker and Sharon Olds

APOLOGUES OF WINTER LIGHT

by CHRISTOPHER BUCKLEY

from POETRY

Street lamps streaming on, and the grey
suspiration of the cold flossing the invisible
tides of air, full with all our lost breath . . .

Soon the heavens will span out—and though
I've learned everything is falling outward,
the galaxies still come set like pin feathers
spired on the dark's spread wings . . .

This time of year, before a brief twilight
turns away, I think of Tiepolo's cherubim,
all countenance and wing, bodiless among
the clouded wisps, breaking away, floating
off like anything souls might be—I think
of our lives drifting out there too, like slow
light through these blue and trembling trees.

Only a hundred thousand years ago
mastodons grazed in Central Park,
and the constellations spun over them
gently as shining leaves—the dark pools,
the staves of ice singing back the mild
ostinato of the stars . . .

             We've tried to figure
our place in the far backwaters and
sequinned outskirts of time, tried to pin down
that one background note reverberating
even in the rocks. But the tumbling
geometry of the sky resolves little more
than those chiseled blocks of light,
those overlays of rust and amber
that were all of an autumn thickening
the air, absolving some distance until we felt
we could take that burning it into us.

                        Nonetheless,
I'm watching Venus rise through the diminished
atmosphere of New Jersey, red as a maple leaf
I've taped above the window to keep my hope
in perspective, for still I'm not much beyond
that feeling at age two when my father,
on a fire escape in east Missouri, lifted me
into the cool, blue night of the 50s,
and I pointed saying, *moon, moon,*
as it basked there large and white
as a beach ball spinning just beyond
my arm's reach . . .

                        And each year now
we know more, but we know no better—
what we see in the sky is simply
the softened gloss of the past sifting
back to us, and likewise, every atom
down the body's shining length
was inside a star, and will be again.

Nominated by Richard Jackson and Sherod Santos

WEJUMPKA

fiction by RICK BASS

from THE CHARITON REVIEW

W HEN WEJUMPKA WAS eleven, and Vern was forty-eight, and
I was thirty, Vern made me be Wejumpka's godfather. We were
drinking, playing cards, and Vern's health had been going down
fast, all that fall. We were playing that ridiculous game of Liar's
Poker, and got down to where the bet was that I had to be
Wejumpka's godfather if I called and lost; but if Vern was
bluffing—he said I had *eight* ones—then he had to marry the
girl he was seeing. She was twenty, plump, with a pear-shaped
face and orange hair: she had a nice laugh and two children, already, but no husband. The reason I made that bet was hoping
she could do something with him; straighten him up, as I knew
women could sometimes do.

Her father was thirty-five, he'd been in my high school (failed
two years), a senior when I was a freshman; we'd played football
together one year, and he was, or had been, a wiry little halfback
who'd gotten even wirier since, working on cars in his garage out
near the Pearl River. His name was Zachary and he would collect
insurance money each spring when the rains brought the river
right into his garage, and on up into his house. Sometimes he
didn't even move out, when it flooded—just waded around, doing his chores, making sure all the circuit breakers were off: waiting for the water to go back down.

When the rains began, each March, he would sit up on the
roof of his garage and listen to the weather station, praying for
more and more rain: each foot of water in his shop was worth

451

about ten thousand dollars. It's cruel, but I don't even know what his daughter's name is; and just as cruelly, I don't even think Dale did, either. We called her Zachary's girl. It was a serious hand of poker. It was only about midnight, but we'd started drinking at four in the afternoon.

Vern wasn't bluffing, it turned out, and, I suspected later, wasn't even drunk. It was a set-up. It was sort of like I'd killed him, as in one of those hunting accidents where a best buddy trips and pulls the trigger, shooting his partner; by winning, by assuming responsibility for Wejumpka, I'd given Vern the last go-ahead he needed to let go of everything, and let his spiral have its way with him, the shortened wick of his life.

I'd really hoped to win the bet, and at least hope for Zachary's girl to take a strong hand with him, if indeed she had said yes. Vern wasn't the same any more, wasn't really fun to be around— I was playing cards with him more out of a sense of duty than anything, and that was probably why I got so drunk, and won Wejumpka—because I'd had duty before, and had not done so well—in fact, I'd fucking struck out—and later that year, when Vern got the old stop-drinking-or-you-only-have-one-year-to-live speech from his doctor, and when he did not stop drinking, not much, anyway—that was when I felt young and stupid for having called an older man's bluff.

I'm a bit in the middle, now, and think I have it figured, too late of course, that the young may bluff *or* charge, and that the guys in the middle, like me—guys just for the first time beginning to lose things—we're the bluffers—but that the ancients, like Vern and beyond, never bluff.

Like I said, too late.

About the boy I have won: Wejumpka. His Christian name is Montrose, but when he was six he went on one of those father-&-son campouts with the scouts, with Vern, and they roasted marshmallows, had canoe races; sang songs around the campfire, farted chili farts, and gave each other Indian names, drawn from a wooden box, very serious, very immortal.

The moon, high and silver over the lake. Bullfrogs drumming, bats chittering and swooping over the water. The cool sweet sound of a whippoorwill, back in the bushes, down in the reeds by the lake. Vern still married.

Everyone else forgot their name, or was less than flattered by it, and threw it in the fire.

Wejumpka remembered his; he embraced it.

About the boy I have inherited, or almost-inherited: he is a hugger.

He's wild about puppies. Cats, parrots, guinea pigs—he loves all animals, even other children—even the mean ones who pushed him down and ran away when he tried to embrace them.

He's always been that way—always holding on. Perhaps even when he was in Ann's womb—and I do not mean to speak so personally, but now that she is Vern's ex-wife, instead of wife, I can say that word—perhaps even then, with some prenatal sonar, casting out into the future, he could see and feel the dark shape of that future, of what would come when he was seven, the divorce—not anything specific, not knowing anything, but just feeling a certain end to things, or rather, the absence of the thing—maybe like Zachary on his roof, watching the storms come in off the Gulf, laughing in the rain, getting filthy rich, cackling and listening to his radio with lightning popping all around him, lightning bouncing off the trees in his front yard—maybe even then Wejumpka could tell that very soon, not long at all after he was born, there would be a jumping-off spot.

Maybe Vern said unkind words to Ann, while Wejumpka was forming in her womb.

Maybe Ann had unkind thoughts about Vern; or maybe she, too, a woman—even more so than a child—could see into the future, could feel the absence of a thing; perhaps she held on to Vern more tightly than ever, then, being wise and clairvoyant and scared in her pregnancy; and perhaps thusly she secreted an excess number of holding-on hormones, of frantic hormones, as would any sane person, and they affected the unborn child, made him be the same way.

Perhaps.

Wejumpka is a hugger.

When he was six, the year before the divorce, he dressed as Porky Pig for Halloween. The other children were dressed as devils, witches, Green Berets with rubber knives clenched in their teeth, scars tattooed on their arms, their faces; but Wejumpka was Porky Pig, and went around hugging people, when they answered the door: not asking for candy, not quite

453

understanding that part of it, but instead just running into these strange people's houses and latching on to their legs, giving them a tight thigh hug. Vern and Ann were having some sort of dinner party, one of the famous ones in which they would end up insulting each other in front of all the guests, maybe even throwing things, and it was my job to babysit Wejumpka, to take him around to all the houses and bring him safely back home.

Vern and Ann had been drinking a little, when we got back, but had not started their fight yet. It's possible that they were even still a little in love, or thought that they were; when they answered the door, and saw Porky Pig, their own little Porky Pig, standing in front of them, they smiled, and felt all those feelings.

"Trick or treat!" Wejumpka shouted through his plastic mask, hopping up and down. I had explained to him how it worked; that sometimes it was best not to hug. He had to be overjoyed, in all the running chaos of the night, all the hurried darkness, at having found his way back home, at seeing his mother and father standing there in the doorway, with all the bright good light of the party behind them, all the safe noise.

"Trick or treat!" he shouted again, jumping up and down once more, and Ann frowned and took a step back.

"Why, you're *scary*," she said, and Wejumpka stopped hopping, and looked at me.

"Whose little boy are *you?*" Vern asked, bending down and peering into the mask. "I don't believe I *know* any little Porky Pig boys," he said, shaking his head, and then—I know they had been drinking—they closed the door!

"It's me!" Wejumpka screamed, struggling to get out of the hot costume and the elastic-string mask. "It's me!" he screamed. "It's your little *boy!*"

They opened the door, then, and everyone was gathered around it, all the guests were laughing too, and Wejumpka, in tears, flew into Ann's arms, crying, and she patted him on the back, did all the right things . . .

So Vern has won this bet. His little sports car has broken down, hasn't run in over a year, and sits idle in the small woodshed-garage behind his apartment. Mice have built their nests in and around the engine, have nibbled the insulation off of the electrical wiring. There are birds living in the rafters of the little shed, nesting there, and they have dappled the car with what seems to be a hearty enthusiasm. Vern walks to work, on the days he goes now; a blueprint for destruction! There he goes! The town drunk! Drunk in the morning!

Sometimes Zachary's girl come by and picks him up in her red '69 Chevy Imperial: bald tires, no muffler, dice, all of it. Vern slumps down in the seat and drinks rum from the bottle, still wearing his suit, still reporting to and from work.

Ann wants the BMW, it's one of two or three things she didn't get in the divorce, and I think that's why he refuses to fix it—I think. I hope that's the reason. He says it's gone too far to be fixed; that's what he tells me. He sounds sad about it, and we both know he's right, but still, I have to say all the right things, have to protest. . . . Aww, hayull, Vern, just throw some money at it, they can fix it . . .

Sometimes I drive Vern over to Zachary's, and they invite me in. Zachary and his daughter and Vern and I play cards at a little linoleum table that rocks whenever you lean your elbows on it. Zachary's girl and Vern drink from the same bottle, but Zach and I drink from jelly glasses. Zachary buries the insurance money.

"Lot of bad shit goin' around," Zach says, shaking his head, studying his hand as if it is the first game of cards he has ever played in his life; as if not knowing quite what to do, not wanting to, or unsure of, making the first move—and Zach's girl and Vern start to giggle, looking at each other's hands, and Zach and I start to talk about football, about how it was—talking as if it's going to happen again, for Chrissakes, talking, in our rum, with hope; hope and idiocy—and Zach's girl and Vern are sliding to the floor, sort of becoming rum themselves, spilling, tangled, twined; and Zach sighs and looks out the window, thinking about how Vern has money too, a little anyway, now that the divorce is almost paid off, and thinking too, perhaps, about Vern's rotting sports car, which Zach would dearly love to get his hands on—he could fix it, he thinks, or at least by damn get it out of that dark garage and out into the daylight, maybe weld it to the top of a tower, run some 8–5/8" drill pipe into the sky out in the front yard and weld rungs to the pipe so that it was a sort of a ladder; and he could climb up into it each day after work, sit behind the steering wheel like a sailor in a crow's nest, look out over the swamp and maybe have a few drinks, lean the front seat back and turn the radio on, maybe listen to some football games in the fall . . .

When Wejumpka entered junior high school, he finally stopped hugging people. The authorities simply made him stop: they told Ann that he couldn't come to school any more, otherwise. He was hugging the teachers, other students, the custodians and maids; it was getting to be a discipline problem.

Also, he changed his name then. He was getting too old for Wejumpka—though it's what Vern and I still call him—but God knows, Montrose was certainly nothing to fall back on. In the end he decided upon Vern Jr. I gave him a wooden bowl with a lot of names mixed up in it, and that was the one he pulled out. Fate; a lucky boy.

He is luckier than Zach's girl, for sure; luckier even than Zach, who has some malaise in his blood, some stun-slugging chemical that makes him have to lie down and rest, every time the wind changes direction; luckier than his mother, Ann, who has also laid down and quit early, gained forty pounds in a year, instead of losing the twenty she needed to: luckier than me, too, me not knowing when to bluff and when to charge, when to commit and when not to—all this bad shit going on!—and feeling, as I watch it all go by, that even though I am away from it, several steps back, I'm still moving along with it all, too, being drawn along, as is everything, everyone. Wejumpka, Vern Jr., knows none of this, has never had this feeling yet. That is how he is lucky.

He knows when and when not to hug. He knows that he has gone through a dark spot, gone into an absent place, and has come out on the other side; and he knows that he can do it again, then, next time, when it comes, again and again; already, he knows that: to just close his eyes, and hold on, and he'll come on through.

For his eleventh birthday, I took him and his brother, Austin, who was sixteen, water skiing for the first time. I rented a little boat with a pretty good engine, and some skis, and we went out on the reservoir in it. Neither of the boys had skiied before, and for a long time we just sat out there, feeling the warmth of the sun, looking at how far away the shore was. Zachary had come and towed the BMW away, had indeed welded it to the top of a tower, and we were so far away from the shore that we had to use binoculars to even see the white speck of it, rising out of the swamp.

We took turns looking at it through the binoculars.

"I pissed in that car the day they got the divorce," Austin bragged, proud and tough, wearing his gold earring in one ear, a dirty blue jean jacket, though it was 100°. He smelled like a night club, like the boy's restroom at school, soggy sour pee-stained cigarette butts, and I wanted him to ski first, so that he would have to get cleaned off.

"I pooted in it," Wejumpka in a small voice, meekly, and the two brothers looked at each other, as far away as planets, and then broke up laughing, and I laughed too, laughed at old Zachary sitting up there in the car that had years-old poot and other in it, but I didn't laugh as much as Wejumpka and Austin; and I was thinking about how good it would be to start the boat up, to push the throttle all the way in and feel the power of it, all the roar, right there in the back of the boat, beneath me, driving me forward, raising the boat's nose into the air, it would be such a powerful thrust.

Wejumpka, in an odd gesture of bravery, wanted to ski first. It's possible that he was just showing off for Austin; or maybe he thought his father had not yet abandoned him, that he was being given one last chance, and that even as he was climbing down into the lake, buoyed by his life vest, slipping his feet into the oversized skis—even then in his staggered, hugging-poet's imagination, his father was climbing up into the car with Zachary, watching him through binoculars, giving him a final chance, maybe even elbowing Zachary and pointing to him and saying, "That's my little boy. That's my Wejumpka."

I started the motor and jockeyed the boat from side to side, getting the tow rope lined up, making sure Wejumpka had his skis ready.

He's stout; he's a strong little ruffian, something of a muscleman these days. He popped right up, a surprised look on his face that was half joy, and half anger.

457

I glanced back over my shoulder once and could see that he was not watching the boat, but the shore: the tops of the trees, as if waiting for something to appear—squinting, and I guessed he was trying to make out the BMW.

"He says he wants to go faster!" Austin shouted, amazed, with his long hair blowing in the wind, and he was excited for his little brother, and I felt badly for having thought of Austin as being a street punk, and hoped it was only a phase.

"He's pointing his thumb up, he wants to go faster!"

I looked back again and it was so, Wejumpka was leaning back like a pro, he was a natural, and already he was relaxed, had sort of a cocky but determined smirk on his face, and he was jabbing his thumb at the sky, as if trying to poke out the bottom of something, skiing with just one hand, and I eased the throttle in.

The boat raised its nose, surged forward, a lion, trying to escape, but Wejumpka was the pursuer, and would not easily be lost: I looked back once more, and he was a little pale, we had the throttle all the way in—he was crouched down again, bucking the wake, no longer showboating, but just trying to hang on— and the wall of blue trees seemed closer, then, and almost without realizing it, I noticed that we could see now the far-off white dot of the car, sitting on top of the trees, looking like the most natural thing in the world.

We skimmed over the chop of summer-wind waves. The wind was blowing my hair, too, and it felt great. The sun was beginning to burn my cheeks and shoulders. I felt like I was sixteen, like I could go through anything, and come out the other side, too.

The white dot was getting larger in the trees; we could tell now that it was a car, could even see that it was a sports car; that's how close we were.

When I looked back, Wejumpka was gone. Austin was staring openmouthed at the lake behind us.

Then we saw that he was still on the end of the rope, his skis knocked off by the fall, but that he was still holding on: submarining, like some kind of crazy, diving fishing lure—holding on, though, occasionally raising his head above the mysterious roostertail of water, his mouth a tiny, frightened "Oh," to gulp some air.

The force had to be tremendous.

"Let go!" I shouted, easing back on the throttle. "Wejumpka, LET GO!"

But he couldn't hear me, underwater. I could feel the strain on the boat—it was like pulling an anchor around the lake. But he wouldn't let go, he stayed with it, and I had to shut the engine off and coast to a stop, before he understood that it was over.

Nominated by The Chariton Review *and Chris Spain*

ASCENSION ON FIRE ISLAND

by HENRI COLE

from ANTAEUS

No octopus-candelabra
    or baby Jesus adorns
the summerhouse we gather in
    to sing a hymn of forgiveness.
No churchbells bronzed overhead
    ring and set our little mob free
when the service is said.
    Only curtains in a strong wind,

billowing like spinnakers
    upon us, seem a godly sign,
or almost so. Sharp as a new pin,
    the day begins around us,
a speckled doe nibbling
    petunias as we pray,
an excess of elementals
    piloting us forward, like Polaris,

into the gospel's verbal cathedral.
    As when Jesus appeared
to the eleven as they sat at meat
    and upbraided them with their
unbelief and hardness of heart,
    our congregation seems unknowing

at first of goodness yet to come:
      Is there a god unvexed to protect us?

What pious groups wouldn't have it so!
      The floor creaks beneath us
like the hull of a ship,
      and the surf purrs in the distance,
confounding us with place,
      till a cardinal alights, twig-flexing,
anchoring us with his featherweight.
      Listen for the passing stillness . . .

In the harbor a man floats
      portside of his sloop, his purple
windbreaker flashing in a sunburst.
      Let him be forgiven, this once,
who put him there. The family squabble,
      the bruised cranium, piece by piece,
will face up to the light of day.
      And the body, its brief

unimmaculate youth, will be hoisted
      from the water's patina of calm.
The nervous deer, the cardinal,
      our perfect citizen, even invisible
bells aloft, press in upon us
      with sheltering mystery,
as in the distance a throng gathers
      and the yellow death-blanket unfolds.

Nominated by John Drury and David Wojahn

A VACANT LOT

by GIBBONS RUARK

from YARROW

One night where there is nothing now but air
I paused with one hand on the bannister
And listened to a film aficionado's
Careless laughter sentence poetry to death.

It's twenty gone years and a few poems later,
The house demolished, the film man vanished,
The friend who introduced us to him dead.

I side with one old master who loves to tell
His film buff friends that film is *like* an art form,
And yet my eyes keep panning the empty air
Above the rubble, as if, if I could run

The film back far enough, I might still start
For home down the darkened street from the newsstand
And turn a corner to the house still standing,

A faint light showing in an upstairs window.
Is someone reading late? Or is it the night
Our newborn lies burning up with fever,
And all the doctor can say is plunge her

In cold water, wrap her up and hold her,
Hold her, strip her down and plunge her in again
Until it breaks and she is weak but cooling?

Is it the night they call about my father
And I lay the mismatched funeral suit
In the back seat with the cigarettes and whiskey
And drive off knowing nothing but Death and South?

Somewhere a tree limb scrapes at a gutter.
The wind blows. Late trucks rattle the windows.
Never you mind, I say out loud to the girls

Away at school, there's nothing there to hurt you.
The sky is thickening over a vacant lot,
And when I leave there is a hard rain drumming
With the sound of someone up in the small hours,

Thirsty, his palm still warm from a sick child's
Forehead, running the spigot in the kitchen
Full force till the water's cold enough to drink.

Nominated by Yarrow

MY LORD BAG OF RICE

fiction by CAROL BLY

from THE LAUREL REVIEW

W HEN VIRGIL HAD been healthy and mean, Eleanor had loved him; now that he was dying, in his pain grinding shoulders and hips into the bed, she sometimes found herself daydreaming, *If Virgil died this week instead of next, I could start everything that much sooner.* "Do you feel guilty?" B. J. at the Women's Support Group asked. "You have a right to your own life." It sounded nineteen-eighties-OK to have a right to your own life; it did not sound so good to say, If Virgil Grummel would only die this week instead of next, or tonight instead of tomorrow night, she could inherit the farm and the engine repair service all the sooner. She could sell it all and take the $183,000 cash which their neighbor, Almendus Leitz, said it was probably worth. She would start a boarding house in St. Paul and never, never again hear cruel language around her. *Never,* she thought, patting Virgil's ankle skin.

It was three in the morning, the hour when she usually visited Virgil at Masonic Hospital because then the drugs didn't cover the pain. She drove over from St. Paul twice a day. Sometimes, like tonight, when she walked right into the hot, wide doorway of the hospital, no one sat guard at Reception. The flowers leaned on their stems in the shadowy glass cooler. The crossword puzzle kits waited motionless in the gift case. Someone could perfectly well walk in and hurt people, and steal things, and trot back out into the August night. Eleanor always walked past the dark counters to the elevator and came up to Three.

Despite his morphine Virgil was awake and in pain. He wanted to talk about the good old days. His agonized, liquid eyes

464

watched her as she cut in half each sock of a new woolen pair. Then she slipped the toe-half over his icy feet. Whole socks didn't work because of the styrofoam packed around Virgil's insteps to prevent bedsores.

He pled with her to mention the good old days. In his wispy, throttled voice he said, "Do you remember how we went to Monte to get you your stone?" Dawson was their town, but Montevideo was the town that counted, the place for buying major things like wall-to-wall carpeting and diamond rings. Eleanor smiled down at Virgil's face in the shadowy hospital room, but she was thinking how he had never called the ring an engagement ring: he called it a "stone," just as meals were "chow" and love was "your medicine." One day their older neighbor lady, Mrs. Almendus Leitz, had come over and told Eleanor how Almendus was always telling her to "just roll over and take your medicine." Mrs. Leitz was sick of it. She and Eleanor stood on the stoop, both of them with their work-strong arms folded, squinting out over Virgil's steaming acreage of corn and beans. It crossed Eleanor's mind at the time that all over the whole breathless prairie, with farm places at half-mile intervals, men were telling women to roll over and take their medicine, but she decided not to think about it.

"Yes, but you *should* have been thinking about it," they all said firmly, down at the Women's Support Group which she now belonged to in Minneapolis. Not just B.J. said so. All of them. B.J. said she fervently hoped that now Eleanor was in the Twin Cities she would become sexually active. Eleanor let her talk.

As soon as they were married, Virgil put in a bid for the old District 73 Country School and won it; he dragged it over to their place on the flatbed, laid down a concrete floor for it, and set it down. He never yanked the old school cupboards and bookshelves off the walls. There were dozens of Elson-Gray Readers and some children's books. There was a book of Japanese fairy tales which Eleanor took up whenever she had a moment.

Now Virgil wanted her to recall how he'd be repairing machinery out there in the shop, and he'd call her on the two-way to come out, and how they worked together out there. "Do you remember," he whispered, "how you'd quit whatever you was doing in the house and come on out and help me in the shop?" She remembered: the two-way crackled and growled all the time in

465

the kitchen. She could hear the field hands from Almendus's west half-section swearing because they'd dropped a furrow wheel or a lunchbox out in the plowing somewhere. Then, very loud and close, Virgil's voice would cut in, "Hey, Little Girl, this is Big Red Chief, get your butt out here a minute," and he would go off without waiting for her to answer. He had fixed up both the laundry area and the kitchen for radio reception, so he knew she'd hear him, wherever she was, canning or what. She would go out to the shop, arms crossed across her breasts if it was cold, running if it was summer, looking out over the fields past Almendus's place towards Dawson Mills. Virgil was fond of the radio. Sometimes he wanted to make love in the shop; he would lay out the hood dropcloth on the station wagon back seat which he never did get back into the station wagon. When the wagon finally threw a rod, the backseat stayed in the shop. Each time he was through making love, he said, "This is Big Red Chief, over and out," and gave her a little slap on the temple.

Eleanor knew she was lucky. All her childhood her father had gone on every-six-months beating binges. He beat up her mother and then he forced her sister. "You don't have to look so owlly," he told Eleanor when she stood dumb, watching, "your big sister is a real princess." She was so lucky to be married to a good man like Virgil, who didn't drink much. It was boring helping a man in the shop, though. Much of the time he would say, "Don't go away, Little Girl, I might need you." He didn't care whether she had quart jars boiling in the processor. So she would give his feet a glance (he had dollied himself underneath someone's Buick now) and she carried the Japanese fairy tale book over to one of the old schoolroom windows. Virgil's FARM AND ENGINE REPAIRS sign creaked outside, the corn tattered in the wind, and Eleanor found a story that she read over and over.

"Hey," Virgil shouted from under the Buick he was fixing. "Get that V-belt and hand it to me." Then he said, "No, dang it all, not that one—the other one!" Then she would open the book again.

"Hey, get your ass over here," Virgil cried. "Hand me all this stuff when I tell you, one by one in order."

She wiped the grease off her hands and went back to the story. A young Japanese hero had a retinue of servants. Watercolor illustrations showed him mustachioed, with slant eyes and nearly white skin. All his servants wore sashes with thin swords tucked

466

into them. They looked a little like middle-aged, effeminate Americans in dressing gowns who had chosen to arm themselves. Eleanor couldn't keep her eyes off the pictures. The hero was travelling through Japan, looking for adventure, when he came to a high, rounded bridge over a river which ran to the sea. As he began to cross it, he saw that a frightful dragon slept at the top of its arch. The dragon's scales and horns and raised back ridge were everything a child would count on when it came to dragons. No one was around to sneer at a grown woman reading a child's book when she was supposed to be helping her husband.

The young Japanese started to step right across the dragon, and it suddenly reared up. His servants dropped back, aghast, but the hero held his ground. Then the dragon took the form of a beautiful woman, who explained that she was ruler of a sea king-dom under the bridge. Each night a centipede of gigantic size slid down from the mountain to the north (she pointed) and ate dozens of her subjects, who were fishes and sea-animals. They realized they needed a man—but not an ordinary man. "You can imagine what fright an ordinary man would feel," the sea princess said.

Dusk was falling. She pointed again to the mountain, which now showed only its black profile before the green, darkening sky. Some sort of procession of people carrying lanterns seemed to descend the near slope of the mountain. "Those are not peo-ple," the sea princess said. "Those are the eyes of the centipede."

"I will kill it," the young Japanese said simply.

"I think you are brave enough," the princess said. "I took the form of a dragon and placed myself on this bridge, pretending to sleep. You are the only man who hasn't fled at the sight of me."

The hero drew a light green arrow from the quiver on his shoulder. He sent it at one of the centipede's eyes. That eye went out, but the monster kept coming. He took another arrow—a pale pink one this time—but it only put out another eye. Then he recalled a proverb of the Japanese people: human saliva is poi-son to magical enemies. He licked the tip of an arrow the color of a bird's egg and sent it off into the thick dusk. It went true. It put out the creature's foremost eye—and then the princess and the hero were joyous to see all the eyes darken to red, then grey, like worn coals.

The princess clapped. "Wait, O hero!" she cried. She clapped again. Fishes dressed in silk robes rose from the river. They carried gigantic vases from earlier, greater times. They brought hundreds of yards of hand-embroidered silks and linens. They handed everything to the hero's servants to carry.

Finally, a sea serpent brought a large plain bag. In the watercolor illustration it was light brown like a gunnysack gone pale. The sea princess said, "The other gifts are for you and your court, since obviously you are a prince. But this bag is for your people. Even if famine comes to your country, your people will never be hungry. This bag full of rice will never empty."

"Then I will carry it myself," he told her. But before raising it to his shoulder, he bowed very low, and the sea princess bowed low back to him. Then she faded.

In his own country, the young man was forever after known as My Lord Bag of Rice.

In the first year of her marriage, Eleanor Grummel read through all the books left in the District 73 schoolhouse. She would hand Virgil what he needed—the snowblower sprocket, the fan belt, the lag-screw, or the color-coded vacuum tubing—and then lean against the wall or sometimes sit on the old station wagon back seat and read. She read all the books, but returned over and over to My Lord Bag of Rice.

Now, eighteen years later, she held Virgil's hand while he whispered to her, his memories blurred by drugs, getting the times wrong, getting the occasions wrong, his eyes weeping from illness and recollection. Eleanor saw herself again standing at the old schoolhouse window, sometimes glancing out at the fields, sometimes studying the illustrations in the fairy tale book. Now she thought that she read in an enchanted way, because she had been too unconscious to know she lived in misery.

Twice each day, throughout Virgil's dying, Eleanor drove happily from Masonic, a building of the University of Minnesota hospital system, back to Mrs. Zenobie's boarding house in St. Paul. On her night run, generally at about three in the morning, Eleanor recited aloud in the car whole passages from the King James translation. Aloud she cried, "And the darkness comprehendeth it not!" or she shouted in the car, "And none shall prevent Him!" She remembered to add "Saith the Lord" after any pronouncements she could remember from Genesis.

468

August changed to early fall; she still drove with the windows open. The air was dusty and smooth, its blackness so thorough she felt as if it lay all over the Middle West—as if even the Twin Cities, a polite place, hardly made a pinprick of light in all the blackness. Of course the Twin Cities were not really a polite place: Mrs. Zenobie, the landlady at her boarding house, was not polite—but in the Twin Cities politeness was possible.

In the normal course Eleanor would have lodged nearer the hospital where Virgil was dying. The University people explained that all the special housing for people like Eleanor happened to be full. Mrs. Zenobie was not the greatest, they explained, and Eleanor would have to drive across to St. Paul, but she was reasonable. They gave her a map and highlighted her route from I-94 to Newell Avenue, St. Paul. They urged her to join a certain Women's Support Group, since she was under stress and was new in the city. They told her she could visit her husband any hour of the night or day she liked.

The night runs brought her back to Mrs. Zenobie's at about four in the morning. No matter how quietly Eleanor turned the key and tiptoed past the roomers' coat hooks, Mrs. Zenobie always woke and came out from behind the Japanese room divider. She slept downstairs, she told Eleanor, because of the crime. If crooks ever realized no one was on the ground floor, especially when it was a woman who ran the household, they would take advantage. And once they robbed a woman they'd rob her again. The police right now were looking for LeRoy Beske, the low-life who had owned 1785 Newell, three houses over, and then sold it to someone who never moved in. "You got to learn these things," Mrs. Zenobie told Eleanor, "if you're serious about wanting to start a rooming house. Also I wanted to say I'd be the last not to be grateful you have brought us so many doughnuts from the bakery, but I can't give you anything off the rent for that."

"I didn't expect it," Eleanor said.

"It doesn't matter how many men boarders you got," Mrs. Zenobie said. "It doesn't do any good. Crime is crime."

Mrs. Zenobie had five elderly male boarders, four of whom were not so polite as Eleanor hoped to find for clientele whenever she finally got her own house. Her idea was to have a five o'clock social hour: they would all gather in the living room

469

before dinner and she would give each boarder some wine or cider, so it would be like home. Eleanor herself had never seen a home like the one she had in mind, but the image was clear to her.

Eleanor started up the staircase, exhausted.

"If you're serious about wanting a house," Mrs. Zenobie whispered fiercely up after her, "I heard that 1785 is for sale again now. It'd be big enough." Mrs. Zenobie's eyes glared up as steady as bathroom nightlights. "I wouldn't feel you were cutting into my prospects," she said. "There's so many people wanting boarding houses these days there's enough for everyone."

Eleanor slept well all that late August and early September. She felt the grateful passion for sleep of people whose lives are a shambles. Only sleep was completely reliable. She dreamed. Every morning she woke up haunted and mystified by the dreams.

In the mornings Alicia Fowler, a realtor recommended by B.J. at the Support Group, picked her up. Eleanor felt cared for in Alicia's car. They ignored the big sun-dried thoroughfares— Snelling, Cleveland, Randolph. Alicia knew every house in St. Paul or Minneapolis and what it likely was worth. Eleanor said, "My idea is three stories, homey, decently built. I can't afford Summit Avenue, but I don't want a dangerous part of town."

After the morning's searches with Alicia, Eleanor took her own (or still Virgil's) car over to the hospital for an hour or so. If Virgil was sleeping, she daydreamed beside his tubings. Once a technician came in to get Virgil ready to wheel down for X-rays. Eleanor realized that, whatever the X-rays would teach Virgil's doctor, these trips were not for Virgil's sake but for other patients after Virgil's death. They were making a lab rat out of Virgil. She pointed out that it was painful for Virgil to be moved onto the stretcher table and off again. The technician said he was only following orders. Eleanor did not dare oppose the doctor's orders. After they wheeled Virgil down, she thought of how she should have protected him from that extra pain. Her fist shook as she held his drip stand.

After an hour she left and drove courteously home on Oak and Fulton streets, onto 94, and east towards St. Paul. She waved to drivers backed up at Erie Street and let them onto the road in front of her. They waved back. She waved to let people from parking lots enter the column of cars. She was delighted to be courteous to strangers. For eighteen years she had shrunk in her seat while Virgil gave the finger to anyone who honked when Virgil crossed lanes. On their few Twin Cities junkets, he would pull ahead two feet into the pedestrian crossing when he had to wait for a stoplight. It forced pedestrians to walk around the front of the car. When a pedestrian gave Virgil a hostile glance Virgil would gun the engine, which made the pedestrian jump. Eleanor always looked out the right-hand window in order not to see Virgil smile. When Virgil was caught speeding, he would not look up as he passed his driver's license out the window to the officer. While the man asked him a question or told Virgil his computer reading, Virgil stared steadily at the steering wheel and kept both hands on it, as if to drive off. His face looked full and stung with blood. The moment the officer turned away, initialed the citation, and wound up the invariably courteous request to keep it down, Virgil came to life: he snarled, "I took your number, fellow! If you ever, like *ever*, try to drive through Chippewa or Lac Qui Parle County, I know the right people that'll put you up so high by the time you hit the ground eagles will have made a nest in your ass!"

Now Eleanor enjoyed driving under the speed limit: she played at imagining other drivers having their lives saved by her carefulness. She even formed a mental image of those in the oncoming traffic saying to themselves, "At least *there's* a car not driven by some natural killer!" as they whipped past on their side of the white line.

On Tuesdays she went to St. Swithin's Episcopal Church confirmation class for instruction. There were three men in the group, and an innumerable, changing roster of women—all of them older than Eleanor. One of the youngish men spoke wrathfully and weakly about one issue or another. Two of the women kept saying, "I'm not sure this is relevant," a remark that caused the young priest to tremble. Eleanor felt at odds with all of them since her aim in church instruction was not relevance but beauty. She wanted to learn polite ideas, whatever they were. She memorized a good deal of what Father said. Once—only once—she repeated one of the phrases she had memorized. The group looked astonished and then disgusted. She stayed on but only because the group met in a room called the Lady Chapel where the royal and navy blue stained-glass windows pleased her.

471

On Thursdays she had the Women's Support Group. They were people so different from herself that she didn't like to think about it. B.J.—all of them—had been sympathetic when she told them about her father's abuse. When her thoughts grew more and more centered around getting a boarding house, they turned indifferent. Anyone in pain was a priority. In October a recently sexually-assaulted woman joined them. After that, Eleanor felt unseen. She knew these women were more intelligent than she was; on the other hand, she felt stung when they wouldn't rejoice with her over having found a house she could buy.

In the week of Virgil's death and the weeks following it, Eleanor had so much to think of that she forgot to tell B.J. and the others that she was widowed at last. When they found out, B.J. threw her arms around Eleanor, crying "You are so wonderfully centered!"

Eleanor blushed. She felt stupid. People had emotions which meant nothing to her; they used words she never used— "centered" and "on top of your shit."

Eleanor stayed on at Mrs. Zenobie's. There was no social hour before dinner, as Eleanor planned for her own boarding house, but now and then Mrs. Zenobie's niece brought in a group of Sunday school students for what was announced as a very, very special occasion. One October Saturday, the children came to explain some small kits to Mrs. Zenobie's boarders. If the boarders would be good enough to assemble these kits, the children would pick them up on St. Andrew's Day.

Eleanor perked up a little at hearing "St. Andrew's Feast," since memorizing trivia about saints was a favorite part of her new church life. Each kit was a plastic sandwich bag in which lay two tongue depressors, a plastic twister, and a plastic baby poinsettia. The idea was to use the twister to attach the tongue depressors at right angles to make a cross, then jam the poinsettia's stem into the twist as well. While it made a good Christmas present for shut-ins, you could trade the poinsettia for a lily and, presto, you had an Easter symbol, too, which was the kind of thing that shut-ins could relate to.

Eleanor backed around the room divider as discreetly as possible and made for the staircase.

Suddenly a man's voice said, "Oh, no, you don't, Eleanor! No one gets out of this!"—with a laugh. He came out to the hallway where she hovered. "I have seen many cultural atrocities in my life," he said to her, not only not lowering his voice but raising it slightly, and even, as she had heard him do any number of times at the dinner table, adding a slight British inflection—"but I think this one surpasses them all!" It was Jack Lackie, the retired Episcopal priest, a mysterious member of Mrs. Zenobie's household.

"The mystery is, what was he really?" Mrs. Zenobie later said, gouging a used kleenex into her apron pocket. "Janitor, maybe. Not a priest. You get wise to what people used to be and what they say they used to be. To hear it, I've had boarders who invented the atom bomb and I've had CIA operatives and I've had three hundred of President Kennedy's cousins. He wasn't all *that* Catholic."

Eleanor felt endeared to Jack Lackie because he never once lifted his trouser cuff to show the ribbing of long underwear. Mrs. Zenobie's other men liked to explain that now winter had set in they put on their long underwear and that was it until spring. Two of them shoved their wooden chairs back, bent over and lifted the bottoms of their trouser legs in case Eleanor didn't believe them. Jack Lackie was the only man not to do it, and Eleanor had made up her mind that she would have him for a boarder in her home when she got it.

Now she smiled at him. It would give such a classy tone to the place if someone spoke of "cultural atrocities!"

She lay on her bed upstairs, hearing the children's voices singing from below. Under the house the ground throbbed from the parked Amtrak train on Transfer Street, throbbing gently through the concrete basement and wooden studs. Eleanor smiled in the dark: this was her favorite mood. She felt simple, full of plans, and not confused. It was true that nearly everyone she talked to that day was so different from her that they could never be friends. She passed quickly over the idea that she might be lonely the rest of her life. She raced to make image after image of her boarding house. There would never, never be any church groups allowed into it. There would be a wood-burning stove in the living room. There would be a wine and cider hour before dinner each night. If anyone sneered or shouted, she would ask them to leave. There would be an outside barbeque. There

473

would be climbing roses. She would tell Alicia the realtor that she definitely wanted 1785 Newell Avenue.

It seemed like a million years since Big Red Chief's voice crackled at her from the speakers in the farmhouse kitchen. Was it true that you needed to be widowed in order to lead a courteous life? She didn't pause to think that idea through but happily imagined the stained-glass window at 1785 and thought how holy it looked even if what it lighted was a staircase, not a church. It made her feel holy and unconfused. Months ago Father said, "It is always a risk to take your soul into real life!" The others nodded, as if wakened and strengthened by his remark. Eleanor made nothing of it but she memorized it, another graceful phrase, even if "risk" to her meant only the risk of borrowing against her inheritance to buy a three-story house. Her mind drifted back to the house.

On the third Sunday in November, Alicia hurried Eleanor to an office building in downtown St. Paul, where they crowded into a small room with a conference table and vinyl chairs. There were four other people. Alicia sat close by Eleanor, bending right over the papers in front of Eleanor, making sure she signed nothing that wasn't right. A man at the opposite end of the crowded table, presumably the owner of 1785 Newell Avenue, was being similarly coached by his real estate agent. Eleanor supposed she would shake hands with him at the end, but for now each avoided the other's eyes. The closing agent's dull energetic voice kept explaining terms. There was some cloud on the title, but it was cleared. The police had asked that if Ms. Grummel ever saw Le-Roy Beske to call them immediately: he had been seen hanging around several times since he sold the house.

Eleanor was in a dream. She looked affectionately at Alicia's permanented head: it was back-combed and sprayed as stiff as a howitzer shell. If you touched it surely your hand would come away with tiny cuts. Eleanor had two feelings: affection for this tough person who had helped her get her life's dream, and the memory of her mother, who wore dark glasses when she went to the beauty parlor for a permanent. Even if she had to cover bruises with pancake, she never missed a hair setting: the time she had three stitches in her right cheek, she postponed her hairdo by two hours. Eleanor kept signing in exactly the places where Alicia pointed a Lee's press-on nail to show her.

474

Keys tinkled across the table. Smiles. The men stood up: people's hands reached across to shake. Then they were back out into the cold street. Alicia said, "Come on. We'll drive to Mrs. Zenobie's and walk to your new house."

Eleanor was learning the small graces of the rich. They brought each other small but ceremonial presents. Women brought just a few rosebuds for other women when they had a meeting together; the Support Group people sometimes arrived with newspaper cones full of flowers, to celebrate someone getting their shit together. At instruction classes, Father kept a good sherry for the confirmands. Women drank with women. No one talked about "hen parties." Now Eleanor opened a bottle of champagne.

The previous owners had left a dining room table and two chairs. Alicia held two styrofoam cups securely, as Eleanor poured. Then they both heard scrabbling below them.

"Not rats," Alicia said quickly and firmly. "I checked that out before. Everything else, of course—but not rats."

"I'm not afraid of rats," Eleanor said. "I'm a farm girl." She was about to tell Alicia about how Virgil would lift up a bale of hay, sometimes, and when the rats burst out she whacked as many as she could.

"Down we go," Alicia said, rising.

As they moved through the fine old kitchen, Eleanor realized with surprise that she had paid no attention to the basement. It was the third floor that had fascinated her: one finished room, church-like, with steep eaves going up to the ridge-pole and a charming dilapidated balcony at the peak-end. The other half of the third floor was not finished. Boarders could store their luggage there. The second floor was like all second floors of abused houses: radiators with paint chipped off, smudgy windows, deeply checked sills and mullions.

Alicia turned on the basement light. They trotted about the basement, between the abandoned coal room and the laundry room, around the monstrous octopus of a furnace spray-painted aluminum like ship's equipment. Behind the worktable there sat against the wall a very thin, old, dirty woman. Her awful eyes gleamed. One skinny hand plucked at her blouse buttons.

Alicia said, "OK, both together . . . . " They raised the woman up. "Nope—she's too weak to stand." Alicia paused.

"Here," Eleanor said. She bent down, her back to Alicia. All that farm work. "Just put her on my back." They got the woman upstairs and laid her on the floor in the living room, which had carpet.

"Police first," Alicia said.

"I'll run to Mrs. Zenobie's," Eleanor said.

Mrs. Zenobie herself frankly listened while Eleanor called 911. She rubbed an elbow and smiled. "You're getting into the problems of running a rooming house even faster than I did! You haven't been there even one night and already you got a nonpaying-type tenant hiding in the basement! Karsh!"

Eleanor riffled through Mrs. Zenobie's directory. She ordered one chicken-onions-snowpeas and rice and gave the address.

"Unsuitable tenants is the second greatest pain next to taxes," Mrs. Zenobie offered.

The police car was already parked at 1785 when Eleanor ran back.

"It's Sunday, so the only social workers on are the primary-interventions. We'll just take her to jail for the night," one of the two young men explained.

Alicia said she had to beat it, since the situation seemed to be under control.

Eleanor said, "I'll keep her for the night." She added, "I run a boarding house."

"Doesn't look like one yet," the other young cop said. "We've been kind of keeping a watch on this house. There was a real bad-news type here. This lady probably needs a doctor. We'll take her, and we'll get a social worker around to you tomorrow."

The policeman looked down at the old woman. "Can you talk, lady?" he said gently.

He waited a second. "OK, we'll wait for the ambulance." One of them went out to radio.

"This the kind of customer you going to have in this house?" the remaining policeman asked with a grin.

There was a knock. Eleanor paid the oriental foods delivery man and brought in her little white paper buckets with their wire handles.

The policeman got the idea. He and Eleanor both knelt on the floor. "If you can eat, lady, it's the best thing you can do," the officer said. He said to Eleanor, "Show it to her."

476

Eleanor said, "We're going to help you lean up against the wall." She opened one of the packets, and the old woman suddenly dug her whole hand into the rice. She put a palm full of it into her own face and began to chew slowly. She reached in again and again.

"She needs chopsticks like I need chopsticks," the young officer said comfortably. Eleanor leaned on her heels. The woman finished all the rice. Eleanor offered her the chicken. "This is going to be a mess," the policeman said. He stood up and ambled into the kitchen. "Someone at least left you some paper towels." Together they wiped the woman's face. Then Eleanor wiped her neck where the Cantonese sauce and a few onions had run down. The ambulance came. The policeman left a number to call if there was any trouble. Eleanor walked over to Mrs. Zenobie's for the last time. *Tomorrow night I'll homestead,* she thought.

When the social worker came the next day, he explained that he was Rex, from Primary Intervention. He told Eleanor that none of the women's shelters had any room for a new person. Eleanor and he sat at the dining room table together, while he told her that there used to be an office especially for cases like this woman's. Now there wasn't the dollars. He told Eleanor that he thought this woman was named Eunice something. She was a victim of the second-to-last owner here, this LeRoy Beske, who'd run a racket of diverting old people's welfare checks to himself. Then Rex looked at his hands.

"I don't know how you'd feel about this," he said. "I don't know what kind of house you want to have, but if you could take care of Eunice on a temporary basis, we could offer you the Difficult Care rate. That is, we'd pay you $22 a day to feed and shelter her. The hospital says she is OK. She's just in shock and can't talk. They don't think there is anything organically wrong except she's nearly starved to death. If you wanted to take her in four or five days . . . ."

Eleanor said to herself fast, *I could still get five or six courteous people who would have polite conversations at the table. It shouldn't be too hard: it'd still be a house where no one told anyone else to get their butt over here or there.*

The truck finally came from Dawson with the furniture. Eleanor bought three more beds from Montgomery Ward. She interviewed prospective tenants. She put Mercein, Mrs. Solstrom, Dick, Carolyn, and George on the second floor. She put Eunice in the room she had imagined for herself, behind the kitchen on the ground floor. She slept on the sofa for several weeks. She kept the third floor bedroom untenanted until the second floor was filled.

"Here," Mrs. Zenobie said. "They've got that racket on the TV so loud I can't hear myself think. Come in the kitchen."

She watched Eleanor with eyes blazing.

"Have I got this straight?" she said finally. "You want to trade one of your tenants for one of mine? What kind of crap is that?" She paused. "I don't want to get tough with you. I know you are mourning your husband. But you're in business, too, and you and I are doing business on the same street. So naturally I am looking at everything carefully. Let me just give this back to you and you tell *me*. You want me to take someone named Mrs. Joanne Solstrom into my house and then you want Mr. Jack Lackie to move to your house? You're going to pay them $100 each for the inconvenience?"

Eleanor nodded.

Mrs. Zenobie looked at her fingernails with the finesse of an actress. Since they were cut to just above the quick, there couldn't be much to discover about them. "I never paid any money to have some man move into any house of mine," she remarked.

There are some things you can't explain to some people, Eleanor thought. You can't tell the Support Group that you're *not* going through "the grief process" for your husband but you are furious at the State of Minnesota for chipping tax out of your late husband's engine repair service inventory before you inherited it. You couldn't tell Mrs. Zenobie that you wanted a retired Episcopal priest in your boarding house because he talked about history and culture and that you did *not* want a perfectly nice woman named Mrs. Solstrom because she constantly sneered. On Sundays, during wine and cider hour, she sneered that if Tommy Kramer couldn't learn to move his butt out of the pocket, he deserved every sack he got.

"I don't get it," Mrs. Zenobie said. "She pays her rent? She's clean? OK. But if you think you're going to get any help out of that Lackie, think again. He's retired. He never picked up a leaf in the yard, not around this place, he didn't."

478

Their lives went smoothly through the winter. Eunice still didn't speak, but everyone fed her. Mercein and Dick brought her Whopper Burgers, Carolyn brought her doughnuts, George brought her take-out Italian food from a place near his plant. Jack brought her cans of Dinty Moore Beef Stew and helped her stack them up in the unfinished part of the attic. She grew fat. Rex, the cordial social worker, thought it might be months before Eunice could speak again.

She followed Jack everywhere; he talked to her all the time. Eleanor began to feel happy. She moved Eunice to the north end of the second floor; she herself took the downstairs bedroom. Jack arranged his few possessions—his oddly old-fashioned clothes, his set of Will and Ariel Durant—in the third-floor room. Jack took over laying and lighting the fire in the living room stove which Eleanor bought at an auction on Fulton Street. Each late afternoon, they all watched the dull, comfortable flame through the isinglass while Jack served the wine and cider. Whenever he rose to refill someone's glass, Eunice stood up too. If he left the room, she followed him. He had to turn directly to her and say, "No," when he wanted to be alone.

The other tenants were grateful that she followed Jack instead of driving them crazy. Eleanor was glad because she needed the hour before dinner to cook, she needed the hour after dinner to plan the next day's work, and she liked to sit alone in the kitchen at night. The dishwasher chugged through its hissing cycles. Eleanor wrote out lists of repairs needed, hardware to buy, meals for the rest of the week. She could hear Jack's voice rising and falling in the living room. He was apparently telling Eunice everything that ever happened in human history.

As the weather warmed, Jack took on some outside chores. He renailed the rose trellis to the house while Eunice passed nails up to him. He sorted through the loose bricks lying in the backyard, dividing wholes from brokens. Whenever he lifted a brick, Eunice picked one up, watching his face. When he set his down, she set hers down. When her hands were free, she ate. There was always food in her jacket pockets—a wrapped ham-and-cheese or Mushroom and Swiss from Hardee's. Sometimes Jack let her into the third-floor storage area to count her cans of stew and soup. Eunice arranged and rearranged them into pyramids, straight walls, squares. Her eyes lost the terrible glint they

479

had at first. The boarders decided that probably she was only sixty or sixty-five, not eighty or ninety. She bathed, dressed, cleaned her teeth, and followed Jack everywhere.

In March, on a Saturday, it was Eleanor's turn to manage the food shelves at St. Swithin's. By now she was a confirmed church member.

Just before she left home, someone outside threw something through the first-floor stained-glass window. Glass and wood splinters scattered all over the base of the stairs. Sharp, normal sunlight broke in. George, Eunice, and Jack had been clearing the breakfast table. Now they stood still. Then Eunice moved towards the mess of glass and smashed sash-work: she bent and picked up a brick. Jack immediately took it from her, in case there were glass shards stuck to it. Eleanor called the police.

"Go on to church," Jack told her. "I'll sweep this up and George can go outside to see if he can see anybody."

Like most people who have done plain work in their lives, Eleanor could separate events at home from the job. All day she worked hard, instructing volunteers, making quick judgments about clients. She knew now who were the few people who picked up food and sold it later. When they showed up and explained what they wanted, Eleanor looked them right in the face, with a deliberate smile, and said, "I'm so sorry, we're fresh out of that." If the person pointed angrily to where that very item stood on the shelf, Eleanor smiled and said, "I know it looks as if we have it. The funny thing is we're out of it."

She was happy to get out of her car and start up the sidewalk to her boarding house. Since it was still March, Jack would have lighted a fire, and they could all gather as usual and speculate about who had broken their stained-glass window.

Her neighbor from across the street called, "Big trouble, huh, Eleanor?"

He was coming after her to talk. "In a way I'm glad that happened, Eleanor," he said in a kind tone. "I know it doesn't seem like the right thing to say, but at least now that guy'll get what's coming to him."

Eleanor said slowly, "LeRoy Beske you mean."

"That creep," the neighbor said. "Hanging around here. Trouble whenever he shows up. I'm sorry it had to happen at your place, Eleanor, but all of us along the street feel relieved." He paused. "Cops came of course," he said. "They wanted to talk to you and said they'd be back around now or so."

Then a last word from the neighbor: "That Jack Lackie, that tenant of yours! I'll say one thing for him! If a job needs doing, he does it!"

Eleanor looked and saw that the paper towelling she had suggested Jack stuff into the broken window wasn't there: the whole window was reglazed, although only in clear glass now.

Inside the house the living room was empty and dark.

"Hello?" Eleanor called up the staircase.

"Hello!" Jack called down in an odd tone.

Eleanor turned back to the door, since someone had rung the bell. It was the two policemen Eleanor remembered from months ago.

"Finally you got home," one of them said. "We've knocked and rung your bell—but no one would let us in."

"It's never locked!" Eleanor said.

"Locked today, Ms. Grummel," the other policeman said. As soon as Eleanor straightened from putting her key in, both policemen were right in the doorway.

"I hated losing that stained-glass window," Eleanor told them.

"That's the last window Beske'll bust in a long time," one man told her. The other loped over to the staircase and called upstairs, "Everybody down! Police!"

"Well," Eleanor said, preening a little, "I think it is very nice of you men to be so concerned about it."

Then they told her what had happened. LeRoy Beske had thrown the brick through her window, all right. Then he had hung around and the boarders had seen him in the yard. He went around to the side of the house. They heard a sharp cry: Dick and George ran outside and found Beske bleeding severely from a head wound. A blood-splashed brick lay near him. They glanced around a little—and then upward at the little balcony off Jack's third-story room. There was no one there. Both men hurried into the house to call the police. They both noticed that neither Jack nor Eunice was in the living room, where the other boarders began to huddle, overhearing the telephone call to 911.

Eleanor said to herself that her boarding house, her polite structure, had fallen into violence just as quickly as any other

481

household in a crime-filled country. The man she had designated to be the cultural leader had assaulted someone right in her own side yard.

One after another the boarders denied any knowledge. Jack's turn came. Eleanor nearly shuddered. His voice denied knowledge just as flatly as the others had.

"Now this lady: your name is?" The policemen were now looking at Eunice. She was forty pounds heavier than when they had seen her three months ago.

George said, "That's Eunice. We can pretty much answer for her, officer."

The officer said, "She'll have to speak for herself. Eunice," he said, "what did you see and where were you?"

Eunice opened her mouth. Her voice croaked and squealed like equipment long unused; phlegm caught in her throat and stopped a vowel now and then, but Eunice talked. When she started in, Eleanor remembered My Lord Bag of Rice and how the hero helped the sea princess. For the moment, Eleanor forgot that her reason for having Jack in her boarding house was that he should provide cultivated conversation. Now she believed that she had intuitively spotted Jack as a kind figure who would stand guard when they needed him. She thought, *well—Well!—now he'd done it*, so she had been canny. Her mind felt large and nervous.

Eunice was not ratting on Jack. Eunice said, "In the beginning the human race needed strong leaders. The Jews in Egypt needed a leader to get them out. When medieval farmers had their lands stolen by the church or the state or by their landlords, they needed brave people to get them their freeholds."

She kept talking. When Eunice got to the Reformation, she switched to Chinese history. She explained that the Chinese invented watertight doors for ships, so that no enemy could rake through the entire hold and sink a ship. Any leader knew it was devastating for a man to be trapped in a watertight compartment with the sea pouring in. Nonetheless, a leader told men on the other sides to turn the battens on the watertight doors. They heard the doomed man's screams, but the leader could save the whole. A leader could do desperate acts while others froze.

Then there was a brief pause in which Eleanor could see that Eunice was going to switch to another culture. She explained how painful it was to learn that the world was not terracentric—so painful a truth thousands couldn't bear it.

"OK, lady, OK," one policeman said.

"For now, that's enough," the other said to Eleanor. "You all have your dinner. We'll come back tomorrow, and anyway, they will know by then if LeRoy Beske is going to live or not."

Before the door had closed behind the policeman, Eunice began again. She explained that in every age of bullies, a leader shows up to give the people respite. She told them about John Ball, a sixteenth-century agricultural reformer. She explained the Odal Law of Norway. Jack declined to have wine with the others, and Eunice followed him upstairs, telling him about how Captain Cook used psychology to induce his men to eat sauerkraut. It saved them from scurvy.

Those down below could still hear her hoarse, unaccustomed voice, less distinct, as she and Jack rounded the landing and started up the reverse flight. They heard her close the door of her room. Jack's steps continued up on the third-floor stairs. Then they heard Eunice speaking to herself in her room.

Eleanor lighted the stove, listening to the boarders' various exclamations. Gradually they told each other their versions over and over, more and more quietly. After a while, Eleanor put the crock pot of stew onto the dining room table. She called to Jack and Eunice. Everyone sat quietly, whispering now and then, "Would you please pass the rolls?" "Would you send the carrot sticks down here?"—with a good deal of glancing at Eunice.

Her face was full of color. She looked fifty now, not sixty. She kept facing Jack and she kept talking. She had got to the nineteenth century. Chinese grandmothers were certainly sorry to see their granddaughters' feet bound the first time. Eunice described how the mothers and daughters cried as they removed their clogs at night, unwinding the bloodied cloths from their toes—yet, they, more than the men, made certain the practice was kept up.

One by one the boarders finished eating, nodded to Eleanor, and left the table. Eleanor and Jack and Eunice remained at the strewn tablecloth.

At last Jack rose. Eunice followed him immediately, in her usual way. She was explaining what the Marines did in Mexico in 1916. Eleanor set the dishwasher growling over its first load.

483

When she went upstairs, she could hear Eunice, alone in her room behind her door, saying that the Michigan National Guard helped Fisher Body Plant #1 defeat union workers in 1937. Eunice's voice, getting exercise, was sounding smoother now. Eleanor paused on the landing, decided to go back downstairs to bed, then noticed Jack sitting on a stair on the flight above.

"You're listening," she whispered to him, going up a few steps. They regarded each other in the weak night light.

"How can I help it!" he said in a whispered laugh. "Amazing! Amazing!"

Eleanor said, "She's not so amazing! It isn't her! *You're* the one that's amazing!" She didn't mind if her enormous happiness showed in her whisper. She felt out of her class, somehow—but this much she knew: it is amazing when a man uses all that violence that's in men to help people instead of just pushing people around! Virgil would never drop a brick on a friend's enemy. Her father never defended anyone. She realized that some time between dinner and this minute she had decided to lie for Jack if she had to. She would say what was necessary to keep the police from cornering him. It would be something new for her: she had not even been able to prevail on the X-ray technicians to leave poor Virgil in peace. She had underestimated Jack, admiring only his ability to talk courteously.

Now she whispered, "You have actually saved her life!"

He said, "You don't even know what happened."

Eleanor ignored that idiotic modesty and whispered, "What's more, she half-saved yours, too. When she rattled on and on all that history to the police, they obviously decided she was out of her head and they got up and went home! Of course, " Eleanor added, feeling very sage the way bystanders do when they double-guess the police, "they had been looking for that awful LeRoy Beske for a long time anyway."

"She didn't save my life, either," Jack now said.

Behind her door Eunice was moving away from Max Planck and introducing Marilyn French and Ruth Bleier.

Jack said from his stair slightly above Eleanor's: "I want you to listen now. I did not, repeat, did *not* drop or throw a brick onto LeRoy Beske from that balcony. You know who goes around this house carrying cans of beef stew and books and bricks."

Eleanor was still. "I don't believe you," she said then.

Jack said, "LeRoy Beske swiped her welfare check for over two years. At the end he hid her and then nearly starved her to death and dumped her in your basement when he couldn't figure out anything more convenient. She was mad at him. Then he made a mistake. He was drunk when he came around here this morning. For the fun of it he tossed a brick through your window. He didn't figure Eunice right: she was on the balcony when he ambled by a few hours later. He shouted, 'Hi, little girl!' to her when he saw her. People on the other side of the house heard him. He probably didn't recognize her. He shouted, 'Hi, princess!' Her rage made her very clean-cut. She had a brick with her because she and I were going to build the barbeque today. Anyway," Jack finished up in a satisfied, brutal way, "she got him good."

He whispered down at Eleanor, "Another thing. You had better know. I am not a retired priest. I am a retired janitor. What you have here is a retired janitor who has read a lot of history."

By now Eunice's voice had almost the lilt and ease of ordinary women's voices. She described the hole widening in the Antarctic ozone. Then she said that Eskimos' teeth had caries from eating American-made candy bars. She said Eskimos were listening to reggae, on the ice floes.

Eleanor and Jack lingered on the staircase. Eleanor imagined the Eskimos looking out over the ice-filled water. But she also remembered the watercolor illustration of the hero with his huge bag of rice: he was looking out over water; his robe was painted in baby colors—pink and light-blue—his quiver dusty-yellow, and the Sea of Japan was pale green, a shade you might choose for a child's nursery.

Nominated by Carolyn Kizer

FOR THE MISSING IN ACTION

by JOHN BALABAN

from PLOUGHSHARES

Hazed with harvest dust and heat
the air swam with flying husks
as men whacked rice sheaves into bins
and all across the sunstruck fields
red flags hung from bamboo poles.
Beyond the last treeline on the horizon
beyond the coconut palms and eucalyptus
out in the moon zone puckered by bombs
the dead earth where no one ventures,
the boys found it, foolish boys
riding their buffaloes in craterlands
where at night bombs thump and ghosts howl.
A green patch on the raw earth.
And now they've led the farmers here,
the kerchiefed women in baggy pants,
the men with sickles and flails, children
herding ducks with switches—all
staring from a crater berm; silent:
In that dead place the weeds had formed a man
where someone died and fertilized the earth, with flesh
and blood, with tears, with longing for loved ones.
No scrap remained; not even a buckle
survived the monsoons, just a green creature,

486

a viny man, supine, with posies for eyes,
butterflies for buttons, a lily for a tongue.
Now when huddled asleep together
the farmers hear a rustly footfall
as the leaf-man rises and stumbles to them.

Nominated by Bruce Weigl

DUST
(Ars Poetica)

by ALLEN GROSSMAN

from AGNI REVIEW

This is Spring for the last time. And poetry
Is dead—as when the Great Mind of the world
Or the mind in fact of the one man or woman
Among us who can speak has suppressed a momentous
Theme and nothing comes to mind in its place
And nothing is heard and nothing is seen
And the field is empty. Or it is like
An old ballad written down, or foot prints
Under the ice of time: the trace of one
Foot fall and in that print another print
Of foot falling and perished in the air
(And thus began the motive of our endless
Patience—the waiting for the sound a thousand years
Of the one foot fall and to hear it again
To hear it is the reason of our art
By which the greatest poet makes the deepest silence
In the empty heart of the strongest song);
But in earth remained the writing of the path
Of two—human, or partly human—who were
Walking on a bare flat plain at the dark hour
The far mountain threw down this dust. Now read
The story of the day or night the far
Mountain threw down the dust and the two wrote

And wrote (the one following the other across
The plain) until they were home. And then lay
Down in one another's arms and the dust
Covered them and the hot rains sealed the scroll
With the seven seals of oblivion.
In time the fires of the mountain cooled.
And a lens of ice began the gathering of
This light by which we read (the two of us),
Which is now a large light, a love of light,
As one might follow with the eyes alone
The words of a song that was written down,
Already written under the ice of time,
An ancient path across a bare flat plain,
Our sentence to the end.—What mercy of heaven,
Then, has sent these signs of the slaughtered dead
To unknot the tongue? There are so many unlaid
Ghosts in the world. Surely, one among them,
Not yet inconsolable, will let us hear
(A young one who is still patient with us
And eagerly descants upon the momentous theme)
A sound of foot fall—human, or partly human—
Out of the empty heart of the long forgotten
Composing the silence of the strongest song:
"Always like a new husband await the night,
And like a bride the rising of the light,"
Who wakens and walks out into the field at dawn
After a dream haunted by weeping animals
To find the patient spider has been brilliantly
At work and left a web articulate with dew,
Like mind a fragile theater of light,
A consolation to all of us who breathe
(And some, perhaps, of those who have no breath)
This Spring for the last time, the foot fall of
Summer, long awaited, passing toward our death.

Nominated by Cleopatra Mathis and David Wojahn

THE BATTLE OF MANILA

fiction by LAURA KALPAKIAN

from THE IOWA REVIEW

THE ICEMAN BROUGHT me to that day, woke me, I mean. He usually brought me two, but this day he didn't bring me nothing, just woke me where I sat on the porch having my dream when he knocked on the rail and said, "Afternoon, Mrs. Dance, I come to collect."

I lifted one eye at him, hardly able to see him at all in the glare of his white uniform and the sunlight shuddering in and out of the foxtails in the yard and the heat baking down in waves underneath the tin roof. I asked him what I owed.

"Two dollars thirty-five, same as ever, Mrs. Dance."

"You're robbing me same as ever," I say, but I got up and went in the house, that dog sniffing at my heels and got my coin purse off the piano where I always keep it between all the pictures and took it back out. "The ice melts too fast in this heat," I say. "Maybe you better bring me an extra cake. I need some for the icebox and some to cool off."

He looks strange for a minute, scratches a pimple on his chin and asks if I got his note, the one he left with the last delivery. "It was the last delivery, Mrs. Dance, the very last one. No more ice no more. No more iceboxes. Everyone in St. Elmo's got refrigerators nowadays and they don't need no ice."

"I got an icebox," I tell him.

He counts me back my change. "Well you get one of your boys to buy you a refrigerator, why don't you? Will and Archie are making good money. They can buy you a refrigerator. Why, some

490

of them fridges have little freezers up top and you can make your own ice." He tips his hat and starts to leave me, to fight his way back up through the foxtails to where I know the fence is and after that, the sidewalks and the icewagon. I hear the squeal of the gate before I call out after him. "What day is it?"

"Tuesday, like ever, Mrs. Dance. I always come—used to come—on Tuesday."

"What Tuesday?" I holler.

"Tuesday the 17th of August," he cries back.

"But what's the year?"

Over the chug of the ice wagon, he shouts, "It's 1948, Mrs. Dance and everyone has a refrigerator and don't need no more ice."

And that's how the iceman brought me to and I knew time was passing and it was years since the Luzon campaign and the battle of Manila Bay.

I got back inside, dog at my heels and put the coin purse back up top of the piano between the picture of my son Will and Mrs. Will and their children, and my son Archie and Mrs. Archie and their children. They're twins, Will and Archie and they had joined up the Navy together and they was at Pearl Harbor when the Japs blowed it up, but they wasn't neither of them killed or even injured when it happened. But this whole house might just as well have been atop the Arizona that day because my husband Hank had the radio on and my youngest Ben was reading the funny paper and I was fixing breakfast when the news of Pearl Harbor come on. Ben drops the paper and screams. I drop the dishes and scream and peed my pants, but Hank, he did not scream. He gasps and moans out the bitterest note I ever heard, a long ragged groan and then a sharp, high one and he crumples over, falls forward out of his chair to the floor. He had a heart attack and died in Ben's arms. The only victim of Pearl Harbor to be living in California.

They give Hank a veteran's funeral, not for his being the first California victim of the second war, but for having fought in the first. Hank had joined up in May, 1917, even though he was a married man and didn't have to go. He said he hated the Hun and owed it to his country. So his country owed it to him to bury him and they did. Hank's no sooner in the grave than Ben's telling me how he hates the Japs and owes it to his country to quit school and join up. I said: Will and Archie will save the world,

491

you stay home with me till they call you. They'll call you soon enough. You're only eighteen. I told him that and Connie told him that and between us we kept him in St. Elmo till after high school graduation, but then he joins up to be like his brothers. He joins the army to be different from them.

But Ben wasn't like his brothers. They both lived and come home and got married and had families and now, just like the ice man said, they're doing real well. Will's manager of the St. Elmo Feed and Seed and he can't string two words together without he talks about diversifying and expansion and hard goods and profit. Archie, he goes to law school. Good thing Hank was already dead because Hank hated lawyers. Hank was a union man. Hank loved the union the way some folks love God or baseball. But Archie's a lawyer and him and his family live over in the new part of town and they even got a television set. They want me to come over and watch their television set, but I say no, I'll just stay here and watch my old dog and whatever flies come to roost and the honeysuckle when it cares to flower. Now, though, I know I'll have to call Archie and Will and say something about a refrigerator because I can't live without ice. I go in and check the icebox and the cake has got another day, maybe more, so I can wait to phone. I chip me off some ice and go back out to the porch and my dream.

It's a new dream. Not real new, but since Christmas, maybe, or some holiday like that. Before, I only dreamed of Ben little, running up these steps and falling and hurting his knee and his little arms around my neck while I carry him into the house and wash the blood and mud off him, my lips against his sweet cheek. Or little Ben in the bathwater taking the suds from his hair and putting them on his chin and saying to me, ho ho ho, like he was Santy Claus. Or little Ben all dressed up to be a pirate on Halloween and coming into the kitchen where I am making popcorn balls, coming up behind me and saying "Boo!" and scaring me out of my wits. But in this new dream, I am in the middle of the amphibious assault on Manila Bay. The fighting is going on all around me, but it don't notice me and I don't pay no mind to the shocks and shells, the blast and shriek all around while I am looking for my son. I am in my old dress like the one I got on now and my old green checked apron that's wore through here and there and I kneel in the mud beside a body I know is Ben. I pull him into my lap and turn him over slowly. The first few times I have this dream, that's all I do: just kneel and turn him over, glad to see his face is only muddy, no blood or nothing. I am glad they have not shot up his face. But lately in my dream I find fresh water from somewheres and I bathe that mud from his face and I am so happy that with the mud washed off, it is still perfect.

Maybe Ben didn't die in the mud, but that's the way I dream it, so that's how it is, even if that ain't how it was. I rock on this porch and suck on the ice and wait for the dream to come get me, even though I can hear the dog snuffling and kids' voices somewheres, kids up to no good, no doubt, and the foxtails rasping against one another and the weight of this honeysuckle vine sagging down on the porch and pretty soon I don't hear no kids or dog, nor nothing but the fighting going on all around me in Manila Bay and I scrape the mud from my son's beautiful young face, his nice tanned skin and fine mouth, his sandy colored hair and I bathe his closed eyes with fresh water. I kiss his eyes.

After a time the sun squints under that tin roof and lights up my eyelids bright and I know it's time to quit the dream and go in and get supper for me and this old dog. I heave my bones out of the rocker and the dog follows me to the kitchen. I don't worry about losing the dream. It will come back and it don't scare me in the least because I know it means I have accepted Ben's death and God's will and I am not fighting God any longer.

Ben's death near killed me. They said I was wild with grief. They said they couldn't figure it because I had took Hank's death so well. Well, of course I did. Hank and me, we had our good times, we had our family and our laughs and our cries and a few beers after the boys were abed, our days on this porch, our nights in that old bed for nearly twenty-five years and always, even in the worst of the Depression, Hank always had work with the railroad and our boys never knew the cramp of hunger in the gut. Me and Hank, we had all of that, but Ben was only twenty-two. Ben had nothing unless you count that slut Connie, which I don't.

I didn't always think she was a slut. I used to like her. A pretty girl. Plump and pink and blue-eyed and mad for Ben. She set her cap for him and she went after him and if Connie Frett had been my daughter, I'd have tanned her hide before I'd let her run after a boy like that, but she got him. They was in love and they

493

couldn't keep their eyes off one another—or their hands neither is my guess. After Ben died I kept watch on Connie Frett, hoping I'd see her sprout a big belly, but I told myself it wouldn't be Ben's baby anyway. He had been gone too long. But Connie was a good girl in her way and after Ben died, she couldn't do enough for me. She was over here all the time, like we had to be together because we was the only ones who loved Ben that much. I shared her grief, but I couldn't let her share mine. She and me, we'd come out on this porch in the evenings and sit on the steps together and I'd say, thank you for cooking supper, Connie, and for cleaning up, or thank you for sweeping the porch and dusting up the place, Connie. And then she'd put her head in my lap and weep and I'd pat her back. We'd stay that way for a long time, but I couldn't let her share my grief. That was all my very own.

After a while she quit coming over so regular and folks said Connie was coming out of it and wasn't that good and I said, yes it was. They said the war was over and the boys all home and wasn't that good and I said yes. But I got lonely after Connie quit coming and it was just me and Ben and this old dog left here and no more Connie flinging herself into my lap, sobbing her eyes out and needing me.

Then one night, I get a knock on my door and it's Connie Frett. She looks real pretty with a gardenia in her hair and a yellow cotton dress on. She leans down and pats this old dog and then she smiles up at me and says: Hi Manila.

That's my lawful name, Manila. I was born the same time Admirable Dewey took Manila Bay, when we whipped them Spanish and showed them what real Americans was made of. My mother told me folks was mad with victory and she could hear my father telling Dr. Tipton that he was going to name me Admirable Dewey and that the doctor pointed out that no girl could go around St. Elmo being called Admirable Dewey. It was the doctor suggested Manila and everyone agreed that was just the perfect name for a baby girl.

I said: What brings you by, Connie? I took two Coca-Colas out of the icebox and we sat on the front porch step, her pink arm next to my brown one, her yellow dress next to my green checked apron and the smell of her gardenia washing over us. She told me she was getting married in a week and she didn't

494

want me hearing it from nobody else. "I'm marrying Michael Kehoe. He fought in Europe and he's home now. He was on the football team with Ben. Maybe you remember him, Manila."

"I don't remember no one but the quarterback."

"Ben was the quarterback."

"I know."

"Ben and Mike Kehoe were very good friends, Manila. They loved cars and football. They were a lot alike."

"No one was like Ben."

"No," she says, slow, pulling the word out taut, like bread dough till it frays and tatters in the middle. "I thought I would die when Ben died. I wanted to die." Connie swallows hard. I hear it. "If I couldn't die, then I wanted to grieve for him my whole life. But I can't."

"Who says you should?" I ask, swilling my Coca-Cola.

"I'm young," she goes on. "I love Michael Kehoe, not like I loved Ben, but I love him and I'm going to marry him and be a good wife to him."

"You never deserved Ben anyway," I say, hating myself, but saying it just the same. "You were a slut."

Connie stood and handed me back the Coke bottle. She brushed off the seat of her yellow dress and started to walk down the path to the gate which you could see in them days because the foxtails hadn't yet growed over it. She gets halfway to the gate and she calls back, sad-like, "I guess Ben is all yours now, Manila."

I don't say nothing. I stay where I am and keep hold on the dog so he don't go after her. I want to ask Connie if she had ever made love with my boy Ben. I'd like to know he had a girl's love before he died. That isn't so much to ask. But I don't say nothing. I just sit here on the step and watch her yellow dress go out of the gate when you could still see the gate because the foxtails hadn't growed over it yet.

"I can't have the new fridge delivered, Ma, until you get these foxtails cut down." That's what Archie says to me, standing on the front porch, popping sweat and I tell him he wouldn't be so hot if he didn't wear vests and wool suits in summer. He laughs. He says, "Ma, that's part of my job. Who ever heard of a lawyer in overalls?"

495

"A mule in a party dress is still a mule."

"Yes, well, what about these foxtails? Let me send a boy over here to cut them down. Hell, Ma, I'll do it myself if you'd let me, but I'm telling you, they won't deliver the fridge until they can get through the yard."

"Then you do it," I tell him. "Only don't wear no suit."

So Archie and Will both come over and cut down my nice foxtails and pretty soon some men come into my kitchen and push the icebox in the corner and puff and huff and bring in a refrigerator and plug it in. I tell them: all I want is some ice. They show me these little trays that you put fresh water in and put them in the freezer and wait a long time and you get ice.

Real nice ice and lots of it. Enough for my Coca-Cola and some for me to drop down my dress and a square or two for the dog so's we can come out here on the porch and rock and let my dream come back to me: the mud of Manila Bay soaking over my skirt and up my knees as I kneel with Ben in my arms and the battle shrieking around us, guns booming and men screaming and mud. Me with my fresh water bathing Ben's beautiful young face, his hair, opening the collar of his uniform and washing the mud from his neck. I pull him tighter into my arms and put my weathered cheek against his perfect one.

Then one day, sometime later, I know it must have been later because my dream wasn't new anymore, but an old dream, I was sitting on the porch, in summer. Anyway, it was hot. I was having my dream when I hear voices and I think it's the soldiers in the battle and I think it's strange I can hear them at last, but it's not soldiers and pretty soon I know it. Other voices. Calling at me. *Manila Dance has ants in her pants . . . Manila Dance has ants* I come to and the dog is barking and snarling and I smell the smoke from the battle all around me. The dog don't leave my side, but sniffs and squeals and looks up at me and barks when I say, "Holy Frijole, they've set us afire!" The smoke was thick everywhere now, but I couldn't see no flames, just a curtain of smoke and that awful chant to cut through it *Manila Dance has ants in her*

Me and the dog run into the house. He must have run under a bed, but I go straight to the piano and snatch all Ben's pictures off, the one in his football uniform and holding his helmet, his graduation picture and the other one of him when he joined up

496

the army, so smart looking and beautiful. Then I grab the wedding picture of me and Hank and my coin purse with all my money. I pull off my green apron and make a bag of it and throw the pictures in and I see I got room for the pictures of Will and Archie when they was little, before Ben came along. I tie it all up quick and make a run for the kitchen and the back door. I can see flames in the service porch and burnt my hand on the back doorknob and I could see the wringer washing machine starting to pop and crackle with the heat, so I run back to Ben's bedroom, but the window is locked. I break it with my elbow and throw my pictures out and call for the dog and he comes bounding and we leap out, me getting a long jagged cut down my leg which I don't notice just then because I hear sirens coming from all directions, blasting and blaring through the smoke. By the time me and the dog have got to the street, the fire department has got their hoses pumping and spraying the house and drowning the yard, fighting their way in the front door through the smoke. I stay as close by the house as they'll let me. I see the blood pouring out my leg. I kneel there and hold my dog and my pictures and I think: this is how it was in my dream, the smoke and ash and soot and blood, the mud, even, of Manila Bay.

Me and the dog have to stay with Will and Mrs. Will and their three children that night and Archie comes over, growling and snarling about how the police have already caught the little bastards that done it and how Archie is going to see they get their little bastard asses locked up for good and always.

But it didn't happen that way. Me and Will and Archie sat in court and listened to the judge rap them boys' little knuckles a few times and say they was never to come near my place again. Then he turns it on the parents and gives them a lot of ragging about their children being a menace to the public safety and how their children was their responsibility and then he says Case Dismissed. Just then one of the little bastards' fathers stands up and says to the Judge. "While you're at it, Your Honor, why don't you do something about her?" (He points to me.) "I ask you, is she responsible? Is anyone who lives in a fire trap and a pig sty and never comes out, who looses her dog on little children, isn't she a menace to the public safety? That woman is crazy, Your Honor, and a threat to property! She's forcing us all out of the neighborhood! She's crazy and she ought to be locked up for good and always!"

497

"Stuff it where the sun don't shine!" I yell, but then Will gets hold of my arm and marches me out of the courtroom and tells me for Chrissake to shut up.

He drives me to his house, a new one with a lot of other new ones all around it and skinny little trees in front and a pool out back. We all sit by the pool and drink lemonade. (Mrs. Will don't allow no Coca-Cola in her house. She says it will rot nails and just think what it will do to your teeth and brains.) They say they want me to come and live with them. Which I say no. Then Archie and Mrs. Archie drive up and come out to the pool too. They say: Why don't we get you a nice apartment, Ma? You don't need that big house anymore, living all by yourself. The yard is just too much for you. There's lots of nice apartments in St. Elmo nowadays, new ones. You could have neighbors and live close to shopping and not have Shirley do your shopping for you.

"I never asked Mrs. Will to do nothing for me," I tell them. "She just does it and she won't never take no for an answer. I'm not moving. Hank bought that house and that's where he lived till he died and that's where I'll live till I die."

Will says: "The house is ruint now, Ma."

"It's just blacked up a little from the smoke and the service porch gone, that's all. No more washing machine. I don't wash too much anyway."

Archie says: "Ma, fifty years ago Guadalupe Street might have been a good neighborhood, even twenty or thirty years ago, but it's just not anymore. That man was right, Ma. All the nice people are moving out."

"What do I care? I don't have no dealings with the neighbors and once the foxtails grow back, I don't even have to see them. Why, once them foxtails grow back, I could live next door to the White House and not see President Roosevelt."

"Roosevelt?" said Mrs. Archie with a little gag. "Roosevelt's dead, Mom. Roosevelt's been dead for ten years. Eisenhower's the President now."

"Eisenhower's the general."

They all look from one to the other. They tell me about how the general got to be the President. Then they go back to talking about the apartment I should live in and neighbors and shopping, but I don't have to hear it. I crunch on my ice and it fills up my ears. I drink my lemonade, wishing I had a Coke and wondering

498

how it could be that so much time had passed since they quit delivering the ice and wondering if my refrigerator still worked and how long it would take the foxtails to grow back and if I could bear to sit on the porch till they did.

They all shout and snuffle at me, but the next day I get Mrs. Will to drive me back to my own house. I won't let her come in. I am glad to be rid of her. Of all of them. A week at Will's is like a year and a half anywhere else. Maybe I been there longer than a week. My house still stinks of smoke, but the wet's almost all dried up, everything except the couch and the chair; they are still wet and they are starting to smell. The television set don't work either.

I tell the dog, let's get to work. First thing is to open all the windows and get the smell of battle out. Then I undo the knot on my green apron and take my pictures out and use the apron to give the piano a nice dust up, to get the ash and cinders off. The wood is all buckled up, but I don't play anyhow. It was always Ben like to thump the piano and grin at Connie Frett while she swooned alongside him. The pictures I left on the piano, they got wet, but not burnt and that's all I really care about anyway.

First I put my wedding picture back up and then I put the one of Will and Archie when they was little. I look at it. I move it so it sits between the one of Will and Mrs. Will, and their family and the one of Archie and Mrs. Archie and their family. Look at that, will you? Will and Archie are getting old! I wonder why I never noticed it in the flesh. Then I say to myself: Manila, it's because you never much look at them in the flesh. But I think on them now, think on them hard, on what they look like now. Will's hair is all pepper and salt and he's got one more chin than God gave him. Archie's hair clings alongside his ears, but it has deserted the top of his head and Archie has a paunch. Will and Archie never was no beauties (and their children ditto and their wives the same), but I had never before noticed that they are getting old.

I reach down and pick up Ben's pictures and set them on the piano, first the football one and then high school graduation and then Ben in his uniform. I touch his beautiful young face. Ben will never grow old, Ben will never be bald or have a paunch or gray hair. Everyone else will change, but not Ben. I pick up the uniform picture and press it to me, but I have to sit down at the piano bench because I get dizzy when I think how it's been ten years since Roosevelt died, since all the boys come home. I get weak when I think how pretty soon everyone will forget all about the boys that didn't come home. No one will remember them. They won't have no children to look like them. The dead don't have no law offices with their names on shingles, don't have their pictures in the paper cutting ribbons for new stores. The boys that didn't come home don't have friends and families and boys of their own who will go to high school and court girls in yellow cotton dresses with gardenias in their hair. Ben won't have none of that. Ever. I hold Ben's picture but I won't cry because I have accepted his death and God's will. I hear a voice come into my ear, steady as the drone of a gnat. *Ben has you, Manila. You're all Ben's got, Manila. Ben and you will live in this house till you die.* I start to cry then and the dog comes over and rubs against my bandaged leg. He thinks I am crying for Ben's death, but I have accepted Ben's death. I am crying because Ben won't have no life. I am crying because I am all the life Ben has and he deserves better than me. I am crying because I know when I die, Ben will die too. He will stay forever young and beautiful and die when I do and no one will ever know he once lived. No one will remember how he filled my arms with his baby body, how he said ho ho ho in the bathwater and Boo at Halloween, that he brought in the newspaper or teased me for the cherries on my hat, that he grinned at Connie Frett while he sat on this piano bench. I slide to the floor with the dog. I cry into his dog smell and promise Ben that when I die they'll put Ben's name on the stone too. Ben don't have no stone in St. Elmo. Ben's buried in the Philippines, but he won't die till I do. Ben Dance 1923–1945, Manila Dance, 1898 to whenever she dies. Ben and Manila, they died together, knee deep in the mud and blood and smoke and stink of battle, the last battle of Manila, the one they fought in St. Elmo, California.

The dog died first. He was old and he just went peaceful in his sleep, but I couldn't lift him so I waited until Mrs. Will come with my groceries and then I told her the dog died and she said she would call Will at the Home Center.

"The what?" I say.

"Sit down, Mom, and relax and I'll make you a cup of coffee." While she's making the coffee, she goes on about how there ain't no Feed and Seed anymore, but the St. Elmo Home Center which carries everything for the Do-It-Yourselfer. She leaves me in the kitchen with the coffee and I hear her go into the living-room and dial the phone and tell Will how he better bring the Home Center truck for the dog, how he better do it fast because she don't know exactly when the dog died. Then she waits for a bit and adds that I might go round the bend if I see the Humane Society truck. I wonder what bend she's talking about since I never leave this house.

Mrs. Will comes back in the kitchen and pours herself a cup of coffee and sits at the table with me and starts to gab like she always does about her kids and what fine things they're doing. Like I could care. I can't even keep their names straight, or which one's got foil all over his teeth and which ones don't. I am wondering what I will do without that old dog. I never liked him and he was mangy and ugly, but we got on and he was a good watch dog. He always heard the kids nosing about the place and he'd snarl and take after them till he got too old. He was mangy, but he was useful. And in the middle of my thinking about the dog, I hear Mrs. Will say something about Connie. "Connie? Connie Frett? Ben's girlfriend?"

"Connie Kehoe, Mom. She came into the Home Center the other day with her husband and we had a real nice chat. She's got three kids now, a boy and two little girls. Mike's going to re-light the kitchen for her, fluorescent light, the latest thing, and they've just poured a new patio too.

"Connie asked after you, Mom. She was real concerned, you living here all by yourself in this bad neighborhood. She said she read in the newspaper about the fire. I told her how we've been trying to get you to move for years now and how stubborn you are." Mrs. Will stopped there like I am supposed to laugh or apologize or say how nice that was. I wipe my nose with my hand. "Connie says she keeps meaning to come over and see you one day, but with all those kids, she just can't—"

"I don't want to see her or no one. You tell her. You tell her she better not come around Guadalupe Street, not her, or no one else. Bad enough I have to jaw and pass the time of day with the meter reader and the mailman, though I don't get no mail no

501

more, just stuff for occupant. I don't even get no bills anymore, come to think of it. I can't remember the last time I got a bill or anything with my real name on it. Manila Dance. I miss the ice man."

Mrs. Will pats my hand and says that was because all my bills now went to Will and Archie and they pay them and wasn't I lucky to have two such fine sons.

"I got three sons," I tell her. "Three and don't you forget it. Don't none of you forget Ben just because he's dead and you're not."

"I didn't mean it like that, Mom. I'm sure if Ben had lived—"

But I get up and go to the fridge for a Coke because I can't stand to hear it from her lips, what Ben might have done if he'd lived. He didn't live. He didn't grow old and fat like Will or fat and bald like Archie. Ben died in Manila Bay. Ben lives in Manila Dance. And then I heard Connie Frett's voice float back to me, past all the years and foxtails, *I guess Ben is all yours now, Manila*. And I thought: she knew it, even then, that little slut of a girl, she knew what would happen to Ben and I did not.

I go to the sink and wash my face and Mrs. Will says she's real sorry about the dog.

Then one day in the spring, they all come over, all the grandchildren and Will and Archie and their wives all dressed up and they brung me a cake and a puppy and told me Happy Birthday. They told me I was sixty and they got me this dog for my birthday. They said his name was Lucky.

I hated the little bastard. He peed on everything and got under my feet and was always climbing up on the bed like it was his. I kicked him off, but he always come back and pretty soon I got so's I couldn't remember the other dog that much and I sort of liked this frisky one, but I told him he wasn't getting nothing special from me and he'd have to earn his keep just like the old one done.

One morning I wake up to hear him barking like a sonofabitch. I put on my robe and open the door so he can go out and pee, but he tears up through the foxtails and then I hear an "Ooof! Ouch! Help! Call off this damn dog! Ow!"

I wait a little, maybe count to ten. Maybe twelve. Then I call the dog off. I go out to this bimbo and ask him what he's doing in

502

my yard. He points to the sign he has just hammered in amongst the foxtails, just about buried in foxtails and right next to the fence. It says:

PUBLIC NOTICE

These premises constitute a public hazard. They will be cleared within thirty (30) days of the date hereon in accordance with Civic Code #452-12-J, Article 5. The owners of title shall clear said property or be fined appropriate to Property Code 21569.

I say: "What the hell does that mean?"

He says: "It means you clean up this pigsty, lady, or they're going to cart you off to the funny farm."

I make like I am going to let go of the dog. He leaves.

Archie come over that night and he says the sign don't mean that exactly. Archie says the City of St. Elmo was very concerned for the fire hazard my house and yard presented. I said there wouldn't be no fire, nor no hazard as long as no bastard brats torched my place, but Archie says that's all five years ago now and that this summer's been especially hot and dry and that the city was afraid that if a passer-by flicked his cigarette into my foxtails, the whole neighborhood would go up in flames. He said of course I wouldn't want that on my conscience.

I said I didn't give a good goddamn. I didn't know any of my neighbors and anyway, they was all a long ways from my house. "Least I got a real yard," I told Archie, "One half acre of real yard, not like that postage stamp with a pool you call your back yard."

Archie started to go on about the city some more, but I watch the electric light gleaming off the top of his head. He don't have no hair there at all anymore. Is Archie just about the same age Hank was when he died? Is he? He don't look like Hank. Hank always had hair. Maybe Archie looks like me, but I reach up top of my head and I got hair too and then remember that I don't know what I look like anymore so how could I know who Archie looks like? My face swims up to Archie's for a closer look, but all I can tell for certain is that Archie don't look like Ben. Ben is still

503

twenty-two and in the mud and I start to tell Archie about my old dream, about how it was scaring me now because even though I had accepted Ben's death and God's will, I was scared, too scared to go on with my dream where I have got Ben's shirt unbuttoned, open, but I can't do nothing more. What if I get his shirt off and find him all bloody and blasted? No, God, please God, no, don't let his flesh be shredded before my eyes. What if I get my son's shirt off his shoulders and back and find he don't have no back, no shoulders, no body that's not bloodied into pulp? Oh, Archie, what if the mud turns red? I can't remember where Ben took the bullets, Archie, or how it was he died at all except for Manila Bay and I . . .

"Now, Ma, let me call the doctor, Ma. Please. Better yet, let me take you to the hospital. They can help you, Ma. Really. They can help you get along with other people. Just a little stay at the hospital, that's all you need. Just to get away from this house and stay where the doctors can help you forget the past and get on with your life."

Well what could I do but laugh out loud? I laughed so hard that dog jumped up and waved its little black tail like I was about to throw him a bone and when I was through laughing, I said, "The first person who comes here to cut them weeds gets shot. And the first doctor who comes near me, he gets shot too. My life is getting on just fine, Archie Dance, without no doctors and without no hospitals and your life is getting on too, Archie, and if you once looked in the mirror you'd see it. You're old, Archie. You're old and fat and you won't never be young and beautiful again."

Archie took his hat off the table and jammed it on his bald head. He said: "That's the way it happens to the living, Ma."

I told him to save it for the jury and leave me be.

They come to cut the foxtails and just like I promised, I holler out the window that I have a shotgun and I am about to blow them to bits. I didn't have no gun, but it sounded good.

The guy hollers back that he was leaving, but that he'd be back with a court order signed by my own son, Judge Archibald Dance.

I turned to the little dog and I said, "Just imagine Archie being a judge and never telling me." The little dog looked at me funny and that's when I thought maybe Archie had told me. I went to the piano and asked Ben what he thought of Archie being a judge and Ben give me his old boyish grin and said this was our foxtail foxhole, our fortress and wouldn't no one get in, judge or no judge. I laughed and turned Ben's picture so he could see the TV. We like the game shows and cartoons best of all. I eat my lunch with Sheriff Sam and the Cartoon Corral.

I must have fell asleep because there was something else on the TV, the picture sputtering up and down when I woke to the sound of a knock on my door. The dog woke up too. (He never was as good a watchdog as the old one.) I go to the door and there stands this blond kid, pink and pale and kind of fat, his blue eyes big with fright. He keeps licking his lips. He says: "I'm Danny Kehoe." He looks over his shoulder. "My mother's down the walk, there, just outside the gate."

I say: "Tell it to the marines. I don't want any."

"My mother, Connie Kehoe, she wants to know if you want me to cut your grass. You talk to her."

He makes like he's going to call her, but I say, real quick, I say, "No, I don't want to see her." I stare at this boy and I can see Connie Frett all over him, but the foxtails are so nice and high that I can't see Connie down at the gate. The boy is thirteen or fourteen, maybe, fat like Connie was when she first set her cap for Ben. I say: "I don't have no grass and I like the foxtails just as they are."

He looks like he wants to run or pee his pants, but he licks his lips again and says, "My mother said I was to do for you whatever might need doing here. She says I'm to do it for you and your boy."

"For Ben?" I say, "For Ben?"

"I don't know his name."

"For Ben," I say again and this time I smile.

Twice a month that boy come. I wouldn't let him touch the foxtails, but he cleared off the tumbleweeds and picked up the trash and cleared away the last of the wreck from the fire, the wringer washer and a mattress I had throwed out too. He said he didn't think there'd be another war and I didn't have to save my tin cans no more and if I got rid of them, maybe I wouldn't have so much mice. He said, if I wanted the mice, he'd leave the cans be. I let him use Ben's little red wagon to gather them cans all up and put them in bags and take them out to the street so the trashmen could come and get them. He said the trash people come Monday on Guadalupe Street and when he come on Saturday, he'd put my trash out. Those Saturdays he didn't come, the trash don't go out. Then one day he shows up hauling a bright trash can, so shiny it makes you blink and he says he got it at the Home Center, that Will give it to him. Connie's boy trimmed back the honeysuckle so it didn't weigh so heavy on the tin roof over the porch, then he put some props alongside the railings and said he would fix the raingutters, but then he looked at them and they were too rotted to fix. He even fixed the window in Ben's room, the one I'd put my elbow through escaping from the fire. I always just stuffed newspapers there to keep out the wind and cold and animals, but he fixed it up with glass and he said Will told him he could have whatever he needed to fix my place up. Danny said since Will was giving away, why not some new raingutters? I said: Why not? Then Danny said: "I'll do the raingutters, Manila, and then I'll trim the foxtails."

While Connie's boy was working I'd remember how Connie used to moon about this yard waiting for Ben to finish his chores so he could take her to the matinee and then out for a soda. When Connie's boy finished up his chores, me and him always had a Coke if it was hot, or coffee if it was cold. He liked his coffee just the way Ben did, with sugar and milk and lots of it. I started having Mrs. Will buy more sugar and milk and asked for some cookies too. Danny said Oreos were his favorite.

One afternoon while we was having coffee, Danny flips on the TV Archie got me after the fire. Danny asks me what's wrong with it. Nothing, I tell him. It works fine. Danny says I'd get a lot more channels if I'd let him put an aerial up, but I didn't know what that was. He said it was no never mind and he'd get it from Will at the Home Center. Even though the next day was Sunday, Danny come back over and he spends the whole afternoon on the roof handing me down wire and calling back and forth while we slid the wire in the window and he used some little pliers to diddle the back of the TV. Then, up he goes again, back on the roof and tells me to holler when the picture is the best. "Just imagine," I said when he come back down, "just imagine all that was going on TV all the time and I never got nothing but Channel 11 and Channel 13."

506

"Now you can watch the football games, Manila," Danny said, but I told him I hadn't been to a football game since Ben graduated from high school and he said they had them on TV now and you could watch football and not leave the comfort of your own home.

After that, Danny'd come earlier and stay later and watch the football games with me. He explained the game. I didn't get it, but I pretended I did. I asked a lot of questions because it was so nice to hear a boy talk about football like Ben used to do. One day Danny asked me why I didn't get some beer so I put it on my list for Mrs. Will and she near puked when she read it. Next thing I know I got Archie in my living room ragging on me about buying beer for miners.

"There's no miners in St. Elmo," I tell him. "St. Elmo's a railroad town."

Archie's face rumples up like a baked potato. "Ma," he says, "we are all very pleased at what Danny Kehoe has been able to do for you. We are very pleased that you will let him help out around here and you ought to know that I have offered both him and Connie money and they won't take it."

"Money for what?"

"There's been a great transformation in you and in this place in the last two years, Ma."

"Years?" I say, "*two years?*"

"But if he is going to ask you to buy beer for him, I must tell him to quit coming, it's against the law and—"

"Don't you dare, Archie Dance! Don't you dare! What's it to you, Mr. Judge Dance, if I have a couple of beers? I'm not buying it for Danny. I'm buying it for me and Ben. We like a beer now and then and who are you to tell us we can't have one?"

So a six pack of beer come with the groceries, but only once a month. Mrs. Will said that was all I needed. I didn't like the beer as much as I like Coke, but it was nice to have a beer with Danny while we watched football after he done the chores. He even painted the porch and the smell come all over the house. I breathed it in. Ben painted the porch once, just before he joined up.

One afternoon I hear a knock and I go to the door and it's Danny and he's wearing a gorilla mask. Scared the living Bejesus out of me. He has a sack of candy in his hand. "It's Halloween,

507

Manila," says Danny, lifting his mask. "And I think I'll just sit here this year and hand out the candy and keep trouble away. We don't want any trouble like last year when those kids broke your window, do we?"

"There's no beer, Danny," I tell him. "We drunk it all up."

"Well, I'll stay here and hold down the fort and you go to Garcia's and get us a six pack."

"I couldn't."

"Sure you could, Manila. Garcia's store is just down the street three blocks. This side. You can't miss it."

"No." I start to back away, but Danny comes up to me and I see that he's taller than me. I come to the same place on Danny that I used to come to on Ben. Danny is still pink and blond like Connie but he's not fat anymore. He's tall.

He takes my old coat off the hook and helps me into it. "What's Halloween without a few beers, Manila? Don't worry, I'll fight off the troops."

That's what I said to Garcia (or whoever it was behind the till). I said: What's Halloween without a few beers? And Garcia says *Si Si* and rolled his eyes toward heaven. He says: Very happy to help you, Manila and I say: How'd you know my name? And he says: Everyone knows you, Manila. You are the crazy lady of Guadalupe Street. Crazy Manila, our lady of Guadalupe.

I squint at Garcia and at one or two others squatting on their haunches near the counter. I say: Boo!

We had a good laugh over that and I go back with the beer. When the kids come to the door, I say: Boo! while Danny stands behind me in his gorilla mask handing out the candy and them kids don't know whether to laugh or run or blubber. We don't get no little kids. Just big ones and when Danny tells them no funny stuff this year, they look at one another and say: Funny stuff? Funny stuff? Oh, I laughed over and over and when Danny left, I told him that was the best Halloween since Ben was a pirate and I was sorry it wouldn't come around again for another year.

After that I went to Garcia's pretty often for beer and maybe twice a week besides, just to get some little thing, some animal crackers for the dog and a box of Cheez-its for me, a bar of Palmolive. Mrs. Will would ask where I got these little things when she brung my regular groceries and I told her I bought them

508

myself. She said that was very good. She said Danny and Garcia were good for me. She said I was getting better. I told her I wasn't sick.

Still, I might have been getting better, but it certainly didn't have nothing to do with Danny or Garcia. It was my dream that was making me happy. I didn't have the dream so often now, but when I did, I could peel Ben's shirt from his shoulders, from his arms, and back and not find no blood nor blasted flesh. He hadn't been shot to bits anywhere. He was still whole and perfect. I washed the mud off him and pulled him into my arms and put his head against my shoulder and held him, my cheek pressed close to his hair, and sang. And sometimes, even though the mud stayed in my dream, the battle didn't. All I could hear was myself singing, no shriek and blast, no groans of others dying, no shot and shell, just my singing to Ben. And when I'd wake, I'd go in to the piano and look at Ben and it made me happy to know that he hadn't been bloodied up and blown apart, that he was still perfect and young and nothing could ever touch him. And I was happy for me too because me and Ben, we had a good life together and he needed me and I was always here for him.

Danny asked me about him once and I showed him Ben's picture on the piano. Danny said Connie told him they'd been friends in high school. "You wouldn't recognize the place anymore, Manila."

"What place?" I asked, all ready to tell him more about Ben.

"St. Elmo High. They got a new auditorium now and a Senior Quad and a new cafeteria and they're fixing up the boys' gym with a new wing. Mom says she doesn't recognize it, except for some of the old teachers." He winks at me. "Some of them are just about as old as you can get and still draw breath."

"You think they might remember Ben?"

"Hell, Manila, they remember Moses. Anyway, you ought to come to my graduation and see the old place."

"I haven't been to a graduation since Ben's."

"Then you come to mine. I'll see you get an invite."

I went to the St. Elmo High graduation, but not because of Danny. One of Archie's boys was Valedictorian of the Class of 1965. I listened to the speeches, but I was looking for Danny amongst the 700 up there. "Seven hundred," I said to Mrs. Archie. "Just imagine St. Elmo High so big they have 700 graduates."

"There's two other high schools too, you know, Mom," she whispers.

"There is? They got 700 too?"

"Hush, Mom. Here comes Ronald. It's Ronald's turn to speak."

I tried to remember how many had graduated with me, but I couldn't even remember my graduating at all. But Ben's, I could remember that. How many graduated with the Class of 1942? They didn't have no auditorium in those days. They had the graduation on the grass out front of the school. Hotter than hell it was. I remember the cherries on my hat clacking when I clapped for the speeches they give, lots of talk about the vile Japs who snuck up and bombed Pearl Harbor and who beat General MacArthur out of the Philippines and everyone that day was talking about the war and the great destiny these boys was going off to and how they would fight in the name of freedom and give their lives and sacred honor and I clapped like everyone else. But I didn't believe it. I didn't believe a word of it. I didn't believe it for a minute that Ben would die in the mud at Manila. Not Ben Dance. Ben's life lay all before him. *Yes, all three years of it.*

"Stop it, Mom. Stop. Archie, do something with her."

"Hand me a handkerchief. Hush, Ma. We want to hear Ronald. Hush, dammit, Ma, hush!"

"Archie, do something!"

The next thing I know we are out of the auditorium and standing by a drinking fountain and Archie wets down the handkerchief and mops my face and says he knew they shouldn't have brung me.

There was a war after Danny's graduation too. Sometimes I watched it on TV now that I get a lot of stations. Danny joined up the Army, but he told me not to worry. He said they would send him to Germany where he could drink all the beer he wanted. I told him Germany was enemy, same as the Japs. Danny said, "Not this time, Manila. The Germans and Japs are our friends now."

"Not my friends."

"It's the gooks who are the enemy now. Gooks for enemies. Gooks for allies. Can't tell the difference anymore."

"Where are they fighting?"

"In Vietnam."

"Is that close to Manila?"

"Hell no, you don't have to worry. You're safe here in St. Elmo."

They sent Danny to Manila and he sent me a lot of post cards which I taped to the piano. He wrote on them he thought I'd like to see the city I was named for. It looked pretty and green and tropical and moist and not at all like St. Elmo which is dry and dusty and brown except for two weeks in the winter when it floods.

St. Elmo is dry and dusty and brown as leather, I wrote in my first letter in a thousand years. I didn't have no pen, just the stub of a pencil I use for my grocery list and the paper Mrs. Will leaves me to write on. I found an envelope back of my bureau and I wrote out Danny's name and his address which was just a lot of numbers mainly. Course I don't have no stamps so I put on my coat to walk to the post office, the one near my house, or what I remember near my house, but there was a parking lot and a Sav-On drug there and no one ever heard of a post office. I thought I probably turned the wrong way and I would just go back, and I turned the wrong way again, and maybe again after that, because I couldn't find my house, couldn't find nothing, only the Dairy Queen and 7-11, the Lotus Blossom and Jolly Burger and Quik Photo and cars. Lots of cars. Cars everywhere. How could St. Elmo be so big and bright and ugly and have so much noise? No more oleanders and the palms all so tall I couldn't see the tops. I hang onto my letter like it is Danny's hand, but there is no one to lead me and I am loster and loster in St. Elmo where I have lived my whole life. A girl finds me in the dark, a Jap girl wearing a shirt that says Lotus Blossom and she wants to know what I am doing by the dumpster where it is so dark and cold. I push my face into the dark of my hands till my hands light up bright with flashing lights whirling around, red and blue and dizzy. A policeman comes up. I hear leather creak and squeal when he kneels down, before I hear his voice asking where I live. He takes hold my hand, the one with the letter, but I tell him that letter is mine and he gives me back my hand and

511

takes my elbow to stand me up. Where do you live, he says again and again. Where do you live, old lady? I tell him I am our crazy lady of Guadalupe Street. He puts me in the car where there is a lot of squawking and squealing. He drives to the Dairy Queen and tells me to wait. He comes back with a hamburger in a little white bag and a Coke. I drink the Coke all up before we get to the police station.

Pretty soon I see Archie. All the police say: Sorry, Your Honor, we didn't know she was your mother.

Archie says: I commend you all for the care you've taken of her.

The police all seem to line up and open doors for us as bald Archie leads me out to his big black car. He says he is taking me home with him. He says he has moved and how he lives up in the hills and out of the smog. I pull my coat around me. "I don't care where you live now," I tell him. "I don't want to go home with you. I want to go home with me. Take me to my house. And mail this letter on the way."

"Who could you be writing to, Ma?"

"I have a friend in Manila," I tell him. "That's where Ben died, you know."

"I know Ben died, Ma, but you don't."

I am glad to see he turns the car around, but I don't say nothing more till we get to my house and the little dog is glad to see me. Archie walks in and turns on all the lights. Then he says: "You ever pull a stunt like that again, Ma, and I swear, I'll have you committed. I should have had you committed years and years ago. This is a warning. You better heed me or it's the state hospital for you. The loony bin, Ma. You understand? The funny farm."

After that I put stamps on my shopping list for Mrs. Will. I quit going to Garcia's. (Though one New Year's Garcia brung me some tamales which I thanked him for, but they were too weird for me. I fed them to the dog who farted all night.) The foxtails started growing back up and I thought: I'll just wait for Danny to get back from Manila before I cut them, but a long time must have passed because they grew up over the fence again and Will and Archie come over with their boys and they spend one whole day cutting them down and not taking no for an answer. The paint chipped off the porch Danny painted and the raingutter fell

512

off again and when Halloween came around, I didn't say Boo to no one. I sat in the dark, in the corner between the piano and the wall, holding my picture of Ben and hoping them kids would go away and not set fire to my house again.

I waited for the mailman to bring me some more post cards from Manila, but Danny didn't send no more. One or two letters, scribbled so bad it looked like I might have wrote them. No pictures. In my letter I said: Please send me some more picture post cards for my piano. Then Danny wrote me a letter. He said there wasn't no post cards where he was now, only heat and rain and mud.

"Mud?" I said to the dog. "Mud?" I held on to the porch rail and stood up slow. *Mud?* I felt my heart quicken and thud in my breast, hard thuds like dirt clods flying and spraying in my eyes and mouth. I got to my bed and the dog followed and loaded his old bones on the bed at my feet to keep them warm, but the rest of me was cold. I lay there and I wondered if I was going to die. I prayed to God I wouldn't die, prayed not for me, but for Ben. Ben was still too young to die and I am all that keeps him alive. Keeping him alive is my life, but it's hard on you, this living for and loving the dead, it's hard, harder because you can't love death. You have to hate the death while you love the dead and keeping them alive is hard for an old woman like me. I tried to think how old I was, but give it up and went back to praying, praying like hell that God would spare me and God would spare Danny too because I knew I didn't have enough life in me to go on living for Ben and Danny too.

The next morning I was real glad to find myself alive. The dog and me, just as we were, me still dressed, so that saved time and I got up and made us some coffee and told the dog it was going to be a hot one today. We go out on our porch, but before noon the smog comes creeping up underneath the tin roof and the honeysuckle vine and sticking it's little yellow fingers in my eyes. I have to go inside and watch Sesame Street till it cools off, but it don't seem to. I take the dog back out and hose him down and hose me down too and then we drip dry on the porch till it was time for cartoons and a couple Cokes. After cartoons it's the news. I listen for word of Manila Bay, but there's nothing, so I turned off the TV and said to the dog: Suppertime. He don't even get up and pad after me. He is getting real old.

I go into the kitchen, but it's too hot to fire up the stove, even for a can of beans, so I get another Coke out of the fridge and some ice and an extra ice cube for the dog. I run ice over my face and neck and then drop it in my glass, pour the Coke and I'm taking the dog's ice in to him when I hear the gate squeal. The dog starts up. We go to the screen door and watch the foxtails swish and whisper like they do when so much as a cat prowls through them, but this is no cat. I can see a body moving through them. It's too late for the mailman and then I see it's a woman's body, but it's not Mrs. Will or Mrs. Archie because the dog starts to growl. I squint into the sun, lowering itself into the foxtails, lighting them up like a thousand torches, flickering in the desert wind. And then I see it's Connie Frett. Connie Frett or someone like her.

Someone pink and puffy and fat. No yellow dress. No gardenia in the hair. The hair is gray and short and the woman is gray and short and fat, but underneath all that I know it's Connie Frett, though she don't say anything. She just comes up to the porch and we sit down together. I ask her the question, the one I wanted to ask all those years ago before her yellow dress disappeared up the walk. "Did you make love with him, Connie?" I ask. "Did he have that much? Did he know a girl's love?"

"Yes. He had that much. I loved him."

"I didn't mean what I said, Connie, about your not deserving him. Calling you a slut. I don't know why I said such a mean thing. I'm sorry. I apologize." I start to wonder how long ago it was, but Connie lowers her head into my lap and I know it doesn't matter, the years, the time. There isn't any years or time, there's only living and dying and laughing and grieving and you keep doing them over and over like the seasons. "You keep living and dying and laughing and grieving." I tell Connie, "but the one thing you don't do, not more than once anyway, is forget. If you once forget, then you have forgot forever and for all time."

"He's only missing in action, Manila. He might come back. Don't you think?" Connie raises up her fat, tear-stained face, the lips chewed raw with grief.

"He might," I say. "There might be someone we don't know about, Connie, someone who finds him in the mud, lying there, face down in the mud and maybe, probably, they turn him over. They bathe his face and eyes unbutton his shirt and wash the mud off his chest and his shoulders and they find he isn't bloody or mangled at all. Just stunned, Connie. That's all. He's just stunned and he's not dead. Someone will touch his eyes, kiss them, and he'll open his eyes and smile, Connie."

"Yes," says Connie, laying her graying head back in my lap. "He's stunned and separated from the rest of his unit, but he's not dead, is he, Manila?"

"No."

"Tell me again, Manila. Tell me how it happens."

I stroke her hair and back. My grief is not my own anymore. I hold her and tell her over and over about the battle for Manila and the mud and finding the body and how someone will lift Danny from the mud, bathe his face, and find he isn't bloody in the least, just muddy and how when the mud is washed off, he is still perfect and young and beautiful. I tell how she will pull him into her arms and hold him against her shoulder, sing maybe. I tell how he will smile, how he will know the touch even if he don't know the person. I hold Connie Frett and I tell her over and over and we stay on the porch till it's long past dark and the dry red moon rises slow in the night sky.

Nominated by Joyce Carol Oates

SPECIAL MENTION

(The editors also wish to mention the following important works published by small presses last year. Listing is in no special order.)

FICTION

At The Back of the World—Amy Herrick (Indiana Review)
High Street—Jane Ruiter (The Florida Review)
The Other Anna—Barbara Esstman (Union Street Review)
In the Form of a Person—Ann Pyne (The Quarterly)
Defeat—Arnost Lustig (Confrontation)
Balancing Accounts—Madeline DeFrees (Helicon Nine)
Bear, Dancing—Wayne Johnson (Story)
Les Femmes Creoles—Bob Shacochis (Hayden's Ferry Review)
Slinkers—Patricia Henley (Sycamore Review)
Taking the Fall—Susan Yankowitz (Parnassus)
Naked—Joyce Carol Oates (Witness)
Shelter—Charles Baxter (The Georgia Review)
Amnesia—Antonya Nelson (River City)
Einstein's Daughter—Claudia Smith Brinson (Kalliope)
Going Out—Dan Chaon (TriQuarterly)
Silver Maple—Catherine Browder (Shenandoah)
Boy Up A Tree—William Hoffman (Shenandoah)
Comedy—Barry Targan (MSS)
The Hat—Diana Chang (North Atlantic Review)
Blue Skies—Joyce Carol Oates (*The Invisible Enemy*, Graywolf)
The Intruder—Mary McGarry Morris (Ontario Review)
Blue Taxis—Eileen Drew (*Blue Taxis*, Milkweed Editions)
The Trogon Dish—Kent Nelson (Virginia Quarterly Review)
Mr. Morning—Siri Hustvedt (Ontario Review)
A Good Shape—Helen Norris (Boulevard)

Money Honey—Binnie Kirshenbaum (New England Review/ Bread Loaf Quarterly)

The Great Black Houdini—Louis Berney (New England Review/ Bread Loaf Quarterly)

Dead Man's Things—Reginald Gibbons (Pacific Review)

from Tinian—Charlie Smith (Bomb)

Conveniences—Ewing Campbell (Kenyon Review)

The Christmas Cathedral—Brad Owens (Threepenny Review)

Accidents—Todd Lieber (Crazyhorse)

Love Out of Bounds—Ami Sands Brodoff (TriQuarterly)

The Eleventh Edition—Leo Litwak (TriQuarterly)

Lorraine—Kathleen Ford (Southern Review)

A Little Piece of Star—Barbara Croft (Kenyon Review)

Between Stations—John Blades (The Quarterly)

A Minor Fatality—Nancy Zafris (Black Warrior Review)

Jesus and Isolt—Robert Pinsky (Representations)

Two Points of A Blue Star—Robert Nelsen (Quarterly West)

A Preponderance of the Small—Meredith Steinbach (Tyuonyi)

Sugar River—Cori Jones (Iowa Review)

How Jimmy Lake Went—Jere Hoar (Southern Review)

In Memory of Jane Fogarty—Jay Neugeboren (Tikkun)

The Invisible Girl—David Madden (Southern California Anthology)

A Flight of Bones—H. E. Francis (The Missouri Review)

Parfum—Jonathan Penner (Manoa)

The Natural Condition of the World—François Camoin (Manoa)

Number Cruncher Suit—M. E. McMullen (The New Renaissance)

Upright and Unbranched—Lisa Teasley (The New Renaissance)

Chicken Skin—Dan Leone (The Florida Review)

Crow Man—Thomas Bailey (Greensboro Review)

Ronnie Big Wolf Tooth—Robert Nelsen (North Dakota Quarterly)

Fireflies—Ronald Rindo (*Suburban Metaphysics*, New Rivers)

Rat Man—George Minot (Union Street Review)

Acapulco Gothic—Frank Ward (Space & Time)

Women—Barbara Mujica (Perceptions)

If You Lived Here—Leslee Becker (River Styx)

Dead Weight—Timo Koskinen (*Sampo*, New Rivers)

The Cow Game—John McNally (Sou'wester)

Spook Light—David Williams (Beloit Fiction Journal)

Fedora—Daniel Wallace (High Plains Literary Review)
Bebe Khomee—Deborah Najor (Indiana Review)
Tule Fogs—Erin McGraw (The Laurel Review)
Killing Color—Charlotte Watson Sherman (Crossing)
Informing—Slawomir Mrozek (Threepenny Review)
Something In Her Instep High—Peter Taylor (Key West Review)
Elephant Day—Francine Prose (Western Humanities Review)
The Psychopathology of Everyday Life by Sigmund Freud—
    Daniel Stern (Paris Review)
Four Times My Sister Cried—Cooley Windsor (Ploughshares)
A Baker—Ned Bachus (Calliope)
The Year Of The Zinc Penny—Rick DeMarinis (Grand Street)
selections from Maya Red—J. R. Humphreys (Cane Hill Press)
Dog Stories—Barbara Nodine (Ploughshares)
The Company—Josephine Jacobsen (Ontario Review)
Magister Luni—Geoffrey Becker (Crazyhorse)
Sleep Tight—Alice Hoffman (Ploughshares)
Callie—Sheila M. O'Connor (Helicon Nine)
Period Sets—John Domini (Witness)
Finding My Niche—Mark Costello (Iowa Review)
The Angel Thomas—Lisa Lenzo (Alaska Quarterly Review)
Up The Gatineau—Elizabeth Spencer (Boulevard)
Ice Skating At the North Pole—Sena Jeter Naslund (Alaska
    Quarterly Review)
The French Revolution—Niccolo Tucci (Paris Review)
The Shopper—Jeanne Wilmot (Ontario Review)
The Running Score—Roland Sodowsky (Epoch)
Man Stabbed In Heart Runs 3 Blocks—Pat Rushin (Kansas
    Quarterly)
Ritter's Crime—James Brantingham (ZYZZYVA)
Traveling—Marcia Stucki (Epoch)
The Girl Painted—Eve Shelnutt (Chariton Review)
Frog Restarts—Stephen Dixon (StoryQuarterly)
Punk: 1969—Greg Jones (Writers' Forum)
White Birds—Dinty Moore (Writers' Forum)
The Moon Will Be Bleeding—Madison Smartt Bell (Hudson
    Review)
Friends—Glenda Adams (The Hottest Night of the Century,
    Cane Hill)
The 20-Breath Snake—Russ Riviere (ZYZZYVA)

ESSAYS

Beloved Juggler—Dennis Vannatta (Antioch Review)

Notes from Yaak—Rick Bass (Antaeus)

Clocking Dollars—Wanda Coleman (Epoch)

The Action of Paradise—Simeon Dreyfuss (Pequod)

When Money Doesn't Talk: Reflections on Business, Poetry and Audience—Dana Gioia (Epoch)

Influences—Seamus Heaney (Boston Review)

The Naming and Blaming of Cats—John Hollander (Raritan Review)

The Homesick Novels of Harriette Arnow—Bette Howland (The American Voice)

A Universe of Sentences II—Richard Kostelanetz (Asylum)

Dr. Rapallo—Stephen Menick (Yale Review)

To Feel These Things—Leonard Michaels (Salmagundi)

Déjà Vu: Thoughts on The Fifties and Eighties—Vern Rutsala (American Poetry Review)

Method Writing—George Singleton (Chattahoochee Review)

As I Sauntered Out, One Mid-Century Morning—W. M. Spackman (Southwest Review)

Portrait of the Artist As a Lion On Stilts—Paul West (Triquarterly)

POETRY

Lofty Calling—A. R. Ammons (Michigan Quarterly Review)

Back Then—James Applewhite (The Chattahoochee Review)

Mercy—David Baker (Poetry)

While Making a Pencil Sketch of Eggs with the Sun so Perfectly Burning—Savana Blue (Primavera)

First Voices—Stephen Bluestone (Greensboro Review)

The Green Diamonds of Summer—Joe Bolton (Apalachee Quarterly)

Provisions—Philip Booth (American Poetry Review)

The Second Coming—Daniel Bosch (Zone 3)

The Past—Christopher Buckley (Poetry)

One More—Raymond Carver (Hayden's Ferry Review)

Lessons of the Past—Judith Ortiz Cofer (The Georgia Review)

521

Trespass—Stefanie Marlis (Floating Island)
Giants In The Earth—Donna Masini (High Plains Literary
    Review)
Nabokov's Blues—William Matthews (Poetry)
Phonic—Gail Mazur (Agni Review)
The Genius of Industry—Campbell McGrath (Witness)
Bad Mother Blues—Sandra McPherson (American Poetry
    Review)
Havana Birth—Susan Mitchell (Ploughshares)
Yahrzeit—Larry Moffi (A Citizen's Handbook)
Barrio Landmark—Jose Montoya (Quarry West)
Always at Aachen—Andrea Moorhead (Osiris)
Spanish—Herbert Morris (Crazyhorse)
The Beginning of Raspberry Summer—Kay Murphy (Mississippi
    Valley Review)
Homage to the Tao Te Ching—Neil Myers (The Chariton Review)
Cradle Song—Alice Connelly Nagle (Zone 3)
The Six-Cornered Snowflake—John Frederick Nims (Poetry)
Decoys—Leslie Norris (The New Criterion)
Znamenskaya Square, Leningrad, 1941—Sharon Olds (Poetry)
The Founder—Gerald Stern (Antaeus)
As I Remember—Ruth Stone (American Poetry Review)
June 5, 1987—Lucien Stryk (American Poetry Review)
Raising Steel—Eric Trethewey (The Missouri Review)
One Physics—Chase Twichell (New England Review/Bread Loaf
    Quarterly)
Willi, Home—Jean Valentine (Alicejamesbooks)
The House on Moscow Street—Marilyn Nelson Waniek (South-
    ern Review)
Meditation at Pearl Street—Bruce Weigl (The Ohio Review)
Laundromat—Kyle Weinandy (Jeopardy)
Saturday Morning—Roger Weingarten (Ploughshares)
KZ—Carolyne Wright (Seattle Arts Image)
Looking Outside the Cabin Window, I Remember a Line by Li
    Po—Charles Wright (Field)
The Grandmothers—Robert Wrigley (Poetry Northwest)

PRESSES FEATURED IN THE PUSHCART PRIZE EDITIONS (1976–1990)

Acts
Agni Review
Ahsahta Press
Ailanthus Press
Alcheringa/Ethnopoetics
Alice James Books
Ambergris
Amelia
American Literature
American PEN
American Poetry Review
American Scholar
The American Voice
Amnesty International
Anaesthesia Review
Another Chicago Magazine
Antaeus
Antietam Review
Antioch Review
Apalachee Quarterly
Aphra
The Ark
Ascensius Press
Ascent
Aspen Leaves
Aspen Poetry Anthology
Assembling

Barlenmir House
Barnwood Press
The Bellingham Review
Beloit Poetry Journal
Bennington Review
Bilingual Review
Black American Literature Forum
Black Rooster
Black Scholar
Black Sparrow
Black Warrior Review
Blackwells Press
Bloomsbury Review
Blue Cloud Quarterly
Blue Unicorn
Blue Wind Press
Bluefish
BOA Editions
Bookslinger Editions
Boulevard
Boxspring
Brown Journal of the Arts
Burning Deck Press
Caliban
California Quarterly
Callaloo
Calliope

Calliopea Press
Canto
Capra Press
Carolina Quarterly
Cedar Rock
Center
Chariton Review
Charnel House
Chelsea
Chicago Review
Chouteau Review
Chowder Review
Cimarron Review
Cincinnati Poetry Review
City Lights Books
Clown War
CoEvolution Quarterly
Cold Mountain Press
Colorado Review
Columbia: A Magazine of Poetry
    and Prose
Confluence Press
Confrontation
Conjunctions
Copper Canyon Press
Cosmic Information Agency
Crawl Out Your Window
Crazyhorse
Crescent Review
Cross Cultural Communications
Cross Currents
Cumberland Poetry Review
Curbstone Press
Cutbank
Dacotah Territory
Daedalus
Decatur House
December
Denver Quarterly
Domestic Crude
Dragon Gate Inc.
Dreamworks
Dryad Press

Duck Down Press
Durak
East River Anthology
Ellis Press
Empty Bowl
Epoch
Exquisite Corpse
Fiction
Fiction Collective
Fiction International
Field
Firebrand Books
Firelands Art Review
Five Fingers Review
Five Trees Press
Frontiers: A Journal of Women
    Studies
Gallimaufry
Genre
The Georgia Review
Gettysburg Review
Ghost Dance
Goddard Journal
David Godine, Publisher
Graham House Press
Grand Street
Granta
Graywolf Press
Green Mountains Review
Greenfield Review
Greensboro Review
Guardian Press
Hard Pressed
Hermitage Press
Hills
Holmgangers Press
Holy Cow!
Home Planet News
Hudson Review
Icarus
Iguana Press
Indiana Review
Indiana Writes

Intermedia
Intro
Invisible City
Inwood Press
Iowa Review
Ironwood
Jam To-day
The Kanchenjuga Press
Kansas Quarterly
Kayak
Kelsey Street Press
Kenyon Review
Latitudes Press
Laughing Waters Press
Laurel Review
L'Epervier Press
Liberation
Linquis
The Little Magazine
Living Hand Press
Living Poets Press
Logbridge-Rhodes
Lowlands Review
Lucille
Lynx House Press
Magic Circle Press
Malahat Review
Mānoa
Manroot
Massachusetts Review
Mho & Mho Works
Micah Publications
Michigan Quarterly
Milkweed Editions
Milkweed Quarterly
The Minnesota Review
Mississippi Review
Missouri Review
Montana Gothic
Montana Review
Montemora
Mr. Cogito Press
MSS

Mulch Press
Nada Press
New America
New American Review
The New Criterion
New Delta Review
New Directions
New England Review and Bread
    Loaf Quarterly
New Letters
New Virginia Review
Nimrod
North American Review
North Atlantic Books
North Dakota Quarterly
North Point Press
Northern Lights
Northwest Review
O. ARS
Obsidian
Oconee Review
October
Ohio Review
Ontario Review
Open Places
Orca Press
Oxford Press
Oyez Press
Painted Bride Quarterly
Paris Review
Parnassus: Poetry In Review
Partisan Review
Penca Books
Pentagram
Penumbra Press
Pequod
Persea: An International Review
Pipedream Press
Pitcairn Press
Ploughshares
Poet and Critic
Poetry
Poetry East

Poetry Northwest
Poetry Now
Prairie Schooner
Prescott Street Press
Promise of Learnings
Puerto Del Sol
Quarry West
The Quarterly
Quarterly West
Raccoon
Rainbow Press
Raritan A Quarterly Review
Red Cedar Review
Red Clay Books
Red Dust Press
Red Earth Press
Release Press
Revista Chicano-Riquena
River Styx
Rowan Tree Press
Russian *Samizdat*
Salmagundi
San Marcos Press
Sea Pen Press and Paper Mill
Seal Press
Seamark Press
Seattle Review
Second Coming Press
The Seventies Press
Sewanee Review
Shankpainter
Shantih
Sheep Meadow Press
Shenandoah
A Shout In The Street
Sibyl-Child Press
Small Moon
The Smith
Some
The Sonora Review
Southern Poetry Review
Southern Review
Southwest Review

Spectrum
The Spirit That Moves Us
St. Andrews Press
Story
Story Quarterly
Streetfare Journal
Stuart Wright, Publisher
Sulfur
Sun & Moon Press
Sun Press
Sunstone
Tar River Poetry
Teal Press
Telephone Books
Telescope
Temblor
Tendril
Texas Slough
13th Moon
THIS
Thorp Springs Press
Three Rivers Press
Threepenny Review
Thunder City Press
Thunder's Mouth Press
Tombouctou Books
Toothpaste Press
Transatlantic Review
TriQuarterly
Truck Press
Tuumba Press
Undine
Unicorn Press
University of Pittsburgh Press
Unmuzzled Ox
Unspeakable Visions of the
    Individual
Vagabond
Virginia Quarterly
Wampeter Press
Washington Writers Workshop
Water Table
Western Humanities Review

Westigan Review
Wickwire Press
Wilmore City
Word Beat Press
Word-Smith
Wormwood Review
Writers Forum

Xanadu
Yale Review
Yardbird Reader
Yarrow
Y'Bird
ZYZZYVA

CONTRIBUTING SMALL PRESSES

(These presses made or received nominations for this edition of *The Pushcart Prize*. See the *International Directory of Little Magazines and Small Presses*, Dustbooks, Box 1056, Paradise, CA 95969, for subscription rates, manuscript requirements and a complete international listing of small presses.)

A.

Abraxas, 2518 Gregory St., Madison, WI 53711

Acadia Press, P.O. Box 170, Bar Harbor, ME 04609

ACTS: A Journal of New Writing, 514 Guerrero St., San Francisco, CA 94110

Adastra Press, 101 Strong St., Easthampton, MA 01027

Advocacy Press, P.O. Box 236, Santa Barbara, CA 93102

Agni Review, Boston Univ. Creative Writing Prog., 236 Bay St., Boston, MA 02215

Ahsahta Press, English Dept., Boise State Univ., Boise, ID 83725

Alabama Literary Review, English Dept., Troy State Univ., Troy, AL 36082

Alaska Quarterly Review, Univ. of Alaska, 3211 Providence Dr., Anchorage, AK 99508

The Albany Review, 4 Central Ave., Albany, NY 12210

Alicejames Books, 33 Richdale Ave., Cambridge, MA 02140

Alpha Beat Press, 5110 Rue Adam, Montreal, Que. CANADA H1V 1W8

Amador Publishers, P.O. Box 12335, Albuquerque, NM 87195

Amaranth Review, P.O. Box 56235, Phoenix, AZ 85079
Ambergris, P.O. Box 29919, Cincinnati, OH 45229
Amelia, 329 "E" St., Bakersfield, CA 93304
Amherst Writers & Artists Press, P.O. Box 1076, Amherst, MA 01004
American-Canadian Publishers, Inc., P.O. Box 4595, Santa Fe, NM 87502
American Poetry Review, 1704 Walnut St., Philadelphia, PA 19103
American Studies Press, Inc., 13511 Palmwood Lane, Tampa, FL 33624
The American Voice, 332 W. Broadway, Ste. 1215, Louisville, KY 40202
Ampersand Press, Creative Writing Prog., Roger Williams College, Bristol, RI 02809
Anna's House, P.O. Box 438070, Chicago, IL 60643
Another Chicago Magazine (& Press), P.O. Box 11223, Chicago, IL 60611
Antaeus, 26 West 17th St., New York, NY 10011
Antietam Review, 82 W. Washington St., Hagerstown, MD 21740
The Antioch Review, P.O. Box 148, Yellow Springs, OH 45387
Apalachee Quarterly, P.O. Box 20106, Tallahassee, FL 32304
Arbiter Press, P.O. Box 592540, Orlando, FL 32859
The Archer, 2285 Rogers Lane NW, Salem, OR 97304
Arizona Coast Magazine, 912 Joshua Ave., Parker, AZ 85344
Arrowwood Books, Inc., P.O. Box 2100, Corvallis, OR 97339
Artful Dodge, English Dept., College of Wooster, Wooster, OH 44691
Ascensius Press, 20 Danforth St., Portland, ME 04102
Asylum, P.O. Box 6203, Santa Maria, CA 93456
AWP Chronicle, Assoc. Writing Prog., Old Dominion University. Norfolk, VA 23529

B.

Ball State University Forum, see Forum
Barnwood Press, 600 E. Washington St., Muncie, IN 47305
Bay Windows, 62 Chandler St., #1, Boston, MA 02116

Bear House Publishing, 2711 Watson, Houston, TX 77009

Bellowing Ark, P.O. Box 45637, Seattle, WA 98145

Beloit Fiction Journal, P.O. Box 11, Beloit College, Beloit, WI 53511

Beloit Poetry Journal, Box 154, RFD 2, Ellsworth, ME 04605

Bitterroot, P.O. Box 489, Spring Glen, NY 12483

BkMk Press, 5216 Rockhill Rd., Rm. 204, Kansas City, MO 64110

Black Mountain Review, P.O. Box 1112, Black Mountain, NC 28711

Black River Review, 855 Mildred Ave., Lorain, OH 44052

Black Warrior Review, P.O. Box 2936, Tuscaloosa, AL 35487

Blue Bird Publishing, 1713 E. Broadway, #306, Tempe, AZ 85282

Blue Buildings, English Dept., Drake University, Des Moines, IA 50311

Blue Scarab Press, 243 S. 8th Ave., Pocatello, ID 83201

Blue Unicorn, 22 Avon Rd., Kensington, CA 94707

Bold Print, c/o Kyle Hogg, 2211 Stuart Ave., Richmond, VA 23220

Bolton Press, 3606 El Camino Ct., Largo, FL 35641

Book Weaver Publishing Co., P.O. Box 30072-AA, Indianapolis, IN 46230

The Boston Review, 33 Harrison Ave., Boston, MA 02111

Boulevard, 2400 Chestnut St., #3301, Philadelphia, PA 19103

Broken Moon Press, P.O. Box 24585, Seattle, WA 98124

Brooding Heron Press, 3618 Oakes Ave., Anacortes, WA 98267

Brook House Press, Mills Pond House, P.O. Box 52, St. James, NY 11780

The Bunny & The Crocodile Press, Forest Woods Ct., Rt. 3, Box 139A, Hedgesville, W.VA 25427

Burning Deck, 71 Elmgrove Ave., Providence, RI 02906

By No Means, 191 Golden Gate Ave., San Francisco, CA 94102

C.

Cafe Solo, P.O. Box 2814, Atascadero, CA 93422

Cliban, P.O. Box 4321, Ann Arbor, MI 48106

Callaloo, English Dept., Wilson Hall, Univ. of Virginia, Charlottesville, VA 22903

Calliope, see Ampersand Press

Calyx, P.O. Box B, Corvallis, OR 97339

Camel Press, Big Cove Tannery, PA 17212

Cane Hill Press, 225 Varick St., 11th fl., New York, NY 10014

Canoe Press, 1587 Lake Dr., Traverse City, MI 49684

Capra Press, P.O. Box 2068, Santa Barbara, CA 93120

Caprice, 229 No. Fountain, Wichita, KS 67208

The Caribbean Writer, Univ. of the Virgin Islands, RR-2, Box 10,000, Kingshill, St. Croix, VI 00850

Carolina Quarterly, Greenlaw Hall, 066A, Univ. of North Carolina, Chapel Hill, NC 27514

Centering, Years Press, College of Arts & Letters, Michigan State Univ., East Lansing, MI 48824

Central Park, P.O. Box 1446, New York, NY 10023

Charioteer Press, 337 West 36th St., New York, NY 10018

The Chariton Review, Northeast Missouri State Univ., Kirksville, MO 63501

The Chattahoochee Review, DeKalb College, 2101 Womack Rd., Dunwoody, GA 30338

Chelsea, Box 5880, Grand Central Sta., New York, NY 10163

Chiron Review, Rt. 2, Box 111, St. John, KS 67576

Chockstone Press, Inc., P.O. Box 3505, Evergreen, CO 80429

Cicada Magazine, 329 "E" St., Bakersfield, CA 93304

Cimarron Review, 205 Morill Hall, Oklahoma State Univ., Stillwater, OK 74078

The Clamshell Press, 160 California Ave., Santa Rosa, CA 95405

Claycomb Press, Inc., P.O. Box 70822, Chevy Chase, MD 20813

Cleveland State Univ. Poetry Center, English Dept., Rhodes Tower, Rm. 1815, Cleveland, OH 44115

Coffee House Press, P.O. Box 10870, Minneapolis, MN 55440

College English, Drawer AL, Univ. of Alabama, Tuscaloosa, AL 35487

Colorado Review, English Dept., Colorado State University, Ft. Collins, CO 80523

Community Council for the Arts, P.O. Box 3554, Kinston, NC 28502

Concho River Review, English Dept., Angelo State Univ., San Angelo, TX 76909

Conference of Calif. Historical Societies, Univ. of the Pacific, Stockton, CA

Confluence Press, Inc., Lewis & Clark State College, 8th Ave. & 6th St., Lewiston, ID 83501

Confrontation, English Dept., C. W. Post Campus, Long Island Univ., Brookville, NY 11548

Conjunctions, 33 West 9th St., New York, NY 10011

Cornfield Review, 1465 Mt. Vernon Ave., Marion, OH 43302

Coyote Love Press, 294 Spring St., Portland, ME 04102

Crab Creek Review, 4462 Whitman Ave. N, Seattle, WA 98103

Crazyhorse, English Dept., Univ. of Arkansas, Little Rock, AR 72204

Cream City Review, English Dept., P.O. Box 413, Univ. of Wisconsin, Milwaukee, WI 53201

Creeping Bent, 433 W. Market St., Bethlehem, PA 18018

Creighton-Morgan Publ. Group, P.O. Box 855, Santa Cruz, CA 95061

The Crescent Review, P.O. Box 15065, Winston-Salem, NC 27113

Crossing Press, P.O. Box 1048, Freedom, CA 95019

Cumberland Poetry Review, P.O. Box 120128, Acklen Sta., Nashville, TN 37212

Curbstone Press, 321 Jackson St., Willimantic, CT 06226

CutBank, English Dept., Univ. of Montana, Missoula, MT 59812

D.

D & J Press, 7475 Callaghan, Ste. 205, San Antonio, TX 78229

Dalkey Archive Press, 1817 79th Ave., Elmwood Park, IL 60635

Damascus Works, 1101 N. Calvert St., Baltimore, MD 21202

John Daniel & Co., Publishers, P.O. Box 21922, Santa Barbara, CA 93121

Dawn Valley Press, see Sunrust

Dead of Night, P.O. Box 682, East Long, MA 01028

Deinotation 7 Press, c/o A. A. Stella, Susquehanna, PA 18847

Denver Quarterly, Univ. of Denver, University Park, Denver, CO 80208

The Dog Ear Press, 132 Water St., Gardiner, ME 04345

Dolphin-Moon Press, P.O. Box 22262, Baltimore, MD 21203

DorPete Press, P.O. Box 238, Briarcliff Manor, NY 10510
The Duckabush Journal, P.O. Box 2228, Sequim, WA 98382

E.

Ecco Press, 26 West 17th St., New York, NY 10011
Edgeworth & North Books, P.O. Box 812, West Side Sta., Worcester, MA 01602
the eleventh MUSE, P.O. Box 2413, Colorado Springs, CO 80901
Elmwood Park Publishing Co., P.O. Box 35132, Elmwood Park, IL 60635
Eotu, 1810 W. State, #115, Boise, ID 83702
Epiphany, P.O. Box 14727, San Francisco, CA 94114
Epoch, 251 Goldwin Smith Hall, Cornell Univ., Ithaca, NY 14853
Eschar Publications, P.O. Box 1196, Waynesboro, VA 22980
Event, P.O. Box 2503, New Westminster, B.C. CANADA V3L 5B2
Exile Editions, 69 Sullivan St., Toronto, CANADA
Exit 13 Magazine, 22 Oakwood Court, Fanwood, NJ 07023
Expresso Tilt, 37 Wharton, Philadelphia, PA 19147
Exquisite Corpse, Box 25051, Baton Rouge, LA 70894

F.

Fiction International, English Dept., San Diego State Univ., San Diego, CA 92182
Fiction Network, P.O. Box 5651, San Francisco, CA 94101
Field, English Dept., Rice Hall, Oberlin College, OH 44074
Fielder Books, 264 San Jacinto Dr., Los Osos, CA 93402
Fine Madness, P.O. Box 15176, Seattle, WA 98115
Firebrand Books, 141 The Commons, Ithaca, NY 14850
First Ink Publishing House, P.O. Box 1267, Rancho Cordova, CA 95741
Five Fingers Press, 553 25th Ave., San Francisco, CA 94121
Floating Island Publications, P.O. Box 516, Point Reyes Station, CA 94956
The Florida Review, English Dept., Univ. of Central Florida, Orlando, FL 32816
Folio, Dept. of Literature, Gray Hall, American Univ., Washington, DC 20016

Footwork, Cultural Affairs, Passaic Co. Community College, College Blvd., Paterson, NJ 07509

Forced Exposure, P.O. Box 1611, Waltham, MA 02254

Forum, Ball State Univ., Muncie, IN 47306

Frogpond, 970 Acequia Madre, Santa Fe, NM 87501

G.

GT Publications, P.O. Box 29293, Oakland, CA 94604

Gaff Press, P.O. Box 1024, Astoria, OR 97103

Gaia Press, P.O. Box 56094, Madison, WI 53705

Galileo Press, 15201 Wheeler Lane, Sparks, MD 21152

Galley Sail Review, 1630 University Ave., Ste. 42, Berkeley, CA 94703

Garric Press, P.O. Box 5723, Berkeley, CA 94705

Gateways, P.O. Box 370, Nevada City, CA 95959

Georgia Review, Univ. of Georgia, Athens, GA 30602

Geryon Press, Ltd., P.O. Box 770, Tunnel, NY 13848

The Gettysburg Review, Gettysburg College, Gettysburg, PA 17325

Gibbs Smith, Publisher, P.O. Box 667, Layton, UT 84041

Graham House Review, Box 5000, Colgate Univ., Hamilton, NY 13346

Grand Street, 50 Riverside Dr., New York, NY 10024

Graywolf Press, P.O. Box 75006, St. Paul, MN 55175

Green Mountain Trading Post, Box 11, East Charleston, VT 05833

Green Mountains Review, Johnson State College, Johnson, VT 05656

Greenhouse Review Press, 3965 Bonny Doon Rd., Santa Cruz, CA 95060

The Greensboro Review, English Dept., Univ. of North Carolina, Greensboro, NC 27412

Groundswell, P.O. Box 13013, Albany, NY 12212

Gulf Coast, English Dept., Univ. of Houston, 4800 Calhoun, Houston, TX 77004

Gulf Stream Magazine, Florida Internat'l Univ., English Dept., N. Miami, FL 33181

Gypsy, P.O. Box 370322, El Paso, TX 79937

H.

Hanging Loose Press, 231 Wyckoff St., Brooklyn, NY 11217

Hard-Press Publications, 210 White Rd., Watsonville, CA 95076

Harvest, 2322 Latona Dr., NE, Salem, OR 97303

Haunts, see Nightshade Publications

Hayden's Ferry Review, Matthews Center, Arizona State Univ., Tempe, AZ 85287

Haypenny Press, 211 New St., West Paterson, NJ 07424

Heaven Bone Press, P.O. Box 486, Chester, NY 10918

Helicon Nine, P.O. Box 22412, Kansas City, MO 64113

Heresies, P.O. Box 1306, Canal St. Sta., New York, NY 10013

Heritage Trails Press, see Prophetic Voices

High Plains Literary Review, 180 Adams St., #250, Denver, CO 80206

Hippo, 28834 Boniface Dr., Malibu, CA 90265

Hiram Poetry Review, Box 162, Hiram, OH 44234

Hobo Jungle, Roxbury, CT 06783

Hubbub, 5344 S.E. 38th, Portland, OR 97202

The Hudson Review, 684 Park Ave., New York, NY 10021

Humerus, Box 222, Piermont, NY 10968

Hurricane Alice, 207 Lind Hall, 207 Church St., SE, Minneapolis, MN 55455

Hutton Publications, P.O. Box 1870, Hayden, ID 83835

I.

Icarus Books, 1015 Kenilworth Dr., Baltimore, MD 21204

Ice River, 953 N. Gale, Union, OR 97883

Illuminations Press, 2110-B 9th St., Berkeley, CA 94710

Images, English Dept., Wright State Univ., Dayton, OH 45435

India Currents, P.O. Box 21285, San Jose, CA 95151

Indiana Review, 316 N. Jordan Ave., Bloomington, IN 47405

Infinity Limited, c/o G. Lester, P.O. Box 2713, Castro Valley, CA 94546

Inroads, P.O. Box 14944, Minneapolis, MN 55414

Integral Publishing, P.O. Box 1030, Lower Lake, CA 95457

Interim, English Dept., Univ. of Nevada, 4505 Maryland Pkwy, Las Vegas, NV 89154

Iowa Review, 308 EPB, Univ. of Iowa, Iowa City, IA 52242

Iowa Woman, P.O. Box 680, Iowa City, IA 52244

Iris, 123 Minor Hall, Univ. of Virginia, Charlottesville, VA 22903

Ironwood, P.O. Box 40907, Tucson, AZ 85717

J.

J & T Publishing, P.O. Box 6520, Ventura, CA 93006

The Jacaranda Review, English Dept., UCLA, Los Angeles, CA 90024

The Jailfish Review, 124½ Broadway E, #16, Seattle, WA 98122

Jam Today, 372 Dunstable Rd., Tyngsboro, MA 01879

Jeopardy, CH 132, Western Washington Univ., Bellingham, WA 98225

The Journal, English Dept., Ohio State Univ., 164 W. 17th Ave., Columbus, OH 43210

Journal of New Jersey Poets, County College of Morris, Randolph, NJ 07869

Journal of Regional Criticism, 1025 Garner St., Space 18, Colorado Springs, CO 80905

K.

Kaleidoscope, 326 Locust St., Akron, OH 44302

Kalliope, FCCJ, 3939 Roosevelt Blvd., Jacksonville, FL 32205

Kansas Quarterly, Denison Hall, Kansas State Univ., Manhattan, KS 66506

Karamu, English Dept., Eastern Illinois Univ., Charleston, IL 61920

The Kelsey Review, Mercer Co. Community College, P.O. Box B, Trenton, NJ 08690

Kelsey St. Press, P.O. Box 9235, Berkeley, CA 94709

Kenyon Review, Kenyon College, Gambier, OH 43022

Michael Kesend Publishing Ltd., 1025 Fifth Ave., New York, NY 10028

Key West Review, 9 Avenue G, Key West, FL 33040

Kingfisher, P.O. Box 9783, N. Berkeley, CA 94709

L.

Lactuca, c/o Mike Selender, P.O. Box 621, Suffern, NY 10901

Lake Street Review, Box 7188, Powderhorn Sta., Minneapolis, MN 55407

Lapis Press, 589 N. Venice Blvd., Venice, CA 90291

Latin American Review Press, 2300 Palmer St., Pittsburgh, PA 15218

Laughing Waters Press, 864-18th St., Boulder, CO 80302

Laurel Review, English Dept., Northwest Missouri State Univ., Maryville, MO 64468

The Ledge, 64–65 Cooper Ave., Glendale, NY 11385

Liberty, P.O. Box 1167, Port Townsend, WA 98368

Life-Link Books, 31- Hope St., Stamford, CT 06906

Lilliput Review, 4 Huddy Ave., Highlands, NJ 07732

Limelight Editions, 118 E. 30th St., New York, NY 10016

LIPS, P.O. Box 1345, Montclair, NJ 07042

Little River Press, 10 Lowell Ave., Westfield, MA 01085

Loom Press, P.O. Box 1394, Lowell, MA 01853

Lorien House, see Black Mountain Review

Lost & Found Times, 137 Leland Ave., Columbus, OH 43214

Lost Generation Journal, Rte. 5, Box 134, Salem, MO 65560

Lost Roads Publishers, P.O. Box 5848, Providence, RI 02903

Lucidity, see Bear House Publishing

Lyceum Press, 2442 N.W. Market St., Ste. 51, Seattle, WA 98107

Lynx House Press, c/o 1326 West St., Emporia, KS 66801

M.

MRK Publishing, 448 Seavey, Petaluma, CA 94952

MSS, SUNY, Binghamton, NY 13901

The Madison Review, English Dept., Univ. of Wisconsin, 600 N. Park St., Madison, WI 53706

The Mage, Student Assoc., Colgate Univ., Hamilton, NY 13346

Magnificat Press, P.O. Box 365, Avon, NJ 07717

The Malahat Review, Univ. of Victoria, P.O. Box 1700, Victoria, BC CANADA V8W 2Y2

manic d press, 1853 Stockton St., San Francisco, CA 94133

Manoa, Univ. of Hawaii, 1733 Donaghho Rd., Honolulu, HI 96822

Maryland Poetry Review, Drawer H, Catonsville, MD 21228

Massachusetts Review, Memorial Hall, Univ. of Massachusetts, Amherst, MA 01003

McDonald & Woodward Publishing Co., P.O. Box 10308, Blacksburg, VA 24062

McFarland & Company, Inc., Publishers, Box 611, Jefferson, NC 28640

Melior Publications, W. 1727 14th Ave., Spokane, WA 99204

Mercury House, 201 Filbert St., Ste. 400, San Francisco, CA 94133

Mho & Mho Works, Box 33135, San Diego, CA 92103

Michigan Quarterly Review, 3032 Rackham Bldg., Univ. of Michigan, Ann Arbor, MI 48109

Mickle Street Review, 328 Mickle St., Camden, NJ 08103

Midwest Villages & Voices, 3220 10th Ave. S, Minneapolis, MN 55407

Milkweed Editions, P.O. Box 3226, Minneapolis, MN 55403

Mindprint Review, P.O. Box 62, Soulsbyville, CA 95372

Mississippi Mud, 1336 S.E. Marion St., Portland, OR 97202

Mississippi Review, Univ. of So. Mississippi, Southern Sta., Box 5144, Hattiesburg, MS 39406

The Missouri Review, 107 Tate Hall, Univ. of Missouri, Columbia, MO 65211

Modern Haiku, P.O. Box 1752, Madison, WI 53701

Moveable Feast Press, P.O. Box 5057, El Dorado Hills, CA 95630

Mr. Cogito, Box 627, Pacific Univ., Forest Grove, OR 97116

Mudfish, 184 Franklin St. New York, NY 10013

Muse, P.O. Box 45, Burlington, NC 27216

N.

Negative Capability, 62 Ridgelawn Dr. East, Mobile, AL 36608

New Age Publishing Co., P.O. Box 01–1549, Miami, FL 33101

New American Writing, 2920 W. Pratt, Chicago, IL 60645

New Chapter Press, Inc., 381 Park Avenue S, Ste. 1122, New York, NY 10016

New Criterion, 850 Seventh Ave., New York, NY 10019

New Delta Review, English Dept., Louisiana State University, Baton Rouge, LA 70803

New Directions for Women, 108 W. Palisade Ave., Englewood, NJ 07631

New England Review & Bread Loaf Quarterly, Middlebury College, Middlebury, VT 05753

New Letters, Univ. of Missouri, 5100 Rockhill Rd., Kansas City, MO 64110

New Mexico Humanities Review, Humanities Dept., New Mexico Tech., Socorro, NM 87801

New Poets Series, Inc., 541 Piccadilly Rd., Baltimore, MD 21204

The New Press, 75–28 -6th Dr., Middle Village, NY 11379

the new renaissance, 9 Heath Rd., Arlington, MA 02174

New Rivers Press, 420 N. 5th St., Ste. 910, Minneapolis, MN 55401

New Sins, 70 Fulmer St., Indiana, PA 15701

Night Roses, P.O. Box 393, Prospect Heights, IL 60070

Nightshade Publications, P.O. Box 3342, Providence, RI 02906

Nimrod, Arts & Humanities Council of Tulsa, 2210 S. Main, Tulsa, OK 74114

North American Review, Univ. of Northern Iowa, Cedar Falls, IA 50614

North Atlantic Review, 15 Arbutus Lane, Stony Brook, NY 11790

North Country Press, P.O. Box 440, Belfast, ME 04915

North Dakota Quarterly, P.O. Box 8237, Univ. of North Dakota, Grand Forks, ND 58202

The Northern Review, Acad. Achiev. Ctr., Univ. of Wisconsin, Stevens Point, WI 54481

Northwest Review, 369 PLC, Univ. of Oregon, Eugene, OR 97403

Nostalgia, P.O. Box 2224, Orangeburg, SC 29116

Now and Then, Box 19180A, Eastern Tennessee State Univ., Johnson City, TN 37614

O.

Oblong Press, 2280 Sunset. Los Osos, CA 93402

Occident Press, Rhetoric Dept., Univ. of California, Berkeley, CA 94720

Ocean View Books, P.O. Box 4148, Mountain View, CA 94040
The Ohio Review, 346 Ellis Hall, Ohio Univ., Athens, OH 45701
Omega Cottonwood Press, P.O. Box 524, Alma, NE 68920
Ontario Review, 9 Honey Brook Dr., Princeton, NJ 08540
Orchises Press, P.O. Box 20602, Alexandria, VA 22320
Organica Press, 4419 N. Manhattan Ave., Tampa, FL 33614
Osiris, Box 297, Deerfield, MA 01342
The Other Side, 1225 Dandridge St., Fredericksburg, VA 22401
Other Voices, 820 Ridge Rd, Highland Park, IL 60035
Out of Ashes Press, c/o A. Smith, 515 Bay, #254, San Francisco, CA 94133
Oxalis, Stone Ridge Poetry Soc., P.O. Box 3993, Kingston, NY 12401
Oxford Magazine, English Dept., Miami Univ., Oxford, OH 45056
Oyez Review, Roosevelt Univ., 430 S. Michigan Ave., Chicago, IL 60605

P.

PWJ Publishing, P.O. Box 238, Tehama, CA 96090
Painted Bride Quarterly, 230 Vine St., Philadelphia, PA 19106
Papaloa Press, 362 Selby Lane, Atherton, CA 94025
Paper Air, c/o Singing Horse Press, P.O. Box 40034, Philadelphia, PA 19106
Paper Bag, P.O. Box 268805, Chicago, IL 60626
Papier-Mache Press, 795 Via Manzana, Watsonville, CA 95076
The Paris Review, 541 East 72nd St., New York, NY 10021
Parnassus, 41 Union Sq. W, Rm. 804, New York, NY 10003
Parnassus Literary Journal, P.O. Box 1384, Forest Park, GA 30051
Parting Gifts, 3006 Stonecutter Terrace, Greensboro, NC 27405
Partisan Review, 236 Bay State Rd., Boston, MA 02215
Passages North, William Bonifas Fine Arts Center, 7th St. & 1st Ave. S, Escanaba, MI 49007
Paterson Literary Review, see Footwork
Pearl, 3030 East Second St., Long Beach, CA 90803
Pegasus Review, P.O. Box 134, Flanders, NJ 07836

The Pennsylvania Review, English Dept., 526 CL, Univ. of Pittsburgh, Pittsburgh, PA 15260

Pequod, English Dept., 19 University Pl., New York, NY 10003

Perceptions, 1945 S. 4th W, Missoula, MT 59801

Peregrine, see Amherst Writers & Artists Press

Permafrost, English Dept., Univ. of Alaska, Fairbanks, AK 99775

Persephone Press, 22-B Pine Lake Dr., Whispering Pines, NC 28327

Personabooks, 6542 Dana St., Oakland, CA 94609

Phoebe, George Mason Univ., 4400 University Dr., Fairfax, VA 22030

The Pikestaff Press, P.O. Box 127, Normal, IL 61761

Pittenbruach Press, 15 Walnut St., P.O. Box 553, Northampton, MA 01060

Pivot, 250 Riverside Dr., #23, New York, NY 10025

Plainsong, Box U245, Western Kentucky Univ., Bowling Green, KY 42101

Ploughshares, Box 529, Cambridge, MA 02139

Pocahontas Press, 2805 Wellesley Court, Blacksburg, VA 24060

Poet & Critic, 203 Ross Hall, Iowa State Univ., Ames, IA 50011

Poetpourri, Box 3737, Taft Rd., Syracuse, NY 13220

Poetry, 60 West Walton St., Chicago, IL 60610

Poetry Around, 436 Elm, Norman, OK 73069

Poetry East, English Dept., DePaul Univ., 802 W. Belden Ave., Chicago IL 60614

Poetry/New York, English Dept., CUNY, 33 W. 42nd St., New York, NY 10036

Poetry Northwest, Dept. English, SIU, Carbondale, IL 62901

The Poetry Peddler, P.O. Box 250, W. Monroe, NY 13167

Potato Eyes, P.O. Box 76, Troy, ME 04987

Prairie Schooner, 201 Andrews, Univ. of Nebraska, Lincoln, NE 68588

Primal Publishing, 107 Brighton Ave., Allston, MA 02134

Primavera, 1212 E. 59th St., Chicago, IL 60637

Prism International, E-455—1866 Main Mall, Univ. of Brit. Col., V6T 1W5 CANADA

Progressive Press, 7320 Colonial, Dearborn Heights, MI 48127

Prophetic Voices, 94 Santa Maria Dr., Novato, CA 94947

Provincetown Arts, P.O. Box 35, Provincetown, MA 02657

Puckerbrush Review [and Press], 76 Main St., Orono, ME 04473

Puerto Del Sol, Box 3E, NMSU, Las Cruces, NM 88003
Pygmy Forest Press, P.O. Box 591, Albion, CA 95410

Q.

Quarry West, Porter College, Univ. of California, Santa Cruz, CA 95064
The Quarterly, 201 East 50th St., New York, NY 10022
Quarterly West, 317 Olpin Union, Univ. of Utah, Salt Lake City, UT 84112
Queen's Quarterly, Queen's Univ., Kingston, Ont. CANADA K7L 3N6
Quimby, P.O. Box 281, Astor Sta., Boston, MA 02123

R.

Ramalo Publications, 2107 N. Spokane St., Post Falls, ID 83854
Raritan, Rutgers Univ., 165 College Ave., New Brunswick, NJ 08903
Raw Dog Press, 128 Harvey Ave., Doylestown, PA 18901
Read Me, 1118 Hoyt Ave., Everett, WA 98201
Real Comet Press, 3131 Western Ave., #410, Seattle, WA 98121
Real Fiction, 298 9th Ave., San Francisco, CA 94118
The Reaper, 325 Ocean View Ave., Santa Cruz, CA 95062
Rebis Press, P.O. Box 2233, Berkeley, CA 94702
Red Dust, Inc., P.O. Box 630, New York, NY 10029
Reflections, P.O. Box 368, Duncan Falls, OH 43734
Regardie's, 1010 Wisconsin Ave., NW, Ste. 600, Washington, DC 20007
Resonance, P.O. Box 215, Beacon, NY 12508
Review: Latin American Lit. & Arts, 630 Park Ave., New York, NY 10021
Rhododendron, 2958 E. Louise Ave., Salt Lake City, UT 84109
River Rat Review, P.O. Box 24198, Lexington, KY 40524
River Styx, 14 S. Euclid, St. Louis, MO 63108
Riverrun, c/o Glen Oaks Comm. College, 62249 Shimmel Rd., Centreville, MO 49032

Rock Steady Press, 2750 Market St., #102, San Francisco, CA 94114

The Rotkin Review, 1607 Broadway at 53rd St., New York, NY 10019

Rowan Tree Press, 124 Chestnut St., Boston, MA 02108

Runaway Publications, P.O. Box 1172, Ashland, OR 97520

S.

SPSM & H Magazine, 329 "E" St., Bakersfield, CA 93304

ST Publications, 407 Gilbert Ave., Cincinnati, OH 45202

Salmagundi, Skidmore College, Saratoga Springs, NY 12866

Salthouse, English Dept., Univ. of Wisconsin, Whitewater, WI 53190

Samisdat, Box 129, Richford, VT 05476

San Francisco Flier, Box 400, 1550 California St., San Francisco, CA 94109

Sandscript, Cape Cod Writers Inc., Box 333, Cummaquid, MA 02637

Santa Clara Review, Box 1212, Santa Clara Univ., Santa Clara, CA 95053

Santa Monica Review, Santa Monica College, 1900 Pico Blvd., Santa Monica, CA 90405

Score, 491 Mandana Blvd., #3, Oakland, CA 94610

Scream Magazine, P.O. Box 10363, Raleigh, NC 27605

The Seal Press, 3131 Western Ave., #410, Seattle, WA 98121

Seems, Lakeland College, Box 359, Sheboygan, WI 53081

Seneca Review, Hobart & William Smith Colleges, Geneva, NY 14456

Seventh Wing Publications, 515 E. Washington St., Colorado Springs, CO 80907

Sewanee Review, Univ. of the South, Sewanee, TN 37375

Shenandoah, Box 722, Lexington, VA 24450

Shepherd Books, P.O. Box 2290, Redmond, WA 98073

Silver Wings, P.O. Box 1000, Pearblossom, CA 93553

Silverfish Review, P.O. Box 3541, Eugene, OR 97403

Simplicity Press, 1064 Ardmore Circle, Redlands, CA 92374

Singular Speech Press, 10 Hilltop Dr., Canton CT 06019

Skylark, 2233 171st St., Hammond, IN 46323

Slipstream, Box 2071, New Market Sta., Niagara Falls, NY 14301

Snowy Egret, RR 1, Box 354, Poland, IN 47868

The Socratic Press, P.O. Box 66683, St. Petersburg Beach, FL 33736

Sojourner, 1050 Commonwealth Ave., Ste. 305, Boston, MA 02215

Soleil Press, Box 452, RFD #1, Lisbon Falls, ME 04252

Sonoma Mandala, English Dept., SSU, Rohnert Park, CA 94928

Sonora Review, English Dept., Univ. of Arizona, Tucson, AZ 85721

The South Carolina Review, English Dept., Clemson Univ., Clemson, SC 29634

Southern Calif. Anthology, c/o Master of Prof. Writing Program, WPH 404, USC, Los Angeles, CA 90089

Southern Poetry Review, English Dept., Univ. of North Carolina, Charlotte, NC 28223

The Southern Review, 43 Allen Hall, Louisiana State Univ., Baton Rouge, LA 70803

Southern Trails Publishing, P.O. Box 34–7009, San Francisco, CA 94134

Southwest Review, Box 4374, 6410 Airline Rd., Southern Methodist Univ., Dallas, TX 75275

Sou'wester, English Dept., Southern Illinois Univ., Edwardsville, IL 62026

Space and Time, 138 West 70th St., 4-B, New York, NY 10023

Sparrow Press, 103 Waldron St., W. Lafayette, IN 47906

Spinsters/Aunt Lute Book Co., P.O. Box 410687, San Francisco, CA 94147

Spirit that Moves Us Press, P.O. Box 820, Jackson Heights, NY 11372

Spitball, 6224 Collegeville Pl., Cincinnati, OH 45224

St. Giles Press, Box 1416, Lafayette, CA 94549

Star Dust Books, 15 Lenox Rd., Kensington, CA 94707

Star Route Journal, P.O. Box 1451, Redway, CA 95560

Still Waters Press, 112 W. Duerer St., Galloway, NJ 08201

Stories, 14 Beacon St., Boston, MA 02108

Story, 1507 Dana Ave., Cincinnati, OH 45207

Story Quarterly, P.O. Box 1416, Northbrook, IL 60065

Studia Hispanica Editors, 5626 W. Bavarian Pass, Fridley, MN 55432

Sun and Moon Press, 6148 Wilshire Blvd., Los Angeles, CA 90048

Sun Dog, 406 Williams, Florida State Univ., Tallahassee, FL 32306

Sunrust, c/o Dawn Valley Press, P.O. Box 58, New Wilmington, PA 16142

Swamp Root, Rt. 2, Box 1098, Jacksboro, TN 37757

T.

Talisman, Box 1117, Hoboken, NJ 07030

Tampa Review, Univ. of Tampa, PO. Box 19F, Tampa, FL 33606

Tapjoe, P.O. Box 104, Grangeville, ID 83530

Teal Press, P.O. Box 4098, Santa Fe, NM 87502

Ten Star Press, P.O. Box 2325, Inglewood, CA 90503

Terata Publications, P.O. Box 810, Hawthorne, CA 90251

The Texas Review, English Dept., Sam Houston State Univ., Huntsville, TX 77341

Thema, c/o Bothomos Enterprises, P.O. Box 72109, Metairie, LA 70033

Third Lung Press, P.O. Box 361, Conover, NC 28613

Thorntree Press, 547 Hawthorn Lane, Winnetka, IL 60093

Threepenny Review, P.O. Box 9131, Berkeley, CA 94709

TIKKUN, 5100 Leona St., Oakland, CA 94619

Timberline Press, Rt. 1, Box 1621, Fulton, MO 65251

Timbuktu, P.O. Box 469, Charlottesville, VA 22902

Tioga Publishing Co., P.O. Box 50490, Palo Alto, CA 94303

To-the-Point Press, Drawer 546, Dana Point, CA 92629

Tough Dove Books, P.O. Box 528, Little River, CA 95456

Treetop Panorama, RR.1, Box 160, Payson, IL 62360

TriQuarterly, Northwestern Univ., 2020 Ridge Ave., Evanston, IL 60208

Trivia, P.O. Box 606, N. Amherst, MA 01059

Tucumcari Literary Review, 3108 W. Bellevue Ave., Los Angeles, CA 90026

Turnstile, 175 Fifth Ave., ste. 2348, New York, NY 10010

Twisted, 22071 Pineview Dr., Antioch, IL 60002

2 A M Magazine, P.O. Box 6754, Rockford, IL 61125

U.

Unicorn Press, Inc., P.O. Box 3307, Greensboro, NC 27402
Union Street Review, P.O. Box 19078, Alexandria, VA 22320
Unity Publications, see GT Publications
Univ. of Illinois Press, 54 E. Gregory Dr., Champaign, IL 61820
Univ. of North Texas Press, P.O. Box 13856, Denton, TX 76203

V.

Village Voice Literary Supplement, 842 Broadway, New York, NY 10003
Virginia Quarterly Review, One West Range, Charlottesville, VA 22903
Visions-International, 4705 South 8th Rd., Arlington, VA 22204

W.

Washington Writers Publishing House, P.O. Box 15271, Washington, DC 20003
Webster Review, Webster Univ., 470 E. Lockwood, Webster Groves, MO 63119
Wesleyan Univ. Press, 110 Mt. Vernon St., Middletown, CT 06457
West Anglia Publications, P.O. Box 8638, LaJolla, CA 92038
West Wind Review, English Dept., South Oregon State College, Ashland, OR 97520
West/Word, Writers' Program, UCLA Extension, 10995 Le Conte Ave., Los Angeles, CA 90024
Westburg Associates Publishers, 1735 Madison St., Fennimore, WI 53809
Western Humanities Review, Univ. of Utah, Salt Lake City, UT 84112
Westgate Press, 8 Bernstein Blvd., Center Moriches, NY 11934
What, Box 338, Sta. J, Toronto, Ont. M4J 4Y8 CANADA
Whetstone, BAAC, P.O. Box 1266, Barrington, IL 60011
The Widener Review, Widener Univ., Chester, PA 19013
Wind Magazine, RFD 1, Box 809-K, Pikeville, KY 41501

Windfall, English Dept., Univ. of Wisconsin, Whitewater, WI 53190

The Windless Orchard, English Dept., Indiana Univ., Fort Wayne, IN 46805

Window Publications, see Amaranth Review

Without Halos, P.O. Box 1342, Point Pleasant Beach, NJ 08742

Witness, 31000 Northwestern Hghwy, Ste. 200, Farmington Hills, MI 48018

Woman of Power, P.O. Box 827, Cambridge, MA 02238

Wood Thrush Books, 25 Lafayette Place, Apt. C, Burlington, VT 05401

Woodhenge Press, N2493 Kunz Rd, Fort Atkinson, WI 53538

Wordcraft, c/o D. Memmott, 953 N. Gale, Union, OR 97883

The Wordworks, P.O. Box 42164, Washington, DC 20015

The Wormwood Review, P.O. Box 8840, Stockton, CA 95208

The Writers' Bar-B-Q, 924 Bryn Mawr, Springfield, IL 62703

Writers' Forum, P.O. Box 7150, Univ. of Colorado, Colorado Springs, CO 80933

Y.

The Yale Review, 1902A Yale Sta., New Haven, CT 06520

Yarrow, English Dept., Kutztown State University, Kutztown, PA 19530

Z.

Zilzal Press, 126 N. Milpas St., Santa Barbara, CA 93103

Zone 3, P.O. Box 4565, Austin Peay State Univ., Clarksville, TN 37042

Zwitter Press, 302 Carlton Dr., Syracuse, NY 13214

ZYZZYVA, 41 Sutter St., Ste. 1400, San Francisco, CA 94104

INDEX

The following is a listing in alphabetical order by author's last name of works reprinted in the first fifteen *Pushcart Prize* editions.

549

552

557

559

570

571

CONTRIBUTORS' NOTES

DONALD W. BAKER is the author of three poetry collections, all available from Barnwood Press. He lives in East Brewster, Massachusetts.

WILL BAKER's numerous books of fiction and nonfiction include *Mountain Blood* (1985), *Backward* (1983) and *Chip* (1979). He teaches at the University of California, Davis.

JOHN BALABAN is the MFA director at Penn State University. His memoir, *Remembering Heaven's Face*, will be published by Poseidon Books in 1991.

RICK BASS' story collection, *The Watch*, was published in 1989 by W. W. Norton & Co. His essay collection, *Oil Notes*, came out from Seymour Lawrence/Houghton Mifflin recently. He lives in Montana.

CAROL BLY teaches at the University of Minnesota. Her books, *Bad Government & Silly Literature* and *Backbone* were published by Milkweed Editions.

MICHAEL BOWDEN teaches sixth grade in Arizona. His work has appeared in *Crazyhorse, Sonora Review* and elsewhere.

CHRISTOPHER BUCKLEY's fifth book of poems, *Blue Autumn*, was just published by Copper Beech Press. He teaches at West Chester University, Pennsylvania.

BARRY CALLAGHAN is the author of *The Black Queen Stories* and *Stone Blind Love*, a poetry collection. He is the founding editor of *Exile* and Exile Editions, published in Toronto.

KEN CHOWDER has published three novels with Harper & Row. He was born in New York, raised in New England and now lives in San Francisco.

JUDITH ORTIZ COFER published her first novel, *The Line of The Sun* in 1989 (University of Georgia Press). "More Room" was also published as part of her collection *Silent Dancing: A Partial Remembrance of A Puerto Rican Childhood* (Arte Publico Press, 1990).

HENRI COLE is the author of two poetry collections, *The Marble Queen* (Atheneum, 1986) and *The Zoo Wheel of Knowledge* (Knopf, 1989). He lives in New York City.

MICHAEL COLLIER is the author of two poetry collections from Wesleyan University Press. He directs the Creative Writing Program at the University of Maryland, College Park.

RICHARD CURREY is the author of a novel and a short story collection, both from Seymour Lawrence. He is at work on a novel titled *Lost Highway*.

LYDIA DAVIS is at work on a novel. Her most recent collection was *Break It Down* (Farrar, Straus and Giroux).

TOI DERRICOTTE teaches at Old Dominion University. The poem published here appeared in a slightly different form in her book *Captivity* (University of Pittsburg Poetry Series, 1989). Her other books have been published by Crossing Press and Lotus Press.

KAREN FISH lives in Pasadena, Maryland. Her work has appeared in *American Poetry Review* and elsewhere.

JOSEPH GEHA was born in Zahleh, Lebanon and moved with his family to Toledo, Ohio in 1946. He now teaches at Iowa State University and will soon publish his collection of stories *Through and Through: Toledo Stories* (Graywolf Press).

SARAH GLASSCOCK's first novel, *Anna L.M.N.O.*, was published by Random House. Her work has appeared in *Descant, Sequoia, Boulevard* and elsewhere.

ALBERT GOLDBARTII teaches at Wichita State University and is the author of five volumes of poetry including a collection of essay-poems forthcoming from Coffee House Press.

ALLEN GROSSMAN received a MacArthur Grant in 1989. He has published two collections with New Directions.

JOY HARJO is the author of four poetry collections, most recently *Mad Love and War* (Wesleyan University Press, 1990). She teaches at The University of Arizona.

DANIEL HAYES lives in Los Angeles. His stories have appeared in *Epoch, Malahat Review, Western Humanities Review* and elsewhere.

ROBIN HEMLEY teaches at The University of North Carolina, Charlotte. His first collection, *All You Can Eat,* was published by Atlantic Monthly Press in 1988. He is at work on a novel.

KIM HERZINGER teaches at The University of Southern Mississippi where he is at work on a biography of Donald Barthelme. "The Day I Met Buddy Holly" is his first piece of short fiction.

LYNDA HULL is the author of *Ghost Money,* which won the Juniper Prize in 1989. She teaches at Vermont College.

T. R. HUMMER edits *New England Review/Bread Loaf Quarterly.* His fourth volume of poetry, *The 18,000 Olympic Dream,* is just out from Morrow.

RODNEY HALE JONES lives in Taipei, Taiwan and is working on a novel about China.

LAURA KALPAKIAN's second collection of stories, *Dark Continent and Other Stories* is just out in paperback from Penguin. She is the author of a previous collection from Graywolf and three novels.

MARY KARR was a winner of the 1989–90 Whiting Award. She will be a Bunting Fellow at Radcliffe next year.

THOMAS E. KENNEDY's novel, *Crossing Borders,* will soon be issued by Watermark Press. He has published critical works on Robert Coover and André Dubus, and he lives with his family in Denmark.

JANE KENYON has published most recently in *Atlantic* and *The New Yorker.* Her forthcoming book of poems is *Let Evening Come.* She lives in Danbury, New Hampshire.

JUDITH KITCHEN has just published a critical study of William Stafford. Her essays, poems and reviews have appeared in many periodicals.

NATALIE KUSZ's essay is part of her collection to be published soon by Farrar, Straus and Giroux.

WALLY LAMB has recently completed his first novel, *Whales*. "Astronauts" is his first published story.

DAVID LEHMAN is series editor for *Best American Poetry* (Scribners). He writes essays on poetry, baseball and detective fiction. His most recent poetry collection is *Operation Memory* (Princeton).

CLARENCE MAJOR is the author of seven novels and eight collections of poetry. Holy Cow! Press just issued his latest collection of fiction, *Fun And Games*, which includes "My Mother and Mitch."

KATHY MANGAN's poems have appeared in *Shenandoah, Georgia Review, Antioch Review, The Southern Review* and elsewhere. She teaches at Western Maryland College.

LOU MATHEWS works as a free-lance journalist in Los Angeles and teaches at UCLA extension. He is at work on a connected series of stories titled "Shaky Town."

LYNNE MCMAHON's collection, *Faith*, was published by Wesleyan University Press. She teaches at The University of Missouri.

CHRISTOPHER MERRILL is the author of *Workbook* (Teal Press) and he is the editor of the Peregrine Smith Poetry series. He directs the Santa Fe and Taos writers conferences.

LEONARD MICHAELS is the author of *Going Places, I Would Have Saved Them If I Could,* and *The Men's Club*.

DAVID MURA is the author of *After We Lost Our Way* (Dutton/National Poetry Series 1989) and *Turning Japanese* (Atlantic Monthly Press, forthcoming.) He lives in St Paul.

KENT NELSON's fiction has appeared in many journals and also in *Best American Short Stories* 1988. His novel, *All Around Me Peaceful*, is published by Delacorte/Delta.

JOSIP NOVAKOVICH emigrated to the United States from Yugoslavia at age twenty. He is a graduate of Yale Divinity School and has published in *Ploughshares, London Magazine, Antaeus* and elsewhere. Paris Review editions will soon publish his collection, *Salvation and Other Disasters*.

FRANKIE PAINO's poems have appeared in *Crazyhorse, Indiana Review, Louisville Review* and elsewhere. Her first collection is just completed.

WALTER PAVLICH's latest poetry collection is *Theories of Birds and Water* (Owl Creek). He lives in Davis, California.

PADGETT POWELL is the author of *Edisto* and *A Woman Named Drown*, both from Farrar, Straus and Giroux.

KENNETH ROSEN directs the Stonecoast Writer's Conference at the University of Southern Maine. He is the author of two collections—*Whole Horse* and *Black Leaves*.

GIBBONS RUARK's new book of poems, *Rescue The Perishing*, will be published next year by LSU press. He has authored three previous collections.

SHARMAN APT RUSSELL's essay will be part of a collection to be published next year by Addison-Wesley. She lives in Mimbres, New Mexico.

LAURIE SHECK's second book of poems is out soon from Knopf. She teaches at Rutgers University.

JAMES SOLHEIM is finishing a book-length poem. He has published in *Poetry, Tendril, The Iowa Review, Kenyon Review* and elsewhere. He lives in Carbondale, Illinois.

MOLLY BEST TINSLEY teaches at the U.S. Naval Academy. Her stories have appeared in *West Branch, Prairie Schooner* and *New England Review/Bread Loaf Quarterly*.

DENNIS VANNATTA's first prose collection is due out in 1991. He has published in *The Quarterly* and elsewhere.

MICHAEL WATERS has published two poetry collections and a third, *Bountiful*, is forthcoming from Carnegie-Mellon University Press. He lives on the Eastern Shore of Maryland.

RICHARD WATSON is professor of philosophy at Washington University in St Louis. He is the author of several novels, most recently *The Breakdown of Cartesian Metaphysics* (1988).

DAVID WOJAHN was a co-poetry editor of *Pushcart Prize XI*. His third poetry collection is *Mystery Train*, forthcoming from University of Pittsburgh Press.

SHAY YOUNGBLOOD's work has appeared in *Amethyst, Catalyst, Common Lives, Conditions* and *Essence*. Her play "Shakin' The Mess Outta Misery" has been performed in Atlanta, Georgia and Albany, New York.

LITERATURE AND BREAKFAST CEREAL

THINK YOU KNOW what's happening in literature today? Maybe you've been missing something.

"Approximately 2,000 alternative publishers now exist in the United States and their number is mushrooming," announced *The New York Times Book Review*. Most of these small independent presses have appeared in the last decade. During the same period many large commercial publishing houses have been absorbed by conglomerates more interested in parking lots, television, motion pictures and, it was gravely rumored for a forthcoming takeover (and gravely denied), in breakfast cereal.

Not since the Paris of Hemingway, Pound and Joyce has so much talent been invested in small presses in every country of the world. The modern small presses publish because of enlightened individualism or, in a few instances, sheer cussedness. They also answer a variety of situations, such as political oppression— the Russian *samizdat* network that nourished Solzhenitsyn for instance—or because of commercial exclusion: the American do-it-yourself tradition that encouraged Anaïs Nin and Stewart Brand and small press immortals such as Thomas Paine, Edgar Allan Poe, Walt Whitman, Stephen Crane, Upton Sinclair and Carl Sandburg.

The result is a galaxy of important authors that most readers have never heard of, let alone read. *The Pushcart Prize* is the first and only collection that annually will bring to a general audience the finest in short fiction, non-fiction, poetry, translation and literary what-not—the classics of tomorrow by today's multitude of small press talents.

—from Bill Henderson's introduction to *The Pushcart Prize, I*
(1976)

In 1971 Bill Henderson founded the Pushcart Press, for which he later won *Publishers Weekly*'s Carey-Thomas Award for creative publishing. He is the author of a memoir, a novel, and several short stories. The Pushcart Press is based on Long Island, New York.